ADA® AS A SECOND LANGUAGE

McGraw-Hill Series in Software Engineering and Technology

Consulting Editor

Peter Freeman, *University of California, Irvine*

Charette: *Software Engineering Environments*
Cohen: *Ada as a Second Language*
Fairley: *Software Engineering Concepts*
General Electric Company: *Software Engineering Handbook*
Jones: *Programming Productivity*
Kolence: *An Introduction to Software Physics: The Meaning of Computer Measurement*
Pressman: *Software Engineering: A Practitioner's Approach*
Wallace: *Practitioner's Guide to Ada*

ADA® AS A SECOND LANGUAGE

Norman H. Cohen

SofTech, Inc.

McGraw-Hill Book Company

New York St. Louis San Francisco Auckland Bogotá Hamburg Johannesburg
London Madrid Mexico Montreal New Delhi Panama Paris
São Paulo Singapore Sydney Tokyo Toronto

This book was set in Times Roman by Publication Services.
The editor was Gerald A. Gleason;
the production supervisor was Leroy A. Young;
the cover was designed by Mark Wieboldt.
Project supervision was done by Publication Services.
Arcata Graphics/Halliday was printer and binder.

ADA® AS A SECOND LANGUAGE

1 2 3 4 5 6 7 8 9 0 HALHAL 8 9 8 7 6

Library of Congress Cataloging-in-Publication Data
Cohen, Norman H.
ADA® as a second language.
1. Ada (Computer program language) I. Title.
QA76.73.A35C64 1986 005.13'3 85-2946
ISBN 0-07-011589-3

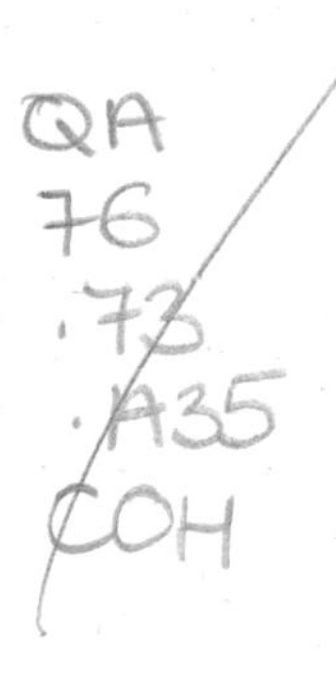

ABOUT THE AUTHOR

Norman H. Cohen is a system consultant for SofTech, Inc. and author of numerous articles on the Ada language. He led the development of major parts of the U.S. Army Ada Curriculum and teaches Ada language and software engineering classes. Dr. Cohen was a principal contributor to a series of case studies on the use of the Ada language, chief designer of an Ada-based program design language, and leader of a research project on the formal verification of Ada programs. He has chaired the Philadelphia area chapter of SIGAda (the Association for Computing Machinery's Special Interest Group on Ada) and a government-sponsored working group on Ada formal semantics. He received his B.A. in computer science from Cornell University and his M.S. and Ph.D. in computer science from Harvard University.

To Dianne; and to David,
Ilana, and Aviva

CONTENTS

PREFACE

Ada as a Second Language is designed to fulfill a wide range of needs. The only prerequisite is an introductory programming course or equivalent practical experience. The book may be used to obtain a reading knowledge of the Ada language, to obtain a writing knowledge of the Ada language, or to serve as a programming reference for someone who is already writing Ada programs. It may be used as a textbook in a course or to learn the Ada language on one's own.

Ada as a Second Language is at once a tutorial introduction to the Ada language and a complete reference. In teaching the language, the book takes time to explain complicated matters in a patient, reassuring manner, with generous explanations. The exposition emphasizes the concerns of the practicing programmer, not theoretical principles of programming languages. As a reference, the book contains a complete description of the nitty-gritty details a programmer needs to write practical, working Ada programs, not just the general principles needed to convey the "flavor" of the language. The blemishes of the language, and their practical implications for the programmer, are described along with the language's graceful contours. There are abundant cross-references to the sections in which concepts are introduced.

WHAT IS THE FIRST LANGUAGE?

The book is entitled *Ada as a Second Language* because it is an introduction to the Ada programming language, but not an introduction to programming. We assume the reader is familiar with certain fundamental programming notions—variables, arrays, loops, conditional statements, and subprograms, for example. The first language can be any statement-oriented high-level language. However, we pay particular attention to FORTRAN, PL/I, and Pascal.

The Ada language is based on programming and software-engineering concepts that may be new to a FORTRAN, PL/I, or Pascal programmer. We take care to make the reader comfortable with programming concepts like programmer-defined types, recursion, pointers, exception handling, and concurrency before the corresponding Ada language feature is introduced. Furthermore, software-engineering concepts like abstract data types, information hiding, and loose coupling, which do not find direct expression in the FORTRAN, PL/I, and Pascal programming languages, must be well understood in order to use the Ada programming language properly. We explain such software-engineering concepts in depth before considering the associated Ada features.

Ada as a Second Language frequently compares the Ada language's features to similar features of FORTRAN, PL/I, and Pascal, to help readers recognize those instances where the Ada language provides a new notation for a familiar concept. For example, the Ada language's `FOR` loop is compared to the `DO` loops of FORTRAN and PL/I and the **for** loop of Pascal. Of course the exposition of an Ada feature never relies on a reader's familiarity with another language.

We also point out circumstances in which familiarity with FORTRAN, PL/I, or Pascal may confuse students of the Ada language or prejudice them to program in a manner that is not appropriate for the Ada language. For example, there is a subtle difference between the treatment of loop control variables in the Ada language and their treatment in the other three programming languages, and this difference can lead to enigmatic errors; entities known as *constants* in FORTRAN and PL/I are called *literals* in the Ada language, and the term *constant* has a quite different meaning; packages can be used in the Ada language in the same way as `COMMON` blocks are used in FORTRAN, but this is rarely appropriate; the exceptions of the Ada language bear strong similarity to the `ON`-conditions of PL/I, but there are important differences that make PL/I condition handling approaches inappropriate in Ada programs.

While the comparative study of programming languages is fascinating, it is not the subject of this book. Our emphasis is overwhelmingly on the Ada language. Other languages are discussed only to the extent that the discussion is likely to help the reader learn the Ada language.

APPROACH

A programming language cannot be taught simply by enumerating rules. Therefore, *Ada as a Second Language* is replete with realistic examples of Ada programming. One-line examples have their place, but extended examples are also necessary, to illustrate how features fit together and the contexts in which they ought to be used. The reader will benefit from over 200 complete Ada compilation units that have been compiled by a validated Ada compiler to verify their legality. Examples have been carefully crafted to be neither too simplistic nor too complicated. The examples are substantial enough to give a realistic idea of how features should be used, but not so involved that they detract from the point being made. Our primary goal, after all, is to teach the Ada language, not particular algorithms or applications.

Just as one cannot learn to play bridge well simply by learning the rules of the game, one cannot learn to program well simply by learning the rules of the programming language. *Ada as a Second Language* explains the basic concepts underlying the features of the Ada language—data abstraction (which it has recently become fashionable to call "object-oriented design"), modularity, the distinction between interfaces and implementations, information hiding, portability, and concurrency, for example—before explaining the features themselves. The book offers specific practical advice on how and why to use each feature, and warns about pitfalls to be avoided.

Good programming style is emphasized throughout the text. Guidelines are provided, for example, on the use of long, descriptive identifiers; the formatting of program text; the appropriate use of exceptions; and the minimization of recompilation costs. The examples consistently practice what the text preaches.

STRUCTURE OF THE BOOK

The typical chapter begins with a discussion of the programming and software-engineering concepts underlying a language feature, then goes on to discuss the essential aspects of the feature itself. Detailed rules about the feature follow later in a separate section. These details must be learned to write correct Ada programs but are best deferred until the reader has become comfortable with general principles. These details can be skipped entirely by the reader who seeks only a general familiarity with the Ada language or the ability to understand Ada programs written by others. Each chapter ends with a summary of the major points and a set of exercises. The exercises include drills on fundamental concepts as well as programming problems.

Chapters 1 and 2 contain introductory material. Chapter 1 briefly recounts the concerns and events that led to the creation of the Ada programming language. This chapter is not essential for learning to read or write Ada programs, but it does provide perspective on the motivation for various language features. Chapter 2 provides a high-level overview of the entire language. In addition, the Ada language's lexical rules and the notation we use for describing Ada syntax are presented there. It is the most important chapter in the book, providing an overall framework within which the specific information in subsequent chapters can be understood. In particular, this chapter introduces the crucial Ada notions of separate compilation units and packages.

Chapters 3 through 6 are concerned with the predominant issue in Ada programs, data types. Chapter 3 introduces the notion of an abstract data type as a set of abstract values plus operations on those values, independent of the underlying physical representation; and describes how the FORTRAN, PL/I, Pascal, and Ada languages provide increasingly comprehensive support for data abstraction. This chapter provides the background needed to appreciate the role of data types in the Ada language, and particularly the role of private types. Chapter 4 describes object and type declarations and discusses six classes of types in detail—integer, floating-point, fixed-point, enumeration, array, and record types. Access types are deferred until Chapter 5 to permit a thorough discussion of the underlying concepts, which will be new to FORTRAN programmers. Chapter 6 introduces the notion of subtypes. The distinction between subtypes and types, a common stumbling block for newcomers to the Ada language, is carefully explained. Derived types are introduced in this chapter to illustrate the concept of strong typing.

Chapters 7 through 9 describe the traditional algorithmic features found in all procedural languages. These features are used in earlier chapters and the reader will already be intuitively familiar with them, but specific rules, caveats, and guidelines are provided here. Chapter 7 describes in detail the statements used in nonconcurrent programming. Chapter 8 gives detailed rules about expressions. Chapter 9 treats subprograms.

The discussion on record types in Chapter 4 is confined to record types without discriminants. Record types with discriminants are introduced in Chapter 10. We deliberately separate this discussion from the earlier coverage of data types. The reader can then master the basic principles of data types before tackling the more intricate topic of discriminants. Furthermore, the thorough treatment of subprograms in Chapter 9 permits more complete and realistic illustrations of how discriminants are used.

The first ten chapters contain all the information necessary for writing small Ada programs and individual subprograms. For some programmers, this may be sufficient. However, it is the features described in the second half of the book—particularly support for programming in the large, exceptions, generic program units, and concurrency—that make the Ada language unique.

Chapters 11 through 13 describe the features that make it possible to write large Ada programs while managing their complexity. Though packages are introduced in Chapter 2 and used in subsequent chapters, Chapter 11 covers them in detail, relating packages to the notions of modularity and information hiding. Chapter 12 describes private and limited private types and relates them to the discussion of data abstraction in Chapter 3. Chapter 13 discusses separate compilation. Each of these chapters includes abundant advice on the appropriate use of language features, for example, when it is appropriate to make a private type limited and how to reduce potential recompilation costs.

Nested program units are introduced as early as Chapter 2, and by this point the reader should have a strong intuitive notion of the Ada language's scope and visibility rules. Chapter 14 builds on this intuition to provide a formal set of rules. The idea is to solidify the reader's understanding of scope and visibility and to enable him to answer scope and visibility questions in unusual situations where the answer might not be intuitively obvious. The rules are applied to specific examples to illustrate how they lead to the conclusions that the reader expects. This will help the reader apply the rules in other situations.

Chapter 15 deals with exceptions. This chapter includes an optional section for PL/I programmers, comparing Ada exceptions to PL/I `ON`-conditions. A considerable portion of the chapter is devoted to guidelines for the appropriate use of exceptions.

Chapter 16 covers generic units. The need for generic units is described by example and the basic notions of template and instance are then discussed. The mechanics of writing and using generic units are illustrated by examples that convey the power of generic units and the variety of ways in which they can be used. A section on generalization provides the thoughtful reader with insights on the appropriate role for generic units in the design process.

Chapter 17 discusses the predefined file input and output facilities of the Ada language. Until this point, all input and output is performed using a simplified package, `Basic_IO`, whose text is given in the Appendix. `Basic_IO` provides a subset of the predefined facilities, consisting of the rudimentary facilities required for interesting examples and exercises. The Ada language's predefined input and output facilities consist not of additional language features, but rather program units written using the features already in the language. A description of these facilities is really a description of a particular set of Ada software components. Therefore, while Chapter 17 contains many details provided for the programmer's reference, it also serves as an extended illustration of the use of packages, generic units, and exceptions.

Chapters 18 and 19 deal with Ada tasks. The reader interested in only a general overview of the language's multitasking features can confine his attention to Chapter 18. That chapter discusses fundamental notions of concurrency and asynchronism, the concept of task objects and task types, and simple rendezvous that do not involve selective waits. Two examples of multitask programming are provided—excerpts from a video game program, to illustrate fundamental real-time programming techniques, and a text processing example, to show how multitasking can simplify apparently sequential problems. Chapter 19 deals with more advanced aspects of tasking, including activation and termination of tasks, selective waits, priorities, entry families, abortion of tasks, and variables shared by multiple tasks. The interaction between tasks and exceptions is also discussed in this chapter.

Chapter 20 deals with low-level and implementation-dependent programming. The approach is necessarily general, since details vary from one Ada compiler to another. Rather than focusing on a particular compiler, we carefully define a variety of hypothetical Ada implementations to illustrate implementation-dependent features and the ways they may differ under different compilers. The hypothetical compilers are for real machines and devices, so the examples are authentic.

NOTES ON STYLE

Ada as a Second Language capitalizes reserved words and uses a mixture of upper and lower case for other identifiers. This differs from the style found in most publications about the Ada language, but it is a more appropriate style for the practicing programmer. The habit of writing identifiers entirely in upper case is a vestige of the day when all programs were entered by keypunch. Given modern-day keyboards, it makes sense to reserve the use of upper case for highlighting abbreviations and the beginnings of words. By mixing upper and lower case, we make our identifier names more expressive and informative. Reserved words should be written in a way that distinguishes them from other identifiers and makes them stand out, so that the underlying program structure is apparent. In many publications, this is done by setting the reserved words in boldface type. For the many programmers who do not have boldface available to them, however, this effect is best achieved by writing reserved words entirely in upper case.

The text uses masculine pronouns in a generic sense, in accordance with conventional English practice. For example, we speak of how a programmer can hide the data in *his* package from other programmers. I am confident that no reader will seriously interpret this as an assertion that women are not programmers. Indeed, as Chapter 1 explains in greater detail, the Ada language is named after the woman generally regarded as the world's first programmer.

ACKNOWLEDGMENTS

This book has benefited from the detailed attention that several devoted friends have paid to it. The comments of Christine Ausnit, Fredric Cohen, and Frank Pappas led to significant improvements. I am further honored to have had the manuscript reviewed by two of the Distinguished Reviewers who officially reviewed the design of the Ada language itself—John Goodenough and Nico Lomuto. Nico deserves special thanks, both for excellent pedagogical and technical advice and for his enthusiastic encouragement. Finally, I am indebted to Jorge Rodriguez for making the facilities of SofTech, Inc., available to me to compile the book's examples.

Ada as a Second Language is the outgrowth of a twenty-session continuing education course on the Ada language. I told my wife and son that, with a few months' effort, I could transform my lecture notes into a textbook. As soon as I sat down and started writing, taking care to introduce underlying concepts and to describe language features completely, it became obvious that I had grossly underestimated the effort involved. Perhaps a textbook on the Ada language can be written in so short a time (in fact I suspect some have been), but not a textbook worth reading. Three years and two daughters later, as I complete this "few months' effort," I thank Dianne for her patience when I needed patience, for her impatience when I needed prodding, and for her loving support throughout. The role of author's spouse is not an enviable one, but Dianne accepted the burdens, above and beyond her already awesome responsibilities, with composure and valor.

Norman H. Cohen

ADA® AS A SECOND LANGUAGE

CHAPTER

ONE

THE DEVELOPMENT OF THE ADA LANGUAGE

1.1 THE DEFENSE DEPARTMENT'S SOFTWARE CRISIS

The programming language Ada is the result of an effort by the U.S. Department of Defense to control the increasing cost of its software. A study conducted between 1973 and 1974 revealed that the department was spending $3 billion each year on computer software, over half of it for *embedded* computers. An embedded computer is one that forms part of a larger system, such as a radar system or a communications system. The primary function of the computer is to monitor and control devices.

Programs for U.S. Defense Department embedded computers are more complex than ordinary commercial programs. The programs for embedded computers are generally huge—between one hundred thousand and one million lines long. The staffs that work on them typically consist of more than fifty programmers. The programs must be able to respond sensibly to a wide range of stimuli from the surrounding environment. They must also provide sophisticated man-machine interfaces. Both the speed and the size of the programs are subject to severe constraints. The programs have a long life span—generally from ten to fifteen years—during which time the system requirements change frequently. Over its life span, a program may have to be adapted to a wide variety of computers. Most importantly, these programs must be reliable. Lives may depend on their functioning correctly.

According to the 1973–1974 study, software was accounting for a growing portion of the total cost of such systems. Most of this cost was in the maintenance of old software rather than in the development of new software. The overwhelming majority of this work was performed by contractors rather than by government personnel, and the greater part of the work was so specialized that the original developers of a system controlled the market for all future contracts to maintain that system.

Many of the Defense Department's high costs arose from the fact that it was using obsolete languages to program embedded computers. These languages, developed in the early 1960s, did not support modern software engineering methods such as structured programming, data abstraction, top-down program development, and re-use of general-purpose components. They provided no way of checking that separately compiled pieces of a program were consistent. A modern programming language was needed to provide (1) support for program specification and validation; (2) better error checking and therefore more reliable programs; and (3) device-level input and output, real time operations, and parallel operations without assembly language inserts.

Besides using obsolete languages, the Department of Defense used too many languages. Many projects used their own languages or special variations of existing languages. This virtually locked the department into contracting the original developers of a system for all maintenance work arising during the life of that system. (The 1973–1974 study found that 61 percent of the Defense Department's embedded computer software expenditures were "captive.") Because so many languages were being developed for a single use, tools that could reduce the cost of developing and maintaining programs in a particular language were very rarely built. Those tools that were built—compilers, linkers, editors, and configuration control tools, among others—were rarely shared by several different projects.

1.2 THE EFFORT TO FIND A STANDARD LANGUAGE

In the early 1970s, military software managers concluded that they could better control their costs by limiting the number of languages used to program embedded computers. The U.S. Air Force, Army, and Navy each began to look for its own standard language. In fact, if only a single language were allowed, there would be additional benefits. The Defense Department could then expect its hardware vendors to provide compilers for that language and perhaps even microcoded hardware tailored to the language. The language could become popular for nonmilitary applications, especially once a large set of tools was developed for the language. It would then be widely taught. This would increase the supply of programmers qualified to work on department software, thus helping to keep the cost of that software down.

Following the 1973–1974 cost study, the Higher Order Language Working Group (HOLWG) was formed in 1975. It included representatives of the Office of the Secretary of Defense, the Air Force, the Army, the Navy, the Defense Communications Agency, the National Security Agency, and the Defense Advanced Research Projects Agency. Its goal was a standard military language, tentatively named DoD–1 (for Department of Defense). DoD–1 would be used for all new software, but the millions of lines of existing software would not be recoded in DoD–1.

DoD–1 could be either an existing language or a new language developed especially for this purpose. However, it would have to be a language worthy of recognition as *the* standard real-time programming language, just as FORTRAN and COBOL were recognized as the standard scientific and commercial programming languages.

The Higher Order Language Working Group replaced the efforts of the individual military services. In addition, the Defense Department halted all funding for programming language research and development not related to the DoD–1 program. Five existing military languages were approved for use in embedded systems until DoD–1 became available, and the definitions of these five languages were standardized and strictly controlled by the military services.

In April 1975, the Higher Order Language Working Group issued a set of sample requirements for DoD–1. The requirements were intended primarily as an illustration of the level of detail the group deemed appropriate, rather than as actual programming language design recommendations. The requirements were given the name "Strawman" and circulated within the government and among programming language experts. Based on the response to the Strawman requirements, the Higher Order Language Working Group drew up a tentative set of actual language requirements in August 1975 and circulated them widely under the name "Woodenman." The responses to Woodenman were used to draft the official requirements for DoD–1. These requirements, named "Tinman," were announced in January 1976.

In formulating the series of requirements that culminated in Tinman, the Higher Order Language Working Group consulted with organizations involved in a wide variety of real-time applications, including avionics, guidance, command and control, and training simulators. Because these different application areas were currently each using a different language, the group expected that different organizations would come up with widely varying sets of language requirements. They were pleasantly surprised to discover that the various organizations had essentially the same requirements. An even greater surprise was that the Tinman requirements also met the needs of scientific and commercial applications.

The Higher Order Language Working Group then proceeded to determine whether these requirements, so agreeable to everybody, could be met by an existing language. In the summer of 1976, the Defense Department contracted with six teams of language experts to review twenty-three languages and determine whether they satisfied Tinman. The twenty-three included languages used in industry (FORTRAN, COBOL, PL/I, and Algol 60), existing military/aerospace languages (HAL/S, TACPOL, CMS–2, CS–4, SPL/1, JOVIAL J3B, JOVIAL J73, and CORAL 66), and languages that were at the time used almost exclusively in universities (Algol 68, Pascal, Simula 67, LIS, Euclid, and EL1). (Other languages considered were LTR, RTL/2, PDL/2, PEARL, and MORAL. APL was summarily excluded from consideration.) In addition, a workshop was held at Cornell University in September 1976 to study the feasibility of a language satisfying Tinman.

In January 1977, the Higher Order Language Working Group announced their conclusion that none of the twenty-three languages met the Tinman requirements closely enough to be anointed DoD–1. Nonetheless, it was both feasible and desirable to develop a new language that did. In particular, Pascal, PL/I, or Algol 68 could be used as the basis of such a new language.

1.3 THE DESIGN OF THE ADA LANGUAGE

Once it was concluded that a new programming language would be needed, the Tinman requirements were reorganized in the form of a language specification and renamed "Ironman." In April 1977, proposals were solicited for language designs based on Pascal, PL/I, or Algol 68 that fulfilled the Ironman requirements. The proposals were to be judged according to the criteria of reliability, maintainability, and efficiency. Reliability would be promoted by language rules that made it possible to catch errors before a program was run, constructs that encouraged good programming practices, and constructs that made it easy to re-use correctly working components from one software system when constructing another software system. Maintainability would be promoted by a language that made programs easy to read, even if this required making them harder to write. Efficiency would be promoted by a language that could be compiled quickly to produce compact object programs that ran quickly.

Development of DoD–1 would take place in three phases. Phase I would be a competition among four contractors to produce prototype languages. Two of these contractors would be asked to develop their prototypes into rigorous language definitions in Phase II. One of these languages would be selected to undergo final revisions in Phase III, resulting in DoD–1.

Seventeen proposals were received by June 1977. All the proposals were based on Pascal except for IBM's, which was based on PL/I. Phase I contracts were awarded to teams headed by Jean Ichbiah of CII Honeywell Bull, Ben Brosgol of Intermetrics, John Goodenough of SofTech, and Jay Spitzen of SRI International. To foster impartial judgment of the four prototype languages, the competitors were known to the Department of Defense only by the code names Green, Red, Blue, and Yellow, respectively. Ironman was revised to remove certain inconsistencies in July 1977, and Phase I ran from July 1977 to January 1978. (The revised Ironman requirements can be found in the December 1977 issue of the Association for Computing Machinery's *SIGPLAN Notices.*)

The four prototype languages were reviewed during February and March of 1978. This included public review of the prototypes by 125 teams and face-to-face questioning of the design teams by a panel of programming language experts appointed by the Higher Order Language Working Group. The Ironman requirements were modified once again in light of experience gained during Phase I, yielding the "Steelman" requirements. The Red and Green languages were chosen as finalists in April 1978; and Phase II ran from the time of this selection until April 1979. Each finalist was required to produce a reference manual, a rationale, a test translator, and a formal semantic specification for its language. These products were subjected to public review during March and April of 1979. In May, the Green language was chosen as the winner.

It was at this time that the name "DoD–1" was replaced by the name "Ada." The name was suggested by Jack Cooper of the U.S. Navy, in honor of Ada Augusta, the Countess of Lovelace. Lady Lovelace, who lived from 1815 to 1852, wrote what some consider to be the world's first computer programs, to run on Charles Babbage's "Analytic Engine." The Analytic Engine was a mechanical computing device that—despite its theoretically correct design—was never built because of the limitations of nineteenth-century manufacturing technology.

The reference manual and rationale for the Green language—now known as "Preliminary Ada"—were published in the June 1979 issue of *SIGPLAN Notices*. This marked the beginning of Phase III, in which comments were solicited and the language was revised. Revisions were executed by the winning contractor, CII Honeywell Bull, under the guidance of a panel of "distinguished reviewers" appointed by the Higher Order Language Working Group. Phase III ran through June 1980.

A proposed standard reference manual for the Ada language, incorporating major changes to Preliminary Ada, was published in July 1980. It was formally accepted by the Higher Order Language Working Group in August, and a ceremony marking the "debut" of the language took place in September. The Higher Order Language Working Group, believing the language to be in its final form at this point, encouraged implementers to begin work on compilers. In December, the Higher Order Language Working Group was dissolved and reconstituted as the Ada Joint Program Office (AJPO). The Ada language reference manual was adopted as Military Standard 1815. The name "Ada" was registered as a trademark of the Ada Joint Program Office, to ensure the Defense Department's continuing control over the language. Nonetheless, because of the great interest in the Ada language outside the defense community, the military standard was submitted to the American National Standards Institute (ANSI) for adoption as an American national standard.

The Department of Defense expected that ANSI consideration of the reference manual would yield suggestions for improving the organization and wording of the manual. However, when the proposed ANSI standard was submitted for public review between April and October of 1981, the language itself came under scrutiny. Over 400 pages of comments, containing over 750 questions, were received. Both editorial and language design issues were raised. There were many strong objections that the language was too complex.

The reference manual was overhauled as a result of the ANSI review. Many corrections, clarifications, and simplifications were made, but the definition of a legal Ada program and its meaning changed only slightly. The revised manual was published in July 1982 under the designations "Draft Revised Military Standard 1815A" and "Draft Proposed ANSI Standard Document for Editorial Review."

Following a second review extending from July to October of 1982, further changes were instituted. With a few notable exceptions (such as new precedence levels for certain operators), these changes were quite minor. Finally, on January

22, 1983, the reference manual was fixed as Military Standard 1815A. Standardization by ANSI followed on February 17, 1983. This book is based on the 1983 revision, the standard definition of the Ada programming language.

The purpose of the standard is to establish a fixed definition of the Ada language. The standard clearly defines those areas in which implementations may vary, such as the size of the largest integer. However, it is possible to write programs that are guaranteed to be *portable*. That is, they will produce equivalent results with any implementation capable of processing the program. An implementation must reject any program it is not capable of processing (for instance, because the program uses integers larger than those supported by the implementation). Portability of software for embedded computers was one of the main goals of the common high-order language effort.

Other standardized languages, like FORTRAN and COBOL, have many divergent implementations supporting different dialects. It is very unusual to be able to move a successfully compiled FORTRAN program to another compiler without making some changes. The Ada Joint Program Office has taken steps to prevent the emergence of independent Ada dialects.

One such step has been to register the name "Ada" as a trademark. The Ada Joint Program Office will only allow the use of the name "Ada" as the name of a programming language in connection with the language described by the military and ANSI standards. A compiler that does not conform to the standard may not be called an Ada compiler. In particular, the name Ada may not be used in connection with compilers implementing supersets or subsets of the standard. (An exception is made for an interim compiler developed as a stepping stone to a standard Ada compiler.)

Of course, it is meaningless to insist that all programs described as Ada compilers conform to the standard unless there is a way to test conformance. This is the purpose of the Ada Compiler Validation Capability, developed by SofTech for the Ada Joint Program Office. The Ada Compiler Validation Capability consists of a set of rigorous test programs for determining conformance with the standard and documenting the allowed implementation-dependent variations; procedures and tools for running the tests; and an Implementer's Guide. The Implementer's Guide describes subtle ramifications of language rules, areas where more than one interpretation of the standard is possible, and misunderstandings that should be avoided. The actual validation of Ada compilers is performed independently by the Ada Validation Office, an agency of the Ada Joint Program Office, under a validation policy developed by the Mitre Corporation.

1.4 OTHER ASPECTS OF THE ADA EFFORT

One driving force behind the development of a single high-order language was the desire to develop a common set of language-oriented tools. An early concern of the Ada program was the development of specifications for an *Ada Programming Support Environment*, or *APSE*. In March 1978, John Buxton of Systems Designers,

Ltd., drew up a set of preliminary APSE requirements, named "Sandman." This was followed two months later by a refined set of requirements named "Pebbleman," and a workshop was held at the University of California at Irvine in June 1978 to discuss Pebbleman. Pebbleman was revised in January 1979 and replaced in February 1980 by "Stoneman," the official Ada Programming Support Environment requirements.

The purpose of an Ada Programming Support Environment is to provide support for the entire project team throughout the life of a system. An APSE might include design tools, an editor, compilers for a variety of target machines, debugging aids, test drivers, management support tools, configuration tools, and program analysis aids ranging from a simple cross-reference program to a checker for proofs of program correctness. Among the goals of the APSE requirements are tools tailored to the Ada language, the ability of an APSE to grow or to be customized for a particular project, and portability. In this case, portability means the ability to move an existing APSE to a new host machine relatively easily, the ability to generate a compiler for a new target machine fairly easily, and the ability of programmers familiar with one APSE to use another similar APSE with minimal retraining.

Another area of Defense Department activity has been research into software engineering methodologies compatible with its new programming language. The Ada language supports many modern software engineering methodologies directly. It also provides fertile ground for the development of new methodologies. New methodologies, in turn, will lead to new APSE tools.

Finally, the Department of Defense is actively supporting training in the use of the Ada language. In addition to its courses for its own personnel, the department is supporting courses for industry and for colleges and universities. The benefits envisioned for the Ada language will not materialize without a sufficient pool of people competent to use the language.

1.5 SUMMARY

The Ada programming language was developed on behalf of the U.S. Department of Defense to help control the cost of software for computers embedded in larger systems. Programs for embedded computers are generally huge and complex. They are developed by large teams and undergo many changes over a long life span. It is imperative that these programs be reliable.

The Defense Department sought a standard programming language both because it was using too many specialized languages and because the languages it was using were technically obsolete. The first step was to identify and refine the requirements for the standard language. After determining that these requirements were feasible but not met by any existing programming language, the Defense Department awarded contracts for the design of a new language.

The language that came to be named "Ada" (after Ada Augusta, the Countess of Lovelace) was chosen from among four competitive designs. The winning design was published as "Preliminary Ada" in June 1979. It underwent major changes during a public review that resulted in the July 1980 version of the Ada language, adopted as Military Standard 1815. The effort to win approval as an ANSI standard resulted in further changes. Most, but not all, of these changes are reflected in the proposed revised Military Standard 1815A published in July 1982. The Ada language was adopted as a revised Military Standard in January 1983 and as an ANSI standard in February 1983. It is the 1983 revised standard that is described in this book.

The standard definition of the Ada language is strictly enforced. The programming language name "Ada" is a trademark owned by the Defense Department, and no compiler may be called an Ada compiler unless its conformance to the standard is validated. Conformance is tested by the rigorous test programs of the Ada Compiler Validation Capability. This strict control of the language should make it easier to re-use software developed using one Ada compiler in a program developed using another compiler.

The design of a new language was only one aspect of the Ada effort. Other aspects include the development of Ada Programming Support Environments, or APSEs; the development of software engineering methodologies to be used in conjunction with the language; and an expanded training effort in the use of the language.

CHAPTER

TWO

AN INTRODUCTION TO THE ADA LANGUAGE

It is hard to appreciate a feature in a programming language until you know how that feature fits in with the rest of the language. This observation leads to a paradox: No programming language feature can be explained well until most of the language has already been explained.

The purpose of this chapter is to circumvent this paradox. The chapter summarizes most of the features of the Ada language. You will not see nearly enough details to begin writing Ada programs, but you will get a sense for the flavor of the Ada language and the perspective necessary to understand the details in later chapters.

Section 2.1 presents the basic rules for composing Ada text. This is the only place these rules are discussed. Section 2.2 defines the notation used in the remainder of the book to describe Ada syntax. Section 2.3 is an overview of the language. Do not be concerned with mastering Section 2.3, since later chapters give detailed explanations of everything presented there. It will suffice for you to come away with a general understanding of features such as assignment statements and subprograms, a high-level picture of the structure of the Ada language, and some sense of the philosophy behind the design of the language.

2.1 THE TEXT OF AN ADA PROGRAM

Below is a simple Ada program. The first eleven lines of the program explain what it does.

```
-------------------------------------------------------------
-- Program to read a sequence of numbers and report:       --
--     - the number of positive items in the sequence      --
--     - the number of negative items in the sequence      --
--     - the number of zeroes in the sequence              --
--     - the sum of the positive items                     --
--     - the sum of the negative items                     --
--                                                         --
-- The user enters the length of the sequence followed     --
--     by the numbers making up the sequence.              --
-------------------------------------------------------------

WITH Basic_IO;
PROCEDURE Print_Totals IS

   Number_Of_Positives,
      Number_Of_Negatives,
      Number_Of_Zeroes :
         Integer := 0;
   Sum_Of_Positives, Sum_Of_Negatives : Integer := 0;
   Number_Of_Items                    : Integer;
   Item                               : Integer;

BEGIN

   Basic_IO.Put ("How many items?");
   Basic_IO.New_Line;
   Basic_IO.Get (Number_Of_Items);

   FOR i IN 1 .. Number_Of_Items LOOP

      Basic_IO.Put ("Enter item: ");
      Basic_IO.New_Line;
      Basic_IO.Get (Item);

      IF Item > 0 THEN
         Number_Of_Positives := Number_Of_Positives + 1;
         Sum_Of_Positives := Sum_Of_Positives + Item;
      ELSIF Item < 0 THEN
         Number_Of_Negatives := Number_Of_Negatives + 1;
         Sum_of_Negatives := Sum_of_Negatives + Item;
      ELSE   -- Item = 0
         Number_Of_Zeroes := Number_Of_Zeroes + 1;
      END IF;

   END LOOP;

   Basic_IO.Put ("Number of positive items: ");
   Basic_IO.Put (Number_Of_Positives);
   Basic_IO.New_Line;

   Basic_IO.Put ("Number of negative items: ");
   Basic_IO.Put (Number_Of_Negatives);
   Basic_IO.New_Line;

   Basic_IO.Put ("Number of zeroes: ");
   Basic_IO.Put (Number_Of_Zeroes);
   Basic_IO.New_Line;

   Basic_IO.Put ("Sum of positive items: ");
   Basic_IO.Put (Sum_Of_Positives);
   Basic_IO.New_Line;
```

```
      Basic_IO.Put ("Sum of negative items: ");
      Basic_IO.Put (Sum_Of_Negatives);
      Basic_IO.New_Line;
   END Print_Totals;
```

An Ada program is a sequence of words, special symbols, and other elements. The points at which this sequence of elements is divided into lines, and the position of the elements within the lines, are irrelevant to an Ada compiler. For example, the three lines

```
IF Item > 0 THEN
   Number_Of_Positives := Number_Of_Positives + 1;
   Sum_Of_Positives := Sum_Of_Positives + Item;
```

could also have been written as

```
IF Item >
0 THEN Number_Of_Positives
:=Number_Of_Positives      +1;Sum_Of_Positives
:=Sum_Of_Positives+        Item;
```

(Of course the first arrangement is much easier to read.) Any number of spaces may appear between elements. However, spaces may not appear within an element, except within elements like

```
"Number of positive items: "
```

representing specific characters or strings of characters. The following two-character combinations are all elements of the Ada language, so no spaces are allowed between the two characters of each combination:

```
=>    ..    **    :=    /=    >=    <=    <<    >>    <>
```

At least one space is required between a word and a numeral that follows it.

The designers of the Ada language have recommended particular conventions for dividing a program into lines and indenting certain lines relative to other lines. Wide use of these conventions will make it easier for one Ada programmer to read a program written by another. The recommended conventions are used in the full program above and throughout the rest of this book.

Two consecutive hyphens in an Ada program mark the beginning of a *comment*. The comment extends from the two hyphens to the end of the line. Comments are not considered part of the sequence of elements constituting the program. They are ignored by a compiler and used only to convey information to another person reading the program. Each of the first eleven lines of the preceding program above consists entirely of a comment. The program also contains a line consisting of the element `ELSE` followed by a comment.

An Ada program may contain both upper-case and lower-case letters. A sequence of characters surrounded by double quotes, such as

```
"How many items?"
```

is a *string literal.* It denotes the exact string of characters appearing between the quotes, except that a double-quote character within the string is denoted by two consecutive double quotes in the string literal. A single character surrounded by apostrophes, such as `'a'`, is a *character literal* corresponding precisely to that individual character. (The `Print_Totals` program does not contain any character literals.) Except within string literals and character literals, corresponding upper-case and lower-case characters are interchangeable: The lines

```
IF Item > 0 THEN
   Number_Of_Positives := Number_Of Positives + 1;
```

could also have been written

```
if ITEM > 0 then
   NUMBER_OF_POSITIVES := Number_Of_Positives + 1;
```

As with the positioning of elements within lines, the use of a standard convention for capitalization makes a program easier to read. Capitalization conventions generally distinguish between sequences of letters used to name things and special sequences, such as `LOOP`, `ELSE`, and `END`, which express the syntactic structure of a program. The latter are called *reserved words,* because the language designates special purposes for them and a programmer cannot use them for any other purpose. Many Ada language references print names in upper case and reserved words in boldface lower case, like this:

```
for I in 1 .. NUMBER_OF_ITEMS loop
   BASIC_IO.PUT("Enter item: ");
   BASIC_IO.NEW_LINE;
   BASIC_IO.GET(ITEM);
   if ITEM > 0 then
      NUMBER_OF_POSITIVES := NUMBER_OF_POSITIVES + 1;
      SUM_OF_POSITIVES := SUM_OF_POSITIVES + ITEM;
   elsif ITEM < 0 then
      NUMBER_OF_NEGATIVES := NUMBER_OF_NEGATIVES + 1;
      SUM_OF_NEGATIVES := SUM_OF_NEGATIVES + 1;
   else -- ITEM = 0
      NUMBER_OF_ZEROES := NUMBER_OF_ZEROES + 1;
   end if;
end loop;
```

This book uses a different convention, compatible with the input/output devices most commonly available to programmers: Reserved words are written in upper case, and names are in mixed case. Generally, the first letter of each word in the name will be in upper case and all other letters will be in lower case (as in `Number_Of_Items`). However, single-letter names (like `i`) will be written in lower case, and initials appearing in names will be capitalized (as in `Basic_IO`, in which the initials `IO` stand for "input/output"). The advantages of this convention are threefold:

1. Programs will appear in the book as you are likely to see them in your listings and on your terminal screen.
2. Reserved words stand out, making the structure of the program evident.
3. Mixing upper and lower case allows programmers to be more expressive in writing descriptive, easily-understood names. (`Channels_Allocated_To_CBs` is an appropriate name for the number of channels allocated for use by citizens band radios. However, if we were restricted to spelling names only in upper case, this name would not convey this meaning as clearly. `CHANNELS_ALLOCATED_TO_CBS` can also be read as the number of television channels allocated to the CBS network.)

The words in a program, or *identifiers,* may consist of letters, digits, and underscores (_). However, the first character must be a letter, and an underscore may only occur between two nonunderscores. There is no restriction on the length of an identifier, except that it must all fit on one line. This means you can use long, descriptive names, consisting of several English words separated by underscores. FORTRAN programmers become skilled at encoding the meaning of a variable in a six-character name. Ada programmers should strive to unlearn this skill. Using names like `Number_Of_Positives` and `Sum_Of_Positives` rather than `NUMPOS` and `POSSUM` makes a program much easier to understand.

Ada has sixty-three reserved words:

```
ABORT     CONSTANT    EXIT       NEW         RAISE      TERMINATE
ABS       DECLARE     FOR        NOT         RANGE      THEN
ACCEPT    DELAY       FUNCTION   NULL        RECORD     TYPE
ACCESS    DELTA       GENERIC    OF          REM        USE
ALL       DIGITS      GOTO       OR          RENAMES    WHEN
AND       DO          IF         OTHERS      RETURN     WHILE
ARRAY     ELSE        IN         OUT         REVERSE    WITH
AT        ELSIF       IS         PACKAGE     SELECT     XOR
BEGIN     END         LIMITED    PRAGMA      SEPARATE
BODY      ENTRY       LOOP       PRIVATE     SUBTYPE
CASE      EXCEPTION   MOD        PROCEDURE   TASK
```

Ada programs are built out of *declarations, statements,* and *pragmas.* Declarations define the meanings of identifiers. Statements specify the steps of a computation. Pragmas provide the compiler with information that may affect the way a program is listed, the way a program is translated into machine language, or the order in which a program performs certain actions. All declarations, statements, and pragmas in a program end with semicolons. (This is different from Pascal, in which statements are *separated* by semicolons. In the Ada language, the last statement in a sequence of statements ends with a semicolon, just like the other statements in the sequence.)

A sequence of statements can appear anywhere in a program that a single statement can appear. For instance, the program shown earlier contains a loop of the form

```
FOR i IN 1 .. Number_Of_Items LOOP
    sequence of statements
END LOOP;
```

The reserved word `LOOP` and the reserved words `END LOOP` mark the beginning and end of the sequence of statements executed during each repetition of the loop. This sequence of four statements ends with an `IF` statement of the form

```
IF Item > 0 THEN
    sequence of statements
ELSIF Item < 0 THEN
    sequence of statements
ELSE
    sequence of statements
END IF;
```

The beginnings and ends of the statement sequences inside the `IF` statement are marked by the reserved words `THEN`, `ELSIF` (one word), `ELSE`, and `END IF` (two words). The sequence of statements following `ELSE` happens to consist of a single statement.

Compound statements like the `DO;` ... `END;` group of PL/I and the "**begin** ... **end**" statement of Pascal—which serve only to form a single statement out of a sequence of statements—are unnecessary in the Ada language. This makes programs easier to modify. When a PL/I programmer is required to change

```
IF A > B
   THEN MAXIMUM = A;
   ELSE MAXIMUM = B;
```

to

```
IF A > B
   THEN DO;
           MAXIMUM = A;
           A_BIGGER = A_BIGGER + 1;
        END;
   ELSE DO;
           MAXIMUM = B;
           B_BIGGER = B_BIGGER + 1;
        END;
```

an Ada programmer need only insert two lines in

```
IF a > b THEN
   Maximum := a;
ELSE
   Maximum := b;
END IF;
```

to obtain

```
IF a > b THEN
   Maximum := a;
   A_Bigger := A_Bigger + 1;
ELSE
   Maximum := b;
   B_Bigger := B_Bigger + 1;
END IF;
```

When a Pascal programmer changes

```
while Line[i] = Blank do
    i := i + 1;
```

to

```
while Line[i] = Blank do
    begin
        i := i + 1;
       NumBlanks := NumBlanks + 1
   end
```

an Ada programmer inserts one line in

```
WHILE Line (i) = Blank LOOP
   i := i + 1;
END LOOP;
```

to obtain

```
WHILE Line (i) = Blank LOOP
   i := i + 1;
   Number_Of_Blanks := Number_Of_Blanks + 1;
END LOOP;
```

Two pragmas, List and Page, control the appearance of the source listing produced by a compiler. The pragma

```
PRAGMA List (Off);
```

instructs the compiler not to list anything following the pragma until the pragma

```
PRAGMA List (On);
```

is encountered. The List pragma itself is always listed, whether it specifies Off or On. The pragma

```
PRAGMA Page;
```

causes a new page of the listing to be started just after the pragma. List and Page pragmas are allowed at the beginning of a compilation, anywhere a declaration is allowed, anywhere a statement is allowed, and in certain other places that will be described in Chapter 13.

2.2 NOTATION FOR ADA SYNTAX

To explain any more about the structure of Ada programs we will need a notation specifying the form of declarations, statements, and other components of Ada programs. The notation described in this section will be used throughout the book. Let's begin with an example:

The form of a procedure specification is

```
PROCEDURE identifier
 ...................................................................
 : ( parameter specification ; ~~~ ; parameter specification ) :
 ...................................................................
```

This means that a procedure specification always begins with the word **PROCEDURE** followed by some identifier. Optionally, the identifier may then be followed by a left parenthesis, a sequence of one or more "parameter specifications" separated by semicolons, and a right parenthesis.

In general, a word appearing in upper case will represent a reserved word. An italicized word appearing in lower case will represent some other component of an Ada program that has already been described or is about to be described. Anything appearing in a dotted box is optional. A wavy line is used to represent a sequence of one or more similar items, perhaps separated by some kind of symbol. Special characters such as semicolons and parentheses stand for themselves.

The descriptions of parts of Ada programs will reflect the formatting conventions of the language's designers. When it is recommended that a statement be split over several lines, the *description* of that statement will be split accordingly. If it is recommended that some of these lines be indented farther than others, the description of the statement will be indented accordingly.

2.3 AN OVERVIEW OF THE ADA LANGUAGE

2.3.1 Compilation Units

Independently developed parts of Ada programs can be used as building blocks. The two most important kinds of building blocks are *subprograms* and *packages*. Subprograms in the Ada language are similar to those in FORTRAN, PL/I, and Pascal. Packages are collections of related subprograms and other entities. The subprograms and other entities are *provided* by the package for use by other building blocks in a program.

Because the Ada language was designed for very large programs, the building blocks can be compiled separately. Furthermore, the individual building blocks can be broken into smaller, separately compilable pieces. The pieces of a program that can be compiled separately are called *compilation units*.

FORTRAN and PL/I, as well as some versions of Pascal, allow subprograms to be compiled separately, but their compilers have no way of checking that a subprogram defined in one compilation unit is used properly in other compilation units. For example, a subprogram may be called from a different compilation unit using the wrong number of parameters or parameters of the wrong type. An Ada compiler is required to enforce consistency between the way subprograms and other entities are defined in one compilation unit and the way they are used in another.

The compiler enforces consistency by referring to a *library* of information about the compilation units of a program. Compilers for most languages read a source program and produce an object program (i.e., a machine-language translation of the source program). They may also produce other information, such as source listings and cross-reference listings. In addition to producing an object program, an Ada compiler adds information about the unit it just compiled to the library, as shown in Figure 2.1. When a new compilation unit uses entities defined in older, separately compiled units, the new unit must begin with a *context clause* naming the older units. When the compiler sees a context clause at the start of a compilation, it retrieves information about the named compilation units from the library. It uses this information to check that entities defined in earlier compilation units are used consistently in the current compilation unit. Thus consistency between the definition and use of an entity is enforced as strictly across two separate compilations as within a single compilation.

The simple Ada program given earlier is a compilation unit. It begins with the context clause `WITH Basic_IO;`, indicating that it will make use of entities provided by the separately compiled package `Basic_IO`. In this case, the entities are subprograms named `Basic_IO.Put`, `Basic_IO.Get`, and `Basic_IO.New_Line`. The library contains enough information about these subprograms to make sure that all the subprogram calls appearing in the program `Print_Totals` are legal. We shall consider the package `Basic_IO` in greater detail shortly.

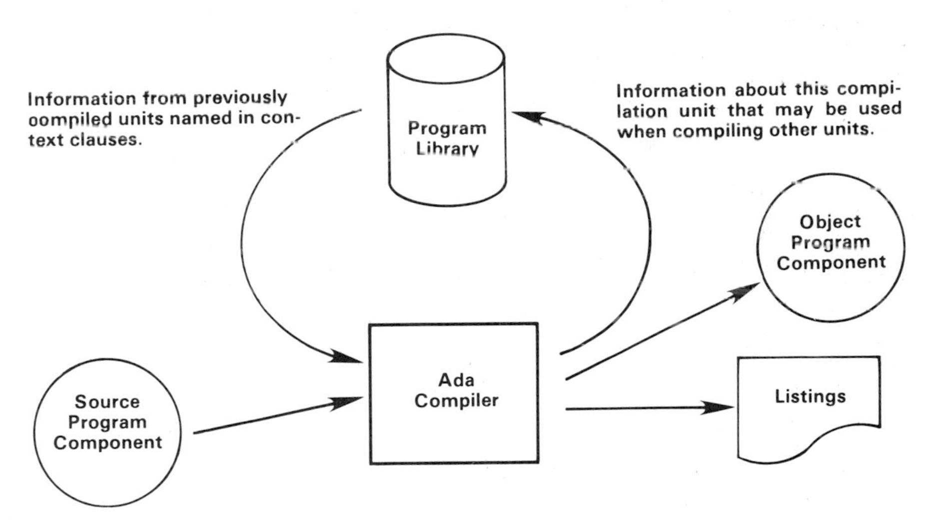

Figure 2.1 Like compilers for other languages, an Ada compiler reads source code and produces object code and listings. However, an Ada compiler also places information about the unit being compiled in a *program library*. Another compilation unit, naming this one in a context clause, may be compiled later. Then the information will be retrieved from the program library so that the compiler can check that the two compilation units are consistent.

2.3.2 Subprograms and Main Programs

Like FORTRAN, PL/I, and Pascal, the Ada language provides two kinds of subprograms, called *procedures* and *functions.* (In FORTRAN, procedures are known as subroutines.) Executing a *procedure call statement* causes a procedure subprogram to be executed. The procedure call statement may specify *parameters,* which are values to be used or variables to be changed by the subprogram. Evaluating an expression containing a *function call* causes a function subprogram to be executed. The function call may contain parameters specifying values to be used by the subprogram. The function subprogram completes by *returning* some value which it computed. The returned value is then used as the value of the function call in the expression containing the function call.

An Ada program is simply a subprogram. The only difference between a main program and any other subprogram is that the main program need not be invoked by a procedure statement or the evaluation of an expression. Rather, the main program is "called" by the operating system when you request that the program be run. The rules of the Ada langage do not specify how a particular subprogram is prepared by an operating system to be run as a main program, or what it means for a main program to have parameters or to return a result. These rules will vary from one compiler and operating system to another. In some cases, parameters to a main program may correspond to files or character strings given in the command language or job control language commands that invoke the program. A function result may correspond to a status code that can be set by any program and then tested by the command or job control language to determine whether any other programs should be run. In any event, every Ada compiler is required to allow a procedure subprogram with no parameters—like the procedure `Print_Totals` presented earlier—as a main program. This is the only kind of main program that will be considered in this book.

A typical Ada main program consists of a context clause followed by the *body* of a subprogram. A typical *procedure body* has the following form:

```
PROCEDURE identifier [ ( formal parameter list ) ] IS
   declarative part
BEGIN
   sequence of statements
END identifier ;
```

The form of a typical *function body* is similar, except for the first line:

```
FUNCTION identifier [ ( formal parameter list ) ] RETURN result type IS
   declarative part
BEGIN
   sequence of statements
END identifier ;
```

(There are variations on these forms that we shall describe later.) The identifier appearing in the first line is the name of the subprogram. The formal parameter list specifies the type of each parameter and the name by which it will be known inside the subprogram. The formal parameter list and surrounding parentheses are omitted when the subprogram has no parameters. The identifier in the last line must be the same as the identifier in the first line.

The *declarative part* is a sequence of zero or more declarations defining names that will be used in the subprogram. In the case of the subprogram `Print_Totals`, all the declarations are *variable declarations,* specifying that `Number_Of_Positives`, `Number_Of_Negatives`, `Number_of_Zeroes`, `Sum_Of_Positives`, `Sum_Of_Negatives`, `Number_Of_Items`, and `Item` are all variables of type `Integer`. A variable declaration may specify an initial value for the variable. The `:= 0` in the first two declarations specifies that `Number_Of_Positives`, `Number_Of_Negatives`, `Number_Of_Zeroes`, `Sum_Of_Positives`, and `Sum_Of_Negatives` are all *initialized* to zero. With a few specific exceptions, all the names used in a subprogram and not declared elsewhere must be declared in the subprogram. (One exception is the name `i`, which is implicitly declared by its appearance following the word `FOR`.)

Section 2.3.3 sketches some of the statements most frequently found in the sequence of statements.

2.3.3 Statements

The kind of statement occurring most frequently in the program `Print_Totals` is the *procedure call statement.* Its form is simply

procedure name (*list of parameters*) ;

(A list of parameters always contains at least one parameter. When a procedure is called without parameters, the list and the surrounding parentheses are omitted. This is the case in calls on the procedure `Basic_IO.New_Line`.) Each of the procedure call statements in `Print_Totals` has a procedure name consisting of two identifiers separated by a period. The meaning of a name of this form will be explained later. The first statement of `Print_Totals` calls the procedure `Basic_IO.Put` with one parameter—the string literal

```
"How many items?"
```

The second statement of `Print_Totals` calls the procedure `Basic_IO.New_Line` with no parameters. The third statement calls `Basic_IO.Get` with one parameter—the variable `Number_Of_Items`.

There are no input or output statements in the Ada language. All input and output is done by calling subprograms. The language provides predefined packages of input, output, and file management subprograms. However, you must use some very advanced features of the language simply to make these subprograms available for use in your program. In order to avoid explaining these features too early, this book uses its own input/output subprograms in the early chapters. These subprograms are defined in the separately compiled package `Basic_IO` and can be used in any other compilation unit by including `WITH Basic_IO;` in the context clause.

The package `Basic_IO`, in turn, defines its subprograms in terms of the standard Ada subprograms, using these advanced features. The text of the program unit `Basic_IO` is provided in the Appendix. You should compile a copy of `Basic_IO` so that you can use it in your own programs and try out the examples in the book. If you are using this book as the textbook in a course, your instructor may already have done this for you.

The subprograms defined in `Basic_IO` are restricted versions of the standard Ada input/output subprograms. The subprogram `Print_Totals` uses subprograms named `Basic_IO.Put`, `Basic_IO.New_Line`, and `Basic_IO.Get`. `Basic_IO.Put` with a string as a parameter writes that string starting in the next available space of the current line of the standard output file. (The standard output file is typically a terminal display or a printer.) `Basic_IO.Put` with an integer as a parameter writes that integer starting in the next available space of the current line of the standard output file. `Basic_IO.New_Line` skips to the next line of the standard output file. `Basic_IO.Get` with an integer variable as a parameter finds the next number in the standard input file and places its value in that integer variable. (The standard input file is typically a terminal keyboard or a card reader.)

The other statement used frequently in `Print_Totals` is the assignment statement, which all FORTRAN, PL/I, and Pascal programmers will find familiar. Its form is

```
variable := expression ;
```

The `:=` can be read aloud as "gets the value of." The effect of the assignment statement is to evaluate the expression to the right of the `:=` and place its value in the variable on the left (replacing any value previously held in that variable).

`Print_Totals` also contains an `IF` statement. The general form of an `IF` statement is:

```
IF condition THEN
     sequence of statements
.........................
: ELSIF condition THEN   :
:      sequence of statements :
:      ~~~               :
: ELSIF condition THEN   :
:      sequence of statements :
.........................

.........................
: ELSE                   :
:      sequence of statements :
.........................

END IF ;
```

Each condition is an expression whose value is either `True` or `False`. The `IF` statement causes at most one of the sequences of statements inside it to be executed, depending on which, if any, of the conditions are true.

A similar statement, not used in `Print_Totals`, is the `CASE` statement. An example is

```
CASE Month_Number IS
   WHEN 4 | 6 | 9 | 11 =>
      Days := 30;
   WHEN 2 =>
      Basic_IO.Put ("What year is it?");
      Basic_IO.New_Line;
      Basic_IO.Get (Year);
      IF Year MOD 4 = 0 THEN -- leap year
         Days := 29;
      ELSE -- ordinary year
         Days := 28;
      END IF;
   WHEN OTHERS =>
      Days := 31;
END CASE;
```

This `CASE` statement executes one of three sequences of statements, depending on the value of `Month_Number`. The first sequence is executed when `Month_Number` has the value 4, 6, 9, or 11, the second when `Month_Number` has the value 2, and the third when `Month_Number` has any other value.

There are three kinds of loop statements in the Ada language. The one in `Print_Totals` is a `FOR` loop, analogous to the **for** loop of Pascal and the `DO` loop of FORTRAN and PL/I. The *loop parameter* `i`—which only exists within the `LOOP` statement—takes on every value in the range `1` to `Number_Of_Items` in turn, and the sequence of statements between `LOOP` and `END LOOP` is executed once for each of these values. Another kind of loop (also found in PL/I and Pascal) is the `WHILE` loop. In the Ada programming language, the general form of a `WHILE` loop is

```
WHILE condition LOOP
   sequence of statements
END LOOP ;
```

The sequence of statements is executed repeatedly as long as the condition remains true at the beginning of the repetition. Both a `FOR` loop and a `WHILE` loop can be executed zero times. The third kind of loop is a *basic loop*. Its form is

```
LOOP
   sequence of statements
END LOOP ;
```

It calls for the sequence of statements to be repeated indefinitely. The sequence of statements itself may contain a statement that breaks out of the loop. For example, the statement

```
EXIT WHEN condition ;
```

—occurring as part of the sequence of statements of a loop—causes the loop to terminate if the condition is true and to continue if it is false.

A statement breaking out of the loop is not required. This may seem strange. Recall, however, that the Ada language was designed primarily for "embedded" applications. In programs meant to control some kind of device, an infinite loop often makes more sense than a terminating loop!

FORTRAN, PL/I, and Pascal all have `GOTO` statements that cause control to be transferred to some other labeled statement. During the late 1960s and early 1970s, it was acknowledged that unrestrained use of `GOTO` statements makes programs hard to understand. A controversy ensued about whether `GOTO` statements are *ever* appropriate, and if so, whether more restricted statements could be designed to cover such cases. The Ada language's `IF` statement, `CASE` statement, `FOR`, `WHILE`, and basic loop statements, and `EXIT` statement—as well as a special facility we shall examine later for handling exceptional conditions—make `GOTO` statements unnecessary virtually everywhere they are used in other programming languages. However, the Ada language provides a `GOTO` statement to cover the extremely rare situations in which it remains the most appropriate feature. Its form is

```
GOTO identifier ;
```

where the identifier corresponds to a very noticeable label of the form

```
<< identifier >>
```

occurring in front of some statement.

2.3.4 A Closer Look at Subprograms

The length of the program `Print_Totals` is primarily due to the large number of calls on input and output procedures. A separate procedure call is required for each item read or printed and each passage to a new line. The program can be made more succinct by writing more powerful subprograms that perform a combination of input and output operations. The version below contains two procedure subprograms, named `Prompt_For_Input` and `Write_Labeled_Number`. The call

```
Prompt_For_Input (Prompt, x);
```

where `Prompt` is a `String` value and `x` is an `Integer` variable, prints `Prompt`, goes to a new line, reads an integer, and places that integer in `x`. The call

```
Write_Labeled_Number (Explanation, x);
```

where `Explanation` is a string and `x` is an `Integer` value, writes `Explanation` and `x` on the same line and then goes to a new line.

```
------------------------------------------------------------
-- Program to read a sequence of numbers and report:      --
--    - the number of positive items in the sequence      --
--    - the number of negative items in the sequence      --
--    - the number of zeroes in the sequence              --
--    - the sum of the positive items                     --
--    - the sum of the negative items                     --
--                                                        --
-- The user enters the length of the sequence followed    --
--    by the numbers making up the sequence.              --
------------------------------------------------------------

WITH Basic_IO;
PROCEDURE Print_Totals_Version_2 IS

   Number_Of_Positives,
      Number_Of_Negatives,
      Number_Of_Zeroes                  : Integer := 0;
   Sum_Of_Positives, Sum_Of_Negatives : Integer := 0;
   Number_Of_Items                      : Integer;
   Item                                 : Integer;

   PROCEDURE Prompt_For_Input
      (Message : IN String; Value : OUT Integer) IS
   BEGIN
      Basic_IO.Put (Message);
      Basic_IO.New_Line;
      Basic_IO.Get (Value);
   END Prompt_For_Input;

   PROCEDURE Write_Labeled_Number
      (Message : IN String; Value : IN Integer) IS
   BEGIN
      Basic_IO.Put (Message);
      Basic_IO.Put (Value);
      Basic_IO.New_Line;
   END Write_Labeled_Number;

BEGIN

   Prompt_For_Input ("How many items?", Number_of_Items);

   FOR i IN 1 .. Number_Of_Items LOOP
      Prompt_For_Input ("Enter item: ", Item);
      IF Item > 0 THEN
         Number_Of_Positives := Number_Of_Positives + 1;
         Sum_Of_Positives := Sum_Of_Positives + Item;
      ELSIF Item < 0 THEN
         Number_Of_Negatives := Number_Of_Negatives + 1;
         Sum_Of Negatives := Sum_Of_Negatives + Item;
      ELSE -- Item = 0
         Number_Of_Zeroes := Number_Of_Zeroes + 1;
      END IF;
   END LOOP;
```

```
      Write_Labeled_Number
         ("Number of positive items: ", Number_Of_Positives);
      Write_Labeled_Number
         ("Number of negative items: ", Number_Of_Negatives);
      Write_Labeled_Number
         ("Number of zeroes: ", Number_Of_Zeroes);
      Write_Labeled_Number
         ("Sum of positive items: ", Sum_Of_Positives);
      Write_Labeled_Number
         ("Sum of negative items: ", Sum_Of_Negatives);
   END Print_Totals_Version_2;
```

The declarative part of the `Print_Totals_Version_2` procedure body now consists of four variable declarations followed by two other procedure bodies. The declarative parts of both inner procedure bodies are empty—that is, they contain no declarations—so the word `IS` is followed immediately by `BEGIN` in both cases.

The identifier `Message` in the first line of `Prompt_For_Input` indicates that the first parameter will be known by the name `Message` throughout the procedure body. The *parameter mode* `IN` specifies that the parameter will be used to transmit information from the calling program in to the subprogram. The identifier `String` indicates the type of the parameter. Similarly, the second parameter, known by the name `Value`, is used to transmit information from the subprogram back out to the calling program (as indicated by the parameter mode `OUT`), and its type is `Integer`. In addition to the parameter modes `IN` and `OUT`, there is a parameter mode `IN OUT`, indicating that a procedure may make use of the original value of the parameter and then change that value. A simple example of a program with `IN OUT` parameters is one that exchanges the values of its two parameters:

```
PROCEDURE Exchange
   (First : IN OUT Integer; Second : IN OUT Integer) IS
   Original_Value_Of_First : Integer;
BEGIN
   Original_Value_Of_First := First;
   First := Second;
   Second := Original_Value_Of_First;
END Exchange;
```

(In FORTRAN and PL/I, only the names of parameters are given in the subprogram heading, not their types; parameters must also appear in variable declarations in order to specify their types. In the Ada language, all information about a parameter is given in the subprogram heading, and there is no separate variable declaration.)

The types of the variables and expressions appearing in a subprogram call must match the types specified in the heading of the subprogram body. However, it is possible to declare more than one subprogram with the same name, provided they do not have the same parameter and result types. This is called *overloading* the subprogram name. When an overloaded subprogram name appears in a subprogram call, an Ada compiler examines the types of the parameters—and, in the case of a function call, the types of result that are legal at the place of the function call—to determine which subprogram is to be called. The compilation unit `Basic_IO` actually has two different procedures named `Basic_IO.Put`. The first is used for writing `String` values and the second for writing `Integer` values. In `Print_Totals_Version_2`, the top statement of `Write_Labeled_Number` calls a subprogram named `Basic_IO.Put` using a `String` value. Thus it calls the first subprogram named `Basic_IO.Put`. The middle statement of `Write_Labeled_Number` calls a subprogram named `Basic_IO.Put` using an `Integer` value. Thus it calls the second subprogram named `Basic_IO.Put`. Because these two subprograms behave similarly, the user of the `Basic_IO.Put` procedures can imagine them as one procedure that can be called either with an `Integer` parameter or a `String` parameter. However, a writer of Ada subprograms must realize that this is only an illusion. In fact, there are separate subprograms with the same name, each of which can only be called with a parameter of a particular type.

2.3.5 Defining New Types

A variable declaration specifies the *type* to which the variable belongs. Like FORTRAN, PL/I, and Pascal, the Ada language provides several types, such as `Integer` and `String`. However, unlike FORTRAN and PL/I, the Ada language allows programmers to define new types. A programmer can create a type consisting of numbers that lie in a specified range and are represented with a specified minimum accuracy. He can also create a type consisting of abstractly named values, such as a type `Day_Type` consisting of the seven values `Sunday`, `Monday`, `Tuesday`, `Wednesday`, `Thursday`, `Friday`, `Saturday` or a type `State_Type` consisting of the fifty values `Alabama`, `Alaska`, `Arizona`, ..., `Wisconsin`, `Wyoming`. A type can consist of values providing indirect access to objects in some other specified type. Finally, types can be defined as combinations of values in other types. An *array* is a combination of values all belonging to the same type, with each value in the combination identified by *index values* computed when a program runs. (Index values are called subscripts in FORTRAN and PL/I.) A *record* is a combination of values possibly belonging to different types, with each value identified by a fixed *component name*. (Records are similar to PL/I structures.) Types are defined by *type declarations,* which appear in declarative parts along with variable declarations. Programmer-defined types will be explained more completely in Chapter 3.

Here is an example of a program with type declarations. The program reads in ten integers and prints them out in reverse order, one per line.

```
----------------------------------------------------------------
-- Program to read in ten integers and print them            --
-- out in reverse order.                                     --
-- The program uses a last-in/first-out stack.               --
----------------------------------------------------------------

WITH Basic_IO;
PROCEDURE Reverse_Integers IS

   TYPE Integer_List_Type IS ARRAY (1 .. 10) OF Integer;
   TYPE Stack_Type IS
      RECORD
         Top      : Integer RANGE 0 .. 10 := 0;
         Elements : Integer_List_Type;
      END RECORD;

   Stack : Stack_Type;
   x     : Integer;

   PROCEDURE Push
      (Item : IN Integer; Stack_Object : IN OUT Stack_Type) IS
   BEGIN
      Stack_Object.Top := Stack_Object.Top + 1;
      Stack_Object.Elements (Stack_Object.Top) := Item;
   END Push;

   PROCEDURE Pop
      (Item : OUT Integer; Stack_Object : IN OUT Stack_Type) IS
   BEGIN
      Item := Stack_Object.Elements (Stack_Object.Top);
      Stack_Object.Top := Stack_Object.Top - 1;
   END Pop;
BEGIN

   FOR i IN 1 .. 10 LOOP
      Basic_IO.Get (x);
      Push (x, Stack);
   END LOOP;

   FOR i IN 1 .. 10 LOOP
      Pop (x, Stack);
      Basic_IO.Put (x);
      Basic_IO.New_Line;
   END LOOP;

END Reverse_Integers;
```

The first type declaration declares `Integer_List_Type` to be the name of a type consisting of arrays of ten integers. The second type declaration declares `Stack_Type` to be a type consisting of records with two components: a component of type `Integer` named `Top` and a component of type `Integer_List_Type` named `Elements`. (The declaration also specifies that the `Top` component of a `Stack_Type` object normally starts out with the value zero.) `Integer_List_Type` and Stack_Type are not variables, but types, like Integer. Stack is a variable whose type is Stack_Type.

The second parameter of Push, named Stack_Object, is of type Stack_Type. Thus it has components named Top (of type Integer) and Elements (of type Integer_List_Type). These are denoted by the names Stack_Object.Top and Stack_Object.Elements, respectively. If A is a variable of type Integer_List_Type, then A is an array and A (3) is the third component of A. Thus if Stack_Object.Top 3, then

```
Stack_Object.Elements (Stack_Object.Top)
```

refers to the third element of the array Stack_Object.Elements. A call on Push stores the value of an integer on a stack. A call on Pop retrieves and removes the most recently stored integer remaining on a stack. The Top component of a Stack_Type object indicates how many values are stored in the stack, and the Elements component contains those values in the order in which they were stored.

Now let us consider another example of a programmer-defined type. The following type declaration defines a type named Fraction_Type. A value of type Fraction_Type consists of two components of type Integer, named Numerator and Denominator.

```
TYPE Fraction_Type IS
   RECORD
      Numerator   : Integer;
      Denominator : Integer;
   END RECORD;
```

Values in this type are exact representations of rational numbers. For instance, the number 9/16 could be represented by a Fraction_Type value with a Numerator component of 9 and a Denominator component of 16. The following function subprogram takes two parameters of type Fraction_Type and returns a Fraction_Type value equal to the sum of the parameters. It is based on the fact that $n1/d1+n2/d2=(n1\cdot d2+n2\cdot d1)/(d1\cdot d2)$.

```
FUNCTION Add_Fractions
   (A : Fraction_Type; B : Fraction_Type)
   RETURN Fraction_Type IS

   Result : Fraction_Type;

BEGIN

   Result.Numerator :=
      A.Numerator * B.Denominator +
      B.Numerator * A.Denominator;

   Result.Denominator := A.Denominator * B.Denominator;

   RETURN Result;

END Add_Fractions;
```

(The list of formal parameters for Add_Fractions does not specify parameter modes. When parameter modes are omitted, the mode IN is assumed by default. Unlike procedures, functions may *only* have parameters of mode IN.)

2.3.6 Extending the Meanings of Operators

The arithmetic operator + can be thought of as a function taking two parameters and returning their sum. The only difference is that the call on the function is written as x+y rather than, say, Sum (x,y). Similarly, the operator * can be thought of as a function taking two parameters and returning their product, but with calls written as x*y rather than, say, Product (x,y). Thus an expression such as A*B+C*D can be viewed as a combination of function calls:

```
Sum ( Product (A, B), Product (C, D) )
```

Of course the operators + and * are a much more succinct and familiar notation. The Ada language allows operators to be used for programmer-defined functions as well. The programmer simply uses a string (like "+") rather than an identifier (like Add_Fractions) to name the function. The string specifies the operator that is to denote a call on the function. For example, the function Add_Fractions could be rewritten with the name "+":

```
FUNCTION "+"
   (A : Fraction_Type; B : Fraction_Type)
   RETURN Fraction_Type IS
   Result : Fraction_Type;
BEGIN
   Result.Numerator :=
      A.Numerator * B.Denominator +
      B.Numerator * A.Denominator;
   Result.Denominator := A.Denominator * B.Denominator;
   RETURN Result;
END "+";
```

This has the effect of overloading the operator +. (Just as there were multiple versions of the procedures Basic_IO.Put and Basic_IO.Get in Section 2.3.4, there are now multiple versions of the operator +.) If F1 and F2 have been declared to be of type Fraction_Type, the expression F1+F2 denotes the result of a call on the function above with parameters F1 and F2. If I1 and I2 have been declared to be of type Integer, I1+I2 continues to denote the ordinary integer sum of I1 and I2. As with any overloaded subprogram name, an Ada compiler examines the types of the expressions to which + is applied and the expected type of the result in order to determine which meaning of + is intended. Only the operators that have meanings in the Ada language can be used as function names in this way; it is not possible to create new operator symbols.

2.3.7 Handling Unexpected Situations

Programming is an error-prone process. Large, complex programs often contain errors even after they have been thoroughly tested. Even a program that has been mechanically proven correct may malfunction if it is given inputs it is not designed to handle. In programs controlling a mechanical device, errors can result from a mechanical failure of the device. The Ada language was designed for programs whose reliability is essential. Such programs must be capable of responding in a sensible way to unexpected situations. Depending on the application, this sensible response may entail terminating in a well-defined state, issuing a warning and continuing normal execution, retrying some computation using a different algorithm, or continuing execution in a degraded mode, for example.

In the Ada language, an unexpected situation is called an *exception*. The language defines several exceptions, corresponding to situations like an attempt to divide by zero, an attempt to assign an out-of-range value to a variable, or a request to use more storage when none is available. The response to an exception is specified by a *handler* for that exception. (Exceptions are similar to PL/I "conditions," and handlers are similar in some ways to PL/I "ON-units.") Handlers can be specified at the end of a procedure or function body, following the word EXCEPTION. A procedure body may take the following form:

```
PROCEDURE identifier [ (formal parameter list) ] IS

   declarative part
BEGIN
   sequence of statements
[ EXCEPTION
   list of handlers ]
END identifier ;
```

A function body may take the following form:

```
FUNCTION designator [ (formal parameter list) ] RETURN result type IS

   declarative part
BEGIN
   sequence of statements
[ EXCEPTION
   list of handlers ]
END designator ;
```

(A designator is either an identifier or a string consisting of an operator symbol). The form of a list of handlers is as follows:

```
WHEN exception name | ~~~ | exception name =>
     sequence of statements
     ~~~
WHEN exception name | ~~~ | exception name =>
     sequence of statements
```

```
WHEN OTHERS =>
     sequence of statements
```

However, at least one of these two optional parts must be present whenever the word **EXCEPTION** appears.

If an exception occurs during the execution of a sequence of statements following the **BEGIN**, execution of that sequence of statements is abandoned. If the exception is named in one of the handlers, the sequence of statements in that handler is executed, completing the subprogram call. The word **OTHERS** acts like an exception list consisting of all the exceptions not listed earlier. If the exception name does not occur in any list and there is no **WHEN OTHERS** handler, the exception is *propagated* to the point at which the subprogram was invoked. This means that the procedure call statement or the expression containing the function call is treated as if it caused the exception directly. This may cause a handler in the calling program to be executed, or it may cause the calling subprogram to propagate the exception yet another level, to *its* caller. When an unhandled exception occurs in (or has been propagated to) the main program, execution terminates.

Programmers can define their own exceptions by declarations of the form

```
identifier , ~~~ , identifier : EXCEPTION ;
```

A **RAISE** statement of the form

```
RAISE exception name ;
```

causes the named exception to occur. Given the type `Fraction_Type` declared earlier, we can declare an exception

```
Zero_Denominator : EXCEPTION ;
```

and then write a subprogram to invert a fraction:

```
FUNCTION Inverse
   (Fraction : Fraction_Type) RETURN Fraction_Type IS
   Result : Fraction_Type;
```

```
BEGIN
   IF Fraction.Numerator = 0 THEN
      RAISE Zero_Denominator;
   ELSE
      Result.Numerator := Fraction.Denominator;
      Result.Denominator := Fraction.Numerator;
      RETURN Result;
   END IF;
END Inverse;
```

Because `Inverse` contains no handler for `Zero_Denominator`, it always propagates that exception when `Fraction.Numerator = 0`. Just as the expression `x/y` either evaluates to the quotient of `x` and `y` or causes an exception (when `y` is zero), so the expression `Inverse (z)` either evaluates to the inverse of `z` or raises an exception.

2.3.8 Packages

One of the goals of the Ada language is to make it possible to write huge programs. Such programs cannot be understood all at once. Rather, the program must be broken into smaller pieces, or *modules*. Each module acts as a "black box," possibly very complicated on the inside, but simple on the outside. When attempting to understand part of a program that uses a module, one only must consider the abstract external view of the module, not all its internal workings. Another major goal of the language is to make it possible to write general *software components* that can be used in many different programs. Such components must have well-defined behavior that can be explained abstractly, without describing how the components are implemented. Both of these goals—division of a large program into manageable modules and provision of reusable software components—are met in the Ada language by *packages*.

A package is a collection of related entities that can be used by other parts of the program. These entities may include, among other things, variables, subprograms, type declarations, and exception declarations. For example, a fractional numbers package could include the type declaration for `Fraction_Type`; several subprograms, such as `"+"` and `Inverse` for manipulating `Fraction_Type` variables; and exceptions, such as `Zero_Denominator`, that can be raised by those subprograms. In a very large program, that portion of the program dealing with the manipulation of fractions could all be confined to one package. This package could be understood in isolation from the rest of the program. The rest of the program could be understood by viewing operations on fractions in their abstract, mathematical sense rather than as manipulations of records.

In fact, one can develop and market a separately compiled general fractional numbers package that could be used by any Ada programmer needing such a component to write a program. In this sense, an Ada package is very much like an "accounting package," a "word processing package," or a "statistics package." It is an independently developed, complete, and general collection of software that can be incorporated in many different systems to fulfill particular needs.

The Ada language draws a sharp distinction between the external appearance of a package and its internal workings. The external appearance of a package, or the package *interface*, includes the types and exceptions provided by the package; the variables provided by the package; and the names, parameter types, and result types of the subprograms provided by the package. The internal workings of the package, or the package *implementation*, may include the bodies of the subprograms provided by the package; internal subprograms never called directly from outside the package but used to implement the other subprograms; variables and exceptions referenced only within the the package body; and types used only within the package body. Only the package interface is relevant to the user of the package.

When a large program is divided into packages, it can be understood in a series of steps. The first step is to determine the purpose of each entity in the package interface (for instance, that a variable of type `Fraction_Type` represents the exact value of a fraction and that the function `Inverse` returns the reciprocal of a fraction). The second step is to study the package implementation to understand how the implementation fulfills these purposes. Once you are convinced that the implementation fulfills the requirements of the interface, you can forget about the implementation and proceed to the third step. The third step is to study the parts of the program that use the package. In doing so, you only need to consider the intended purpose of each entity of the package interface.

The description of a package in the Ada language consists of a *package specification* describing the interface and, in most cases, a *package body* describing the implementation. In its simplest form, a package specification consists of a sequence of declarations:

```
PACKAGE identifier IS
   declaration
      ~~~
   declaration
END identifier ;
```

The form of a package body is similar to the form of a subprogram body, except for the heading and the fact that the sequence of statements is optional:

```
PACKAGE BODY identifier IS

      declarative part
 ..............................
 : BEGIN                      :
 :     sequence of statements :
 : ...................        :
 : : EXCEPTION       :        :
 : :   list of handlers :     :
 : ...................        :
 ..............................
END identifier ;
```

The term "package" is sometimes used to refer to the package specification and package body collectively.

An entity E declared in the *specification* of a package P can be referred to outside of the package by the *expanded name* P.E and within the package by the *simple name* E. An entity declared only in the declarative part of the package *body* can only be referred to within the package body. A subprogram to be called from outside of the package is declared in the package specification by a *subprogram declaration* of one of the following forms:

```
PROCEDURE identifier  [ (formal parameter list) ]  ;

FUNCTION designator   [ (formal parameter list) ]  RETURN result type ;
```

In addition, the subprogram body must appear within the declarative part of the package body.

The program Reverse_Integers, presented earlier, can be partitioned into smaller pieces by placing parts of the program concerned with the type Stack_Type in a separate package. The package specification might read as follows:

```
PACKAGE Stack_Package IS
   TYPE Integer_List_Type IS ARRAY (1 .. 10) OF Integer;
   TYPE Stack_Type IS
      RECORD
         Top      : Integer RANGE 0 .. 10 := 0;
         Elements : Integer_List_Type;
      END RECORD;
   PROCEDURE Push
      (Item : IN Integer; Stack : IN OUT Stack_Type);
   PROCEDURE Pop
      (Item : OUT Integer; Stack : IN OUT Stack_Type);
END Stack_Package;
```

Thus the package Stack_Package provides two types that can be referred to outside the package as Stack_Package.Integer_List_Type and Stack_Package.Stack_Type, as well as two procedures that can be referred to outside the package as Stack_Package.Push and Stack_Package.Pop. The package body describes the implementation of these procedures:

```
PACKAGE BODY Stack_Package IS
   PROCEDURE Push
      (Item : IN Integer; Stack : IN OUT Stack_Type) IS
   BEGIN
      Stack.Top := Stack.Top + 1;
      Stack.Elements (Stack.Top) := Item;
   END Push;
```

```
      PROCEDURE Pop
         (Item : OUT Integer; Stack : IN OUT Stack_Type) IS
      BEGIN
         Item := Stack.Elements (Stack.Top);
         Stack.Top := Stack.Top - 1;
      END Pop;

   END Stack_Package;
```

A package specification and a package body may each be compiled separately. Compilation of the package specification places information about the package's interface into the program library. Other compilation units naming the package in a context specification may then refer to the entities declared in the package specification by their expanded names. The specification of the separately compiled package `Basic_IO` includes declarations for procedures named `Put`, `Get`, and `New_Line`. In a compilation unit with the context specification

```
   WITH Basic_IO;
```

these procedures may be referred to by the expanded names `Basic_IO.Put`, `Basic_IO.Get`, and `Basic_IO.New_Line`.

If the package `Stack_Package` is separately compiled, the program `Reverse_Integers` can be rewritten as follows:

```
   ---------------------------------------------------------
   -- Program to read in ten integers and print them      --
   -- out in reverse order.                               --
   -- The program uses a last-in/first-out stack.         --
   ---------------------------------------------------------

   WITH Basic_IO, Stack_Package;
   PROCEDURE Reverse_Integers_Version_2 IS
      Stack : Stack_Package.Stack_Type;
      x     : Integer;
   BEGIN
      FOR i IN 1 .. 10 LOOP
         Basic_IO.Get (x);
         Stack_Package.Push (x, Stack);
      END LOOP;
      FOR i IN 1 .. 10 LOOP
         Stack_Package.Pop (x, Stack);
         Basic_IO.Put (x);
         Basic_IO.New_Line;
      END LOOP;
   END Reverse_Integers_Version_2;
```

Reverse_Integers_Version_2 uses stacks as if they were a "built-in" feature of the Ada language, like integers. The procedure itself does not describe how stacks are represented and how the operations on stacks are implemented, but uses stacks abstractly.

An entity declared in either the specification or body of a separately compiled package exists throughout the execution of the program. A variable declared in the package retains its values between calls on the package's subprograms. The sequence of statements in the body of a separately compiled package is executed once, before execution of the main program begins. These statements typically compute the initial values of the variables declared in the package specification and the declarative part of the package body.

Because the program Reverse_Integers uses only one stack, it is not really necessary for the package dealing with stacks to provide a *type* for stacks. Instead, we might use the following package, which provides operations for manipulating a single stack. Calls on Push and Pop specify only the item to be pushed or popped, not the stack. All calls on Push and Pop implicitly refer to the same stack. The stack itself is hidden within the package body:

```
PACKAGE Stack_Object IS
   PROCEDURE Push (Item : IN Integer);
   PROCEDURE Pop (Item : OUT Integer);
END Stack_Object;

PACKAGE BODY Stack_Object IS
   TYPE Integer_List_Type IS ARRAY (1 .. 10) OF Integer;
   Stack_Elements : Integer_List_Type;
   Stack_Index    : Integer RANGE 0 .. 10;
   PROCEDURE Push (Item : IN Integer) IS
   BEGIN
      Stack_Index := Stack_Index + 1;
      Stack_Elements (Stack_Index) := Item;
   END Push;
   PROCEDURE Pop (Item : OUT Integer) IS
   BEGIN
      Item := Stack_Elements (Stack_Index);
      Stack_Index := Stack_Index - 1;
   END Pop;
BEGIN
   -- Package initialization:
   Stack_Index := 0;
END Stack_Object;
```

The following program uses this package:

```
--------------------------------------------------------
-- Program to read in ten integers and print them     --
-- out in reverse order.                               --
-- The program uses a last-in/first-out stack.         --
--------------------------------------------------------

WITH Basic_IO, Stack_Object;
PROCEDURE Reverse_Integers_Version_3 IS
   x : Integer;
BEGIN
   FOR i IN 1 .. 10 LOOP
      Basic_IO.Get (x);
      Stack_Object.Push (x);
   END LOOP;
     FOR i IN 1 .. 10 LOOP
        Stack_Object.Pop (x);
        Basic_IO.Put (x);
        Basic_IO.New_Line;
     END LOOP;
  END Reverse_Integers_Version_3;
```

The only entities in package `Stack_Object` that may be referred to outside the package are the procedures `Push` and `Pop`. The type `Integer_List_Type` and the variables `Stack_Elements` and `Stack_Index` declared in the declarative part of the package body may only be referred to within the package body. (The type `Integer_List_Type` is referred to in the declaration of the variable `Stack_Elements`. The variables are referred to in the two procedure bodies and in the package body's sequence of statements.)

The sequence of statements in the package body—in this case the single statement

```
Stack_Index := 0;
```

—is executed before the main program begins, and only at that time. The variables `Stack_Elements` and `Stack_Index` remain in existence throughout the execution of `Reverse_Integers_Version_3`. Although they cannot be referred to outside of the package, the values left in those variables at the end of a call on `Push` or `Pop` will all be found there at the beginning of the next call on `Push` or `Pop`.

2.3.9 Private Types

Suppose we really do want to use several stacks in a program. Then the original `Stack_Package` is more appropriate. However, as written, `Stack_Package` provides more than just a type named `Stack_Type` and two operations named `Push` and `Pop` for manipulating `Stack_Type` objects. It also provides a type named `Integer_List_Type`, used in the definition of type `Stack_Type`. Furthermore, it allows operations other than `Push` and `Pop` on objects of type Stack_Type. For instance, if S is declared as a variable of type Stack_Package.Stack_Type, operations like

```
S.Top := S.Top + 3;
```

and

```
S.Elements (S.Top) := S.Elements (S.Top - 1);
```

are possible. The first operation above places S in a state in which a call on Pop will place an unpredictable value in the Item parameter. In general, Push and Pop cannot be guaranteed to work sensibly on stacks that have been subjected to operations other than Push and Pop.

To give more precise control over the entities provided to the outside world, the Ada language allows a package specification to contain a *private part,* which begins with the word PRIVATE and extends to the end of the package specification:

```
PACKAGE Stack_Package_2 IS
   TYPE Stack_Type IS PRIVATE;
   PROCEDURE Push
      (Item : IN Integer; Stack : IN OUT Stack_Type);
   PROCEDURE Pop
      (Item : OUT Integer; Stack : IN OUT Stack_Type);
PRIVATE
   TYPE Integer_List_Type IS ARRAY (1 .. 10) OF Integer;
   TYPE Stack_Type IS
      RECORD
         Top      : Integer RANGE 0 .. 10 := 0;
         Elements : Integer_List_Type;
      END RECORD;
END Stack_Package_2;
```

That part of the package specification preceding the private part is called the *visible part.* Only the information contained in the visible part is provided to the outside world. The declaration

```
TYPE Stack_Type IS PRIVATE;
```

stipulates that the internal representation of a Stack_Type value is not known outside of the package. The *only* operations that may be applied to a stack outside of the package are Push, Pop, assignment of a Stack_Type value to a Stack_Type variable, and testing whether two stacks are identical. (Even these last two possibilities can be eliminated by declaring Stack_Type to be *LIMITED* PRIVATE.) A type can only be declared private in the visible part of the package specification. An ordinary declaration for that type must appear in the private part of the package specification. Any other entities that must be referred to by the ordinary declaration, but which should not be available to the outside world, may also appear in the private part. The type Integer_List_Type is such an entity.

Logically, the private part of a package specification describes aspects of the implementation of a package rather than its interface. In this sense, the private part acts more like an extension of the package body than a part of the package specification. The rules of the Ada language put the private part in the package specification rather than in the package body only because this provides greater flexibility in compiling pieces of a program separately.

When a package specification is separately compiled, information in the private part is incorporated in the program library. It is then possible—even before the corresponding package body is compiled—to compile a subprogram that declares an object belonging to one of the package's private types. The compiler consults the program library to determine how much storage such an object should occupy. If the specification had not contained a private part with an ordinary type declaration, this information would not be available.

2.3.10 Generic Program Units

Stacks have many uses in computer programs. The program Reverse_Integers uses a stack holding up to *ten integers.* Another program might use a stack holding up to *255 characters.* We could write another package almost identical to Stack_Package_2:

```
PACKAGE Character_Stack_Package IS
   TYPE Stack_Type IS PRIVATE;
   PROCEDURE Push
      (Item : IN Character; Stack : IN OUT Stack_Type);
   PROCEDURE Pop
      (Item : OUT Character; Stack : IN OUT Stack_Type);
PRIVATE
   TYPE Character_List_Type IS ARRAY (1 .. 255) OF Character;
   TYPE Stack_Type IS
      RECORD
         Top      : Integer RANGE 0 .. 255 := 0;
         Elements : Character_List_Type;
      END RECORD;
END Character_Stack_Package;
```

The only changes are the name of the package, the type of the Item parameter of Push and Pop, the definition and use of the type Character_List_Type in place of Integer_List_Type, and the use of the number 255 in place of 10. The package body would be identical to the Stack_Package body presented earlier, except for the type of the Item parameter of Push and Pop.

Rather than forcing the programmer to write a new, almost identical, version of the package for each type to be stacked and each stack size to be used, the Ada language allows the programmer to write a *generic package:*

```
GENERIC
   Stack_Size : IN Integer;
   TYPE Item_Type IS PRIVATE;
PACKAGE Generic_Stack_Package IS
   TYPE Stack_Type IS PRIVATE;
   PROCEDURE Push
      (Item : IN Item_Type; Stack : IN OUT Stack_Type);
   PROCEDURE Pop
      (Item : OUT Item_Type; Stack : IN OUT Stack_Type);
PRIVATE
   TYPE Item_List_Type IS
      ARRAY (1 .. Stack_Size) OF Item_Type;
   TYPE Stack_Type IS
      RECORD
         Top      : Integer RANGE 0 .. Stack_Size := 0;
         Elements : Item_List_Type;
      END RECORD;
END Generic_Stack_Package;

PACKAGE BODY Generic_Stack_Package IS

   PROCEDURE Push
      (Item : IN Item_Type; Stack : IN OUT Stack_Type) IS
   BEGIN
      Stack.Top := Stack.Top + 1;
      Stack.Elements (Stack.Top) := Item;
   END Push;

   PROCEDURE Pop
      (Item : OUT Item_Type; Stack : IN OUT Stack_Type) IS
   BEGIN
      Item := Stack.Elements (Stack.Top);
      Stack.Top := Stack.Top - 1;
   END Pop;

END Generic_Stack_Package;
```

The word `GENERIC` in the first line indicates that `Generic_Stack_Package` is not really a package, but a *template* for a package. The next two lines declare `Stack_Size` and `Item_Type` to be *generic formal parameters.* An *instance* of a generic package is a copy of the template with each occurrence of a given generic formal parameter replaced by a specified value, variable, type, or subprogram. An instance of a generic package is a full-fledged package. In the case of Generic_Stack_Package, the generic formal parameter Stack_Size stands for an integer value, and the generic parameter Item_Type stands for a type. An instance of a generic package is specified by a *generic package instantiation,* like these:

```
PACKAGE Boolean_Stack_Package IS
   NEW Generic_Stack_Package
      (Stack_Size => 36, Item_Type => Boolean);
PACKAGE Character_Stack_Package IS
   NEW Generic_Stack_Package
      (Stack_Size => 255, Item_Type => Character);
PACKAGE Integer_Stack_Package IS
   NEW Generic_Stack_Package
      (Stack_Size => 10, Item_Type => Integer);
```

The first instantiation declares a package named Boolean_Stack_Package for stacks holding up to 36 values of type Boolean, the second declares a package named Character_Stack_Package for stacks holding up to 255 values of type Character, and the third declares a package named Integer_Stack_Package for stacks holding up to ten values of type Integer. The effect of these instantiations is the same as if three packages had been written out in full at that point. In particular, there are procedures named Boolean_Stack_Package.Push, Character_Stack_Package.Push, and Integer_Stack_Package.Push for pushing Boolean values onto values of type Boolean_Stack_Package.Stack_Type, Character values onto values of type Character_Stack_Package.Stack_Type, and Integer values onto values of type Integer_Stack_Package.Stack_Type, respectively.

In addition to generic packages, the Ada language allows the definition of individual generic subprograms. Generic packages and generic subprograms may be separately compiled. A separately compiled generic package or subprogram may be instantiated by any compilation unit naming the generic unit in a context specification. If Generic_Stack_Package were separately compiled, the Reverse_Integers program could be written as follows:

```
---------------------------------------------------------
-- Program to read in ten integers and print them      --
-- out in reverse order.                                --
-- The program uses a last-in/first-out stack.          --
---------------------------------------------------------

WITH Basic_IO, Generic_Stack_Package;
PROCEDURE Reverse_Integers_Version_4 IS
   PACKAGE Integer_Stack_Package IS
      NEW Generic_Stack_Package
         (Stack_Size => 10, Item_Type => Integer);
   S : Integer_Stack_Package.Stack_Type;
   x : Integer;
```

```
BEGIN
   FOR i IN 1 .. 10 LOOP
      Basic_IO.Get (x);
      Integer_Stack_Package.Push (x, S);
   END LOOP;
   FOR i IN 1 .. 10 LOOP
      Integer_Stack_Package.Pop (x, S);
      Basic_IO.Put (x);
      Basic_IO.New_Line;
   END LOOP;
END Reverse_Integers_Version_4;
```

The original Stack_Package was written specifically for use in the program Reverse_Integers. It was clear that this program would not try to push more than ten elements onto a stack or pop an element off an empty stack. However, a generic package is written as a general software component that may be used in unforeseen ways. To be truly general, a generic package should provide subprograms that perform sensibly for any combination of calls. The following version of Generic_Stack_Package provides two exceptions named Empty_Stack_Error and Full_Stack_Error. When Push is called with a stack having no more room, it raises Full_Stack_Error. When Pop is called with a stack having no elements to pop, it raises Empty_Stack_Error. In all other cases, the subprograms perform their normal functions.

```
GENERIC
   Stack_Size : IN Integer;
   TYPE Item_Type IS PRIVATE;
PACKAGE Generic_Stack_Package_Version_2 IS
   TYPE Stack_Type IS PRIVATE;
   PROCEDURE Push
      (Item : IN Item_Type; Stack : IN OUT Stack_Type);
   PROCEDURE Pop
      (Item : OUT Item_Type; Stack : IN OUT Stack_Type);
   Empty_Stack_Error, Full_Stack_Error : EXCEPTION;
PRIVATE
   TYPE Item_List_Type IS
      ARRAY (1 .. Stack_Size) OF Item_Type;
   TYPE Stack_Type IS
      RECORD
         Top      : Integer RANGE 0 .. Stack_Size := 0;
         Elements : Item_List_Type;
      END RECORD;
END Generic_Stack_Package_Version_2;
```

```
PACKAGE BODY Generic_Stack_Package_Version_2 IS

   PROCEDURE Push
      (Item : IN Item_Type;Stack : IN OUT Stack_Type) IS
   BEGIN
      IF Stack.Top = Stack_Size THEN
         RAISE Full_Stack_Error;
      ELSE
         Stack.Top := Stack.Top + 1;
         Stack.Elements (Stack.Top) := Item;
      END IF;
   END Push;

   PROCEDURE Pop
      (Item : OUT Item_Type;Stack : IN OUT Stack_Type) IS
   BEGIN
      IF Stack.Top = 0 THEN
         RAISE Empty_Stack_Error;
      ELSE
         Item := Stack.Elements (Stack.Top);
         Stack.Top := Stack.Top - 1;
      END IF;
   END Pop;
END Generic_Stack_Package_Version_2;
```

2.3.11 Concurrent Computations

Typical computer programs specify steps to be carried out in sequence. An Ada program can specify operations that are to occur concurrently. An Ada *task* carries out a sequence of steps one after the other, but an Ada program may contain several tasks operating at the same time. In a program controlling some physical device, for example, different tasks might monitor different parts of the device. In a program to be run on a computer system with more than one processor, two independent parts of the computation can be performed by different tasks at the same time, allowing the computation to proceed more quickly than if one part of the computation were to start only after the other had finished. In a system with one processor, an operating system generally causes the processor to interleave the execution of the various active tasks. The processor alternately executes a few instructions from one task, then a few instructions from another, giving the *appearance* that the tasks are executing simultaneously.

Most often, tasks do not operate completely independently, but rather in cooperation with each other. This means that there must be a way for tasks to communicate. In the Ada language, tasks communicate through *entries.* One task executes an *entry call,* which looks very much like a procedure call. Another task *accepts* the entry call. For instance, a task named `Counter` might have an entry declared as follows:

```
ENTRY Increment
   (Amount : IN Integer; New_Total : OUT Integer);
```

This means that calls on the entry `Increment` can have the same form as calls on a procedure with two parameters of type `Integer`, the first of mode `IN` and the second of mode `OUT`. Another task can communicate with task `Counter` by issuing an entry call like

```
Counter.Increment (x,y);
```

The task `Counter` accepts this entry by executing an `ACCEPT` statement such as the following:

```
ACCEPT Increment
   (Amount : IN Integer; New_Total : OUT Integer) DO

   Total := Total + Amount;
   New_Total := Total;

END Increment;
```

The `ACCEPT` statement is then executed with Amount representing the value of `x` and with `y` receiving the value assigned to `New_Total`. This process is called a *rendezvous*. Once the `ACCEPT` statement is complete, the task issuing the entry call `Counter.Increment(x,y)` can proceed to the following statement.

Thus a rendezvous is much like a procedure call, with the `ACCEPT` statement behaving much like a procedure body. The crucial difference is that the `ACCEPT` statement is one of the steps executed in sequence by the task `Counter`. The completion of the entry call can only occur when the task `Counter` reaches the `ACCEPT` statement. If a task executes a call on the entry `Counter.Increment` before `Counter` has reached the `ACCEPT` statement, the task executing the entry call is forced to wait. Similarly, if `Counter` reaches the `ACCEPT` statement before an entry call has been executed, it waits for some task to call the appropriate entry. A rendezvous between two Ada tasks is similar to a rendezvous between two people: Whichever arrives at the appointed meeting place first waits for the other; once the meeting is complete, each continues about its own business independently.

In many applications, there is a need for several tasks to do the same thing simultaneously (such as to monitor the states of identical devices or to perform the same analysis of different sets of data). For this reason, the Ada language provides *task types*. Every task belongs to some task type, and all tasks belonging to the same type have identical entries and identical sequences of operations to execute. A task type declaration describes the task's entries. An example is:

```
TASK TYPE Counter_Task_Type IS

   ENTRY Increment
      (Amount : IN Integer; New_Total : OUT Integer);

END Counter_Task_Type;
```

A task type declaration must be accompanied by a *task body* describing the sequence of operations to be executed by the task. An example is:

```
TASK BODY Counter_Task_Type IS
   Total : Integer := 0;
BEGIN
   LOOP
      ACCEPT Increment
         (Amount : IN Integer; New_Total : OUT Integer) DO
         Total := Total + Amount;
         New_Total := Total;
      END Increment;
   END LOOP;
END Counter_Task_Type;
```

The form of a task body is identical to the form of a subprogram body, except for the heading. (In particular, it may contain exception handlers.) Once a task type has been defined, individual tasks belonging to that type can be declared just as ordinary variables are declared to belong to some type. The declaration

```
Counter_1, Counter_2 : Counter_Task_Type;
```

declares `Counter_1` and `Counter_2` to be two tasks each independently executing the task body above. Each task has its own copy of the variables declared in the task body (the variable `Total` in the example above). The effect is as if each task were executing a separate copy of the task body. A third task can call the entry `Counter_1.Increment` to communicate with the first task or `Counter_2.Increment` to communicate with the second task.

2.3.12 Low-Level Interfaces

A high-level language allows programmers to think in terms of the problems they are solving rather than the machines they are using. However, programs that control hardware directly or that share data with programs written in another language often require high-level algorithms and data declarations to be translated in a particular way. An Ada program can contain *representation specifications* stipulating low-level properties such as the address of a variable or subprogram, the size of a variable, the bit-by-bit arrangement of the components of a record, and whether a variable or component must be aligned on some kind of boundary (such as a word or double-word boundary). There is a way to specify that when a particular hardware interrupt takes place, it should appear to the Ada program as if a particular entry has been called. Then that class of interrupts can be handled by the task containing an `ACCEPT` statement for that entry.

The presence of representation specifications does not affect the way an entity may be used in an Ada program, only the way in which uses of the entity are translated into machine language. It is both possible and appropriate to write high-level, abstract programs containing entities with low-level representation specifications.

Some programs may have to execute special-purpose machine-language instructions at some point. The Ada language allows subprograms consisting entirely of descriptions of machine-language instructions. The intent of the Ada language's designers is that this facility be used rarely, and only for incorporating very short sequences of machine-language instructions in an Ada program. An Ada compiler may provide a separate facility for allowing an Ada program to call a subprogram written in assembly language or some other language. An Ada compiler may also provide a package for describing device-level input/output operations.

2.4 SUMMARY

An Ada program is a sequence of words, special symbols, and other elements. These elements may be grouped into lines in any manner and separated by any number of spaces (although at least one space is required between a word and a numeral). Spaces are not allowed within an element (except when the element is the *character literal* `' '` or a *string literal* like `"Here are spaces!"`). Two consecutive hyphens mark the beginning of a comment, and the comment extends to the end of the line. This book follows the formatting recommendations of the Ada language's designers.

An *identifier* is a sequence of letters, digits, and underscores beginning with a letter. Underscores are allowed only between two characters that are not underscores. There is no limit on the length of an identifier. Sixty-three identifiers are *reserved words* that play special roles in an Ada program and may not be given other meanings by the programmer. Corresponding upper-case and lower-case letters are equivalent, except in character literals and string literals. This book uses upper case for reserved words and a mixture of upper case and lower case for other identifiers.

The elements of a program can be combined to form *declarations* specifying the meaning of identifiers, *statements* specifying actions, and *pragmas* specifying information for the compiler. Declarations, statements, and pragmas always end with semicolons. A sequence of statements is allowed anywhere in a program that a single statement is allowed. The `List` and `Page` pragmas are used to control the source listing produced by a compiler.

This book uses the following notation to specify how elements can be combined to form declarations, statements, pragmas, and other program structures:

Upper-case letters denote reserved words.
Special characters like semicolons and parentheses denote themselves.
Lower-case italicized words name program structures embedded in the program structure being defined.

A dotted box indicates that whatever it surrounds is optional.
Similar constructs separated by a wavy line denote a sequence of one or more of those constructs, perhaps separated by a specified kind of symbol.

The two most important kinds of building blocks in Ada programs are *subprograms* and *packages.* Large programs can be built by combining such building blocks. These building blocks, in turn, consist of one or more *compilation units.*

The compilation units of an Ada program may be compiled separately, but they must be consistent with each other. An Ada compiler enforces consistency among separately compiled units by placing relevant information about a compilation unit in the *program library* when the compilation unit is compiled and by retrieving that information when other compilation units are compiled. Retrieval is controlled by a *context clause* at the beginning of a compilation unit. The context clause starts with the word WITH and lists the other building blocks referred to inside the compilation unit.

A subprogram may be either a *procedure* invoked by a procedure call statement to perform some action or a *function* invoked by evaluation of an expression to compute some value. A main program is simply a subprogram that is "called" from the outside world in some manner that varies from one system to another. The simplest form of a procedure is:

```
PROCEDURE identifier  [(formal parameter list)]  IS
   declarative part
BEGIN
   sequence of statements
END identifier ;
```

The declarative part contains zero or more declarations defining names that are used in the subprogram. These include *variable declarations* such as:

```
x    : Character;
y, z : Integer := 10;
```

Two or more subprograms may be declared with the same name, provided that they do not have identical parameter and result types. This is called *overloading.* The types of the actual parameters in a procedure or function call, and the expected type of the result in a function call, determine which of the subprograms with a given name is being called.

A function with two parameters can be given a name such as "+" or "*" (an operator symbol enclosed in quotation marks). This overloads the corresponding operator. Then occurrences of the operator in an expression become calls on that function, provided that the operand and result types match.

The most basic statements in a program are *procedure call statements* of the form *procedure name* (*list of parameters*) ;

and assignment statements of the form

variable := *expression* ;

All input and output is specified by procedure calls. Subprograms adequate for simple input and output operations are provided by the package `Basic_IO`, which may be copied out of this book's Appendix. Other packages, provided by the Ada language and described in Chapter 17, offer more sophisticated input and output operations.

These basic statements can be combined into compound statements. Compound statements include `CASE` statements, `IF` statements, and loops. There are three kinds of `LOOP` statements in the Ada language—`FOR` loops, `WHILE` loops, and basic (indefinitely repeating) loops. Although the Ada language has a `GOTO` statement, its use is almost never appropriate. Most of the uses of `GOTO` statements in other languages are made unnecessary by the Ada language's other statements.

The Ada language was designed for writing programs that must function sensibly even when unexpected situations, or *exceptions,* arise. Programs can contain *exception handlers,* specifying responses to exceptions. A programmer can declare his own exceptions, besides those defined by the language, and raise exceptions explicitly.

A programmer may define new types to supplement types such as `Integer` and `String` that are defined by the Ada language. A *type declaration* describes the values in a type. For example, it may indicate that values in a type for lists of integers are arrays with components of type `Integer`. It may indicate that a type for positions of a switch consists of four values named `Off`, `Low`, `Medium`, and `High`. Once a type has been defined, variables may be declared to belong to that type.

Large programs are usually composed of *modules.* In the Ada language, these modules are called *packages.* A package has an *interface* providing facilities to its users and an *implementation* of those facilities. The facilities typically include new types, subprograms for manipulating values of those types, and exceptions that can be raised by those subprograms. Besides breaking a large program into more manageable pieces, packages provide a vehicle for general-purpose off-the-shelf software components.

A package usually has two parts, called the *package specification* and the *package body.* Generally speaking, the package specification describes the package's interface, and the package body describes the implementation. Only the package specification, containing the interface, is relevant to users of the package. If an entity `E` is declared in the specification of package `P`, then `P` provides `E` to its users. `E` (which may be a subprogram or a type, for example) may be referred to outside the package as `P.E`. An entity declared inside a package body can only be referred to inside the package body.

A type provided by a package may be a *private type.* This means that the structure of the type is not part of the package's interface. The structure of a private type is defined by a type declaration in the *private part* of a package specification. Values in a private type can be manipulated according to their structure only from within the package. From outside of the package, values in a private type may be manipulated only by copying them, checking whether two values are equal, and calling subprograms provided by the package. This limits the amount of information about the type that is relevant outside the package, simplifying the interconnections between modules of a large program.

Generic program units are templates for packages and subprograms. Certain information in these templates is left unspecified. A template can be *instantiated* by supplying this unspecified information. The resulting *instance* of the template can be used like an ordinary package or subprogram. A single template can have several instances in which different information is specified. This facility allows the construction of general-purpose software components that can be instantiated to solve a variety of similar but not identical problems.

A program may contain several *tasks*. Each task is a sequence of actions performed one after the other, but several tasks may execute concurrently. Tasks communicate when one task calls an *entry* of the other, and the other task *accepts* this entry call. This process is called a *rendezvous*.

Programs that deal directly with hardware or with assembly language software often require data to be represented internally in a specific way. The Ada language provides mechanisms for exerting this kind of low-level control. Such mechanisms are intended to be used only rarely. If used properly, they do not cause low-level concerns to be reflected throughout a program. To the contrary, they allow data to be manipulated abstractly, without regard to its internal representation, once its internal representation has been specified.

Chapter 1 described the problems that led to the development of the language: concern with controlling the complexity of mammoth programs, allowing large teams of programmers to work together, reusing software, maintaining software, and making software reliable. The language's design directly addresses these concerns.

EXERCISES

2.1 Which of the following identifiers are illegal, and why?

(*a*) `Ada`
(*b*) `Ada_Language`
(*c*) `ADA`
(*d*) `ADA__LANGUAGE`
(*e*) `Ada_`
(*f*) `Reverse_Version_1`
(*g*) `Reverse`
(*h*) `1_More_Reverse`
(*i*) `$Reverse`
(*j*) `_Version_2`

2.2 What is wrong with each of the following programs?

(*a*)
```
WITH Basic_IO;

PROCEDURE Sum_3_Inputs IS
   -- This program reads in three numbers
      and prints out their sum. --
   a, b, c : Integer;
BEGIN
   Basic_IO.Get (a);
   Basic_IO.Get (b);
   Basic_IO.Get (c);
   Basic_IO.Put (a+b+c);
END Sum_3_Inputs;
```

(*b*)
```
WITH Basic_IO;

PROCEDURE Compute_Difference_Of_Products IS
   a, b, c, d : Integer;
BEGIN
   Basic_IO.Get (a);
   Basic_IO.Get (b);
   Basic_IO.Get (c);
   Basic_IO.Get (d);
   Basic_IO.Put (a *--Multiply first number
                b ---by second number and subtract
                c *--product of third number and
                d -- fourth number.
                 );
END Compute_Difference_Of_Products;
```

(*c*)
```
WITH Basic_IO;

PROCEDURE Echo IS
   x : Integer;
BEGIN
   Basic_IO.Get (x);
   Basic_IO.Put (x)
END Echo;
```

2.3 The following is a formal description of the syntax of the selective wait, which is an advanced feature for multitask programs. Describe the syntax of the selective wait in words.

```
SELECT
   . . . . . . . . . . . . . . .
   : WHEN expression =>        :
   . . . . . . . . . . . . . . .
        selective wait alternative

OR

   ~~~

OR

   . . . . . . . . . . . . . . .
   : WHEN expression =>        :
   . . . . . . . . . . . . . . .
        selective wait alternative

. . . . . . . . . . . . . . . . . .
: ELSE                            :
:      sequence of statements     :
. . . . . . . . . . . . . . . . . .

END SELECT;
```

2.4 Use the syntactic notation explained in section 2.2 to describe the syntax of a FORTRAN, PL/I, or Pascal procedure header.

2.5 Write an Ada program that reads two integers from the standard input file and writes the larger of them to the standard output file.

2.6 Write an Ada program that reads integers until the number zero is read in, then reports how many times the number five was read in.

CHAPTER

THREE

PROGRAMMER-DEFINED DATA TYPES

3.1 WHAT IS A DATA TYPE?

Although most people who have programmed in a high-level language can give examples of data types, many would have difficulty giving a precise definition of a data type. You can program in FORTRAN or PL/I without ever giving much thought to this question. However, the Ada language gives programmers the ability to construct their own data types to supplement those provided by the language. To understand what this ability means and how to use it effectively, we must give careful consideration to what a data type is.

A data type consists of a set of values and a set of operations that can be applied to those values. For instance, the FORTRAN data type `INTEGER` consists of the set of whole numbers within a certain range and a set of operations for manipulating whole numbers. These operations include addition, subtraction, multiplication, and division. They include comparisons between two `INTEGER` values. Assignment, input, and output of `INTEGER` values are also operations on the FORTRAN data type `INTEGER`.

The PL/I data type `CHARACTER (3) VARYING` consists of the set of all sequences of zero, one, two, or three characters and a set of operations on those sequences. Among these operations are comparisons to check whether two sequences of characters are identical or which one comes before the other in alphabetical order. Other operations take the form of built-in functions like `SUBSTR`, which extracts a subsequence from a sequence of characters, and `INDEX`, which determines the position at which one sequence of characters first occurs within a second sequence of characters. Input, output, and assignment of `CHARACTER (3) VARYING` values are also operations of this data type.

Programming can be simplified by thinking in terms of data types besides those defined by the programming language. Let's consider a hypothetical checker-playing program. The program uses eight-by-eight arrays of integers to represent checkerboards. Each integer in the array corresponds to a square of the checkerboard, with -2 representing a red king, -1 representing an uncrowned red checker, 0 representing an empty square, 1 representing an uncrowned black checker, and 2 representing a black king. These arrays are manipulated as follows: One subroutine sets up the initial arrangement of a checkerboard. Another examines a checkerboard and determines the next move the program should make. A third subroutine executes a specified move on one arrangement of checkers to obtain a new arrangement. Finally, there is a subroutine to display an arrangement on a terminal.

We have, in effect, invented a new data type. The type's values are arrangements of checkerboards. The type's operations are the creation of an initial arrangement, the determination of a move, the execution of a move, and the display of a checkerboard. Although this type may seem different from types such as `INTEGER` and `CHARACTER (3) VARYING`, it is really quite similar. Even the values in language-defined types are represented in terms of other values. For example, a FORTRAN `INTEGER` is typically represented as a sequence of bits forming a binary number. Addition and subtraction operations manipulate this representation. The only difference is that the representation and manipulation of an `INTEGER` value are provided automatically by the FORTRAN compiler and hidden from the programmer.

An *abstract data type* is one that can be completely characterized by the way in which the values of the data type are related to each other by the operations. In an abstract data type, we are concerned with abstract values (for instance, numbers viewed as mathematical entities) rather than their representations (for instance, numbers viewed as bit patterns). It is possible to define an abstract data type mathematically without ever writing a computer program or referring to a computer. However, we can *implement* an abstract data type on a computer by choosing a representation for the values and writing subprograms that manipulate that representation.

Consider an abstract data type, `IntegerSetType`, whose values are sets of numbers from one to ten and whose operations are the following functions:

Singleton (*i*), where *i* is one of the numbers one through ten, is the set containing the number *i* and no other number.

Union (*a, b*), where *a* and *b* are `IntegerSetType` values, is the set containing every number contained in either *a* or *b,* but no other number.

Member (*i, a*), where *i* is one of the numbers one through ten and *a* is an `IntegerSetType` value, is equal to *true* if *a* contains *i* and *false* otherwise.

These descriptions of *Singleton, Union,* and *Member* completely describe the data type `IntegerSetType`. To implement the data type on a computer, we first must choose a representation for `IntegerSetType` values in terms of the primitive data objects available to us. If we are programming in FORTRAN, for instance, these primitive data types include arrays of integers. Since the sets we are dealing with contain at most ten integers, we can represent an `IntegerSetType` value as a ten-element array in which members of the set are held in the leftmost elements of the array and each array element not holding a member of the set contains a zero (see Figure 3.1).

8	4	10	2	6	0	0	0	0	0

Figure 3.1 Representation for the set {2, 4, 6, 8, 10} as an array of integers. The members of the set are stored at the beginning of the array and the remaining array elements are set to zero.

Next, we must implement the *Singleton, Union,* and *Member* operations in FORTRAN. Since FORTRAN functions cannot return arrays, we might write subroutines `SINGLE (I, S)` to set `S` to the value of *Singleton* (`I`) and `UNION (A, B, S)` to set `S` to the value of *Union* (`A, B`). `MEMBER` can be written directly as a `LOGICAL` function. These subprograms could take the following form:

```
      SUBROUTINE SINGLE (I, S)
      INTEGER I, S(10)
      INTEGER J
      S(1) = I
      DO 100 J = 2, 10
         S(J) = 0
100   CONTINUE
      RETURN
      END
      SUBROUTINE UNION (A, B, S)
      INTEGER A(10), B(10), S(10)
      INTEGER SPTR, APTR, BPTR, ASIZE, I
      SPTR = 1
C COPY NONZERO ELEMENTS FROM A TO S:
      APTR = 1
100   IF (APTR .GT. 10) GO TO 200
      IF (A(APTR) .EQ. 0) GO TO 200
      S(SPTR) = A(APTR)
      APTR = APTR + 1
      SPTR = SPTR + 1
      GO TO 100
200   ASIZE = APTR - 1
C COPY TO S EACH NONZERO ELEMENT IN B THAT DID NOT ALSO
C  OCCUR IN A:
      BPTR = 1
300   IF (BPTR .GT. 10) GO TO 400
      IF (B(BPTR) .EQ. 0) GO TO 400
      DO 310 I = 1, ASIZE
         IF (B(BPTR) .EQ. A(I)) GO TO 320
310   CONTINUE
      S(SPTR) = B(BPTR)
      SPTR = SPTR + 1
320   BPTR = BPTR + 1
      GO TO 300
C FILL IN REMAINING ELEMENTS OF S WITH ZERO
400   DO 410 I = SPTR - 1, 10
         S(SPTR) = 0
410   CONTINUE
      RETURN
      END
```

```
      LOGICAL FUNCTION MEMBER (I, A)
      INTEGER I, A(10)
      INTEGER J
      MEMBER = .TRUE.
      DO 100 J = 1, 10
         IF (A(J) .EQ. I) RETURN
100   CONTINUE
      MEMBER = .FALSE.
      RETURN
      END
```

We could also have represented `IntegerSetType` values using arrays of ten `LOGICAL` (true/false) values. The ith element of the array representing the `IntegerSetType` value a would be true if i were a member of a and false otherwise (see Figure 3.2). Then the `IntegerSetType` operations would be implemented differently:

```
      SUBROUTINE SINGLE (I, S)
      INTEGER I
      LOGICAL S(10)
      INTEGER J
      DO 100 J = 1, 10
         S(J) = .FALSE.
100   CONTINUE
      S(I) = .TRUE.
      RETURN
      END

      SUBROUTINE UNION (A, B, S)
      LOGICAL A(10), B(10), S(10)
      INTEGER J
      DO 100 J = 1, 10
         S(J) = A(J) .OR. B(J)
100   CONTINUE
      RETURN
      END

      LOGICAL FUNCTION MEMBER (I, A)
      INTEGER I
      LOGICAL A(10)
      MEMBER = A(I)
      RETURN
      END
```

1	2	3	4	5	6	7	8	9	10
.FALSE.	.TRUE.	.FALSE.	.TRUE.	.FALSE.	.TRUE.	.FALSE.	.TRUE.	.FALSE.	.TRUE.

Figure 3.2 Representation for the set {2,4,6,8,10} as an array of `LOGICAL` values. The numbers above the boxes are subscript values. The ith element of the array is `.TRUE.` if i is a member of the set and `.FALSE.` if i is not a member of the set.

The two choices of representation for sets lead to two different implementations of the same abstract operations. No matter which representation we choose, the statements

```
CALL SINGLE (1, S1)
CALL SINGLE (2, S2)
CALL UNION (S1, S2, S12)
M1 = MEMBER (1, S12)
M2 = MEMBER (3, S2)
```

leave `.TRUE.` in `M1` and `.FALSE.` in `M2`, for example. That is why it makes sense to say that the `INTEGER` array together with its subprograms and the `LOGICAL` array together with its subprograms are two different implementations of the same abstract data type.

Just as an abstract data type can be represented by more than one combination of components belonging to other data types, a given combination of components can serve as the representation for many different abstract data types. As we have seen, an array of ten integers can represent a set. But it can also represent the distribution of grades in a class, with the ith element of the array holding the number of grades between $10i-9$ and $10i$, inclusive. The operations on this data type would be different, perhaps consisting of an operation to initialize the distribution so that it holds no grades, an operation to add a grade to the distribution, and an operation to print a bar graph of the distribution.

3.2 TREATMENT OF DATA TYPES IN THE FORTRAN, PL/I, PASCAL, AND ADA LANGUAGES

Designing a program in terms of data types natural to the problem being solved (such as `CheckerboardType` or `IntegerSetType`) is called *data abstraction.* Programming languages have evolved over the years to make data abstraction easier. To better appreciate the data abstraction facilities of the Ada language, let's compare them with those of earlier programming languages.

FORTRAN, as revised in 1978, provides the primitive data types `INTEGER`, `REAL`, `DOUBLE PRECISION`, `COMPLEX`, `LOGICAL`, and `CHARACTER*`*n* (where *n* is some fixed positive integer), as well as single-dimensional and multidimensional arrays of these types. Often the representation of a value in one of the programmer's abstract data types consists of a *group* of distinct variables, each belonging to one of the primitive FORTRAN data types. For instance, consider a data type whose values are batting records of baseball teams. One of the operations of the data type might be to print the names of all the players on the team with batting averages of .300 or more; another might be to calculate the number of such players on the team. In FORTRAN, a value of this type might be represented by an array of `CHARACTER*20` values containing the players' names and an array of `REAL` values containing the corresponding batting averages in the same order. In a program dealing with batting records of several baseball teams, it would be necessary to declare one CHARACTER*20 array and one REAL array for each team batting record. The programmer would have to remember which CHARACTER*20 array went with which REAL array.

FORTRAN does not protect programmers from mistakes in the use of their own data types in the same way that it protects them from mistakes in the use of the primitive data types. If a programmer writes a statement to divide an INTEGER variable by a CHARACTER*20 variable, we would expect a FORTRAN compiler to issue an error message. However, if the programmer passes the REAL array containing a baseball team's batting averages to a subroutine meant to manipulate some other kind of REAL array, the compiler will find nothing wrong.

It is often desirable to define a data type using several *levels of abstraction*. For instance, the programmer might first define two data types in terms of the primitive data types of the language and then define a third data type in terms of these two. There is no way to distinguish these levels of abstraction in a FORTRAN program. If we wanted to define a data type whose components were a baseball team's name, the team's home city, and the team's batting record, we could use two CHARACTER*20 variables (to represent the team name and the city name) and the CHARACTER*20 and REAL arrays described earlier (to represent the batting record). However, there is no distinction between a data type represented directly by two CHARACTER*20 variables, a CHARACTER*20 array, and a REAL array, and a data type represented by two CHARACTER*20 variables and a value in some other type that is *internally* represented by a CHARACTER*20 array and a REAL array (see Figure 3.3).

If we want to represent a new data type using an array of values in some data type we have defined earlier, FORTRAN is especially unhelpful. For instance, if we want to represent a league batting record as an array of team batting records, the best we can do in FORTRAN is to use a two-dimensional CHARACTER*20 array and a two-dimensional REAL array. One row of the CHARACTER*20 array together with the corresponding row of the REAL array represent a single team's batting record. Suppose we must implement an operation for league batting records that determines the number of teams in the league with five or more players batting .300 or better. This operation is reminiscent of the operation on a team batting record that determines the number of players on that team batting .300 or better. In fact, if a league batting record were truly represented by an array of team batting records, it would be simple to implement the new operation in terms of the old one:

```
          COUNT = 0
          DO 100 I = 1, NUMTMS
             IF (NGE300(LEAGUE(I)) .GE. 5) COUNT = COUNT + 1
    100   CONTINUE
```

(LEAGUE is presumed to be the array of team batting records, so that LEAGUE(I) is a single team batting record. NGE300 is a function taking a team batting record and returning the number of batters with averages greater than or equal to .300. NUMTMS is the number of teams in the league.) We cannot really do this in FORTRAN. Since the only way to represent an array of team batting records is to

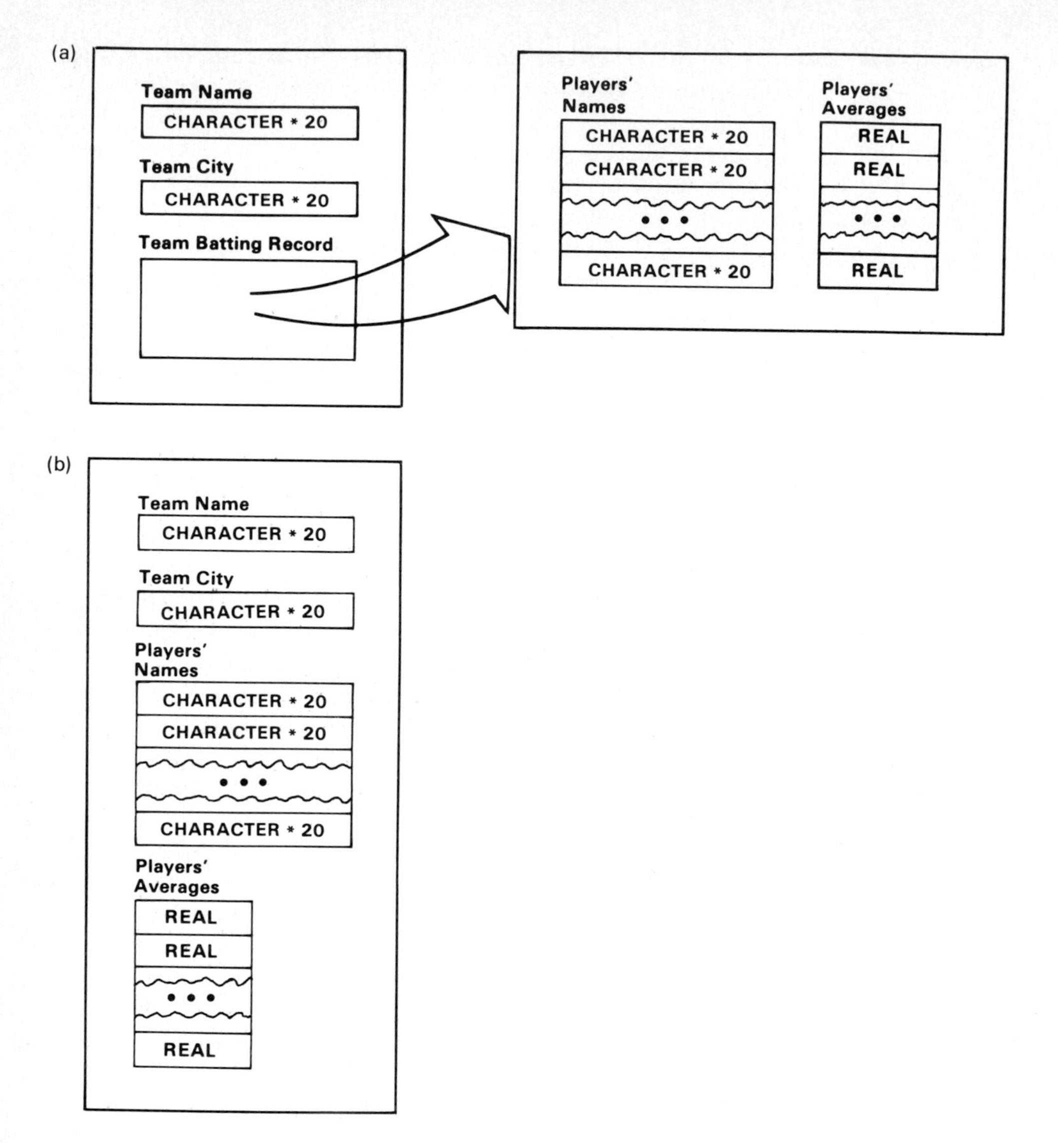

Figure 3.3 Levels of abstraction. (a) The logical view of the data type as built out of previously defined data types. (b) The flat view imposed by FORTRAN.

put all the names and batting averages in two-dimensional arrays, `NGE300` must be rewritten to use two subscripts instead of one.

Many of the inadequacies of FORTRAN data types are remedied by PL/I *structures*. A structure is a collection of *components* defined by the programmer. A component may be a variable belonging to a primitive PL/I data type, an array, or another structure with its own components. Just as a structure may have a component that is an array, so an array may have components that are instances of some structure. A team batting record can be declared in PL/I as follows:

```
DECLARE
   1 TEAM_BATTING_RECORD,
      2 PLAYER_BATTING_RECORD (25),
         3 PLAYER_NAME      CHARACTER (20),
         3 PLAYER_AVERAGE   FLOAT;
```

This declaration states that the structure TEAM_BATTING_RECORD consists of 25 player batting records, each of which consists of a player's name and batting average. The representation of a team batting record is declared as a single entity. It can also be passed as a single entity to a subroutine operating on team batting records. If we want to represent several team batting records in a PL/I program, we can declare other structures to be "LIKE TEAM_BATTING_RECORD" without repeating the entire declaration above. Thus, in many ways, PL/I structures can be used in the same manner as the primitive data types of the language.

PL/I structures make it easy to define data types at several levels of abstraction. To define the data type whose values consist of a team's name, home city, and batting record, we simply define a structure with three components:

```
DECLARE
   1 TEAM,
      2 NAME              CHARACTER (20),
      2 CITY              CHARACTER (20),
      2 BATTING_RECORD    LIKE TEAM_BATTING_RECORD;
```

This declaration clearly separates the levels of abstraction. We can represent a league batting record as an array of structures representing team batting records:

```
DECLARE
   1 LEAGUE_BATTING_RECORD (12) LIKE TEAM_BATTING_RECORD;
```

Any operation that we implemented earlier for team batting records can be applied directly to a component of this array:

```
COUNT = 0;
DO I = 1 TO NUMBER_OF_TEAMS;
   IF NUM_BATTING_GE_300 (LEAGUE_BATTING_RECORD (I)) > 5
      THEN COUNT = COUNT + 1;
END;
```

As we define the representation of a new data type in terms of simpler data types, we can define the operations on the new data type in terms of the operations on these simpler data types.

PL/I retains a major weakness of FORTRAN data types: If a PL/I programmer designs two different data types with the same representation, PL/I does not bar the programmer from applying an operation of the first data type to the representation of a value in the second data type. It does not matter if two structures, or their components, have different names; if they have the same kinds of components, the language treats them as belonging to the same type.

The language Pascal helps programmers think in terms of their own data types. A Pascal program may contain *data type definitions,* in which the programmer specifies the name of a data type and its representation in terms of other data types. Once a data type has been defined in this way, its name can be used in the same way as the names of the language-defined data types. The names of programmer-defined data types may appear in variable declarations, in the headings of procedures and functions (to indicate the types of the parameters and function results), and in subsequent data type definitions. In effect, the data type definition adds a new data type to the language.

Values in separately defined Pascal data types are not interchangeable, even if they have the same representation. For example, if `IntegerSetType` and `GradeDistributionType` are both defined to be the names of types whose values are represented by arrays of ten integers, an `IntegerSetType` variable cannot be assigned to a `GradeDistributionType` variable or passed to a subprogram that has a `GradeDistributionType` parameter.

A Pascal data type only specifies the name of a data type and a representation for its values. It does not specify the operations on the data type. Suppose that a programmer defines the data type `IntegerSetType` to be represented by an array of ten integers and writes subprograms to implement the *Singleton, Union,* and *Member* operations. There is nothing in the Pascal language to prevent another programmer, working on a different part of the program, from manipulating an `IntegerSetType` variable directly as an array of integers rather than calling these subprograms.

This presents two problems. First, it is not safe to change the representation of the data type later simply by rewriting the type definition and the subprograms implementing the operations; other parts of the program may be dependent on the original representation. Second, the programmer manipulating an `IntegerSetType` variable directly as an array may make the array invalid as a representation of an `IntegerSetType` value.

The original programmer might have written subprograms that only worked correctly for sorted arrays, for example. As long as the subprograms implementing *Singleton* and *Union* only produced sorted arrays, and as long as the rest of the program only manipulated `IntegerSetType` variables by calling the subprograms implementing *Singleton, Union,* and *Member,* it would be safe to assume that all `IntegerSetType` variables would always be sorted. However, a second programmer, manipulating `IntegerSetType` variables directly as arrays, could generate unsorted arrays, unwittingly causing the first programmer's subprograms to fail.

In some ways, the data type definitions of Pascal are too restrictive. When the values of a type are to be represented using arrays, the type definition must specify the number of elements in the arrays. Since subprograms must specify the types of their parameters, a subprogram manipulating arrays can only manipulate arrays of one specific size. One cannot write a general Pascal subroutine to find the largest integer in a one-dimensional array, for instance. (A feature has been added to the International Standards Organization definition of Pascal to remedy this problem.

However, this feature has not been accepted as part of the American National Standards Institute's definition of the language.)

Another problem in Pascal is the need to write duplicate versions of the same algorithm to work with different types. After a programmer has written a data type definition and a set of subprograms for a data type of sets of integers, there is no way to specify that a data type for sets of characters is to be implemented "in the same way." Rather, we must write a second, almost identical data type definition and set of subprograms.

The Ada language's data abstraction facilities are based on Pascal's, but there are significant improvements. Like Pascal, the Ada language has type definitions that specify the representation of a data type. In the Ada language, however, the type definitions and the subprograms implementing the operations of the data type can be *encapsulated*. That is, they can be isolated in one package in such a way that the rest of the program cannot manipulate variables of the data type except by calling those subprograms. The representation of a data type and the implementation of the operations can be changed safely without ever looking at the part of the program outside this package. If the subprograms in the package rely on some assumption about the form of the variables of the data type (such as the assumption that an array is sorted), no other part of the program can invalidate that assumption.

When an Ada type is to be represented as an array, one may—but need not—specify the number of elements in the array. If the number is not specified, different values in the data type may be represented by arrays of different sizes. Subprograms with parameters belonging to such data types can manipulate all these arrays. Furthermore, an Ada programmer can write a *generic definition* describing the representation and operations of a data type like "set of objects of type ______," where the blank is filled in later with names of different types of set elements to create different types of sets.

Just as one can extend the language by providing new data type names, one can extend the language by defining new meanings for operators used in expressions. The Ada expression "$x + y$" already applies one kind of operation to x and y when x and y are integers and another when x and y are floating-point (real) numbers. (We think of both of these operations as "addition," but because integers and floating-point numbers have different internal representations, integer addition and floating-point addition are generally implemented using different machine-language instructions.) After defining the data type `IntegerSetType`, we can stipulate that when x and y are `IntegerSetType` values, $x + y$ will apply the `IntegerSetType` *Union* operation to x and y.

3.3 CLASSES OF ADA DATA TYPES

Ada has eight classes of data types:

integer types
floating-point types

fixed-point types
enumeration types
array types
record types
access types
task types

Integer, floating-point, and fixed-point types are known collectively as *numeric types.* Array types and record types are known collectively as *composite types.*

3.3.1 Integer Types

An *integer type* is a type whose values are whole numbers and whose operations include the familiar arithmetic operations. If you are used to a programming language providing *an* integer type, you may be puzzled by the fact that the Ada language provides a class of potentially *many* integer types. What does it mean to have more than one integer type?

A program can use whole numbers to represent several different kinds of information. For instance, a program manipulating information about cities could use whole numbers to represent both the population of a city and the number of hours difference between local time and Greenwich Mean Time. But it would not be meaningful to compute the sum of a city's population and its time difference or to store a city's population in a variable meant to hold a time difference. In the Ada language, you can define one integer type for populations and another for time differences. Then the compiler will report an error if your program tries to add a population value to a time-difference value or to store a population value in a time-difference variable. (This is precisely what a FORTRAN compiler does if a program tries to add a character string and an integer or if it tries to assign a character string to a logical variable.)

The purpose of defining more than one integer type is to distinguish between integer values with different meanings and to enable the Ada compiler to enforce this distinction. Each integer type definition specifies the range of integer values that the type includes. The appropriate range for a given type depends on the meaning of the values in the type. The integers from -12 to 12 can be used to represent the difference between a city's local time and Greenwich Mean Time. To represent the population of a city, one might want to use the range of integers from zero to twenty million.

3.3.2 Floating-Point Types

Floating-point types are analogous to the FORTRAN and Pascal types named `REAL` and the PL/I type named `FLOAT`. That is, values in a floating-point type include both whole and fractional numbers ranging from very large numbers (say 10^{75}) to numbers very near zero (say 10^{-75}); negative numbers with these magnitudes; and the number zero.

Most real numbers can be represented only approximately on a computer. The values of a floating-point type are approximations that can be thought of as containing no more than some maximum number of nonzero digits (called the *number of digits of precision* or the *number of significant digits*). The decimal point may "float" from far to the left of these digits (assuming that the digits are preceded by zeroes), to someplace within the digits, to far to the right of these digits (assuming that the digits are followed by zeroes). This is the origin of the term *floating point*. Approximations of small numbers, such as 0.00000123 and 0.00000124, are crowded close together; and approximations of large numbers, such as 12300000 and 12400000, are spread far apart.

As with integer types, the Ada language allows a programmer to define different floating-point types for floating-point values with different meanings. Each floating-point type definition specifies the number of significant digits in that type's floating-point values. The definition may also specify the range of values in the type.

3.3.3 Fixed-Point Types

Fixed-point types also contain approximations to real numbers. Unlike the approximations in floating-point types, the approximations in fixed-point types are evenly spaced. It follows that values in a fixed-point type approximate real numbers to within a fixed number of decimal places. That is why these types are called *fixed-point types*.

You can define different fixed-point types for fixed-point values with different meanings. Each fixed-point type definition specifies the size of the interval between approximations and the range of the values in the type.

3.3.4 Enumeration Types

Some data types contain few enough values that all values can be conveniently listed. *Enumeration types* are types containing values whose names are *enumerated* (that is, *listed*) in the type definition. For instance, an enumeration type called `Day_Type` could contain seven values named `Sunday`, `Monday`, `Tuesday`, `Wednesday`, `Thursday`, `Friday`, and `Saturday`. An enumeration type named `Grade_Type` could contain four values named `Fail`, `Low_Pass`, `Pass`, and `High_Pass`. Except for their positions in the list, the values of an enumeration type have no intrinsic meaning as far as the Ada language is concerned. It is up to the programmer to provide such meanings. Character values are represented in the Ada language by an enumeration type containing one value for each possible character. Logical values are represented by an enumeration type containing a value named `False` and a value named `True`.

In other languages, integers are sometimes used to encode values such as days of the week. An enumeration type is essentially such an encoding, but the details are handled by the compiler. From the programmer's point of view, values in an enumeration type are not numbers, but unique abstract entities. In fact, arithmetic operations like addition and multiplication cannot be applied to enumeration types.

3.3.5 Array Types

The values of an *array type* are arrays of one or more dimensions. All the components of a given array have the same type. The index values (i.e., subscripts) used to select components of an array may be integers, as in FORTRAN and PL/I, or they may be values in enumeration types. For instance, a 52-week calendar can be represented by an array in which a row is identified by one of the integers one through 52 and a column is identified by one of the values in the enumeration type `Day_Type` described in Section 3.3.4.

Each array type definition specifies the type of the array components. In addition, for each dimension of the array, the array type definition specifies the type of the index values in that dimension. The definition may specify the lowest and highest index values in each dimension (in which case all arrays in the type have the same size), or it may leave these values unspecified (in which case the type contains arrays of different sizes).

3.3.6 Record Types

A value in a *record type* is a combination of components that may belong to several different types. The record type definition specifies the name and type of each component. It is possible to manipulate the components of a record type value individually or to treat the entire value as a single entity. In some record types, different values in the type can have different kinds of components.

3.3.7 Access Types

Access types are somewhat similar to the types `POINTER` and `OFFSET` in PL/I and very similar to pointer types in Pascal. That is, the values in an access type are *pointers* to variables of some other type. (In other words, they provide *access* to these variables.) The type definition defining an access type specifies the type of the variables to be pointed to. The values in one access type might point to variables in some integer type, and the values in a second access type might point to variables in some array type, for example. The internal representation of the pointers is of no concern to the programmer because Ada programs do not manipulate them directly. (In particular, they are not numeric values and cannot be added.) Rather, if `A` is a variable in an access type, a notation meaning "the variable pointed to by the value contained in `A`" can appear anywhere a variable name can appear in an Ada program.

3.3.8 Task Types

The values of a *task type* correspond to tasks all performing their own computations at the same time. The definition of a task type specifies the computation to be performed by all tasks of that type. The task type definition also specifies the interface through which that computation can communicate with other computations occurring simultaneously. Task types are different from other types because the values of the type are not data in the usual sense of the word.

3.3.9 Private Types

Normally, the kinds of operations that can be performed on a variable are determined by the class of the variable's data type. If A is a variable belonging to an array type, then you can use index values (subscripts) to name a component of A any place in the program where you can refer to A. If A is a variable belonging to an integer type, then you can compute the value of A+1 anywhere in the program where you can refer to A.

However, as explained in Section 3.2, it is preferable to use a value in some data type by invoking that type's operations rather than by manipulating the representation of the value directly. A *private type* is a data type whose definition is "kept secret" from most of the program. A private data type always belongs to one of the eight classes of types described above. However, the class of a private type is considered unknown except in one package containing the type definition and the subprograms implementing the operations of the data type. Outside of this package, the values in the private type can only be manipulated by invoking these subprograms.

3.4 SUMMARY

A *data type* consists of a set of values plus a set of operations on those values. Programming problems can be solved more easily by characterizing the solution in terms of data types arising naturally from the problem. This is called *data abstraction.* In languages such as FORTRAN and PL/I, problem-oriented data types are simulated using data types provided by the language. In the Pascal and Ada languages, problem-oriented data types are defined by the programmer to be bona fide data types.

An *abstract data type* can be completely characterized by the way in which the type's values are related to each other by the type's operations. *Implementation* of an abstract data type involves selecting a representation for each abstract value and formulating the data type's operations in terms of manipulations on this representation. There may be many ways to implement an abstract data type. Similarly, a given data structure may serve as the representation of values in different abstract data types with different operations.

Trends in programming language design reflect an increasing concern with data abstraction. FORTRAN provides virtually no support for data abstraction. PL/I provides structures, which allow several variables representing a single abstract value to be treated as a single entity. Structures also allow groups of data to be described hierarchically and given names. Pascal expands upon this concept, allowing the programmer to define new types that can be used in the same way as predefined types. Pascal distinguishes between type and structure: Distinct types that happen to have the same structure cannot be used interchangeably. The Ada language goes further, providing for the definition of types that can *only* be manipulated according to the type's abstract operations. Thus the Ada language provides direct support for the idea of an abstract data type. (Other improvements of the Ada language over Pascal include array types that may include arrays of different sizes, generic definition, and the ability to extend operators such as + and * to work on programmer-defined types.)

The Ada language has eight classes of data types. An *integer type* consists of whole numbers in a specified range. *Floating-point types* and *fixed-point types* consist of approximations to real numbers. In floating-point types, approximations are accurate to within a specified number of decimal digits; approximations for smaller numbers are more closely spaced than approximations for larger numbers. In fixed-point types, approximations are evenly spaced and accurate to within the specified distance between approximations. *Enumeration types* consist of values individually listed in the type definition. An *array type* consists of arrays having a specified type for index values in each dimension and a specified type for components. The values in a *record type* are combinations of values in other types. An *access type* consists of pointers to variables in some other specified type. A *task type* consists of values corresponding to concurrently executing tasks.

In the next chapter, we shall discuss integer, floating-point, fixed-point, enumeration, array, and record types in greater detail and explain how to define them. Access types will be discussed in Chapter 5. Record types will be revisited in Chapter 10 and private types will be discussed in Chapter 12. Task types will not be mentioned again until Chapter 18.

CHAPTER

FOUR

OBJECT AND TYPE DECLARATIONS

A *declaration* specifies the meaning of an identifier used in a program. There are different forms of declarations for the many different kinds of entities named by identifiers. This chapter discusses *object declarations* and *type declarations*. Object declarations introduce identifiers that are associated with values during a computation. They are analogous to the variable declarations of FORTRAN and PL/I and to the variable and constant declarations of Pascal. Type declarations associate identifiers with data types defined by the programmer. (Pascal also has type declarations, but there is nothing analogous in FORTRAN and PL/I.) Except in a few special contexts, and except for identifiers whose meanings in the Ada language are *predefined,* every identifier naming a type or an object must first be introduced by a declaration. FORTRAN and PL/I have rules determining the meaning of an identifier that is used without being declared, but the Ada language treats the use of an undeclared identifier as an error.

In some languages, declarations play no role once a program is running. The information provided by the declarations is used when translating the program and then discarded. In the Ada language, declarations are processed as they are encountered during program execution. A declaration may refer to values computed earlier in the program. The act of processing a declaration is called *elaboration.* In a simple Ada program of the form

```
PROCEDURE identifier IS
    declaration
        ~~~
    declaration
BEGIN
    statement
        ~~~
    statement
END identifier ;
```

each of the declarations is elaborated in turn and then each of the statements is executed in turn.

4.1 OBJECT DECLARATIONS

Objects hold the values used in a computation. There are two kinds of objects in Ada—*variables* and *constants*. A program may change the value of a variable, but a constant holds the same value for as long as it exists. Except for the fact that variables can be changed and constants cannot, variables and constants are very much alike. (In some languages, numbers such as 10 and 3.5 and character strings such as "THE ANSWER IS" are called constants. In the Ada language, these are called *literals*, and the term *constant* means *constant valued object*.)

The following program prints out the first 100 numbers of the Fibonacci sequence:

```
WITH Basic_IO;
PROCEDURE Print_Fibonacci_Numbers IS
   Next                       : Integer;
   One_Earlier, Two_Earlier   : Integer := 1;
   Amount_Printed             : Integer RANGE 0 .. 100;
BEGIN
   Basic_IO.Put (1);
   Basic_IO.Put (1);
   Amount_Printed := 2;
   WHILE Amount_Printed < 100 LOOP
      Next := One_Earlier + Two_Earlier;
      Basic_IO.Put (Next);
      Amount_Printed := Amount_Printed + 1;
      Two_Earlier := One_Earlier;
      One_Earlier := Next;
   END LOOP;
END Print_Fibonacci_Numbers;
```

(The first two numbers in the Fibonacci sequence both have the value one, and every other number in the sequence is the sum of the two previous numbers.) The three lines

```
Next                       : Integer;
One_Earlier, Two_Earlier   : Integer := 1;
Amount_Printed             : Integer RANGE 0 .. 100;
```

are *variable declarations*. They declare Next, One_Earlier, Two_Earlier, and Amount_Printed to be variables of type Integer. One_Earlier and Two_Earlier both have initial values of one, but the initial values of Next and Amount_Printed are not specified in their declarations. The variable Amount_Printed is *constrained* to hold values in the range zero to 100.

The general form of a variable declaration is

identifier **,** ~~~ **,** *identifier* **:**
typemark [*constraint*] [**:=** *expression*] **;**

The identifiers to the left of the colon name the variables being declared. The *typemark* is an identifier specifying the data type of the values that can be held by these variables. For now, you can think of a typemark as a name declared in a type declaration, although we shall see another kind of typemark in Chapter 6.

The *constraint* may be omitted in many cases. When present, it specifies further restrictions on the values that may be held by the variables, besides the restriction that the values must belong to the type specified by the typemark. Different forms of constraints apply to different classes of types. We shall discuss each form when we discuss the class of types to which it applies. The type of the variables being declared determines whether a certain kind of constraint is required, optional, or forbidden in a particular variable declaration.

The **:=** symbol together with the expression following it are also optional. If they are present, the value of the expression specifies the initial value of each of the variables named in the declaration. The expression must, of course, be of the appropriate data type. If the variable declaration contains a constraint, the initial value is also restricted by the constraint.

The following program reads in integers until a zero is encountered and then prints out the sum of the integers read:

```
WITH Basic_IO;
PROCEDURE Print_Sum IS
   Sum            : Integer := 0;
   Input_Value    : Integer;
   Stopping_Value : CONSTANT Integer := 0;
BEGIN
   Basic_IO.Get (Input_Value);
   WHILE Input_Value /= Stopping_Value LOOP
      Sum := Sum + Input_Value;
      Basic_IO.Get (Input_Value);
   END LOOP;
   Basic_IO.Put ("The sum is ");
   Basic_IO.Put (Sum);
   Basic_IO.New_Line;
END Print_Sum;
```

The line

```
Stopping_Value : CONSTANT Integer := 0;
```

is a *constant declaration*. It declares `Stopping_Value` to be a constant of type `Integer` that will always hold the value zero.

The general form of a constant declaration is similar to that of a variable declaration:

```
identifier , ~~~ , identifier :
      CONSTANT typemark [ constraint ]  := expression ;
```

The differences are the presence of the word `CONSTANT` after the colon and the fact that the initial value *must* be specified. In a constant declaration, the "initial value" is, in fact, the permanent value of the constant.

Constant declarations can be used to provide meaningful names for values. For instance, if we have previously declared a floating-point type named `Distance_Type`, the constant declaration

```
Meters_Per_Inch : CONSTANT Distance_Type := 0.0254;
```

allows the name `Meters_Per_Inch` to be used in place of the literal `0.0254` in the rest of the program to represent the number of meters in an inch. This makes the program easier to understand, because the name `Meters_Per_Inch` conveys the significance of the value it stands for, while the literal `0.0254` does not. Meaningful names are especially useful for values that are likely to be changed in future revisions of a program. For instance, given the constant declaration

```
Zip_Code_Size : CONSTANT Field_Size_Type := 5;
```

(where `Field_Size_Type` is some previously declared integer type), the program can be written to refer to `Zip_Code_Size` rather than `5` every place the size of a zip code is used. These places might include the definition of a data type for mailing addresses and loops manipulating the digits of zip codes. Then the program can be adapted to handle nine-digit zip codes simply by changing the constant declaration. It will not be necessary to search the program for each occurrence of the literal `5` and to determine which of these occurrences refer to the length of a zip code.

As in the program `Print_Sum`, constant declarations may also be used in place of variable declarations simply to document the fact that an object retains its initial value for as long as it exists. This may make a program easier to understand or allow a compiler to generate a more efficient machine-language program. When more than one person is working on a program, one programmer can declare an object constant to be sure that its value is not modified by other programmers. Any statement attempting to change the value of a constant is treated as an error by an Ada compiler.

4.2 TYPE DECLARATIONS

The usual form of a type declaration is

```
TYPE identifier IS type definition ;
```

The form of the type definition following the word `IS` differs for each class of types. Forms for integer, floating-point, fixed-point, enumeration, array, and record types are explained in this section. The type declaration specifies that the identifier following the word `TYPE` is the name of a data type whose representation is specified by the type definition.

Although the rules of the Ada language do not require it, we shall always use identifiers ending with the characters "`_Type`" to name the types we declare. This clarifies the meaning of the identifier in the rest of the program. It also makes it easy to come up with distinct names for types and objects belonging to those types (such as a variable `Distance` of type `Distance_Type`).

4.2.1 Integer Type Declarations

An integer type declaration may be written

`TYPE` *identifier* `IS RANGE` *low* `..` *high* `;`

where the numbers *low* and *high* indicate the lowest and highest values of the type being declared. The symbol `..` is meant to be suggestive of an ellipsis ("..."), often used in mathematical writing to denote a sequence of values. Thus the Ada text "*low* `..` *high*" can be read as "the range of values from *low* up to *high.*"

For example, the type declaration

```
TYPE Year_Type IS RANGE 1901 .. 2099;
```

declares `Year_Type` to be the name of an integer type whose values range from 1901 to 2099. Following this type declaration, a program may have declarations for objects of type `Year_Type`, such as the following:

```
Current_Year, Year_Of_Birth : Year_Type;
Next_Leap_Year : Year_Type := 1988;
Turn_Of_Century : CONSTANT Year_Type := 2000;
```

The identifier `Year_Type` occurs as the typemark in these object declarations. The object declaration

```
Starting_Year : CONSTANT Year_Type := 1776;
```

is in error, since `Year_Type` was declared to include only the values 1901 through 2099, and the initial value 1776 does not fall into this range.

A declaration of an object belonging to an integer type may contain a *range constraint* that further restricts the range of values the object can hold. This range constraint is always optional. The form of a range constraint is

`RANGE` *low* `..` *high*

where *low* and *high* are expressions whose values belong to the type of the object being declared. Here are examples of object declarations with range constraints:

```
Activation_Date : Year_Type RANGE 1975 .. 1990 := 1980;
Expiration_Date : Year_Type RANGE 1980 .. 1995;
```

The first declaration states that `Activation_Date` is a variable of type `Year_Type` that can take on only those `Year_Type` values from 1975 to 1990, and whose initial value is 1980. The second declaration states that `Expiration_Date` is a variable of type `Year_Type` that can take on only those `Year_Type` values from 1980 to 1995. Every value placed in either of these variables during the execution of the program will be checked to make sure it obeys the range constraint. The declaration

```
Activation_Date : Year_Type RANGE 1975 .. 1990 := 1995;
   --INCORRECT
```

is in error because the initial value violates the range constraint. The declaration

```
Expiration_Date : Year_Type RANGE 1800 .. 2000;
   --INCORRECT
```

is in error because the lower value in the range constraint is not a value of type `Year_Type`.

The Ada language has a predefined integer type named `Integer`. In other words, the class of types known as "the integer types" includes one particular type, defined by the language, named `Integer`. The use of the same name for a class of types and for one of the types in the class may be confusing at first, but consider these analogies:

Automobiles made by the Chrysler Corporation may be referred to collectively as Chrysler cars; but there are three kinds of Chrysler cars—Dodges, Plymouths, and Chryslers.

In the United States, democrats—that is, believers in democracy—may choose to join one of the two major political parties. Such democrats include both Republicans and Democrats.

The state named New York contains many cities, one of which is also named New York. In fact, that city contains five counties, one of which is named New York.

Similarly, the Ada language has a *class* of types named "integer" containing a *type* named "`Integer`." (Throughout this book we shall capitalize the name of the type, but we shall not normally capitalize the name of the class of types. In some loose sense, "`Integer`" is to "integer" as "Democrat" is to "democrat.")

The predefined type `Integer` has a range of values defined independently by each Ada implementation. Typically, this will be the range of whole numbers that can be represented in a word on the machine that will run the program. An implementation may also provide a predefined type named `Short_Integer` (typically containing the range of integers that can be represented in a half word) and a predefined type named `Long_Integer` (typically containing the range of integers that can be represented in a double word.)

4.2.2 Floating-Point Type Declarations

The values of a floating-point type are approximations to real numbers. The form of a floating-point type declaration is

```
TYPE identifier IS DIGITS precision [RANGE low .. high] ;
```

The positive whole number *precision* specifies the accuracy of the approximations in terms of significant decimal digits: If *n* digits of precision are specified, then two real numbers that differ somewhere in their first *n* significant digits are guaranteed to be approximated by different values of the floating-point type. (The significant digits of a numeral start at the leftmost nonzero digit.) A compiler may provide more digits of precision than are required by the declaration, but not fewer. If the declaration includes a range, the range specifies the lowest and highest real numbers approximated by values in the floating-point type. If the declaration does not include a range, the Ada compiler selects a range on its own.

Here is a floating-point type declaration followed by the declaration of two variables in that type:

```
TYPE Distance_Type IS DIGITS 6;
x, y : Distance_Type;
```

If a program assigns `0.000123456` to `x` and `0.000123457` to `y`, `x` and `y` are guaranteed to contain distinct values. If a program assigns `0.0001234561` to `x` and `0.0001234562` to `y`, `x` and `y` may actually be given the same value—the value in the type that approximates `0.000123456`. In the first case, `x` and `y` differ in their six most significant digits; in the second case, they do not.

A declaration of an *object* in a floating-point type may include a constraint of one of the following forms:

a *floating-point accuracy constraint* of the form

```
DIGITS precision
```

a range constraint of the form

```
RANGE low .. high
```

a combination of the form

```
DIGITS precision RANGE low .. high
```

(in which the `DIGITS` part must always precede the `RANGE` part)

Alternatively, the object declaration may specify no constraint at all. (A floating-point *type* declaration always specifies a precision and may also specify a range. An *object* declaration for a floating-point type may specify a range, a precision, both, or neither.)

A floating-point accuracy constraint in an object declaration specifies that the objects being declared need not be represented with as much precision as is required for the floating-point type as a whole. Thus the number of digits specified in the accuracy constraint must be less than or equal to the number of digits specified in the corresponding type declaration. As with the number of digits specified in a floating-point type declaration, an implementation may choose to provide more precision than that stipulated in a floating-point accuracy constraint, but not less.

Given the floating-point type declaration

```
TYPE Capacity_Type IS DIGITS 10 RANGE 0.0 .. 10_000.0;
```

the object declarations

```
Container_1_Capacity : Capacity_Type DIGITS 6 := 10.33333;
Container_2_Capacity : Capacity_Type DIGITS 6 := 10.33334;
```

are both allowable, even though both initial values contain seven digits. The floating-point accuracy constraint does not restrict the values that may be approximated by `Container_1_Capacity` and `Container_2_Capacity`, only the minimal guaranteed accuracy of the approximation. Some implementations may initialize these two variables to the same approximation, while others may not.

A range constraint for an object in a floating-point type declaration is similar to a range constraint for an object in an integer type. The values given for *low* and *high* must both lie within the type's range of values. That is, they must lie within the range specified by the type declaration or within the range chosen by the compiler if the programmer does not specify a range in the type declaration. Here are examples of floating-point object declarations specifying ranges:

```
a : Capacity_Type DIGITS 5 RANGE 0.0 .. 10.0;
b : Capacity_Type RANGE 7.5 .. 20.0;
c : Capacity_Type RANGE 0.0 .. 10.0 := 0.0;
```

There is a predefined floating-point type named `Float`, whose range and precision are determined independently by each Ada implementation. Typically, the range and precision of the type `Float` will be the range and precision of the standard floating-point representation on the machine that is to run the program. (Type `Float` is the Ada counterpart to the FORTRAN type `REAL`, the Pascal type `Real`, and the PL/I type `FLOAT`.) Some implementations may also have a predefined floating-point type `Short_Float` with much less precision than `Float` or a floating-point type `Long_Float` with much greater precision than `Float`.

4.2.3 Fixed-Point Type Declarations

The form of a fixed-point type declaration is

TYPE *identifier* **IS DELTA** *precision* **RANGE** *low* **..** *high* **;**

The range must always be specified, unlike the range in floating-point type declarations. The precision specifies the maximum distance between approximations to real values. An implementation may use a smaller distance. It will normally use a positive or negative power of two less than or equal to the specified distance.

The type declaration

```
TYPE Batting_Average_Type IS DELTA 0.001 RANGE 0.0 .. 1.0;
```

specifies that `Batting_Average_Type` is a fixed-point type whose values are evenly spaced approximations to real numbers in the range from zero to one, and that the distance between approximations is no more than one one-thousandth. (The actual distance between approximations may be 1 / 1024, which is two raised to the power -10.)

An *object* in a fixed-point type may optionally be declared with a constraint of one of the following forms:

a *fixed-point accuracy constraint* of the form

DELTA *precision*

a range constraint of the form

RANGE *low* **..** *high*

a combination of the form

DELTA *precision* **RANGE** *low* **..** *high*

Alternatively, the object declaration may specify no constraint at all. (A fixed-point *type* declaration always specifies both a precision and a range. An *object* declaration for a fixed-point type may specify a range, a precision, both, or neither.)

Like a floating-point accuracy constraint, a fixed-point accuracy constraint can only specify less precision than the type declaration, not more. That is, the number following the word **DELTA** in a fixed-point object declaration must be greater than or equal to the number following the word **DELTA** in the corresponding type declaration. (A higher number means a greater distance between approximations and thus less precision.) Given the declaration of `Batting_Average_Type` above,

```
Batting_Category : Batting_Average_Type DELTA 0.100;
```

would be a legal object declaration, but

```
Four_Digit_Average : Batting_Average_Type DELTA 0.0001;
```

would not. The range in a fixed-point object declaration is completely analogous to the range in a floating-point object declaration.

4.2.4 Enumeration Type Declarations

An enumeration type is a type consisting of a relatively small number of distinct values. Each of these values is named in the enumeration type declaration. The form of an enumeration type declaration is

```
TYPE identifier IS ( enumeration literal , ~~~ , enumeration literal ) ;
```

Typically, an *enumeration literal* is an identifier. (You will see another form of enumeration literal later.) The enumeration literals denote the values of the enumeration type. For example, the declaration

```
TYPE Suit_Type IS (Clubs, Diamonds, Hearts, Spades);
```

specifies that `Suit_Type` is the name of an enumeration type with four values, denoted by the identifiers `Clubs`, `Diamonds`, `Hearts`, and `Spades`. `Clubs`, `Diamonds`, `Hearts`, and `Spades` are not *variables* of type `Suit_Type`, but *literals*, just as `1` and `3.14` are literals. The object declarations

```
Longest_Suit : Suit_Type := Diamonds;
Old_Maid_Suit : CONSTANT Suit_Type := Spades;
Trump_Suit : Suit_Type;
```

declare a variable `Longest_Suit` and a constant `Old_Maid_Suit` of type `Suit_Type`. The initial value for each of these objects is specified by a `Suit_Type` enumeration literal. The declaration of `Suit_Type` gives meaning to five identifiers—the name of the type and the four enumeration literals.

4.2.4.1 Manipulation of enumeration types. The order in which the enumeration literals are listed in an enumeration type is significant. One value in an enumeration type is considered to be "less than" another value in that type if it is denoted by an enumeration literal occurring earlier in the list. In `Suit_Type`, the value `Clubs` is less than the value `Diamonds`, and the value `Diamonds` is less than the value `Spades`. Given two expressions whose values belong to the same enumeration type, a program can test whether the value of the first expression is less than (or greater than, less than or equal to, or greater than or equal to) the value of the second. For example, the statement

```
IF Longest_Suit < Hearts THEN
   Basic_IO.Put ("Longest suit is a minor suit.");
   Basic_IO.New_Line;
END IF;
```

prints a message when the variable Longest_Suit holds the value Clubs or the value Diamonds, but not when it holds the value Hearts or the value Clubs.

Given any two values in an enumeration type, there is a *subrange* of the type consisting of all values in the type greater than or equal to the first value and less than or equal to the second. For example, the subrange Clubs .. Hearts consists of the three values Clubs, Diamonds, and Hearts, in that order. There is a convenient way to write a loop that performs some action once for each value in a subrange of an enumeration type, taking each value of the subrange in order:

```
FOR Suit IN Clubs .. Hearts LOOP
   [some sequence of statements]
END LOOP;
```

(We will examine this kind of loop more closely in Chapter 7.)

Subranges of an enumeration type may appear in range constraints for object declarations of that type. An example is

```
Longest_Minor_Suit : Suit_Type RANGE Clubs .. Diamonds;
```

This declaration states that Longest_Minor_Suit is a variable of type Suit_Type that can hold only those values greater than or equal to Clubs and less than or equal to Diamonds.

A program can compute the *predecessor* or *successor* of a value in an enumeration type. The predecessor of a value denoted by a given enumeration literal is the value denoted by the preceding enumeration literal; the successor of a value denoted by a given enumeration literal is the value denoted by the following enumeration literal. For example, if x is a Suit_Type variable, Suit_Type'Pred(x) denotes the Suit_Type value just before x and Suit_Type'Succ(x) denotes the Suit_Type value just after x. This notation will be described more fully in Chapter 8. (The first value in an enumeration type has no predecessor, and the last value has no successor.)

4.2.4.2 Overloading enumeration literals. In the Ada language, the same enumeration literal may appear in more than one enumeration type declaration. (This is prohibited in Pascal.) For instance, the following two declarations both contain the enumeration literal Diamonds:

```
TYPE Suit_Type IS (Clubs, Diamonds, Hearts, Spades);
TYPE Commodity_Type IS
   (Pork_Bellies, Wheat, Silver, Diamonds, Gold);
```

The second Suit_Type value and the fourth Commodity_Type value are completely distinct values that happen to be denoted by the same enumeration literal. Their relationship is analogous to the relationship between two different people named John Smith: They are two different people denoted in the same way. This is why we have been careful to say that enumeration literals *denote* the values of enumeration types rather than that they *are* the values of enumeration types. An enumeration literal that denotes more than one value is said to be *overloaded.* Although the same enumeration literal may appear in several enumeration type declarations, no enumeration literal may occur more than once in a single declaration. Consequently, overloaded enumeration literals never denote more than one value of the *same* enumeration type.

We may talk about "John Smith" in a context that makes it clear to which John Smith we are referring. (For instance, if one John Smith is one year old and the other is 31, one such context is the sentence "All purchase orders must be signed by John Smith.") If the context is one that could apply to either John Smith (as in the sentence "John Smith's shirt is dirty."), we must *qualify* the term "John Smith" with additional information to indicate whom we are talking about (as in the sentence "*Baby* John Smith's shirt is dirty.")

The situation is quite similar in the Ada language. An overloaded enumeration literal may appear in a context in which only one of the values it denotes is legal. For example, in the declaration

```
Longest_Suit : Suit_Type := Diamonds;
```

the initial value is required to be of type `Suit_Type`, so the meaning of `Diamonds` is clear. In a context where more than one of the values denoted by an enumeration type would be legal, an Ada program must *qualify* the enumeration literal with additional information. For example, the *qualified expression* `Suit_Type'(Diamonds)` always names `Suit_Type`'s value `Diamonds`. (Qualified expressions will be covered in Chapter 8.)

4.2.4.3 Predefined enumeration types. The FORTRAN data type `LOGICAL` and the Pascal data type `Boolean` consist of the values *true* and *false.* (In PL/I, bit strings consisting of a single bit are used for this purpose.) In the Ada language, there is a predefined enumeration type named `Boolean`. Its definition is:

```
TYPE Boolean IS (False, True);
```

This predefined type has special properties that programmer-defined enumeration types do not have. For instance, values of type `Boolean` control which part of an `IF` statement will be executed.

PL/I and the 1977 version of FORTRAN have data types whose values are strings of characters. Pascal has a data type whose values are individual characters; character strings are represented in Pascal by arrays of characters. The Ada language follows the approach of Pascal, providing a predefined enumeration type named `Character` whose values are individual characters.

The American Standard Code for Information Interchange, or ASCII, defines a sequence of 128 characters. (Thirty-three of these characters are *control characters* that have no written representation. The other 95 characters, called *graphic charac-*

ters, include the space, 10 digits, 26 upper-case letters, 26 lower-case letters, and 32 special characters such as `+`, `-`, `!`, and `=`.) The predefined enumeration type `Character` has values corresponding to the 128 ASCII characters, in order. Each of the 95 values corresponding to graphic characters is denoted by a *character literal,* consisting of that character surrounded by apostrophes. For example, the 66th ASCII character is an upper-case *A,* and the enumeration literal `'A'` denotes the 66th value of type `Character`. `'A'` and `'a'` are two distinct character literals, each denoting a different value of type `Character`. (`'''` is a valid character literal denoting the apostrophe character.)

4.2.5 Discrete Types

Integer types and enumeration types are known collectively as *discrete types.* Among the properties of a discrete type are the following:

The type has a first and a last value.

Each value other than the first has a unique predecessor, and each value other than the last has a unique successor. A value is *greater than* its predecessor and *less than* its successor. The successor of a value's predecessor and the predecessor of a value's successor are the value itself. (The predecessor and successor of an integer x are the integers $x - 1$ and $x + 1$, respectively.)

By starting with the first value and repeatedly computing successors, or by starting with the last value and repeatedly computing predecessors, we eventually encounter every value in the type.

The type represents a finite set of abstract values, and contains an exact representation for each of these values. (This is in contrast to floating-point and fixed-point types, which represent infinitely many abstract values by a finite number of approximations.)

Given two values in the type, there is a subrange consisting of those values greater than or equal to the first and less than or equal to the other. The number of values in this range is well defined. (In contrast, the number of values in a floating-point or fixed-point type that lie between two given values of the type depends on the internal representation of the type and will vary from implementation to implementation.)

There are many contexts in which Ada programs refer to a subrange of a discrete type. One of these is in the declaration of an array type, as we shall see in Section 4.2.6. Such a subrange is specified by a *discrete range*. The general form of a discrete range is

typemark **RANGE** *low* .. *high*

This subrange consists of all the values in the discrete type specified by the typemark that are greater than or equal to *low* and less than or equal to *high*. For example, the discrete range

```
Integer RANGE -5 .. 5
```

consists of eleven consecutive values of type `Integer`, starting with -5 and ending with 5. A discrete range in which *high* is less than *low* is permissible but contains no values. Such a subrange is called a *null range.*

There are two shorthand notations for discrete ranges. If *low* and *high* are, respectively, the first and last values associated with the given typemark, the "`RANGE` *low* `..` *high*" part may be omitted, so that the discrete range consists only of the typemark. For example, given the declaration of `Suit_Type` in Section 4.2.4, the discrete range

```
Suit_Type
```

is equivalent to

```
Suit_Type RANGE Clubs .. Spades
```

If there is no more than one discrete range that both *low* and *high* might belong to, the "*typemark* `RANGE`" part may be omitted, so that the discrete range is simply "*low* `..` *high.*" Thus the discrete range above can also be abbreviated as

```
Clubs .. Spades
```

If, as shown in Section 4.2.4, the enumeration literal `Diamonds` is overloaded with a literal of type `Commodity_Type`, then the abbreviation

```
Diamonds .. Diamonds
```

is not allowed because it could mean either

```
Suit_Type RANGE Diamonds .. Diamonds
```

or

```
Commodity_Type RANGE Diamonds .. Diamonds
```

However, the discrete range

```
Clubs .. Diamonds
```

has only one possible interpretation (since there is no `Commodity_Type` value named `Clubs`), and it is allowed. An abbreviation of the form *low* `..` *high* is also allowed when both *low* and *high* are integer literals. Even though integer literals can usually be used as values of *any* integer type, they are assumed in this context to represent values of the predefined type `Integer`. Thus the discrete range

```
1 .. 10
```

is a shorthand for

```
Integer RANGE 1 .. 10
```

However, the discrete range

```
-5 .. 5
```

may not be used as an abbreviation for

```
Integer RANGE -5 .. 5
```

because the expression -5 is not an integer literal.

4.2.6 Array Type Declarations

An array in the Ada language is essentially like an array in FORTRAN, PL/I, or Pascal. It is a collection of values all belonging to the same type. These values are called the *components* of the array. The components of an array are identified by one or more subscripts. In the Ada language, subscripts are called *index values*. There is one index value for each *dimension* of the array. The index values in a given dimension must all belong to the same type, called the *index type* for that dimension. This may be any discrete type—either an integer type or an enumeration type. Index values in different dimensions may belong to different discrete types.

An *array type* is a type whose values are arrays. All the arrays in a given array type share certain characteristics in common, including the type of the components, the number of dimensions, and the type of the index values in a given dimension. There are two kinds of array types—constrained and unconstrained.

In a *constrained array type*, the lowest and highest permitted index values in a given dimension are the same for all arrays in the type. (These values are called the *bounds* of the array.) All arrays in a constrained array type have the same size and shape.

In an *unconstrained array type*, different arrays may have different bounds. The index type for a given dimension is the same for all arrays in the type, but different arrays may have index values belonging to different subranges of the type. That is, different arrays in an unconstrained array type may have different sizes. Because these different-sized arrays belong to the same type, however, it is possible to write general-purpose subprograms that manipulate arrays of different sizes. (Chapter 9 will explain this.)

4.2.6.1 Constrained array types. The declaration

```
TYPE Table_Type IS
   ARRAY (1 .. 10, 0 .. 10) OF Float RANGE 0.0 .. 100.0;
```

declares Table_Type to be a two-dimensional array type. The index values in the first dimension are values of type Integer ranging from one to ten. The index values in the second dimension are values of type Integer ranging from zero to ten. The components belong to type Float and lie in the range 0.0 to 100.0.

The general form of a constrained array type declaration is

```
TYPE identifier IS
    ARRAY ( discrete range , ~~~ , discrete range ) OF
        typemark [ constraint ] ;
```

One discrete range is specified for each dimension. Any value in the specified range may be used as an index value in that dimension. (Three forms of discrete ranges were given at the end of Section 4.2.5.) The typemark following the word OF specifies the component type of the arrays in the array type. The component type may be any predefined or previously declared type, including another array type. The constraint, if provided, restricts the values of the array components. The form of the constraint depends on the typemark: If the typemark can be followed by a particular constraint in an object declaration, it can be followed by that constraint in an array type declaration. For example, if the typemark names an integer type, only a range constraint is permitted; if the typemark names a floating-point type, either a range constraint, a floating-point accuracy constraint, or a combination of the two is permitted.

The following sequence of declarations culminates in the declaration of an array type to represent sets of playing cards:

```
TYPE Suit_Type IS (Clubs, Diamonds, Hearts, Spades);

Jack  : CONSTANT Integer := 11;
Queen : CONSTANT Integer := 12;
King  : CONSTANT Integer := 13;
Ace   : CONSTANT Integer := 14;

TYPE Card_Set_Type IS ARRAY (2 .. Ace, Suit_Type) OF Boolean;
```

The first dimension of a Card_Set_Type array has index values of type Integer in the range two to fourteen. The second dimension has all four Suit_Type values as index values. Thus a Card_Set_Type array has 52 components of type Boolean, each corresponding to a different pair of index values. The value corresponding to a given pair can be set to True if the card specified by that pair is a member of the set being represented, and to False otherwise.

Given this type declaration, we can declare Card_Set_Type objects as follows:

```
North, South, East, West : Card_Set_Type;
```

North, South, East, and West are each two-dimensional arrays of Boolean components, with index values as described above. Equivalently, North, South, East, and West each contain a Card_Set_Type value. Although a Card_Set_Type value is composed of 52 Boolean values, we can view it as a single value in its own right. For example, the assignment

```
North := South;
```

replaces each component of `North` with the corresponding component of `South`.

Each component of an array can be named by an *indexed component* of the form

array name (*expression* , ~~~ , *expression*)

There must be exactly one expression for each dimension of the array. The value of each expression must be a valid index value for the corresponding dimension. For example, the indexed component

```
North (Ace, Spades)
```

names the component of the array `North` corresponding to the pair of index values fourteen and `Spades`.

Now let us consider a complete program using an array. The program is to read all characters from the standard input file and report how many times each capital letter occurred in the file.

```
WITH Basic_IO;
PROCEDURE Count_Letters IS
   TYPE Frequency_Table_Type IS
      ARRAY ('A' .. 'Z') OF Integer;
   Frequency_Table : Frequency_Table_Type;
   Next_Char       : Character;
BEGIN
   FOR c IN 'A' .. 'Z' LOOP
      Frequency_Table (c) := 0;
   END LOOP;
   WHILE NOT Basic_IO.End_Of_File LOOP
      Basic_IO.Get (Next_Char);
      IF Next_Char IN 'A' .. 'Z' THEN
         Frequency_Table (Next_Char) :=
            Frequency_Table (Next_Char) + 1;
      END IF;
   END LOOP;
   FOR c IN 'A' .. 'Z' LOOP
      Basic_IO.Put (c);
      Basic_IO.Put (" occurred ");
      Basic_IO.Put ( Frequency_Table (c) );
      IF Frequency_Table (c) = 1 THEN
         Basic_IO.Put (" time.");
      ELSE
         Basic_IO.Put (" times.");
      END IF;
      Basic_IO.New_Line;
   END LOOP;
END Count_Letters;
```

`Frequency_Table_Type` is declared to be an array type with one dimension. The index values in this dimension are values of type `Character` in the range `'A' .. 'Z'`. (All the capital letters occur consecutively in the ASCII character set and thus in the predefined type `Character`.) `Frequency_Table` is an array belonging to this type. The first `FOR` loop is repeated with `c` taking on each value in the range `'A' .. 'Z'` in turn, so that each component of the array is initialized to zero. (We will see a better way to do this in Chapter 8.) The `WHILE` loop is executed once for each character in the standard input file. The expression

```
Next_Char IN 'A' .. 'Z'
```

is true when `Next_Char` contains a capital letter and false otherwise. Thus the `IF` statement guarantees that the program refers to `Frequency_Table (Next_Char)` only when `Next_Char` contains a valid index value for `Frequency_Table`. When it does, the corresponding component of `Frequency_Table` is increased by one. The final `FOR` loop is also repeated once with `c` taking on each value in the range `'A' .. 'Z'` in turn. Each repetition of the loop prints the value of `c`, the contents of the component of `Frequency_Table` indexed by `c`, and explanatory text.

4.2.6.2 Unconstrained array types. The declaration

```
TYPE Matrix_Type IS
   ARRAY (Integer RANGE <>, Integer RANGE <>) OF Float;
```

declares `Matrix_Type` to be a two-dimensional array type. Index values in both dimensions belong to type `Integer`, and components belong to type `Float`. Although index values for all `Matrix_Type` objects belong to type `Integer`, the lowest and highest bounds in each dimension may vary from one `Matrix_Type` object to another. For example, the object declarations

```
Matrix_1 : Matrix_Type (1 .. 10, 1 .. 5);
Matrix_2 : Matrix_Type (0 .. 4, 0 .. 4);
```

declare `Matrix_1` and `Matrix_2` to be `Matrix_Type` arrays. For `Matrix_1`, index values in the first dimension may range from one to ten, and index values in the second dimension may range from one to five. For `Matrix_2`, index values in both dimensions may range from zero to four.

The general form of an unconstrained array type declaration is as follows:

```
TYPE identifier IS
   ARRAY ( typemark RANGE <> , ~~~ , typemark RANGE <> )
      OF typemark  : constraint :  ;
```

The symbol `<>`, pronounced "box," means *unspecified.* The form

```
typemark RANGE <>
```

can be viewed as a dummy discrete range, in which the bounds of the range have been left blank. The typemark and constraint following the word OF are just like their counterparts in the constrained array type declaration. The two forms of array type declarations may not be combined. For instance, it is illegal to write

```
TYPE Impossible_Type IS
   ARRAY (Character RANGE 'A' .. 'Z', Integer RANGE <>)
      OF Boolean; -- INCORRECT!
```

because the form

```
Character RANGE 'A' .. 'Z'
```

is only allowed in a constrained array type declaration and the form

```
Integer RANGE <>
```

is only allowed in an unconstrained array type declaration.

In an unconstrained array type, different objects may have different index bounds. However, the index bounds of each object remain fixed for the life of the object. Matrix_1 (declared above) will always have index bounds of 1 .. 10 and 1 .. 10 ; Matrix_2 will always have index bounds of 0 .. 4 and 0 .. 4.

The index bounds of an object in an unconstrained array type are generally specified by an *index constraint* in the object declaration. The form of an index constraint is:

(*discrete range* , ~~~ , *discrete range*)

The index constraint must have precisely one discrete range for each dimension of the unconstrained array type. The bounds of each discrete range must be compatible with the typemark specified for that dimension in the array type declaration.

A declaration of a variable in an unconstrained array type *must* contain an index constraint. A declaration of a constant in an unconstrained array type need not contain an index constraint. (If there is no index constraint, the bounds of the constant are inferred from the initial value.) Assuming that c is a previously declared Matrix_Type constant with index bounds 1 .. 5 and 1 .. 7, the following declarations are all legal:

```
Matrix_3 : Matrix_Type (1 .. 5, 1 .. 7) := c;
Matrix_4 : CONSTANT Matrix_Type := c;
Matrix_5 : CONSTANT Matrix_Type (1 .. 5, 1 .. 7) := c;
```

The declarations of Matrix_3 and Matrix_4 demonstrate that an index constraint is neither required nor forbidden when declaring constants of an unconstrained array type. The declaration

```
Bad_Matrix : Matrix_Type := c; -- INCORRECT!
```

is illegal because a variable in an unconstrained array type must be declared with an index constraint whether or not it has an initial value. A declaration of an object in a *constrained* array type *must not* contain an index constraint, since the index bounds are already specified in the array type declaration. For example, given the declaration of the constrained array type `Card_Set_Type` in section 4.2.6, the declaration

```
Bad_Card_Set : Card_Set_Type (2 .. Ace, Suit_Type);
   -- INCORRECT!
```

is illegal.

It is possible to declare an array type whose component type is itself a previously declared array type. When the previously declared array type is unconstrained, the new array type declaration must include an index constraint specifying the bounds of the component arrays. For example, the declaration

```
TYPE Matrix_List_Type IS
   ARRAY (Integer RANGE <>)
      OF Matrix_Type (1 .. 10, 1 .. 10);
```

is legal, but the declaration

```
TYPE Bad_Array_Type IS ARRAY (1 .. 10) OF Matrix_Type;
   -- INCORRECT!
```

is illegal.

There is a predefined unconstrained array type named `String`, whose values are sequences of characters. Specifically, `String` values are one-dimensional arrays whose index type is the predefined type `Integer` and whose components belong to the predefined enumeration type `Character`. (For reasons that will be explained in Chapter 6, the index values of a `String` object are always positive.) Each declaration of a `String` variable must contain an index constraint with one discrete range, as in the following declaration :

```
Message : String (1 .. 80);
   -- an array with 80 components of type Character
```

Normally, both the lower and upper bounds of a `String` variable must be positive `Integer` values. A declaration like

```
Null_String : String (1 .. 0);
```

is permitted for declaring a `String` variable with no components (a string of length zero).

A sequence of consecutive components in a one-dimensional array can be viewed as an array in its own right. For example, given the declarations

```
Message      : String (1 .. 80);
Message_Code : String (1 .. 4);
```

the assignment statement

```
Message_Code := Message (1 .. 4);
```

copies the four components of `Message` whose index values are encompassed by the discrete range `(1 .. 4)`. The expression

```
Message (1 .. 4)
```

is called a *slice* of the array `Message`. It is a four-component value of type `String`. The index values of the slice

```
A (I .. J)
```

start at `I` and end at `J`. Thus components of the slice are indexed by the same values as in the array from which the slice is taken.

The following program reads an eighty-character string, exchanges the front and back halves of the string, and prints the resulting string:

```
WITH Basic_IO;
PROCEDURE Flip_String IS
   Input_String : String (1 .. 80);
   Front_Part   : String (1 .. 40);
BEGIN
   Basic_IO.Get (Input_String);
   Front_Part := Input_String (1 .. 40);
   Input_String (1 .. 40) := Input_String (41 .. 80);
   Input_String (41 .. 80) := Front_Part;
   Basic_IO.Put (Input_String);
   Basic_IO.New_Line;
END Flip_String;
```

The operator `&` can be used to *catenate* two values in the same array type, that is, to join them together end-to-end to form a larger array. The program `Flip_Strings` above could also be written as follows:

```
WITH Basic_IO;
PROCEDURE Flip_String IS
   Input_String : String (1 .. 80);
   Front_Part   : String (1 .. 40);
BEGIN
   Basic_IO.Get (Input_String);
   Basic_IO.Put
      (Input_String (41 .. 80) & Input_String (1 .. 40));
   Basic_IO.New_Line;
END Flip_String;
```

Further discussion of catenation can be found in Chapter 8.

4.2.7 Record Type Declarations

A value in a record type consists of a combination of *components*. Each component has a distinct name and holds a value of a particular type. Different components may hold values of different types. The declaration

```
TYPE Buffer_Type IS
   RECORD
      Length_Part   : Integer RANGE 0 .. 128;
      Contents_Part : String (1 .. 128);
   END RECORD;
```

declares `Buffer_Type` to be a record type. Each value *v* in `Buffer_Type` has two components: a value of type `Integer` in the range `0 .. 128` named *v*`.Length_Part` and a 128-component array of type `String` named *v*`.Contents_Part`. A value in a record type is called a *record.*

There are two different kinds of record types, with and without *discriminants.* All objects in a record type without discriminants, like `Buffer_Type`, have the same kinds of components. In a record type with discriminants, different objects may consist of different kinds of components. Record types with discriminants will be discussed in Chapter 10. In this chapter, discussion will be confined to record types without discriminants.

The declaration of a record type without discriminants takes the following form:

```
TYPE identifier IS
   RECORD
      component declaration
         ~~~
      component declaration
   END RECORD ;
```

A *component declaration* has exactly the same form as a variable declaration:

```
identifier , ~~~ , identifier :
     typemark [ constraint ] [ := expression ] ;
```

The identifier preceding the word `IS` in the type declaration becomes the typemark identifying the record type. Each identifier listed before the colon in a component declaration names a component. The typemark determines the type of these components; and the constraint, if present, further restricts the values that these components may hold.

A particular kind of constraint may be required, optional, or forbidden in a given component declaration, depending on the typemark. The restrictions on constraints in variable declarations also apply to constraints in component declarations. For example, a record component of type `Integer` may optionally have a range constraint; a record component of type `String` *must* have an index constraint.

The declaration

```
TYPE Complex_Type IS
   RECORD
      Real_Part, Imaginary_Part : Float;
   END RECORD;
```

declares Complex_Type to be a record type whose values consist of two components of type Float. One component is named Real_Part and the other is named Imaginary_Part. The type declaration is equivalent to one in which the two components are declared in separate component declarations:

```
TYPE Complex_Type IS
   RECORD
      Real_Part      : Float;
      Imaginary_Part : Float;
   END RECORD;
```

The ability to combine declarations of similar components into a single component declaration is simply a convenient shorthand.

The optional ":= *expression*" part of the component declaration is used to specify a *default initial value* for the listed components. If it is present, all objects belonging to the record type have the corresponding components initialized to the specified value, except when the object declaration specifies an initial value for the entire record. Record types are the only kinds of types for which the programmer can specify a default initial value.

Suppose the declaration of Buffer_Type were modified so that the component Length_Part had a default value of zero:

```
TYPE Buffer_Type IS
   RECORD
      Length_Part   : Integer RANGE 0 .. 128 := 0;
      Contents_Part : String (1 .. 128);
   END RECORD;
```

If Buffer_1 were a previously declared Buffer_Type record, then the declarations

```
Buffer_2 : Buffer_Type;
Buffer_3 : Buffer_Type := Buffer_1;
```

initialize Buffer_2.Length_Part to zero (because of the default initial value in the type declaration for Buffer_Type) but leave the initial value of Buffer_2.Contents_Part undefined. The record Buffer_3 is explicitly initialized to the value of Buffer_1. This means that Buffer_3.Length_Part starts out with the value of Buffer_1.Length_Part (overriding the default initial value) and Buffer_3.Contents_Part starts out with the value of Buffer_1.Contents_Part.

PL/I and common nonstandard implementations of Pascal support varying length character strings. In the Ada language, `String` is an unconstrained array type. Although different variables of type `String` may have different lengths, each individual variable must be declared with an index constraint that determines the permanent length of that variable. However, an Ada programmer can implement his own varying length character strings using the record type `Buffer_Type`.

We can view a `Buffer_Type` variable *b* as representing a varying length character string as follows: *b*`.Length_Part` holds the current length of the string (which may vary from zero to 128). The first *b*`.Length_Part` components of *b*`.Contents_Part` represent the contents of the string, and the remaining components of *b*`.Length_Part` are considered meaningless. The default initial value of zero for the `Length_Part` component means that a `Buffer_Type` variable is initialized by default to the representation of the empty string.

The following program assumes that the standard input file contains 100 sentences, one sentence per line. Each sentence contains up to 128 characters and ends with either a period or a question mark. The program prints out first all sentences ending with a period (*statements*) and then all sentences ending with a question mark (*questions*), one sentence per line.

```
WITH Basic_IO;
PROCEDURE Print_Sentences IS
   TYPE Buffer_Type IS
      RECORD
         Length_Part   : Integer RANGE 0 .. 128 := 0;
         Contents_Part : String (1 .. 128);
      END RECORD;
   TYPE Buffer_List_Type IS ARRAY (1 .. 100) OF Buffer_Type;
   Input_Sentence, Output_Sentence : Buffer_Type;
   Statement_List, Question_List   : Buffer_List_Type;
   Statement_Count, Question_Count : Integer := 0;
BEGIN
   FOR i IN 1 .. 100 LOOP
      Basic_IO.Get_Line
         (Input_Sentence.Contents_Part,
          Input_Sentence.Length_Part);
      IF Input_Sentence.Contents_Part
            (Input_Sentence.Length_Part) = '.' THEN
         Statement_Count := Statement_Count + 1;
         Statement_List (Statement_Count) := Input_Sentence;
      ELSE
         Question_Count := Question_Count + 1;
         Question_List (Question_Count) := Input_Sentence;
      END IF;
   END LOOP ;
```

```
      FOR i IN 1 .. Statement_Count LOOP
         Output_Sentence := Statement_List (i);
         Basic_IO.Put
            (Output_Sentence.Contents_Part
               (1 .. Output_Sentence.Length_Part));
         Basic_IO.New_Line;
      END LOOP;
      FOR i IN 1 .. Question_Count LOOP
         Output_Sentence := Question_List (i);
         Basic_IO.Put
            (Output_Sentence.Contents_Part
               (1 .. Output_Sentence.Length_Part));
         Basic_IO.New_Line;
      END LOOP;
   END Print_Sentences;
```

Basic_IO.Get_Line is a procedure with two parameters, the first of type String and the second of type Integer. Assuming the String parameter has at least one component for each character in the current line of the standard input file, the call on Basic_IO.Get_Line reads the characters on the current line into the components of its first parameter (perhaps leaving certain components at the end of the array unfilled) and sets its second parameter to the index value of the component containing the last character. In this program, the two components of the record Input_Sentence are used as parameters. This has the effect of reading a line from the standard input file into the representation of a varying length character string.

In the IF statement, the condition

```
Input_Sentence.Contents_Part
   (Input_Sentence.Length_Part) = '.'
```

tests whether the last character of the varying length string in Input_Sentence is a period. The record component Input_Sentence.Contents_Part is an array of type String. The record component Input_Sentence.Length_Part is a value of type Integer used as an index into this array.

Buffer_List_Type is a constrained array type with 100 Buffer_Type components. We use Buffer_List_Type variables to hold lists of sentences. In manipulating these lists, we can view each Buffer_Type component as a single abstract value representing a sentence. For example, the assignment statement

```
Statement_List (Statement_Count) := Input_Sentence;
```

assigns the value of the Buffer_Type variable Input_Sentence to a component of the Buffer_List_Type array Statement_List. At this level of abstraction, we view the assignment statement as copying a single Buffer_Type value, even though this involves copying two different record components,

In the statement

```
Basic_IO.Put
   (Output_Sentence.Contents_Part
      (1 .. Output_Sentence.Length_Part));
```

the discrete range

```
1 .. Output_Sentence.Length_Part
```

is the range of index values corresponding to "filled in" parts of the array. Thus

```
Output_Sentence.Contents_Part
   (1 .. Output_Sentence.Length_Part)
```

is a slice of the `String` value `Output_Sentence.Contents_Part` containing the characters of the sentence. This slice, itself of type `String`, is written by `Basic_IO.Put`.

4.3 DETAILS

It is now time to consider some details about object and type declarations that we avoided earlier to concentrate on the basic ideas. This section discusses restrictions on the expressions that may appear in object and type declarations, the issue of when those expressions are evaluated, and further details about each class of types discussed earlier.

4.3.1 Static and Dynamic Expressions

Every expression is either *dynamic* or *static*. A dynamic expression may have different values at different times during the execution of a program. The value of a static expression never changes and can be determined without running the program. If `x` is a variable, the following expressions are dynamic:

```
x    3 * x + 17    Basic_IO.End_Of_File
```

Given the constant declarations

```
Pi     : CONSTANT Float := 3.141593;
Radius : CONSTANT Float := 1.76;
```

the following expressions are static:

```
1    Pi    (4.0 / 3.0) * Pi * Radius ** 3
```

A precise definition of static expressions, in terms of the elementary pieces making up the expression, will be given in Chapter 8.

A good compiler will evaluate static expressions while compiling the program and use only the values of the expressions in generating machine language instructions. For example, given the declaration

```
Maximum : Integer := 2 ** 21 - 1;
```

a compiler can calculate while compiling the program that `2 ** 21 - 1` is 2,097,151 and avoid generating instructions to perform the calculation while the program is running.

The programmer's intent is often more clearly conveyed by writing a static expression than by writing the value of that expression. The declaration above makes it clear that `Maximum` is being initialized to the largest value that can be represented in twenty-one binary digits. Had the declaration been written as

```
Maximum : Integer := 2_097_151;
```

this would not have been clear. Furthermore, the programmer could make a mistake while performing the calculation himself.

4.3.2 Numeric Literals and Universal Expressions

A numeric literal without a fractional part, such as `10`, is called an *integer literal.* An integer literal may be interpreted as a value in any integer type with an appropriate range. A numeric literal containing a fractional part, such as `3.5` or `4.0`, is called a *real literal.* A real literal may be interpreted as a value in any floating-point or fixed-point type with an appropriate range.

Literals may be combined using arithmetic operators to form *universal expressions.* Here are some examples:

```
25 * 80     3.14159 * 10.0 * 10.0     2 ** 16 - 1
```

A universal expression containing only integer literals is a *universal integer expression.* It may be interpreted as a value in any integer type with an appropriate range. A universal expression containing only real literals is a *universal real expression.* It may be interpreted as a value in any floating-point or fixed-point type with an appropriate range. Integer and real literals can be combined in certain restricted ways to form a universal real expression. Details will be presented in Chapter 8.

There is a variation of the constant declaration called a *number declaration.* Its form is

identifier **,** ~~~ **,** *identifier* **:**
    CONSTANT := *static universal expression* **;**

Unlike a constant declaration, a number declaration does not contain a typemark or a constraint. The sole purpose of a number declaration is to provide a meaningful name for the value following the `:=` . The declared identifiers are known as *named numbers*. The *constant* declaration

```
Pi : CONSTANT Float := 3.1415926536;
```

declares `Pi` to be an *object* of type `Float` that can only be used as a value of that type. The *number* declaration

```
Pi : CONSTANT := 3.1415926536;
```

declares `Pi` to be a universal real named number. Given the second declaration, `Pi` can be interpreted as a value in *any* floating-point or fixed-point type with the appropriate range.

A named number declared with a universal integer expression can be used anywhere an integer literal can be used; a named number declared with a universal real expression can be used anywhere a real literal can be used. In particular, named numbers can be used in the universal expressions of later number declarations:

```
Radians_Per_Degree : CONSTANT := Pi / 180.0;
Degrees_Per_Radian : CONSTANT := 1.0 / Radians_Per_Degree;
Number_Of_Bits     : CONSTANT := 21;
Highest_Number     : CONSTANT := 2 ** Number_Of_Bits - 1;
```

4.3.3 Expressions Allowed in Declarations

Until now, virtually all of the numeric values you have seen in type declarations have been numeric literals. In fact a wider class of expressions is permitted. In integer, floating-point, and fixed-point type declarations, any static expression of an appropriate type may be used. Appropriate types are as follows:

In the declaration of an integer type, each bound of the range may be an expression of any integer type.

In the declaration of a floating-point or fixed-point type, each bound of the range may be an expression of any floating-point or fixed-point type. An expression of a floating-point type may be used in declaring a fixed-point type, and vice versa.

In the declaration of a floating-point type, the number of digits of precision can be given by an expression of any integer type.

In the declaration of a fixed-point type, the delta can be given by an expression of any floating-point or fixed-point type.

In each case, the expression must be static. The upper and lower bounds of a range are not required to belong to the same type. Furthermore, a universal integer expression (such as an integer literal or an integer named number) may be used where an expression of any integer type is allowed; a universal real expression (such as a real literal or a real named number) is allowed where an expression of any floating-point or fixed-point type is allowed.

Consider the following examples:

```
Digits_In_Account_Number : CONSTANT := 10;
Required_Precision       : CONSTANT := 5;
Speed_Of_Light           : CONSTANT Float := 2.9979E8;
Pi                       : CONSTANT := 3.1415926536;

TYPE Account_Number_Type IS
   RANGE 0 .. Digits_In_Account_Number;

TYPE Speed_Type IS
   DIGITS Required_Precision
   RANGE -Speed_Of_Light .. Speed_Of_Light;

TYPE Angle_Type IS
   DELTA (2 * Pi) / 1000.0 RANGE 0.0 .. 2.0 * Pi;
```

Like all these expressions in integer, floating-point, and fixed-point type declarations, the universal expressions in number declarations must be static. (There are universal expressions that are not static, but we will not examine them until Chapter 8.) All other expressions in the kinds of declarations we have seen so far may be dynamic expressions:

The initial value expression in a variable or constant declaration may be either a static or dynamic expression. (This is another difference between number declarations and constant declarations.)

The index bounds in an array type declaration may be either static or dynamic expressions.

The expressions appearing in range constraints, accuracy constraints, and index constraints may be either static or dynamic. These constraints may appear in variable declarations, in constant declarations, following the component type in an array type declaration, and in the component declarations of a record type declaration.

Assume in each of the examples below that the function call

```
User_Input (Low, High)
```

queries the operator of the program for an integer between `Low` and `High`, prompts as many times as necessary until valid input is obtained and returns the valid value. This function call is a dynamic expression. The following sequence of declarations is legal:

```
Number_To_Process :
   Integer RANGE 1 ..10 := User_Input (1, 10);

Number_Of_Samples : CONSTANT Integer := User_Input (0, 100);

TYPE Sample_List_Type IS
   ARRAY (1 .. 2 * Number_Of_Samples) OF Float;

Approximation : Float DIGITS User_Input (3, 10);

TYPE ID_List_Type IS
   ARRAY (Integer RANGE <>) OF
      Integer RANGE 1 .. User_Input (1, 1000);

ID_List : ID_List_Type (1 .. Number_To_Process);
```

(Besides the calls on `User_Input`, expressions referring to `Number_To_Process` and `Number_Of_Samples` are dynamic.)

This raises the question of when and how often expressions in declarations are evaluated. Recall that declarations are *elaborated* while a program is running. In general, the dynamic expressions in a declaration are evaluated at the time the declaration is elaborated. Given the sequence of declarations above, `User_Input` would be called at the time the declaration of `Number_To_Process` was elaborated, and the value entered by the program operator, say four, would become the initial value of that variable. At the time the declaration of `ID_List` was elaborated, `Number_To_Process` would still contain this value, so four would be used as the upper bound in the index constraint. It is the value of the expression at the time it is evaluated that is used as the upper bound. `ID_List` will continue to have four components even if the variable `Number_To_Process` is given a different value.

An exception to this rule is made in the case of record-type declarations. Expressions giving default initial values for record components are evaluated not when the record-type declaration is elaborated, but *each time* a new record in the type is created without an explicit initial value. Consider the following declarations:

```
TYPE Work_Item_Type IS
   RECORD
      ID_List_Part : ID_List_Type (1 .. User_Input (1, 10));
      Count_Part   : Integer := User_Input (0, 50);
   END RECORD;

Work_Item_1 : Work_Item_Type;
Work_Item_2 : Work_Item_Type;
Work_Item_3 : Work_Item_Type := Work_Item_1;
```

The dynamic expression in the index constraint for `ID_List_Part` is evaluated at the time the declaration of `Work_Item_Type` is elaborated, resulting in `ID_List_Part` components of the same length for objects `Work_Item_1`, `Work_Item_2`, and `Work_Item_3`. The dynamic expression giving a default initial value for `Count_Part` is evaluated once when the declaration of `Work_Item_1` is elaborated and once when the declaration of `Work_Item_2` is elaborated. It is not evaluated when the declaration of `Work_Item_3` is elaborated, because Work_Item_3 has an explicit initial value. In all, there are three calls on User_Input, each of which may return a different value.

An object declaration or a record component declaration can contain a list of identifiers all being declared together, as in the following examples:

```
a, b, c : Integer;

TYPE Complex_Type IS
   RECORD
      Real_Part, Imaginary_Part : Float;
   END RECORD;
```

Such a declaration is equivalent to a sequence of identical declarations for individual identifiers:

```
a : Integer;
b : Integer;
c : Integer;

TYPE Complex_Type IS
   RECORD
      Real_Part      : Float;
      Imaginary_Part : Float;
   END RECORD;
```

This equivalence holds precisely, even for declarations containing dynamic expressions. For example,

```
a, b, c : Integer := User_Input (1, 30);
```

is equivalent to

```
a : Integer := User_Input (1, 30);
b : Integer := User_Input (1, 30);
c : Integer := User_Input (1, 30);
```

The initial value expression is evaluated once for each identifier. In this case, that means the program operator is queried for input three times.

4.3.4 Predefined Numeric Types and Portability

The predefined integer types Integer, Short_Integer, and Long_Integer should be used with restraint. You can easily fall into the habit of using the type Integer for all objects that will hold whole numbers, especially if you are used to a language with a single integer type. However, you will fail to take advantage of an important feature of the Ada language—the ability to distinguish between different uses of whole numbers.

Furthermore, the use of the predefined integer types is detrimental to *portability*, that is, the ability to transfer a correctly running program from one kind of computer to another. This is because the ranges of the predefined types vary from one compiler to another. For example, integers in the range -10,000,000,000 to 10,000,000,000 can fit in a 36-bit word but not in a 32-bit word. Assuming compilers for both a machine with 32-bit words and a machine with 36-bit words use a single word to represent values of type `Integer`, a variable holding values in this range can be declared `Integer` on the first machine, but not on the second. On the second machine, some type represented with two words (perhaps `Long_Integer`) may be required.

If you declare an integer type with the range of values required by your program, as in

```
TYPE Count_Type IS RANGE -10_000_000_000 .. 10_000_000_000;
```

each compiler will automatically choose the appropriate representation for that type on its own target machine. If you try to move to a machine that cannot handle integers as large as some your program uses, you are stuck; but at least you have the consolation of finding this out when you try to recompile your program and an error message tells you that your integer type declaration specified too large a range. If you simply use the type `Integer`, your program may appear to be running successfully on the new machine until the first time it computes a value that belongs to the type `Integer` on the old machine but not on the new one.

Similar considerations apply to the use of the predefined floating-point types `Float`, `Short_Float`, and `Long_Float`. Furthermore, when you omit the optional range on a floating-point type declaration, the implementation chooses a range for you. The range chosen varies from compiler to compiler. Thus the omission of a range in a floating-point type declaration is also detrimental to portability. It may cause a program well tested on one machine to appear to work correctly on a new machine but then to fail unexpectedly when the range chosen by the new machine's compiler is exceeded.

4.3.5 Enumeration Types with Character Literals

All enumeration type declarations we have seen until now have used identifiers as enumeration literals. The predefined enumeration type `Character` seemed extraordinary, since it contains values denoted by character literals like `'X'` rather than by identifiers. Actually, a character literal is just a special kind of enumeration literal. An enumeration literal in an enumeration type declaration may be either an identifier or a character literal. Both kinds may appear in the same declaration.

This capability is primarily useful in defining enumeration types that correspond to character sets other than the ASCII character set. For example, Figure 4.1 depicts the Fieldata character set devised by the U.S. Army in 1960. Here is a declaration for an enumeration type corresponding to this character set:

```
TYPE Fieldata_Character_Type IS
   ('@', '[', ']', '#', Delta_Symbol, ' ', 'A', 'B',
    'C', 'D', 'E', 'F', 'G', 'H', 'I', 'J',
    'K', 'L', 'M', 'N', 'O', 'P', 'Q', 'R',
    'S', 'T', 'U', 'V', 'W', 'X', 'Y', 'Z',
    ')', '-', '+', '<', '=', '>', '&', '$',
    '*', '(', '%', ':', '?', '!', ',', '\',
    '0', '1', '2', '3', '4', '5', '6', '7',
    '8', '9', ''', ';', '/', '.',
    Lozenge_Symbol, Not_Equal_Symbol);
```

This declaration specifies that `Fieldata_Character_Type` is the name of an enumeration type with 64 values. Given the declaration

```
Next_Character : Fieldata_Character_Type;
```

the comparison

```
Next_Character < 'A'
```

is based on the Fieldata collating sequence rather than the ASCII collating sequence.

@	[	]	#	△		A	B
C	D	E	F	G	H	I	J
K	L	M	N	O	P	Q	R
S	T	U	V	W	X	Y	Z
)	-	+	<	=	>	&	$
*	(	%	:	?	!	,	\
0	1	2	3	4	5	6	7
8	9	'	;	/	.	⌑	≠

Figure 4.1 The Fieldata character set.

Except for the way it is written, a character literal is no different from an enumeration literal that is an identifier. Every time you declare an enumeration type with a character literal, you are overloading an enumeration literal of the predefined enumeration type `Character`. The `Fieldata_Character_Type` value `'A'` (the seventh value of `Fieldata_Character_Type`) has no more of a relationship to the `Character` value `'A'` (the 66th value of type `Character`) than the `Commodity_Type` value `Diamonds` had to the `Suit_Type` value `Diamonds`. They are just two values that both happen to be called `'A'`. (In the comparison

```
Next_Character < 'A'
```

it is the type of `Next_Character` that determines the interpretation of `'A'`.)

Do not confuse an enumeration literal consisting of a single-character identifier with a character literal. The declaration

```
TYPE Silly_Type IS (A, 'A', 'a');
```

declares `Silly_Type` to be an enumeration type consisting of three values, one of which is denoted by the identifier `A`, one of which is denoted by the character literal `'A'`, and one of which is denoted by the character literal `'a'`. `A`, `'A'`, and `'a'` are distinct enumeration literals.

4.3.6 More on Array Types

4.3.6.1 Null arrays. An index constraint or a constrained array type declaration may contain a null discrete range (i.e., a discrete range in which the lower bound is greater than the upper bound). In such a case, the array declared is a *null array,* consisting of no elements. In particular,

```
Empty_String : String (1 .. 0);
```

declares `Empty_String` to be a sequence of zero characters.

Most often, null arrays arise when algorithms designed to work for any number of input values are applied to zero input values. For example, a program to read some number of integers specified by the user and process them in some way might contain the following declarations:

```
Number_Of_Inputs : Integer := User_Input (0, 30);
TYPE Integer_List_Type IS
   ARRAY (1 .. Number_Of_Inputs) OF Integer;
Input_List, Output_List : Integer_List_Type;
```

When the call on `User_Input` returns zero, `Input_List` and `Output_List` are null arrays.

4.3.6.2 Multidimensional arrays versus arrays of arrays. In Pascal, multidimensional arrays are defined as being equivalent to arrays of arrays. This is not so in the Ada language. Consider the following array type declaration:

```
TYPE String_Matrix_Type IS
   ARRAY (1 .. 25, 1 .. 100) OF String (1 .. 20);
```

A `String_Matrix_Type` object can only be considered a 25-by-100 array whose elements are 20-component arrays of `Character` values. It cannot be treated as a 25-by-100-by-20 array of characters or as a 25-component array whose components are 100-component arrays of 20-character strings. Given the declaration

```
String_Matrix : String_Matrix_Type;
```

the indexed component

```
String_Matrix (24, 50) (10)
```

is valid. It names the tenth component of the 20-character string `String_Matrix (24, 50)`. However, the indexed components

```
String_Matrix (24, 50, 10)
```

and

```
String_Matrix (24) (50, 10)
```

are not valid.

4.3.6.3 "One of a kind" arrays. Many programs have individual arrays that are never used in conjunction with other arrays having the same index and component types. Because it is cumbersome to declare an array type only to use it in a single object declaration, the Ada language offers a shortcut for "one of a kind" arrays: An array variable declaration may take the form

```
identifier , ~~~ , identifier :
    ARRAY ( discrete range , ~~~ , discrete range ) OF
        typemark [ constraint ] [ := expression ] ;
```

as in the example

```
Input_List : ARRAY (1 .. Number_Of_Inputs) OF Integer;
```

(Essentially, the typemark and constraint of the object declaration are replaced by a constrained array *type definition*.) An array constant declaration may take the form

```
identifier , ~~~ , identifier :
   CONSTANT ARRAY ( discrete range , ~~~ , discrete range ) OF
      typemark [ constraint ] := expression ;
```

as in this example:

```
TYPE Month_Type IS
   (January, February, March, April, May, June, July,
    August, September, October, November, December);
Days_In_Month :
   CONSTANT ARRAY (Month_Type) OF Integer :=
      (31, 28, 31, 30, 31, 30, 31, 31, 30, 31, 30, 31);
```

(The array's initial value is specified by a list of component values called an *aggregate.* Aggregates will be discussed in Chapter 8.)

An array object declared in this way does not have the same type as any other array object. The variable declaration

```
Input_List : ARRAY (1 .. Number_Of_Inputs) OF Integer;
```

has the same effect as the two declarations

```
TYPE One_Of_A_Kind_Type IS
   ARRAY (1 .. Number_Of_Inputs) OF Integer;
Input_List : One_Of_A_Kind_Type;
```

except that the typemark `One_Of_A_Kind_Type` is not available for use elsewhere in the program. Because the type of an array declared in this way cannot be named, the array is said to belong to an *anonymous array type.*

A declaration of this form declaring several objects at once is equivalent to a sequence of individual declarations. For example,

```
Input_List, Output_List :
   ARRAY (1 .. Number_Of_Inputs) OF Integer;
```

is equivalent to

```
Input_List  : ARRAY (1 .. Number_Of_Inputs) OF Integer;
Output_List : ARRAY (1 .. Number_Of_Inputs) OF Integer;
```

This means that `Input_List` and `Output_List` belong to two *different* anonymous array types!

This kind of shortcut cannot be used with other classes of types. For instance, you *cannot* declare a variable of an "anonymous integer type" by writing

```
Number_Of_Inputs : RANGE 0 .. 100; -- ILLEGAL SYNTAX!
```

or a variable in an "anonymous enumeration type" by writing

```
Result : (Success, Failure); -- ILLEGAL SYNTAX!
```

Furthermore, the shortcut for anonymous array types cannot be used in record-component declarations. Instead of writing

```
TYPE Stack_Type IS
   RECORD
      Top_Part      : Integer RANGE 0 .. 100 := 0;
      Elements_Part : ARRAY (1 .. 100) OF Float;
         -- ILLEGAL SYNTAX!
   END RECORD;
```

you must explicitly declare an array type:

```
TYPE Element_List_Type IS ARRAY (1 .. 100) OF Float;

TYPE Stack_Type IS
   RECORD
      Top_Part      : Integer RANGE 0 .. 100 := 0;
      Elements_Part : Element_List_Type;
   END RECORD;
```

4.4 SUMMARY

Objects and types must, with a few specific exceptions, be declared. Declarations are, in effect, processed one after the other at the time a program runs. The processing of a declaration is called *elaboration*.

For some classes of types, certain expressions appearing in the type declaration must be *static*. This means essentially that the expression has a fixed value that can be determined without running the program. (A more exact definition of static expressions will be given in Chapter 8.) In object declarations and in certain places in some type declarations, any expression of an appropriate type is allowed.

There are two kinds of *objects*—*variables* and *constants*. The value of a variable can change during a computation, but the value of a constant cannot. The form of a variable declaration is:

identifier , ~~~ , *identifier* :
   typemark [*constraint*] [:= *expression*] ;

The form of a constant declaration is:

identifier , ~~~ , *identifier* :
   CONSTANT *typemark* [*constraint*] := *expression* ;

The identifiers are the names of the objects being declared; the typemark indicates the type of the objects; the constraint further restricts the values that the object may hold; and the expression gives the initial value of the object. (In the case of constants, the expression is required and the initial value of the object is its permanent value.) Different constraints are required, allowed, or forbidden in declaring objects of different types. The expressions used in constraints and for the initial value may be dynamic expressions. They are evaluated at the time the declaration is elaborated.

Named number declarations are similar to constant declarations but contain no typemark or constraint:

```
identifier , ~~~ , identifier :
    CONSTANT := static universal expression ;
```

Universal expressions include, among other things, integer literals (which have no decimal point), real literals (which always have a point), and combinations of literals and arithmetic operators. (A more complete definition will be given in Chapter 8.) Depending on whether or not it contains real literals, a universal expression is either a *universal integer* expression or a *universal real* expression. Universal integer expressions may be used in contexts where an expression of some integer type is required, and universal real expressions may be used in contexts where an expression of some floating-point or fixed-point type is required. The identifiers declared in a number declaration are called *named numbers* and can be used as if they were numeric literals. In particular, they may be used in universal expressions of later number declarations.

Type declarations usually take the form

```
TYPE identifier IS type definition ;
```

where the form of the type definition depends on the class of the type being declared.

The form of an integer type declaration is:

```
TYPE identifier IS RANGE low .. high ;
```

The static expressions *low* and *high* belong to integer types and give the range of values that must be included in the type being declared. There is a predefined integer type name `Integer` and, with some compilers, predefined integer types named `Short_Integer` and `Long_Integer`. The declaration of an object in an integer type can contain a *range constraint* of the form

```
RANGE low .. high
```

further restricting the values that that object may hold. In the range constraint of an object declaration, the expressions *low* and *high* need not be static but must belong to the type of the object being declared.

The form of a floating-point type declaration is:

TYPE *identifier* **IS DIGITS** *precision* [**RANGE** *low* **..** *high*] **;**

The precision is a positive static expression of some integer type indicating the number of significant decimal digits required for approximating values in the type. Each bound of the optional range is a static expression of some floating-point or fixed-point type. There is a predefined floating-point type named `Float` and, with some compilers, predefined floating point types named `Short_Float` and `Long_Float`. The declaration of an object in a floating-point type may have a *floating-point accuracy constraint* indicating that not as much precision is required for that particular object, a range constraint indicating that the object's values will lie within a subrange of the type's values, or a combination:

DIGITS *precision*

RANGE *low* **..** *high*

DIGITS *precision* **RANGE** *low* **..** *high*

In the constraint of an object declaration, the expression *precision* must be a positive static expression of some integer type; the expressions *low* and *high* need not be static but must belong to the type of the object being declared.

The form of a fixed-point type declaration is:

TYPE *identifier* **IS DELTA** *precision* **RANGE** *low* **..** *high* **;**

Each of the expressions *precision, low,* and *high* is static, and each belongs to some floating-point or fixed-point type. The value of *precision* is positive and gives the maximum distance between approximations in the fixed-point type being declared. Unlike the range in a floating-point type declaration, the range in a fixed-point type declaration can never be omitted. The declaration of an object in a fixed-point type may have a *fixed-point accuracy constraint* indicating that not as much precision is required for that particular object (in other words, that a larger delta may be used), a range constraint indicating that the object's values will lie within a subrange of the type's values, or a combination:

DELTA *precision*

RANGE *low* **..** *high*

DELTA *precision* **RANGE** *low* **..** *high*

In the constraint of an object declaration, the expression *precision* must be a positive static expression of some floating-point or fixed-point type; the expressions *low* and *high* need not be static but must belong to the type of the object being declared.

The form of an enumeration type declaration is:

> TYPE *identifier* IS
>   (*enumeration literal* , ~~~ , *enumeration literal*) ;

Each enumeration literal is either an identifier like `Spades` or a character literal like `'A'`. The enumeration literals listed in the type declaration denote the values in the enumeration type. Values whose literals occur later in the list are considered *greater than* values whose literals occur earlier. Each value is the *successor* of the value that comes before it and the *predecessor* of the value that follows it. The predefined type `Boolean` is an enumeration type consisting of the two values `False` and `True`. The predefined type `Character` is an enumeration type with the list of values corresponding, in order, to the characters in the ASCII character set. The declaration of an object in an enumeration type may contain a range constraint specifying the smallest and largest values that will be held in that object. The same enumeration literal may appear in more than one enumeration type declaration, causing the enumeration literal to be *overloaded.* The values denoted by an overloaded enumeration literal are distinct values that are not related to each other in any way except by the fact that they have the same name. An overloaded enumeration literal may only appear in a context that makes clear what its type is. Each character literal appearing in an enumeration type declaration overloads a literal of the predefined type `Character`.

A *discrete type* is any type that is either an integer type or an enumeration type. All discrete types have a first and last value, a predecessor for each value other than the first, a successor for each value other than the last, a way to compare two values in the type to determine which is greater than the other, and subranges containing well-defined numbers of values. A subrange of a discrete type is described by a construct called a *discrete range.* There are three forms of discrete ranges:

> *typemark* RANGE *low* .. *high*
>
> *typemark*
>
> *low* .. *high*

In the first form, the expressions *low* and *high* need not be static but must be of the type specified by the typemark. The second form can be viewed as an abbreviation for the first form when the range includes every value specified by the typemark. The third form can be viewed as an abbreviation for the first form when there is only one type to which the expressions *low* and *high* can be viewed as belonging. In addition, the third form is allowed when each of *low* and *high* is either an integer literal or an integer named number. In this case, the discrete range is assumed to specify a subrange of the predefined type `Integer`.

One place discrete ranges are used is in declaring array types and array objects. There are two kinds of array types—*constrained* array types, in which all arrays have the same bounds for a given dimension, and *unconstrained* array types, in which different arrays may have different bounds. Whether the type is constrained or unconstrained, all arrays in the type have the same number of dimensions, the same discrete type used for index values in a given dimension, and the same type for components. The form of a constrained array type declaration is:

```
TYPE identifier IS
    ARRAY ( discrete range , ~~~ , discrete range ) OF
        typemark  ...........
                  : constraint : ;
                  ...........
```

There is one discrete range in each dimension, indicating the type and range of values that may be used as index values for that dimension. The form of an unconstrained array type declaration is:

```
TYPE identifier IS
    ARRAY ( typemark RANGE <> , ~~~ , typemark RANGE <> )
        OF typemark  ...........
                     : constraint : ;
                     ...........
```

The typemarks inside the parentheses specify the discrete *types* that the index values for each dimension must belong to, but the <> symbol indicates that the *range* for each dimension is left unspecified. In each case, the typemark following the word OF specifies the type of the components. The optional constraint may further restrict the values held by the array components. The constraints allowed or required with a particular typemark in an array type declaration are exactly those that are allowed or required with that typemark in an object declaration. The two forms of array type declarations may not be combined. The expressions in the discrete ranges and in the constraint may be dynamic. They are evaluated at the time the array type declaration is elaborated. There is a predefined one-dimensional unconstrained array type named String whose index values are positive values of type Integer and whose components are of type Character. The declaration of an object in a constrained array type never contains any kind of constraint. The declaration of a variable in an unconstrained array type *must* contain an *index constraint* of the form

```
( discrete range , ~~~ , discrete range )
```

(with one discrete range of the appropriate type in each dimension) indicating the index bounds that the variable will always have. The declaration of a constant in an unconstrained array type may have an index constraint, or it may be omitted, with the index bounds inferred from the constant's initial value. If one of the discrete ranges in an index constraint has an upper bound that is less than its lower bound, the array is a *null array*, containing no elements. Special shorthand forms of variable and constant declarations are allowed for declaring one-of-a-kind arrays:

```
identifier , ~~~ , identifier :
    ARRAY ( discrete range , ~~~ , discrete range ) OF
        typemark  ...........  ...............
                  : constraint : : := expression : ;
                  ...........  ...............
```

```
identifier , ~~~ , identifier :
    CONSTANT ARRAY ( discrete range , ~~~ , discrete range ) OF
        typemark [ constraint ]    := expression ;
```

An object declared in this way belongs to an *anonymous array type*. No other array in the program belongs to the same type. Similar shorthands do not exist for the other types covered in this chapter. A component of an array object is named by an *indexed component* of the form

```
array name ( expression , ~~~ , expression )
```

If the named array is a variable, the indexed component may be used as a variable belonging to the component type. A subarray consisting of consecutive components in a one-dimensional array may be named by a *slice* of the form

```
array name ( discrete range )
```

If the named array is a variable, the slice may be used as a variable belonging to the array type. The *catenation* operator & may be used to join two one-dimensional arrays together to form a larger array.

A record type may or may not have *discriminants*. In a record type without discriminants, all records in the type have the same form. Chapter 10 discusses record types with discriminants, in which different records of the same type may take different forms.

A record type without discriminants is declared as follows:

```
TYPE identifier IS
   RECORD
      component declaration
               ~~~
      component declaration
   END RECORD ;
```

The form of a component declaration is:

```
identifier , ~~~ , identifier :
    typemark [ constraint ] [ := expression ] ;
```

The identifiers give the names of the components being declared; the typemark indicates the type of the components; the constraint may further restrict the values that may be held by the components; and the optional expression determines the default initial value for the components. The constraints allowed or required with a given typemark are those that would be allowed or required with that typemark in an object declaration. The default initial value expression need not be static. It is evaluated not when the record type declaration is elaborated, but every time a record in the type is created and no initial value is specified for the record as a whole. If more than one component is declared in the same component declaration, the expression is reevaluated once for each component. If `x` is a record in a type in which all records have a component named `c`, the corresponding component of `x` is named `x.c`. No constraint may appear in the declaration of an object in a record type without discriminants.

EXERCISES

4.1 Write a declaration for a variable that can hold values of type `Integer` in the range zero to 999 and that initially holds the value 100.

4.2 A program processes fragments of text that end with the character `'#'`. Write a declaration that allows this value to be referred to by the name `End_Mark`.

4.3 Acceleration due to gravity at the earth's surface, called *g* in physics textbooks, is 9.78049 meters per second per second. Write declarations establishing a floating-point type with five digits of precision and values ranging from zero to *g* and a fixed-point type with values ranging from -4.5 times *g* to 4.5 times *g*, accurate to within 0.01. The declarations should be written in a way that makes clear the relationship between the range of each type and the value of *g*.

4.4 Given the type declarations

```
TYPE Zip_Code_Type IS RANGE 0 .. 99999;
TYPE Resistance_Type IS DIGITS 8;
TYPE Speed_Type IS DELTA 1.0 RANGE 0.0 .. 99.0;
TYPE City_List_Type IS ARRAY (1 .. 100) OF String (1 .. 25);
TYPE Data_List_Type IS ARRAY (Integer RANGE <>) OF Float;
```

indicate which of the following object declarations have appropriate constraints and what is wrong with the declarations that do not have appropriate constraints:

```
(a) Zip_Code_1 : Zip_Code_Type (0 .. 9999);
(b) Zip_Code_2 : Zip_Code_Type DIGITS 5;
(c) Resistance_1 : Resistance Type DIGITS 10;
(d) Resistance_2 : Resistance_Type RANGE 0 .. 1000;
(e) Resistance_3 : Resistance_Type DIGITS 6 RANGE 0.0 .. 1.0;
(f) Speed_1 : Speed_Type RANGE 0.0 .. 55.0;
(g) Speed_2 : Speed_Type DELTA 0.5;
(h) Speed_3 : Speed_Type DELTA 5.0 RANGE 0.0 .. 150.0;
(i) City_List_1 : City_List_Type (1 .. 100);
(j) City_List_2 : City_List_Type RANGE 1 .. 25,
(k) Data_List_1 : Data_List_Type (-3.0 .. 3.0);
(l) Data_List_2 : Data_List_Type RANGE -3.0 .. 3.0;
(m) Data_List_3 : Data_List_Type (1 .. 50);
(n) Data_List_4 : Data_List_Type RANGE 1 .. 50;
```

4.5 Declare a type whose values are the floor numbers in a 52-story building, assuming the lowest floor is numbered 1. Then declare a variable in this type that can only hold numbers of the top 26 floors.

4.6 Declare a type for representing distances up to ten meters to an accuracy of three decimal digits. Then declare a variable in this type that can only hold distances greater than or equal to one meter.

4.7 Declare a type for representing distances up to 100,000 feet to within half a foot. Then declare a variable in this type for which accuracy to within ten feet is sufficient.

4.8 Declare a type for representing the possible settings of an automatic transmission. Then declare a variable in this type that can only hold the settings that produce forward motion.

4.9 A program to control an elevator needs a table to indicate which call buttons have been pushed. In general, there are three buttons associated with a floor: the *up* call button on that floor, the *down* call button on that floor, and the button for that floor on the elevator itself. The table should have one entry for each combination of a floor and a kind of button. (You may ignore the facts that the bottom floor does not have a *down* call button and the top floor does not have an *up* call button.) Write all declarations needed to declare a type for such tables. Then declare two such tables, one for the elevator at the north end of the building and one for the elevator at the south end of the building. You may reuse the declaration written for Exercise 4.5.

4.10 Replace the declarations given in the previous exercise with declarations that create a single table, assuming that there is no need for other objects of the same type.

4.11 Declare a type for three-dimensional arrays with components of type `Float`. Index values in each dimension are of type `Integer`, but the bounds may vary from object to object. Also declare a typical object in this type.

4.12 Declare a type for representing an angle as a number of degrees between zero and 359, a number of minutes between zero and 59, and a number of seconds between zero and 59.

4.13 Declare the types needed for representing checkerboards. A checkerboard has eight rows and eight columns of squares, and each square may be either empty, occupied by a red checker, occupied by a red king, occupied by a black checker, or occupied by a black king. Ignore the fact that the rules of checkers cause every other square always to be empty.

4.14 Section 3.1 described two representations for sets of integers in the range one to ten. Give Ada type declarations for both these representations.

4.15 Write Ada type declarations to represent each of the following types described in Section 3.2:

(*a*) a type for a baseball player's batting record, consisting of his name (thirty characters long) and batting average (in the range 0.000 to 1.000, accurate to within 0.001)

(*b*) a type for a team batting record, consisting of 25 individual players' batting records

(*c*) a type for teams, consisting of the team's name (ten characters long), the team's home city (fifteen characters long), and the team's batting record

(*d*) a type for leagues, consisting of fourteen values in the type for teams

4.16 Write statements that, given a variable `Team_Batting_Record` in the type declared in Exercise 4.15 (*b*), set a variable `Count` (of type `Integer`) to the number of players on the team with batting averages of 0.300 or higher. Then write statements that, given a variable `League` of the type declared in Exercise 4.15 (*d*), print out the name of each team in the league with five or more players batting 0.300 or better.

4.17 Given the declarations

```
TYPE Switch_Setting_Type IS (Off, On);
Setting           : Switch_Setting_Type;
Initial_Stock     : CONSTANT := 100;
Remaining_Items : Integer := Initial_Stock;
```

indicate whether each of the following expressions is static and whether it is universal:

(*a*)	`Off`	(*f*)	`97 ** 2 + 97`
(*b*)	`Setting`	(*g*)	`Initial_Stock - 1`
(*c*)	`100`	(*h*)	`Initial_Stock - Remaining_Items`
(*d*)	`Initial_Stock`	(*i*)	`Remaining_Items + 3`
(*e*)	`Remaining_Items`		

4.18 The standard input file contains 200 integers, with pairs of consecutive integers representing the numerator and denominator of a fraction. Write a program that reads the 100 pairs of integers into a two-dimensional array row-by-row and then writes the same 100 pairs to the standard output file column-by-column. That is, all numerators should be written first, then all denominators.

4.19 Modify the program written for the previous exercise to use a one-dimensional array of records. Each record should have a component for the numerator and a component for the denominator.

CHAPTER

FIVE

ACCESS TYPES

An access type contains values, called *access values,* that point to variables. Figure 5.1 depicts a variable x belonging to an access type. This variable contains an access value pointing to another variable that holds the value 100. (We depict variables by boxes. We depict an access value pointing to a variable by an arrow pointing to that variable's box.) Access values are equal if they point to the same variable and unequal otherwise. (Two arrows depict the same access value if and only if they point to the same box.) In Figure 5.2, a and b are equal to each other but not to c, because a and b point to the same variable, but c points to another variable. Even though both variables contain zero, they are two different variables, and the access values pointing to them are two different access values.

There are two kinds of variables in an Ada program—*declared variables* and *dynamically allocated variables.* Until now, we have seen only declared variables, which come into existence as a result of variable declarations and can be referred to by their declared names. Dynamically allocated variables are typically created during the execution of a statement. *Dynamic allocation* is the process of setting aside storage for such a variable and providing the program with an access value pointing to the variable. The dynamically allocated variable has no identifier naming it, so the program can refer to the variable only by using this access value.

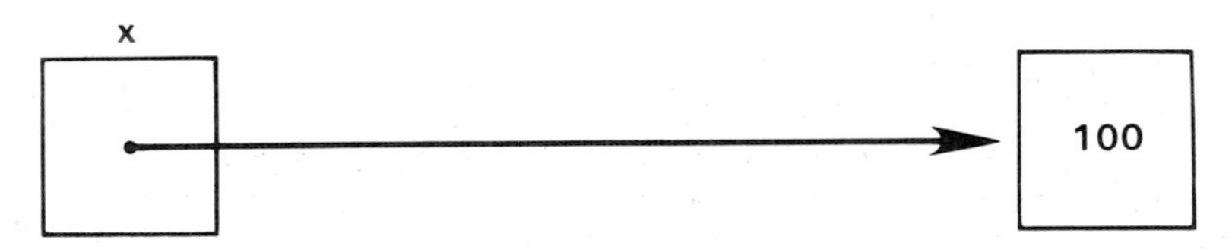

Figure 5.1 An acess type variable x containing a value thats points to a variable holding 100. The boxes represent variables. An access value pointing to a variable is represented by an arrow pointing to the corresponding box.

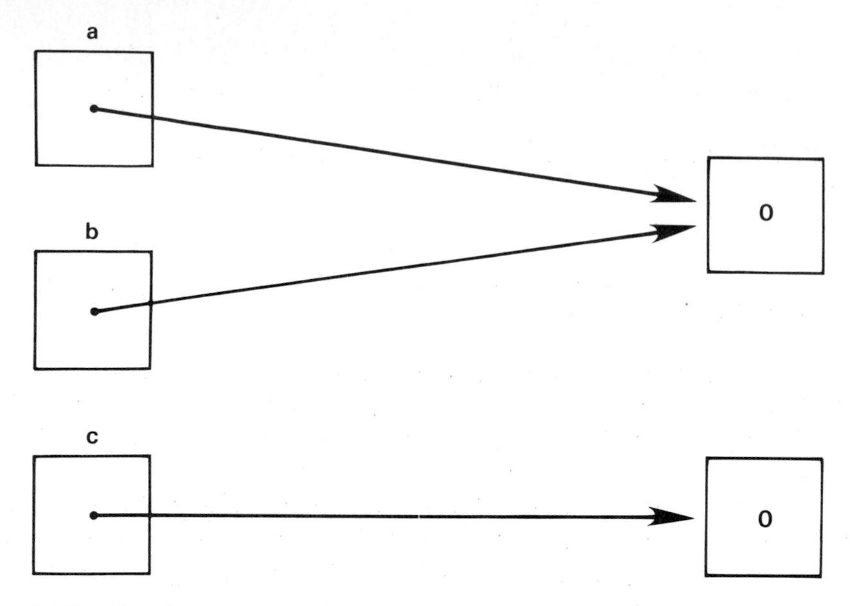

Figure 5.2 Equality of access values. Two access values are equal if they point to the same variable, not just to variables with identical contents. Thus `a = b`, but `a /= c` and `b /= c`. Arrows represent the same access value if and only if they point to the same box.

Just as dynamically allocated variables may only be referred to in terms of access values, declared variables may only be referred to by identifiers. Access values only point to dynamically allocated variables, never to declared variables.

5.1 ACCESS TYPE DECLARATIONS

The values in an access type point to dynamically allocated variables of a particular type, called the *designated type*. (An access value is said to *designate* the variable to which it points.) An access type is declared by a declaration of the following form:

TYPE *identifier* IS ACCESS *typemark* [*constraint*] ;

The typemark names the designated type. The optional constraint further restricts the values that may be held by the dynamically allocated variables to be pointed to by values in the access type. The constraint may be any kind that can be used with the given typemark, as in the following examples:

```
TYPE Letter_Pointer_Type IS
   ACCESS Character RANGE 'A' .. 'Z';

TYPE Phone_Number_Pointer_Type IS ACCESS String (1 .. 10);
```

However, a constraint is never required in an access type declaration. For example, the following declaration is legal even though `String` is an unconstrained array type:

```
TYPE Name_Pointer_Type IS ACCESS String;
```

`Phone_Number_Pointer_Type` consists of pointers to dynamically allocated `String` values of length ten. `Name_Pointer_Type` consists of pointers to dynamically allocated `String` variables of arbitrary length.

Every access type has a special value, called `NULL`, that does not point to any variable. Every variable in an access type is initialized to `NULL` unless another initial value is specified explicitly. (Just as record types are the only types for which a programmer can specify a default initial value, access types are the only types for which the language rules specify a default initial value.) The values in an access type consist entirely of the value `NULL` and the values produced by dynamic allocation.

There is a separate *collection* of dynamically allocated variables associated with each access type. The values of an access type only point to the dynamically allocated variables in that type's collection. Values in two different access types can never point to the same variable. Given the declarations

```
Phone_Number_Pointer : Phone_Number_Pointer_Type;
Name_Pointer         : Name_Pointer_Type;
```

the assignment statement

```
Name_Pointer := Phone_Number_Pointer;
```

is illegal. It purports to assign a value in one access type to a variable in another access type.

5.2 DYNAMIC ALLOCATION

Dynamic allocation is performed when a special kind of expression called an *allocator* is evaluated. Evaluation of this expression consists of two steps:

1. A variable is dynamically allocated.
2. An access value pointing to the dynamically allocated variable becomes the value of the expression.

The simplest form of an allocator is

`NEW` *typemark*

Evaluation of this expression creates a dynamically allocated variable of the type specified by the typemark. The contents of the dynamically allocated variable are left undefined. The initial value of the dynamically allocated variable can be specified by an allocator of the form

`NEW` *typemark* `' (` *expression* `)`

The value of the expression is copied into the dynamically allocated variable. (If a constraint was specified in the access type declaration, the initial value must obey this constraint.) Given the declarations

```
TYPE Integer_Pointer_Type IS ACCESS Integer;
Integer_Pointer : Integer_Pointer_Type;
```

the assignment statement

```
Integer_Pointer := NEW Integer;
```

leaves `Integer_Pointer` pointing to a dynamically allocated variable of type `Integer` with unknown contents. The assignment statement

```
Integer_Pointer := NEW Integer'(0);
```

leaves `Integer_Pointer` pointing to a dynamically allocated variable of type `Integer` containing the value zero.

Just as a declaration creating a variable in an unconstrained array type must specify the index bounds for that variable, so an allocator creating a variable in an unconstrained array type must specify the index bounds for that variable. One way to do this is by specifying the initial value of the variable. Given the declaration of `Name_Pointer_Type` in Section 5.1 and the declarations

```
Name_Pointer : Name_Pointer_Type;
Greeting     : String (1 .. 5) := "Hello";
```

the assignment statement

```
Name_Pointer := NEW String'(Greeting);
```

allocates a `String` variable of length five, initializes it to the contents of `Greeting`, and copies a pointer to it into `Name_Pointer`.

Another way to specify the index bounds of a dynamically allocated array is with a third form of allocator:

`NEW` *typemark index-constraint*

This allows a program to allocate a variable in an unconstrained array type without specifying its contents, as in the following assignment statement:

```
Name_Pointer := NEW String (1 .. 5);
```

(Observe that in the form of allocator specifying an initial value there is an apostrophe between the typemark and the left parenthesis; however, in the form specifying an index constraint there is not an apostrophe.)

When a variable in an unconstrained array type is allocated, the bounds must be specified by the allocator (by either an initial value or an index constraint), even if the corresponding access type declaration contained an index constraint. Even given the declarations

```
TYPE Phone_Number_Pointer_Type IS ACCESS String (1 .. 10);
Phone_Number_Pointer : Phone_Number_Pointer_Type;
```

the following assignment statement is illegal:

```
Phone_Number_Pointer := NEW String; --ILLEGAL!
```

We must write something like

```
Phone_Number_Pointer := NEW String'("2125551212");
```

or

```
Phone_Number_Pointer := NEW String (1 ..10);
```

instead.

Because each evaluation of an allocator creates an access value pointing to a new variable, care must be taken when initializing several access type objects at once. As explained in Section 4.3.3, the declaration

```
IP1, IP2 : Integer_Pointer_Type := NEW Integer'(0);
```

is equivalent to the sequence of declarations

```
IP1 : Integer_Pointer_Type := NEW Integer'(0);
IP2 : Integer_Pointer_Type := NEW Integer'(0);
```

Thus `IP1` and `IP2` are initialized to point to two *different* dynamically allocated variables each containing the number zero. To initialize `IP1` and `IP2` to point to the same allocated variable, you must perform the allocation before the declaration of `IP1` and `IP2`:

```
Pointer_To_Zero :
   CONSTANT Integer_Pointer_Type := NEW Integer'(0);
IP1, IP2 : Integer_Pointer_Type := Pointer_To_Zero;
```

5.3 NAMING DYNAMICALLY ALLOCATED VARIABLES

If the variable `x` contains an access value, the notation `x.ALL` names the dynamically allocated variable pointed to by that access value, as shown in Figure 5.3. This

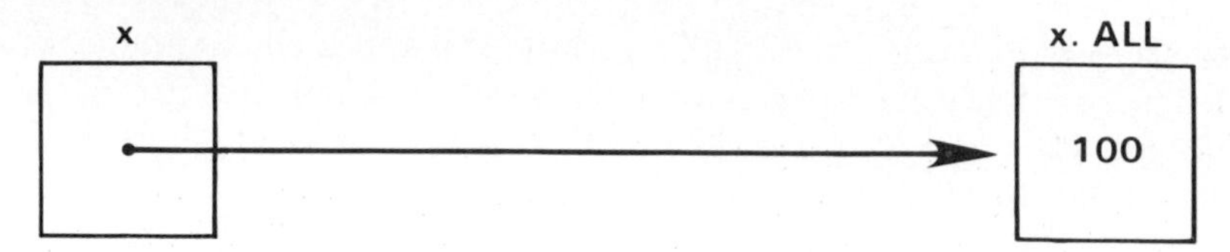

Figure 5.3 Notation for the dynamically allocated variable pointed to by an access value.

notation may appear anywhere a variable of the designated type may appear, such as in an expression or on the lefthand side of an assignment statement. Given the declarations

```
TYPE Integer_Pointer_Type IS ACCESS Integer;

Integer_Pointer_1 : Integer_Pointer_Type := NEW Integer'(1);
Integer_Pointer_2 : Integer_Pointer_Type := NEW Integer'(2);
```

the statement

```
Integer_Pointer_1.ALL := Integer_Pointer_2.ALL;
```

copies the contents of the variable *pointed to by* the access value in `Integer_Pointer_2` into the variable *pointed to by* the access value in `Integer_Pointer_1`. In contrast, the statement

```
Integer_Pointer_1 := Integer_Pointer_2;
```

copies the access value in `Integer_Pointer_2` into `Integer_Pointer_1`, so that `Integer_Pointer_1` and `Integer_Pointer_2` point to the same allocated variable. In the first case, a value of type `Integer` is copied, while in the second case, a value of type `Integer_Pointer_Type` is copied. See Figure 5.4.

We stated earlier that given the declarations

```
TYPE Phone_Number_Pointer_Type IS ACCESS String (1 .. 10);
TYPE Name_Pointer_Type IS ACCESS String;

Phone_Number_Pointer : Phone_Number_Pointer_Type;
Name_Pointer         : Name_Pointer_Type;
```

the statement

```
Name_Pointer := Phone_Number_Pointer;
```

is an illegal attempt to assign a `Phone_Number_Pointer_Type` value to a `Name_Pointer_Type` variable. However, the statement

```
Name_Pointer.ALL := Phone_Number_Pointer.ALL;
```

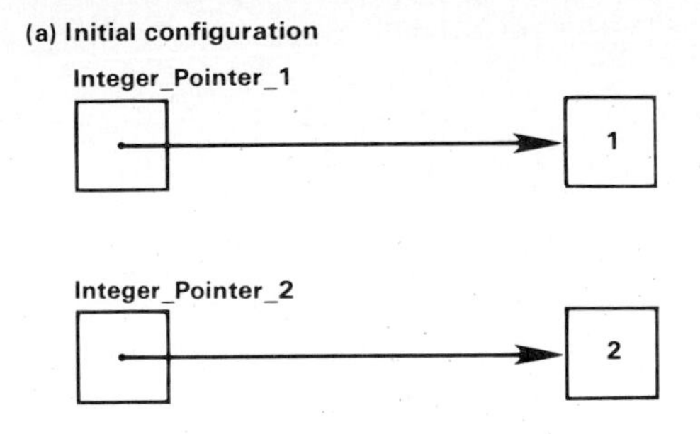

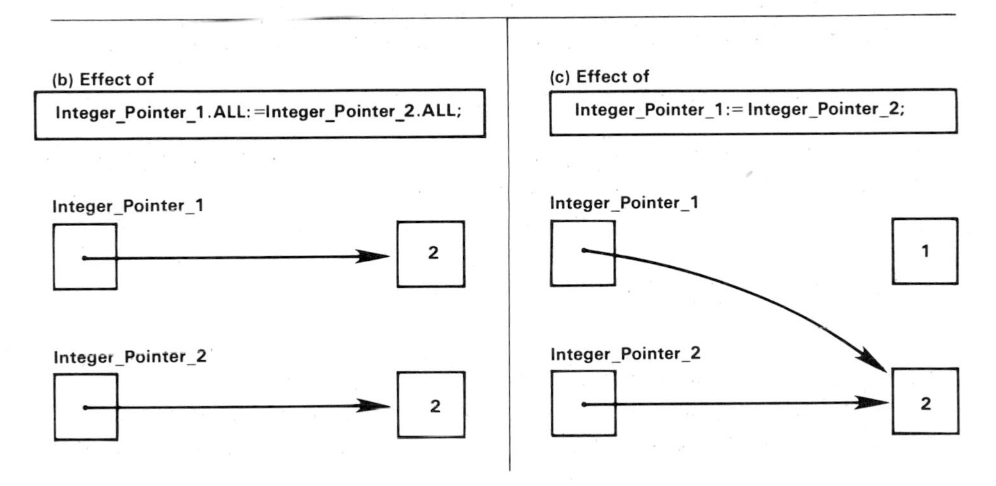

Figure 5.4 Assignment of access values versus assignment of values pointed to by access values. (a) Initial configuration. (b) Effect of assigning the integer in `Integer_Pointer_2.ALL` to the `Integer` variable `Integer_Pointer_1.ALL`. (c) Effect of assigning the access value in `Integer_Pointer_2` to the access type variable `Integer_Pointer_1` starting from the configuration in (a).

is perfectly legitimate, provided that the dynamically allocated variable initially pointed to by `Name_Pointer` is ten characters long. This assignment copies a value of type `String` into a variable of the same type.

A constant in an access type always contains the same access value. That is, it always points to the same dynamically allocated variable. However, the contents of the dynamically allocated variable itself may change. Given the declaration

```
Integer_Pointer_3 :
   CONSTANT Integer_Pointer_Type := NEW Integer'(0);
```

the assignment

```
Integer_Pointer_3 := Integer_Pointer_1;
```

is illegal, because it attempts to update a constant. In contrast, the assignment

```
Integer_Pointer_3.ALL := Integer_Pointer_1.ALL;
```

is perfectly legal. It leaves the value in `Integer_Pointer_3` intact but changes the contents of the variable pointed to by that value.

The name `Name_Pointer.ALL (1)` names the first component of the array `Name_Pointer.ALL`, that is, the first component of the array pointed to by the access value in `Name_Pointer`. However, there is a convenient shorthand for naming components of a dynamically allocated array or record. The name

```
Name_Pointer.ALL (1)
```

may be abbreviated as

```
Name_Pointer (1)
```

Since `Name_Pointer` belongs to an access type rather than to an array type, `Name_Pointer` itself does not have components identified by index values. Therefore, we take the name `Name_Pointer (1)` to mean the first component of the array *pointed to by* `Name_Pointer`. A similar shorthand applies to slices of allocated arrays. The name

```
Phone_Number_Pointer.ALL (1 .. 3)
```

(which denotes the slice consisting of the first three characters in the string variable pointed to by `Phone_Number_Pointer`) can be abbreviated as

```
Phone_Number_Pointer (1 .. 3)
```

Given the declarations

```
TYPE Buffer_Type IS
   RECORD
      Length_Part   : Integer RANGE 0 .. 128 := 0;
      Contents_Part : String (1 .. 128);
   END RECORD;
TYPE Buffer_Pointer_Type IS ACCESS Buffer_Type;
Buffer_Pointer : Buffer_Pointer_Type;
```

the components of the record pointed to by `Buffer_Pointer` can be named by similar abbreviations:

```
Buffer_Pointer.ALL.Length_Part
```

can be abbreviated as

```
Buffer_Pointer.Length_Part
```

and

```
Buffer_Pointer.ALL.Contents_Part
```

can be abbreviated as

```
Buffer_Pointer.Contents_Part
```

This, in fact, is the origin of the `.ALL` notation for the dynamically allocated variable pointed to by an access value: `Buffer_Pointer.Length_Part` names one component of the record pointed to by `Buffer_Pointer`; `Buffer_Pointer.Contents_Part` names another component of the record pointed to by `Buffer_Pointer`, and `Buffer_Pointer.ALL` names *all* of the record pointed to by `Buffer_Pointer`.

5.4 THE USE OF ACCESS TYPES

Access values are useful in a variety of programming situations. This section illustrates some of the most important ones:

In some algorithms, different variables play different roles at various times. A particular access type variable can be used to point to the dynamically allocated variable currently playing a certain role.

Access values allow the same data to be shared by several parts of a data structure. Rather than keeping several copies of the data, we can keep one copy in a dynamically allocated variable pointed to from several places. This makes it unnecessary to update several copies when the data changes. Furthermore, if the data take up more space than an access value, this reduces the amount of space required to represent the data.

Many programs can be speeded up by copying pointers to large data structures rather than the data structures themselves.

As explained in Section 4.2.6, an object in an unconstrained array type can only hold arrays of one particular length, specified by its index constraint. However, the effect of a variable holding different-sized arrays at different times can often be simulated by a variable that *points to* different-sized arrays at different times.

Access types make it possible to declare *recursive types*, which are types defined in terms of themselves. An array or record type cannot have a component of the same array or record type, but it can have a component *pointing to* objects of the same type.

5.4.1 Variables with Changing Roles

Some algorithms call for actions to be repeated several times with the roles played by certain variables interchanged each time. Consider an animation program that is to display an image moving across a screen. The image is represented by a 25-by-80 array of `Boolean` values, and there is a procedure `Display` that takes such an array and displays the corresponding image. `Display` is to be called fifty times, with the `True` values in the representation of the image moved one column to the left each time. (`True` values in column one are discarded in the process.) The following algorithm can be used:

```
FOR i IN 1 .. 50 LOOP

   --Copy the image in Source into Target, shifted one
   --    column to the left:

   FOR Column IN 1 .. 79 LOOP
      FOR Row IN 1 .. 25 LOOP
         Target (Row, Column) := Source (Row, Column+1);
      END LOOP;
   END LOOP;

   FOR Row IN 1 .. 25 LOOP
      Target (Row, 80) := False;
   END LOOP;

   -- Display the shifted image:
   Display (Target);

   [exchange the roles of Source and Target]

END LOOP;
```

The last step in the outer loop, exchanging the roles of `Source` and `Target`, can be accomplished by using dynamically allocated arrays in place of `Source` and `Target`. One access type variable points to the array playing the role of `Source` during a given iteration and another points to the array playing the role of `Target` during that iteration. At the end of each iteration, the contents of the two access type variables are exchanged.

Declarations like the following are needed:

```
TYPE Image_Type IS ARRAY (1 .. 25, 1 .. 80) OF Boolean;
TYPE Image_Pointer_Type IS ACCESS Image_Type;

Source_Pointer     : Image_Pointer_Type := NEW Image_Type;
Target_Pointer     : Image_Pointer_Type := NEW Image_Type;
Old_Source_Pointer : Image_Pointer_Type;
```

Then the loop can be rewritten as follows:

```
FOR i IN 1 .. 50 LOOP

   -- Copy the image in Source into Target, shifted one column
   --   to the left:

   FOR Column IN 1 .. 79 LOOP
      FOR Row IN 1 .. 25 LOOP
         Target_Pointer (Row, Column) :=
            Source_Pointer (Row, Column+1);
      END LOOP;
   END LOOP;
```

```
      FOR Row IN 1 .. 25 LOOP
         Target_Pointer (Row, 80) := False;
      END LOOP;

      -- Display the shifted image:
      Display (Target_Pointer.ALL);

      -- Exchange the roles of the source array and the target
      --   array by exchanging the contents of Source_Pointer
      --   and Target_Pointer:

      Old_Source_Pointer := Source_Pointer;
      Source_Pointer := Target_Pointer;
      Target_Pointer := Old_Source_Pointer;

   END LOOP;
```

Remember that in this loop, names like

```
Target_Pointer (Row, Column)
```

and

```
Source_Pointer (Row, Column+1)
```

really mean

```
Target_Pointer.ALL (Row, Column)
```

and

```
Source_Pointer.ALL (Row, Column+1)
```

respectively. This is the only possible interpretation, since access values do not have components. In the call on the procedure `Display`, however, the `.ALL` must be written explicitly so that the array pointed to by `Target_Pointer`, rather than the access value `Target_Pointer` itself, will be used as a parameter.

5.4.2 Shared Data

Suppose an office has 100 different forms processed by 20 different people. Each person knows how to process several different kinds of forms, but each kind of form can be processed by only one person. There is a program that, given a form number, prints out a mailing label for the person who processes that form. However, to control the flow of work, no more than 25 labels for a given person will be printed out in a given day. Subsequent requests will be denied.

The program could use a data structure like the following, depicted in Figure 5.5:

```
TYPE Mailing_Label_Type IS
   RECORD
      Name_Part         : String (1 .. 30);
      Mail_Station_Part : String (1 .. 10);
   END RECORD;
TYPE Worker_Type IS
   RECORD
      Label_Part         : Mailing_Label_Type;
      Forms_So_Far_Part : Integer := 0;
   END RECORD;
TYPE Worker_Pointer_Type IS ACCESS Worker_Type;
TYPE Form_Number_Type IS RANGE 1 .. 100;
Form_Assignments :
   ARRAY (Form_Number_Type) OF Worker_Pointer_Type;
```

When a form number is read into the variable `Form_Number` (of type `Form_Number_Type`), the program performs the following actions:

```
Worker := Form_Assignments (Form_Number);
IF Worker.Forms_So_Far_Part < 25 THEN
   Print_Label (Worker.Mailing_Label_Part);
   Worker.Forms_So_Far_Part :=
      Worker.Forms_So_Far_Part + 1;
ELSE
   Deny_Request;
END IF;
```

(`Print_Label` and `Deny_Request` are procedures that do just what their names suggest.) The variable `Worker` is of type `Worker_Pointer_Type` , so the names

```
Worker.Forms_So_Far_Part
```

and

```
Worker.Mailing_Label_Part
```

are equivalent to

```
Worker.ALL.Forms_So_Far_Part
```

and

```
Worker.ALL.Mailing_Label_Part
```

respectively.

An alternative approach would have been to declare `Form_Assignments` as follows:

```
Form_Assignments : ARRAY (Form_Number_Type) OF Worker_Type;
```

In this case, we use an array of `Worker_Type` records instead of an array of pointers to `Worker_Type` records. The original approach, using access values, is better because it allows a single `Worker_Type` record to be shared by all the array components to which it applies.

This sharing has two advantages. First, when the `Forms_So_Far_Part` count corresponding to one form is incremented, the count is instantaneously incremented for all forms processed by the same person. Second, the forty characters of `Mailing_Label_Part` information are stored once for each person. The alternative approach requires copies of the same information to be stored once for each form that is processed by a person.

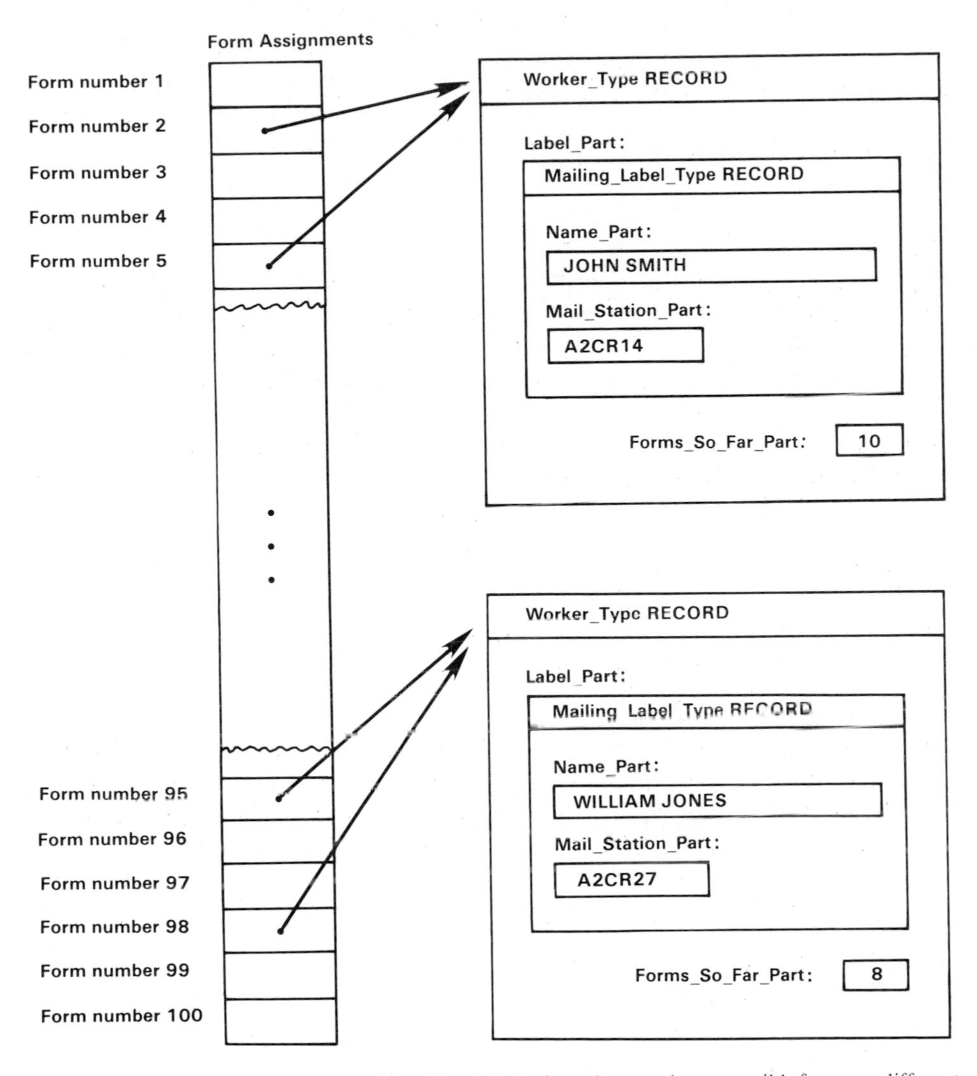

Figure 5.5 Data structure for processing mailing labels. A worker may be responsible for many different kinds of forms, but each form is handled by only one worker. This data structure has only one allocated `Worker_Type` record for each worker, avoiding duplication of data while retaining direct access to information about a worker responsible for a given kind of form

5.4.3 Reducing Copying of Data

Algorithms that move a lot of data, like sorting algorithms, often can be speeded up by having them move pointers to the data instead. For example, suppose the standard input file contains groups of three eighty-character lines, with the first line in each group containing a person's name, last name first; the second line containing the person's street address; and the last line containing the person's city, state, and zip code. Assuming there are no more than 1,000 groups of lines in the standard input file, the following program uses the data in that file to produce a directory alphabetized by name:

```
WITH Basic_IO;

PROCEDURE Print_Directory IS

   TYPE Directory_Entry_Type IS
      RECORD
         Name_Part, Street_Part, City_Part :
            String (1 .. 80);
      END RECORD;
   New_Entry            : Directory_Entry_Type;
   Length               : Integer RANGE 0 .. 80;
   Out_Of_Place_Entry   : Directory_Entry_Type;
   Number_Of_Entries    : Integer RANGE 0 .. 1000 := 0;
   No_Exchanges         : Boolean;
   Entry_List : ARRAY (1 .. 1000) OF Directory_Entry_Type;
BEGIN
   -- Read data into Entry_List:
   WHILE NOT Basic_IO.End_Of_File LOOP
      Basic_IO.Get_Line (New_Entry.Name_Part, Length);
      Basic_IO.Get_Line (New_Entry.Street_Part, Length);
      Basic_IO.Get_Line (New_Entry.City_Part, Length);
      Number_Of_Entries := Number_Of_Entries + 1;
      Entry_List (Number_Of_Entries) := New_Entry;
   END LOOP;
   -- Sort Entry_List using a bubble sort:
   LOOP
      No_Exchanges := True;
      FOR i IN 1 .. Number_Of_Entries - 1 LOOP
         IF Entry_List (i).Name_Part >
            Entry_List (i+1).Name_Part THEN
            Out_Of_Place_Entry := Entry_List (i+1);
            Entry_List (i+1) := Entry_List (i);
            Entry_List (i) := Out_Of_Place_Entry;
            No_Exchanges := False;
         END IF;
      END LOOP;
      EXIT WHEN No_Exchanges;
   END LOOP;
```

```
      -- Write the sorted data:

      FOR i IN 1 .. Number_Of_Entries LOOP
         Basic_IO.Put (Entry_List (i).Name_Part);
         Basic_IO.New_Line;
         Basic_IO.Put (Entry_List (i).Street_Part);
         Basic_IO.New_Line;
         Basic_IO. Put (Entry_List(i).City_Part);
         Basic_IO.New_Line;
         Basic_IO.New_Line;
      END LOOP;

   END Print_Directory;
```

The bubble sort works by repeatedly scanning `Entry_List` for adjacent elements that are out of order and exchanging those two elements, until finally the array is scanned and no out-of-order elements are found. In the process, `Directory_Entry_Type` values may be exchanged several times, with each exchange involving three assignments of a record containing 240 characters.

There are more sophisticated sorting algorithms that sharply reduce the number of exchanges. However, the simplicity of the bubble sort can be retained while greatly reducing the amount of data movement by using an array of *pointers to* `Directory_Entry_Type` records in place of the array of `Directory_Entry_Type` records. Whenever two large records would have been exchanged, pointers to these records are exchanged instead:

```
   WITH Basic_IO;
   PROCEDURE Print_Directory IS
      TYPE Directory_Entry_Type IS
         RECORD
            Name_Part, Street_Part, City_Part :
               String (1 .. 80);
         END RECORD;
      TYPE Directory_Entry_Pointer_Type IS
         ACCESS Directory_Entry_Type;

      New_Entry            : Directory_Entry_Type;
      Length               : Integer RANGE 0 .. 80;
      Out_Of_Place_Entry   : Directory_Entry_Pointer_Type;
      Number_Of_Entries    : Integer RANGE 0 .. 1000 := 0;
      No_Exchanges         : Boolean;
      Entry_Pointer_List :
         ARRAY (1 .. 1000) OF Directory_Entry_Pointer_Type;
   BEGIN
      -- Read data into Entry_List:

      WHILE NOT Basic_IO.End_Of_File LOOP
         Basic_IO.Get_Line (New_Entry.Name_Part, Length);
         Basic_IO.Get_Line (New_Entry.Street_Part, Length);
         Basic_IO.Get_Line (New_Entry.City_Part, Length);
         Number_Of_Entries := Number_Of_Entries + 1;
         Entry_Pointer_List (Number_Of_Entries) :=
            NEW Directory_Entry_Type'(New_Entry);
      END LOOP;
```

```
      -- Sort Entry_List using a bubble sort:
      LOOP
         No_Exchanges := True;
         FOR i IN 1 .. Number_Of_Entries - 1 LOOP
            IF Entry_Pointer_List (i).Name_Part >
               Entry_Pointer_List (i+1).Name_Part THEN
               Out_Of_Place_Entry := Entry_Pointer_List (i+1);
               Entry_Pointer_List (i+1) :=
                  Entry_Pointer_List (i);
               Entry_Pointer_List (i) := Out_Of_Place_Entry;
               No_Exchanges := False;
            END IF;
         END LOOP;
         EXIT WHEN No_Exchanges;
      END LOOP;
      -- Write the sorted data:
      FOR i IN 1 .. Number_Of_Entries LOOP
         Basic_IO.Put (Entry_Pointer_List (i).Name_Part);
         Basic_IO.New_Line;
         Basic_IO.Put (Entry_Pointer_List (i).Street_Part);
         Basic_IO.New_Line;
         Basic_IO.Put (Entry_Pointer_List (i).City_Part);
         Basic_IO.New_Line;
         Basic_IO.New_Line;
      END LOOP;
   END Print_Directory;
```

In this version, the input loop dynamically allocates a record for each group of three input lines and places a pointer to that record in the next component of `Entry_Pointer_List`. The sorting loop compares the records pointed to by adjacent components of this array and exchanges these pointers if the record pointed to by the lower component has a greater `Name_Part` component than the record pointed to by the higher component. The output loop traverses the array of pointers in order, printing out the data in the record pointed to by each component. (In the `IF` statement of the sorting loop, the name

```
Entry_Pointer_List (i).Name_Part
```

is a shorthand for

```
Entry_Pointer_List (i).ALL.Name_Part
```

A similar shorthand occurs in the output loop.)

5.4.4 Pointing to Arrays of Various Sizes

Consider the problem of reading each line in the standard input file, assuming that there are no more than 100 lines and that no line contains more than 132 characters, and writing these lines to the standard output file in reverse order. This requires us to save the lines in some data structure before writing them out.

The most obvious data structure to use is an array of String values. However, because String is an unconstrained array type, the following declaration is illegal:

```
TYPE String_List_Type IS ARRAY (1 .. 100) OF String;
   -- ILLEGAL USE OF AN UNCONSTRAINED ARRAY TYPE FOR THE
   --   COMPONENT TYPE OF ANOTHER ARRAY TYPE!
```

An array cannot have components that are arrays of various sizes. However, an array can have components that are pointers to arrays of various sizes, as shown in Figure 5.6. Thus the following declarations are legal:

```
TYPE String_Pointer_Type IS ACCESS String;

TYPE String_List_Type IS
   ARRAY (1 .. 100) OF String_Pointer_Type;
```

An unconstrained array type can be used as the designated type in an access type declaration without providing an index constraint. Furthermore, an access type is permitted as the component type of an array type.

Here is how String_Pointer_Type can be used to solve the problem:

```
WITH Basic_IO;

PROCEDURE Reverse_Lines IS

   TYPE String_Pointer_Type IS ACCESS String;

   Line_List  : ARRAY (1 .. 100) OF String_Pointer_Type;
   Line_Count : Integer := 0;
   Input_Line : String (1 .. 132);
   Line_Size  : Integer;

BEGIN

   -- Read and store lines:

   WHILE NOT Basic_IO.End_Of_File LOOP
      Basic_IO.Get_Line (Input_Line, Line_Size);
      Line_Count := Line_Count + 1;
      Line_List (Line_Count) :=
         NEW String'(Input_Line (1 .. Line_Size));
   END LOOP;

   -- Write the stored lines in reverse order:

   FOR i IN REVERSE 1 .. Line_Count LOOP
      Basic_IO.Put (Line_List (i).ALL);
      Basic_IO.New_Line;
   END LOOP;

END Reverse_Lines;
```

In the WHILE loop, the call on Basic_IO.Get_Line sets Line_Size to the number of characters in the line and places those characters in the first Line_Size characters of Input_Line. Thus the slice Input_Line (1 .. Line_Size) is a value of type String with the same length and contents as the line just read. This slice is used as the initial value in an allocator. The allocator creates a dynamically allocated array with the same number of characters as the initial value. A pointer to this array is inserted in `Line_List`. The `FOR` loop is executed with `i` taking on each value between one and `Line_Count` in reverse order. Each time around the loop, the string pointed to by the `i`th component of `Line_List` is written.

5.4.5 Recursive Data Types

A *recursive type* is a type defined in terms of itself. The only way to define a type in terms of itself is with access types. For example, an object in a recursive type *t* may contain an access value whose designated type is *t*.

A simple example of a recursive type is one of *singly linked lists*. A singly linked list is a set of *list cells* that are chained together by access values. In a singly linked list of integers, each list cell contains an integer and an access value pointing to the next cell on the list. The last cell on the list is marked by the special access value `NULL` in place of a pointer to another cell. An entire list is represented by a pointer to its first cell. Figure 5.7 depicts a singly linked list containing the numbers one, three, and five.

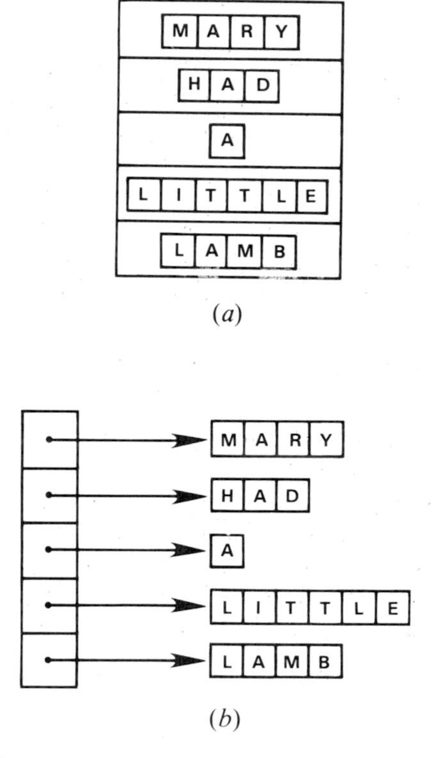

Figure 5.6 (*a*) A hypothetical array containing arrays of different sizes. *Such arrays do not exist in the Ada language.* (*b*) The use of access values to achieve the effect of arrays containing arrays of different sizes.

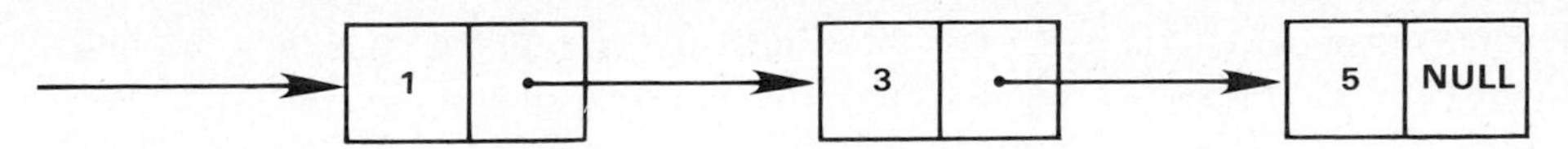

Figure 5.7 A singly linked list containing the numbers 1, 3, and 5. Each rectangle is a dynamically allocated *list cell* containing an element of the list and, except in the last cell, a pointer to the next cell on the list. The last cell contains the access value `NULL` in place of a pointer to another cell. The entire list is represented by the access value pointing to the first cell.

To represent singly linked lists, we must declare a record type for list cells (which we shall call `List_Cell_Type`) and an access type for pointing to these records (which we shall call `List_Cell_Pointer_Type`). Assuming that the list contains integers, the record type could be declared as follows:

```
TYPE List_Cell_Type IS
   RECORD
      Integer_Part   : Integer;
      Next_Cell_Part : List_Cell_Pointer_Type;
   END RECORD;
```

The access type could be declared as follows:

```
TYPE List_Cell_Pointer_Type IS ACCESS List_Cell_Type;
```

There is a problem here. The definition of `List_Cell_Type` refers to `List_Cell_Pointer_Type` in the second component declaration, so this definition must occur after the declaration of `List_Cell_Pointer_Type`. However, the definition of `List_Cell_Pointer_Type` refers to `List_Cell_Type` as the designated type, so this definition must occur after the declaration of `List_Cell_Pointer_Type`!

Such a vicious circle occurs with any recursive type. The solution is an *incomplete type declaration*, of the form

`TYPE` *identifier* `;`

A declaration of this form is a promise that a full declaration of the named type will follow later. In the meantime, the declared identifier can be used as the designated type in an access type declaration. Thus the types needed to represent a singly linked list of integers can be declared as follows:

```
TYPE List_Cell_Type;
TYPE List_Cell_Pointer_Type IS ACCESS List_Cell_Type;
TYPE List_Cell_Type IS
   RECORD
      Integer_Part   : Integer;
      Next_Cell_Part : List_Cell_Pointer_Type;
   END RECORD;
```

The incomplete declaration for List_Cell_Type allows that type to be declared without giving its definition. Therefore, it can be declared before List_Cell_Pointer_Type, breaking the vicious circle. Once List_Cell_Type is declared, albeit incompletely, it can be used to declare List_Cell_Pointer_Type. Once List_Cell_Pointer_Type is declared, it can be used in the full declaration of List_Cell_Type.

It is an error if an incomplete type declaration is not followed eventually by a full declaration for the same type. After the incomplete type declaration and before the full type declaration, the *only* permitted use of the type is the one illustrated above—as the designated type in an access type declaration. After the full type declaration, the type can be used in the same way as an ordinary type.

To illustrate the use of List_Cell_Type and List_Cell_Pointer_Type (and typical methods for manipulating singly linked lists), let us solve another reversal problem. This time the standard input file contains a sequence of *integers* to be written to the standard output file in reverse order. However, we do not know in advance how many numbers the input contains, so we cannot declare an array to hold the numbers.

Linked lists are often a good representation for lists whose maximum lengths are not known *a priori*. This is because new list cells can be dynamically allocated and added to the list as the need arises. When lists are represented as arrays, the number of array components must be known before declaring the array.

Singly linked lists are also convenient for reversal. It is easy to add new list cells to the front of the list as new numbers are read in. This builds a list containing the numbers of the input file in reverse order. The desired output then can be produced by traversing the list from front to back.

Here is the program:

```
WITH Basic_IO;
PROCEDURE Reverse_Numbers IS
   TYPE List_Cell_Type;
   TYPE List_Cell_Pointer_Type IS ACCESS List_Cell_Type;
   TYPE List_Cell_Type IS
      RECORD
         Integer_Part   : Integer;
         Next_Cell_Part : List_Cell_Pointer_Type;
      END RECORD;
   New_Cell   : List_Cell_Type;
   Input_List : List_Cell_Pointer_Type; --Initially NULL
BEGIN
   -- Read and store numbers:
   WHILE NOT Basic_IO.End_Of_File LOOP
      Basic_IO.Get (New_Cell.Integer_Part);
      New_Cell.Next_Cell_Part := Input_List;
      Input_List := NEW List_Cell_Type'(New_Cell);
   END LOOP;
```

```
      -- Write the stored lines in reverse order:
      WHILE Input_List /= NULL LOOP
         Basic_IO.Put (Input_List.Integer_Part);
         Basic_IO.New_Line;
         Input_List := Input_List.Next_Cell_Part;
      END LOOP;
   END Reverse_Numbers;
```

The `WHILE` loop builds up the reversed list of input values. `Input_List` starts out holding `NULL`, which is the default initial value for all variables in an access type and also the representation of an empty list. As each value is read in, a new cell containing that value is added to the front of the list in three steps.

1. The declared variable `New_Cell` is initialized to the record value that the new list cell should hold. The `Integer_Part` component is set to the value read in, and the `Next_Cell_Part` component is set to point to the old front cell.
2. A new list cell is allocated and initialized to the value of `New_Cell`.
3. The access value pointing to the newly allocated cell is assigned to `Input_List`, making it the new front cell of the list.

(The first step is accomplished by the first two statements inside the `WHILE` loop. The second and third steps are both accomplished by the third statement inside the loop.)

The second `WHILE` loop writes out the integers in the list. On each passage through the loop, `Input_List` points to the first cell whose contents have not yet been written. After each cell's contents are written, the assignment statement

```
Input_List := Input_List.Next_Cell_Part;
```

which is shorthand for

```
Input_List := Input_List.ALL.Next_Cell_Part;
```

moves `Input_List` up to point to the next cell on the list. `Input_List` can also be viewed as representing the list beginning with the cell to which it points. Each time the front number on the list is written, `Input_List` is updated to represent a list of numbers that have not yet been written. From this point of view, the loop terminates when the list of numbers remaining to be written becomes empty (null).

(Pascal also has recursive types. The vicious circle described previously does not arise in Pascal because a Pascal pointer type definition can refer to a still-undeclared type. The usual way to declare a recursive type in Pascal is to first declare the pointer type, then the type to which it points. To declare an Ada recursive type, you begin with an incomplete declaration of the type being pointed to, then declare the access type, and then provide a full declaration for the type being pointed to.)

5.5 ACCESS TYPES AND INDEX CONSTRAINTS

If the designated type in an access type declaration is an unconstrained array type, an index constraint may be provided, as in the declaration

```
TYPE Phone_Number_Pointer_Type IS ACCESS String (1 .. 10);
```

or omitted, as in the declaration

```
TYPE Name_Pointer_Type IS ACCESS String;
```

When the index constraint is omitted from the access type declaration, it may be provided in the declarations of individual objects in the access type, as in the following declarations:

```
Name_Pointer_1, Name_Pointer_2 : Name_Pointer_Type (1 .. 15);
Name_Pointer_3, Name_Pointer_4 : Name_Pointer_Type (1 .. 25);
```

The variables `Name_Pointer_1` and `Name_Pointer_2` may only contain `Name_Pointer_Type` values that point to strings with a lower index bound of one and an upper index bound of fifteen. `Name_Pointer_3` and `Name_Pointer_4` may contain only `Name_Pointer_Type` values that point to strings of with a lower index bound of one and an upper index bound of 25. (In addition, each of these four variables may contain the value `NULL`.) Given the declaration

```
Name_Pointer_5 : Name_Pointer_Type;
```

`Name_Pointer_5` may point to strings with any index bounds. The assignment statement

```
Name_Pointer_5 := Name_Pointer_1;
```

always succeeds. The assignment statement

```
Name_Pointer_1 := Name_Pointer_5;
```

succeeds only when `Name_Pointer_5` contains the value `NULL` or a pointer to a string with bounds of one and fifteen.

Of the constraints we have seen so far—range constraints, floating-point accuracy constraints, fixed-point accuracy constraints, and index constraints—index constraints are the only ones that may appear in the declarations of objects in an access type. This is allowed only when the designated type is an unconstrained array type (like `String`) and the access type declaration does not contain an index constraint. The declaration

```
Phone_Number_Pointer : Phone_Number_Pointer_Type (1 .. 10);
```

is illegal because the declaration of `Phone_Number_Pointer_Type` contains an index constraint.

5.6 SUMMARY

Values in an access type are pointers to dynamically allocated variables of a particular type. In addition, each access type contains a special value called `NULL`. Unlike declared variables, which are created by object declarations and referred to by their declared names, dynamically allocated variables are created by the evaluation of allocators and referred to in terms of the access values that point to them. Access values never point to declared variables.

An access type is declared by a type declaration of the following form:

`TYPE` *identifier* `IS ACCESS` *typemark* [*constraint*] `;`

The type named by the typemark is called the designated type. The allowable constraints are determined by the kind of type being used as the designated type. When the designated type is an unconstrained array type, an index constraint is optional. When it is omitted, an index constraint is also allowed (but not required) in the declaration of an object in the access type.

An allocator is an expression whose evaluation causes dynamic allocation of a variable. An access value pointing to this dynamically allocated variable becomes the value of the allocator. An allocator may take any of the following forms:

`NEW` *typemark*

`NEW` *typemark* `' (` *expression* `)`

`NEW` *typemark index-constraint*

The first form allocates a variable but does not specify its contents. The second form allocates a variable and specifies its initial value. The third form, allowed only when allocating an array in an unconstrained array type, specifies the index bounds but not the initial contents of the array. So that the size of the allocated array can be determined, only the second or third form may be used when allocating an array in an unconstrained array type.

The notation `x.ALL` names the variable pointed to by the access value `x`. It can appear anywhere a variable of the designated type is allowed, including on the lefthand side of an assignment statement. `x.ALL` can be a variable in the designated type (able to assume new values) even if `x` is a constant in the access type (required always to point to the same variable). If `x.ALL` is an array, `x(i)` can be used as a shorthand for the component `x.ALL(i)`, and `x(i .. j)` can be used as a shorthand for the slice `x.ALL(i .. j)` Similarly, if `x.ALL` is a record with a component named `c`, `x.c` can be used as a shorthand for the component `x.ALL.c`.

Access types can be used for the following purposes:

to allow different variables to play different roles at various times, by having certain access type variables point to the dynamically allocated variables currently playing certain roles
to allow the same data to be shared by several parts of a data structure, so that only one copy needs to be kept up to date and only one copy takes up space
to allow pointers to large data structures to be copied rather than the data structures themselves
to construct arrays whose components point to arrays of different sizes
to declare recursive types

A recursive type is one declared in terms of itself. An object in a recursive type can never contain another object of the same type, but it might contain a pointer to another object of the same type. For example, linked lists can be built out of list cells that contain pointers to other list cells.

Typically, recursive type declarations involve two types—an access type and a designated type—each declared in terms of the other. Because a type cannot be referred to in a type declaration until after its own declaration, these types cannot be declared without an incomplete type declaration. An incomplete type declaration takes the following form:

TYPE *identifier* ;

An incomplete type declaration must be followed eventually by a full declaration for the same type. After its incomplete declaration but before its full declaration, the type may be used only as the designated type in an access type declaration. This allows typical recursive types to be declared in three steps:

1. An incomplete declaration for the designated type;
2. The declaration of the access type in terms of the designated type; and
3. The full declaration for the designated type, in terms of the access type.

EXERCISES

5.1 Assume that a, b, c, and d are all variables in an access type designating the type Integer. Draw a picture showing the result of the following statements:

```
a := NEW Integer'(3);
b := NEW Integer'(3);
c := a;
d := NEW Integer;
d.ALL := a.ALL;
c.ALL := 1;
```

5.2 Following the assignment statements in Exercise 5.1, which of the following conditions are true?

(*a*) a = b
(*b*) a = c
(*c*) a = d
(*d*) a.ALL = b.ALL
(*e*) a.ALL = c.ALL
(*f*) a.ALL = d.ALL
(*g*) b.ALL = d.ALL

5.3 Each component of a two-dimensional array has up to eight *neighbors* in the row above, the row below, the column to the left, and the column to the right. Given a two-dimensional array of `Boolean` components, there is a *successor array* of the same dimensions defined as follows: For each component *c* equal to `True`, the corresponding component in the successor array is `True` if *c* has two or three neighbors equal to `True`; otherwise the corresponding component in the successor array is `False`. For each component *c* equal to `False`, the corresponding component in the successor array is `True` if *c* has three neighbors equal to `True`; otherwise the corresponding component in the successor array is `False`.

An eighty-by-eighty array of `Boolean` values can be represented in text files as a sequence of eighty lines, each eighty characters long, in which the character `'X'` stands for `True` and a space stands for `False`. Write a program that reads in such a representation from the standard input file and writes the representation of ten consecutive successor arrays to the standard output file. Use two arrays that take turns playing the role of the original array and the successor array.

(Counting the number of neighbors equal to `True` will be simplified if each array is given extra rows at the beginning and end and extra columns at the beginning and end, all containing only the value `False`. Thus the eighty-by-eighty array will be imbedded in the middle of an 82-by-82 array. Only the inner eighty rows and columns must be recomputed, and the first and last of these eighty rows and eighty columns need not be treated as special cases. They all have eight neighbors.)

5.4 Declare a data type for representing a person's name, home address, and mailing address. When the two addresses are the same, the data should be represented only once in storage. Nonetheless, the procedure for printing out the home address should not depend on whether the two addresses are the same and neither should the procedure for printing out the mailing address.

5.5 Give data type declarations for a one-week appointment calendar. Each week contains seven days and there may be zero or more appointments on a given day. For each appointment, there should be a time and an eighty-character description. Once a calendar for a given week is constructed, the number of appointments for a given day will not change. Do not use a linked list in your solution.

5.6 Give data type declarations for the one-week appointment calendar described in the previous exercise, but use a linked list this time.

5.7 A doubly linked list is a linked list in which each cell contains not only an access value pointing to the next cell on the list, but also one pointing to the previous cell on the list. (The previous cell pointer for the first cell on the list is set to `NULL`.) Write type declarations for a doubly linked list of fifteen-character strings.

5.8 A *tree* is a data structure consisting of *nodes* that contain information and have parent-child relationships to other nodes. Each node has one parent (except for a node called the *root*, which has no parents) and zero or more children. A *binary tree* is one in which every node has at most two children. Write type declarations for representing a binary tree in which each node contains a value of type `Integer`. It should be possible, given a node, to determine the node's children. It is not necessary, given a node, to be able to determine the node's parent.

5.9 Give the type declarations for a data structure used to keep track of which students are enrolled in which classes. The data structure is built from three kinds of records:

A record giving information about a student, including a name of up to thirty characters and a student number in the range zero to 999,999

A record giving information about a course, including a three-character department code, a three-digit course number, and a fifty-character course name

A record giving information about the enrollment of a particular student in a particular course, including a pointer to the record describing the student and a pointer to the record describing the course

A record giving information about a course, including a three-character department code, a three-digit course number, and a fifty-character course name

A record giving information about the enrollment of a particular student in a particular course, including a pointer to the record describing the student and a pointer to the record describing the course

The records describing students form one linked list, and the records describing courses form another. In addition, each record describing a student contains a linked list of enrollments for that student, and each record describing a course contains a linked list of enrollments for that course. (When we say that a record *contains* a linked list, we mean that it contains a pointer to the first record on that list.) This means that each record describing the enrollment of a student in a course is simultaneously a part of two different linked lists: a list of all enrollments for that student and a list of all enrollments for that course. This can be accomplished by giving each enrollment record *two* components pointing to other enrollment records. One points to the next enrollment record for the same student, and the other points to the next enrollment record for the same course.

5.10 Given the type declarations in the previous exercise, write a loop that prints out, for each course, the department code, the course number, and the student numbers of all students enrolled in that course. Then write a loop that prints out, for each student, the student's name and the names of all courses in which that student is enrolled.

5.11 Write a program that reads consecutive sequences of 500 integers (until the end of the standard input file is encountered) and then prints the sequence with the greatest sum. Use an access type to avoid copying 500 values every time a new largest sequence is found.

5.12 Write a program that reads integers until the end of the standard input file is encountered and then prints them out again in ascending order. Each integer should be inserted in the appropriate position of a linked list when it is read in. The output can be produced by scanning the list from beginning to end.

5.13 Why can't the previous exercise be solved using an array instead of a linked list?

CHAPTER

SIX

SUBTYPES AND TYPE EQUIVALENCE

6.1 TYPE RESTRICTIONS ON THE USE OF DATA

The Ada language has strict rules requiring values of a particular type to appear in a particular context. In an assignment statement, for example, the type of the variable on the lefthand side must be identical to the type of the expression on the righthand side. In subprogram calls, parameters must belong to the types specified in the subprogram. Violations of rules such as these are detected when an Ada program is compiled.

FORTRAN, PL/I, and Pascal are more lenient, allowing *implicit conversion* of a value in one type to a value in another type. In FORTRAN and Pascal, it is legal to write an expression such as **I+R**, where **I** is an integer variable and **R** is a real variable. The value of **I** is implicitly converted to a real number and then added to the value of **R**. Furthermore, FORTRAN allows an assignment statement in which the lefthand side is of type **REAL** and the righthand side is of type **INTEGER**, or vice versa. In either case, the value of the righthand side is implicitly converted to the type of the lefthand side. PL/I allows a wide assortment of implicit conversions that occur when an expression of one type appears in a context where a value of another type is needed.

As explained in Section 4.3.2, the Ada language allows a universal integer literal expression to be used anywhere a value in some integer type is needed, and a universal real expression anywhere a value in some floating-point or fixed-point type is needed. Except in these cases, however, there are no implicit type conversions in the Ada language. When a value of a particular type is expected at some point in an Ada program, only an expression of that type may appear there. To obtain a value in one type corresponding to some value in another type, the programmer must write an *explicit conversion*. For example, given the declarations

```
I : Integer;
F : Float;
```

the assignment

```
F := I;
```

is illegal. To convert the value of `I` to a value of type `Float` and then assign that value to `F`, the programmer must write

```
F := Float (I);
```

The expression `Float (I)` is a *type conversion* denoting a value of type `Float` corresponding to the value of `I`. Type conversions are described in Chapter 8.

Every Ada type declaration introduces a distinct type. Even two *identical* type declarations introduce different types that happen to have the same representation. Thus, given the declarations

```
TYPE Frame_Number_Type IS RANGE 1 .. 10;
TYPE Bowling_Pin_Type IS RANGE 1 .. 10;

Current_Frame : Frame_Number_Type;
Front_Pin     : Bowling_Pin_Type;
```

it is illegal to assign `Current_Frame` to `Front_Pin`. Even though the values in `Frame_Number_Type` and the values in `Bowling_Pin_Type` are both *represented* by integers in the range from one to ten, values in the two types have different meanings.

In effect, all values in the Ada language are "tagged" as belonging to some type. The fifth value in type `Frame_Number_Type` consists of the integer five and the tag of type `Frame_Number_Type`. The fifth value in type `Bowling_Pin_Type` consists of the integer five and the tag of type `Bowling_Pin_Type`. Because their tags are different, these are two different values.

6.2 SUBTYPES

An object declaration containing a constraint specifies that the values of the declared object are restricted not only to a certain type but to a particular subset of the values in that type. Consider the following declarations:

```
TYPE Day_Type IS
   (Sunday, Monday, Tuesday, Wednesday, Thursday, Friday,
    Saturday);

Pay_Day : Day_Type RANGE Thursday .. Friday;
```

The range constraint in the declaration of `Pay_Day` restricts the values of `Pay_Day` to the subset of `Day_Type` values in the range `Thursday` through `Friday`. Given the declarations

```
TYPE Hours_Type IS RANGE 0 .. 24;
TYPE Time_Distribution_Type IS
   ARRAY (Day_Type RANGE <>) OF Hours_Type;
TYPE Time_Distribution_Pointer_Type IS
   ACCESS Time_Distribution_Type;
Weekday_Hours : Time_Distribution_Type (Monday .. Friday);
Weekday_Hours_Pointer :
   Time_Distribution_Pointer_Type (Monday .. Friday);
```

the index constraint in the declaration of `Weekday_Hours` restricts the values of `Weekday_Hours` to the subset of `Time_Distribution_Type` values with index bounds of `Monday .. Friday`. The index constraint in the declaration of `Weekday_Hours_Pointer` restricts the values of `Weekday_Hours_Pointer` to the subset of `Time_Distribution_Pointer_Type` values that *point to* allocated variables with index bounds of `Monday .. Friday`.

(Floating-point and fixed-point accuracy constraints behave slightly differently. They do not necessarily restrict the values that a variable will hold, only the approximations that the implementation is *required* to be able to store in the variable. An implementation may provide greater accuracy, but the programmer should not rely on this.)

The subsets of types defined by constraints are called *subtypes*. The type from which a subtype is taken is called the *base type* of the subtype. For instance, `Pay_Day` belongs to a subtype of `Day_Type` consisting of the values `Thursday` and `Friday`. `Day_Type` is the base type of this subtype.

Because any set is a subset of itself, any type can be viewed as a subtype of itself. For instance, the declaration

```
Today : Day_Type;
```

declares `Today` to belong to the subtype of `Day_Type` containing all seven `Day_Type` values. It follows that we can use the term *subtype* to mean "type or subtype."

Objects (i.e., variables and constants) are containers that hold *values*. Objects have subtypes, but values do not. The subtype of an object is specified by the typemark and optional constraint in its object declaration. (Sometimes this is a subtype containing every value in its base type.) A value may belong to only one type—the type indicated by its imaginary "tag"—but it may belong to many subtypes. Given the declarations

```
A : Integer RANGE 0 .. 10;
B : Integer RANGE 5 .. 15;
C : Integer;
```

the `Integer` values from five to ten belong to the subtype of `A`, the subtype of `B`, *and* the subtype of `C`.

Thus it is always meaningful to talk about the subtype of an object and never meaningful to talk about the subtype of a value. It is meaningful to talk about the *type* of either a variable or a value. The relationships among types, subtypes, objects, and values are summarized in Figure 6.1.

	Objects (Variables and constants)	**Values (stored in objects, computed in expressions)**
Types	Every object is declared as belonging to some type.	Every value has an imaginary "tag" naming a unique type.
Subtypes	Every object is declared as belonging to a particular subtype of its type.	A value belongs to many subtypes of its type.

Figure 6.1 Relationships among types and subtypes, objects and values.

The subtype of a variable may restrict the values stored in the variable, but not the ways in which the value of the variable may be used. For example, given the declaration of `A` above, the assignment

```
A := 11;
```

is in error. However, the expression `A + 11` is perfectly legitimate. It computes the `Integer` value resulting from the addition of the `Integer` value stored in `A` and the `Integer` value eleven. In general, the subtype of a variable is irrelevant in an expression. When the name of variable occurs in an expression, the name really signifies the current *value* stored in that variable, and values have no subtypes.

6.2.1 Subtype Declarations

Programs often refer to the same subtype in many places. For instance, you might declare several variables, constants, or record components belonging to the same subtype; you might define an array type with components in the subtype, an access type designating allocated objects in the subtype, or a subprogram with parameters in the subtype. *Subtype declarations* give names to subtypes, and thus make it easier to refer to the same subtype in many places. The form of a subtype declaration is

SUBTYPE *identifier* IS *typemark* [*constraint*] ;

This declares the identifier to be a name for the subtype indicated by the typemark and constraint. In fact, the identifier becomes a typemark itself and may appear anywhere typemarks are allowed in an Ada program. Each appearance of a typemark defined in a subtype declaration of the form

SUBTYPE *identifier* IS *typemark constraint* ;

stands for the *"typemark constraint"* combination following the word `IS`. For example, given the declaration

```
SUBTYPE State_Abbreviation_Subtype IS String (1 .. 2);
```

the typemark State_Abbreviation_Subtype stands for

```
String (1 .. 2)
```

each time it occurs afterward. A subtype declaration of the form

SUBTYPE *identifier* IS *typemark* ;

simply defines a new typemark that is synonymous with the typemark following the word IS.

Now you have seen two kinds of typemarks—those declared in type declarations (described in Chapter 4) and those declared in subtype declarations. Since a type is also a subtype of itself, you can think of all typemarks simply as names of subtypes.

A subtype declaration is appropriate whenever naming a subtype would make a program easier to read. For example, a program to manipulate eighty-column card images might have many variables, constants, array components, and record components declared as String (1 .. 80). The subtype declaration

```
SUBTYPE Card_Image_Subtype IS String (1 .. 80);
```

provides a one-symbol shorthand for String (1 .. 80). In declarations, the typemark Card_Image_Subtype documents the intended use of the declared objects more precisely than String (1 .. 80). (Still, Card_Image_Subtype names a subtype of type String rather than a separate type. Any operations defined for values of type String can be applied directly to Card_Image_Subtype values.)

There are certain places in Ada programs where a subtype can only be described by a typemark, not by a full subtype indication. One such place is before the word RANGE in an unconstrained array type declaration. To indicate that Card_Field_Type consists of arrays whose index bounds may be chosen from the range of Integer values one to eighty, one first must provide a name for that range:

```
SUBTYPE Column_Number_Subtype IS Integer RANGE 1 .. 80;
TYPE Card_Field_Type IS
   ARRAY (Column_Number_Subtype RANGE <>) OF Character;
```

(As we shall see in Chapter 9, this approach is also used to describe the subtypes of subprogram parameters.)

6.2.2 Compatibility Between Typemarks and Constraints

A typemark followed by a constraint is called a *subtype indication.* A subtype indication specifies a subtype that is a subset of the subtype named by the typemark.

The subtype specified by the subtype indication and the subtype named by the typemark are subtypes of the same base type. For example, after the declaration

```
SUBTYPE Weekday_Subtype IS Day_Type RANGE Monday .. Friday;
```

the subtype indication

```
Weekday_Subtype RANGE Monday .. Wednesday
```

specifies a subtype that is a subset of `Weekday_Subtype`. Both the subtype `Weekday_Subtype` and the subtype

```
Weekday_Subtype RANGE Monday .. Wednesday
```

are subtypes of type `Day_Type`. That is, values in subtype `Weekday_Subtype` and values in subtype

```
Weekday_Subtype RANGE Monday .. Wednesday
```

have the same imaginary tags—the tags of the base type `Day_Type`.

The kinds of constraints that may follow a typemark depend on the kind of subtype named by the typemark. Figure 6.2 summarizes the rules for using constraints. An "integer subtype" means a subtype of an integer type, an "enumeration subtype" means a subtype of an enumeration type, and so forth. Record subtypes and access subtypes designating them will be addressed in Chapter 10.

6.2.2.1 Range constraints.

In a subtype indication

typemark **RANGE** *lower* **..** *upper*

where *lower* ≤ *upper*, *lower* and *upper* must both belong to the subtype named by the typemark. Thus the sequence of subtype declarations

```
SUBTYPE From_0_To_100 IS Integer RANGE 0 .. 100;
SUBTYPE From_10_To_80 IS From_0_To_100 RANGE 10 .. 80;
SUBTYPE From_40_To_50 IS From_10_to_80 RANGE 40 .. 50;
```

defines successively narrower subtypes of type `Integer`. The declaration of `From_10_To_80` is equivalent to the declaration

```
SUBTYPE From_10_To_80 IS Integer RANGE 10 .. 80;
```

and the declaration of `From_40_To_50` is equivalent to either of the following declarations:

```
SUBTYPE From_40_To_50 IS Integer RANGE 40 .. 50;
SUBTYPE From_40_To_50 IS From_0_To_100 RANGE 40 .. 50;
```

Type of constraint

Kind of subtype named by typemark	Range constraint	Floating-point accuracy constraint	Fixed-point accuracy constraint	Index constraint
integer subtype	integer subtype	constraint not allowed	constraint not allowed	constraint not allowed
floating-point subtype	floating-point subtype	floating-point subtype	constraint not allowed	constraint not allowed
fixed-point subtype	fixed-point subtype	constraint not allowed	fixed-point subtype	constraint not allowed
enumeration subtype	enumeration subtype	constraint not allowed	constraint not allowed	constraint not allowed
constrained subtype of an array type	constraint not allowed	constraint not allowed	constraint not allowed	constraint not allowed
unconstrained subtype of an array type	constraint not allowed	constraint not allowed	constraint not allowed	constrained subtype of an array type
access subtype designating a constrained array subtype	constraint not allowed	constraint not allowed	constraint not allowed	constraint not allowed
access subtype designating an unconstrained array subtype	constraint not allowed	constraint not allowed	constraint not allowed	access subtype designating a constrained array subtype
access subtype designating a noncomposite type	constraint not allowed	constraint not allowed	constraint not allowed	constraint not allowed

Figure 6.2 Rules for using constraints. A subtype indication consists of a typemark optionally followed by a constraint. The allowable constraints depend on the kind of subtype named by the typemark. The typemark and constraint taken together name a new subtype of the kind indicated in the table.

However, the following subtype declaration would be in error, because neither twenty nor thirty belongs to the subtype `From_40_To_50`:

```
SUBTYPE From_20_To_30 IS From_40_To_50 RANGE 20 .. 30;
   -- INCORRECT!
```

6.2.2.2 Accuracy constraints. A floating-point or fixed-point accuracy constraint may not specify greater accuracy than the subtype named by the typemark, although it may specify less. A floating-point accuracy constraint must specify a number of digits *less* than or equal to the number of digits associated with the typemark. A fixed-point accuracy constraint must specify a delta *greater* than or equal to the delta associated with the typemark. The following sequence of subtype declarations defines successively less precise subtypes of the predefined type `Float`:

```
SUBTYPE Five_Digits IS Float DIGITS 5;
SUBTYPE Four_Digits IS Five_Digits DIGITS 4;
SUBTYPE Three_Digits IS Four_Digits DIGITS 3;
```

The declaration of `Four_Digits` is equivalent to

```
SUBTYPE Four_Digits IS Float DIGITS 4;
```

and the declaration of `Three_Digits` is equivalent to either of the following declarations:

```
SUBTYPE Three_Digits IS Float DIGITS 3;
SUBTYPE Three_Digits IS Five_Digits DIGITS 3;
```

The following subtype declaration is in error because it calls for more precision than subtype `Five_Digits` is required to have:

```
SUBTYPE Seven_Digits IS Five_Digits DIGITS 7;
   -- INCORRECT!
```

6.2.2.3 Index constraints. Given the following declarations, both `Quadruple_Type` and `List_Of_5_Subtype` are typemarks naming constrained array subtypes:

```
TYPE Quadruple_Type IS ARRAY (1 .. 4) OF Integer;
TYPE Integer_List_Type IS ARRAY (Integer RANGE <>) OF Integer;
SUBTYPE List_Of_5_Subtype IS Integer_List_Type (1 .. 5);
```

The declaration

```
List : List_Of_5_Subtype;
```

is equivalent to the declaration

```
List : Integer_List_Type (1 .. 5);
```

In specifying array subtypes, an index constraint may only be applied to an unconstrained array subtype, resulting in a constrained array subtype. In other words, an index constraint may only appear once in the sequence of type and subtype declarations defining successive array subtypes.

Every individual *object* designated by an access value is constrained at the time it is allocated. However, a *subtype* of an access type designating array objects is considered unconstrained if different access values in the subtype may designate array objects with different index bounds. In defining a subtype of an access type, an index constraint may only be applied to an unconstrained access subtype designating array objects. The result is a constrained access subtype consisting only of values designating array objects with the given index bounds. The following examples are based on the type and subtype declarations above:

```
TYPE Quadruple_Pointer_Type IS ACCESS Quadruple_Type;
TYPE Integer_List_Pointer_Type IS ACCESS Integer_List_Type;
TYPE List_Of_5_Pointer_Type IS ACCESS List_Of_5_Subtype;
SUBTYPE Constrained_List_Pointer_Subtype IS
   Integer_List_Pointer_Type (1 .. 5);
```

Of these four declarations, only the second declares an unconstrained access type. `Quadruple_Pointer_Type` values and `List_Of_5_Pointer_Type` values designate objects in constrained array subtypes. `Constrained_List_Pointer_Subtype` values designate objects in an unconstrained array subtype, but only those values with a particular index constraint. Thus `Constrained_List_Pointer_Subtype` itself is a constrained access subtype. An index constraint may appear following the typemark `Integer_List_Pointer_Type` (as shown in the fourth declaration), but not following the typemark `Quadruple_Pointer_Type`, `List_Of_5_Pointer_Type`, or `Constrained_List_Pointer_Subtype`.

6.2.3 Discrete Ranges of Subtypes

Any subtype of an integer or enumeration type may be named by the typemark in a discrete range. In a discrete range of the form

typemark RANGE *low* .. *high*

where *low* ≤ *high*, the lower and upper bounds must be values in the subtype named by the typemark. (In the case of a null range, that is, one where *low* > *high*, the requirement is less stringent, as will be explained in Section 6.2.5.) A discrete range consisting only of a typemark specifies the range extending from the lowest value in the named subtype to the highest value in that subtype. Given the declarations

```
TYPE Day_Type IS
   (Sunday, Monday, Tuesday, Wednesday, Thursday, Friday,
    Saturday);
SUBTYPE Weekday_Subtype IS Day_Type RANGE Monday .. Friday;
```

the discrete range

```
Weekday_Subtype RANGE Tuesday .. Thursday
```

is equivalent to the discrete range

```
Day_Type RANGE Tuesday .. Thursday
```

The discrete range

```
Weekday_Subtype
```

is equivalent to

```
Day_Type RANGE Monday .. Friday
```

(and to

```
Weekday_Subtype RANGE Monday .. Friday
```

as well). The discrete range

```
Weekday_Subtype RANGE Sunday .. Wednesday
  -- INCORRECT!
```

is incorrect because `Sunday` is not contained in the subtype `Weekday_Subtype`.

Chapter 4 explained that an array type declaration specifies the index type associated with each dimension. However, an array type specifies more than just the type of an index; it also specifies the subtype of the index, known as the *index subtype*. Consider the following declaration:

```
TYPE Weekday_Calendar_Type IS
   ARRAY (Weekday_Subtype, Integer RANGE 1 .. 5) OF Integer;
```

The index subtype in the first dimension is the subtype of the index type `Day_Type` consisting of the values `Monday` through `Friday`. The index subtype in the second dimension is the subtype of the index subtype `Integer` consisting of the values one through five.

Unconstrained array type declarations also specify index subtypes. Given the subtype declaration

```
SUBTYPE Week_Number_Subtype IS Integer RANGE 1 .. 52;
```

the type declaration

```
TYPE General_Calendar_Type IS
   ARRAY (Day_Type RANGE <>, Week_Number_Subtype RANGE <>)
      OF Integer;
```

specifies that the index subtype in the first dimension is the subtype Day_Type (i.e., the subtype consisting of all seven Day_Type values), and the index subtype in the second dimension is the subtype Week_Number_Subtype. A non-null index constraint appearing in the declaration of a General_Calendar_Type object must specify index bounds that belong to the index subtypes. The declaration

```
February_Weekdays:
   General_Calendar_Type (Monday .. Friday, 1 .. 4);
```

is correct, but

```
Next_Two_Years:
   General_Calendar_Type (Sunday .. Saturday, 1 .. 104);
   -- INCORRECT!
```

is in error, because the upper bound for the second dimension does not belong to Week_Number_Subtype.

6.2.4 Subtypes of Array and Record Components

An array type declaration specifies not only the type but the subtype of the components. The type General_Calendar_Type could also have been defined as

```
TYPE General_Calendar_Type IS
   ARRAY (Day_Type RANGE <>, Week_Number_Subtype RANGE <>)
      OF Integer RANGE 1 .. 31;
```

In this case, the components of General_Calendar_Type objects would be required to belong to the subtype of type Integer consisting of the values one through 31. Equivalently, we could have defined the subtype

```
SUBTYPE Day_Of_Month_Subtype IS Integer RANGE 1 .. 31;
```

and declared General_Calendar_Type as

```
TYPE General_Calendar_Type IS
   ARRAY (Day_Type RANGE <>, Week_Number_Subtype RANGE <>)
      OF Day_Of_Month_Subtype;
```

The component declarations of a record type declaration consist of a typemark (naming a subtype) followed by an optional constraint (perhaps specifying a smaller subtype). Thus record type declarations specify not only the type but the subtype of each component. The declaration

```
TYPE Indexed_Card_Image_Type IS
   RECORD
      Index_Part : Integer RANGE 0 .. 999999;
      Image_Part : String (1 .. 80);
   END RECORD;
```

is equivalent to the declarations

```
SUBTYPE Image_Index_Subtype IS Integer RANGE 0 .. 999999;
SUBTYPE Card_Image_Subtype IS String (1 .. 80);
TYPE Indexed_Card_Image_Type IS
   RECORD
      Index_Part : Image_Index_Subtype;
      Image_Part : Card_Image_Subtype;
   END RECORD;
```

6.2.5 Predefined Subtypes

Two subtypes of type `Integer`, named `Positive` and `Natural`, are predefined. `Positive` is the subtype consisting of all positive values of type `Integer` and `Natural` is the subtype consisting of all nonnegative values of type `Integer`. The only difference between these subtypes is that the `Integer` value zero belongs to `Natural` but not to `Positive`. Type `String` was described in Section 4.2.6 as a one-dimensional unconstrained array type whose index type is `Integer` and whose component type is `Character`. We can now be more specific: The index *sub*type of type `String` is `Positive`. That is, `String` is defined as

```
TYPE String IS ARRAY (Positive RANGE <>) OF Character;
```

That is why an index constraint for a non-null `String` object can only specify positive bounds.

(Section 6.2.3 alluded to an exception to the rule requiring the bounds in a discrete range to belong to the subtype indicated by the discrete range's typemark. In the case of a null range, the bounds must still belong to the same *type* as that subtype, but they need not belong to the subset defined by the typemark. This makes it possible, for example, to declare a null string with the subtype indication `String (1 .. 0)`, even though zero does not belong to subtype `Positive`. A string of length *n* can be therefore always declared as `String (1 .. n)`.)

6.3 DIFFERENCES BETWEEN TYPES AND SUBTYPES

Each type declaration introduces a new set of values. The types defined by the declarations

```
TYPE Camera_Number_Type IS RANGE 1 .. 3;
TYPE Channel_Type IS RANGE 2 .. 83;
```

do not overlap. The value consisting of the number three and the tag Camera_Number_Type is distinct from the value consisting of the number three and the tag Channel_Type. A subtype simply defines a subset of an existing type. The subtypes defined by the declarations

```
SUBTYPE VHF_Channel_Subtype IS Channel_Type RANGE 2 .. 13;
SUBTYPE Low_VHF_Channel_Subtype IS
   Channel_Type RANGE 2 .. 6;
```

do overlap. For instance, the value consisting of the number five and the tag Channel_Type belongs to both these subtypes. (The tag implicitly associated with a value indicates its type, not its subtype, since a value may belong to many subtypes of the type.)

Although each type declaration introduces a new type, even in the case of identical declarations, it is possible for two subtype declarations to specify different names for the same subtype. The subtype declarations need not be identical. Consider the following floating-point type and subtype declarations:

```
TYPE Trigonometric_Function_Value IS DIGITS 7;
SUBTYPE Approximate_Trigonometric_Value IS
   Trigonometric_Function_Value DIGITS 3;
SUBTYPE Sine_Cosine_Value IS
   Trigonometric_Function_Value RANGE -1.0 .. 1.0;
```

Trigonometric_Function_Value consists of floating-point approximations with at least seven digits of precision. Approximate_Trigonometric_Value is a subset of this type whose approximations need only be accurate to three digits. Sine_Cosine_Value consists of the set of seven-digit Trigonometric_Function_Value approximations whose values lie in the range of the sine and cosine functions (i.e., the interval from -1.0 to 1.0). The following three subtype declarations all define the subtype consisting of the intersection of these two subsets, approximations of type Trigonometric_Function_Value accurate to three digits and within the range -1.0 to 1.0:

```
SUBTYPE Approximate_Sine_Cosine_Value_1 IS
   Trigonometric_Function_Value DIGITS 3 RANGE -1.0 .. 1.0;
SUBTYPE Approximate_Sine_Cosine_Value_2 IS
   Approximate_Trigonometric_Value RANGE -1.0 .. 1.0;
SUBTYPE Approximate_Sine_Cosine_Value_3 IS
   Sine_Cosine_Value DIGITS 3.0;
```

The following six object declarations contain equivalent subtype indications:

```
U : Trigonometric_Function_Value DIGITS 3 RANGE -1.0 .. 1.0;
V : Approximate_Trigonometric_Value RANGE -1.0 .. 1.0;
W : Sine_Cosine_Value DIGITS 3;
X : Approximate_Sine_Cosine_Value_1;
Y : Approximate_Sine_Cosine_Value_2;
Z : Approximate_Sine_Cosine_Value_3;
```

Whenever two subtype indications specify the same subset of values, one can be replaced by the other without affecting the meaning of the program.

Type declarations should be used when defining a new meaning for data. Suppose we are writing a program dealing with points and lines on a plane. We can define a fixed-point type `Coordinate_Type` to express the distance of a point from the X-axis or Y-axis:

```
TYPE Coordinate_Type IS DELTA 0.1 RANGE -50.0 .. 50.0;
```

(This declaration assumes that the program will never deal with any point more than fifty units from either axis and that it is sufficient to approximate coordinates to within one-tenth of a unit.) We can represent a point as a pair of `Coordinate_Type` values using a record type:

```
TYPE Point_Type IS
   RECORD
      X_Coordinate, Y_Coordinate : Coordinate_Type;
   END RECORD;
```

If our program never deals with lines parallel to the X or Y axes or going directly through the point (0,0), a line can also be represented uniquely in terms of a pair of `Coordinate_Type` values—the X-coordinate at which the line intercepts the X-axis and the Y-coordinate at which the line intercepts the Y-axis. It is possible, but inappropriate, simply to define another subtype name for the record type declared earlier:

```
SUBTYPE Line_Type IS Point_Type;
```

This declaration states that `Line_Type` is a subtype consisting of every value in `Point_Type`. Because lines and points are different abstract notions, they should be described by different types. A second type declaration would be more appropriate:

```
TYPE Line_Type IS
   RECORD
      X_Intercept, Y_Intercept : Coordinate_Type;
   END RECORD;
```

One effect of the type declaration is to define more appropriate names for the components of `Line_Type` records. A more important effect is to prevent

Point_Type representations and Line_Type representations from being used interchangeably. The Point_Type record containing the Coordinate_Type values 1.0 and 3.0 has an implicit tag of type Point_Type, and the Line_Type record containing the Coordinate_Type values 1.0 and 3.0 will have an implicit tag of type Line_Type. This reflects the fact that the point (1,3) and the line passing through (1,0) and (0,3) are two distinct entities, even though they happen to have the same underlying representation. Given the separate type definitions, an Ada compiler will not allow a value of type Line_Type to be assigned to a variable of type Point_Type, or vice versa. If a subprogram is designed to manipulate a line in some way, it will not be possible to call that subprogram to manipulate a point instead. Any attempt to violate these type restrictions will be detected by an Ada compiler while the program is being compiled.

This protection is not provided by subtype declarations. The declaration

```
SUBTYPE Line_Type IS Point_Type;
```

would simply have made Line_Type another name for the set of values in type Point_Type. The set of variable declarations

```
A : Point_Type;
B : Line_Type;
```

would then have precisely the same meaning as the set of declarations

```
A : Line_Type;
B : Point_Type;
```

The assignment A := B; would be permitted with either set of declarations.

This is not to suggest that you should declare as many different types as possible. It is possible to define too many types, declaring values with similar meanings to be different. Then the protective type restrictions become cumbersome, making it difficult to do reasonable things in a straightforward manner. For example, a programmer might reason that a number indicating distance from the X-axis and a number indicating distance from the Y-axis have two different meanings, and might declare two separate types in place of the single type Coordinate_Type:

```
TYPE X_Coordinate_Type IS DELTA 0.1 RANGE -50.0 .. 50.0;
TYPE Y_Coordinate_Type IS DELTA 0.1 RANGE -50.0 .. 50.0;

TYPE Point_Type IS
   RECORD
      Ordinate : X_Coordinate_Type;
      Abscissa : Y_Coordinate_Type;
   END RECORD;
```

Now suppose P and P_Reflection are variables of type Point_Type and the programmer wishes to assign P_Reflection the point that is the reflection of of P along the line $y=x$. That is, if P is the point (a,b), the desired value of P_Reflection is the point (b,a). The program cannot simply perform the assignments

```
P_Reflection.Ordinate := P.Abscissa;
P_Reflection.Abscissa := P.Ordinate;
```

because the Abscissa and Ordinate components of Point_Type values belong to two different types. Furthermore, the program cannot test whether a point is above, on, or below the line $y=x$ simply by checking whether the point's Abscissa component is greater than, equal to, or less than its Ordinate component, because the operators >, =, and < are ordinarily defined only for two values of the same type. There are ways to get around these problems (by writing explicit conversions between X_Coordinate_Type and Y_Coordinate_Type or by defining new versions of > and < to compare an X_Coordinate_Type value with a Y_Coordinate_Type value), but they make the program more complicated and more difficult to read.

It is a matter of judgment whether two uses of a certain kind of value constitute two distinct meanings or two variations of the same meaning. In making this judgment, you should consider the operations that will be applied to the values and how often these operations will intermix the two uses. If intermixing is frequent, you will be better off using a single type, like Coordinate_Type, for both uses. If intermixing is infrequent, two type declarations may be preferable. Then, in the few places where operations must be applied to values in different types, you can write an explicit conversion. Everywhere else, the type restrictions enforced by the compiler will protect you from confusing the two uses.

The expressions in constraints need not be static. Therefore, the set of values contained in a subtype cannot always be known before a program begins execution. (Consider the declaration

```
Elapsed_Time : Float RANGE 0.0 .. Square_Root (2.0 * d / g);
```

where Square_Root is a function.) Errors resulting from *type* mismatches are always determined when a program is compiled, but errors resulting from *subtype* mismatches can sometimes only be detected during program execution. In cases of obvious subtype mismatches, such as

```
x : Integer RANGE 1 .. 10 := 11;
```

a good compiler will issue a *warning* that execution of the program is sure to result in a subtype mismatch. However, the compiler must still compile the program and allow it to begin execution.

6.4 DERIVED TYPES

A derived type declaration is used to define a new type in which each value is represented by a single value in some previously declared type. The form of a derived type declaration is

TYPE *identifier* IS NEW *typemark* *constraint* ;

After elaboration of this declaration, the identifier names a subtype that is essentially a copy of the subtype indicated by the typemark and optional constraint. The values in the new subtype are identical to the values in the old subtype, except that the values in the new subtype have a different implicit tag. It is because the implicit tags are different that we say that the identifier names a copy of the old subtype rather than the old subtype itself. Values in the old and new subtypes cannot be used interchangeably because the two subtypes are subsets of distinct types.

Certain operations on the old type—including both operators defined by the language and subprograms defined by programmers—are called *derivable subprograms.* When a derived type is declared, new versions of the derivable operations are also implicitly declared. These new versions work in exactly the same way as the old versions, except that they operate on values of the derived type rather than on values of the old type. We shall discuss derivable subprograms further in Chapter 11.

Suppose we have declared a type named `Table_Type` to represent a set of thirty-character strings with an integer between zero and 9,999,999 associated with each string:

```
TYPE Table_Entry_Type IS
   RECORD
      Key   : String (1 .. 30);
      Value : Integer RANGE 0 .. 9_999_999;
   END RECORD;
TYPE Entry_List_Type IS
   ARRAY (Positive RANGE <>) OF Table_Entry_Type;
TYPE Table_Type IS
   RECORD
      Entry_Count_Part : Natural := 0;
      Entry_List_Part  : Entry_List_Type (1 .. 100);
   END RECORD;
```

Suppose we have also declared subprograms to add a new string and associated integer to a table and to look up the integer currently associated with a given string.

Different `Table_Type` objects can hold different kinds of data. One might hold people's names and telephone numbers. Another might hold names of inventory items and the number of each item currently in stock. In a program containing several `Table_Type` objects used as telephone directories and several used as inventory records, it would be desirable to distinguish between these two uses. The following derived type declarations establish this distinction:

```
TYPE Telephone_Directory_Type IS NEW Table_Type;
TYPE Inventory_Record_Type IS NEW Table_Type;
```

The declarations create two new types. Each value in the derived type Telephone_Directory_Type is *represented* by a value of type Table_Type. So is each value in the derived type Inventory_Record_Type. However, a Telephone_Directory_Type value and the corresponding Inventory_Record_Type value are distinct from each other and from the underlying Table_Type value. Variables in these three types cannot be used interchangeably.

The relationship between type Telephone_Directory_Type and type Inventory_Record_Type is quite similar to the relationship between types Point_Type and Line_Type in Section 6.3. In fact, it would have been possible to define those two types as follows:

```
TYPE Point_Type IS
   RECORD
      X_Coordinate, Y_Coordinate : Coordinate_Type;
   END RECORD;
TYPE Line_Type IS NEW Point_Type;
```

However, this formulation is misleading, because it suggests that a line is represented by a point. Actually, both a line and a point are represented by a pair of coordinates, but in different ways. Therefore, the following formulation is more appropriate:

```
TYPE Coordinate_Pair_Type IS
   RECORD
      First_Coordinate, Second_Coordinate : Coordinate_Type;
   END RECORD;
TYPE Point_Type IS NEW Coordinate_Pair_Type;
TYPE Line_Type IS NEW Coordinate_Pair_Type;
```

6.5 SUMMARY

A value of some particular type is required at many places in a program. If a value of some other type appears instead, the program will be marked illegal when it is compiled. In particular, the value supplied is not automatically converted to the required type. Conversions from one type to another (other than conversions of universal expressions such as 3 and 4.5 to ordinary numeric types) take place only when they are explicitly specified by the programmer. Every type declaration introduces a new type whose values are not shared by any other type.

A constraint in an object declaration restricts the object to hold only values in a certain subset of its type. The subset is called a *subtype*, and the type itself is called the *base type* of the subtype. A type can be viewed as a subtype consisting of every value in its base type. An object belongs to a particular subtype—the one specified by the typemark and (optionally) the constraint in its declaration. A value, in contrast, belongs to one type but, in general, to many subtypes of that type.

A subtype declaration of the form

SUBTYPE *identifier* IS *typemark* *constraint* ;

provides a new name for a subtype. This name stands for the *subtype indication*

typemark *constraint* ;

in the subtype declaration. The subtype name may be used as a typemark. It may appear, for instance, in object declarations, in other subtype indications, in discrete ranges, and to specify the subtypes of components in array or record type declarations.

The typemark and constraint in a subtype indication must be compatible. Only a range constraint may follow a typemark naming an integer subtype or an enumeration subtype. A range constraint or a floating-point accuracy constraint may follow a typemark naming a floating-point subtype. A range constraint or a fixed-point accuracy constraint may follow a typemark naming a fixed-point subtype. In each case, the subtype named by the subtype indication is the same kind of subtype as that named by the typemark. An index constraint may follow a typemark naming an array subtype only if the array subtype is unconstrained. When an index constraint appears, the subtype indication specifies a constrained array subtype. If an access subtype designates an unconstrained array subtype, an index constraint may follow a typemark naming the access subtype. The subtype indication then specifies an access subtype designating a constrained array subtype.

There are two predefined subtypes of the predefined type `Integer`. The subtype `Natural` extends from zero to the highest value of type `Integer`. The subtype `Positive` extends from one to the highest value of type `Integer`. `Positive` is the index subtype of the predefined type `String`:

```
TYPE String IS ARRAY (Positive RANGE <>) OF Character;
```

Although each type declaration introduces a new type, subtype declarations may introduce overlapping or identical subtypes. Separate type declarations should be used for data with distinct meanings, so that a compiler can catch inadvertent intermixing of the two meanings. Separate types should not be used for data with similar meanings if it is reasonable and likely that the meanings will be intermixed frequently.

A *derived type* is a *copy* of another type. A derived type contains a value corresponding to each value in the other type. It also has operations corresponding to operations in the other type. However, uses of the two types cannot be intermixed. A derived type is declared as follows:

TYPE *identifier* **IS NEW** *typemark* [*constraint*] **;**

The declaration causes the identifier to name a copy of the subtype specified by the typemark and optional constraint.

EXERCISES

6.1 What is wrong with the following declaration?

```
TYPE Week_Number_Type IS Integer RANGE 1 .. 52;
```

Show how to make this into a legal integer type declaration, a legal derived type declaration, and a legal subtype declaration.

6.2 Consider the following declarations:

```
TYPE Hour_Number_Type IS RANGE 1 .. 12;

SUBTYPE Late_Hour_Number_Subtype IS
   Hour_Number_Type RANGE 7 ..12;

TYPE Month_Number_Type IS RANGE 1 .. 12;

SUBTYPE Late_Month_Number_Subtype IS
   Month_Number_Type RANGE 7 .. 12;

Hour_Number       : Hour_Number_Type;
Late_Hour_Number  : Late_Hour_Number_Subtype;
Month_Number      : Month_Number_Type;
Late_Month_Number : Late_Month_Number_Subtype;
```

Which of the following assignment statements are legal?

(*a*) `Hour_Number := Late_Hour_Number;`
(*b*) `Hour_Number := Month_Number;`
(*c*) `Hour_Number := Late_Month_Number;`
(*d*) `Month_Number := Late_Hour_Number;`
(*e*) `Month_Number := Late_Month_Number;`
(*f*) `Late_Month_Number := Late_Hour_Number;`

6.3 Consider the following declarations:

```
TYPE Sign_Type IS (Negative, Zero, Positive);

SUBTYPE Non_Negative_Sign_Subtype IS
   Sign_Type RANGE Zero .. Positive;

SUBTYPE Non_Positive_Sign_Type IS
   Sign_Type RANGE Negative .. Zero;

Sign              : Sign_Type;
Non_Negative_Sign : Non_Negative_Sign_Subtype;
Non_Positive_Sign: Non_Positive_Sign_Subtype;
```

Say all you can about the correctness of the following assignments:

(*a*) `Sign := Non_Negative_Sign;`
(*b*) `Non_Negative_Sign := Sign;`
(*c*) `Non_Negative_Sign := Non_Positive_Sign;`

6.4 Section 6.2 contained a series of subtype declarations for increasingly narrower integer subtypes named `From_1_To_100`, `From_10_To_80`, and `From_40_to_50`, and a similar series of floating-point subtypes named `Five_Digits`, `Four_Digits`, and `Three_Digits`. Provide another such series of subtype declarations for subtypes of the following fixed-point type:

```
TYPE Thousandths IS DELTA 0.001 RANGE 0.0 .. 1.0;
```

Also provide an example of a fixed-point subtype declaration that would be illegal because of the size of its accuracy constraint.

6.5 The following declarations are taken from Section 6.2.2:

```
TYPE Integer_List_Type IS ARRAY (Integer RANGE <>) OF Integer;

TYPE Integer_List_Pointer_Type IS ACCESS Integer_List_Type;
SUBTYPE Constrained_List_Pointer_Subtype IS
   Integer_List_Pointer_Type (1 .. 5);

SUBTYPE List_Of_5_Subtype IS Integer_List_Type (1 .. 5);
TYPE List_Of_5_Pointer_Type IS ACCESS List_Of_5_Subtype;
```

Do `Constrained_List_Pointer_Subtype` and `List_Of_5_Pointer_Type` name the same subtype? Why or why not?

6.6 Consider the following declarations:

```
SUBTYPE Alpha IS Integer RANGE 1 .. 10;
TYPE Beta IS NEW Integer RANGE 1 .. 10;

A : Alpha;
B : Beta;
```

Give examples of operations legal for both `A` and `B`, legal for `A` but illegal for `B`, and illegal for both `A` and `B`. What are the implicit tags of `A` and `B`?

CHAPTER

SEVEN

STATEMENTS

A *statement* specifies an action to be performed by a program. This chapter describes most of the statements used in single-task Ada programs (programs that do only one thing at a time). Statements used only in multitask Ada programs (programs executing multiple sequences of statements simultaneously) will be discussed in Chapters 18 and 19. The procedure call statement will be discussed only briefly in this chapter, and the **RETURN** statement will not be discussed at all, since Chapter 9 covers procedure calls in detail. The **RAISE** statement will be discussed in Chapter 15.

Certain statements contain *variable names* or *expressions*. An identifier declared in a variable declaration is a variable name. In addition, indexed components of array variables and selected components of record variables are variable names (see Sections 4.2.6 and 4.2.7). An expression is a description of a value. An expression may be an object name, a literal, a function call, a combination of expressions connected by operators such as +, –, **AND**, and **OR**, or one of several other constructs. Every expression belongs to a particular type. A Boolean expression is an expression describing a value in the predefined type `Boolean`, which consists of the values `True` and `False`. Assuming that `Array_Is_Sorted` is declared as a variable of type `Boolean`, the following are all Boolean expressions:

```
True
Array_Is_Sorted
x = 0
0 < i AND i < n
```

Expressions will be described more completely in Chapter 8.

7.1 ASSIGNMENT STATEMENTS

An *assignment statement* changes the value of a variable. Its form is:

variable-name := *expression* ;

The current value of the variable named by the variable name is replaced by the value of the expression. Except in the case of assignments to an array variable (which we will consider shortly), the value of the expression must belong to the subtype of the variable. This means that

1. The type of the expression must be the same as the type of the variable, and
2. The value of the expression must belong to the subset of that type stipulated in the declaration of the variable.

A violation of condition 1 will be detected by a compiler when it is trying to compile a program. However, a violation of condition 2 will generally be detected only once the program is running, since it depends on the value of the expression at the moment the assignment statement is executed. For example, assume the following declarations:

```
TYPE Hour_Type IS RANGE 1 .. 24;
TYPE Minute_Type IS RANGE 1 .. 60;

Hours   : Hour_Type RANGE 1 .. 12;
Minutes : Minute_Type;
```

The assignment statement

```
Hours := Minutes;
```

violates condition 1 because `Hours` and `Minutes` belong to distinct types. It will be rejected by a compiler. The assignment statement

```
Hours := Hours + 1;
```

(which increases the current value of `Hours` by one) is syntactically valid. Both the variable `Hours` and the expression `Hours + 1` are of type `Hour_Type`. However, the statement violates condition 2 when executed while `Hours` has the value twelve. In such a case, the value of `Hours + 1`—thirteen—does not belong to the subtype of variable `Hours`—`Hour_Type RANGE 1 .. 12`.

In the case of assignment to an array variable, the rules are a little more lenient. The expression and the variable must belong to the same type. However, they may belong to different subtypes, provided that both subtypes have the same *length* in each dimension. For example, given the declarations

```
TYPE Matrix_Type IS
   ARRAY (Integer RANGE <>, Integer RANGE <>) OF Integer;
A : Matrix_Type (1 .. 5, 1 .. 10);
B : Matrix_Type (0 .. 4, 0 .. 9);
```

the assignment statement

```
A := B;
```

is legal. Both `A` and `B` are arrays with five rows and ten columns, but a component of `A` does not have the same index values as the component in the same relative position in `B`. The components are assigned according to their position relative to the initial position in each dimension, not according to the index values of the component. For example, the value of `B (0, 0)` is assigned to `A (1, 1)`; the value of `B (4, 9)` is assigned to `A (5, 10)`.

7.2 PROCEDURE CALL STATEMENTS, INPUT, AND OUTPUT

7.2.1 Procedure Call Statements

A procedure call statement causes a procedure subprogram to be executed. A simple form of the procedure call statement is

procedure-name (*parameter* , ~~~ , *parameter*) ;

Execution of the procedure call statement consists of execution of the named procedure using the given parameters. A *parameter* is either an *expression* whose value is *used* by the procedure or a *variable* whose value may be *updated* by the procedure. Since a variable is one form of an expression, it is possible for one parameter to play both these roles. Chapter 9 will teach you how to write subprograms, and the full form of the procedure call statement will be given there.

7.2.2 Input and Output

The Ada programming language does not have any input or output *statements*. However, there is a set of standard input and output *subprograms* that are provided by every Ada implementation. Some of these subprograms are provided in *generic packages*. However, generic packages are one of the most advanced features of the Ada language, and you will not learn how to use them until Chapter 16. In the meantime, you can use a simplified set of input and output subprograms provided in the compilation unit `Basic_IO`.

`Basic_IO` is not a standard part of the Ada language, but a package written expressly to be used in this book. The text of `Basic_IO` is given in the Appendix. You should make a copy of `Basic_IO` and compile it if your instructor has not already done this for you. Then the simplified input and output subprograms will be available for use in any program that begins

```
WITH Basic_IO;
```

(This line is a *context clause* indicating that your program is making use of another compilation unit compiled earlier. Context clauses and other aspects of separate compilation will be discussed in Chapter 13.)

Each implementation of the Ada language has a *standard input file* and a *standard output file*. On batch systems, the standard input file is typically a set of data cards in the job deck, and the standard output file is typically a line printer. On interactive systems, the standard input file is typically a terminal keyboard, and the standard output file is typically a terminal display. The procedures in `Basic_IO` read from the standard input file and write to the standard output file.

The procedures in `Basic_IO` are named `Basic_IO.Get`, `Basic_IO.Put`, `Basic_IO.Get_Line`, `Basic_IO.New_Line`, and `Basic_IO.New_Page`. The procedure call

```
Basic_IO.Get (x);
```

where *x* is a variable of type `Integer` or type `String`, reads data from the standard input file and places it in *x*. When *x* is an `Integer` variable, `Basic_IO.Get` skips over blanks if necessary and then reads as many characters as can be interpreted as an Ada integer literal optionally preceded by a plus or minus sign. The value of the number read is placed in *x*. When *x* is a `String` variable, `Basic_IO.Get` reads the number of characters corresponding to the length of *x*, skipping to a new line when necessary. The characters read are placed in *x*.

The procedure call

```
Basic_IO.Put (x);
```

where *x* is an expression of type `Integer`, type `String`, or type `Character`, writes the value of *x* to the standard output file. `Integer` values are written as decimal numbers possibly preceded by minus signs, without leading or trailing blanks. `String` values are written without any surrounding double quotes. `Basic_IO.Put` does not begin a new line as long as there is still room on the line written to last.

The procedure call

```
Basic_IO.Get_Line (s, n);
```

where *s* is a `String` variable and *n* is an `Integer` variable, reads up to a line from the standard input file. Input stops when either the end of the line is reached or *s* is filled. The variable *n* is set to the index of the last character read into *s*, or to one less than the first index position of *s* if an empty line is read. When the first index position of *s* is one—which it will be whenever *s* is declared as `String (1 .. k)` for some value *k*—this simply means that *n* is always set to the number of characters read, possibly zero.

The procedure call

```
Basic_IO.New_Line;
```

skips to the beginning of the next line of the standard output file. The procedure call

```
Basic_IO.New_Page;
```

skips to the beginning of the next page of the standard output file.

In addition to these procedures, the package `Basic_IO` provides a parameterless function named `Basic_IO.End_Of_File`. The Boolean expression `Basic_IO.End_Of_File` is true when there are no more characters (including blank characters) left to be read in the standard input file. Otherwise it is false. (Many interactive operating systems have special character sequences that can be entered at the terminal to indicate the end of the standard input file.)

The standard set of Ada input and output subprograms is covered in Chapter 17. All the subprograms in `Basic_IO` have counterparts in the standard set that will behave exactly as described above when called as shown previously. However, the standard subprograms can be called with different numbers and types of parameters as well, to perform other functions. There are many programs in the standard set that do not have counterparts in `Basic_IO`.

`Basic_IO` provides the bare minimum input and output operations needed to write interesting programs while learning the language. The facilities described in Chapter 17 can do much more. They can use files other than the standard input and output files and can use types other than `Integer`, `String`, and `Character`. They provide greater control over formatting, including the ability to skip over lines and pages in an input file. Operations reading from or writing to files have counterparts that read from or write to `String` variables instead. Finally, files can be viewed as collections of records rather than as streams of characters divided into lines and pages. These records can be accessed either in order or randomly.

7.3 IF STATEMENTS AND CASE STATEMENTS

`IF` statements and `CASE` statements execute at most one of several possible sequences of statements contained within them. An `IF` statement chooses a sequence of statements by evaluating one or more Boolean expressions. A `CASE` statement examines the value of an expression in some integer or enumeration type and stipulates which sequence of statements is to be executed for each possible value of the expression.

7.3.1 IF Statements

The simplest kind of IF statement resembles the following:

```
IF Units = 10 THEN
   Tens := Tens + 1;
   Units := 0;
END IF;
```

If Units has the value ten when this statement is encountered, the two assignment statements within it are executed. Otherwise, no action is taken. The following IF statement executes one sequence of statements when the value of Units is less than ten, and another otherwise:

```
IF Units < 9 THEN
   Units := Units + 1;
ELSE
   Tens := Tens + 1;
   Units := 0;
END IF;
```

Statements contained in an IF statement may themselves be IF statements:

```
IF Year1 = Year2 THEN
   Same_Year := True;
   IF Month1 < Month2 THEN
      Earlier_Date_Month := Month1;
   ELSE
      Earlier_Date_Month := Month2;
   END IF;
   Earlier_Date_Year := Year2;
ELSE -- Year1 /= Year2
   Same_Year := False;
   IF Year1 < Year2 THEN
      Earlier_Date_Month := Month1;
      Earlier_Date_Year := Year1;
   ELSE
      Earlier_Date_Month := Month2;
      Earlier_Date_Year := Year2;
   END IF;
END IF;
```

The inner IF statements are said to be *nested* in the outer one.

Nested IF statements can be used to check a series of conditions in turn and to select one of many possible sequences of statements:

```
IF Score >= 95 THEN --  >= means "greater than or equal to"
   Grade := A;
ELSE
   IF Score >= 85 THEN
      Grade := B;
   ELSE
      IF Score >= 75 THEN
         Grade := C;
      ELSE
         IF Score >= 65 THEN
            Grade := D;
         ELSE
            Grade := F;
         END IF;
      END IF;
   END IF;
END IF;
```

However, this is a cumbersome way to express a rather straightforward sequence of decisions. The program looks more complicated than the algorithm it expresses. Despite the indentation, it is hard for both the writer and readers of the program to match up the `IF`, `ELSE`, and `END IF` lines that go together. Furthermore, the nested `IF` statements divide the problem of assigning letter grades to numeric scores in an unnatural way. They split the problem into cases of A grades and non-A grades, then split the case of non-A grades into B grades and non-B grades, and so forth. We normally think of the five possible letter grades as forming five symmetric cases.

To solve these problems, the Ada language provides a way to write a sequence of conditions without nesting. The following `IF` statement has the same effect as the preceding one:

```
IF Score >= 95 THEN
   Grade := A;
ELSIF Score >= 85 THEN
   Grade := B;
ELSIF Score >= 75 THEN
   Grade := C;
ELSIF Score >= 65 THEN
   Grade := D;
ELSE
   Grade := F;
END IF;
```

The single word `ELSIF` is meant to be pronounced as "else if." However, unlike the two words `ELSE IF`, the single word `ELSIF` is used to specify additional conditions at the same level of nesting. A single `END IF` at the bottom matches the `IF` at the top. The conditions now appear to form a list rather than a hierarchy with certain conditions subordinate to others. The use of `ELSIF` makes this `IF` statement much more straightforward. It is easier to read and easier to write.

It is also possible to write an `IF` statement that has `ELSIF` branches but no `ELSE` branch:

```
IF Month = January THEN
   Quarter := 1;
   Year := Year + 1;
ELSIF Month = April THEN
   Quarter := 2;
ELSIF Month = July THEN
   Quarter := 3;
ELSIF Month = October THEN
   Quarter := 4;
END IF;
```

This `IF` statement does nothing when `Month` has a value other than `January`, `April`, `July`, or `October`.

The form and meaning of an `IF` statement may be summarized as follows. The general form of an `IF` statement is:

```
IF Boolean expression THEN
    sequence of statements
...............................
: ELSIF Boolean expression THEN :
:     sequence of statements    :
:                               :
: ~~~                           :
:                               :
: ELSIF Boolean expression THEN :
:     sequence of statements    :
...............................
...............................
: ELSE                          :
:     sequence of statements    :
...............................
END IF;
```

Each of the Boolean expressions is evaluated in turn, until one having the value `True` is found or until they all turn out to have the value `False`. If a Boolean expression having the value `True` is found, the sequence of statements following it is executed, completing the execution of the `IF` statement. If all the Boolean expressions are false and the `ELSE` is present, the sequence of statements following `ELSE` is executed. If all the Boolean expressions are false and the `ELSE` is not present, the `IF` statement simply completes without performing any further actions. The `IF` statement only evaluates as many Boolean expressions as necessary. Once a true one is found, the remaining Boolean expressions are not processed.

7.3.2 CASE Statements

The following `IF` statement updates the `X` and `Y` coordinates of a point to move the point one unit north, south, east, or west, depending on the value of `Direction`:

```
IF Direction = North THEN
   y := y + 1;
ELSIF Direction = South THEN
   y := y - 1;
ELSIF Direction = East THEN
   x := x + 1;
ELSE  -- Direction = West
   x := x - 1;
END IF;
```

When `Direction = North`, the program finds that the first Boolean expression in the `IF` statement is true and executes the first assignment statement. However, when `Direction = West`, the program first checks whether `Direction = North`, whether `Direction = South`, and whether `Direction = East`. Only after finding that none of these conditions holds does the program finally execute the fourth assignment statement.

A more appropriate way to express this computation is with a `CASE` statement. The following `CASE` statement has the same ultimate effect as the `IF` statement above:

```
CASE Direction IS
   WHEN North =>
      y := y + 1;
   WHEN South =>
      y := y - 1;
   WHEN East =>
      x := x + 1;
   WHEN West =>
      x := x - 1;
END CASE;
```

A `CASE` statement is used when the actions a program is to perform depend on the value of some expression in a discrete type. (A discrete type is either an integer type or an enumeration type. It consists of a finite sequence of consecutive values.) The `CASE` statement specifies which sequence of statements is to be executed for each possible value of the expression. The order in which the possible values are listed is immaterial.

The rules of the Ada language do not *require* that a compiler translate the `CASE` statement in a particular way. However, they do *allow* a translation of the `CASE` statement that generally executes faster than the translation of an `IF` statement. A `CASE` statement does not require the actual value of an expression to be compared with each possible value in turn. The appropriate sequence of statements can be chosen directly and immediately. Executing an `IF` statement containing a sequence of `ELSIF`'s is like leafing through a dictionary page by page until you reach the beginning of the words starting with a certain letter. Executing a `CASE` statement is like using a thumb tab to open the book directly to that page.

The general form of a `CASE` statement is as follows:

```
CASE expression IS
   WHEN choice list =>
      sequence of statements
   ~~~
   WHEN choice list =>
      sequence of statements
  .........................
  :WHEN OTHERS =>         :
  :   sequence of statements:
  .........................
END CASE;
```

We shall describe the form of a choice list momentarily. Each choice list specifies one or more of the possible values of the expression. `OTHERS` acts as a choice list specifying every possible value of the expression that was not specified earlier in the choice list. Every possible value of the expression must be specified by exactly one of the actual choice lists or by `OTHERS`. In particular, no value may be specified by more than one choice list; and, if the `WHEN OTHERS` part is omitted, each possible value of the expression must be specified in a choice list. (At the end of this section we shall explain just what is meant by "every possible value.") The `CASE` statement determines the value of the expression and then executes the one sequence of statements that corresponds to that value.

A choice list consists of one or more "choices" separated by vertical bars:

choice | ~~~ | *choice*

The simplest form of a choice is a static expression—for instance, an integer literal or an enumeration literal. (In the `CASE` statement given earlier, each choice list consists of a single choice, and each choice is one of the enumeration literals `North`, `South`, `East`, and `West`.) To make it easier to specify several consecutive values in a choice list, the Ada language also allows a choice to be a discrete range whose bounds are static expressions.

Here are some more examples of `CASE` statements:

```
CASE Month IS
   WHEN September | April | June | November =>
      Days_In_Month := 30;
   WHEN February =>
      IF Leap_Year THEN
         Days_In_Month := 29;
      ELSE
         Days_In_Month := 28;
      END IF;
   WHEN OTHERS =>
      Days_In_Month := 31;
END CASE;
```

```
CASE Today IS
   WHEN Monday .. Friday =>
      Pay_Rate := Normal_Rate;
   WHEN Saturday | Sunday =>
      Pay_Rate := 1.5 * Normal_Rate;
END CASE;

CASE Next_Character IS
   WHEN 'A' .. 'Z' | 'a' .. 'z' =>
      Character_Class := Alphabetic;
   WHEN '0' .. '9' =>
      Character_Class := Numeric;
   WHEN '*' | '+' | '-' | '/' | '<' .. '>' =>
      Character_Class := Operator;
   WHEN OTHERS =>
      Character_Class := Invalid;
END CASE;
```

We conclude the discussion of `CASE` statements with a more precise explanation of the rule that a `CASE` statement must account for each possible value of the expression between the words `CASE` and `IS`. In general, this means that, in the absence of the `WHEN OTHERS` part, *every value in the type* of the expression must be accounted for in one of the choice lists. However, if the expression is a declared variable or constant, it is sufficient to account only for *every value in the subtype* in which this object is declared, provided that the upper and lower bounds of the subtype have been specified by static expressions.

7.4 NULL STATEMENTS

Each sequence of statements in an `IF` statement or a `CASE` statement must itself contain at least one statement. Occasionally, a branch of an `IF` or `CASE` statement corresponds to a circumstance in which no action is to be taken. In such cases, the sequence of statements on that branch should consist of a single `NULL` *statement*. The form of a `NULL` statement is simply

```
NULL;
```

A `NULL` statement serves as a "place holder" and does not call for any action to be performed.

The following `IF` and `CASE` statements contain `NULL` statements:

```
IF Divisor <= 0 THEN
   Error_Flag := True;
ELSIF Divisor = 1 THEN
   NULL;
ELSE
   Result := Result / Divisor;
   Divisions := Divisions + 1;
END IF;
```

```
CASE Month IS
   WHEN January =>
      Quarter := 1;
      Year := Year + 1;
   WHEN April | July | October =>
      Quarter := Quarter + 1;
   WHEN OTHERS =>
      NULL;
END CASE;
```

NULL statements are often found inside CASE statements because a CASE statement must associate a sequence of statements with all possible values of the CASE expression, even those values for which no action is to be performed.

7.5 LOOP STATEMENTS

LOOP statements are used to specify that a sequence of statements is to be executed repeatedly. LOOP statements come in three varieties—WHILE loops, FOR loops, and basic loops. All of them have the same general form:

```
[ identifier : ]
 [ iteration scheme ] LOOP
      sequence of statements
   END LOOP [ identifier ] ;
```

If an identifier followed by a colon is present at the top of the loop, the same identifier must appear at the bottom, following the words END LOOP. If no identifier appears at the top, no identifier may appear at the bottom. The *iteration scheme* has one form in WHILE loops and another in FOR loops. It is omitted in basic loops. (PL/I programmers should note that the first occurrence of the word LOOP is not a statement in itself, but is part of the structure of the LOOP statement. Therefore, it is not followed by a semicolon.)

7.5.1 WHILE Loops

The Ada language's WHILE loop is similar to those of PL/I and Pascal. A WHILE loop has an iteration scheme of the form

WHILE *Boolean expression*

The Boolean expression is evaluated before each repetition of the loop, and the loop terminates when the expression turns out to be false. If the Boolean expression turns out to be false the first time it is evaluated, the statements inside the loop are repeated zero times.

The following program reads a nonnegative integer and writes the lowest integer greater than or equal to the square root of the number read.

```
WITH Basic_IO;
PROCEDURE Integer_Square_Root IS
   x, Root : Natural;
BEGIN
   Basic_IO.Get (x);
   Root := 0;
   WHILE Root ** 2 < x LOOP   -- Root ** 2 is Root squared.
      Root := Root + 1;
   END LOOP;
   Basic_IO.Put (Root);
END Integer_Square_Root;
```

If `x = 5`, the assignment statement incrementing `Root` is repeated three times. The Boolean expression following the word `WHILE` is evaluated four times, with `Root` equal to zero, one, two, and then three. The first three times, the Boolean expression is true, causing `Root` to be incremented to one, two, and then three. The fourth time, it is false, causing the `LOOP` statement to terminate. Then the statement following the `LOOP` statement writes the value three. If `x = 0`, the Boolean expression is false the first time it is evaluated. This terminates the `WHILE` loop immediately, `Root` is never incremented, and the value zero is printed.

7.5.2 FOR Loops

`FOR` loops in the Ada language are similar to `DO` loops in FORTRAN and PL/I and **for** loops in Pascal. They have an iteration scheme of one of the following forms:

> `FOR` *identifier* `IN` *discrete range*
>
> `FOR` *identifier* `IN REVERSE` *discrete range*

The identifier names an object called the *loop parameter.* (Do not confuse the loop parameter with subprogram parameters, which are entirely different entities.) For each value in the discrete range, the sequence of statements is executed with the loop parameter set to that value. If the discrete range is a null range, the statements are repeated zero times. For the first form of the iteration scheme, the loop parameter takes on the values of the discrete range in ascending order. For the second form of the iteration scheme, the loop parameter takes on the values of the discrete range in descending order. (Unlike FORTRAN and PL/I, the Ada language does not provide for the specification of a "step" by which the loop parameter is advanced after each repetition. Neither may the lower or upper bounds be fractional numbers.)

The program

```
WITH Basic_IO;
PROCEDURE For_Loop_Demo IS
BEGIN
   Basic_IO.Put("Hello");
   Basic_IO.New_Line;
```

```
    FOR i in 1 .. 3 LOOP
       Basic_IO.Put(i);
       Basic_IO.New_Line;
    END LOOP;

    Basic_IO.Put("Goodbye");
    Basic_IO.New_Line;

END For_Loop_Demo;
```

produces the following output:

```
Hello
1
2
3
Goodbye
```

Replacing the iteration scheme `FOR i IN 1 .. 3` by the iteration scheme `FOR i IN REVERSE 1 .. 3` would produce the following output:

```
Hello
3
2
1
Goodbye
```

Changing the iteration scheme to `FOR i IN 3 .. 1` would produce the following output:

```
Hello
Goodbye
```

(The discrete range `3 .. 1` is a null range. The statements inside the loop are executed once for each value in this range—that is, not at all.) The iteration scheme

```
FOR i IN REVERSE 3 .. 1
```

would also produce the output

```
Hello
Goodbye
```

("`REVERSE 3 .. 1`" means that the values of the range `3 .. 1`—of which there are none—should be taken in reverse order.)

A `FOR` loop can range over values in an enumeration type. Suppose a program contains the following type declaration:

```
TYPE Day_Type IS
   (Sunday, Monday, Tuesday, Wednesday, Thursday, Friday,
    Saturday);
```

The following loop calls a subprogram named `Get_Hours` for each of the values `Monday` through `Friday`:

```
FOR d IN Day_Type RANGE Monday .. Friday LOOP
   Get_Hours (d);
END LOOP;
```

If there is no other discrete type with values named Monday and Friday, the discrete range Day_Type RANGE Monday .. Friday can be abbreviated as Monday .. Friday. Given the subtype declaration

```
SUBTYPE Weekday_Subtype IS Day_Type RANGE Monday .. Friday;
```

the FOR loop can be written simply as

```
FOR d IN Weekday_Subtype LOOP
   Get_Hours(d);
END LOOP;
```

Here, Weekday_Subtype is a discrete range consisting only of a typemark.

The loop parameter is declared implicitly—that is, automatically—by its appearance in the iteration scheme. This implicit declaration applies within the loop, but not outside of it. There is no way to refer to the loop parameter outside of the loop.

The loop parameter cannot be altered by the statements inside a FOR loop. In particular, it may not appear as the lefthand side in an assignment statement or as a parameter to be changed by a procedure call. Although the loop parameter takes on different values from one repetition of the loop to the next, it acts as a constant during the course of a single repetition.

7.5.3 Basic Loops

A WHILE loop terminates when the Boolean expression in the iteration scheme is false at the beginning of the sequence of statements. A FOR loop terminates when the loop parameter has taken on every value in the range of the iteration scheme. A basic loop does not contain an iteration scheme specifying how the loop terminates.

Consider a device consisting of a digital temperature sensor, a warning light to be lit when the temperature exceeds eighty degrees Fahrenheit, and a warning light to be lit when the temperature falls below sixty degrees Fahrenheit. Suppose a package named Hardware_Interface provides subprograms named Read_Sensor, Set_Too_Hot_Light, and Set_Too_Cold_Light. Read_Sensor takes a single Integer parameter that it sets to the current reading of the temperature sensor; Set_Too_Hot_Light and Set_Too_Cold_Light each take a Boolean parameter, causing the respective warning light to be turned on when the parameter is True and off when it is False. (Chapter 20 will explain how such subprograms, providing an interface with electronic devices, can be written in the Ada language.) A computer controlling this device should keep running until its power supply is turned off. Thus the program running on that computer could contain a basic loop to be repeated indefinitely:

```
WITH Hardware_Interface;

PROCEDURE Monitor_Temperature IS
   Lower_Limit : CONSTANT := 60;
   Upper_Limit : CONSTANT := 80;
   Temperature : Integer;
```

```
BEGIN
   LOOP
      Hardware_Interface.Read_Sensor(Temperature);
      IF Temperature > Upper_Limit THEN
         Hardware_Interface.Set_Too_Cold_Light(False);
         Hardware_Interface.Set_Too_Hot_Light(True);
      ELSIF Temperature < Lower_Limit THEN
         Hardware_Interface.Set_Too_Hot_Light(False);
         Hardware_Interface.Set_Too_Cold_Light(True);
      ELSE
         Hardware_Interface.Set_Too_Cold_Light(False);
         Hardware_Interface.Set_Too_Hot_Light(False);
      END IF;
   END LOOP;
END Monitor_Temperature;
```

A basic loop need not be nonterminating. The execution of the loop can be broken by one of the statements in the loop. The statements discussed in the next two sections—`EXIT` statements and `GOTO` statements—are both capable of breaking the execution of a loop. Loops can also be terminated by `RETURN` statements (see Chapter 9), exceptions (see Chapter 15), and the completion of the task executing the loop (see Chapter 19).

7.6 EXIT STATEMENTS

An `EXIT` statement is used to break out of a loop. A simple form of the `EXIT` statement is

```
EXIT [ WHEN Boolean expression ] ;
```

The statement may only occur within a loop. If the Boolean expression is true, or if the `WHEN` part is omitted, this statement terminates execution of the loop.

A `WHILE` loop terminates based on a condition tested at the beginning of each repetition. If you want a loop to terminate based on a condition tested at some other point in the repetition, you can write a basic loop statement containing an `EXIT` statement. For instance, the effect of Pascal's **repeat** ... **until** loop, which tests a condition at the bottom of a loop, can be achieved by a basic loop whose last statement is an `EXIT` statement:

```
Root := 0;
LOOP
   Root := Root + 1;
   EXIT WHEN Root ** 2 >= x;
END LOOP;
```

The difference between this loop and the similar `WHILE` loop presented in procedure `Integer_Square_Root` in Section 7.5.1 is that the basic loop will always be executed at least one time, even if the value of `x` is zero.

Sometimes a loop must do significant processing just to determine whether to terminate and then some additional processing if it is not to terminate. (Such loops are sometimes called loops with "*n* and a half" repetitions.) Such a loop can be written easily and naturally as a basic loop with an EXIT statement in the middle. The following program contains such a loop. The program reads in a series of numbers representing progress toward a "goal" of 100. After each number is read in, the program either announces the amount left to go to reach the goal or announces that the goal has been reached and terminates. Here is a sample interactive run of the program:

```
Enter progress towards goal.
20
80 left to go.
Enter progress towards goal.
30
50 left to go.
Enter progress towards goal.
55
You have reached your goal.
```

Here is the program itself:

```
WITH Basic_IO;
PROCEDURE Reach_Goal IS
   Goal       : CONSTANT := 100;
   Left_To_Go : Integer := Goal;
   Progress   : Positive;
BEGIN
   LOOP
      Basic_IO.Put("Enter progress towards goal.");
      Basic_IO.New_Line;
      Basic_IO.Get(Progress);
      Left_To_Go := Left_To_Go - Progress;
      EXIT WHEN Left_to_Go <= 0;
      Basic_IO.Put(Left_To_Go);
      Basic_IO.Put(" left to go.");
      Basic_IO.New_Line;
   END LOOP;
   Basic_IO.Put("You have reached your goal.");
   Basic_IO.New_Line;
END Reach_Goal;
```

An EXIT statement can also appear in a WHILE loop or a FOR loop. This produces a loop that can terminate at more than one point. The following program reads and sums integers, stopping either when ten integers have been processed or when the number -1 has been read, whichever happens first. The -1 is not to be included in the sum.

```
WITH Basic_IO;
PROCEDURE Read_And_Sum IS
   Sum          : Integer := 0;
   Next_Number : Integer;
BEGIN
   FOR i IN 1 .. 10 LOOP
      Basic_IO.Get(Next_Number);
      EXIT WHEN Next_Number = -1;
      Sum := Sum + Next_Number;
   END LOOP;
   Basic_IO.Put("The sum is ");
   Basic_IO.Put(Sum);
   Basic_IO.New_Line;
END Read_And_Sum;
```

The loop in this program terminates either at the end of the tenth iteration (because of the iteration scheme) or in the middle of a repetition that reads -1 (because of the `EXIT` statement).

When you interrupt a `FOR` loop with an `EXIT` statement, it is important to remember that you cannot refer to the loop parameter outside of the loop to determine the point at which the loop is interrupted. For instance, the program below purports to read a number and print its lowest divisor greater than one. (A divisor of a number n is a number that leaves no remainder when n is divided by it. The Ada expression n `MOD` m gives the value of the remainder when n is divided by m. The `EXIT` statement below is guaranteed to be executed on the last repetition of the `FOR` loop if it is not executed earlier, since every positive number is a divisor of itself.) The program is illegal because it refers to the loop parameter `Divisor` outside of the `FOR` loop. An Ada compiler will view the occurrence of `Divisor` in the call on `Basic_IO.Put` not as the loop parameter, but as an undeclared variable.

```
WITH Basic_IO;
PROCEDURE Illegal_Lowest_Divisor_Program IS
   Dividend : Positive;
BEGIN
   Basic_IO.Get(Dividend);
   IF Dividend = 1 THEN
      Basic_IO.Put("1 has no divisors greater than 1.");
```

```
      ELSE
         FOR Divisor IN 2 .. Dividend LOOP
            EXIT WHEN Dividend MOD Divisor = 0;
         END LOOP;
         Basic_IO.Put(Divisor);
            -- ILLEGAL REFERENCE TO
            -- LOOP PARAMETER OUTSIDE OF LOOP!
         Basic_IO.Put(" is the lowest divisor of ");
         Basic_IO.Put(Dividend);
         Basic_IO.Put(" greater than 1.");
      END IF;
      Basic_IO.New_Line;
   END Illegal_Lowest_Divisor_Program;
```

Adding a declaration for a variable `Divisor` of subtype `Positive` will make the program syntactically correct. It will be acceptable to an Ada compiler, but it still will not behave correctly when run. That is because the program will then have two objects named `Divisor`—the loop parameter that exists while the loop is running and a variable that is used only in the call on `Basic_IO.Put`, without ever having been initialized.

The program can be made to work correctly by assigning the value of the loop parameter to an ordinary variable before leaving the loop. Note the use of an `EXIT` statement without a Boolean expression:

```
WITH Basic_IO;
PROCEDURE Print_Lowest_Divisor IS
   Dividend, Solution : Positive;
BEGIN
   Basic_IO.Get (Dividend);
   IF Dividend = 1 THEN
      Basic_IO.Put ("1 has no divisors greater than 1.");
   ELSE
      FOR Divisor IN 2 .. Dividend LOOP
         IF Dividend MOD Divisor = 0 THEN
            Solution := Divisor;
            EXIT;
         END IF;
      END LOOP;
      Basic_IO.Put (Solution);
      Basic_IO.Put (" is the lowest divisor of ");
      Basic_IO.Put (Dividend);
      Basic_IO.Put (" greater than 1.");
   END IF;
   Basic_IO.New_Line;
END Print_Lowest_Divisor;
```

In fact, the program would be clearer if the FOR loop were replaced by a WHILE loop that incremented an ordinary variable explicitly:

```
WITH Basic_IO;
PROCEDURE Print_Lowest_Divisor IS
   Dividend, Divisor : Positive;
BEGIN
   Basic_IO.Get(Dividend);
   IF Dividend = 1 THEN
      Basic_IO.Put("1 has no divisors greater than 1.");
   ELSE
      Divisor := 2;
      WHILE Dividend MOD Divisor /= 0 LOOP
         Divisor := Divisor + 1;
      END LOOP;
      Basic_IO.Put (Divisor);
      Basic_IO.Put (" is the lowest divisor of ");
      Basic_IO.Put (Dividend);
      Basic_IO.Put (" greater than 1.");
   END IF;
   Basic_IO.New_Line;
END Print_Lowest_Divisor;
```

A FOR loop is not really appropriate because we do not know before the loop starts how many times it will be executed. In fact, the FOR loop never terminates by virtue of having been repeated for every value in the discrete range of the iteration scheme; even when the loop terminates with Divisor equal to Dividend, it does so by executing the EXIT statement. We are only using the FOR loop to avoid writing the assignment statement incrementing Divisor. Unlike PL/I's DO loop, which can be written without an upper bound   DO I = 1 BY 1;—the Ada languages's FOR loop is designed specifically for iterating over a specified range. When a loop is to terminate based on the value of a Boolean expression, it should be written as a WHILE loop or a basic loop.

If one loop is nested inside another, an EXIT statement in the inner loop can terminate the outer loop. The outer loop must be *named*. That is, an identifier must appear at the top of the outer loop (followed by a colon) and at the bottom of the outer loop (between END LOOP and the semicolon ending the LOOP statement). The full form of the EXIT statement is

EXIT [*identifier*] [WHEN *Boolean expression*] ;

If the identifier is present, it must be the name of a loop that directly or indirectly surrounds the EXIT statement. It is that loop that will be terminated by the EXIT statement when the Boolean expression turns out to be false. When no identifier is present (as in all the examples we have seen so far), the EXIT statement refers to the innermost loop surrounding it.

An example of exiting two loops at once is provided by a program to decode and print messages encoded as integers. Suppose that 0 stands for a space character, the integers 1 through 26 stand for the upper-case letters of the alphabet in order, 27 marks the end of a line, and 28 marks the end of the message. The program is to print the message in its proper format, with the character '#' marking the end of the message. If the end-of-message code is not preceded by an end-of-line code, the '#' should appear on the same line as the preceding text. For example, the input

```
12 9 14 5 0 15 14 5 27 12 9 14 5 0 20
23 15 27 12 9 14 5 0 20 8 18 5 5 28
```

should produce the following output:

```
LINE ONE
LINE TWO
LINE THREE#
```

A separately compiled procedure named Write_Letter takes any integer from 0 to 26 as a parameter and writes the corresponding character (either a letter or a space) in the next position in the standard output file. (Like packages, subprograms can be compiled separately. Naming the subprogram in another compilation unit's WITH clause allows the subprogram to be called from that other compilation unit. These points will be explained more fully in Chapter 9.) The main procedure of the decoding program is primarily responsible for processing the end-of-line and end-of-message codes. The program contains a loop that processes one line of the message during each repetition. Nested inside this loop is a loop that processes one character of the message during each repetition. When the inner loop detects the end-of-message code, it exits both loops, aborting normal processing of the current line.

```
WITH Basic_IO, Write_Letter;
PROCEDURE Decode IS
   SUBTYPE Code_Subtype IS Integer RANGE 0 .. 28;
   End_Of_Line_Code    : CONSTANT Code_Subtype := 27;
   End_Of_Message_Code : CONSTANT Code_Subtype := 28;
   Next_Code           : Code_Subtype;
```

```
BEGIN
   Line_Loop:                -- Process each line in the message.
      LOOP
         Character_Loop: -- Process each character in the line.
            LOOP
               Basic_IO.Get (Next_Code);
               EXIT Character_Loop
                  WHEN Next_Code = End_Of_Line_Code;
               EXIT Line_Loop
                  WHEN Next_Code = End_Of_Message_Code;
               Write_Letter (Next_Code);
            END LOOP Character_Loop;
         Basic_IO.New_Line; -- Handle the end-of-line code.
      END LOOP Line_Loop;
   Basic_IO.Put ("#"); -- Handle the end-of-message code.
   Basic_IO.New_Line;
END Decode;
```

It is not really necessary to name the inner loop, since the first `EXIT` statement is equivalent to

```
EXIT WHEN Next_Code = End_Of_Line_Code;
```

However, the name `Character_Loop` makes the program easier to understand.

7.7 GOTO STATEMENTS

Like FORTRAN, PL/I, and Pascal, the Ada language has a `GOTO` statement that causes the program to continue execution at the statement following a specified *label.* Any Ada statement may be preceded by zero or more labels of the form

<< *identifier* >>

The form of a `GOTO` statement is

`GOTO` *identifier* `;`

Unlike Pascal, the Ada language does not require—or even provide for—the explicit declaration of labels. An identifier is implicitly declared as a label name simply by its appearance between << >> brackets or in a GOTO statement.

(Labels should not be confused with the *loop name* that can occur at the beginning and end of a loop. A label, which is surrounded by the brackets "<<" and ">>," enables a GOTO statement to refer to the statement bearing the label. A loop name, which occurs followed by a colon before the word LOOP and followed by a semicolon after the words END LOOP, enables an EXIT statement inside the loop to refer to the loop. The LOOP statement

```
<< Statement_Label >>
   Loop_Name:
      FOR i IN 1 .. Command_Quota LOOP
         Read_Command (Command);
         IF Command = "Quit" THEN
            EXIT Loop_Name;
         ELSIF Command = "Restart" THEN
            GOTO Statement_Label;
         ELSE
            Execute_Command(Command);
         END IF;
      END LOOP Loop_Name;
```

has both a label—Statement_Label—and a loop name—Loop_Name. The statement EXIT Loop_Name; causes control to pass to the point just after the loop, while the statement GOTO Statement_Label; causes the FOR loop to start over again with i equal to one.)

A GOTO statement may not branch *into* a sequence of statements. However, it may branch out of the sequence directly containing the GOTO statement, to a label in a surrounding sequence of statements. For example, the statement GOTO Statement_Label; above branches out of the sequence of statements in the second arm of the IF statement into the surrounding sequence of statements containing the FOR loop. However, the following statement is illegal, because it contains a GOTO to a label in a nonsurrounding sequence of statements:

```
LOOP

   IF x < Minimum_Value THEN

      Error_Message := "Too small.";
      x := Minimum_Value;
      GOTO Error_Processing; -- ILLEGAL GOTO STATEMENT!

   ELSIF x > Maximum_Value THEN

      Error_Message := "Too large.";
      x := Maximum_Value;

      << Error_Processing >> -- Intended target of GOTO

      Error_Count := Error_Count + 1;
      Basic_IO.Put(Error_Message);
      Basic_IO.New_Line;
      y := 0;
```

```
   ELSE
      y := f(x);
   END IF;
   EXIT WHEN y > a AND y < b;
   x := (x + y) / 2.0;
END LOOP;
```

Another use for the NULL statement, besides those described in Section 7.4, is to provide a place to hang a label when you want to branch to the end of a sequence of statements:

```
FOR i IN 1 .. Number_Of_Students LOOP
   Get_Student_Information
      (Student_Number, Student_Grade, Grading_System);
   IF Student_Grade >= 65 THEN
      IF Grading_System = Pass_Fail THEN
         GOTO Done_With_This_Student;
      ELSE
         Compute_Letter_Grade
            (Student_Grade, Letter_Grade);
      END IF;
   ELSE
      Letter_Grade := F_Grade;
   END IF;
   Record_Letter_Grade (Student_Number,Letter_Grade);
   << Done_With_This_Student >>
      NULL;
END LOOP;
```

GOTO statements usually make a program harder to follow. Fortunately, the Ada language provides constructs that make the GOTO statement unnecessary in most cases. For example, the sequence of actions that is coded in FORTRAN IV as

```
      IF (I .LT. 0) GO TO 10
      J = K
      GOTO 20
   10 J = L
   20 M = J
```

can be coded in the Ada language without branches:

```
IF i >= 0 THEN
   j := k;
ELSE
   j := l;
END IF;
m := j;
```

The use of a GOTO statement to exit from the middle of a loop rather than the top or bottom is made unnecessary by the EXIT statement. The basic loop eliminates the need to write

```
<< Top_Of_Loop >>
  ...
  GOTO Top_Of_Loop;
```

to construct a loop without a termination test at the top. In other languages, GOTO statements are sometimes used to escape from the normal sequence of action when an unexpected condition is detected. In the Ada language, this can be done with exceptions (described in Chapter 15).

Thus Ada programs should almost never contain GOTO statements. There are some situations in which it may actually be simpler and clearer to write a GOTO statement than to avoid it. However, such situations are extremely rare.

7.8 DELAY STATEMENTS

As its name suggests, a DELAY statement causes a computation to pause for some amount of time before performing the next action. DELAY statements are used in *real-time* programs, that is, programs in which the timing of a computation is critical. Although they are most often used in multitask programs, there are occasional applications for DELAY statements in single-task programs.

The form of the DELAY statement is

DELAY *expression* ;

The expression belongs to a predefined fixed-point type named Duration, representing amounts of time measured in seconds. The DELAY statement causes execution to pause for at least the number of seconds specified by the expression. The delay may in fact be longer than that specified. (This is because the computer may be doing something else when the specified delay expires.)

The exact definition of the type Duration varies from compiler to compiler. However, the type must include values as high as 86,400—the number of seconds in a day. The Ada standard *requires* that the distance between approximations be no more than 0.02 (twenty milliseconds) and strongly *recommends* that it be no more than 0.00005 (fifty microseconds). In some implementations, the approximations making up type Duration may correspond to the values that can be held in the hardware clock. However, the rules of the Ada language do not require this.

7.9 BLOCK STATEMENTS

A *block statement* of the form

```
: identifier : :
      DECLARE
         declarative part
      BEGIN
         sequence of statements
      END  : identifier :  ;
```

can be used to group a sequence of statements together with its own declarative part. If an identifier appears at the top of the block statement (preceding **DECLARE**) the same identifier must appear at the bottom (following **END**). (This is the same rule as for loop names.) When an identifier does appear at the top and bottom of a block statement, it is called a *block name*. The full form of a block statement is more general; it will be explained in Chapter 15.

A block statement is executed by first elaborating the declarations in the declarative part and then executing the sequence of statements with those declarations in effect. The declarations only remain in effect during the execution of the block statement. If the block statement is reentered several times, the declarations are elaborated anew each time. This means that a variable declared in a block statement does not retain its value between different executions of the block statement. In fact, the variable ceases to exist after one execution of the block statement, and a new variable with the same name is created during the next execution.

Consider the following program, which reads in two numbers and then prints out the smaller one followed by the larger one:

```
WITH Basic_IO;

PROCEDURE Print_In_Order IS

   A, B : Integer;

BEGIN

   Basic_IO.Get(A);
   Basic_IO.Get(B);

   IF A < B THEN

      Exchange_Values:
         DECLARE
            Old_A : Integer := A;
         BEGIN
            A := B;
            B := Old_A;
         END Exchange_Values;

   END IF;

   Basic_IO.Put(A);
   Basic_IO.New_Line;
   Basic_IO.Put(B);
   Basic_IO.New_Line;

END Print_In_Order;
```

The IF statement in this program contains a sequence of statements consisting of a single block statement. The declarative part of the block statement contains a single declaration, for the Integer variable Old_A. Old_A is initialized to the value that is in A when the declaration is elaborated. The sequence of statements inside the block statement refers to Old_A. However, it would be illegal to refer to Old_A outside the block statement.

The declarations of A and B, located in the declarative part of procedure Print_In_Order, remain in effect inside the block statement. That is why A and B can be referred to there. If a variable named B had been declared in the block statement, however, it would have *hidden* the outer declaration of B. There would then be two variables named B. Outside the block statement, the identifier B would name the variable declared in the declarative part of Print_In_Order. Inside the block statement, B would refer to the variable declared in the declarative part of the block statement. We will examine the issue of hidden declarations more closely in Chapter 14.

The program above could also have been written without a block statement, as follows:

```
WITH Basic_IO;
PROCEDURE Print_In_Order IS
   A, B, Old_A : Integer;
BEGIN
   Basic_IO.Get(A);
   Basic_IO.Get(B);
   IF A < B THEN
      Old_A := A;
      A := B;
      B := Old_A;
   END IF;
   Basic_IO.Put(A);
   Basic_IO.New_Line;
   Basic_IO.Put(B);
   Basic_IO.New_Line;
END Print_In_Order;
```

The block statement in the first version *localizes* the declaration of Old_A. That is, it serves to document the fact that Old_A is only used in a small part of the program. It limits the area you must scan to determine how A is declared and all the ways in which Old_A is used. It avoids inadvertent use of one variable for different and possibly conflicting purposes at different places in a long sequence of statements.

In a program as small as Print_In_Order, the benefits of localizing a declaration are marginal. In fact, the block statement may be more of a distraction than an aid to readability. However, localization can make a large program, containing many variables interacting in complex ways, easier to read and modify. Declaring a constant within a block statement is a particularly effective way to document your knowledge that an object will retain the same value throughout some region of the program.

A block statement may be used to declare an array whose length is determined during execution of the program. For instance, the following program repeatedly reads a number *n* followed by *n* additional integers and writes those *n* integers in reverse order. It terminates when a value of zero is read for *n*.

```
WITH Basic_IO;
PROCEDURE Reverse_Sequences IS
   n : Natural;
BEGIN
   LOOP
      Basic_IO.Get (n);
      EXIT WHEN n = 0;
      DECLARE
         List : ARRAY (1 .. n) OF Integer;
      BEGIN
         FOR i IN 1 .. n LOOP
            Basic_IO.Get (List (i));
         END LOOP;
         FOR i IN REVERSE 1 .. n LOOP
            Basic_IO.Put (List (i));
         END LOOP;
      END;
   END LOOP;
END Reverse_Sequences;
```

7.10 SUMMARY

A simple Ada program has the following form:

```
: context clause :

PROCEDURE identifier IS
   declarative part
BEGIN
   sequence of statements
END identifier ;
```

The declarative part consists of zero or more declarations, and the sequence of statements specifies actions to be performed by the program. The sequence of statements may include assignment statements, procedure call statements, conditional statements, LOOP statements, DELAY statements, and block statements. Each statement in the sequence ends with a semicolon.

An assignment statement has the form

variable name **:=** *expression* **;**

It copies the value of the expression into the named variable. The expression and the variable must be of the same type, or an error will result when the program is being compiled. Normally, the value of the expression must also belong to the subtype of the variable, or an error will result while the program is running; in the case of array types, it is sufficient for the variable and the array specified by the expression to have the same number of index values in each dimension, even if the corresponding index ranges start at different lower bounds.

A procedure call may take the form

```
procedure-name  ⁞ ( parameter , ~~~ , parameter ) ⁞  ;
```

If you have compiled the package `Basic_IO` given in the Appendix, simple input and output can be achieved by calling the subprograms provided by that package:

```
Basic_IO.Put
Basic_IO.Get
Basic_IO.Get_Line
Basic_IO.New_Line
Basic_IO.New_Page
```

There are two kinds of conditional statements, `IF` statements of the form

```
IF Boolean expression THEN
     sequence of statements
.................................
: ELSIF Boolean expression THEN :
:      sequence of statements   :
: ~~~                           :
: ELSIF Boolean expression THEN :
:      sequence of statements   :
:::::::::::::::::::::::::::::::::
: ELSE                          :
:      sequence of statements   :
.................................
END IF ;
```

and `CASE` statements of the form

```
CASE expression IS
     WHEN choice | ~~~ | choice =>
          sequence of statements
     ~~~
     WHEN choice | ~~~ | choice =>
          sequence of statements
.................................
:    WHEN OTHERS =>             :
:         sequence of statements:
.................................
END CASE ;
```

where each choice is either a static expression or a discrete range with static bounds. For an `IF` statement, the first sequence of statements preceded by a true Boolean expression, if any, is executed; otherwise the sequence of statements preceded by the word `ELSE`, if any, is executed. For a `CASE` statement, every possible value of the expression must be reflected by exactly one choice (or by `WHEN OTHERS`). The sequence of statements corresponding to that choice is executed. A statement of the form

```
NULL;
```

which specifies no action at all, may be used as a sequence of statements in an `IF` statement or a `CASE` statement.

The general form of a `LOOP` statement is

```
: identifier : :
   : iteration scheme :   LOOP
       sequence of statements
   END LOOP : identifier : ;
```

If an identifier is specified at the top of the loop, the same identifier must be specified at the bottom of the loop. This is the *loop name*. If no identifier is specified at the top of the loop, none may appear at the bottom. A `WHILE` loop has an iteration scheme of the form

```
WHILE Boolean expression
```

The Boolean expression is tested before each repetition of the loop, and the loop is exited if the value is `False`. A `FOR` loop has an iteration scheme of the form

```
FOR identifier IN discrete range
```

or

```
FOR identifier IN REVERSE discrete range
```

specifying that the loop is to be repeated with the loop parameter taking on each value of the discrete range in turn. In the absence of the word `REVERSE`, it takes on these values in ascending order; in the presence of the word `REVERSE`, it takes on these values in descending order. A loop parameter exists only within the `FOR` loop and should not be declared in an object declaration. A basic loop has no iteration scheme and specifies continual repetition. An `EXIT` statement of the form

```
EXIT : identifier : :WHEN Boolean expression: ;
```

can be used to break out of some or all of the loops surrounding it. The identifier is the name of the outermost loop to be exited. If it is omitted, the `EXIT` statement breaks out of the immediately surrounding loop only. If the Boolean expression is present, the loop is exited only when the Boolean expression is true.

A statement may be preceded by zero or more labels of the form

```
<< identifier >>
```

A GOTO statement of the form

```
GOTO identifier ;
```

branches to the statement with the specified label. It cannot branch into a sequence of statements from outside that sequence. Because of the Ada language's rich control structures, GOTO statements are almost never necessary in Ada programs.

A block statement has the following form:

```
[ identifier : ]
    DECLARE
        declarative part
    BEGIN
        sequence of statements
    END [ identifier ] ;
```

It groups a sequence of statements together with its own declarative part. Each declaration in the declarative part is elaborated upon entry to the block statement, and each entity created in this way ceases to exist upon completion of the block statement. An identifier may appear at the top of the block statement only if the same identifier appears at the bottom of the block statement.

EXERCISES

7.1 If the IF statement

```
IF x = 1 THEN
   y := a + b;
ELSIF x = 2 THEN
   y := a * b;
ELSIF x = 3 THEN
   y := a ** b;
END IF;
```

is rewritten as

```
IF x = 3 THEN
   y := a ** b;
ELSIF x = 2 THEN
   y := a * b;
ELSIF x = 1 THEN
   y := a + b;
END IF;
```

it will have the same effect. However, the IF statement

```
IF Score > 20 THEN
   Rating := Excellent;
ELSIF Score > 15 THEN
   Rating := Good;
ELSIF Score > 10 THEN
   Rating := Fair;
ELSE
   Rating := Poor;
END IF;
```

does not have the same effect as

```
IF Score > 10 THEN
   Rating := Fair;
ELSIF Score > 15 THEN
   Rating := Good;
ELSIF Score > 20 THEN
   Rating := Excellent;
ELSE
   Rating := Poor;
END IF;
```

Why not? In general, when is the order of the branches of an `IF` statement relevant, and when is it irrelevant? What about the branches of a `CASE` statement?

7.2 Rewrite the program below using a `WHILE` loop in place of the `FOR` loop. Then rewrite it again using a basic loop with an `EXIT` statement in place of the `WHILE` loop.

```
WITH Basic_IO;

PROCEDURE Count_To_10 IS

BEGIN

   FOR i IN 1 .. 10 LOOP
      Basic_IO.Put (i);
      Basic_IO.New_Line;
   END LOOP;

END Count_To_10;
```

7.3 Rewrite the program `Read_And_Sum` given in Section 7.6 so that it reports how many numbers were read (excluding -1) as well as the sum of those numbers.

7.4 Rewrite the program `Decode` given in Section 7.6 by replacing the `IF` statement inside loop `Character_Loop` with a `CASE` statement.

7.5 Write a program that copies lines from the standard input file to the standard output file but does not copy the last of every ten lines read. (Thus the lines printed will be input lines 1 through 9, 11 through 19, 21 through 29, and so forth.) Use the procedure `Basic_IO.Get_Line`, described in Section 7.2.2. You may assume that no line to be read is more than 132 characters long. The number of lines in the input file is not necessarily a multiple of ten.

7.6 Write the following sequence of statements without a `GOTO` statement:

```
Divisor := 2;

WHILE Divisor ** 2 <= Candidate LOOP
   IF Candidate MOD Divisor = 0 THEN
      GOTO Not_Prime;
   END IF;
   Divisor := Divisor + 1;
END LOOP;

-- This point is reached if and only if Candidate has no
--   divisor greater than or equal to 2 and less than or
--   equal to its square root.
-- In such a case, Candidate must be prime.

Primes_Found := Primes_Found + 1;

<< Not_Prime >>

Candidate := Candidate + 1;
```

Under what circumstances might the version with a `GOTO` statement be justified?

7.7 Rewrite the procedure `Reverse_Sequences` in Section 7.9 without a block statement, using an access type and dynamically allocating an array of the appropriate size each time through the loop.

CHAPTER

EIGHT

EXPRESSIONS

An *expression* specifies a formula for calculating a value. Determining the current value of an expression is called *evaluating* the expression. Expressions occur in statements and declarations.

In the Ada language (as in FORTRAN, PL/I, and Pascal), it is impossible to write an expression that yields values of different types at different times. In most cases, it is possible to determine the type of an Ada expression simply by examining the expression. In every other case, the type of the expression can be determined by examining the context in which the expression appears. For example, given the declarations

```
TYPE Suit_Type IS (Clubs, Diamonds, Hearts, Spades);
TYPE Commodity_Type IS
   (Pork_Bellies, Wheat, Silver, Diamonds, Gold);
```

the expression `Diamonds` might belong either to `Commodity_Type` or to `Suit_Type`. However, in the context of the assignment statement

```
A := Diamonds;
```

the expression `Diamonds` must denote a value in the type of the variable `A`. The type of `A` can be discerned by examining `A`'s declaration.

A *variable* is a container in which values can be placed. It may be either an object declared in a variable declaration, an object designated by an access value, or a component of a variable that belongs to to a record or array type. For example, consider the following declarations:

```
TYPE Inning_Score_List_Type IS ARRAY (1 .. 9) OF Integer;
TYPE Scoreboard_Type IS
   RECORD
      Visitor_Part, Home_Team_Part : Inning_Score_List_Type;
   END RECORD;
TYPE Scoreboard_Pointer_Type IS ACCESS Scoreboard_Type;
Scoreboard         : Scoreboard_Type;
Scoreboard_Pointer : Scoreboard_Pointer_Type;
```

Both `Scoreboard` and `Scoreboard_Pointer` are variables. If the value in `Scoreboard_Pointer` is not null, then the allocated variable it designates, `Scoreboard_Pointer.ALL`, is also a variable. The `Visitor_Part` component of `Scoreboard` is a variable of type `Inning_Score_List_Type`, and the nine components of this array variable are themselves variables of type `Integer` (subtype `Natural`). The same applies to the `Visitor_Part` component of the record `Scoreboard_Pointer.ALL` and the nine array components of that record component.

The relationship between variables and expressions is the same in the Ada language as in FORTRAN, PL/I, and Pascal. When the name of a variable occurs in a place where *only* the name of a variable is permitted, it denotes the variable itself, a container. When the name of a variable occurs in a place where an expression is permitted, it denotes the current *value* of the variable, the *contents* of the container.

Section 8.1 describes elementary expressions, which can be combined to form larger expressions. Among these simple expressions are the names of variables. Section 8.2 describes the *operators* of the Ada language, which are used to combine elementary expressions into compound expressions. Section 8.3 provides further details about expressions.

8.1 ELEMENTARY EXPRESSIONS

There are seven kinds of elementary expressions—*literals, names, aggregates, qualified expressions, type conversions, allocators,* and *function calls*. Literals (such as `1` and `"Hello"`) denote specific values. Names are symbols or combinations of symbols denoting variables, constants, and other entities. Aggregates describe values in array and record types in terms of the value of each array or record component. Qualified expressions are expressions explicitly marked as belonging to particular subtypes. Type conversions produce a result in one type corresponding to a specified value in some other type. Allocators, which we have already seen in Section 5.2, create allocated objects and produce access values designating those objects. Function calls cause function subprograms to be executed to produce a result.

8.1.1 Literals

A *literal* is an expression that explicitly names a particular value. There are four kinds of literals—*numeric literals, string literals, enumeration literals,* and the access type literal `NULL`.

8.1.1.1 Numeric literals. A numeric literal is simply a number. In its simplest form, a numeric literal is just a sequence of digits, such as `0` or `1024`. A numeric literal may contain a decimal point, as in `1.0` and `3.141`, but then at least one digit (possibly a zero) must appear on each side of the point. A numeric literal containing a point is called a *real literal,* and one without a point is called an *integer literal.*

The digits of the number may be followed by the letter `E` (or, equivalently, `e`) and an *exponent.* The exponent indicates a power of ten by which the number before the `E` is to be multiplied to obtain the value of the numeric literal. For example, `3E4` represents 3 multiplied by ten to the fourth power, or 30,000; `0.314E1` represents 0.314 multiplied by ten to the first power, or 3.14; `31.4E-1` represents 31.4 multiplied by ten to the power -1, also 3.14. A minus sign may only appear in the exponent if a decimal point appears in the number preceding the exponent. A numeric literal without a decimal point is an integer literal even if it contains an exponent. (This is different from FORTRAN, in which any literal containing *either* a decimal point or an exponent is considered real. The Ada numeric literal `68E3` means exactly the same thing as `68000`, while `68E-3` is illegal.) No spaces may appear anywhere within a numeric literal, even if it contains an exponent.

An underscore may appear between any two digits in a numeric literal. The underscore does not affect the value of the literal, but it may make the program more readable by grouping digits. For example, `12_345_678.9` is equivalent to `12345678.9`.

The Ada language also provides a notation for writing numeric literals in bases other than ten. In particular, it is sometimes easier and clearer to specify numbers in base two, eight, or sixteen when interacting directly with hardware or with program components written in assembly language. Nondecimal numeric literals are described in section 8.3.2.

8.1.1.2 String literals. The value of a character string can be represented by a string literal. A string literal consists of the characters in the string surrounded by double quote symbols ("), except that a double quote character occurring within the string is represented by a pair of double quote symbols in the string literal. Each space in a string literal denotes a space character in the string. Upper-case and lower-case letters have distinct meanings within string literals. Thus `"ABC"` denotes the string consisting of the three characters `'A'`, `'B'`, and `'C'`; `"abc  "` denotes the string consisting of the five characters `'a'`, `'b'`, `'c'`, `' '` (blank), and `' '` (another blank); """" denotes the string consisting of the one character '"' (the double quote character); and "" denotes the string consisting of zero characters (the *empty string*).

8.1.1.3 Enumeration literals. An enumeration literal is one of the items listed in an enumeration type definition. It may be either an identifier or a character literal. Enumeration literals were discussed in sections 4.2.4 and 4.3.5.

8.1.1.4 The literal `NULL`. As explained in Section 5.1, every access type contains a value that does not designate any object. The literal `NULL` denotes these values.

8.1.2 Names

Elementary expressions include *names* that identify variables, constants, and numeric values. The simplest form of a name is an *identifier.* An identifier declared in a variable or constant declaration can be used as the name of that variable or constant. In addition, the identifier occurring after the word `FOR` in a loop statement can be used as the name of the loop parameter. An identifier declared in a number declaration can be used as a named number. An identifier declared in a type or subtype declaration can be used as the name of the declared type or subtype.

There are also more complicated forms of names. These include:

indexed components naming components of arrays. Indexed components were discussed in Section 4.2.6.
slices naming subsections of one-dimensional arrays. Slices were discussed in Section 4.2.6 also.
selected components. Selected components naming record components were described in Section 4.2.7. Selected components are also used to name entities provided by packages, such as the procedure `Basic_IO.Get` provided by the package `Basic_IO`.
attributes, discussed in Section 8.1.3.

Indexed components, slices, selected components, and attributes may be used in combination to form complex names, referring to components of components, slices of components, attributes of components, attributes of slices, and attributes of attributes. (It is also possible, but rarely useful, to name components of slices and slices of slices. It is rarely useful because `A(i .. j)(k)` produces the same result as `A(k)` whenever it produces a result, and `A(i .. j)(m .. n)` produces the same result as `A(m .. n)` whenever it produces a result.) Consider the following declarations:

```
TYPE Simple_Record_1_Type IS
   RECORD
      A1, B1 : Integer;
   END RECORD;
```

```
TYPE Simple_Record_2_Type IS
   RECORD
      A2, B2 : Integer;
   END RECORD;

TYPE Simple_Array_Type IS
   ARRAY (Integer RANGE <>) OF Integer;

TYPE Record_Of_Records_Type IS
   RECORD
      C : Simple_Record_1_Type;
      D : Simple_Record_2_Type;
   END RECORD;

TYPE Record_Of_Arrays IS
   RECORD
      E, F : Simple_Array_Type (1 .. 5);
   END RECORD;

TYPE Array_Of_Records_Type IS
   ARRAY (20 .. 30) OF Simple_Record_2_Type;

TYPE Array_Of_Arrays_Type IS
   ARRAY (40 .. 50) OF Simple_Array_Type (6 ..10);

RR : Record_Of_Records_Type;
RA : Record_Of_Arrays_Type;
AR : Array_Of_Records_Type;
AA : Array_Of_Arrays_Type;
```

Then the following names are all legal:

`RR.C`	(of type `Simple_Record_1_Type`)
`RR.C.A1`	(of type `Integer`)
`RA.E`	(of subtype `Simple_Array_Type (1 .. 5)`)
`RA.E (3)`	(of type `Integer`)
`RA.E (3 .. 5)`	(of subtype `Simple_Array_Type (3 .. 5)`)
`AR (25)`	(of type `Simple_Record_2_Type`)
`AR (25).B2`	(of type `Integer`)
`AA (45)`	(of subtype `Simple_Array_Type (6 .. 10)`)
`AA (45) (8)`	(of type `Integer`)
`AA (45) (7 .. 9)`	(of subtype `Simple_Array_Type (7 .. 9)`)

`AR (24 .. 26).B2` and `AA (44 .. 46) (8)` are not legal names. Why not?

(PL/I and Pascal allow more flexibility than the Ada language in the formation of names. In PL/I, `RR.C.A1` can be abbreviated as `RR.A1`, since there is no other possible interpretation, and `AR(25).B2` can be written equivalently as `AR.B2(25)`. If `AR.A2` were not also an array, PL/I would also accept `AR(25)` as an abbreviation for `AR.B2(25)`. In Pascal, `AA[45][8]` is equivalent to `AA[45,8]`. *Transformations like these are not permitted in the Ada language,* in which the structure of the name must correspond exactly to the type declarations.)

8.1.3 Attributes

An *attribute* of an entity is a value, a range of values, a type, or a function reflecting some property of the entity. Different kinds of entities have different kinds of attributes, identified by *attribute designators.* Attribute designators are identifiers that have a special meaning when used to refer to attributes. If x is the name of an entity, then attributes of that entity have names of the form

x ' *attribute-designator*

The remainder of this subsection describes some of the attributes of the Ada language. Other attributes will be covered later. In addition to the attributes described in this book, an implementation may define its own attributes.

If `T` is the name of a discrete subtype (i.e., a subtype of an integer type or an enumeration type), then `T'First` names the smallest value in `T` and `T'Last` names the largest value in `T`. For example, given the declaration

```
SUBTYPE Digit_Subtype IS Integer RANGE 0 .. 9;
```

`Digit_Subtype'First` names the value zero and `Digit_Subtype'Last` names the value nine. Given the declaration

```
TYPE Tone_Type IS (Low_Do, Re, Mi, Fa, Sol, La, Ti, High_Do);
```

`Tone_Type'First` names the value `Low_Do`, and `Tone_Type'Last` names the value `High_Do`. `Integer'Last` names the highest value of type `Integer`, which varies from one compiler to another. (An attribute such as `T'First` can be pronounced as "T's First." Besides being an accurate description, this pronunciation makes it easy to remember the meaning of the apostrophe.)

If `T` is the name of a discrete subtype, then `T'Pred` names `T`'s *predecessor function*—the function that takes an argument in subtype `T` and returns the next lower value. Similarly, `T'Succ` names `T`'s *successor function*—the function that takes a value in subtype `T` and returns the next higher value. Given the declaration of `Tone_Type` above, the function call `Tone_Type'Pred (Fa)` has the value `Me`, and the function call `Tone_Type'Succ (Fa)` has the value `Sol`. When `T` is an integer subtype, `T'Pred (`x`) = `x`-1` and `T'Succ (`x`) = `x`+1`.

The values listed in an enumeration type declaration have *position numbers,* which are assigned in ascending order starting with zero. If `T` names an enumeration subtype, then `T'Pos` names a function that takes an argument of type `T` and returns its position number. Inversely, `T'Val` names a function that takes an integer (of any integer type) and returns the enumeration value in subtype `T` with that position number. Thus `Tone_Type'Pos (Low_Do) = 0`, `Tone_Type'Pos (High_Do) = 7`, `Tone_Type'Val (0) = Low_Do`, and `Tone_Type'Val (7) = High_Do`. Section 8.1.4 provides a more complete illustration of the use of these attributes.

Just as the `'Pos` and `'Val` attributes establish a correspondence between enumeration values and position numbers, attributes designated `'Image` and `'Value` establish a correspondence between discrete values and values of type `String`. If `T` names an enumeration subtype, then `T'Image` names a function that takes a value in subtype `T` and returns a value of type `String` containing the characters forming the corresponding enumeration literal. If the enumeration literal is an identifier, the string contains the characters forming that identifier, with all letters in upper case; if it is a character literal, the string contains the exact character in the literal, surrounded by apostrophes. In neither case are there leading or trailing spaces. Thus, given the declarations

```
TYPE Fieldata_Character_Type IS
   ('@', '[', ']', '#', Delta_Symbol, ' ', 'A', 'B',
    'C', 'D', 'E', 'F', 'G', 'H', 'I', 'J',
    'K', 'L', 'M', 'N', 'O', 'P', 'Q', 'R',
    'S', 'T', 'U', 'V', 'W', 'X', 'Y', 'Z',
    ')', '-', '+', '<', '=', '>', '&', '$',
    '*', '(', '%', ':', '?', '!', ',', '\',
    '0', '1', '2', '3', '4', '5', '6', '7',
    '8', '9', ''', ';', '/', '.',
    Lozenge_Symbol, Not_Equal_Symbol);
Equal : CONSTANT Fieldata_Character_Type := '=';
Not_Equal :
   CONSTANT Fieldata_Character_Type := Not_Equal_Symbol;
```

the value of

```
Fieldata_Character_Type'Image (Not_Equal)
```

is the sixteen-character string `"NOT_EQUAL_SYMBOL"` and the value of

```
Fieldata_Character_Type'Image (Equal)
```

is the three-character string `"'='"`.

Inversely, if `T` names an enumeration subtype, then `T'Value` names a function that takes a `String` argument and returns the enumeration value in `T` whose enumeration literal is spelled by the characters in the string. The string may have leading or trailing spaces, which are ignored. In the case of identifiers, capitalization is disregarded. Given the declarations above,

```
Fieldata_Character_Type'Value (" NOT_EQUAL_SYMBOL ")
```

and

```
Fieldata_Character_Type'Value ("NOT_equal_symbol")
```

both have the value `Not_Equal_Symbol`, and

```
Fieldata_Character_Type'Value (" '=' ")
```

has the value `'='`.

The `'Image` and `'Value` attributes can also be used with integer subtypes. If `T` is an integer subtype and `X` is a value in `T`, `T'Image (X)` is a string consisting of the digits of `X` preceded by either a minus sign or a single space. (The number is printed in base ten, without any underscores, decimal point, exponent, or trailing spaces.) Inversely, if `S` is a string containing a valid Ada integer literal (as described in Section 8.1.1) optionally preceded by a plus or minus sign, `T'Value (X)` is the numeric value of that literal. `S` may contain underscores, an exponent, or leading or trailing spaces.

We conclude this section with four attributes describing index ranges of arrays. They apply to either a constrained array subtype or to an array object. The attribute designators for these attributes have a special form: an identifier possibly followed by a parenthesized integer literal. This integer literal specifies a dimension of the array. (Actually, any static universal integer expression is allowed between the parentheses, but integer literals are usually most appropriate in this context.)

If `A` names an array variable, an array constant, or a constrained array subtype, then `A'Range(`*n*`)` stands for the range of index values in the nth dimension. This attribute can be used in place of a range of the form *low* `..` *high* in integer type declarations, in subtype indications, and in discrete ranges. For example, given the declarations

```
TYPE Day_Type IS
   (Sunday, Monday, Tuesday, Wednesday, Thursday, Friday,
    Saturday);

TYPE Year_Calendar_Type IS
   ARRAY (0 .. 52, Day_Type) OF Calendar_Entry_Type;
      -- The definition of Calendar_Entry_Type does
      -- not concern us here.

Calendar_For_1980 : Year_Calendar_Type;
```

the subtype declaration

```
SUBTYPE Week_Number_Subtype IS Integer RANGE 0 .. 52;
```

can be rewritten in either of the following ways:

```
SUBTYPE Week_Number_Subtype IS
   Integer RANGE Year_Calendar_Type'Range(1);

SUBTYPE Week_Number_Subtype IS
   Integer RANGE Calendar_For_1980'Range(1);
```

Range attributes can also be used as discrete ranges. One place a discrete range can occur is in the choice list of a `CASE` statement, to indicate a range of consecutive choices:

```
CASE Week_Chosen IS
   WHEN Calendar_For_1980'Range (1) =>
      Entry_Chosen :=
         Calendar_For_1980 (Week_Chosen, Day_Chosen);
   WHEN OTHERS =>
      Basic_IO.Put ("Invalid week chosen.");
      Basic IO.New Line;
      Entry_Chosen := Null_Calendar_Entry;
END CASE;
```

Notice how directly this expresses the idea that one action is to be taken when `Week_Chosen` is a valid first subscript for `Calendar_For_1980` and another action is to be taken when it is not. Similarly, the declaration

```
Working_Days_In_Week :
   ARRAY (Year_Calendar_Type'Range(1)) OF
      Integer RANGE 0 .. 5;
```

conveys that the array `Working_Days` has one component for each row of a `Year_Calendar_Type` array. Discrete ranges also occur in slices, so given the declarations

```
Result_String : String (1 .. 80);
Prefix        : String (1 .. 10);
```

the assignment statement

```
Prefix := Result_String (Prefix'Range(1));
```

assigns the first ten characters of `Result_String` to `Prefix`.

Perhaps the most common use of the `Range` attribute is in the discrete range of the iteration rule in a `FOR` loop. The following nested loops set each component of `Calendar_For_1980` to the value `Default_Calendar_Entry`:

```
FOR w IN Calendar_For_1980'Range(1) LOOP
   FOR d IN Calendar_For_1980'Range(2) LOOP
      Calendar_For_1980 (w,d) := Default_Calendar_Entry;
   END LOOP;
END LOOP;
```

If `A` names an array variable, an array constant, or a constrained array subtype, then `A'First (`*n*`)` and `A'Last (`*n*`)` name the upper and lower bounds in the nth dimension, respectively. Thus `A'Range (`*n*`)` is a shorthand for the range `A'First (`*n*`) .. A'Last (`*n*`)`. The attribute `A'Length(`*n*`)` names the number of values in this range, that is, the number of index values in `A`'s n^{th} dimension. It follows, for instance, that if `A` is a three-dimensional array, then it has `A'Length(1) * A'Length(2) * A'Length(3)` components (where `*` denotes multiplication).

Recall from Section 5.3 that if `AV` is an access value pointing to a dynamically allocated array, `AV(`*n*`)` is an indexed component of the array *pointed to by* `AV`, and `AV(`*m* `..` *n*`)` is a slice of that array. Similarly, `AV'Range(`*n*`)`, `AV'First(`*n*`)`, `AV'Last(`*n*`)`, and `AV'Length(`*n*`)` are attributes of the array pointed to by *the access value* `AV`. For example, consider the following declarations:

```
TYPE String_Pointer_Type IS ACCESS String;
String_Pointer :
   String_Pointer_Type := NEW String (1 .. 10);
```

The access-type variable `String_Pointer` points to a string with index bounds of `1 .. 10`, so the attribute `String_Pointer'Range(1)` denotes the range `1 .. 10`, the attribute `String_Pointer_Type'Length(1)` denotes the value ten, and so forth.

Whether A names an array value, an array type, or an access value pointing to an array, the attributes A'Range(1), A'First(1), A'Last(1), and A'Length(1) can be abbreviated as A'Range, A'First, A'Last, and A'Length, respectively. This provides a more succinct notation for one-dimensional arrays. (It is misleading, and therefore inappropriate, to use this abbreviation when referring to the first dimension of a multidimensional array.) The assignment to Prefix previously would be better written as

```
Prefix := Result_String(Prefix'Range);
```

Since a one-dimensional array has one component for each index position, Result_String'Length gives Result_String's length, eighty. If Count_List is a one-dimensional array with components in some integer type, the loop

```
FOR i IN Count_List'Range LOOP
   Count_List(i) := Count_List(i) + 1;
END LOOP;
```

increments each element of the array.

It is remarkable that this loop could be written without ever referring to the index bounds of Count_List. This style of writing FOR loops makes programs easier to understand. The iteration rule says, simply and directly, "Repeat this loop for each value in the index range of Count_List." The program reader is not burdened with details irrelevant to understanding what the loop does, and the text of the loop can remain unchanged if the bounds of the array are later revised.

The meaning of the names X'First and X'Last depends on the kind of entity named by X. If X names a discrete subtype, the names refer to the first and last values of that subtype. If X names a one-dimensional constrained array subtype, the names refer to the lower and upper index bounds of that subtype. If X names a one-dimensional array variable or constant, the names refer to the lower and upper index bounds of that object.

The First, Last, and Length attributes name values. The Pred, Succ, Val, Pos, Image, and Value attributes name functions. The Range attribute names ranges. However, an attribute never names a variable.

8.1.4 An Extended Example

The following program reads in lines of up to eight letters and digits that are interpreted as a number written in base sixteen, and prints out the number in base ten. In the input, either the lower-case letters 'a' through 'f' or the upper-case letters 'A' through 'F' may be used as hexadecimal digits corresponding to the decimal values ten through fifteen, respectively. In the output, commas will be used to group digits in groups of three. For example, the hexadecimal numeral 12D687 has the same value as the decimal numeral 1234567, so the input "12D687" or "12d687" should generate the output "1,234,567". The program terminates when the value zero is read in. In addition, the program should print an error message and terminate if it reads a line that does not contain a valid hexadecimal number. The empty string is considered to be a valid representation of zero.

```
WITH Basic_IO;
PROCEDURE Hexadecimal_To_Decimal IS
   Zero_Position       : CONSTANT := Character'Pos ('0');
   Capital_A_Position : CONSTANT := Character'Pos ('A');
   Small_a_Position    : CONSTANT := Character'Pos ('a');
   Max_Input_Length    : CONSTANT := 8;
   Max_Output_Length   : CONSTANT := 13;
   Hexadecimal_Input : String (1 .. Max_Input_Length);
   Decimal_Output     : String (1 .. Max_Output_Length);
   TYPE Numeric_Value_Type IS
      RANGE 0 .. 16**Max_Input_Length - 1;
   Numeric_Value : Numeric_Value_Type;
   Digit_Value   : Numeric_Value_Type RANGE 0 .. 15;
   Input_Length : Integer RANGE 0 .. Max_Input_Length;
   Left_End     : Integer RANGE 1 .. Max_Output_Length + 1;
   Digit_Character : Character;
BEGIN
   -- Read input:
   LOOP
      Basic_IO.Get_Line (Hexadecimal_Input, Input_Length);
         -- Reads up to Max_Input_Length characters.
      Numeric_Value := 0;
      -- Examine hexadecimal digits left to right and
      --   determine Numeric_Value:
      FOR i IN 1 .. Input_Length LOOP
         Digit_Character := Hexadecimal_Input (i);
         CASE Digit_Character IS
            WHEN '0' .. '9' =>
               Digit_Value :=
                  Character'Pos (Digit_Character) -
                     Zero_Position;
            WHEN 'A' .. 'F' =>
               Digit_Value :=
                  Character'Pos (Digit_Character) -
                     Capital_A_Position + 10;
            WHEN 'a' .. 'f' =>
               Digit_Value :=
                  Character'Pos (Digit_Character)-
                     Small_a_Position + 10;
            WHEN OTHERS =>
               Basic_IO.Put ("Invalid hexadecimal digit.");
               Basic_IO.New_Line;
               RETURN;
         END CASE;
        Numeric_Value := 16 * Numeric_Value + Digit_Value;
           -- Shift old digits one place to the left and
           -- insert new digit.
      END LOOP;
      -- Now Numeric_Value contains the value of the input.
```

```
      -- Test for termination:
      EXIT WHEN Numeric_Value = 0;
      -- Examine Numeric_Value and produce decimal digits
      --   right to left:
      Left_End := Max_Output_Length + 1;
      Comma_Loop:
         LOOP
            FOR i IN 1 .. 3 LOOP
               Digit_Value := Numeric_Value MOD 10;
                  -- the last decimal digit of Numeric_Value
               Numeric_Value := Numeric_Value / 10;
                  -- Numeric_Value with the last decimal
                  --   digit removed
               Digit_Character :=
                  Character'Val (Zero_Position + Digit_Value);
               Left_End := Left_End - 1;
               Decimal_Output (Left_End) := Digit_Character;
               EXIT Comma_Loop WHEN Numeric_Value = 0;
                  -- No more digits. Don't produce a comma.
            END LOOP;
            -- Three digits have been placed in Decimal_Output,
            --   but higher-order digits remain.
            --   Insert a comma.
            Left_End := Left_End - 1;
            Decimal_Output (Left_End) := ',';
         END LOOP Comma_Loop;
      -- Print output:
      Basic_IO.Put
         ( Decimal_Output (Left_End .. Max_Output_Length) );
      Basic_IO.New_Line;
   END LOOP;
END Hexadecimal_To_Decimal;
```

The first three constant declarations establish `Zero_Position`, `Capital_A_Position`, and `Small_a_Position` as names for the position numbers of `'0'`, `'A'`, and `'a'`, respectively, in the enumeration type `Character`. The values of type `Character` are enumerated in the order given by the ASCII collating sequence, so the position number of each character is identical to its ASCII code.

The next two number declarations establish `Max_Input_Length` and `Max_Output_Length` as names for the length of the longest possible input and output, respectively. The problem statement specifies that the longest possible input is eight hexadecimal digits. The highest value that can be specified in eight hexadecimal digits has ten digits when written in decimal. A ten-digit number will be written with three commas interspersed, bringing the length of the longest possible output to thirteen characters. String variables `Hexadecimal_Input` and `Decimal_Output` are declared long enough to hold these values.

The type Numeric_Value_Type is an integer type whose values are the numbers that can be written using from zero to eight hexadecimal digits. (The number 16**8, or 16 raised to the power 8, is written in hexadecimal as 100000000—a one followed by eight zeroes. The next lower number is written in hexadecimal as FFFFFFFF—eight F's.) This type is used to represent the numeric values that are translated from hexadecimal to decimal. The variable Numeric_Value will hold the value of the string being translated. During the translation process, the variable Digit_Value will hold the value of the decimal or hexadecimal digit currently being processed. Digit_Value is declared to be of type Numeric_Value_Type because it is used in arithmetic operations along with Numeric_Value. It is declared to be of subtype Numeric_Value_Type RANGE 0 .. 15 because that is the range of values that can be represented by a single hexadecimal digit.

The variables Input_Length and Left_End will be used to indicate positions within the strings Hexadecimal_Input and Decimal_Output, respectively. They are declared to be of type Integer because String values are indexed by values of type Integer. Hexadecimal_Input is filled in from left to right, and Input_Length indicates the rightmost position that is filled in by the input (or zero when the input is the empty string). Decimal_Output is filled in from right to left, and Left_End indicates the leftmost position that has been filled in; when Decimal_Output contains no characters, it points one position to the right of the rightmost component of the string. This explains the subtypes of these two variables.

The algorithm consists of a loop that performs the following steps repeatedly: First a line of input is read into Hexadecimal_Input, using the procedure Basic_IO.Get_Line. This procedure also sets Input_Length to the number of characters read. Next, the characters in Hexadecimal_Input are decoded, and the number they represent is placed in Numeric_Value. This decoding step terminates the program if an invalid hexadecimal numeral is read. The loop is exited at this point, terminating the program normally, if Numeric_Value is zero. (This is an excellent example of a loop executed "n and a half times." Considerable processing is required to determine whether the current iteration should be completed.) If the loop is not exited, the value of Numeric_Value is encoded as a decimal numeral with commas. These characters are placed, right-justified, in Decimal_Output and a slice of Decimal_Output, containing only those characters forming the numeral, is printed.

The decoding step begins by setting Numeric_Value to zero and executing a FOR loop that processes each input character in turn, going from left to right. In each iteration, the FOR loop executes a CASE statement and an assignment statement. The CASE statement sets Digit_Value to the numeric value corresponding to the current character or aborts the program if the current character is not a valid hexadecimal digit. The assignment statement replaces Numeric_Value with 16 * Numeric_Value + Digit_Value.

If s is a sequence of hexadecimal digits and n is the corresponding numeric value, then $16n$ is the numeric value corresponding to the digits in s shifted left one place (i.e., the digits in s followed by a zero.) If d is a hexadecimal digit corresponding to numeric value *v*, then 16*n*+*v* is the numeric value corresponding to the digits in *s* followed by *d*. Thus, after *k* iterations of the FOR loop, Numeric_Value holds the numeric value corresponding to the leftmost *k* hexadecimal digits in Hexadecimal_Input. When the FOR loop terminates after Input_Length iterations, Numeric_Value holds the numeric value corresponding to the input.

The CASE statement determining the numeric equivalent of the current character takes advantage of the fact that in the ASCII code, and thus in the enumeration of type Character, the characters '0', '1', '2', ..., '9' occur in consecutive order; the characters 'A', 'B', 'C', 'D', 'E', 'F' occur in consecutive order; and the characters 'a', 'b', 'c', 'd', 'e', 'f' occur in consecutive order. Characters that occur in consecutive order have consecutive position numbers. The first arm of the CASE statement handles a character in the range '0' through '9' by subtracting the position number of '0' from the position number of the character, obtaining the numeric value of the character. The second arm of the CASE statement handles characters in the range 'A' through 'F' by subtracting the position number of 'A' from the position number of the character, obtaining one of the values zero through five, and then adding ten to obtain one of the values ten through fifteen. The third arm of the CASE statement handles characters in the range 'a' through 'f' analogously. The fourth arm of the CASE statement handles any character not in one of these three ranges by printing an error message and halting. (The RETURN statement, explained further in Chapter 9, completes the execution of a subprogram. Its effect in a main subprogram is to halt execution of the main subprogram.)

Decimal encoding is performed right to left by the loop Comma_Loop. Each full iteration of Comma_Loop adds a comma followed by three digits to the left of the characters already produced. Comma_Loop consists of a FOR loop repeated three times followed by statements to add the comma to the left of the characters produced by the FOR loop. Each iteration of the FOR loop determines the rightmost digit in the decimal representation of Numeric_Value, places that digit to the left of the digits just produced, and replaces Numeric_Value by a value that has a similar decimal representation, but with the last digit removed. (For example, 1234 would be replaced by 123 after adding '4' to the output, and 4321 would be replaced by 432 after adding '1' to the output.) When Numeric_Value becomes zero, all digits have been added to the output, and both the FOR loop and Comma_Loop are exited. This aborts the FOR loop regardless of the value of the loop parameter and leaves Comma_Loop before another comma is added to the left of the digits that have been produced.

The numeric value of the rightmost digit of Numeric_Value is simply Numeric_Value MOD 10, the remainder when Numeric_Value is divided by ten. When this digit value is added to the position number of the character '0', the result is the position number of the Character value for the rightmost digit. Applying the function Character'Val to this position number yields the Character value itself. The number that has a similar decimal representation to that of Numeric_Value, but with the last digit removed, is obtained by dividing Numeric_Value by ten and discarding the remainder. As we shall explain in

Section 8.2.3, the Ada operator / behaves in this way when both of its operands are integers.

Since Left_End always points to the leftmost position in Decimal_Output that has received a character (or just past the right end of Decimal_Output when it has not yet received any characters), a character is added to the left of those already produced by decreasing Left_End by one and placing the new character in Decimal_Output (Left_End)—in that order. When Comma_Loop is exited, Decimal_Output (Left_End) is the leftmost character of the desired output, and Decimal_Output (Max_Output_Length) is the rightmost. Thus the slice

```
Decimal_Output ( Left_End .. Max_Output_Length )
```

is a string containing the desired output.

8.1.5 Aggregates

An *aggregate* describes a value in a record or array type. It is possible to describe an entire record or array value directly, without first storing values in individual components of some object and then referring to the object. Thus aggregates can play a role for composite types similar to the roles played by numeric literals for numeric types and enumeration literals for enumeration types.

An aggregate is essentially a list of expressions giving the values of array or record components. The values may be listed in the order of the components, or the aggregate may specify names and values of components in any order the programmer chooses. Aggregates for arrays and records have analogous, but not identical, forms.

8.1.5.1 Array aggregates. Consider a program controlling a digital watch. Internally, hours of the day are represented by the numbers zero through 23, as indicated by the following type declaration:

```
TYPE Hour_Type IS RANGE 0 .. 23;
```

Externally, hours are displayed in either *civilian style* or *military style*. In civilian style, hours are denoted by the numbers one through twelve and followed by a *qualifier* reading either "AM" or "PM"; for hours less than ten, the leftmost digit position is blank. In military style, hours are denoted by the numbers zero through 23 and followed by a qualifier consisting of two blanks; for hours less than ten, the leftmost digit position contains a zero. The program includes the following declarations:

```
TYPE Display_Style_Type IS
   (Civilian_Style, Military_Style);

Display_Style : Display_Style_Type;

Hour_Display_Table, Qualifier_Table :
   ARRAY (Hour_Type) OF String (1 .. 2);
```

Suppose we want to fill in Hour_Display_Table and Qualifier_Table according to the current value of Display_Style. We can use the following CASE statement:

```
CASE Display_Style IS
   WHEN Civilian_Style =>
      Hour_Display_Table :=
         ("12", " 1", " 2", " 3", " 4", " 5",
          " 6", " 7", " 8", " 9", "10", "11",
          "12", " 1", " 2", " 3", " 4", " 5",
          " 6", " 7", " 8", " 9", "10", "11");
      Qualifier_Table := (0 .. 11 => "AM", 12 .. 23 => "PM");
   WHEN Military_Style =>
      Hour_Display_Table :=
         ("00", "01", "02", "03", "04", "05",
          "06", "07", "08", "09", "10", "11",
          "12", "13", "14", "15", "16", "17",
          "18", "19", "20", "21", "22", "23");
      Qualifier_Table := (0 .. 23 => "  ");
END CASE;
```

Each of the four assignment statements assigns an entire array at once. The array value to be assigned is specified by an array aggregate.

An array aggregate may be either *positional* or *named.* The aggregates used in the assignments to `Hour_Display_Table` are positional. Positional array aggregates consist of an ordered list of array components. The aggregates used in the assignments to `Qualifier_Table` are *named.* Named array aggregates allow index values or ranges of index values to be listed to the left of the `=>` symbol, with the corresponding component value given to the right of that symbol.

As the previous example makes clear, named aggregates are more convenient when the same component value is to be repeated regularly throughout an array. More importantly, named aggregates can make a program easier to understand by documenting an important association between index values and component values. For example, the first assignment to `Hour_Display_Table` could have been written equivalently as follows:

```
Hour_Display_Table :=
   (0 | 12 => "12", 1 | 13 => " 1", 2 | 14 => " 2",
     3 | 15 => " 3", 4 | 16 => " 4", 5 | 17 => " 5",
    6 | 18 => " 6", 7 | 19 => " 7", 8 | 20 => " 8",
     9 | 21 => " 9", 10 | 22 => "10", 11 | 23 => "11");
```

This clarifies, for example, that `Hour_Display_Table (0)` and `Hour_Display_Table (12)` are both to be given the value `"12"`. Such information helps a reader understand the meaning of the array.

We shall now give the exact rules for writing array aggregates. We shall begin with aggregates for one-dimensional arrays. Aggregates for multidimensional arrays are built out of nested one-dimensional array aggregates.

A positional aggregate for a one-dimensional array has the following form:

(*expression* , ~~~, *expression* [, OTHERS => *expression*])

Values for components of the array are listed in the order of the components, starting with the lowest index position. If there is not an expression listed for each component of the array, the **OTHERS** part must be present; it specifies the value of all of the remaining components of the array. A positional aggregate of the form

```
( expression )
```

is disallowed because it is indistinguishable from an ordinary parenthesized expression. One-element array aggregates must be given in named notation.

A named aggregate for a one-dimensional array has the form

```
( choice | ~~~ | choice => expression ,
     ~~~
  choice | ~~~ | choice => expression  [ , ]
 [ OTHERS => expression               ] )
```

where each *choice* is either an index value or a discrete range specifying a range of index values. The expressions to the right of the => symbol give the values of the corresponding array components. No index value may appear more than once. **OTHERS** stands for each index value not specified earlier. **OTHERS** is required unless all index values have been specified by the choices.

As a special case, an array aggregate may consist *only* of an **OTHERS** part. This indicates that every component value of the array is to be given by the same expression. For example, the assignment

```
Qualifier_Table := (0 .. 23 => "   ");
```

could have been written equivalently as

```
Qualifier_Table := (OTHERS => "   ");
```

The number of components in an array aggregate containing **OTHERS** depends on how many index values, above, below, and between those specified explicitly, are covered by **OTHERS**. This can only be determined by the context in which the aggregate appears, not by the aggregate itself. Therefore, an array aggregate containing **OTHERS** may only appear in certain restricted contexts in which the set of index values is clearly determined. This is detailed in Section 8.3.9.

Now let's examine aggregates for multidimensional arrays. For the purpose of writing aggregates, an n-dimensional array value v, where, $n>1$, is treated as a one-dimensional array w of (n-1)-dimensional arrays, such that $w(i_1)(i_2, \ldots, i_n) = v(i_1, i_2, \ldots, i_n)$. (Thus a three-dimensional array of `Integer` values is treated as a one-dimensional array, each component of which is a two-dimensional array of `Integer` values.) *This view of arrays is only relevant when writing aggregates.* In all other respects, the Ada language draws a sharp distinction between ($j \times k$)-dimensional arrays and j-dimensional arrays whose components are k-dimensional arrays.

$(j \times k)$-dimensional arrays and j-dimensional arrays whose components are k-dimensional arrays.

Given the declaration

```
TYPE Two_By_Three_By_Four_Type IS
   ARRAY (1 .. 2, 1 .. 3, 1 .. 4) OF Integer RANGE 1 .. 4;
```

the positional array aggregate

```
(
   (  (111, 112, 113, 114),
      (121, 122, 123, 124),
      (131, 132, 133, 134) ),
   (  (211, 212, 213, 214),
      (221, 222, 223, 224),
      (231, 232, 233, 234) )
                              )
```

can be used as a `Two_By_Three_By_Four_Type` expression. It represents the array value such that the component corresponding to the index values `(`*i*`,`*j*`,`*k*`)` has the value `100*`*i*`+10*`*j*`+`*k*. (For instance, the component corresponding to the index values `(1,2,3)` has the value 123.) The following aggregate is equivalent:

```
(
   1 => ( 1 => (111, 112, 113, 114),
          2 => (121, 122, 123, 124),
          3 => (131, 132, 133, 134) ),
   2 => ( 1 => (211, 212, 213, 214),
          2 => (221, 222, 223, 224),
          3 => (231, 232, 233, 234) )
                                       )
```

(This is a two-component named aggregate, in which each component value is a three-component named aggregate. Each component of this three-component named aggregate is a four-component positional aggregate.)

Normally, all *index* values appearing in a named aggregate are required to be static. (The *component* values are not required to be static.) This allows the compiler to check that each index value is specified at most once and also to determine which index values are covered by `OTHERS`. However, a nonstatic index value expression is allowed in a named aggregate consisting of a single choice:

`(` *choice* `=>` *expression* `)`

This allows aggregates such as the one in the declaration

```
Point_List :
   Point_List_Type (1 .. Number_Of_Points) :=
      (1 .. Number_Of_Points => 0.0);
```

where `Point_List_Type` is an unconstrained array type, and `Number_Of_Points` is a variable. It is okay for `Number_Of_Points` to be zero, in which case the aggregate

```
(1 .. Number_Of_Points => 0.0)
```

specifies a null array value. In fact, the only way to write an aggregate for a null array is

(*lower* .. *upper* => *expression*)

where the value of *upper* is less than the value of *lower*.

Since a `String` value is just an array of `Character` values, a string literal is really just a more convenient way of writing an array aggregate. For instance, the string literal `"Hello!"` is equivalent to the positional array aggregate `('H','e','l','l','o','!')`. In fact, whenever the component type of an array is an enumeration type that includes some character literals, string literals may be used in place of an aggregate if all the component values are denoted by character literals.

For example, consider the following declarations:

```
TYPE Fieldata_Character_Type IS
   ('@', '[', ']', '#', Delta_Symbol, ' ', 'A', 'B',
    'C', 'D', 'E', 'F', 'G', 'H', 'I', 'J',
    'K', 'L', 'M', 'N', 'O', 'P', 'Q', 'R',
    'S', 'T', 'U', 'V', 'W', 'X', 'Y', 'Z',
    ')', '-', '+', '<', '=', '>', '&', '$',
    '*', '(', '%', ':', '?', '!', ',', '\',
    '0', '1', '2', '3', '4', '5', '6', '7',
    '8', '9', ''', ';', '/', '.',
    Lozenge_Symbol, Not_Equal_Symbol);
TYPE Fieldata_String_Type IS
   ARRAY (Positive RANGE <>) OF Fieldata_Character_Type;
```

The string literal `"ADA"`, of type `Fieldata_String_Type`, can be used as a shorthand for the aggregate

```
('A', 'D', 'A')
```

(The type of the string literal is determined by the context in which it appears.) A string literal cannot be used to describe a `Fieldata_String_Type` array value containing `Lozenge_Symbol` as a component.

8.1.5.2 Record aggregates. Consider the following declarations:

```
TYPE File_Description_Type IS
   RECORD
      Name_Part      : String (1 .. 8);
      Extension_Part : String (1 .. 3);
      Length_Part    : Natural;
      Location_Part  : Integer RANGE 0 .. 511;
   END RECORD;
```

```
TYPE Directory_Type IS
   ARRAY (Positive RANGE <>) OF File_Description_Type;

Directory             : Directory_Type (1 .. 128);
New_File_Name         : String (1 .. 8);
New_File_Extension    : String (1 .. 3);
New_File_Length       : Natural;
New_File_Location     : Integer RANGE 0 .. 511;
Blank_File_Name       : CONSTANT String := (1 .. 8 => ' ');
Blank_File_Extension : CONSTANT String := (1 .. 3 => ' ');
```

Suppose an empty directory entry is represented by a `File_Description_Type` record with a blank file name, a blank extension, a length of zero, and a location of zero. The following loop finds the first empty entry in `Directory` (assuming there is one) and fills it in with a record having the information contained in the variables `New_File_Name`, `New_File_Extension`, `New_File_Length`, and `New_File_Location`:

```
FOR i IN Directory'Range LOOP
   IF Directory (i) =
      (Blank_File_Name, Blank_Extension, 0, 0) THEN
      Directory (i) :=
         (Name_Part      => New_File_Name,
          Extension_Part => New_File_Extension,
          Length_Part    => New_File_Length,
          Location_Part  => New_File_Location);
      EXIT;
   END IF;
END LOOP;
```

The condition of the `IF` statement and the expression of the assignment statement both contain record aggregates describing values of entire records. The aggregate

```
(Blank_File_Name, Blank_Extension, 0, 0)
```

is a *positional record aggregate*. The component values are listed in the same order as the components appear in the record type declaration. The aggregate

```
(Name_Part      => New_File_Name,
 Extension_Part => New_File_Extension,
 Length_Part    => New_File_Length,
 Location_Part  => New_File_Location)
```

is a *named record aggregate*. The value on the right of each `=>` is assigned to the record component named on the left. Components may be listed in any order in a named record aggregate.

There are other forms as well. Components with the same base type can be specified together if they are to receive the same value. The component names are listed to the left of the `=>` separated by vertical bars. Thus the aggregate

```
(Name_Part                      => Blank_File_Name,
 Extension_Part                 => Blank_File_Extension,
 Length_Part | Location_Part => 0);
```

is equivalent to the positional aggregate above. This record value can also be written as follows:

```
(Name_Part      => Blank_File_Name,
 Extension_Part => Blank_File_Extension,
 OTHERS         => 0);
```

The form

`OTHERS =>` *expression*

is only allowed as the last item in a record aggregate, only if one or more record component values have not been specified earlier in the aggregate, and only if all these unspecified record components have the same base type. `OTHERS` is rarely useful in a record aggregate. Finally, *unlike an array aggregate,* a record aggregate may contain a mixture of named and positional notation:

```
(Blank_File_Name,
 Blank_File_Extension,
 Length_Part | Location_Part => 0)
```

The positional part of the aggregate must come first. After a component value is specified in named notation, all subsequent components must be specified in named notation.

In general, named rather than positional record aggregates should be used because they are more informative. Positional record aggregates should be reserved for cases in which the order of the record components is determined by a well-known convention, making the aggregate self-explanatory. For example, given the declaration

```
TYPE Point_Type IS
   RECORD
      X_Part, Y_Part : Float;
   END RECORD;
```

it is reasonable to use aggregates like `(1.0, 0.0)` and `(4.0, -10.0)` to describe `Point_Type` values.

8.1.6 Qualified Expressions

Certain Ada expressions can be interpreted as belonging to more than one type. For example, given the declarations at the end of the section on array aggregates (see page 206), the character literal `'A'` may be the seventh value of type

`Fieldata_Character_Type` or the 66th value of type `Character`. The string literal `"ADA"` may belong to type `Fieldata_String_Type` or to the predefined type `String`. The aggregate `(1, 2, 3, 4)` may belong to any one-dimensional unconstrained array subtype whose component type is an integer type and whose index subtype includes at least four values.

When an expression that can be interpreted as belonging to more than one type occurs in a context where more than one of these types is legal, you must explicitly indicate which type is intended. This can be done with a qualified expression. A *qualified expression* is simply an expression that is explicitly marked as belonging to a particular type or subtype. Its form is

typemark `'` `(` *expression* `)`

and its value is simply the value of the expression. The type associated with the typemark must be one of the possible types of the expression. Thus the expression `Fieldata_Character_Type'('A')` is `Fieldata_Character_Type`'s character literal `'A'`, and `Fieldata_String_Type'("ADA")` is `Fieldata_String_Type`'s string literal `"ADA"`. (As with attributes, the use of the apostrophe in the Ada programming language is reminiscent of its use in English.)

When the expression is an aggregate, this syntax calls for a double set of parentheses, as in

```
Fieldata_String_Type'(('A', 'D', 'A'))
```

(The outer parentheses come from the qualified expression and the inner ones from the aggregate.) In such a case, there is a special rule allowing the double parentheses to be replaced by single parentheses, as in

```
Fieldata_String_Type'('A', 'D', 'A')
```

8.1.7 Type Conversions

Chapter 6 explained that every value in an Ada program belongs to exactly one type. Nonetheless, it is possible for two types to have values that *correspond* to each other in an obvious way. For example, values in two numeric types correspond to each other if they refer to the same numeric quantity.

A *type conversion* is an Ada expression whose value is a value in a specified type corresponding to a given value in another type. The form of a type conversion is

typemark `(` *expression* `)`

where the typemark names the subtype to which the value of the expression is to be converted. (This is similar to the form of a qualified expression; however the typemark in the qualified expression is followed by an apostrophe, and the typemark in a type conversion is not.) Conversions are allowed between numeric types, between certain array types, and between a derived type and the type from which it was derived.

A value in one numeric type can be converted to a value in any other integer, fixed-point, or floating-point type. Conversion of a fixed-point or floating-point value to a value in an integer type entails *rounding* to the nearest whole number (not truncation toward zero as in FORTRAN, PL/I, and Pascal). The rules of the Ada language do not specify whether a number midway between two integers (such as -3.5) is rounded up (to -3) or down (to -4).

If type `T1` is derived from type `T2` then it is possible to convert a value of type `T1` to the corresponding value in type `T2`, or to convert a value of type `T2` to the corresponding value of type `T1`. In fact, it is possible to convert between any two types that are directly or indirectly derived from the same type. Given the declarations

```
TYPE a IS NEW t;
TYPE b IS NEW t;
TYPE c IS NEW a;
TYPE d IS NEW b;
```

each of the types `t`, `a`, `b`, `c`, and `d` is convertible to each of the others. (See Figure 8.1.)

A value in one array type may be converted to a value in another array type when the types meet the following conditions:

They have the same number of dimensions.

The index types in any given dimension are either the same or convertible to each other. (This means that corresponding index types must both be integer types, be the same enumeration type, or be two enumeration types directly or indirectly derived from the same type.)

They have the same component type; and if the component subtype of one array type is a *constrained* subtype, then the component subtype of the other array has the same constraint.

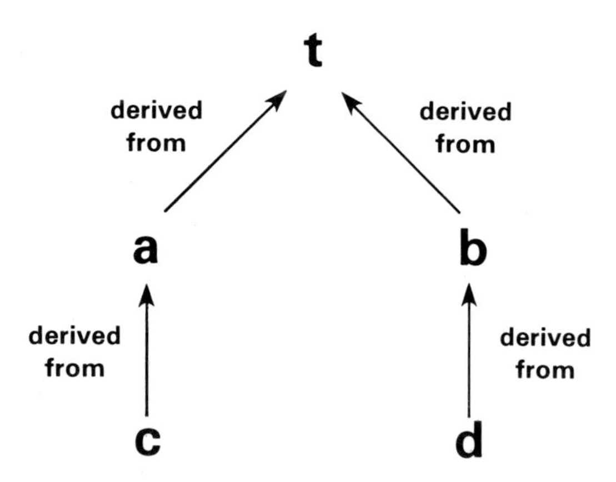

Figure 8.1 Type conversion is allowed in either direction between any two of the types `a`, `b`, `c`, `d`, and `t`

Furthermore, if the array subtype being converted to is constrained, the array being converted must have the appropriate length in each dimension. The result of the conversion is an array containing the same component values in the same relative positions as in the original array. Here is an example:

```
PROCEDURE Array_Conversion IS
   TYPE Array_Type_1 IS ARRAY (0 .. 1, 1 .. 2) OF Integer;
   TYPE Array_Type_2 IS ARRAY (1 .. 2, 0 .. 1) OF Integer;
   A : Array_Type_1 := ( (1, 2), (11, 12) );
   B : Array_Type_2;
BEGIN
   -- A (0,1) = 1, A (0,2) = 2, A (1,1) = 11, A (1,2) = 12
   B := Array_Type_2 (A); -- type conversion
   -- B (1,0) = 1, B (1,1) = 2, A (2,0) = 11, A (2,1) = 12
END Array_Conversion;
```

The assignment `A := B` would have been illegal, because `A` and `B` have different types.

It is easy to confuse qualified expressions and type conversions. Syntactically, they are distinguished by the fact that a qualified expression contains an apostrophe between the typemark and the left parenthesis. (In addition, if a conversion is applied to an aggregate, it is necessary to write one set of parentheses for the type conversion and one for the aggregate. A qualified aggregate expression may be written using a single set of parentheses.) A qualified expression is used to tell the compiler that an expression belongs to a particular type when this is not apparent from the expression itself. It does not call for any new values to be computed while the program is running. A type conversion is an expression that takes a value known to be of a particular type and produces a corresponding value in another type. This may involve some sort of computation when the program is running (for instance, when a value in a floating-point type is converted to a value in an integer type), or it may not (when values in the original type have the same underlying representation as the corresponding values in the resulting type).

8.1.8 Allocators

An *allocator* is an expression that evaluates to an access value designating a new allocated variable. Allocators were discussed in Section 5.2. Allocators differ from the other kinds of expressions we have seen so far in that they specify not only a value, but also an action to be performed—the creation of a new allocated variable.

8.1.9 Function Calls

Function calls will be dealt with only briefly here. Full treatment will be given in Chapter 9. The simple form of a function call is

function name [(*expression* , ~~~ , *expression*)]

Like allocators, function calls specify an action to be performed in the process of producing a value. In this case, the action is execution of the function subprogram named by the function name, using the values of the expressions as parameter values. When the subprogram executes a RETURN statement of the form

```
RETURN expression;
```

the execution of the subprogram completes, and the value of the expression in the RETURN statement becomes the value of the function call.

A function call may be used as a *name* in the sense of Section 8.1.2 to form larger names. Thus, if Identity_Type is a type defined by

```
TYPE Identity_Type IS
   RECORD
      First_Name, Last_Name   : String (1 .. 20);
      Social_Security_Number : Integer RANGE 0 .. 1E9 - 1;
   END RECORD;
```

and Find_Identity is a function taking an argument of some type Person_Type and returning a value of type Identity_Type, the following are all valid *names:*

```
Find_Identity (P).First_Name (1)
Find_Identity (P).First_Name (1 .. 5)
Find_Identity (P).First_Name
```

Similarly, Find_Identity (P).First_Name'Range is the range 1 .. 20.

A function call never names a variable. Thus none of the names above may be used on the lefthand side of an assignment statement. However, if a function returns a non-null access value, then the object designated by that access value is always a variable. Thus a function call returning an access value may appear on the lefthand side of an assignment statement as part of the name of an allocated object. Suppose SSN_Owner is a function taking a social security number as a parameter and returning a pointer to an Identity_Type record containing that social security number. Then the assignment statement

```
SSN_Owner (123_45_6789).Last_Name :=
   "Smith               ";
```

assigns a value to the Last_Name component of the Identity_Type variable

```
SSN_Owner (123_45_6789).ALL
```

8.2 COMPOUND EXPRESSIONS

The seven kinds of elementary expressions—literals, names, aggregates, qualified expressions, type conversions, allocators, and function calls—may be combined using *operators* and parentheses to form compound expressions. An operator may consist of one or two special characters (like `+` or `>=`) or a reserved word (like `AND`). The expressions to which an operator is applied are called the *operands* of the operator. For example, in the expression `A * B`, `A` and `B` are the operands of the operator `*`.

The operators are classified in *levels of precedence.* Operators at a higher level of precedence are associated with their operands before operators at a lower level of precedence. For example, `*` has higher precedence than `+`, so `A+B*C` is the application of the operator `+` to the expressions `A` and `B*C`, not the application of `*` to `A+B` and `C`. Parentheses may be used to associate expressions with an operator that they would not otherwise be associated with. Expressions occurring inside parentheses can only be joined to each other by operators inside those parentheses. Thus `(A+B)*C` is the application of the operator `*` to `(A+B)` and `C`. The six precedence levels of Ada operators are listed in Figure 8.2. (In the official Ada jargon, the combination `AND THEN`, the combination `OR ELSE`, the word `IN`, and the combination `NOT IN` are not called operators. However, they play essentially the same role in expressions that operators do.) When operators at the same level of precedence occur in sequence, they are applied in left-to-right order. Thus `A/B*C` means `(A/B)*C`, not `A/(B*C)`.

8.2.1 Exponentiation

Ada's exponentiation operator, `**`, is more restricted than its counterpart in FORTRAN and PL/I. The right operand of `**` must always belong to the predefined type `Integer`. The left operand may belong to any integer type or any floating point type, but not to a fixed point type. The result is of the same type as the left operand. When the left operand belongs to an integer type, the right operand must be nonnegative.

Suppose *n* is an `Integer` value greater than or equal to zero. The value of *x*`**`*n* is equal to that obtained by starting with one and multiplying by *x* a total of *n* times. The expression *x*`**(`-*n*`)` is equivalent to `1.0/`*x*`**`*n*.

Highest Precedence

`** , ABS , NOT`
`* , / , MOD , REM`
`+ , -` (applied to a single operand)
`+ , - , &` (applied to two operands)
`+ , /= , < , <= , > , >= , IN , NOT IN`
`AND , OR , XOR , AND THEN , OR ELSE`

Lowest Precedence

Figure 8.2 In the absence of parentheses, higher-precedence operators are applied before lower-precedence operators.

An expression of the form *a****b****c* is forbidden in the Ada language. If either the left or the right operand of ** is itself an exponentiation, that operand must be enclosed in parentheses, as in (*a****b*)***c* and *a***(*b****c*).

8.2.2 Absolute Value

The operator ABS is applied to a single operand, as in the expression ABS x, and the result is the absolute value of that operand. The operand may belong to any numeric type. The result is an expression of the same type. An expression combining applications of ABS and ** must contain parentheses. Thus ABS a ** b is illegal. It must be written either as (ABS a) ** b or ABS (a ** b), depending on what is intended.

8.2.3 Multiplication and Division

The symbol * is the multiplication operator and the symbol / is the division operator. In general, the two operands of these operators must belong to the same numeric type, and the result also belongs to that type. However, special rules apply when one or both of the operands belong to a fixed-point type.

In the case of multiplication, if one operand belongs to a fixed-point type then the other operand must belong to a fixed-point type (not necessarily the same one) or to the predefined type Integer. When a value in a fixed-point type is multiplied by a value of type Integer, the result belongs to the fixed-point type. Two fixed-point operands can only be multiplied when the product occurs as the expression inside a type conversion. For example, given the declarations

```
TYPE Tenths_Type         IS DELTA 0.1   RANGE 0.0 .. 1.0;
TYPE Hundredths_Type     IS DELTA 0.01  RANGE 0.0 .. 1.0;
TYPE Thousandths_Type    IS DELTA 0.001 RANGE 0.0 .. 1.0;

F_10  : Tenths_Type;
F_100 : Hundredths_Type;
I     : Integer;
```

the multiplication F_10 * F_100 is legal only in the context of a type conversion, such as

```
Thousandths_Type (F_10 * F_100)
```

The expressions F_10 * I and I * F_10 are legal anywhere an expression of type Tenths_Type is allowed.

When the operands of / belong to the same integer type, the quotient is *truncated toward zero* if necessary to produce a result of that integer type. Thus if I and J belong to the same integer type, I = 10, and J = 3, then I / J = 3; if I = 10 and J = -3 (or I = -10 and J = 3), then I / J = -3. A value in a fixed-point type may be divided by a value in a fixed-point type (not necessarily the same one) or by a value in the predefined type Integer. Like the multiplication of two fixed-point values, the division of one fixed-point value by another may only occur inside a type conversion. The division of a value in a fixed-point type by a value of type Integer produces a result in the fixed-point type and may occur wherever an expression of that type is allowed. A value of type `Integer` cannot be divided by a value in a fixed-point type. Regardless of type, it is always illegal to divide by zero.

(Do not confuse the rule for integer division with the rule for type conversions given in Section 8.1.7. Conversion of a fixed-point or floating-point value to an integer type causes the value to be *rounded* to the nearest integer. Division of one integer by another causes the quotient to be *truncated* toward zero to produce an integer result. Thus `Integer (7.0 / 4.0) = Integer (1.75) = 2`, but `7 / 4 = 1`.

8.2.4 Remainder

There are two slightly different remainder operators, `REM` and `MOD`. Each takes two operands that belong to the same integer type. (`MOD` and `REM` are operators, like `**`, `*`, and `/`, which are written between their operands. They are not functions as in PL/I and FORTRAN.) When x and y are both nonnegative, x `MOD` y and x `REM` y have the same value—the remainder when x is divided by y. `MOD` and `REM` differ in their behavior with negative operands. When x is an exact positive or negative multiple of y, x `MOD` y and x `REM` y are both zero. Otherwise, x `REM` y has the same sign as x and the same magnitude as `ABS` x `REM` `ABS` y; x `MOD` y has the same sign as y and a magnitude less than y's magnitude such that adding some multiple of y to x `MOD` y will yield x. Neither x `MOD` y nor x `REM` y is defined when $y = 0$.

Figure 8.3 illustrates x `MOD` y and x `REM` y with x running from -8 to 8 and y equal to 4 and 4. $(-x)$ `REM` y always equals `-` (x `REM` y), and the sign of y is irrelevant. x `MOD` y repeats the same cycle of y different values as x takes on successive values, regardless of the sign of x. The cycle consists of the values 0, 1, ..., y-1 when y is positive and y+1, ..., -1, 0 when y is negative.

8.2.5 Plus and Minus

The operators `+` and `-` may be applied to either one operand or two. When applied to one operand, they are called *unary* operators. Otherwise, they are called *binary* operators.

Unary `+` and `-` can be applied to an operand in any numeric type, and the result always belongs to the same type. The unary `+` operator simply yields the value of its

x	−8	−7	−6	−5	−4	−3	−2	−1	0	1	2	3	4	5	6	7	8
x REM 4 x REM −4	0	−3	−2	−1	0	−3	−2	−1	0	1	2	3	0	1	2	3	0
x MOD 4	0	1	2	3	0	1	2	3	0	1	2	3	0	1	2	3	0
x MOD −4	0	−3	−2	−1	0	−3	−2	−1	0	−3	−2	−1	0	−3	−2	−1	0

Figure 8.3 Illustrations of the behavior of `REM` and `MOD` with a right operand of -4 or 4. The shading in the lower two rows show the cycle of values returned by `x MOD y` for sucessive values of `x`. When `x` = 4, the cycle consists of the values 0, 1, 2, 3. When `y` = -4, the cycle consists of the values -3, -2, -1, 0.

operand. The unary - operator yields the negation of its operand. The two operands of binary + or - must belong to the same numeric type, and the addition or subtraction produces a result of that type.

8.2.6 Catenation

Catenation is an operation joining two operands together to form an array containing values from the first operand followed by values from the second operand. Usually, the two operands belong to the same one-dimensional array type, and the result is a new array in the same array type: the length of the result is the sum of the lengths of the operands and the components of the result are the components of the first operand followed by the components of the second operand. Catenation was introduced in Section 4.2.6.

Since `String` is a one-dimensional array type, values of type `String` can be catenated. Thus the expression

```
"The value is " & "43" & "."
```

has the same value as the expression

```
"The value is 43."
```

Since a string literal cannot be split across different lines, catenation is useful when a program contains long messages:

```
Basic_IO.Put
   ("Invalid input.  " &
    "Please reenter or press " &
    "control-Q to quit.");
```

It is sometimes useful to apply catenation to one-dimensional array types besides the type `String`. Consider the following declarations:

```
TYPE Player_Type IS
   RECORD
      Player_Name   : String (1 .. 30);
      Player_Number : Integer RANGE 1 .. 99;
      Wins, Losses  : Integer;
      Percentage    : Float RANGE 0.0 .. 0.1;
   END RECORD;

TYPE Player_List_Type IS
   ARRAY (Integer RANGE <>) OF Player_Type;

Division_1, Division_2 : Player_List_Type (1 .. 10);
Finalists              : Player_List_Type (1 .. 8);
```

Assume there is a tournament in which twenty players are divided into two divisions of ten players each. `Division_1` and `Division_2` are lists of the players in each division, sorted in order of descending win-loss ratios. Finalists can be set to a list consisting of the top four players in each division by the following statement:

```
Finalists := Division_1 (1 .. 4) & Division_2 (1 .. 4);
```

A basket with one orange in it is not the same as one orange. Similarly, an array with one component having the value *x* is not the same value as *x* itself. Consider the following declarations:

```
TYPE Row_Type IS ARRAY (Integer RANGE <>) OF Integer;

Row_Of_1 : Row_Type (1 .. 1) := (1 => 0);
Zero     : Integer := 0;

Sentence : String (1 .. 80);
```

Based on what we have shown so far, it should not be possible to catenate `Zero` with `Row_Of_1` because `Zero` is not a value of type `Row_Type`. Similarly, the expression `Sentence & '.'` should be illegal because the literal `'.'` represents a value of type `Character`, not type `String`.

However, as a convenience, the Ada language allows a component value to be used in place of an array in a catenation. It is equivalent in that context to an array with one component. Thus `Zero & Row_Of_1` is allowed as an abbreviation for `(1 => Zero) & Row_Of_1`; and `Sentence & '.'` is allowed as a shorthand for `Sentence & (1 => '.')` (equivalently, `Sentence & "."`). A component value may occur as the left operand of `&`, the right operand of `&`, or both.

8.2.7 Relational Operators and Membership Tests

The *relational operators* `=`, `/=`, `<`, `<=`, `>`, and `>=` and the *membership tests* `IN` and `NOT IN` all produce results of type `Boolean`. The relational operators are used to determine whether a certain relationship holds between the values of the left and right operands. Membership tests are used to determine whether the value of the left operand belongs to the subtype described by the right operand. In either case, the result is a value in the predefined type `Boolean`. (Despite the use of the word `IN` and the term *membership test*, the Ada membership tests `IN` and `NOT IN`—which test for membership in a subtype—have nothing to do with the Pascal *set* membership operator `IN`—which tests whether a given value belongs to a given set. The Ada language does not deal directly with sets, although you can define your own type with many of the same operations as Pascal sets.)

The relational operator `=` tests for equality. It is applied to two operands in the same type, producing the result `True` if the operands have the same value and `False` if they do not. The relational operator `/=` stands for *not equal.* (It is suggestive of the mathematical symbol consisting of an equal sign with a slash through it.) Like `=`, `/=` is applied to two operands in the same type. It produces the result `False` if the operands have the same value and `True` if they do not.

The relational operators `<`, `<=`, `>`, and `>=` stand for *less than, less than or equal to, greater than,* and *greater than or equal to,* respectively. These operators may be applied to two operands in the same numeric type. Furthermore, they may be applied to two operands in the same enumeration type. One enumeration value is "less than" a second if it is denoted by an enumeration literal listed earlier in the enumeration type declaration; the other relations are defined accordingly. For example, given the declarations

```
TYPE Suit_Type IS (Clubs, Diamonds, Hearts, Spades);
Suit_1 : CONSTANT Suit_Type := Diamonds;
Suit_2 : CONSTANT Suit_Type := Spades;
```

the following expressions are true:

```
Suit_1 < Suit_2
Suit_1 <= Suit_2
Suit_1 <= Diamonds
```

The following expressions are false:

```
Suit_1 > Suit_2
Suit_1 >= Suit_2
Suit_1 > Diamonds
```

The relational operators may also be applied to two operands in the same one-dimensional array type, provided that the array components belong to either an integer type or an enumeration type. The comparison works as follows: If the two operands have the same number of components and the corresponding components are equal, the two operands are equal. Otherwise, begin comparing corresponding components, starting from the left, until either one operand runs out of components or corresponding components are not equal. If unequal components are found, the operand containing the smaller component at the position at which the difference is found is considered less than the other array. Thus `(1, 3, 8, 5)` is less than `(1, 3, 9, 5)` and also less than `(1, 4)`. Otherwise, one of the operands contains the component values of the other operand followed by one or more additional values. In this case, the shorter array is considered less than the longer array. For example, `(1, 3, 8, 5)` is less than `(1, 3, 8, 5, 4, 7)`, and a null array is less than any non-null array.

These rules are precisely the rules we use to determine whether one word comes before another in a dictionary. In fact, `String` is a one-dimensional array type whose components belong to the enumeration type `Character`, so `String` values may be compared in this way. When two `String` operands consist of all upper-case letters or all lower-case letters, the relational operators correspond to alphabetical order. However, because of the definition of the ASCII character set, all `Character` values corresponding to upper-case letters are less than all `Character` values corresponding to lower-case letters. Thus the following `String` values are in ascending order according to the relational operators:

```
"Alpha"
"Alphabet"
"Alpine"
"ZZZ"
"Zeta"
"aardvark"
"abacus"
"zymurgy"
```

The membership tests `IN` and `NOT IN` are different from the operators we have seen so far because their right operands are not expressions. The right operand of a membership test is either a typemark, a range of the form

lower bound `..` *upper bound*

where *lower bound* and *upper bound* are expressions, or a `'Range` attribute. In an expression of the form

x `IN` *st*

(where *x* is an expression and *st* is a typemark), *x* must belong to the base type of subtype *st*. (This can be checked when the program is compiled.) The expression is true when the value of *x* belongs to the subtype *st*, and false otherwise. (In general, it will be necessary to run the program to determine this.) For instance, given the declarations

```
TYPE Day_Type IS
   (Sunday, Monday, Tuesday, Wednesday, Thursday, Friday,
    Saturday);
SUBTYPE Weekday_Subtype IS Day_Type RANGE Monday .. Friday;
```

the expression

```
Today IN Weekday_Subtype
```

may appear in a program only if `Today` is of type `Day_Type`. The expression is true when `Today` holds one of the values `Monday` through `Friday` and false when it holds the value `Sunday` or the value `Saturday`. Given the declarations

```
TYPE Row_Type IS ARRAY (Integer RANGE <>) OF Integer;
SUBTYPE Row_Of_10_Subtype IS Row_Type (1 .. 10);
```

the expression

```
x IN Row_Of_10_Subtype
```

may appear in a program only if `x` is of type `Row_Type`. The expression is true if `x` has the index bounds `(1 .. 10)` and false otherwise.

In a membership test of the form

```
x IN y .. z
```

x must belong to a numeric type or an enumeration type, and y and z must be expressions in the same type. The expression is true when the expressions y `<=` x and x `<=` z are both true, and false otherwise. Thus

```
Today IN Weekday_Subtype
```

is equivalent to

```
Today IN Monday .. Friday
```

Similarly, in a membership test of the form

```
Today in T'Range(n)
```

`T` must be an array subtype whose n^{th} index type is the type of `Today`, an array object belonging to such a subtype, or an access value designating an array object in such a subtype.

The following program counts the number of lower-case letters, upper-case letters, and other characters occurring in an input file, assuming the file does not contain any lines of more than eighty characters:

```
WITH Basic_IO;
PROCEDURE Count_Letters IS
   Maximum_Line_Length : CONSTANT := 80;
   Input_Line          : String (1 .. Maximum_Line_Length);
   c                   : Character;
   Line_Length         : Natural;
   Lower_Case_Count,
      Upper_Case_Count,
      Non_Letter_Count : Natural := 0;
BEGIN
   WHILE NOT Basic_IO.End_Of_File LOOP
      Basic_IO.Get_Line (Input_Line, Line_Length);
      FOR i IN 1 .. Line_Length LOOP
         c := Input_Line (i);
         IF c IN 'a' .. 'z' THEN
            Lower_Case_Count := Lower_Case_Count + 1;
         ELSIF c IN 'A' .. 'Z' THEN
            Upper_Case_Count := Upper_Case_Count + 1;
         ELSE
            Non_Letter_Count := Non_Letter_Count + 1;
         END IF;
      END LOOP;
   END LOOP;
```

```
      Basic_IO.Put (Lower_Case_Count);
      Basic_IO.Put (" lower case letters.");
      Basic_IO.New_Line;
      Basic_IO.Put (Upper_Case_Count);
      Basic_IO.Put (" upper case letters.");
      Basic_IO.New_Line;
      Basic_IO.Put (Non_Letter_Count);
      Basic_IO.Put (" other characters.");
      Basic_IO.New_Line;
   END Count_Letters;
```

The program works because both the lower-case letters and the upper-case letters occur consecutively in the ASCII character set. Thus `'A' .. 'Z'` names a range of 26 `Character` values containing only the upper-case letters, and `'a' .. 'z'` names a range of 26 `Character` values containing only the lower-case letters. This can be made clearer by adding the declarations

```
SUBTYPE Lower_Case_Subtype IS Character RANGE 'a' .. 'z';
SUBTYPE Upper_Case_Subtype IS Character RANGE 'A' .. 'Z';
```

and changing the `IF` statement to read as follows:

```
IF c IN Lower_Case_Subtype THEN
   Lower_Case_Count := Lower_Case_Count + 1;
ELSIF c IN Upper_Case_Subtype THEN
   Upper_Case_Count := Upper_Case_Count + 1;
ELSE
   Non_Letter_Count := Non_Letter_Count + 1;
END IF;
```

The membership operator `NOT IN` follows the same rules as `IN` but produces the opposite result. Thus

x `NOT IN` *st*

is a convenient shorthand for

`NOT (`*x* `IN` *st*`)`

An expression may not contain two relational operators or membership tests in a row, without intervening parentheses. Thus `A < B = C` is illegal. However, you may write `(A < B) = C` to test whether the Boolean value `C` is equal to the value of the expression `A<B`.

8.2.8 Logical Operators and Short-Circuit Control Forms

The logical operators `AND`, `OR`, and `XOR` and the *short-circuit control forms* `AND THEN` and `OR ELSE` can be applied to two values of type `Boolean` to produce a result of type `Boolean`. The logical operator `NOT` can be applied to a single operand of type `Boolean` to produce a result of type `Boolean`.

8.2.8.1 Logical operators. An expression of the form *x* AND *y* is true when *x* and *y* are both true, and false otherwise. An expression of the form *x* OR *y* is true when *x*, or *y*, *or both* are true, and false otherwise. The operator XOR is pronounced *exclusive or*. It is a variation on OR that "excludes" the case where both operands are true. Thus *x* XOR *y* is true when *x* is true and *y* is false or when *x* is false and *y* is true; but it is false when *x* and *y* are both true or both false. The expression NOT *x* is true when *x* is false and false when *x* is true. The behavior of AND, OR, XOR, and NOT is summarized in Figure 8.4.

(Do not confuse the logical operator AND with the catenation operator & discussed in Section 8.2.6. Similarly, do not confuse the logical operator OR with the symbol | used to separate listed choices in places like CASE statements and aggregates.)

8.2.8.2 Short-circuit control forms. When *x* is false, *x* AND *y* is false regardless of the value of *y*. When *x* is true, *x* OR *y* is true regardless of the value of *y*. However, both operands of an operator are evaluated before the operator is applied, so the second operand gets evaluated even when its value is irrelevant. The short-circuit control forms AND THEN and OR ELSE compute the values we would expect from AND and OR, respectively, but do not evaluate the second operand when the result can be determined from the value of the first operand. AND THEN works as follows:

1. Evaluate the first operand.
2. If it is false, produce a result of False. Otherwise, evaluate the second argument and use its value as the result.

OR ELSE works as follows:

1. Evaluate the first operand.
2. If it is true, produce a result of True. Otherwise, evaluate the second argument and use its value as the result.

Comparison with Figure 8.4 will confirm that AND THEN computes the values we would expect from AND, and OR ELSE computes the values we would expect from OR.

<table>
<tr><th>x</th><th>y</th><th></th><th>x AND y</th><th>x OR y</th><th>x XOR y</th><th>NOT x</th></tr>
<tr><td>True</td><td>True</td><td></td><td>True</td><td>True</td><td>False</td><td rowspan="2">False</td></tr>
<tr><td>True</td><td>False</td><td></td><td>False</td><td>True</td><td>True</td></tr>
<tr><td>False</td><td>True</td><td></td><td>False</td><td>True</td><td>True</td><td rowspan="2">True</td></tr>
<tr><td>False</td><td>False</td><td></td><td>False</td><td>False</td><td>False</td></tr>
</table>

Figure 8.4 Behavior of the logical operators.

The primary purpose of short-circuit control forms is not to reduce execution time, but to let you write expressions such as

```
y = 0  OR ELSE  x / y > 10
```

in which the left operand determines the value of the expression precisely in those cases in which evaluation of the right operand would lead to an error. Even though it looks as though

```
y = 0  OR  x / y = 10
```

should be true when `y = 0`, regardless of the value of `x / y > 10`, an executing program will try to evaluate both `y = 0` and `x / y > 10` before applying `OR`, leading to an error when an attempt is made to divide `x` by zero. When the short-circuit control form is used, the left operand is found to be true and the right operand is never evaluated.

8.2.8.3 An example: Insertion sort. Such logical expressions arise surprisingly often. An example is provided by the following insertion sort program, which reads in ten integers, sorts them, and prints them out in ascending order:

```
WITH Basic_IO;
PROCEDURE Insertion_Sort IS
   Number_Of_Items : CONSTANT := 10;
   New_Item        : Integer;
   Buffer : ARRAY (1 .. Number_Of_Items) OF Integer;
   Candidate_Position :
      Integer RANGE 0 .. Number_Of_Items - 1;
BEGIN
   -- Read data into buffer:
   FOR i IN Buffer'Range LOOP
      Basic_IO.Get( Buffer(i) );
   END LOOP;
   -- Sort buffer:
   FOR Next IN 2 .. Buffer'Last LOOP
      -- Buffer (1 .. Next-1) is already sorted.
      New_Item := Buffer (Next);
      -- Set Candidate_Position to position after which
      --   New_Item should be inserted:
      Candidate_Position := Next - 1;
      WHILE Candidate_Position > 0 AND THEN
               Buffer(Candidate_Position) > New_Item LOOP
         Candidate_Position := Candidate_Position - 1;
      END LOOP;
```

```
         -- Slide other elements to the right to make room and
         --   then insert New_Item at that position:
         Buffer (Candidate_Position+2 .. Next) :=
            Buffer (Candidate_Position+1 .. Next-1);
         Buffer (Candidate_Position + 1) := New_Item;
         -- Now Buffer (1 .. Next) is sorted.
      END LOOP;
      -- Print contents of buffer:
       FOR i IN Buffer'Range LOOP
          Basic_IO.Put( Buffer(i) );
          Basic_IO.New_Line;
       END LOOP;
   END Insertion_Sort;
```

The first FOR loop reads the input data into the array Buffer; the second FOR loop sorts Buffer in ascending order; and the third FOR loop prints the values in Buffer. At the beginning of a repetition of the second FOR loop, the slice Buffer (1 .. Next-1) is already in ascending order. The WHILE loop determines the position within this slice at which Buffer (Next) should be inserted, setting Candidate_Position to the position *after* which the insertion should take place. To make room, the components of the slice

```
Buffer (Candidate_Position+1 .. Next-1)
```

are each moved one position to the right, into

```
Buffer (Candidate_Position+2 .. Next)
```

Then the new value is inserted in Buffer (Candidate_Position+1). This leaves the slice Buffer (1 .. Next) in ascending order. Thus Buffer (1 .. 1) is sorted before the first repetition of the FOR loop (because a slice with one component is always sorted); Buffer (1 .. 2) is sorted after one repetition; Buffer (1 .. 3) is sorted after two repetitions, and so forth.

The WHILE loop works by starting at Buffer(Next-1) and proceeding backwards through the array until either a component less than or equal to Buffer(Next) is found or all components of Buffer (1 .. Next-1) are seen to be greater than Buffer (Next). In the first case, the loop terminates with Candidate_Position set to the index of the component that was found; and in the second case, the loop terminates with Candidate_Position set to zero. Either way, Buffer (Next) should be inserted at position Candidate_Position+1. However, in the second case, evaluation of the expression

```
Candidate_Position > 0 AND
   Buffer(Candidate_Position) > New_Item
```

would cause an error. Even though the Candidate_Position > 0 part is false, and this is enough to determine that the entire expression will be false, the Buffer(Candidate_Position) > New_Item part is also evaluated. It is evaluated with Candidate_Position set to zero, a value that is not a valid index for Buffer. To avoid this error, the WHILE loop is written with the short-circuit control form

```
Candidate_Position > 0 AND THEN
   Buffer (Candidate_Position) > New_Item
```

which evaluates Buffer (Candidate_Position) > Item only when Candidate_Position > 0 is found to be true.

8.2.8.4 Parentheses in logical expressions. You may write expressions in which the same logical operator or short-circuit control form occurs two or more times in succession. However, *different* logical operators or short-circuit control forms can only be combined using parentheses. The operator AND and the short-circuit control form AND THEN are considered different, as are the operator OR and the short-circuit control form OR ELSE. Thus the following expressions are illegal:

```
a >b  AND  b > c  OR  a < c
a /= 0  AND  b /= 0  AND THEN  c/(a*b) > d
```

However,the following expressions are legal:

```
(a > b  AND  b > c)  OR  a < c
a > b  AND (b > c  OR  a < c)
(a /= 0  AND  b /= 0)  AND THEN  c/(a*b) > d
a > b  AND  b > c  AND  c > d
a = 1  AND  (b = 2  OR  b = -2)  AND  c = 1
i /= 0  AND THEN  a(i) /= 0.0  AND THEN  1.0/a(i) > 5.0
```

8.2.8.5 Extensions of the logical operators. The logical operators NOT, AND, OR, and XOR can actually be applied to certain types of operands besides the predefined type Boolean. There are two extensions of these operators, one of which also applies to the short-circuit control forms AND THEN and OR ELSE.

First, NOT can be applied to an operand of any *truth value type,* and AND, OR, XOR, AND THEN, and OR ELSE can be applied to two operands of the same truth value type. A truth value type is either the predefined type Boolean or a derived type derived from a truth value type. (Thus Boolean, types derived from Boolean, types derived from types derived from Boolean, and so forth are all truth value types.) Every truth value type has two values, denoted by the enumeration literals True and False. When a logical operation is applied to one or two operands in a given truth value type, it produces a result in that type. The conditions appearing in IF statements, WHILE loops, and EXIT statements may, in fact, belong to any truth value type. However, the relational operators and membership tests always produce a result of type `Boolean`.

Second, `NOT` can be applied to a one-dimensional array whose components belong to a truth value type, and `AND`, `OR`, and `XOR` can be applied to a pair of such arrays. In the case of `NOT`, the result is an array of the same array subtype in which each component has the opposite value of the corresponding component of the operand. In the case of `AND`, `OR`, and `XOR`, the two operands must belong to the same array type and have the same number of components. The result is an array in the subtype of the left operand in which each component's value is obtained by applying the operator to the corresponding components of the operands. Thus

```
(True, True, False, False) XOR (True, False, True, False)
```

is `(False, True, True, False)`. The short-circuit control forms cannot be applied to arrays of truth values.

8.3 DETAILS

8.3.1 Order of Evaluation of Operands

The rules of the Ada language do not specify the order in which the components of an expression are evaluated. The precedence levels of the operators determine that

```
A * B + C * D
```

adds the value of `A*B` to the value of `C*D` (rather than multiplying the value of `A` by the value of `B+C` and then multiplying the result by `D`). However, the rules do not specify whether the value of `A*B` or the value of `C*D` is computed first.

The only time this really matters is when one of the components of an expression is a function call, and execution of the function subprogram could change the value of another component of the expression. Then the value of the expression could depend on the order in which its components are evaluated. Since this order is not defined by the Ada language, it is incorrect to write a program that depends on a particular order.

8.3.2 Nondecimal Numeric Literals

In programs dealing directly with hardware or with assembly language software, it is often convenient to write numeric literals in some base other than base ten (decimal). An Ada numeric literal may be written in any base from two to sixteen. The usual choices besides base ten are base two (binary), base eight (octal), and base sixteen (hexadecimal), since they allow a number to be written in ways that reflect its internal representation.

An Ada numeric literal written in a base other than ten consists of the representation of the number in the other base, surrounded by number signs (#), preceded by a *base ten* number specifying the base, and optionally followed by an exponent. The numeric literal may not contain a space, but, as in a decimal numeric literal, digits can be separated by underscores. Thus `2#101#` is a numeric literal standing for the number represented in base two by the digits `101`, namely five. `16#28#`, `8#50#`, `2#101000#`, `2#0010_1000#`, `10#40#`, and `40` are all numeric literals with the same value. In bases greater than ten, the letters `A` through `F`, or their lower-case equivalents, are used as "digits" representing the values ten through fifteen, respectively. Thus `16#A1#` and `16#a1#` are alternative ways of denoting the value 161.

The number between the # symbols may contain a point, just like a decimal numeric literal. Positions to the right of the point represent successive decreasing powers of the base. Thus `8#0.24#` stands for `2*8.0**(-1) + 4*8.0**(-2)`, or `2.0/8 + 4.0/64`, or 0.3125 decimal. (Strictly speaking, the point should be called a *radix point* rather than a decimal point when the base is not ten.) As with decimal numeric literals, a numeric literal in another base is a real literal if it contains a point, and an integer literal otherwise.

The exponent represents a power of the base, so that `2#111#E3` is equal to `2#111#` multiplied by two to the third power. The exponent itself is always written in base ten. Assuming that *n* is positive, an exponent of *n* is equivalent to shifting the point *n* places to the right (adding trailing zeroes if necessary), and an exponent of -*n* is equivalent to shifting the point *n* places to the left (adding leading zeroes if necessary). This is true regardless of the base: `111E3` equals `111000`, and `2#111#E3` equals `2#111000#`; `111.0E-3` equals `0.111`, and `2#111.0#E-3` equals `2#0.111#`. An exponent with a minus sign may only occur in a real literal.

If `T` is an integer type, then a string forming a nondecimal numeric literal optionally preceded by a sign may be used as a parameter to the function `T'Value`. For example, `T'Value("-2#1010_0101#")` is -165. If `S` is a string whose characters form an unsigned hexadecimal number, then

```
Integer'Image ( Integer'Value ("16#" & S & "#") )
```

is a string whose characters form the equivalent decimal number.

8.3.3 Accuracy of Fixed-Point and Floating-Point Arithmetic*

The values in fixed-point and floating-point types are approximations to real numbers. A real literal used as a value in a particular fixed-point or floating-point type really denotes a value in that type that approximates the specified number. Furthermore, the exact mathematical product, quotient, sum, or difference of two values in a fixed-point or floating-point type may be a number that is not itself a

*This section is optional. It will be of interest primarily to those concerned with numerical properties of programs.

value of the type. In such a case, the Ada operator `*`, `/`, `+`, or `-` actually computes an *approximation* to the mathematical product, quotient, sum, or difference of the operands.

The following operations involving a fixed-point type have an exact mathematical result that is always another value in the fixed-point type, provided that the result is within the range of the type:

addition or subtraction of two values in the fixed-point type
multiplication of a value in the fixed-point type by a value in the predefined type `Integer`

Multiplication of two values in fixed-point types produces an exact fixed-point result, but this result must be immediately converted to some specified type, and this conversion may involve approximation. Any other operation involving a fixed-point or floating-point type may produce a result that only approximates the exact mathematical result.

Round-off error is a serious problem in programs that control physical devices, especially when reliability is critical. Small errors can accumulate during the course of a computation to give significantly incorrect results. For this reason, the Ada language carefully defines the minimum accuracy you may expect from arithmetic operations in a particular type. It does so in a way that depends on the declarations of fixed-point and floating-point types rather than the characteristics of the computer running the program. This makes it easy to write a program that will run with a guaranteed degree of accuracy on any machine for which the program can be compiled.

We have already explained the basic principles determining the accuracy of fixed-point and floating-point types. A type declaration of the form

```
TYPE identifier IS DIGITS n;
```

declares a floating-point type accurate to *n* decimal digits, and one of the form

```
TYPE identifier IS DELTA d RANGE low .. high;
```

declares a fixed-point type accurate to within plus or minus *d*. However, for those who are concerned with the exact mathematical behavior of their programs, the Ada language provides a precise mathematical definition of what it means for a type to have a certain accuracy.

Based on the `DIGITS`, `DELTA`, and `RANGE` values specified in a fixed-point or floating-point type declaration, there is a set of *model numbers* that must be included among the values in the type. That is, model numbers are those real numbers whose values are guaranteed to be represented exactly. Other real numbers may be either represented exactly or approximated by a value in the type, depending on the implementation. In particular, there is a set of numbers called *safe numbers* for which an implementation may provide exact representations. The safe numbers provide the same degree of precision as the model numbers but may extend over a wider range. The safe numbers of a type always include its model numbers.

Suppose a real literal is used as a value in a particular fixed-point or floating-point type, but the real number named by the literal is not a model number of the type. Assuming that the real number is within the declared range of the type, it is guaranteed to be approximated by either the next lower model number, the next higher model number, or some value in between. Similarly, suppose an arithmetic operation is applied to two values in a fixed-point or floating-point type and the mathematical result is within the declared range of that type but is not represented exactly in the type. The result of the Ada arithmetic operation is guaranteed to be either the model number just below the mathematical result, the model number just above the mathematical result, or some closer approximation.

When two expressions *e1* and *e2* have values that are not guaranteed to have at least one model number between them, *e1* < *e2* may be true in some implementations, *e1* = *e2* may be true in others, and *e1* > *e2* may be true in still others. Thus it is usually risky to make the course of a computation depend on a Boolean expression of the form *e1* = *e2* or *e1* /= *e2*, where *e1* and *e2* belong to a fixed-point or floating-point type. Rather than testing for exact equality, programs generally check for *proximity* between fixed-point or floating-point values. The values of *e1* and *e2* are deemed close enough to be considered equal when `ABS(e1-e2) < Epsilon` for some carefully chosen very small number `Epsilon`.

8.3.3.1 Model numbers of a fixed-point subtype. The model numbers of a fixed-point subtype declared with an accuracy constraint of

```
DELTA d
```

and a range constraint of

```
RANGE low .. high
```

are determined as follows: Let s be the largest positive or negative power of two less than or equal to d. (For instance, $s = 4$ when $d = 5$ and $s = 0.0625 = 2^{-4}$ when $d = 0.1$.) Let n be the smallest power of two such that $-n*s \leq low$ and $n*s \geq high$. Then the model numbers of the subtype are the following $2n$-1 multiples of s:

$$-(n-1)*s,\ -(n-2)*s,\ \ldots,\ -1*s,\ \ldots,\ (n-2)*s,\ (n-1)*s$$

In addition, the implementation may provide safe numbers that are higher and lower multiples of s. For each safe number x, $-x$ must also be a safe number.

For example, consider the following declarations:

```
Pi : CONSTANT := 3.14159;
TYPE Angle_Type IS DELTA 0.1 RANGE 0.0 .. 2*Pi;
```

Since $2^{-3} = 1/8 = 0.125$ is greater than 0.1 and $2^{-4} = 1/16 = 0.0625$ is less than 0.1, 1/16 is chosen as the value for *s*. The model numbers of type `Angle_Type` will be multiples of 0.0625. Now `2*Pi` = 6.28318, so 2^6 * 0.0625, or 4.0000, is less than `2*Pi`, but 2^7 * 0.0625, or 8.0000, is greater than or equal to `2*Pi`. Therefore, $2^7 =$ 128 is chosen as the value for *n*. The model numbers of `Angle_Type` are

-127/16, -126/16, ..., -1/16, 0, 1/16, ..., 126/16, 127/16,

or

-7.9375, -7.8750, ..., -0.0625, 0.0000, 0.0625, ..., 7.8750, 7.9375

The declaration

```
x : Angle_Type := Pi;
```

will initialize `x` to some approximation of `3.14159`. Since 3.1250 = 50/16 is the next lower model number and 3.1875 = 51/16 is the next higher model number, the approximation chosen is guaranteed to be no lower than 3.1250 and no higher than 3.1875. Thus it is within the declared `DELTA` value of `0.1`.

8.3.3.2 Model numbers of a floating-point subtype. The model numbers of a floating-point subtype with an accuracy constraint of

`DIGITS` *d*

are determined as follows: Let *b* be one more than the number of binary digits required to hold as much information as *d* decimal digits. Values of *b* are given in Figure 8.5 for values of *d* ranging from one to twenty. (In each case, the value of *b* is one more than the integer above *d**(log(10)/log(2)). Thus *b* is slightly more than 1 + 3.32*d*.) The model numbers consist of zero and all values that can be written in the form

sign * *mantissa* * $2^{exponent}$

where *sign* is either -1 or +1, *exponent* is an integer in the range `-4*`*b* `..` `4*`*b*, and *mantissa* is a binary fraction consisting of a point followed by *b* binary digits, the first of which is a `1`. For example, if *d* = 1, then *b* = 5, and the possible values of the mantissa, written as base two fractions, are

```
2#0.10000#     2#0.10100#     2#0.11000#     2#0.11100#
2#0.10001#     2#0.10101#     2#0.11001#     2#0.11101#
2#0.10010#     2#0.10110#     2#0.11010#     2#0.11110#
2#0.10011#     2#0.10111#     2#0.11011#     2#0.11111#
```

(or, in decimal notation, 16/32, 17/32, 18/32, and so forth, up to 31/32). In general, the mantissa can be any value of the form $i/2^b$ where i is an integer in the range 2^{b-1} .. 2^b-1. The lowest possible value of the mantissa is always one half and the largest is slightly less than one.

(Any number greater than one can be repeatedly halved, or any number less than one half repeatedly doubled, to obtain a number greater than or equal to one half and less than one. The number obtained is the original number times a positive or negative power of two. Thus any positive real number can be written in the form $m \star 2^k$ where k is an integer and $1/2 \leqslant m < 1$. This is equivalent to writing the number as a binary fraction, sliding the binary point just to the left of the leftmost one, and adjusting the exponent accordingly. It is the binary version of scientific notation.)

In addition to the model numbers, an implementation may provide exact representations of *safe numbers.* These are zero and numbers of the form

$$sign \star mantissa \star 2^{exponent}$$

with *sign* and *mantissa* as before, but with *exponent* allowed to range from -*n* to *n* for some value of *n* greater than 4*b*. The model numbers are a subset of the safe numbers.

d	b	mantissa values		exponent range
1	5	i/32,	i = 16,...,31	−20 to 20
2	8	i/256,	i = 128,...,255	−32 to 32
3	11	i/2048,	i = 1024,...,2047	−44 to 44
4	15	i/32768,	i = 16384,...,32767	−60 to 60
5	18	i/262144,	i = 131072,...,262143	−72 to 72
6	21	i/2097152,	i = 1048576,...,2097151	−84 to 84
7	25	i/33554432,	i = 16777216,...,33554431	−100 to 100
8	28	i/268435456,	i = 134217728,...,268435455	−112 to 112
9	31	i/2147483648,	i = 1073741824,...,2147483647	−124 to 124
10	35	i/34359738368,	i = 17179869184,...,34359738367	−140 to 140
11	38	i/274877906944,	i = 137438953472,...,274877906943	−152 to 152
12	41	i/2199023255552,	i = 1099511627776,...,2199023255551	−164 to 164
13	45	i/35184372088832,	i = 17592186044416,...,35184372088831	−180 to 180
14	48	i/281474976710656,	i = 140737488355328,...,281474976710655	−192 to 192
15	51	i/2251799813685248,	i = 1125899906842624,...,2251799813685247	−204 to 204
16	55	i/36028797018963968,	i = 18014398509481984,...,36028797018963967	−220 to 220
17	58	i/288230376151711744,	i = 144115188075855872,...,288230376151711743	−232 to 232
18	61	i/2305843009213693952,	i = 1152921504606846976,...,2305843009213693951	−244 to 244
19	65	i/36893488147419103232,	i = 18446744073709551616,...,36893488147419103231	−260 to 260
20	68	i/295147905179352825856,	i = 147573952589676412928,...,295147905179352825855	−272 to 272

Figure 8.5 Model numbers for floating-point subtypes. The number d is the number of decimal digits of precision specified in the type or subtype declaration. The number b is the number of binary digits needed to achieve that precision. Mantissa values consist of fractions of the form indicated in the third column, with the numerator i taking on values in the specified range. (In each case, the lowest mantissa value is one half and the highest is slightly higher than one.) For a given d, all numbers of the form $s \star m \star 2^e$ are model numbers, where s is −1 or 1, m is one of the mantissa values, and e is an exponent in the indicated range.

When a floating-point subtype has a range constraint, the range constraint is not used in determining the model numbers of the subtype. To the contrary, the model numbers are derived from the accuracy constraint, and any range constraint provided for a floating-point subtype is *then* checked to make sure that the lower and upper bounds are within the range of the lowest and highest safe numbers. If not, the range constraint is illegal.

Let's examine how the literal `3.14159` would be represented in a type with the declaration

```
TYPE Radians_Type IS DIGITS 4;
```

By repeated halving to obtain a mantissa greater than or equal to one half and less than one, we discover that $3.14159 = 1.570795 * 2^1 = 0.7853975 * 2^2$. Thus the model numbers surrounding 3.14159 will have a sign of +1, a mantissa approximating 0.7853975, and an exponent of two. As shown in Figure 8.5, fourteen binary digits are required to represent four decimal digits. The possible mantissa values using fifteen binary digits range from 16384/32768 (or one half) to 32767/32768 (or just less than one) in increments of 1/32768. In particular, 25735/32768, or 0.785367893048675, is just less than 0.7853975, and 25736/32768, or 0.785400390625000, is just greater. Thus the model numbers of `Radians_Type` surrounding 3.14159 are $0.785367893048675 * 2^2$, or 3.141479492187500, and $0.785400390625000 * 2^2$, or 3.141601562500000. The internal representation used to approximate 3.14159 will be one of these two values or some value in between. As expected from the type declaration, the approximation is accurate to four significant decimal digits.

8.3.4 Attributes of Fixed-Point and Floating-Point Subtypes

There are several attributes describing characteristics of fixed-point and floating-point subtypes. These attributes all name numeric values. This section describes seven attributes meaningful for both fixed-point and floating-point subtypes, one attribute meaningful only for fixed-point subtypes, and four attributes meaningful only for floating-point subtypes. These attributes are useful primarily for programmers with a sophisticated understanding of computer arithmetic and numerical analysis.

The attributes meaningful for both fixed-point and floating-point subtypes are designated `'First`, `'Last`, `'Small`, `'Large`, `'Safe_Small`, `'Safe_Large`, and `'Mantissa`. If `T` is the name of a fixed-point or floating-point subtype, then `T'First` is the smallest number with an exact representation in the subtype, and `T'Last` is the largest number with an exact representation in the subtype. While the subtype is required to have an exact representation for each model number, it may have exact representations for other numbers as well, so `T'First` and `T'Last` need not be model numbers. In contrast, `T'Small` and `T'Large` name the smallest and largest *positive model numbers* of the subtype, respectively. The attribute `T'Safe_Small` names the value of the smallest *positive safe number* of subtype `T`, and the attribute `T'Safe_Large` names the largest such number. When

`T` is a fixed-point subtype, `T'Mantissa` is the number of binary digits required to represent n-1, the largest number by which s is multiplied to obtain a model number. (The numbers s and n used in defining the model numbers of a fixed-point subtype were defined in Section 8.3.3. Since n is defined to be a power of two, `T'Mantissa` will always be exactly the logarithm of n to the base two.) When `T` is a floating-point subtype, `T'Mantissa` is the number of binary digits in the mantissa of the model numbers, as described in Section 8.3.3. (This is the number b given in Figure 8.5.)

The attribute meaningful only for fixed-point subtypes is designated `'Delta`. If `T` names a fixed-point subtype, then `T'Delta` names the interval between approximations specified for `T` in a type or subtype declaration. This is the value d of Section 8.3.3. The value s actually used in defining model numbers is the largest power of two less than or equal to d. Since $1*s$ is the smallest positive model number of `T` (by the definition of model numbers), the value of s is given by the attribute `T'Small` described earlier.

The attributes meaningful only for floating-point subtypes are designated `'Digits`, `'Epsilon`, `'EMax`, and `'Safe_EMax`. If `T` names a floating-point subtype, then `T'Digits` names the number of decimal digits of precision specified for `T` in a type or subtype declaration. `T'Epsilon` names the distance from 1.0 to the next higher model number of `T`. If $1/(2k)$ is the increment between mantissa values given in Figure 8.5, then $1.0 = (k/(2k)) * 2^1$, so the next model number above 1.0 is $((k+1)/(2k)) * 2^1$. Thus `T'Epsilon` is equal to $(1/(2k)) * 2^1$, or twice the increment between mantissa values. The attribute `T'EMax` names the exponent part of the highest model number of `T`. By the definition of floating-point model numbers, this is four times `T'Mantissa`. `T'Safe_EMax` names the exponent part `T`'s largest safe number. It is analogous to `T'Safe_Small` and `T'Safe_Large`, described previously.

8.3.5 Static Expressions and Static Subtypes

Section 4.3.1 introduced *static expressions*. In certain contexts where the compiler must know the value of an expression to check the legality of the program or to produce efficient object code, the language rules require an expression to be static. Static expressions always have the same value, and this value can be determined when a program is being compiled. However, not all expressions with these properties are static expressions. This section gives an exact definition of static expressions.

Certain subtype declarations—for instance, those in the declarative part of a block statement—may be elaborated many times during the course of a computation, and the subtype may consist of different values each time. For example, the following program copies each integer in the input file to the output file in a bizarre way:

```
WITH Basic_IO;
PROCEDURE Funny_Copy IS
   n : Integer;
```

```
BEGIN
   WHILE NOT Basic_IO.End_Of_File LOOP
      Basic_IO.Get(n);
      DECLARE
         SUBTYPE Dummy_Subtype IS Integer RANGE 1 .. n;
      BEGIN
         Basic_IO.Put(Dummy_Subtype'Last);
      END;
      Basic_IO.New_Line;
   END LOOP;
END Funny_Copy;
```

The declaration of `Dummy_Subtype` is elaborated anew each time the block statement is entered and each time it defines a new subtype whose last value is the current value of `n`.

Most of the time, however, the bounds in a subtype declaration are static expressions, so the values in the subtype do not vary during the execution of the program. A subtype of a numeric or enumeration type is called a *static subtype* when it consists of every value in the type or when it consists of a subset defined by a range constraint whose lower and upper bounds are both static expressions. `Dummy_Subtype` is *not* a static subtype. However, because enumeration literals are static expressions, the declarations

```
TYPE Day_Type IS
   (Sunday, Monday, Tuesday, Wednesday, Thursday, Friday,
    Saturday);
SUBTYPE Weekday_Subtype IS Day_Type RANGE Monday .. Friday;
```

establish both `Day_Type` and `Weekday_Subtype` as static subtypes.

A static expression is an expression in an *enumeration* type or a *numeric* type in which the elementary expressions connected by the operators are each of one of the following:

A literal (either a numeric literal, a character literal, or another enumeration literal)
A named number
A constant declared in a declaration of the form

```
identifier , ~~~ , identifier :
   CONSTANT subtype indication := expression ;
```

provided that the subtype indication specifies a static subtype and the expression is a static expression

An attribute of the form `T'`*attribute-designator* or a function call of the form `T'`*attribute-designator* `(`*expression*`)`, where `T` is a static subtype (not an array subtype, since only subtypes of numeric and enumeration types can be static), the attribute designator names one of the language-defined attributes (not an implementation-defined one), and the expression, if present, is a static expression

A qualified expression of the form *typemark*' (*expression*), where the typemark names a static subtype and the expression is a static expression

For example, consider the following declarations, where Time_Of_Day is assumed to be a function returning a value of type Integer giving the current time of day in seconds:

```
Seconds_Per_Hour : CONSTANT := 60 * 60;
Present_Time     : CONSTANT Integer := Time_Of_Day;
Closing_Time     : CONSTANT Integer := 17 * Seconds_Per_Hour;

SUBTYPE Time_Subtype IS
   Integer RANGE Present_Time .. Closing_Time;

SUBTYPE Afternoon_Time_Subtype IS
   Integer RANGE 12 * Seconds_Per_Hour .. Closing_Time;

x : CONSTANT Time_Subtype := 43200;
y : Afternoon_Time_Subtype := 46800;
```

The literal 17 and the named number Seconds_Per_Hour are both static expressions; so, therefore, is 17 * Seconds_Per_Hour. Furthermore, the type Integer (viewed as a subtype) is a static subtype. Therefore, the constant Closing_Time is a static expression. However, the function call Time_Of_Day is not a static expression. Therefore, the constant Present_Time cannot be static. It follows that Time_Subtype is not a static subtype. However, 12 * Seconds_Per_Hour is a static expression, so Afternoon_Time_Subtype *is* a static subtype. The constant x is not a static expression, even though its initial value is static, because its subtype is not static; y is not a static expression because it is a variable. Afternoon_Time_Subtype'Last is a static expression, but Time_Subtype'Last is not. (Even though the upper bound of Time_Subtype is given by a static expression, what matters is that the subtype itself is not static.) The expression

```
Afternoon_Time_Subtype'Pred (Afternoon_Time_Subtype'Last)
```

is static, but

```
Afternoon_Time_Subtype'Pred (y)
```

is not. The qualified expression

```
Afternoon_Time_Subtype'(44000)
```

is a static expression, but the qualified expressions

```
Time_Subtype'(44000)
```

and

```
Afternoon_Time_Subtype'(y)
```

are not.

Here are the contexts we have seen so far in which an expression must be static:

The upper and lower bounds of ranges in integer, fixed-point, and floating-point *type* declarations must be static. However, a range constraint in a *subtype* declaration need not have static bounds.

The number *d* in an accuracy constraint of the form `DIGITS` *d* or `DELTA` *d* must be given by a static expression, whether it occurs in a type declaration or a subtype declaration.

The initial value specified in a named number declaration must be a static expression. However, the initial value of a constant declaration (in which a subtype indication follows the word `CONSTANT`) need not be static. Given the function `Time_Of_Day` described earlier,

```
Now : CONSTANT Integer := Time_Of_Day;
```

is legal, but

```
Now : CONSTANT := Time_Of_Day;
```

is not, because `Time_Of_Day` is not a static expression.

In attributes of the form `T'First(`*n*`)`, `T'Last(`*n*`)`, `T'Length(`*n*`)`, and `T'Range(`*n*`)`, where `T` names an array object or a constrained array subtype, the expression *n* must be static. The effect is as if a three-dimensional array `A`, for instance, has three distinct attributes named `T'First(1)`, `T'First(2)`, and `T'First(3)`, each of which can be recognized by the compiler.

Each choice list in a `CASE` statement (see Section 7.3.2) must contain only static expressions. Thus the values for which a given arm of the `CASE` statement will be selected are determined when the program is compiled.

The list of choices in a named array aggregate (see Section 8.1.5) must contain only static expressions and (in discrete ranges) static subtypes. This allows the array positions that will receive the specified component values to be determined when the program is compiled. This restriction applies to the expressions to the left of the `=>` symbol, not those to its right. For example, in the aggregate

```
(A | B => C, D .. E | F => G)
```

the expressions `A`, `B`, `D`, `E`, and `F` must be static, but `C` and `G` need not be.

Other contexts requiring static expressions will be pointed out as those contexts are introduced.

8.3.6 Universal Expressions

Universal expressions were introduced in Section 4.3.2. They include numeric literals, named numbers, and certain other expressions. This section describes universal expressions in greater detail.

Technically, universal integer expressions, including all numeric literals without decimal points, belong to a special type called *universal_integer;* universal real expressions, including all numeric literals with decimal points, belong to a special type called *universal_real.* We write these types in italics because they cannot be named in an Ada program. Thus variable declarations, subtype declarations, and so forth cannot refer to these types. When a *universal_integer* expression occurs in a place where a value in some ordinary integer type is required, the value of the expression is implicitly *converted* to the required type. Similarly, when a *universal_real* expression occurs in a place where a value in some ordinary fixed-point or floating-point type is required, the value of the expression is implicitly *converted* to the required type.

Universal expressions are required in certain contexts. The static expression *n* in the attributes `T'First(`*n*`)`, `T'Last(`*n*`)`, `T'Length(`*n*`)`, and `T'Range(`*n*`)` must be of type *universal_integer.* The static expression giving the initial value of a named number must be either a *universal_integer* or *universal_real* expression. After elaboration of its declaration, the named number may then be used as an expression of the same universal type.

In addition to numeric literals and named numbers, the values named by certain attributes belong to universal types. The attributes `T'Delta`, `T'Small`, `T'Large`, `T'Safe_Small`, `T'Safe_Large`, and `T'Epsilon` all name values of type *universal_real.* The attributes `T'Digits`, `T'EMax`, `T'Safe_EMax`, `T'Mantissa`, `T'Pos`, `T'Length`, and `T'Length(`*n*`)` all name values of type *universal_integer.*

Finally, arithmetic expressions composed entirely of subexpressions in a universal type belong to a universal type themselves. Any arithmetic operation that can be applied to values in an integer type can be applied to *universal_ integer* values to produce a *universal_integer* result. Any arithmetic operation that can be applied to values in a floating-point type can be applied to *universal_real* values to produce a *universal_real* result. In addition, a *universal_real* value and a *universal_integer* value may be multiplied together, a *universal_real* value may be divided by a *universal_integer* value, or a *universal_real* value may be raised to a *universal_integer* power to produce a *universal_real* result.

Whether an expression is static and whether it is universal are two independent properties. Numeric literals are both static and universal, as are named numbers. Numeric constants may be static (if their initial values are given by static expressions), but not universal. (Constants belong to ordinary types, not *universal_integer* or *universal_real.*) Attributes with universal values may or may not be static. (Attributes of static numeric and enumeration subtypes are always static, but by definition, attributes of arrays and array subtypes never are.)

The precision with which a *universal_real* expression is evaluated depends on whether or not it is static. Evaluation of a nonstatic *universal_real* expression is performed with at least as much precision as the corresponding computation in the most precise ordinary floating-point type. Evaluation of a static *universal_real* expression produces an exact result, but implicit conversion of this value to some fixed-point or floating-point type causes the value to be approximated according to the representation for that type.

8.3.7 More on Attributes

Most of the attribute designators are not reserved words, but three—`Delta`, `Digits`, and `Range`—are. Attribute designators that are not reserved words may be used as ordinary identifiers. A program may contain a variable named `Epsilon` or `Pred`, for example. For the sake of uniformity in writing attributes, this book capitalizes the words `DELTA`, `DIGITS`, and `RANGE` when they are used in their reserved sense but only capitalizes the first letter when they are used as attribute designators.

Certain attributes that are functions are not defined for all argument values of the appropriate type. For any numeric or enumeration *base* type `T`, `T'Pred(T'First)` and `T'Succ(T'Last)` are not defined. However, if `T` is a *subtype* of a larger type, it is possible for these expressions to produce well-defined results in the larger type. For example, given the declarations

```
TYPE Day_Type IS
   (Sunday, Monday, Tuesday, Wednesday, Thursday, Friday,
    Saturday);
SUBTYPE Weekday_Subtype IS Day_Type RANGE Monday .. Friday;
```

the expression `Weekday_Subtype'Pred(Weekday_Subtype'First)` is perfectly legitimate, and produces the `Day_Type` value `Sunday`. Similarly, `T'Val (`*n*`)` is not defined if *n* is not a valid position number for the base type of subtype `T`; `T'Value (`*s*`)` is not defined if the string *s* is not a valid enumeration literal or optionally signed integer literal for the base type of subtype `T`. However, `Weekday_Subtype'Val (0)` and `Weekday_Subtype'Value ("Sunday")` are both legitimate `Day_Type` expressions equal to `Sunday`.

The attributes `T'Pos` and `T'Val` are defined not only if `T` is an enumeration subtype, but also if `T` is an integer subtype. The position number of a value in an integer subtype is the number itself. Thus, given the declaration

```
One : CONSTANT Integer := 1;
```

the expression `Integer'Pos (One)` is a universal integer expression with the value one; and `Integer'Val (1) = 1`.

8.3.8 Base Types

There is an attribute, `T'Base`, that names the base type of subtype `T`. This attribute cannot stand alone but must be used as part of a longer attribute, as in

T'Base'First. However, care must be taken in using this attribute, because the base type of a subtype is not always what it appears to be.

Given the enumeration type and subtype declarations

```
TYPE Suit_Type IS (Clubs, Diamonds, Hearts, Spades);
SUBTYPE Major_Suit_Subtype IS
   Suit_Type RANGE Hearts .. Spades;
```

the base type of Major_Suit_Subtype is Suit_Type. Suit_Type can also be viewed as a subtype consisting of all four values Clubs, Diamonds, Hearts, and Spades. The base type of the subtype Suit_Type is Suit_Type itself.

You might expect that for any typemark T declared in a type declaration, the base type of T, viewed as a subtype, is always T itself. Unfortunately, matters are not quite that simple. In some cases, the type declaration for T really declares a larger type that includes all the values specified in the type declaration plus some additional values and then declares T to be a subtype of that type, containing only the values actually specified in the type declaration. The larger type is called an *anonymous* type because there is no identifier naming it. It is this anonymous type that is named by T'Base in an attribute such as T'Base'First.

Most of the time, the programmer need not even be aware of the existence of the anonymous type. If you think of T as being a base type in its own right, you will usually not be surprised by the behavior of a program. The details in this subsection are important only for programs that use the attribute T'Base and programs with arithmetic expressions whose intermediate results exceed the declared bounds of their type.

When you declare a numeric type, the compiler chooses a method for representing the values in that type internally. The method chosen must provide a unique representation for each value required by the type declaration. In the case of an integer type declaration of the form

```
TYPE t IS RANGE a .. b;
```

this includes every integer value from *a* up to *b*. In the case of a fixed-point or floating-point type, this includes every model number of the type, as described in Section 8.3.3. Often, the method chosen will be capable of representing many other numbers as well. For example, given the declaration

```
TYPE Serial_Number_Type IS RANGE 0 .. 9999;
```

a compiler might choose an internal representation using sixteen bits (because the machine that is to run the program has machine-language instructions for performing arithmetic on sixteen-bit integers). However, sixteen-bit signed integers can range from -32768 to 32767.

In general, a numeric type declaration declares a type containing each value in the internal representation chosen by the compiler and then uses the name specified in the type declaration to name a subtype of that type. For instance, with a compiler choosing to represent Serial_Number_Type values as sixteen-bit signed integers, the declaration of Serial_Number_Type is really equivalent to the two declarations

```
TYPE anonymous_base_type IS RANGE -32768 .. 32767;
SUBTYPE Serial_Number_Type IS
    anonymous_base_type RANGE 0 .. 9999;
```

Even though Serial_Number_Type variables may only contain numbers in the range 0 .. 9999, evaluation of a Serial_Number_Type expression may produce an intermediate result that is not in this range. For example, consider the execution of the statement

```
Serial_Number := (Serial_Number + 1) MOD 10_000;
```

where Serial_Number is a Serial_Number_Type variable initially containing the value 9,999. The result of the addition is 10,000, which is not in the subtype Serial_Number_Type, but is in the anonymous base type. Since the MOD operation yields the value zero, which is in Serial_Number_Type, the assignment statement works correctly. The fact that 10,000 is part of the anonymous base type reflects the fact that the compiler is using an internal representation for Serial_Number_Type values that is capable of representing the number 10,000. In contrast, the assignment statement

```
Serial_Number := Serial_Number * 10 MOD 10_000;
```

might not have succeeded if Serial_Number were initially 9,999, even though the ultimate mathematical value of the expression is in Serial_Number_Type, because the intermediate result of the multiplication, 99,990, is not in the anonymous base type. Since the range of the anonymous base type depends on the compiler, you can use the attributes Serial_Number_Type'Base'First and Serial_Number_Type'Base'Last to name the lowest and highest intermediate values that evaluation of Serial_Number_Type expressions may safely produce.

The base type of a derived type is a copy of the base type of the subtype specified in the derived-type declaration. The typemark declared in a derived-type declaration names a subtype of this base type. Thus, if *bt* is a typemark naming a base type and *c* is a constraint, then the derived-type declaration

```
TYPE dt IS NEW bt c;
```

is equivalent to the following two declarations:

```
TYPE anonymous_derived_base_type IS NEW bt;
SUBTYPE dt IS anonymous_derived_base_type c;
```

The same equivalence applies to a derived-type declaration having some other subtype indication equivalent to *bt c*. For example, given

```
TYPE Day_Type IS
   (Sunday, Monday, Tuesday, Wednesday, Thursday, Friday,
    Saturday);
SUBTYPE Weekday_Subtype IS Day_Type RANGE Monday .. Friday;
```

the declaration

```
TYPE Derived_Weekday_Type IS NEW Weekday_Subtype;
```

is equivalent to

```
TYPE anonymous_derived_base_type IS NEW Day_Type;
SUBTYPE Derived_Weekday_Type IS
   anonymous_derived_base_type RANGE Monday .. Friday;
```

A constrained array type declaration declares an array subtype whose base type is an unconstrained array type. Thus the declaration

```
TYPE Matrix IS ARRAY (1 .. 10, 1 .. 10) OF Float;
```

is equivalent to the following two declarations:

```
TYPE anonymous_base_type IS
   ARRAY (Integer RANGE <>, Integer RANGE <>) OF Float;
SUBTYPE Matrix IS anonymous_base_type (1 ..10, 1 .. 10);
```

Technically, there are no constrained array types, only constrained subtypes of unconstrained array types. Given the declarations

```
TYPE Row_Of_10 IS ARRAY (1 .. 10) OF Integer;
R : Row_Of_10;
```

the slices `R (1 .. 3)` and `R (4 .. 10)` belong to different subtypes of the base type of `Row_Of_10`. (Since the slices cannot possibly belong to `Row_Of_10` itself because of their sizes, there is no other way to explain the type of the slices and why the assignment

```
R := R (4 .. 10) & R (1 .. 3);
```

is legal. When the operator `&` is applied to catenate two arrays, both arrays must belong to the same type, and the result is also of that type.)

8.3.9 More on Aggregates

When OTHERS occurs in an array aggregate, it stands for all index positions not specified earlier in the aggregate. However, these positions depend on the lower and upper bounds of the subtype to which the aggregate belongs. For example, given the declarations

```
TYPE Row_Type IS ARRAY (Integer RANGE <>) OF Integer;
A : Row_Type (1 .. 5) := (10, 20, OTHERS => 0);
B : Row_Type (0 .. 10) := (10, 20, OTHERS => 0);
```

the same aggregate stands for two different array values. In the declaration for A, OTHERS is a shorthand for 3 .. 5. In the declaration for B, OTHERS is a shorthand for 2 .. 10.

Because of this potential ambiguity, array aggregates containing OTHERS are only allowed in certain contexts in which the type and index bounds of the aggregate are obvious. Specifically, a *named* array aggregate specifying certain positions by the word OTHERS may occur in the following places:

in a qualified expression whose typemark names a *constrained* array subtype
as a component of a larger array or record aggregate

The second context arises with arrays of arrays and with records containing components that are arrays. When nested array aggregates are used to specify a value in a multidimensional array type, OTHERS is not allowed at any level of nesting unless the entire multidimensional aggregate appears in one of the contexts specified above.

In addition, a *positional* aggregate containing an OTHERS part, or an aggregate containing only an OTHERS part, may appear in the following contexts:

as the expression following the symbol := (in a declaration with an initial value or in an assignment statement, for example)
as a parameter in a procedure call or function call, provided that the subprogram specifies a *constrained* array subtype to which that parameter must belong
as the expression following the word RETURN in a RETURN statement in a function, provided that the function subprogram specifies a *constrained* array subtype to which its result must belong

When a component expression in an aggregate applies to more than one component position, the expression is reevaluated once for each component to which it applies. For example, given the declarations

```
TYPE Integer_Pointer_Type IS ACCESS Integer;
TYPE Integer_Pointer_List_Type IS
   ARRAY (Positive RANGE <>) OF Integer_Pointer_Type;
List :
   Integer_Pointer_List_Type (1 .. 10) :=
      (OTHERS => NEW Integer'(0));
```

ten Integer variables are dynamically allocated.

8.4 SUMMARY

There are seven kinds of elementary expressions:

literals
names, including identifiers, names of array and record components, names of allocated variables, and attributes
aggregates
qualified expressions
type conversions
allocators
function calls

Operators, short-circuit control forms, and membership tests combine these elementary expressions to form compound expressions.

Literals include numeric literals, string literals, enumeration literals, and the literal `NULL`. There are four kinds of numeric literals, depicted in Figure 8.6. String literals such as

```
"I am a string literal."
```

denote sequences of characters, with occurrences of a quotation mark (") within the sequence denoted by two consecutive quotation marks. Enumeration literals may be identifiers or character literals. The literal `NULL` denotes an access value that does not designate any object.

Names include declared identifiers, indexed components, slices, selected components, and attributes. All except attributes were discussed in Chapter 4. (Names for allocated variables and their components were discussed in Section 5.3.) The form of an attribute is

x ' *attribute-designator*

where *x* is the name of some entity such as a variable or a subtype and the attribute designator is an identifier with a special language-defined or implementation-defined meaning. An attribute may stand for a value, a range of values, a type, or a function.

	Integer Literals	Real Literals
Decimal Literals	43210 43_210 4321E1	43_210.0 4.321E4 432100.0E-1
Based Literals	2#11_11#E4 8#260# 16#F0#	2#1.11# 8#0.007#E3 16#ABCD.0#E-2

Figure 8.6 Numeric literals may be integer literals or numeric literals and may be written in decimal or based notation. Examples are given for each of the four possible combinations.

The attributes introduced in this chapter are summarized in Figure 8.7. The range attribute can be used in place of a range of the form

low .. *high*

in range constraints and discrete ranges. In particular, a loop to be executed with i taking on successive index values of the one-dimensional array *x* can be written as follows:

```
FOR i IN x'Range LOOP
  ...
END LOOP;
```

Aggregates are expressions denoting array or record values. A one-dimensional array aggregate may be positional, such as

```
("12", " 1", " 2", " 3", " 4", " 5",
 " 6", " 7", " 8", " 9", "10", "11",
 "12", " 1", " 2", " 3", " 4", " 5",
 " 6", " 7", " 8", " 9", "10", "11");
```

or named, such as

```
(0 .. 11 => "AM", 12 .. 23 => "PM")
```

Attribute	Where...	Meaning
T'First	T is a numeric or enumeration subtype	the first value in T
T'Last	T is a numeric or enumeration subtype	the last value in T
T'Pred	T is an integer or enumeration subtype	a function taking a value in T and returning the previous value
T'Succ	T is an integer or enumeration subtype	a function taking a value in T and returning the next value
T'Pos	T is an enumeration subtype	a function taking a value in T and returning its position number, starting with zero for the first value in T's base type
T'Pos	T is an integer subtype	a function taking a value in T and returning that number itself
T'Val	T is an enumeration subtype	a function taking a position number and returning the value in T with that position number
T'Val	T is an integer subtype	a function taking an integer value and returning that number as a value of type T

Figure 8.7 Attributes of numeric types, enumeration types, array types, and array objects.

In a named array aggregate, index values and ranges of index values must be given by static expressions and static discrete ranges. An aggregate for an n-dimensional array v, where $n > 1$, is written as if it were an aggregate for a one-dimensional array w of (n-1)-dimensional arrays, such that

$$w\ (i_1)\ (i_2,\ \ldots,\ i_n) = v\ (i_1\ i_2,\ \ldots,\ i_n)$$

A positional array aggregate of the form

(*expression* , ~~~, *expression* [, OTHERS => *expression*])

Attribute	Where...	Meaning
`T'Image`	T is an integer or enumeration subtype	a function taking a value in T and returning a string containing a character representation of that value
`T'Value`	T is an integer or enumeration subtype	a function taking a string that contains a character representation of a value in T and returning that value
`A'Range (n)`	A is a constrained array subtype or an array object	the range of index values for A in the nth dimension
`A'First (n)`	A is a constrained array subtype or an array object	the first index value for A in the nth dimension
`A'Last (n)`	A is a constrained array subtype or an array object	the last index value for A in the nth dimension
`A'Length (n)`	A is a constrained array subtype or an array object	the number of index values for A in the nth dimension
`A'Range`	A is a constrained array subtype or an array object (typically one-dimensional)	equivalent to `A'Range (1)`
`A'First`	A is a constrained array subtype or an array object (typically one-dimensional)	equivalent to `A'First (1)`
`A'Last`	A is a constrained array subtype or an array object (typically one-dimensional)	equivalent to `A'Last (1)`
`A'Length`	A is a constrained array subtype or an array object (typically one-dimensional)	equivalent to `A'Length (1)`

Figure 8.7 (*continued*)

may appear inside a qualified expression for a constrained array subtype, as a component of a larger array or record aggregate, following the symbol `:=`, as a parameter in a procedure or function call where the corresponding parameter subtype is constrained, or in a `RETURN` statement of a function whose result type is constrained. A named aggregate of the form

```
( choice | ~~~ | choice => expression ,
     ~~~
  choice | ~~~ | choice => expression ,
  OTHERS => expression )
```

may appear inside a qualified expression for a constrained array subtype or as a component of a larger array or record aggregate. In each case, `OTHERS` stands for every component position not specified earlier in the aggregate.

A record aggregate may be named, like the aggregate

```
(Name_Part      => New_File_Name,
 Extension_Part => New_File_Extension,
 Length_Part    => New_File_Length,
 Location_Part  => New_File_Location)
```

may be positional, like the aggregate

```
(1.0, 0.0)
```

or may be mixed, like the aggregate

```
(Blank_File_Name,
 Blank_File_Extension,
 Length_Part | Location_Part => 0)
```

In the mixed form, components specified in positional notation must come first. In any case, the aggregate may end with

```
OTHERS => expression
```

if there is at least one still unspecified component and if all still unspecified components are of the same type.

A qualified expression has the form

```
typemark ' ( expression )
```

and tells the compiler that the expression should be interpreted as belonging to the specified subtype. A type conversion has the form

```
typemark ( expression )
```

(without an apostrophe) and causes the value of the expression to be *converted* to the specified subtype when the type conversion is evaluated during program execution. Conversion is defined between any two numeric types; between any two types directly or indirectly derived from the same type (including between a derived type and its parent); and between two array types that have the same number of dimensions, corresponding index types that are convertible to each other, and the same component subtype. Conversion of a floating-point or fixed-point value to an integer type causes the value to be rounded.

Allocators, which dynamically create allocated variables, were described in Section 5.2. Function calls, which invoke function subprograms and evaluate to the values returned by those subprograms, will be discussed in detail in Chapter 9. The evaluation of an allocator or function call not only produces a value, but also calls for some actions to be performed.

Elementary expressions can be combined by operators, short-circuit control forms, and relational operators. The allowable forms are summarized in Figure 8.8. Expressions of the form `a ** b ** c` and `ABS a ** b` are illegal; parentheses must be added to indicate which operands go with which operators. Similarly, *different* two-operand logical operators or short-circuit control forms cannot be applied in succession without parentheses. Thus

```
a AND b AND c
```

is legal, but

```
a AND b OR c
```

is not.

Level	Left Operand	Operator	Right Operand	Result	Remarks
6	any integer type	**	subtype `Positive`	type of left operand	
	any floating-point type	**	type `Integer`	type of left operand	
	—	ABS	any numeric type	type of operand	
	—	NOT	`Boolean`	`Boolean`	
	—	NOT	array of truth values	type of operand	Applied component by component.

Figure 8.8 Summary of Ada operators. The leftmost column indicates each operator's level of precedence. Operators at higher levels are bound to operands first. Other columns describe the allowable combinations of operand types and the result type for each combination. (Strictly speaking, IN and NOT IN are not operators, but are *membership tests;* AND THEN and OR ELSE are not operators, but are *short-circuit control forms.*)

Level	Left Operand	Operator	Right Operand	Result	Remarks
5	any integer type	* /	type of left operand	type of operands	Fractional quotients truncated toward zero.
	any floating-point type	* /	type of left operand	type of operands	
	type `Integer`	*	any fixed-point type	type of right operand	No division of an `Integer` value by a fixed-point value.
	any fixed-point type	* /	type `Integer`	type of left operand	
	any fixed-point type	* /	any fixed-point type	(see remarks)	Only allowed inside a type conversion.
	any integer type	`MOD`	type of left operand	type of operands	Result has sign of right operand. Adding some multiple of right operand to result yields left operand.
	any integer type	`REM`	type of left operand	type of operands	Result has sign of left operand. Magnitude of result does not depend on sign of operands.
4	—	+ -	any numeric type	type of operand	
3	any numeric type	+ -	type of left operand	type of operands	
	any one-dimensional array type	&	type of left operand	type of operands	`"ab" & "cd" = "abcd"`
	any one-dimensional array type	&	type of left operand's components	type of left operand	`"ab" & 'c' = "abc"`
	type of right operand's components	&	any one-dimensional array type	type of right operand	`'a' & "bc" = "abc"`
	any type	&	type of left operand	one-dimensional array type with components of the operand type	`'a' & 'b' = "ab"`

Figure 8.8 *(continued)*

Level	Left Operand	Operator	Right Operand	Result	Remarks
	any type	= /=	type of left operand	Boolean	
	any numeric or enumeration type	< <= > >=	type of left operand	Boolean	
2	any one-dimensional array type with integer or enumeration type components	< <= > >=	type of left operand	Boolean	lexicographic ordering
	any type	IN NOT IN	(any range or typemark with the base type of the left operand)	Boolean	Right operand is not really an expression.
	Boolean	AND OR XOR	Boolean	Boolean	
1	one-dimensional array of truth values	AND OR XOR	type of left operand (same length)	type of operands	Applied component by component.
	Boolean	AND THEN	Boolean	Boolean	Right operand not evaluated if left operand is false.
	Boolean	OR ELSE	Boolean	Boolean	Right operand not evaluated if left operand is true.

Figure 8.8 (*continued*)

EXERCISES

8.1 The following declarations were given at the beginning of this chapter:

```
TYPE Inning_Score_List_Type IS ARRAY (1 .. 9) OF Integer;

TYPE Scoreboard_Type IS
   RECORD
      Visitor_Part, Home_Team_Part : Inning_Score_List_Type;
   END RECORD;

TYPE Scoreboard_Pointer_Type IS ACCESS Scoreboard_Type;

Scoreboard         : Scoreboard_Type;
Scoreboard_Pointer : Scoreboard_Pointer_Type;
```

Write down names for the variables below. In (*d*) through (*g*), you may assume that the value of `Scoreboard_Pointer` is not `NULL`.

(*a*) The `Visitor_Part` component of `Scoreboard`.

(*b*) The third array component of the `Visitor_Part` component of `Scoreboard`.

(*c*) The slice consisting of the fourth through sixth array components of the `Visitor_Part` component of `Scoreboard`.

(*d*) The `Scoreboard_Type` variable pointed to by `Scoreboard_Pointer`.

(*e*) The `Home_Team_Part` component of the variable pointed to by `Scoreboard_Pointer`.

(*f*) The first array component of the `Home_Team_Part` component of the variable pointed to by `Scoreboard_Pointer`.

(*g*) The slice consisting of the seventh through ninth array components of the `Home_Team_Part` component of the variable pointed to by `Scoreboard_Pointer`.

8.2 Rewrite the following real literals without an exponent part:

(*a*) `123.0E4` (*d*) `123.45E0`
(*b*) `123.0E-4` (*e*) `123.45E1`
(*c*) `123.0E-3` (*f*) `123.45E2`

8.3 Rewrite the following real literals using an exponent, so that the only digit preceding the decimal point is zero and the first digit following the decimal point is not zero.

(*a*) `123.0` (*d*) `6.02E23`
(*b*) `1.23` (*e*) `6.02E-23`
(*c*) `0.000123` (*f*) `123.45E6`

8.4 (*a*) Write the string literal `"a'b""c'd"` as a positional aggregate of character literals.

(*b*) Write the positional aggregate `('"','"')` as a string literal.

8.5 For any enumeration subtype `T` and any value `X` in that subtype, it is always the case that `T'Value (T'Image (X)) = X`.

(*a*) Explain why this is so.

(*b*) Explain why, even if the `String` variable `S` contains the name of one of the enumeration literals of `T`, it may not be the case that `T'Image (T'Value (S)) = S`.

8.6 Suppose there were no `Length` attribute. Write an expression using the `Pos`, `First`, and `Last` attributes that has the same value as `A'Length(2)`.

8.7 Rewrite the following array aggregate in positional notation:

```
(9 => 6, 1 => 11, 0 => 4, 3 .. 5 => 0, 2 | 10 => 1,
 6 .. 8 | 11 | 13 .. 15 => 2, 12 => 3)
```

8.8 Rewrite the following array aggregate in named notation, using as few index lists as possible:

```
(1, 2, 2, 2, 3, 4, 4, 4, 1, 2)
```

Assume the indexes run from one to ten.

8.9 Write an array aggregate to replace the question marks in the declaration below, such that `Power_Table(i,j)` will equal `i**j` for all appropriate index values `i` and `j`:

```
Power_Table:
   CONSTANT ARRAY (1 .. 3, 1 .. 3) OF Integer := ???;
```

8.10 Write an array aggregate to replace the question marks in the declaration below, such that each component along the edge of `Board` (in other words, each component in row zero, row 101, column zero, or column 101) will equal zero and every other component will equal one:

```
Board : ARRAY (0 .. 101, 0 .. 101) OF Integer := ???;
```

(*Hint:* It is possible to do this quite succinctly, as succinctly as if the index ranges of `Board` were much smaller.)

8.11 Rewrite the program `Count_Letters` of Section 4.2.6 to initialize `Frequency_Table` in its object declaration.

8.12 Indicate which operands the operators are applied to in each of the following expressions. Do this either by inserting parentheses around each operand or by drawing the expressions as trees.

(*a*) `- a ** b * c`
(*b*) `ABS a * b`
(*c*) `NOT a OR b`
(*d*) `a + b * c + d`
(*e*) `a + b MOD c`
(*f*) `NOT a < b`

8.13 Sometimes it is useful to imagine a one-dimensional array as if it were bent into a circle. That is, the first component of the array is viewed as occurring immediately after the last component. Write an *expression* giving the "next" position in the array after position `I`, assuming (*a*) that the array index values are numbered from zero to nine; and (*b*) that the array index values are numbered from one to ten. When `I` is equal to the last index position, the value of the expression should be the first index position. Otherwise, the value of the expression should be one more than the value of `I`.

8.14 Suppose there is a device that processes character strings four characters at a time. When a `String` value is to be processed by this device, it is broken up into chunks of four characters each, and each chunk is processed in turn. If the length of the string is not a multiple of four, from one to three blanks are catenated to the right of the string first so that it will be a multiple of four. Assuming that `L` is the length of a string to be processed in this way, (*a*) write a single expression giving the number of blanks (possibly zero) that must be added to the string to make its length a multiple of four; and (*b*) write a single expression giving the number of four-character chunks in the string once any necessary blanks have been added. (*Hint* for (*b*): What number, when added to `L`, will produce a sum greater than or equal to the next multiple of four if and only if `L` was not already a multiple of four?)

8.15 The components of the expression `a*b/c+d*e/f` may be evaluated in any of the following orders:

1. `a*b, a*b/c, d*e, d*e/f, a*b/c+d*e/f`
2. `a*b, d*e, a*b/c, d*e/f, a*b/c+d*e/f`
3. `a*b, d*e, d*e/f, a*b/c, a*b/c+d*e/f`
4. `d*e, a*b, a*b/c, d*e/f, a*b/c+d*e/f`
5. `d*e, a*b, d*e/f, a*b/c, a*b/c+d*e/f`
6. `d*e, d*e/f, a*b, a*b/c, a*b/c+d*e/f`

List as many evaluation orders as you can for the evaluation of the operands of `(a+b)*(c+d)*(e+f)`.

8.16 Rewrite each of the following decimal literals as a literal in the indicated base:

(*a*) `256` in base sixteen
(*b*) `266` in base sixteen
(*c*) `0.5` in base sixteen
(*d*) `0.5` in base eight
(*e*) `8` in base eight
(*f*) `2` in base two
(*g*) `4.5` in base two
(*h*) `11` in base twelve

8.17 Rewrite each of the following literals as equivalent decimal literals (without the #), and indicate which are integer literals and which are real literals.

(*a*) `2#1.0#E5`
(*b*) `2#1.0#E-1`
(*c*) `3#10#E2`
(*d*) `16#AB#`

8.18 The following program reads in two strings of up to eighty characters that are assumed to consist entirely of upper-case letters and prints them out in alphabetical order:

```
WITH Basic_IO;

PROCEDURE Order_Strings IS

   String_1, String_2 : String (1 .. 80);
   Length_1, Length_2 : Integer;

BEGIN

   Basic_IO.Get_Line ( String_1, Length_1 );
   Basic_IO.Get_Line ( String_2, Length_2 );

   IF String_1 (1..Length_1) < String_2 (1..Length_2) THEN
      Basic_IO.Put ( String_1 (1 .. Length_1) );
      Basic_IO.New_Line;
      Basic_IO.Put ( String_2 (1 .. Length_2) );
      Basic_IO.New_Line;
```

```
      ELSE
         Basic_IO.Put ( String_2 (1 .. Length_2) );
         Basic_IO.New_Line;
         Basic_IO.Put ( String_1 (1 .. Length_1) );
         Basic_IO.New_Line;
      END IF;

   END Order_Strings;
```

Write a program that does the same thing without using a relational operator to compare values of type `String`. You may use relational operators to compare values of type `Character`.

8.19 A palindrome is a string that reads the same when read forward or backward, such as `"ADA"`, `"DoD"`, `"noon"`, `"EE"`, and `""` (the empty string). Write a program that reads in lines from the input file (using `Basic_IO.Get_Line`) and prints only those lines that are palindromes.

8.20 Write a program that reads in a word of up to twenty upper-case and lower-case letters and prints out the same word entirely in upper case.

8.21 Write a program that reads in two strings of up to eighty lower-case and upper-case letters and prints them out in the order in which they would appear in the dictionary. You cannot use the relational operators to compare `String` values, because all upper-case letters precede all lower-case letters in the ASCII sequence, while upper case and lower case are considered equivalent in dictionary ordering. (*Hint:* Combine the approaches of the two immediately preceding exercises.)

CHAPTER

NINE

SUBPROGRAMS

Section 7.2.1 described a simple form of the procedure call statement, which causes a procedure subprogram to be executed. Section 8.1.9 described a simple form of the function call, an expression whose evaluation causes a function subprogram to be executed to compute the expression's value. In this chapter, you will learn how to write the *subprogram bodies* that specify the actions performed by these subprograms. Then you will see the full form of procedure and function calls. You will also learn how to create multiple subprograms with the same name but different definitions and how to extend or redefine the meanings of the operators used in compound expressions.

9.1 PROCEDURE BODIES

A *procedure body* specifies the actions performed by a procedure subprogram. The main programs you have seen so far are all procedure bodies, preceded in most cases by a **WITH** clause. Typically, procedures have *parameters*, which are mechanisms for communication with the calling subprogram. (When a procedure is called, the *calling subprogram* is the subprogram that executes the procedure call statement.) A procedure call statement may contain a list of *actual parameters*, which are values to be used or variables to be set by the procedure. Within the procedure body, identifiers called *formal parameters* stand for the actual parameters specified in the procedure call statement. (Formal parameters are called *dummy arguments* in FORTRAN.)

The typical form of a procedure body is as follows:

```
PROCEDURE identifier
   ( parameter specification ; ~~~ ; parameter specification )   IS
   declarative part
BEGIN
   sequence of statements
END identifier ;
```

The identifier following the word **PROCEDURE** is the name of the subprogram, and the identifier following the word **END** must be identical. The parameter specifications, which name and describe the formal parameters, will be discussed shortly. The declarative part is a sequence of zero or more declarations.

A procedure body is itself a kind of declaration, so it can be placed in another declarative part. Alternatively, a procedure body may be written as an independent compilation unit. Independent compilation units are generally preferable, especially for large programs. However, this chapter will deal primarily with subprogram bodies placed in the declarative parts of other subprogram bodies. Independent compilation units will be considered in detail in Chapter 13.

Certain of the declarations that can be placed in declarative parts are known as *basic declarations,* and others are known as *later declarations.* All of the basic declarations in a declarative part must precede all of the later declarations. The kinds of declarations we have seen until now—variable, constant, named number, type, and subtype declarations—are all basic declarations, but procedure bodies are later declarations. Consequently, in a declarative part, procedure bodies must come after variable, constant, named number, type, and subtype declarations. Additionally, unless special measures are taken, a subprogram body containing a call on another subprogram must be placed somewhere after that other subprogram's body. (The special measures will be described in Section 9.4.) In other words, if a main program contains subprograms **A** and **B**, and **B** calls **A**, the body of **A** must normally occur earlier than the body of **B**.

The general form of a parameter specification is as follows:

```
identifier , ~~~ , identifier :
   mode   typemark   := expression
```

The identifiers are names of formal parameters, and the information following the colon describes the formal parameters listed before the colon. Typically, a parameter specification describes a single identifier; as a shorthand, formal parameters with the same description can be listed together and described by the same parameter specification.

The *mode* describes how the parameter is used to pass information between a procedure and its calling subprogram. There are three possibilities:

`IN` The parameter mode `IN` specifies that the parameters listed are to be used for passing input values from the calling subprogram in to the procedure. The parameter value may be read, but not modified, by the procedure. Thus an `IN` parameter acts as a constant within the procedure body.

`OUT` The parameter mode `OUT` specifies that the parameters listed are to be used for passing results from the procedure back out to the calling subprogram. In a procedure call, the actual parameter corresponding to an `OUT` formal parameter must specify a variable. Within the procedure body, the value of the formal parameter may be set, but not examined (except in a restricted way that will be described later). Upon completion of the procedure, the value held by the formal parameter is used to replace the value previously held by the corresponding actual parameter.

`IN OUT` The parameter mode `IN OUT` specifies that the parameters listed are to pass information in both directions between the procedure and the calling subprogram. In a procedure call, the actual parameter corresponding to an `IN OUT` formal parameter must specify a variable. The procedure body may both examine and modify the value of the formal parameter. The final value of the formal parameter is used to update the value of the corresponding actual parameter upon completion of the procedure.

When no parameter mode is given in a parameter specification, the mode is assumed to be `IN`.

The typemark specifies the subtype of the listed parameters. Unlike FORTRAN and PL/I—in which the procedure heading gives only the names of formal parameters, and ordinary variable declarations (or type defaulting rules) are used to specify the types of the parameters—the Ada language requires the type of the parameters to be given in the procedure heading. Ada formal parameters are described only by parameter specifications and never by a declaration in the declarative part of the procedure body.

Since the typemark in a parameter specification may not be accompanied by a constraint, constraints on the subtypes of parameters must be expressed in a subtype declaration preceding the procedure body. Then the name of the declared subtype can be used as the typemark in the parameter specification. For example, if a procedure `P` is to have one parameter, used to pass an `Integer` value in the range one to five into the procedure body, we could first declare

```
SUBTYPE Low_Positive_Subtype IS Integer RANGE 1 .. 5;
```

and later write

```
PROCEDURE p (x : IN Low_Positive_Subtype) IS
   ...
BEGIN
   ...
END p;
```

A parameter specification of the form

```
PROCEDURE p (x : IN Integer RANGE 1 .. 5) IS
                 -- ILLEGAL PARAMETER SPECIFICATION!
   ...
BEGIN
   ...
END p;
```

is not permitted.

The optional `:=` sign and expression are only allowed for parameters of mode `IN`. The expression specifies a *default value* for the parameters. As Section 9.3 will explain further, a subprogram call need not supply a value for an `IN` parameter that has a default value. If the corresponding actual parameter is omitted from the call, the expression given in the corresponding formal parameter specification is evaluated to determine the value of the formal parameter for that execution of the procedure. The expression is evaluated anew each time that a procedure call statement omitting the corresponding actual parameter is executed, and the expression may have a different value each time it is evaluated. When a parameter specification describes more than one formal parameter for which the corresponding actual parameter has been omitted in a procedure call statement, the expression is reevaluated for each such expression. This is only relevant when the expression is one whose evaluation produces some side effect in addition to producing a value. For instance, given the declaration

```
TYPE Integer_Pointer_Type IS ACCESS Integer;
```

and the procedure declaration

```
PROCEDURE p
   (a, b, c : IN Integer_Pointer := NEW Integer'(0)) IS
   ...
BEGIN
   ...
END p;
```

the procedure call statement

```
p;
```

(in which actual parameters for a, b, and c are omitted) causes the allocator NEW Integer'(0) to be evaluated three times, resulting in the allocation of three Integer variables and the creation of three distinct access values.

The execution of a procedure subprogram consists of two steps. First, the declarations in the procedure body's declarative part are elaborated, in order. Second, the statements of the procedure body are executed, until either the entire sequence of statements is complete or a RETURN statement of the form

```
RETURN ;
```

is executed. It is not necessary for a procedure body to contain such a statement.

Here are two examples of procedure bodies:

```
PROCEDURE Place_Smallest_First
   (First, Second : IN OUT Float) IS

    Old_First : Float;

BEGIN

   IF Second > First THEN
      Old_First := First;
      First := Second;
      Second := Old_First;
   END IF;

END Place_Smallest_First;


PROCEDURE Determine_Order
   (First, Second   : IN Float;
    Smaller, Larger : OUT Float) IS

BEGIN

   IF First < Second THEN
      Smaller := First;
      Larger := Second;
   ELSE
      Smaller := Second;
      Larger := First;
   END IF;

END Determine_Order;
```

The procedure body for Place_Smallest_First has a single parameter specification listing two parameters of mode IN OUT. Its declarative part contains one declaration, for the variable Old_First. When called with two variables, this procedure examines the two values and leaves the smaller value in the first variable and the larger value in the second variable. Thus this procedure examines, and may modify, both of its parameters. For example, if a, b, c, and d are Float variables with the values 3.0, 2.0, 9.0, and 10.0, respectively, then the procedure call statement

```
Place_Smallest_First (a, b);
```

exchanges the values of a and b, leaving 2.0 in a and 3.0 in b; the procedure call statement

```
Place_Smallest_First (c, d);
```

leaves c and d unchanged.

The procedure Determine_Order performs essentially the same function in a slightly different way. The body of Determine_Order has two parameter specifications, the first for two parameters of mode IN and the second for two parameters of mode OUT. The declarative part of the procedure body is empty. Determine_Order examines the values of its first two parameters and copies the smaller of these two values to its third parameter and the larger to the fourth parameter. The first two parameters are examined to determine their value, but not modified, while the last two are given values, but never examined. Assuming again that a and b are variables of type Float, the procedure call statement

```
Determine_Order (1.0, 2.0, a, b);
```

leaves 1.0 in a and 2.0 in b, while

```
Determine_Order (5.0, 3.0, a, b);
```

leaves 3.0 in a and 5.0 in b.

The subtype specified for a formal parameter can be an unconstrained array subtype. On a given call, the formal parameter assumes the constraints of the corresponding actual parameter. This provides a measure of flexibility missing in Pascal—the ability to write a subprogram that can manipulate arrays of any size.

For example, suppose we have defined an array type Data_List_Type as follows:

```
TYPE Data_List_Type IS ARRAY (Integer RANGE <>) OF Float;
```

The following procedure takes a Data_List_Type value as an IN parameter, computes the mean and the variance of the array components, and places those values in OUT parameters. (The variance of a set of values is computed by subtracting the square of their mean from the mean of their squares.)

```
PROCEDURE Analyze
   (Data_Points    : IN Data_List_Type;
    Mean, Variance : OUT Float) IS

   Number_Of_Points :
      CONSTANT Float := Float (Data_Points'Length);
   Sum, Sum_Of_Squares                : Float := 0.0;
   Mean_Of_Points, Mean_Of_Squares : Float;
```

```
BEGIN
   FOR i IN Data_Points'Range LOOP
      Sum := Sum + Data_Points (i);
      Sum_Of_Squares :=
         Sum_Of_Squares + Data_Points (i) ** 2;
   END LOOP;
   Mean_Of_Points := Sum / Number_Of_Points;
   Mean_Of_Squares := Sum_Of_Squares / Number_Of_Points;
   Mean := Mean_Of_Points;
   Variance := Mean_Of_Squares - Mean_Of_Points ** 2;
END Analyze;
```

(At first glance, it appears that the last four assignment statements could be condensed into three as follows:

```
Mean := Sum / Number_Of_Points;
Mean_Of_Squares := Sum_Of_Squares / Number_Of_Points;
Variance := Mean_Of_Squares - Mean ** 2;
```

However, the last of these three assignment statements is illegal because it examines the value of `Mean`, which is an `OUT` parameter. Examination of an `OUT` parameter is forbidden even after the procedure has assigned a value to it.) Since the parameter specification for `Data_Points` names the unconstrained subtype `Data_List_Type`, the procedure will work for arrays of various sizes. For example, given the declarations

```
Sample_1    : Data_List_Type (0 .. 99);
Sample_2    : Data_List_Type (1 .. 256);
m, v        : Float;
Sample_Size : Integer RANGE 0 .. 256;
```

each of the following calls is legal:

```
Analyze (Sample_1, m, v);
Analyze (Sample_2, m, v);
Analyze (Sample_2 (1 .. Sample_Size), m, v);
```

Unlike FORTRAN and PL/I, the Ada language never requires the programmer to provide a separate parameter giving the size of the array being manipulated. The procedure can learn all it has to know about the length and bounds of an array parameter by examining attributes of the array itself, such as `Data_Points'Length` (as in the first declaration in the body of `Analyze`) and `Data_Points'Range` (as in the iteration scheme of the `FOR` loop in `Analyze`).

Although it is generally illegal to examine the value of an `OUT` formal parameter within the procedure body, certain restricted forms of examination are allowed to determine which values the corresponding actual parameter is permitted to assume. It is legal to use the 'First, 'Last, 'Length, and 'Range attributes of an OUT array parameter to determine the bounds of the actual parameter. Components of an OUT parameter may be examined in the same restricted way.

Below is an example of a procedure that has an OUT parameter in an unconstrained array type. It is based on the following type declaration:

```
TYPE Integer_List_Type IS
   ARRAY (Positive RANGE <>) OF Integer;
```

If the length of its parameter is less than four, the procedure sets each component of the parameter to one. Otherwise, the procedure sets the first four components of the parameter to one and each successive component to the sum of the previous four components.

```
PROCEDURE Build_Sequence
   (Result : OUT Integer_List_Type) IS
   Work_Space : Integer_List_Type (Result'Range);
BEGIN

   IF Result'Length <= 4 THEN
      Result := (Result'Range => 1);
   ELSE
      Work_Space
         (Work_Space'First .. Work_Space'First+3) :=
         (1, 1, 1, 1);
      FOR i IN Work_Space'First+4 .. Work_Space'Last LOOP
         Work_Space (i) :=
            Work_Space (i-4) + Work_Space (i-3) +
            Work_Space (i-2) + Work_Space (i-1);
      END LOOP;
      Result := Work_Space;
   END IF;
END Build_Sequence;
```

The bounds of the array value computed by this procedure are those of the actual parameter. In other words, during a call on Build_Sequence, Result inherits the index constraint of that call's actual parameter. The procedure cannot override this index constraint. The algorithm for parameters with more than four components involves examination of previously computed array components. Since examination of an OUT parameter is forbidden, the sequence is computed in the array Work_Space and then copied to the formal parameter once the computation is complete. Although examination of the *contents* of Result is forbidden, examination of the attributes Result'Range, Result'Length, Result'First, and

`Result'Last` is allowed. Indeed, such examination is necessary to write the procedure.

9.2 FUNCTION BODIES

Function bodies are quite similar to procedure bodies. There are three differences, involving the form of the subprogram heading, the mode of the parameters, and the way in which execution of the statements in the body is completed.

The typical form of a function body is as follows:

```
FUNCTION identifier
    ( parameter specification ; ~~~ ; parameter specification )
    RETURN typemark IS
    declarative part
BEGIN
    sequence of statements
END identifier ;
```

The word **PROCEDURE** is replaced by **FUNCTION**, and the word **RETURN** is added, followed by a typemark specifying the *result subtype* of the function. The value returned by an invocation of this function must belong to this subtype. Like the typemark in a parameter specification, the typemark following the word **RETURN** may not be accompanied by a constraint. However, the typemark may be one declared in an earlier subtype declaration that includes a constraint.

When reading a program, people tend to regard expressions simply as specifications of values. Therefore, it is confusing when a function call has the side effect of modifying variables used by the calling subprogram. For this reason, all parameters of a function subprogram must be of mode **IN**. A function subprogram may communicate with the calling subprogram by receiving parameter values and returning a result, but not by modifying its actual parameters.

Since a parameter specification without any mode is equivalent to one with the mode **IN**, the following rule of style is appropriate: In the specification of a *procedure* parameter, which may be of any mode, the mode **IN** should always be written explicitly, to emphasize the mode of each parameter. Since a *function* parameter may only be of mode **IN**, the mode is omitted from the specifications of function parameters. This convention is followed throughout this book.

Since a function must return a value to the calling subprogram, a function body must contain at least one **RETURN** statement of the form

```
RETURN expression ;
```

where the type of the expression is that of the result subtype. All **RETURN** statements in the function body must be of this form. It is an error if the sequence of statements in a function body completes its execution without encountering a **RETURN** statement.

Here is the body of a function that takes two Float parameters and returns the larger of the two parameter values:

```
FUNCTION Maximum (x1, x2 : Float) RETURN Float IS
BEGIN
   IF x1 > x2 THEN
      RETURN x1;
   ELSE
      RETURN x2;
   END IF;
END Maximum;
```

Thus the value of the expression Maximum (3.5, 4.0) is 4.0.

The following function has no parameters. It is meant for use in an interactive environment and returns an integer between one and five supplied by the user. It prompts the user for input, makes sure the value entered is in the proper range, and asks the user to reenter the value if it is not.

```
WITH Basic_IO;
FUNCTION Valid_User_Input RETURN Positive IS
   x : Integer;
BEGIN
   Basic_IO.Put ("Please enter a number between 1 and 5.");
   Basic_IO.New_Line;
   LOOP
      Basic_IO.Get (x);
      EXIT WHEN x IN 1 .. 5;
      Basic_IO.Put ("That is not between 1 and 5.");
      Basic_IO.New_Line;
      Basic_IO.Put ("Please try again.");
      Basic_IO.New_Line;
   END LOOP;
   RETURN x;
END Valid_User_Input;
```

This function can greatly simplify the logic of the calling program. The statement

```
Option := Valid_User_Input;
```

obtains a number from the user and assigns it to Option. The value assigned is guaranteed to be valid, and the surrounding statements can concern themselves entirely with using that value rather than with the process of interacting with the user to obtain it. Behind the scenes, of course, evaluation of the expression Valid_User_Input triggers the execution of the function body to conduct a dialogue with the user.

9.3 SUBPROGRAM CALLS

This section describes the full form of subprogram calls. A subprogram call is either a procedure call statement or a function call occurring in an expression. The form is the same in either case.

A subprogram call with no parameters consists only of the name of a subprogram. For example, the main program below contains calls on the parameterless function `Basic_IO.End_Of_File` and the parameterless procedure `Basic_IO.New_Line`. The program copies the lines in the input file to the output file, assuming that no line in the input file contains more than eighty characters.

```
WITH Basic_IO;
PROCEDURE Copy_Input IS

   Line        : String (1 .. 80);
   Line_Length : Integer RANGE 0 .. 80;

BEGIN

   WHILE NOT Basic_IO.End_Of_File LOOP
      Basic_IO.Get_Line (Line, Line_Length);
      Basic_IO.Put ( Line (1 .. Line_Length) );
      Basic_IO.New_Line;
   END LOOP;

END Copy_Input;
```

(The subprogram names are expanded names, indicating that the subprograms are provided by the package `Basic_IO`.)

When a subprogram call provides one or more parameters, its form is as follows:

name (*parameter association* , ~~~ , *parameter association*)

The name is the name of the subprogram. The parameter associations may be *positional* or *named.* A positional parameter association is simply an actual parameter. A named parameter association has the following form:

formal parameter identifier => *actual parameter*

All of the positional parameter associations in a subprogram call must precede all of the named parameter associations. In the subprogram call

```
Determine_Order (5.0, 3.0, Larger => B, Smaller => A);
```

the first two parameter associations are positional, and the last two are named.

An actual parameter in a positional parameter association is associated with a formal parameter on the basis of its position in the list of parameter associations. The actual parameter in the first positional parameter association corresponds to the first formal parameter specified in the subprogram body, the second corresponds to the second, and so forth. The actual parameter in a named parameter association is associated with a formal parameter on the basis of the formal parameter name in the parameter association. The order in which the named parameter associations are listed need not bear any relationship to the order in which the formal parameters are specified in the subprogram body. No more than one actual parameter may be associated with a given formal parameter in one call.

Named parameter associations can be used to make a program more reliable and more readable. It can make a program more reliable by eliminating the danger of confusing the meaning of two parameter positions. If a programmer thinks that the procedure call

```
Copy_File (File_1, File_2);
```

copies `File_2` into `File_1`, but it really does just the opposite, the consequences may be devastating. However, if the formal parameters are given mnemonic names like `Source_File` and `Target_File`, then the programmer is on safe ground whether he writes

```
Copy_File (Source_File => File_2, Target_File => File_1);
```

or, equivalently,

```
Copy_File (Target_File => File_1, Source_File => File_2);
```

Furthermore, named parameter associations can help a reader understand the meaning of a subprogram call without looking at the subprogram body, provided that the formal parameter names are meaningful. This is particularly important when the number of parameters is large. Compare the obscurity of the statement

```
Itinerary :=
   Cheapest_Route
      ("JFK", "LAX", 730, 2330, "UA", "Y", 2);
```

with the clarity of the statement

```
Itinerary :=
   Cheapest_Route
      (Origin                       => "JFK",
       Destination                  => "LAX",
       Earliest_Possible_Departure=> 730,
       Latest_Possible_Arrival      => 2330,
       Airline_Preference           => "UA",
       Fare_Class_Desired           => "Y",
       Length_Of_Stay               => 2);
```

An actual parameter corresponding to a formal parameter of mode IN may be any expression of the appropriate type. A name may be used as an OUT or IN OUT actual parameter if it would make sense on the lefthand side of an assignment statement. For example, a procedure call statement like

```
Place_Smallest_First (A, 1.0);
```

is illegal because both parameters of Place_Smallest_First (defined in Section 9.1) are of mode IN OUT. It is nonsense to speak of placing the larger of A and 1.0 in 1.0. Similarly, the statement

```
Determine_Order (A, B, 1.0, C);
```

is illegal because the last two parameters of Determine_Order (also defined in Section 9.1) are of mode OUT and exist exclusively for the procedure to place values in them.

In addition to a variable, a *type conversion* may be used as an OUT or IN OUT actual parameter, provided that the expression inside the type conversion is a variable. (Type conversions were described in Section 8.1.7.) The type conversion must specify a subtype whose base type is the same as that of the formal parameter. In the case of an IN OUT parameter, the type conversion is applied in its usual sense to the variable inside it to obtain the value given to the formal parameter. For either an IN OUT or OUT parameter, the value left in the formal parameter at the end of the call is taken to be the new value of the type conversion, and the type conversion is then "reversed" to obtain the value of the variable inside it.

For example, recall the procedure Place_Smallest_First defined in Section 9.1. If f1 and f2 are variables of type Float, the procedure call

```
Place_Smallest_First (f1,f2)
```

places the smaller of their two values in f1 and the larger of their two values in f2. If i1 and i2 are variables of type Integer, then the call

```
Place_Smallest_First (Float (i1), Float (i2));
```

does the same thing for i1 and i2. Assuming that the values in i1 and i2 do not contain more than Float'Digits significant digits, this procedure call places the smaller of their two values in i1 and the larger of their two values in i2. Before the procedure body is executed, the values of Float (i1) and Float (i2) are computed. The values of type Float computed by these type conversions are used as the initial values of the formal parameters. Upon completion of the procedure body, the value of type Float left in the first formal parameter is taken as the new value of the type conversion Float (i1). The inverse type conversion is applied to convert this value to the type of i1 (that is, type Integer) and to update i1 accordingly. The second parameter is treated analogously.

Actual parameter values need not be supplied for any formal parameter of mode `IN` that has a default expression. All formal parameters in positions following the position of an omitted parameter can only be associated with actual parameters through named parameter associations. For example, consider the following function body with default parameter expressions:

```
FUNCTION Final_Position
   (Elapsed_Time, Acceleration         : Float;
    Initial_Velocity, Initial_Position : Float := 0.0)
   RETURN Float IS
BEGIN
   RETURN
      Acceleration * Elapsed_Time ** 2 / 2.0 +
         Initial_Velocity * Elapsed_Time +
         Initial_Position;
END Final_Position;
```

Then the value of the expression `Final_Position(t,a)` is the distance traveled by an object starting at rest and subjected to an acceleration *a* for a time *t*; the value of

```
Final_Position (t, a, Initial_Position => x)
```

is the final position of such an object if it starts out at position *x*. The value of `Final_Position(t,a,v)` is the distance traveled by an object with an initial velocity of *v* subjected to an acceleration of *a* for a time *t*; and the value of `Final_Position(t,a,v,x)` is the final position of such an object if its initial position is *x*. (There is no way to omit the third parameter and supply the fourth without using named notation.) A default parameter expression is most useful when the parameter has a standard value that is appropriate most of the time. Then an actual parameter is needed only when the parameter is to receive a nonstandard value. The function call in the standard case is simple and concise.

9.4 RECURSIVE SUBPROGRAMS

Section 5.4.5 described recursive *types,* which are types defined in terms of themselves. The Ada language also allows *recursive subprograms,* that is, subprograms defined directly or indirectly in terms of themselves. If a subprogram is called while it is already in the process of executing, a separate *activation* of the subprogram is begun. This separate activation has its own version of all formal parameters and all entities declared in the subprogram body's declarative part.

Given the type declaration

```
TYPE Integer_List_Type IS
   ARRAY (Positive RANGE <>) OF Integer;
```

the following procedure to increment each element of an `Integer_List_Type` array is recursive because it contains a procedure call statement calling itself:

```
PROCEDURE Increment_List (List: IN OUT Integer_List_Type) IS
BEGIN
   IF List'Length > 0 THEN
      Increment_List (List (List'First .. List'Last-1));
      List (List'Last) := List (List'Last) + 1;
   END IF;
END Increment_List;
```

When `List'Length = 0` (in other words, when `List` is a null array), the procedure returns without doing anything. Otherwise, `Increment_List` is called recursively with the slice consisting of all components of `List` but the last, to increment every component in that slice, and then the last component is incremented by an assignment statement.

To the reader unfamiliar with recursion, this may seem like black magic, since the definition of `List` appears to be circular. In fact, it is not, because the process of updating an array of some positive length is defined in terms of the process of updating an array with one less component. Eventually, we are faced with the problem of updating an array with no components, and this problem is solved without a recursive call—by doing nothing.

The procedure works correctly for arrays of length zero because no action need be taken to increment each element of such an array. If we *assume that the procedure works correctly for an array of length n,* where *n* is any positive integer—so that the recursive procedure call statement properly increments each component of the slice `List (List'First .. List'Last-1)`—then it is easy to see that the procedure works correctly for arrays of length *n*+1. Thus correctness for arrays of length one follows from correctness for arrays of length zero, correctness for arrays of length two follows from correctness for arrays of length one, and so forth.

If this argument (known as a *proof by induction*) leaves you still not believing that recursion can work, it may help to trace through the operation of a call on `Increment_List`. Suppose that a main program containing the declaration

```
x: Integer_List_Type (1 .. 3);
```

executes the procedure call statement `Increment_List (x)` when `x` contains the value `(10, 20, 30)`. The following steps are depicted in Figure 9.1:

1. Inside the subprogram body, `List'Length` is three, so the statements inside the `IF` statement are executed. First, the recursive call is executed. Since `List'First` is equal to one and `List'Last` is equal to three, the actual parameter is a slice of length two, containing the value `(10, 20)`.
2. The procedure call causes a *separate activation* of `Increment_List` to begin execution *with its own copy of the formal parameter* `List`. In this activation of

Increment_List, List has the value (10, 20). Since List'Length is two, the statements inside the IF statement are executed, beginning with another recursive call.

3. This recursive call starts a third activation of Increment_List, in which List is the one-element array containing the component ten. In this activation, List'Length, List'First, and List'Last are all equal to one. The statements inside the IF statement are executed, beginning with a procedure call statement in which the actual parameter is the slice List(1 .. 0)—a null array. This generates a fourth activation of Increment_List, in which List'Length is equal to zero.
4. In the fourth activation of Increment_List, the statements inside the IF statement are *not* executed, so the activation completes without doing anything.
5. The third activation of Increment_List now picks up where it left off—just after the recursive procedure call statement. It executes the assignment statement incrementing its only component (so that List(1) = 11) and returns.
6. This allows the second activation to pick up where *it* left off. As a result of the recursive call, this activation's version of List contains the value (11, 20). After the assignment statement incrementing List(List'Last), List contains the value (11, 21).
7. Upon the completion of the second activation of Increment_List, the first activation—that created by the procedure call statement in the main program—resumes with List having the value (11, 21, 30). The assignment statement increments List(List'Last) and returns control to the main program with X having the value (11, 21, 31).

Functions can also be recursive. The following function returns the sum of the components of its parameter:

```
FUNCTION List_Sum (List: Integer_List_Type) RETURN Integer IS
BEGIN
   IF List'Length = 0 THEN
      RETURN 0;
   ELSE
      RETURN
         List_Sum ( List (1 .. List'Last-1) ) +
            List (List'Last);
   END IF;
END List_Sum;
```

When the parameter is a null array, List_Sum simply returns zero. Otherwise, it calls itself recursively on the slice consisting of all components of List but the last,

Step 1:

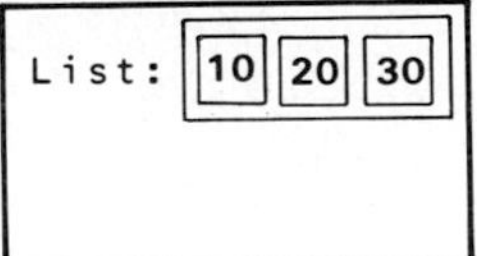

Step 2:

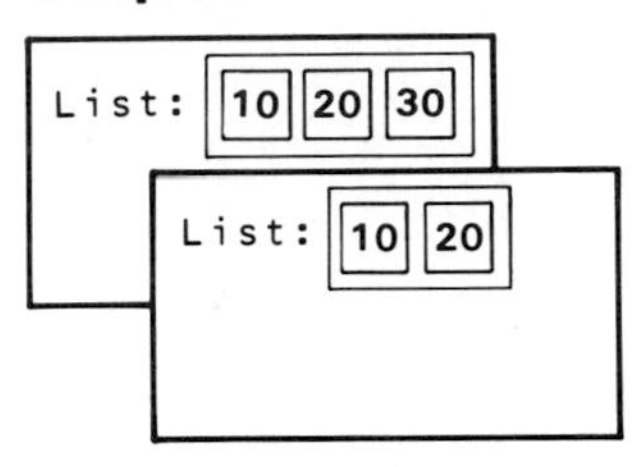

Step 3:

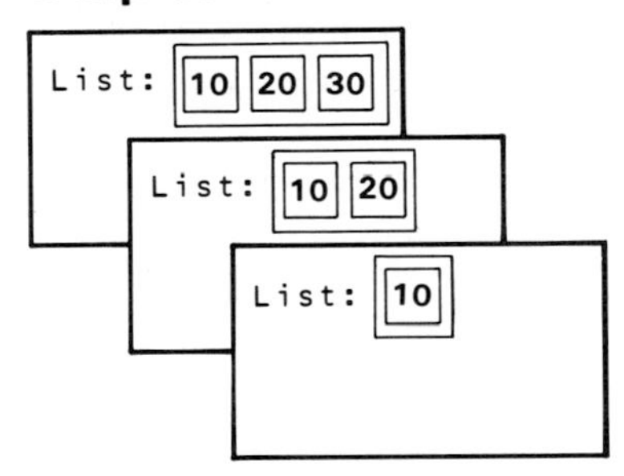

Step 4:

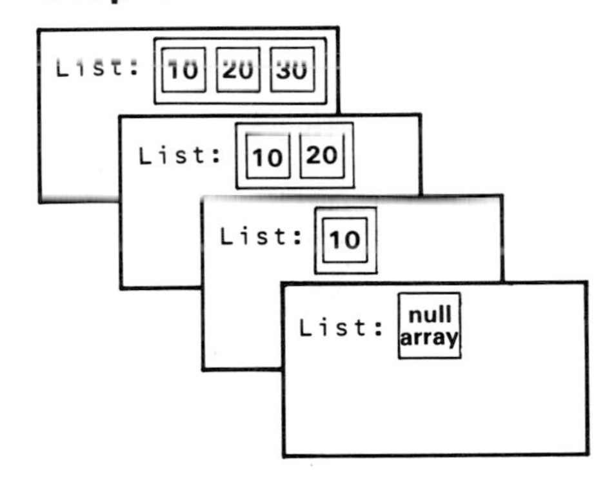

Step 5:

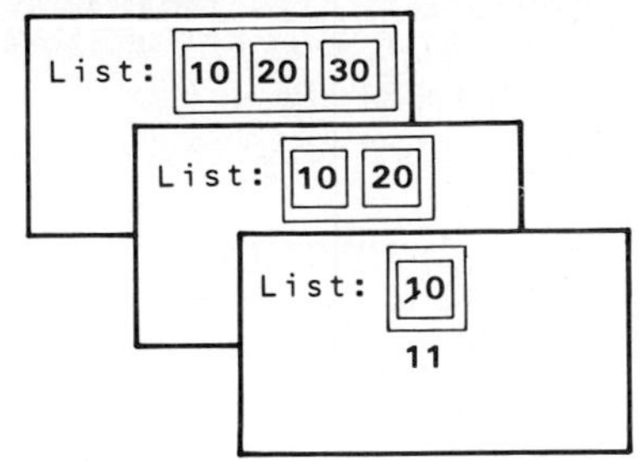

Step 6:

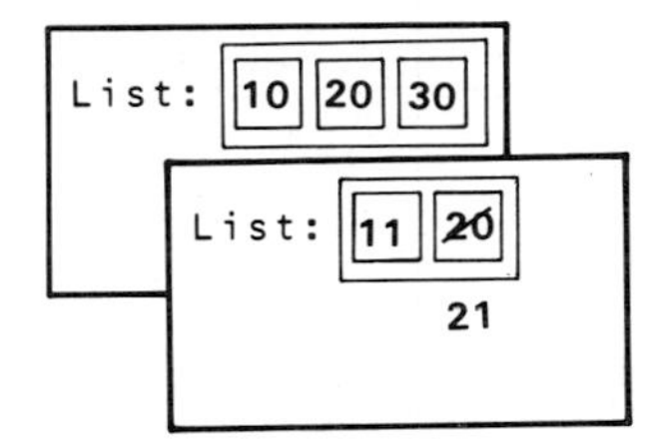

Step 7:

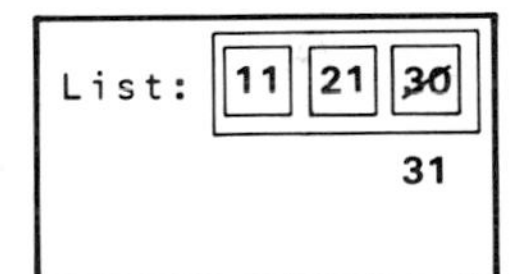

Figure 9.1 The steps involved in completing a call on the recursive procedure `Increment_List`. Each overlapping rectangle represents a currently active invocation. The most recent invocation appears in front of the others. Each invocation has its own copy of the formal parameter `List`.

to obtain the sum of those components, and adds the value of the last component to obtain the sum of all the components of `List`.

If the main program contains the expression `List_Sum( (10, 20, 30) )`, its evaluation proceeds as follows (see Figure 9.2):

1. `List_Sum` is called with `List` set to `(10, 20, 30)`. Since `List'Length` is not zero, the program begins evaluation of the expression in the second `RETURN` statement. This causes `List_Sum` to be called recursively with the actual parameter equal to `List(1 .. 2)`, or `(10, 20)`.
2. A second activation of `List_Sum` begins execution with `List` set to `(10, 20)`. In evaluating the expression in the second `RETURN` statement, this activation calls `List_Sum` recursively with the actual parameter equal to `List(1 .. 1)`, or `(1 => 10)`.
3. A third activation of `List_Sum` begins execution with `List` set to an array whose only component, `List(1)`, is ten. Since `List'Length` is one, the program begins evaluation of the expression in the second `RETURN` statement. This causes `List_Sum` to be called recursively with the actual parameter set to `List(1 .. 0)`—a null array.
4. A fourth activation of `List_Sum` begins execution with `List` set to a null array. Since `List'Length` is zero, this activation executes the first `RETURN` statement and returns zero.
5. Control returns to the third activation of `List_Sum`, which resumes evaluation of the expression in the second `RETURN` statement. The value of the recursive call, zero, is added to the value of `List(List'Last)`, ten, and the value ten is returned.
6. The second activation of `List_Sum` resumes evaluation of the expression in the second `RETURN` statement. The value of the recursive call, ten, is added to the value of `List(List'Last)`, twenty, and the value thirty is returned.
7. Finally, the first activation of `List_Sum` resumes evaluation of the expression in the second `RETURN` statement. The value of the recursive call, thirty, is added to the value of `List(List'Last)`, also thirty, and the value sixty is returned to the main program.

The procedure `Increment_List` and the function `List_Sum` illustrate the mechanism of recursion, but not its usefulness. These two subprograms could have been written just as easily, at least as clearly, and more efficiently using a `FOR` loop instead of a recursive call. In contrast, we shall now see a sorting subprogram that is most easily understood in terms of recursive calls.

The procedure `Merge_Sort` takes a single `IN OUT` parameter of type `Integer_List_Type` and sorts it in ascending order. It does so in most cases by splitting the array into two equal (or, when the number of components is odd, nearly equal) pieces, sorting each piece separately by a recursive call, and merging the two sorted pieces. However, when the length of the parameter is zero or one, `Merge_Sort` simply returns without doing anything. The subprogram begins on page 274.

Step 1:

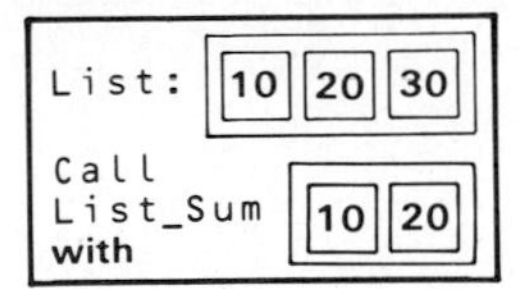

Step 2:

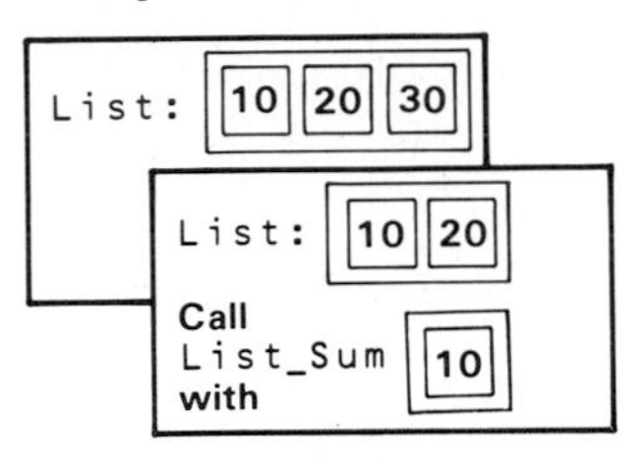

Step 3:

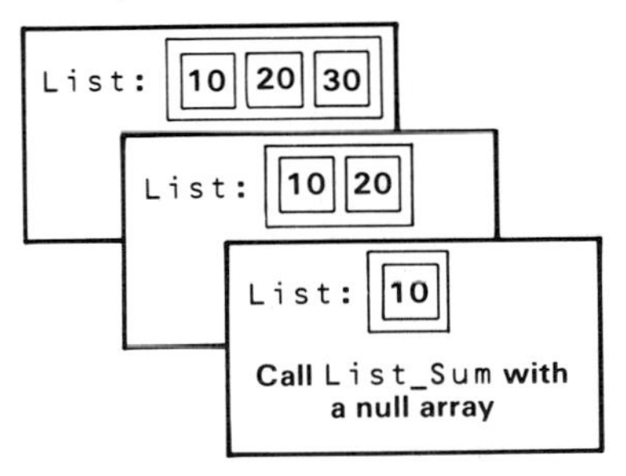

Step 4:

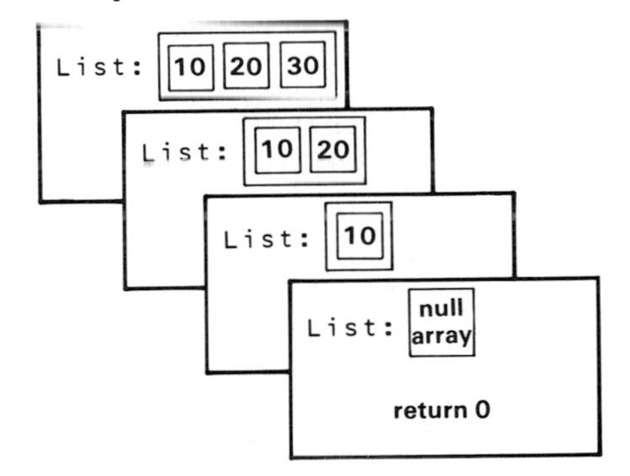

Step 5:

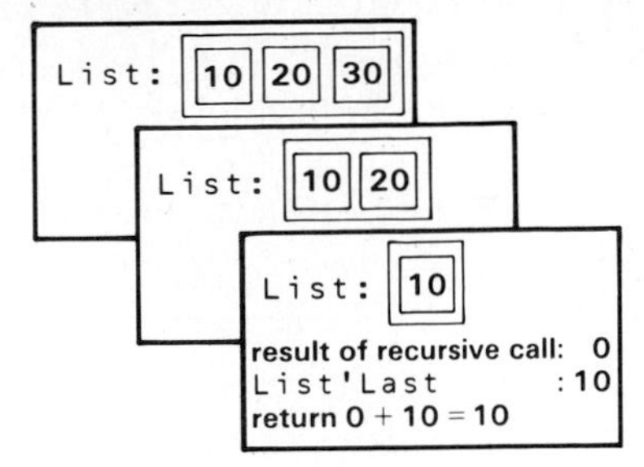

Step 6:

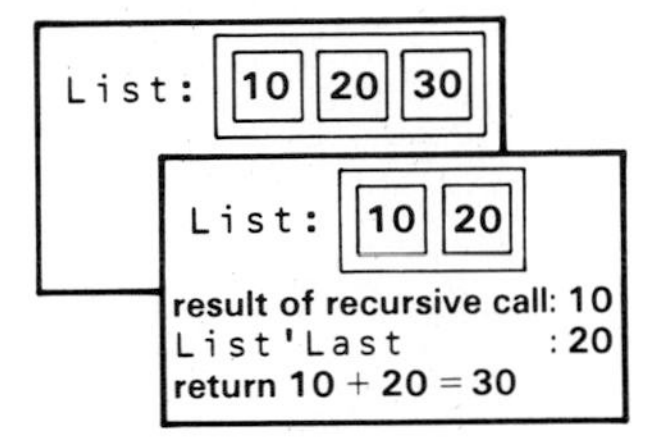

Step 7:

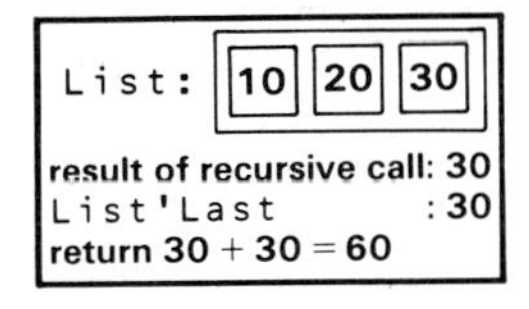

Figure 9.2. The steps involved in completing a call on the recursive function List_Sum.

```
PROCEDURE Merge_Sort (List : IN OUT Integer_List_Type) IS
   Midpoint: CONSTANT := (List'First + List'Last) / 2;
   SUBTYPE Front_Half_Index_Subtype IS
      Integer RANGE List'First .. Midpoint;
   SUBTYPE Back_Half_Index_Subtype IS
      Integer RANGE Midpoint + 1 .. List'Last;
   Front_Half : Integer_List_Type (Front_Half_Index_Subtype);
   Back_Half  : Integer_List_Type (Back_Half_Index_Subtype);
   Front_Half_Pointer :
      Integer RANGE Front_Half'First .. Front_Half'Last+1 :=
         Front_Half'First;
   Back_Half_Pointer :
      Integer RANGE Back_Half'First .. Back_Half'Last+1 :=
         Back_Half'First;
   Result_Pointer : Integer RANGE List'Range := List'First;
BEGIN
   IF List'Length > 1 THEN
      -- Sort each half:
      Front_Half := List (Front_Half_Index_Subtype);
      Back_Half := List (Back_Half_Index_Subtype);
      Merge_Sort (Front_Half);
      Merge_Sort (Back_Half);
      -- Merge the two halves back into List:
   WHILE Front_Half_Pointer <= Front_Half_Index_Subtype'Last AND
         Back_Half_Pointer <= Back_Half_Index_Subtype'Last LOOP
         -- Which half's smallest remaining value is smaller?
         IF  Front_Half (Front_Half_Pointer) <
               Back_Half (Back_Half_Pointer) THEN
            List (Result_Pointer) :=
               Front_Half(Front_Half_Pointer);
            Front_Half_Pointer := Front_Half_Pointer + 1;
         ELSE
            List (Result_Pointer) :=
               Back_Half (Back_Half_Pointer);
            Back_Half_Pointer := Back_Half_Pointer + 1;
         END IF;
         Result_Pointer := Result_Pointer + 1;
      END LOOP;
```

```
      -- Now either the front half or the back half has had
      --   all its components merged into List. Add the
      --   remaining values of the other half to the end of
      --   List:
      IF Front_Half_Pointer > Front_Half_Index_Subtype'Last THEN
         List (Result_Pointer .. List'Last) :=
            Back_Half (Back_Half_Pointer .. Back_Half'Last);
      ELSE
         List (Result_Pointer .. List'Last) :=
            Front_Half (Front_Half_Pointer .. Front_Half'Last);
      END IF;
      END IF; -- List'Length > 1
   END Merge_Sort;
```

The assignments to `Front_Half` and `Back_Half` are slice assignments. (`Front_Half_Index_Subtype` and `Back_Half_Index_Subtype` act as discrete ranges consisting only of typemarks.) The recursive calls on `Merge_Sort` place `Front_Half` and `Back_Half` in ascending order. The `WHILE` loop refills `List` from left to right with values extracted left to right from `Front_Half` and `Back_Half`. `Front_Half_Pointer` is the index of the next component of `Front_Half` that is yet to be extracted, or one more than the last index when all components of `Front_Half` have been extracted. `Back_Half_Pointer` works analogously. Since `Front_Half` and `Back_Half` are both sorted in ascending order, extracting the lesser of `Front_Half(Front_Half_Pointer)` and `Back_Half (Back_Half_Pointer)` each time through the loop guarantees that the smallest not-yet-extracted value is extracted next. This, in turn, guarantees that `List` is refilled in ascending order. When either `Front_Half` or `Back_Half` has had all of its components extracted, the remaining components of the other variable are used, in order, to refill the remaining components of `List`. This is accomplished by one of the two slice assignments inside the final `IF` statement. (The `WHILE` loop ends when either `Front_Half` or `Back_Half` has had all its components extracted. If the condition `Front_Half_Pointer > Front_Half_Index_Subtype'Last` is true, it was `Front_Half`; otherwise, it must have been `Back_Half`.)

In each of the examples you have seen so far, a subprogram was recursive because it contained a call on itself. A subprogram `P` is also recursive if it calls another subprogram `Q` that then calls `P`. In general, when there is a set of subprograms, each of which can directly or indirectly call each of the others, the subprograms are said to be *mutually recursive.*

As an example of mutual recursion, consider a program to read and print restricted Ada expressions followed by semicolons and print the values of the expressions. The expressions consist only of decimal integer literals without underscores or exponents, the operators + and *, and parentheses. To keep the example simple, we assume that there are no spaces embedded in the expression, that the input contains no syntactic errors, and that all expressions have values less than or equal to `Integer'Last`. Given the input

```
1+2*3*(4+5)+6;7*8;9+10;
```

for example, the program should produce the following output:

```
61
56
19
```

To describe the form of the input formally, we can define a *restricted expression* as a sequence of *restricted terms* separated by `'+'` characters, a restricted term as a sequence of *restricted factors* separated by `'*'` characters, and a *restricted factor* as either a decimal integer literal without an exponent part or a restricted expression in parentheses.

We can write three mutually recursive procedures with the names `Process_Expression`, `Process_Term`, and `Process_Factor` to recognize and evaluate restricted expressions, restricted terms, and restricted factors, respectively. Each procedure has an `IN OUT` parameter of type `Character` and an `OUT` parameter of type `Integer`. When one of these procedures is called, the `Character` parameter contains the first character from the input stream to be processed by this call; all subsequent characters remaining to be processed are still in the input file. When the procedure returns, the `Character` parameter contains the first character in the input stream that this call did *not* process—with all subsequent unprocessed characters still in the input file—and the `Integer` parameter contains the value of the restricted expression, term, or factor that was just recognized. Here are the bodies of the three procedures:

```
PROCEDURE Process_Expression
   (Next_Character   : IN OUT Character;
    Expression_Value : OUT Integer) IS

   Sum, Term_Value : Integer;

BEGIN -- Process_Expression

   Process_Term (Next_Character, Sum);
   WHILE Next_Character = '+' LOOP
      Basic_IO.Get (Next_Character);
         -- Advance past '+' to first character of next
         --   term.
      Process_Term (Next_Character, Term_Value);
      Sum := Sum + Term_Value;
   END LOOP;
   Expression_Value := Sum;

END Process_Expression;
```

```
PROCEDURE Process_Term
   (Next_Character : IN OUT Character;
    Term_Value     : OUT Integer) IS

   Product, Factor_Value : Integer;

BEGIN -- Process_Term

   Process_Factor (Next_Character, Product);
   WHILE Next_Character = '*' LOOP
      Basic_IO.Get (Next_Character);
         -- Advance past '*' to first character of next
         --   factor.
      Process_Factor (Next_Character, Factor_Value);
      Product := Product * Factor_Value;
   END LOOP;
   Term_Value := Product;

END Process_Term;


PROCEDURE Process_Factor
   (Next_Character : IN OUT Character;
    Factor_Value   : OUT Integer) IS

   Zero_Pos      : CONSTANT := Character'Pos ('0');
   Literal_Value : Integer := 0;

BEGIN -- Process_Factor

   IF Next_Character  '(' THEN

      Basic_IO.Get (Next_Character);
         -- Advance past '(' to first character of
         --   expression.

      Process_Expression (Next_Character, Factor_Value);

      Basic_IO.Get (Next_Character);
         -- Advance past ')' to first character
         --   following factor.

   ELSE

      WHILE Next_Character IN '0' .. '9' LOOP

         Literal_Value :=
            10 * Literal_Value +
               Character'Pos(Next_Character) - Zero_Pos;

         Basic_IO.Get (Next_Character);
            -- Advance past digit to next character.

      END LOOP;

      Factor_Value := Literal_Value;

   END IF;

END Process_Factor;
```

These three procedures are mutually recursive because `Process_Expression` calls `Process_Term`, `Process_Term` calls `Process_Factor`, and `Process_Factor` sometimes calls `Process_Expression`.

These three bodies are all placed, in some order, in the declarative part of the main program. But what order? Normally, a subprogram body containing a call on another subprogram should come after the body of the other subprogram. It is impossible for the preceding three procedure bodies to each come after one of the others.

To break this vicious circle, the Ada language provides a special kind of declaration called a *subprogram declaration.* A subprogram declaration describes the parameters and results of a subprogram but does not give its body. A subprogram body containing a call on some subprogram `S` need not occur after the *body* of `S` as long as it occurs after the *declaration* of `S`.

A subprogram declaration consists of all the information in a subprogram body preceding the word `IS`—what we have until now referred to as a subprogram heading. Like all declarations, it ends with a semicolon. Thus the subprogram declaration for `Process_Expression` is as follows:

```
PROCEDURE Process_Expression
   (Next_Character   : IN OUT Character;
    Expression_Value : OUT Integer);
```

(Another, more important, use of subprogram declarations will be described in Chapter 11.)

There are no restrictions on the placement of a subprogram declaration within a declarative part. It may occur either as a basic declaration (like type, subtype, and object declarations) or as a later declaration (like subprogram bodies). A declarative part containing a subprogram declaration must also contain the full body for that subprogram later on. Thus one of the many possible arrangements of the main program's declarative part is the following:

1. Declarations of variables used by the main program
2. Declaration of `Process_Expression`
3. Body of `Process_Factor`
4. Body of `Process_Term`
5. Body of `Process_Expression`

When all of this is put together, we get the following main program (depicted schematically in Figure 9.3) to evaluate restricted expressions followed by semicolons and print their values:

```
WITH Basic_IO;
PROCEDURE Process_Expression_List IS

   Next_Character   : Character;
   Expression_Value : Integer;
```

```
PROCEDURE Process_Expression
   (Next_Character   : IN OUT Character;
    Expression_Value : OUT Integer);
   -- Procedure declaration

PROCEDURE Process_Factor
   (Next_Character : IN OUT Character;
    Factor_Value   : OUT Integer) IS

   Zero_Pos      : CONSTANT := Character'Pos ('0');
   Literal_Value : Integer := 0;

BEGIN -- Process_Factor

   IF Next_Character = '(' THEN
      Basic_IO.Get (Next_Character);
         -- Advance past '(' to first character of
         --   expression.
      Process_Expression (Next_Character, Factor_Value);
      Basic_IO.Get (Next_Character);
         -- Advance past ')' to first character
         --   following factor.
   ELSE
      WHILE Next_Character IN '0' .. '9' LOOP
         Literal_Value :=
            10 * Literal_Value +
               Character'Pos(Next_Character)-Zero_Pos;
         Basic_IO.Get (Next_Character);
            -- Advance past digit to next character.
      END LOOP;
      Factor_Value := Literal_Value;
   END IF;

END Process_Factor;


PROCEDURE Process_Term
   (Next_Character : IN OUT Character;
    Term_Value     : OUT Integer) IS

   Product, Factor_Value : Integer;

BEGIN -- Process_Term

   Process_Factor (Next_Character, Product);
   WHILE Next_Character = '*' LOOP
      Basic_IO.Get (Next_Character);
         -- Advance past '*' to first character of next
         --   factor.
      Process_Factor (Next_Character, Factor_Value);
      Product := Product * Factor_Value;
   END LOOP;
   Term_Value := Product;

END Process_Term;
```

```
      PROCEDURE Process_Expression
         (Next_Character   : IN OUT Character;
          Expression_Value : OUT Integer) IS

         Sum, Term_Value : Integer;

      BEGIN -- Process_Expression

         Process_Term (Next_Character, Sum);
         WHILE Next_Character = '+' LOOP
            Basic_IO.Get (Next_Character);
               -- Advance past '+' to first character of next
               --   term.
            Process_Term (Next_Character, Term_Value);
            Sum := Sum + Term_Value;
         END LOOP;
         Expression_Value := Sum;

      END Process_Expression;

   BEGIN -- Process_Expression_List (main program)

      WHILE NOT Basic_IO.End_Of_File LOOP
         Basic_IO.Get (Next_Character);
            -- Advance to first character of next expression.
         Process_Expression (Next_Character, Expression_Value);
            -- Trailing ';' is left in Next_Character.
         Basic_IO.Put (Expression_Value);
         Basic_IO.New_Line;
      END LOOP;

   END Process_Expression_List;
```

```
WITH Basic_IO;

PROCEDURE Process_Expression_List IS

      [declaration of variables used by main program]

      [declaration of Process_Expression]

      [body of Process_Factor]

      [body of Process_Term]

      [body of Process_Expression]

BEGIN

      [statements of main program]

END Process_Expression_List;
```

Figure 9.3. Structure of the main program Process_Expression_List.

The two variables declared at the beginning of the main program are those used in the main program's sequence of statements. Within each subprogram body (including that of the main program), each occurrence of the word `BEGIN` is followed by a comment naming the subprogram whose declarative part ends and whose sequence of statements starts at that point. This convention—in conjunction with indentation—helps clarify the way in which subprogram bodies are nested.

9.5 OVERLOADING SUBPROGRAMS

A subprogram body specifies the type of each parameter and, in the case of functions, the type of the result. It is impossible to invoke that subprogram body with parameters of different types or to use a function result as a value of a different type. For instance, the function body

```
FUNCTION Maximum (i1, i2: Integer) RETURN Integer IS
BEGIN
   IF i1 > i2 THEN
      RETURN i1;
   ELSE
      RETURN i2;
   END IF;
END Maximum;
```

cannot be invoked by a function call containing two parameters of type `Float`, nor can the result of a call on `Maximum` be used as a value of type `Float`.

Nonetheless, the abstract notion of the maximum of two numbers makes just as much sense for two `Float` values, or for an `Integer` value and a `Float` value, as for two `Integer` values. Indeed, it makes just as much sense to talk about the maximum of three numbers. The Ada language allows the simultaneous definition of several functions, each handling a different number or combination of parameter types, all named `Maximum`. The definition of multiple subprograms with the same name is called *overloading*.

A compiler interprets a call on an overloaded subprogram as a call on one of the versions by examining the call and the context in which it occurs. A compiler may use the following clues to determine which overloaded subprogram a particular call refers to:

1. Whether the call is a function call or a procedure call
2. The number of actual parameters appearing in the subprogram call
3. The types of the actual parameters
4. In the case of a function call, the types that are legal for expressions at the place where the function call occurs
5. The names of formal parameters appearing in named parameter associations in the subprogram call

For example, suppose a program contains function bodies for the following six overloaded versions of `Maximum`:

```
-- Version 1:

FUNCTION Maximum (i1, i2: Integer) RETURN Integer IS
BEGIN
   IF i1 > i2 THEN
      RETURN i1;
   ELSE
      RETURN i2;
   END IF;
END Maximum;

-- Version 2:

FUNCTION Maximum (i1: Integer; f2: Float) RETURN Float IS
   f1: CONSTANT Float := Float(i1); -- Type conversion
BEGIN
   IF f1 > f2 THEN
      RETURN f1;
   ELSE
      RETURN f2;
   END IF;
END Maximum;

-- Version 3:

FUNCTION Maximum (f1: Float; i2: Integer) RETURN Float IS
   f2: CONSTANT Float := Float(i2); -- Type conversion
BEGIN
   IF f1 > f2 THEN
      RETURN f1;
   ELSE
      RETURN f2;
   END IF;
END Maximum;

-- Version 4:

FUNCTION Maximum (f1, f2: Float) RETURN Float IS
BEGIN
   IF f1 > f2 THEN
      RETURN f1;
   ELSE
      RETURN f2;
   END IF;
END Maximum;

-- Version 5:

FUNCTION Maximum (i1, i2: Integer) RETURN Float IS
BEGIN
   IF i1 > i2 THEN
      RETURN Float(i1); -- Type conversion
   ELSE
      RETURN Float(i2); -- Type conversion
   END IF;
END Maximum;
```

```
-- Version 6:
FUNCTION Maximum (f1, f2, f3: Float) RETURN Float IS
BEGIN
   IF f1 > f2 THEN
      IF f1 > f3 THEN
         RETURN f1;
      ELSE
         RETURN f3;
      END IF;
   ELSE
      IF f2 > f3 THEN
         RETURN f2;
      ELSE
         RETURN f3;
      END IF;
   END IF;
END Maximum;
```

These versions are summarized in Figure 9.4. Let us assume that there are no other versions of `Maximum` defined. Given the declarations

```
n1, n2, n3 : Integer;
x1, x2, x3 : Float;
```

the assignment statement

```
n1 := Maximum(n2, n3);
```

can only contain a call on version 1. The fact that there are only two parameters rules out version 6. The fact that both parameters are of type `Integer` rules out versions 2, 3, and 4. Because the function result is assigned to a variable of type `Integer`, the version called must return a value of type `Integer`. This rules out version 5. By similar reasoning, the assignment statement

Version	Parameter Types	Result Type
1	`Integer, Integer`	`Integer`
2	`Integer, Float`	`Float`
3	`Float, Integer`	`Float`
4	`Float, Float`	`Float`
5	`Integer, Integer`	`Float`
6	`Float, Float, Float`	`Float`

Figure 9.4 The parameter types and result types of the six versions of function `Maximum`.

```
x1 := Maximum(n1, n2);
```

can only contain a call on version 5. In the assignment statement

```
x1 := Maximum(n1, Maximum(x2, n2));
```

the inner call can only be a call on version 3, since its first parameter is of type `Float` and its second parameter is of type `Integer`. Since version 3 returns a result of type `Float`, the outer call has a first parameter of type `Integer` and a second parameter of type `Float`. Therefore, the outer call must be a call on version 2. Finally, consider the assignment statement

```
x1 := Maximum(x2, Maximum(n1, n2), x3);
```

Taken out of context, the inner call

```
Maximum(n1, n2)
```

could be a call on either version 1 or version 5. However, because the outer call contains three parameters, it can only be a call on version 6. Since the second actual parameter in a call on version 6 can only be of type `Float`, the inner call must be a call on version 5.

Determining which overloaded subprogram a call refers to is called *resolving the overloading.* A call on an overloaded subprogram is illegal if the compiler cannot resolve the overloading using one of the five clues previously listed. For example, the assignment statement

```
x1 := Maximum (x2, Maximum (n1, n2));
```

is illegal because two interpretations are possible:

1. The inner call is a call on version 1, so that the second parameter of the outer call is of type `Integer`. Therefore, the outer call is a call on version 3.
2. The inner call is a call on version 5, so that the second parameter of the outer call is of type `Float`. Therefore, the outer call is a call on version 4.

This is where qualified expressions come in handy. The qualified expression in the assignment statement

```
x1 := Maximum (x2, Float'(Maximum (n1, n2)) );
```

indicates that the second parameter of the outer call is of type `Float`. This determines both the result type of the inner call and the second parameter type of the outer call. The qualified expression does not cause any type conversion to take place. It simply tells the compiler to use the second of the two possible interpretations described. The assignment statement

```
x1 := Maximum (x2, Integer'(Maximum (n1, n2)) );
```

would have told the compiler to use the first interpretation. The most important use of qualified expressions in the Ada language is to make calls on overloaded subprograms unambiguous.

The ambiguity of the assignment statement

```
x1 := Maximum(x2, Maximum(n1, n2));
```

could also have been removed by the use of a named parameter association. In the assignment statement

```
x1 := Maximum(x2, i2 => Maximum(n1, n2));
```

the outer call can only be on version 3, because the second formal parameter of version 4 is named `f2`, not `i2`. It follows that the inner call must be on version 1. Similarly, in the assignment statement

```
x1 := Maximum(x2, f2 => Maximum(n1, n2));
```

the outer call can only be a call on version 4, because of the name specified for the second formal parameter. Thus the inner call is on version 5.

Subprograms may not be overloaded unless there are easy ways to distinguish calls on the various versions. Specifically, two subprograms may not be overloaded unless they have different numbers of parameters, parameters of different types, or, in the case of functions, results of different types. To be more precise, every subprogram has a *parameter and result type profile* consisting of the following information:

whether the subprogram is a procedure or function
if the subprogram is a function, the result type of the function
the number of parameters in the subprogram
the base type of each parameter

Only subprograms with different parameter and result type profiles may be overloaded.

Do not confuse the ways in which subprograms must differ if they are to be overloaded with the clues that a compiler may use to resolve the overloading. The six versions of `Maximum` can be overloaded because they have different parameter and result type profiles, as shown in Figure 9.4. Once subprograms are overloaded, a compiler can use formal parameter names in a named subprogram call to resolve the overloading, as in the two assignment statements above. However, subprograms with the same parameter and result type profile cannot be overloaded, even if they have different formal parameter names.

9.6 DEFINING NEW MEANINGS FOR OPERATORS

Operators such as +, *, XOR, and ABS are really functions. They each take one or two values and use them to compute a result. The only difference between these functions and "ordinary" functions is the form of the function call. A call on an "ordinary" function with one or more parameters consists of the name of the function followed by a parenthesized list of expressions giving the parameter values. A call on an operator with two operands consists of an expression giving the value of the first parameter (the left operand), the symbol naming the function (e.g., +), and an expression giving the value of the second parameter (the right operand). A call on an operator with one operand consists of the symbol naming the function (for instance, -) and an expression giving the value of the parameter.

Thus the expression ABS a + b * c is really a call on the function "+" with parameters ABS a and b * c. The expression ABS a, in turn, is a call on the function "ABS" with parameter a; and b * c is a call on the function "*" with parameters b and c. A compound expression such as ABS a + b * c really represents a combination of function calls such as "+" ("ABS" (a), "*" (b, c)).

In fact, the Ada language allows you to write function bodies in which the identifier naming the function is replaced by a string literal containing an operator symbol. The effect is to overload the predefined functions already represented by that operator symbol. For example the function body

```
FUNCTION "&" (Left, Right: Positive) RETURN Positive IS
   Left_Image     : CONSTANT String := Positive'Image(Left);
                    -- Digits of Left preceded by a blank.
   Right_Image    : CONSTANT String := Positive'Image(Right);
                    -- Digits of Right preceded by a blank.
   Result_Size    : CONSTANT Natural :=
                      Left_Image'Length +
                      Right_Image'Length - 2;
                    --  2 less than sum of lengths because
                    --    blanks are not included.
   Result_Image   : String (1 .. Result_Size);
BEGIN
   Result_Image   : =
         Left_Image (2 .. Left_Image'Last) &
         Right_Image (2 .. Right_Image'Last);
      RETURN Positive'Value (Result_Image);
END "&";
```

overloads the catenation operator & with a function taking two parameters of type Integer (subtype Positive) and returning a value of type Integer (subtype Positive). If A and B are positive integers, the value of A & B is the number whose decimal representation is the catenation of the decimal representation of A and the decimal representation of B. For example, 12 & 34 has the value 1234, and 7 * 8 & 6 * 13 equals 56 & 78, or 5678. (You probably did not realize it was relevant when you read Section 8.2, but * has higher precedence than &. Thus 7 * 8 & 6 * 13 means (7 * 8) & (6 * 13), not 7 * (8 & 6) * 13.)

All of the predefined operators are already implicitly overloaded. An Ada compiler uses the rules for resolution of overloading described in the previous section to determine the function to which a particular occurrence of the operator refers. For example, for each numeric type there is a version of + that takes two parameters in that type and returns a result of the same type. It is as if there were a function body of the form

```
FUNCTION "+"(Left, Right : t) RETURN t IS
BEGIN
   RETURN [the sum of Left and Right];
END "+";
```

already defined for each numeric type *t*. In fact, the internal mechanism used to compute the sum of two Float values is generally different from the internal mechanism used to compute the sum of two Integer values; the + operators for these types are two distinct functions that happen to have the same name. A programmer overloading an operator symbol is simply adding yet another version to the several already defined by the language.

Only *operators,* as defined strictly at the beginning of Section 8.2, may be overloaded. Membership tests and short-circuit control forms may not be. For an operator, a string literal such as "+" or "ABS" is used as the function name in the function body. The quotation marks may not be omitted. The operators **, *, /, MOD, REM, &, <, <=, >, >=, AND, OR, and XOR may each be overloaded by functions with two parameters, with the first parameter corresponding to the left operand and the second parameter corresponding to the right operand. The operators ABS and NOT may each be overloaded by functions with one parameter. The operators + and - may be overloaded either with one-parameter functions (which are called by expressions like +A and -A) or two-parameter functions (which are called by expressions like A+B and A-B). The operators = and /= can sometimes be overloaded with two-parameter functions, but only in special circumstances that will be described in Chapter 12.

Only these operator symbols may appear in string literals used as function names. It is not possible to write functions defining new operator symbols. Overloading does not affect the precedence levels of operators, as given in Section 8.2.

A function named by a string literal may not have default expressions for its parameters. That is because operands of operators may not be omitted in expressions. Except for this, and for the use of a string literal in place of an identifier both after the word FUNCTION and after the word END, a function body overloading an operator symbol has the same form as any other function body.

Good programming practice dictates that operators should only be overloaded with functions whose meaning is analogous to the predefined meaning of the operator. For example, the use of XOR for a function computing the average of two Float values would be misleading and would make a program hard to understand. On the other hand, given the type declaration

```
TYPE Matrix_Type IS
   ARRAY (Positive RANGE <>, Positive RANGE <>) OF Float;
```

there are at least two appropriate ways to define a version of * that "multiplies" two `Matrix_Type` values to produce a `Matrix_Type` result. The function body

```
FUNCTION "*" (Left, Right: Matrix_Type) RETURN  Matrix_Type IS

   Result : Matrix_Type (Left'Range(1), Right'Range(2));
   Sum    : Float;
BEGIN
   FOR i IN Result'Range(1) LOOP
      FOR j IN Result'Range(2) LOOP
         Sum := 0.0;
         FOR k IN Left'Range(2) LOOP
            Sum := Sum + Left (i,k) * Right (k,j);
         END LOOP; -- FOR k
         Result (i,j) := Sum;
      END LOOP; -- FOR j
   END LOOP; -- FOR i
   RETURN Result;
END "*";
```

defines the matrix multiplication operation of linear algebra. The function body

```
FUNCTION "*" (Left, Right: Matrix_Type) RETURN  Matrix_Type IS
   Result : Matrix_Type (Left'Range(1), Left'Range(2));
BEGIN
   FOR i IN Result'Range(1) LOOP
      FOR j IN Result'Range(2) LOOP
         Result (i, j) := Left (i, j) * Right (i, j);
      END LOOP;
   END LOOP;
   RETURN Result;
END "*";
```

defines multiplication of `Matrix_Type` values as component-by-component multiplication of corresponding `Float` values, as in APL and PL/I. Since these two versions of `"*"` have the same parameter and result type profiles, they cannot be overloaded. Only one of them can be made available at a given point in the program.

(Both these functions are only well-defined when the index bounds of their parameters obey certain restrictions. In the case of algebraic matrix multiplication, we have assumed that the bounds in the second dimension of the left operand are the same as the bounds in the first dimension of the right operand. In the case of component-by-component multiplication, we have assumed that the two operands have identical index bounds. Given parameters that do not obey these restrictions, these functions will not work correctly. In practice, a function should be written to raise an exception when it is given incorrect parameters. Chapter 15 will explain how to do this.)

As a final example, consider the following data type for representing exact fractions:

```
TYPE Fraction_Type IS
   RECORD
      Numerator_Part   : Integer;
      Denominator_Part : Positive;
   END RECORD;
```

The arithmetic operations can be overloaded to take two `Fraction_Type` operands and compute a `Fraction_Type` result. In writing the function bodies for these operations, we shall assume the availability of a procedure `Reduce` with one `IN OUT` parameter. Given a `Fraction_Type` variable, this procedure reduces the numerator and denominator to lowest possible terms. The procedure will be used to prevent the components of `Fraction_Type` values from growing too large. The function bodies overloading the arithmetic operators are as follows:

```
-- Unary plus:
FUNCTION "+" (Right: Fraction_Type) RETURN Fraction_Type IS
BEGIN
   RETURN Right;
END "+";

-- Unary minus:
FUNCTION "-" (Right: Fraction_Type) RETURN Fraction_Type IS
BEGIN
   RETURN
      Fraction_Type'
         (Numerator_Part   => -Right.Numerator_Part,
          Denominator_Part => Right.Denominator_Part);
END "-";
```

```
-- Binary plus:
FUNCTION "+"
   (Left, Right: Fraction_Type) RETURN Fraction_Type IS
   Result : Fraction_Type;
BEGIN
   Result.Numerator_Part :=
      Left.Numerator_Part * Right.Denominator_Part +
      Right.Numerator_Part * Left.Denominator_Part;
   Result.Denominator_Part :=
      Left.Denominator_Part * Right.Denominator_Part;
   Reduce (Result);
   RETURN Result;
END "+";

-- Binary minus:
FUNCTION "-"
   (Left, Right: Fraction_Type) RETURN Fraction_Type IS
   Result : Fraction_Type;
BEGIN
   Result.Numerator_Part :=
      Left.Numerator_Part * Right.Denominator_Part -
      Right.Numerator_Part * Left.Denominator_Part;
   Result.Denominator_Part :=
      Left.Denominator_Part * Right.Denominator_Part;
   Reduce (Result);
   RETURN Result;
END "-";

FUNCTION "*"
   (Left, Right: Fraction_Type) RETURN Fraction_Type IS
   Result : Fraction_Type;
BEGIN
   Result.Numerator_Part :=
      Left.Numerator_Part * Right.Numerator_Part;
   Result.Denominator_Part :=
      Left.Denominator_Part * Right.Denominator_Part;
   Reduce (Result);
   RETURN Result;
END "*";
```

```
FUNCTION "/"
   (Left, Right: Fraction_Type) RETURN Fraction_Type IS
   -- This function assumes that Right.Numerator_Part /= 0.
   -- It will not work correctly when this is not the case.
   Result_Numerator, Result_Denominator : Integer;
   Result                               : Fraction_Type;
BEGIN
   Result_Numerator :=
      Left.Numerator_Part * Right.Denominator_Part;
   Result_Denominator :=
      Left.Denominator_Part * Right.Numerator_Part;
   IF Result_Denominator > 0 THEN
      Result :=
         Fraction_Type'
            (Numerator_Part   => Result_Numerator,
             Denominator_Part => Result_Denominator);
   ELSE
      Result :=
         Fraction_Type'
            (Numerator_Part   => - Result_Numerator,
             Denominator_Part => - Result_Denominator);
   END IF;
   Reduce (Result);
   RETURN Result;
END "/";

FUNCTION "**"
   (Left: Fraction_Type; Right: Integer)
   RETURN Fraction_Type IS
BEGIN
    RETURN
       Fraction_Type'
          (Numerator_Part   => ABS Right.Numerator_Part,
           Denominator_Part => Right.Denominator_Part);
 END "ABS";
```

These functions simply implement fraction arithmetic as you learned it in grade school. All results have positive denominators and are reduced if the operands are reduced. (The qualified expressions in the bodies for unary "-", "**", and "ABS" are not required; a simple aggregate would be sufficient. The qualified expressions are present only because they make the function bodies easier for a reader to understand.)

It is also useful to overload "/" to take two parameters of type Integer and return a Fraction_Type value:

```
FUNCTION "/" (Left, Right: Integer) RETURN Fraction_Type IS
   -- This function assumes that Right /= 0.
   -- It will not work correctly when Right = 0.
   Result : Fraction_Type;

BEGIN
   IF Right > 0 THEN
      Result :=
         Fraction_Type'
            (Numerator_Part   => Left,
             Denominator_Part => Right);
   ELSE
      Result :=
         Fraction_Type'
            (Numerator_Part   => - Left,
             Denominator_Part => - Right);
   END IF;
   Reduce (Result);
   RETURN Result;
END "/";
```

Then conventional fraction notation can be used to denote values of type Fraction_Type. For example, the declaration

```
F : Fraction_Type := 6 / 8;
```

would initialize F to a Fraction_Type value with a Numerator_Part component of three and a Denominator_Part component of four. In most contexts, the compiler would be able to distinguish this version of / from the predefined division operator for values of type Integer by looking at the required type of the result. However, the expression (3/4) / (10/2) would be illegal in a context where a Fraction_Type value was expected because there are two possible interpretations:

The division operators enclosed in parentheses refer to the predefined division operation for Integer values, the parenthesized expressions are of type Integer, and the middle division operator represents the new programmer-defined function to compute a Fraction_Type value from two Integer values.

The division operators enclosed in parentheses refer to the new programmer-defined function, the parenthesized expressions are of type Fraction_Type, and the middle division operator represents the function given earlier that divides one Fraction_Type value by another to produce a Fraction_Type result.

Qualified expressions can be used to eliminate the ambiguity: Either

```
Integer'(3/4) / (10/2)
```

or

```
(3/4) / Integer'(10/2)
```

forces the first interpretation, and either

```
Fraction_Type'(3/4) / (10/2)
```

or

```
(10/2) / Fraction_Type'(10/2)
```

forces the second interpretation.

9.7 THE `Inline` PRAGMA

Often, subprograms are used to avoid duplicate programming of similar computations. When the same actions are to be performed at several places in the program, it makes sense to describe those actions in a subprogram body and to call the subprogram at every place the actions are to be performed. This makes the program easier to maintain because revising these actions only requires one part of the program—the subprogram body—to be changed.

Usually, a subprogram called from many places also makes the machine-language translation of the program shorter, because the machine-language instructions carrying out the actions of the subprogram body only occur at one place. Calls on the subprogram are translated into a series of machine-language instructions that perform a number of bookkeeping actions and branch to the instructions for the program body. Returns are translated as branches back to the place from which the subprograms were called, followed by actions to restore the bookkeeping information that was valid before the subprogram call.

There are also excellent reasons to use a subprogram that is only called from one place. Subprograms can make a program easier to understand by dividing the program into several *levels of abstraction.* A subprogram call is a concise, high-level description of the work to be done at a given point in the program. The subprogram body is a low-level description of how the work is to be accomplished. By separating the description of *what* is to be done from the description of *how* it is to be done, subprograms divide large programs into small pieces, each of which can be understood more or less in isolation.

Unfortunately, some programmers, legitimately concerned about the efficiency of their programs, are reluctant to use subprograms for abstraction. They fear that the bookkeeping required when calling and returning from a subprogram will be too time-consuming. Where a well-written program would have contained a subprogram call, these programmers instead write the sequence of statements that would have gone in the subprogram body. As a result of this concern for efficiency, the clarity of the programs suffers.

The pragma `Inline` advises the compiler to translate a subprogram call *as if* the statements of the subprogram body were written directly at the place of the subprogram call. That is, the statements of the program body are translated *inline* at each place the subprogram is called. Nonetheless, the Ada *source* program contains one copy of the subprogram body and a subprogram call at each place the statements in that body are to be invoked.

The `Inline` pragma has no effect on the ultimate meaning of a subprogram or its calls, just the manner in which that meaning is realized. In fact, each compiler is free to follow or ignore the advice given in an `Inline` pragma on a call-by-call basis. When the advice is followed, the programmer worried about efficiency may reap many of the performance benefits of writing the body's statements separately in place of each call, without sacrificing clarity.

The form of the `Inline` pragma is as follows:

```
PRAGMA Inline ( subprogram name , ~~~ , subprogram name ) ;
```

A string constant containing an operator symbol may be used as the name of a function. The pragma must occur in the sequence of declarations containing the declaration or body of each named subprogram, after either the declaration or body. If a subprogram name is overloaded, the pragma refers to all versions whose declarations or bodies have already appeared, but not those yet to be introduced (by either a body or a declaration that will be followed later by a body).

Use of the pragma `Inline` carries a price—the amount of space used by the machine-language translation of the subprogram body. Without the `Inline` pragma, a compiler is likely to generate instructions from the subprogram body only once. If the `Inline` pragma is used, a separate copy of these instructions will be generated for each call for which the pragma is obeyed. In addition, as we shall see in Chapter 13, use of the `Inline` pragma may significantly increase the amount of recompilation that must take place when a large program consisting of many compilation units is modified.

A programmer who decides that an `Inline` pragma will be beneficial is making certain implicit assumptions about the compiler's translation methods, the relative sizes and speeds of the ordinary and inline translations, the number of places the named subprograms are called from, and the number of times calls on the named subprograms will be executed. Often, many of these assumptions turn out to be wrong. Thus the `Inline` pragma should not be used routinely while a program is first being written.

Rather, the program should be tested *once it is complete* to determine whether execution time is really a problem. (Often, programmers are pleasantly surprised to discover that it is not the problem they feared it would be.) If it is a problem, *metering tools* available in Ada Programming Support Environments should be used to determine which subprograms are taking up most of the time. Typically, programs spend most of their time executing a very small part of the program text over and over. Only after a programmer has pinpointed the bottlenecks in his program should he try to improve the program's performance with the `Inline` pragma. The program should then be reexamined to make sure that its running time is really improved and that the size of the machine-language translation is still acceptable.

Perhaps the greatest strength of the `Inline` pragma is that it allows efficiency decisions to be made separately and at the proper time. Subprograms can be written for readability without concern for efficiency. Later, when efficiency becomes an important issue, a program is easily modified to move subprograms inline without distorting the structure of the source program.

9.8 DETAILS

9.8.1 Nested Subprograms and Global Variables

Just as subprogram bodies may appear in the declarative part of a main program, so other subprogram bodies may appear in the declarative part of these subprogram bodies. Subprogram bodies may be *nested* in other subprogram bodies to an arbitrary depth. However, this practice can make a program hard to read. It is difficult to keep track of the pattern of nesting when a subprogram spans several pages. It even may be difficult to recognize which previously started subprogram bodies surround a given program body. Large subprogram bodies in a declarative part increase the distance between the variable declarations at the top of the declarative part and the corresponding sequence of statements following the declarative part. In contrast, placing all subprogram bodies directly in the declarative part of the main program decreases the amount of text that must be examined in order to understand a given subprogram. In fact, by writing subprograms as independent compilation units, as you will learn to do in Chapter 13, it is possible to avoid even this much nesting.

When an inner subprogram body occurs in the declarative part of an outer subprogram body, it may refer to any of the names declared earlier in the declarative part of the outer subprogram body. Because type, subtype, named number, and object declarations are basic declarations and subprogram bodies are later declarations, the inner subprogram may refer to all types, subtypes, named numbers, variables, and constants declared in the outer subprogram. (However, the reverse is not true. Entities declared in the inner subprogram may not be referred to in the outer subprogram.)

When the same identifier is given different meanings at two different levels of nesting, the Ada language usually follows the rule of PL/I and Pascal and uses the inner meaning within the inner subprogram. However, there are exceptions. The rules that determine where you may refer to names declared at a given point, and what those names mean at various places in the program, are called *scope rules*. The scope rules of the Ada language are described in Chapter 14.

A variable declared in an outer subprogram but used in an inner subprogram is said to be *global* to the inner subprogram. Global variables often make a program hard to read by obscuring the ways in which information is passed back and forth between a calling program and a subprogram. When information is passed back and forth through parameters, a subprogram call explicitly states that the action of the subprogram will be based on certain specified values and may affect the values of certain specified variables. When a subprogram refers to global variables, a call on that subprogram does not necessarily name all variables whose values will determine the effect of the subprogram call. Worse yet, if a subprogram changes the value of a global variable, a statement containing a call on that procedure indirectly results in the modification of a variable not even mentioned in the subprogram call. Except in certain restricted contexts that we shall describe in Chapter 11, it is wise to avoid the use of global variables.

Fortunately, it is easy to eliminate global variables from a program. A new formal parameter can be added to a subprogram for each global variable in the subprogram body, and each reference to the global variable can be replaced by the corresponding formal parameter. In the calling program, the variables formerly used as global variables inside the calling program are added to the subprogram call as actual parameters. The mode of the new formal parameters depends on whether the global variables were examined, modified, or both examined and modified by the subprogram.

For example, the following program, to count the number of periods in the standard input file, uses a nested subprogram named `Increment_Count`. `Increment_Count` uses `Number_Of_Periods` as a global variable.

```
WITH Basic_IO;
PROCEDURE Count_Periods IS

   Number_Of_Periods : Natural := 0;
   Next_Character    : Character;

   PROCEDURE Increment_Count IS
   BEGIN
      Number_Of_Periods := Number_Of_Periods + 1;
   END Increment_Count;

BEGIN -- Count_Periods

   WHILE NOT Basic_IO.End_Of_File LOOP
      Basic_IO.Get (Next_Character);
      IF Next_Character = '.' THEN
         Increment_Count;
      END IF;
   END LOOP;

   Basic_IO.Put (Number_Of_Periods);
   Basic_IO.Put (" periods were found.");
   Basic_IO.New_Line;

END Count_Periods;
```

Since Increment_Count both examines and modifies Number_Of_Periods, the global variable can be eliminated by giving Increment_Count a parameter of mode IN OUT:

```
WITH Basic_IO;
PROCEDURE Count_Periods IS
   Number_Of_Periods : Natural := 0;
   Next_Character    : Character;
   PROCEDURE Increment_Count (Count : IN OUT Integer) IS
   BEGIN
      Count := Count + 1;
   END Increment_Count;
BEGIN -- Count_Periods
   WHILE NOT Basic_IO.End_Of_File LOOP
      Basic_IO.Get (Next_Character);
      IF Next_Character = '.' THEN
         Increment_Count (Number_Of_Periods);
      END IF;
   END LOOP;
   Basic_IO.Put (Number_Of_Periods);
   Basic_IO.Put (" periods were found.");
   Basic_IO.New_Line;
END Count_Periods;
```

This makes it easier to find points in the main program where Number_Of_Periods is modified. The program Count_Periods is very small, and either version is relatively easy to understand. In a larger program, the deleterious effect of global variables would be more pronounced.

9.8.2 The Process of Passing Parameters

When a subprogram body is executed, each formal parameter is made to *stand for* one of the actual parameters (or for a default parameter value). In general, this is accomplished as follows. A parameter of mode IN is *evaluated* and *copied* into the formal parameter before the subprogram body is executed. An actual parameter of mode IN OUT is evaluated and copied into the formal parameter before the procedure body is executed, and the value remaining in the formal parameter when the procedure body is complete is copied back into the actual parameter. A formal parameter of mode OUT has an undefined value when execution of a procedure body begins, and the value remaining in the formal parameter when the procedure body is complete is copied to the actual parameter.

Whenever an actual parameter is copied into a formal parameter, the program makes sure that the value copied belongs to the subtype named in the formal parameter specification. Whenever a formal parameter is copied into a variable acting as an actual parameter, the program makes sure that the value copied belongs to the subtype of that variable. Whenever the formal parameter is copied back into a type conversion acting as an actual parameter, the value copied is first converted to the type of the variable inside the type conversion, and the program then checks that the converted value belongs to the subtype of the variable. (Similarly, when a RETURN statement is executed in a function body, the program makes sure that the value to be returned is in the subtype specified after the word RETURN in the function specification.)

If a procedure were to complete without assigning a value to some formal parameter of mode OUT, the formal parameter's initial undefined value would be copied back into the actual parameter. If this initial undefined value happened not to belong to the subtype of the actual parameter, this would result in an error. Thus it is wise to be sure that some value is assigned to each OUT parameter before a procedure returns.

There are some exceptions to the general approach described above. In the case of *access type* formal parameters of mode OUT, the value of the actual parameter is copied into the formal parameter before the procedure body is executed. It is still forbidden to examine the value of the formal parameter within the procedure body, but it is impossible for an undefined access value to be copied into the actual parameter at the end of the call. (If the formal parameter is never updated by the procedure, the actual parameter gets back its original value.) This copy-in rule for parameters of mode OUT also applies to access-type *components* contained, directly or indirectly, in an array or record type parameter.

In the case of array-type and record-type formal parameters, a compiler has the option of using a different mechanism, known as *call by reference,* in which the formal parameter becomes another name for the object named by the actual parameter. Any change to the value of the formal parameter is instantaneously reflected in the value of the actual parameter, and vice versa. (Call by reference is used in typical FORTRAN implementations and in PL/I when the actual parameter is a variable; and in Pascal when the formal parameter is a **var** parameter.) Use of call by reference does not affect the legality of modifying or examining a given formal parameter, which is determined entirely by the parameter mode; internally, however, call by reference may avoid the need to copy large amounts of data.

When the copying option is used for array-type or record-type parameters, at least some information about the actual parameter is copied into the formal parameter, even if the parameter mode is OUT. This information includes the index bounds for arrays, both for the parameters themselves and for any arrays contained directly or indirectly in the parameters.

A compiler may select different parameter passing options for different subprogram calls or for different parameters in the same subprogram call. It is possible to write a program whose effect depends on the option selected by the compiler. *Such a program is incorrect,* even though the compiler is unlikely to detect it. Here is an example of such a program:

```
WITH Basic_IO;
PROCEDURE Erroneous_Program IS
   TYPE Singleton_Array IS ARRAY (1 .. 1) OF Integer;
   X : Singleton_Array;
```

```
      PROCEDURE Print_X (Y : IN OUT Singleton_Array) IS
      BEGIN
         Y(1) := 2;
         Basic_IO.Put ( X(1) );
         Basic_IO.New_Line;
      END Print_X;
   BEGIN
      X(1) := 1;
      Print_X (X);
      Basic_IO.Put ( X(1) );
      Basic_IO.New_Line;
   END Erroneous_Program;
```

If call by reference is used, the assignment to `Y (1)` in `Print_X` immediately changes the value of the actual parameter `X`, so that the value `2` is printed by `Print_X`. If copying is used, the modified value of `Y` is not copied back into `X` until `Print_X` is complete, so `X` still contains one when its component is printed by `Print_X`. Either way, the value of `X` is updated by the time the procedure call statement, `Print_X (X)`, is complete, so the value printed by the main program is `2`.

Unless a subprogram raises an exception, its effect depends on the method of parameter passing only when calls on the subprogram to generate multiple names, or *aliases*, for an actual parameter inside the subprogram body, when the actual parameter is modified by one of its aliases, and when its value is later examined by another one of its aliases. Depending on the way in which parameters are passed, the modified value may or may not be reflected in the other aliases by the time the program refers to these aliases. In the example above, the actual parameter `X` was modified under the name `X` (as a global variable) and then examined under the name of the corresponding actual parameter, `Y`.

Global variables passed as parameters always result in aliases. Similarly, aliases can arise when the same object is used as an actual parameter in more than one position (in which case two or more formal parameters correspond to the same object), when two actual parameters are overlapping slices, or when one actual parameter is contained in another. Access values are also a rich source of aliases.

9.8.3 More On Overloading

In resolving overloading, the compiler must account for the possibility of defaulted parameters. Consider the following functions:

```
   FUNCTION f (x : Integer; y : Integer := 0) RETURN Integer IS
   BEGIN
      RETURN 2 * x + y;
   END f;

   FUNCTION f (z : Integer) RETURN Integer IS
   BEGIN
      RETURN 3 * z;
   END f;
```

Overloading is permitted because the parameter and result type profile of the first version is

```
kind of subprogram:          function
base type of result:         Integer
number of parameters:        2
base types of parameters: (1) Integer, (2) Integer
```

and the parameter and result type profile of the second version is

```
kind of subprogram:          function
base type of result:         Integer
number of parameters:        1
base types of parameters: (1) Integer
```

Nonetheless, assuming `n` is an `Integer` variable, the call in

```
n := f (1);
```

is ambiguous. It may be a call on the first version of `f` with the actual parameter for `y` omitted, or it may be a call on the second version. Unambiguous versions of the assignment statement include the following:

```
n := f (x => 1);
n := f (1, 0);
n := f (z => 1);
```

The only clues that may be used in resolving overloading are those listed in Section 9.5—whether the call is a procedure call or function call, the number and base types of actual parameters, the types that may legally appear at the place that a function call appears, and the names of formal parameters in named parameter associations. In particular, parameter modes and parameter subtypes are never used to resolve overloading. In cases where it would be possible to deduce the meaning of the call using this information, but not without using it, the call is considered ambiguous and therefore illegal.

Like subprograms, enumeration literals can be overloaded. For purposes of resolving overloading, an enumeration literal is treated as if it were a function with no parameters, returning a value in the corresponding enumeration type. (Thus an enumeration literal has a parameter and result type profile.) Enumeration literals can be overloaded with other enumeration literals, subprograms can be overloaded with other subprograms, and subprograms can be overloaded with enumeration literals. However, these are the only forms of overloading. A type cannot be overloaded with a subprogram, for example.

When a string literal is used as the name of a function, it may not contain spaces. However, the case of letters in the string does not matter: `"ABS"`, `"abs"`, `"Abs"`, `"aBs"`, `"abS"`, and so forth are all considered to be the same function name.

Functions named by operator symbols may be called in the conventional format for function calls, although it is rarely useful to do this. For example, `"+" (a,3)` may be used in place of `a+3`, and `"ABS" (a)` in place of `ABS a`. In fact, named parameter associations may be used for such calls. All the two-operand predefined operators have formal parameters named `Left` and `Right`. All the one-operand predefined operators have a formal parameter named `Right`. (Thus we may write

```
"-" (Right => x, Left => y)
```

for `y-x`.)

9.9 SUMMARY

A *subprogram body* may be either a *procedure body* or a *function body*. The typical form of a procedure body is

```
PROCEDURE identifier
    [ (parameter specification ; ~~~ ; parameter specification ) ]   IS
    declarative part
BEGIN
    sequence of statements
END identifier ;
```

where a parameter specification has the form

```
identifier , ~~~ , identifier :
  [ mode ]  typemark  [ := expression ]
```

Similarly, the form of a function body is

```
FUNCTION identifier
  [ ( parameter specifications ; ~~~ ; parameter specification ) ]
    RETURN typemark IS
    declarative part
BEGIN
    sequence of statements
END identifier ;
```

A subprogram body can be placed in a declarative part, following all variable, constant, named number, type, and subtype declarations, or it can be compiled as an independent compilation unit.

The identifiers in a parameter specification name the subprogram's *formal parameters*. The parameter mode may be either `IN`, indicating that the parameter is used to pass data from the subprogram call in to the subprogram; `OUT`, indicating that the parameter is used to pass data from the subprogram out to the call; or `IN OUT`, indicating that the parameter is used to pass data in both directions. If the mode is not given, it is assumed to be `IN`. `IN` is the only mode allowed for functions. The typemark in a parameter specification gives the subtype of the parameter. The optional `:=` and expression, only allowed for parameters of mode `IN`, specify a *default initial value*. An actual parameter may be omitted from a subprogram call if the corresponding parameter specification provides a default value for that parameter. A program may not modify its `IN` parameters or examine the values of its `OUT` parameters.

When a subprogram is called, the declarative part of the subprogram body is elaborated and then the sequence of statements is executed. Execution of a procedure ends when the sequence of statements is finished or a statement of the form

```
RETURN ;
```

is executed. Execution of a function ends when a statement of the form

`RETURN` *expression* `;`

is executed. The value of the expression becomes the value of the function call that invoked the function.

A subprogram parameter may belong to an unconstrained array subtype, in which case arrays of different lengths can be passed during different calls. The subprogram can use the `'Length`, `'Range`, `'First`, and `'Last` attributes to determine the bounds of the array, even if the parameter has mode `OUT`. (Although the *value* of the `OUT` parameter cannot be examined by the subprogram, attributes of the parameter can be.) Unlike FORTRAN and PL/I, the Ada language does not require additional parameters giving the dimensions of the array parameter.

The form of a subprogram call is

name [`(` *parameter association* , ~~~ , *parameter association* `)`]

where a parameter association is either a *named parameter association* of the form

formal parameter identifier `=>` *actual parameter*

or a *positional parameter association* of the form

actual parameter

Positional parameter specifications must come first, and the nth positional actual parameter is associated with the nth parameter in the list of parameter specifications. Named parameter associations may appear in any order, and the actual parameter is associated with the parameter named. If a parameter in a given position is omitted from a subprogram call (because the corresponding parameter specification gives a default value), parameter associations in all subsequent positions must be named.

For parameters of mode **IN**, any expression may be used as an actual parameter. For parameters of mode **OUT** or **IN OUT**, only a variable or a type conversion of a variable may be used as an actual parameter. At the beginning of a subprogram call, the values of **IN** and **IN OUT** actual parameters are copied into the corresponding formal parameters. At the end of the subprogram call, all values of **IN OUT** and **OUT** formal parameters are copied back into the actual parameters and, if the actual parameter is a type conversion, "unconverted" to the type of the variable inside the type conversion.

A subprogram may call itself. This is known as *recursion*. It causes a separate *activation* of the subprogram to begin while the previous activation remains suspended at the point of the call. Each activation has its own copy of the variables declared inside the subprogram body. Similarly, there may be a circle of two or more subprograms, each of which calls the next subprogram in the circle. This is called *mutual recursion*. Normally, one subprogram body may not contain a call on another subprogram whose body appears later. However, such a call is allowed if the body of the first subprogram is preceded by a *declaration* of the second subprogram. A *procedure declaration* has the form

PROCEDURE *identifier*
    (*parameter specification* **;** ~~~ **;** *parameter specification*)   **;**

A *function declaration* has the form

FUNCTION *identifier*
    (*parameter specification* **;** ~~~ **;** *parameter specification*)
    RETURN *typemark* **;**

Mutual recursion would be impossible without subprogram declarations.

Two subprograms may be given the same name, provided they differ in at least one of the following respects:

whether the subprogram is a procedure or function
if the subprogram is a function, the result type of the function
the number of parameters in the subprogram
the base type of each parameter

These properties of a subprogram are collectively called the subprogram's *parameter and result type profile*. Using the same name for multiple subprograms is called *overloading*. Overloading is appropriate for subprograms that perform analogous operations, but on different numbers of parameters or parameters of different types. In a subprogram call with an overloaded subprogram name, a compiler may use the following clues to determine which subprogram is actually being called:

whether the call is a function call or a procedure call
the number of actual parameters appearing in the subprogram call
the types of the actual parameters
in the case of a function call, the types that are legal for expressions at the place where the function call occurs
the names of formal parameters appearing in named parameter associations in the subprogram call

The subprogram call is illegal if the version being called cannot be determined using only these clues.

Expressions with operators such as +, *, XOR, and ABS are really calls on functions with names such as "+", "*", "XOR", and "ABS". (The quotation marks are part of the name.) A function body with an appropriate string literal as a function name overloads the operator named by the literal. Then an expression applying the operator to operands of the appropriate type and producing a result of the appropriate type is interpreted as a call on that function.

The Inline pragma can be used to recommend that a compiler translate a subprogram call by inserting a translation of the subprogram body directly at the point of the subprogram call. For some implementations, this makes subprogram calls more efficient. However, it can also increase the size of the program and the number of program units that must be recompiled when part of a program is changed. The Inline pragma is best used only to improve the performance of working programs once any bottlenecks in those programs have been identified. Its form is:

```
PRAGMA Inline ( subprogram name , ~~~ , subprogram name ) ;
```

EXERCISES

9.1 One of the most famous recursive algorithms is the solution to the Eight Queens Problem. The problem is to find all possible placements of eight queens on a chess board such that no queen is in a position to attack another. In other words, each queen must be the only piece in its row, the only piece in its column, and the only piece along each of its two diagonals. The problem can be solved with a recursive procedure having two parameters—some representation of the chess board and an integer in the range zero to eight. When the procedure is called with the integer parameter having some value *n*, it is assumed that an acceptable placement has been found for queens in the first *n* columns of the chessboard. Thus, if *n* is eight, the procedure should just print out the arrangement of queens on the chessboard and return. If *n* is less than eight, the program should try to place a queen in each of the eight squares of column *n*+1 in turn, and check whether a queen on that square is in the same row, left-to-right ascending diagonal, or left-to-right descending diagonal as a queen in some previous column. If this check reveals no conflicts with any queens in previous columns, the procedure should call itself recursively with the chessboard representation having a queen on that square and the integer parameter equal to *n*+1, to try to fill in the remaining columns.

Code this solution in the Ada language. Write a main program that contains all necessary type declarations, the body for a function that returns a Boolean value indicating whether the queen in a given column conflicts with any queen in a previous column, and the body of the recursive procedure described previously. The main program should contain a call on the recursive procedure with an integer actual parameter of zero and an empty chessboard. (*Hint* for writing the function: The sum of the row number and column number of a square remains constant along each left-to-right ascending diagonal of the board, and each such diagonal has a unique sum; the difference between the row number and the column number of a square remains constant along each left-to-right descending diagonal of the board, and each such diagonal has a unique difference.)

9.2 Generalize the program written for the previous problem so that the main program reads some number k from the standard input file, and all possible arrangements of k queens on a k-by-k board are printed.

9.3 It is inconvenient that the Ada language does not automatically pad string literals with blanks to obtain the string length required in the context of the literal. A variable of subtype `String (1 .. 10)` cannot be assigned the string literal `"ABC"`; you must write `"ABC       "` instead. Write a function named `Padded_String` that takes a parameter of type `String` and a parameter of subtype `Natural` giving the intended length of the string. When the intended length is greater than or equal to the length of the string, `Padded_String` returns a string of the specified length, obtained by adding zero or more blanks to the right end of the string. When the specified length is less than the number of characters in the first parameter, the value of the first parameter is truncated to obtain the result, but this is not the intended use of the function. Here are some examples:

```
Padded_String ("ABC", 10) = "ABC       "
Padded_String ("ABC", 3) = "ABC"
Padded_String ("ABC", 2) = "AB"
```

9.4 Consider the following declarations:

```
SUBTYPE Scalar_Subtype IS Float RANGE -1.0E5 .. 1.0E5;

TYPE Vector_Type IS
   RECORD
      X_Part, Y_Part, Z_Part : Scalar_Subtype;
   END RECORD;

c1, c2         : Scalar_Subtype;
f              : Float;
v1, v2, v3, v4 : Vector_Type;


FUNCTION "*"
   (c: Scalar_Subtype; v: Vector_Type) RETURN Vector_Type IS

   -- scalar multiple of a vector

BEGIN

   RETURN Vector_Type'(c*v.X_Part, c*v.Y_Part, c*v.Z_Part);

END "*";


FUNCTION "*"
   (v1, v2: Vector_Type) RETURN Scalar_Subtype IS

   -- scalar product (dot product) of two vectors

BEGIN

   RETURN
      v1.X_Part * v2.X_Part +
         v1.Y_Part * v2.Y_Part +
         v1.Z_Part * v2.Z_Part;

END "*";
```

```
FUNCTION "*"
   (v1, v2: Vector_Type) RETURN Vector_Type IS
   -- vector product (cross-product) of two vectors
BEGIN
   RETURN
      Vector_Type'
         (X_Part =>
            v1.Y_Part * v2.Z_Part - v1.Z_Part * v2.Y_Part,
          Y_Part =>
            v1.Z_Part * v2.X_Part - v1.X_Part * v2.Z_Part,
          Z_Part =>
            v1.X_Part * v2.Y_Part - v1.Y_Part * v2.X_Part);
END "*";

PROCEDURE p
   (a: IN Vector_Type;
    b: IN Scalar_Subtype := 1.0;
    c: OUT Scalar_Subtype) IS
BEGIN
   c := b * (a.X_Part + a.Y_Part + a.Z_Part);
END p; -- Version 1

PROCEDURE p (a, d : IN Scalar_Subtype; c: IN Float) IS
BEGIN
   f := a * d * c;
END p; -- Version 2

PROCEDURE p (a: IN Vector_Type; b: IN Scalar_Subtype) IS
BEGIN
   f := b * (a.X_Part + a.Y_Part + a.Z_Part);
END p; -- Version 3
```

These declarations establish three overloaded versions of `"*"` and three overloaded versions of `p`. The versions of `"*"` also overload the predefined multiplication operator that takes two operands of type `Float` and returns a result of that type.

(*a*) Describe the parameter and result type profile of each version of `"*"` and each version of `p`.

(*b*) Indicate each possible interpretation of the calls in the statements below. Where only one interpretation is possible, explain how you reached your conclusion and state whether an Ada compiler would also have eliminated all other interpretations.

```
(1) v3 := c1 * v1 * v2;          (7) p (c1*v1*v2, 1.0);
(2) c2 := c1 * v1 * v2;          (8) p (c1*v1*v2, 1.0, f);
(3) v3 := c1 * (v1 * v2);        (9) p (c1*v1*v2, 1.0, 2.0);
(4) c2 := c1 * (v1 * v2);        (10) p (c1*v1*v2, c => f, b => 1.0);
(5) v4 := v1 * v2 * v3;          (11) p (c1*v1*v2, c => f);
(6) c1 := v1 * v2 * v3;
```

9.5 Imagine that the only predefined version of the operator `&` was one that catenated two values of type `String`. Show how you could define for yourself the versions catenating a character to a string, a string to a character, and a character to a character.

9.6 Complex numbers are numbers of the form $a+b*i$, where a and b are real numbers and i is an imaginary number with the property that $i^2 = -1$. The arithmetic operations can be applied to complex numbers to yield results that are complex numbers, as follows:

```
-(a+b*i)              = (-a) + (-b)*i
(a+b*i) + (c+d*i)     = (a+c) + (b+d)*i
(a+b*i) - (c+d*i)     = (a-c) + (b-d)*i
(a+b*i) * (c+d*i)     = a*c + b*c*i + a*d*i + b*d*i*i
                      = (a*c - b*d) + (b*c+a*d)*i
                        (since i*i = -1)
(a+b*i) / (c-d*i)     = ((a+b*i) * (c+d*i)) / ((c-d*i) * (c+d*i))
                      = ((a*c - b*d) + (b*c + a*d)*i) / ((c c+ d* d) + (c*d - c*d)*i)
                      = ((a*c - b*d) / (c**2 + d**2)) + ((b*c + a*d) / (c**2 + d**2)) * i
```

Also, by convention, the absolute value of $a + b*i$ is the square root of a^2+b^2. Define a type to represent complex numbers, and overload each of the arithmetic operations just described to work for complex operands. In overloading `ABS`, you may assume that you have available a function named `Square_Root` that takes a parameter of type `Float` and returns a result of type `Float` whose value is the square root of the parameter.

9.7 Generalize the version of `"*"` in Section 9.6 for linear algebraic matrix multiplication, so that the second dimension of the left operand need not have the same lower and upper bounds as the first dimension of the right operand, just the same length. For example, it should be possible to multiply a value of subtype `Matrix_Type (1 .. 10, 5 .. 7)` by a value of subtype `Matrix_Type (1 .. 3, 0 .. 5)`, obtaining a result of subtype `Matrix_Type (1 .. 10, 0 .. 5)`.

9.8 In general, a compiler cannot be expected to obey an `Inline` pragma applied to a recursive subprogram. What would happen if a compiler tried simplistically to obey the advice of the `Inline` pragma when translating every call on a recursive subprogram?

CHAPTER

TEN

RECORD TYPES WITH DISCRIMINANTS

As Section 4.2.7 indicated, there are two kinds of record types, record types without discriminants and record types with discriminants. Record types without discriminants were introduced in Section 4.2.7. This chapter explains record types with discriminants.

10.1 RECORDS WITH VARYING STRUCTURE

The table in Figure 10.1 shows the airfares for all the flights of Ada Airlines. If Ada Airlines has a flight between two given cities, the corresponding entry in the table shows both the regular and first-class airfares. If there is no flight offered between two given cities, the corresponding entry in the table has an X.

Given the declaration of a type `Table_Entry_Type` for representing a single table entry, a type for tables such as this could be declared as follows:

```
TYPE City_Type IS
   (Boston, Minneapolis, San Francisco, Washington, Paris);
TYPE Airfare_Table_Type IS
   ARRAY (City_Type, City_Type) OF Table_Entry_Type;
```

(`Airfare_Table_Type` is a two-dimensional constrained array type with `City_Type` used as the index type in both dimensions.) But how should `Table_Entry_Type` be declared?

To

From	Boston	Minneapolis	San Francisco	Washington	Paris
Boston	X	X	X	$150 $325	X
Minneapolis	X	X	$675 $1,375	$375 $775	$1,125 $2,275
San Francisco	X	$657 $1,375	X	$1,000 $2,025	X
Washington	$150 $325	$375 $775	$1,000 $2,025	X	$1,000 $2,025
Paris	X	$1,125 $2,275	X	$1,000 $2,025	X

Figure 10.1 A table giving the regular and first-class fares for all flights of Ada Airlines. If there ia a flight from one city to another, the corresponding box in the table contains the regular fare followed by the first-class fare. If there is no flight from one city to another, the corresponding box contains an X.

An obvious solution is a record-type declaration such as:

```
TYPE Table_Entry_Type IS
   RECORD
      Regular_Fare_Part, First_Class_Fare_Part :
         Integer RANGE 0 .. 2000;
   END RECORD;
```

However, this does not provide any way to represent table entries containing an X. (If we revise the range constraint in the declaration of `Regular_Fare_Part` and `First_Class_Fare_Part`, special "fare values" like -1 could be used to signify that a given route is not served, but this is not a natural solution. It does not reflect the abstract meaning of the record components `Regular_Fare_Part` and `First_Class_Fare_Part`.) What is needed is a type whose values can take on two different forms—a form indicating that there is no service between two cities and a form giving the regular and first class airfares between two cities for which there is service.

The following declaration defines `Table_Entry_Type` to be a *record type with discriminants:*

```
TYPE Table_Entry_Type (Route_Serviced : Boolean := False) IS
   RECORD
      CASE Route_Serviced IS
         WHEN True =>
            Regular_Fare_Part, First_Class_Fare_Part :
               Integer RANGE 0 .. 2000;
         WHEN False =>
            NULL;
      END CASE;
   END RECORD;
```

Route_Serviced is a *discriminant*. A discriminant is a record component with the special property that its value affects the structure of the record. There are two different forms of Table_Entry_Type values:

1. Records consisting of a Route_Serviced component equal to True, a Regular_Fare_Part component, and a First_Class_Fare_Part component
2. Records consisting of a Route_Serviced component equal to False and no other component

The following procedure modifies an airfare table to eliminate service for any route with a regular fare of less than $200:

```
PROCEDURE Eliminate_Cheap_Routes
   (Fare_Table : IN OUT Airfare_Table_Type) IS

   Table_Entry : Table_Entry_Type;

BEGIN

   FOR From_City IN City_Type LOOP

      FOR To_City IN City_Type LOOP

         Table_Entry := Fare_Table (From_City, To_City);

         IF Table_Entry.Route_Serviced AND THEN
            Table_Entry.Regular_Fare_Part < 200 THEN

            Fare_Table (From_City, To_City) :=
               (Route_Serviced => False);

         END IF;

      END LOOP;

   END LOOP;

END Eliminate_Cheap_Routes;
```

The short-circuit control form in the IF statement is necessary because it is an error to refer to the component Table_Entry.Regular_Fare_Part if Table_Entry.Route_Serviced is false. The Regular_Fare_Part component does not exist for records with false Route_Serviced components. A record aggregate lists only those components that exist for the record value it describes. Thus the aggregate

```
(Route_Serviced => False);
```

does not give values for `Regular_Fare_Part` or `First_Class_Fare_Part` components.

Besides being a record component, a discriminant acts as a "parameter" for objects in the type: Discriminant names may appear as expressions in certain places in the record-type declaration. A declaration of an *object* in a record type with discriminants may include a *discriminant constraint* that specifies the values to be used for the "parameters" of that object. The values of the discriminants may affect the structure of that object. For example, in the object declaration

```
Fares : Table_Entry_Type (Route_Serviced => True);
```

the discriminant constraint

```
(Route_Serviced => True);
```

restricts the object `Fares` to hold only `Table_Entry_Type` values of the first kind. The declaration

```
Table_Entry : Table_Entry_Type;
```

has no discriminant constraint, so `Table_Entry` can hold different forms of `Table_Entry_Type` records at different times.

One of the possible forms of the discriminant constraint is:

(*identifier* => *expression* , ~~~ , *identifier* => *expression*)

Each identifier names a discriminant of the record type to which the discriminant constraint is being applied. The expression following a discriminant name specifies the value to be used for the corresponding discriminant in the object being declared. This expression must be of the subtype specified for that discriminant in the record-type declaration.

10.2 DECLARING RECORD TYPES WITH DISCRIMINANTS

A type declaration for a record type with discriminants looks different from the type declarations we have seen so far. A list of *discriminant specifications* appears after the name of the type being declared and before the word `IS`. The usual form of the declaration is as follows:

```
TYPE identifier (discriminant specification ; ~~~; discriminant specification ) IS
   RECORD

     ......................
     : component declaration :
     :        ~~~            :
     : component declaration :
     ......................

     ............
     : variant part :
     ............

   END RECORD ;
```

The form of a discriminant specification is:

```
identifier , ~~~ , identifier : typemark  [ := expression ]  ;
```

The typemark in the discriminant specification must name a subtype of a discrete type (i.e., a subtype of an integer type or an enumeration type, perhaps the subtype consisting of the entire type). The optional expression, if present, specifies a default initial value for the discriminant. The optional *variant part* in the type declaration is used to specify components that may exist in some of the objects in the record type and not in others. If the variant part is present, it may be preceded by zero or more component declarations; however, if the variant part is omitted, there must be at least one component declaration.

The typemark in the discriminant specification may not be followed by a constraint. However, the allowable values of the discriminant can be restricted by declaring a new subtype first and using the name of that subtype in the discriminant specification:

```
TYPE Class_Type IS (Freshman, Sophomore, Junior, Senior);
SUBTYPE Upper_Class_Subtype IS
   Class_Type RANGE Junior .. Senior;
TYPE Concentrator_Type
   (Year : Upper_Class_Subtype := Junior) IS
   RECORD
      Name  : String (1 .. 80);
      Major : String (1 ..10);
      CASE Year IS
         WHEN Junior =>
            Junior_Dissertation_Advisor : String (1 .. 30)
         WHEN Senior =>
            Honors_Candidate : Boolean;
      END CASE;
   END RECORD;
```

The declaration of Upper_Class_Subtype allows the declaration of a record type in which the discriminant may assume only the two highest values of Class_Type.

10.2.1 Declaring Record Types with Variants

The form of the variant part is similar to the form of a CASE statement:

```
CASE identifier IS
   WHEN choice list =>
      component list

      ~~~

   WHEN choice list =>
      component list
  ......................
  : WHEN OTHERS =>      :
  :    component list   :
  ......................
END CASE;
```

The form of the choice list is the same as in a CASE statement. (See Section 7.3.2. As in a CASE statement, only static expressions and static discrete ranges are allowed.) In a CASE statement, any expression of a discrete type may follow the word CASE, but in a variant part, it must be the name of one of the record type's discriminants. In a CASE statement, each choice list is followed by a list of statements to be executed for certain values of the expression. In a variant part, each choice list is followed by a list of components that are present in the record type for certain values of the discriminant. Each possible combination of record components is called a *variant* of the record type. All components in a record type must have distinct names, even if they occur in different variants.

For example, if we have already declared an enumeration type named State_Type, containing one value for each of the states in the United States, we can define a type named Mailing_Address_Type as follows:

```
TYPE Mailing_Address_Type (US_Address : Boolean := True) IS
   RECORD
      Name_Part, Street_Part : String (1 .. 30);
      City_Part              : String (1 .. 20);
      CASE US_Address IS
         WHEN True =>
            State_Part    : State_Type;
            Zip_Code_Part : Integer RANGE 0 .. 99999;
         WHEN False =>
            Country_Part : String (1 .. 20);
      END CASE;
   END RECORD;
```

This record type has two variants. One has a `US_Address` component set to `True`, as well as `Name_Part`, `Street_Part`, `City_Part`, `State_Part`, and `Zip_Code_Part` components. The other has a `US_Address` component set to `False`, as well as `Name_Part`, `Street_Part`, `City_Part`, and `Country_Part` components.

It is possible for a variant to have no components. In this case, a component list of the form

```
NULL;
```

is used for that variant. The declaration for `Table_Entry_Type` as a record type with discriminants had a component list of this form:

```
TYPE Table_Entry_Type (Route_Serviced : Boolean := False) IS
   RECORD
      CASE Route_Serviced IS
         WHEN True =>
            Regular_Fare_Part, First_Class_Fare_Part :
               Integer RANGE 0 .. 2000;
         WHEN False =>
            NULL;
      END CASE;
   END RECORD;
```

(In this case, the record-type declaration had *only* a variant part.)

The component list in a variant part can also contain zero or more ordinary component declarations followed by a nested variant part. For example, a personal calendar program might have commands to record an appointment for a particular time and day, along with a description of the appointment; to list all appointments for a given day; and to cancel an existing appointment for a given time and day. These commands may be summarized as follows, where *d* is a day, *t* is a time, and *s* is a string describing the appointment:

```
ADD    d t s
LIST   d
DELETE d t
```

A command could be represented internally by a record type with discriminants. Assume we start with the following declarations:

```
TYPE Date_Type IS
   RECORD
      Month_Part : Integer RANGE 1 .. 12;
      Day_Part   : Integer RANGE 1 .. 31;
      Year_Part  : Integer RANGE 1980 .. 2099;
   END RECORD;
```

```
TYPE Time_Type IS
   RECORD
      Hour_Part   : Integer RANGE 0 .. 23;
      Minute_Part : Integer RANGE 0 .. 59;
   END RECORD;
TYPE Command_Code_Type IS
   (Add_Command, List_Command, Delete_Command);
```

Then the type for commands can be declared as follows:

```
TYPE Command_Type
   (Command_Code : Command_Code_Type := List_Command) IS
   RECORD
      Date_Part : Date_Type;
      CASE Command_Code IS
         WHEN List_Command =>
            NULL;
         WHEN Add_Command | Delete_Command =>
            Time_Part : Time_Type;
            CASE Command_Code IS
               WHEN Add_Command =>
                  Description_Part : String (1 .. 80)
               WHEN OTHERS =>
                  NULL;
            END CASE;
      END CASE;
   END RECORD;
```

The record-type declaration has a component declaration for Date_Part followed by a variant part with two variants. The second variant's component list consists of a component declaration for Time_Part followed by a nested variant part. In all, Command_Type has three variants:

1. a Command_Code component set to List_Command and a Date_Part component
2. a Command_Code component set to Add_Command, along with Date_Part, Time_Part, and Description_Part components
3. a Command_Code component set to Delete_Command, along with Date_Part and Time_Part components

Assuming there are procedures named Get_Command, Process_Add_Command, Process_List_Command, and Process_Delete_Command, the main program might contain statements such as:

```
Get_Command (Command);
CASE Command.Command_Code IS
   WHEN Add_Command =>
      Process_Add_Command
         (Command.Date_Part,
          Command.Time_Part,
          Command.Description_Part);
   WHEN List_Command =>
      Process_List_Command (Command.Date_Part);
   WHEN Delete_Command =>
      Process_Delete_Command
         (Command.Date_Part, Command.Time_Part);
END CASE;
```

To summarize, the component list in a variant part may take one of three possible forms:

1. one or more component declarations optionally followed by a nested variant part:

   component declaration
   ~~~
   *component declaration*
   *variant part* (boxed with dotted lines)

2. a nested variant part not preceded by any component declarations:

   *variant part*

3. a null list:

```
NULL;
```

## 10.2.2 Declaring Record Types with Variable-Length Components

When one of the components of a record type belongs to an unconstrained array type, the component declaration must include an index constraint. However, any of the bounds in this index constraint may be discriminants. This means that the discriminant determines the size of the array. Different values in the record type may have components that are arrays of different sizes.

Consider the type `Buffer_Type` introduced in Section 4.2.7 to represent variable-length strings:

```
TYPE Buffer_Type IS
   RECORD
      Length_Part   : Integer RANGE 0 .. 128 := 0;
      Contents_Part : String (1 .. 128);
   END RECORD;
```
   ~~~

The maximum length of any string represented by a Buffer_Type value is 128. The maximum length is chosen to be adequate for all anticipated strings that will be produced by the program. However, this length may be more than is needed for certain Buffer_Type variables. Since the Contents_Part component always has a 128-character capacity, even when it is representing a shorter string, this can lead to inefficient use of space.

Using discriminants, we can define a type for variable-length strings that allows different objects to have different maximum lengths. This allows a compiler to use only as much space for a given object as is required for that object. The declaration is as follows:

```
TYPE Varying_String_Type (Maximum_Length : Natural) IS
   RECORD
      Current_Length_Part : Natural:= 0;
      Contents_Part       : String (1 .. Maximum_Length);
   END RECORD;
```

A variable declared

```
Input_Image : Varying_String_Type (Maximum_Length => 80);
```

will have a component Input_Image.Maximum_Length set to eighty, a component Input_Image.Current_Length_Part, and a component Input_Image.Contents_Part large enough to hold eighty characters. A variable declared

```
Output_Image : Varying_String_Type (Maximum_Length => 132);
```

will have a component Input_Image.Maximum_Length set to 132, a component Input_Image.Current_Length_Part, and a component Input_Image.Contents_Part large enough to hold 132 characters. (The Maximum_Length component gives the *physical length* of the string—the size of the longest string that the record can *ever* represent. The Current_Length_Part component gives the *logical length* of the string—the size of the string that the record is *currently* representing.)

Varying_String_Type works just like the PL/I type CHARACTER VARYING (*n*): Each object in the type is declared along with a number specifying the length of the longest string that object can hold. At any time, an object can hold any string whose length does not exceed the maximum length. Different objects can be declared with different maximum lengths. A good compiler will set aside only as much space for each object as is required for that object.

10.2.3 Declaring Types Whose Components Have Discriminants

Sometimes a record type *T* may have a component *C* that belongs to another type with discriminants. The component declaration for *C* may have a discriminant constraint. A discriminant of *T* may be used in this discriminant constraint. Viewing discriminants as parameters, one of type *T*'s "formal parameters" is used as an "actual parameter" in the component declaration.

Consider the following example, which uses the type `Mailing_Address_Type` shown in Section 10.2.1:

```
TYPE Directory_Entry_Type (US_Entry : Boolean := True) IS
   RECORD
      Address_Part :
         Mailing_Address_Type (US_Address => US_Entry);
      Phone_Number_Part : String (1 .. 10);
      CASE US_Entry IS
         WHEN True =>
            NULL;
         WHEN False =>
            Country_Code_Part : String (1 .. 3);
      END CASE;
   END RECORD;
```

The discriminant `US_Entry` is used to select a variant, but it is also used in the discriminant constraint of the `Address_Part` component declaration. The discriminant constraint in the declaration of a `Directory_Entry_Type` object determines the discriminant value of that object's `Address_Part` component. Thus there are two different kinds of `Directory_Entry_Type` records. The first kind has the following components:

a `US_Entry` component equal to `False`
an `Address_Part` component consisting of a `Mailing_Address_Type` record
 whose discriminant `US_Address` has the value `False`
a `Phone_Number_Part` component
a `Country_Code_Part` component

The second kind has the following components:

a `US_Entry` component equal to `True`
an `Address_Part` component consisting of a `Mailing_Address_Type` record
 whose discriminant `US_Address` has the value `True`
a `Phone_Number_Part` component

10.2.4 Allowable Uses of Discriminants

We have seen three contexts in which the name of a discriminant may occur in the declaration of other record components:

following the word `CASE` in a variant part
as a bound in the index constraint of a component declaration
as a value in the discriminant constraint of a component declaration

In addition, a discriminant may be used as the default initial value in an *ordinary* component declaration. (One discriminant of a record type may not be used as the default initial value of another discriminant of the same record type.)

These are the *only* ways in which a discriminant may be used inside the record-type declaration. For example, the following variation on the Varying_String_Type declaration given earlier is illegal because the discriminant Maximum_Length is used in the range constraint of Current_Length_Part:

```
TYPE Varying_String_Type (Maximum_Length : Natural) IS
   RECORD
      Current_Length_Part :
         Integer RANGE 0 .. Maximum_Length := 0;
            -- ILLEGAL USE OF A DISCRIMINANT!
      Contents_Part : String (1 .. Maximum_Length);
   END RECORD;
```

When a discriminant appears in a component declaration, the bound in the index constraint, the value in the discriminant constraint, or the default initial value must consist only of the discriminant name. The discriminant may not appear as part of a larger expression. Assuming that Integer_List_Type is an unconstrained array type, for example, the following declaration is illegal:

```
TYPE Triangular_Matrix_Type (Size : Positive) IS
   RECORD
      Component_List :
         Integer_List_Type (1 .. Size * (Size + 1) / 2);
            -- ILLEGAL USE OF A DISCRIMINANT!
   END RECORD;
```

10.3 DISCRIMINANT CONSTRAINTS

Discriminant constraints serve two purposes. First, in the absence of default initial values for discriminants, they ensure that the initial values of a record's discriminants are well defined. Second, they restrict the values that may be stored in the record. A discriminant constraint in the declaration of a record variable stipulates that the variable will only hold values in a particular *subtype* of the record type.

One form of discriminant constraint was described in Section 10.1:

(*identifier* => *expression* , ~~~ , *identifier* => *expression*)

Alternative notation will be described in Section 10.6. However, the form above is usually more conducive to program readability than the alternative forms.

10.3.1 Initial Values of Discriminants

The composition of a record type with discriminants is largely determined by the values of the discriminants. Therefore, it is essential that the values of an object's discriminants be defined throughout the life of the object. The Ada language imposes the following rules to ensure that this is the case:

1. Default initial values must appear in either all or none of the discriminant declarations of the record-type declaration.

2. If the discriminants do not have default initial values, then the typemark naming the record type must be followed by a discriminant constraint in each of the following contexts:

   (a) in a variable declaration
   (b) following the word OF in an array-type declaration (when the record type is being used as the component type of an array type) or in an object declaration for a one-of-a-kind array
   (c) in a component declaration of a record-type declaration (when the record type is being used as a component type for another record type)

   The discriminant constraint specifies the value of the discriminants for that variable, array component, or record component. (The constraint may be omitted in the declaration of a constant, in which case the discriminant values are obtained from the initial value of the constant.)
3. If the discriminants do have default initial values, then a discriminant constraint may still appear in any of the contexts listed above, but it is not required. When the discriminant constraint appears, it determines the value of the discriminants. When it does not appear, the discriminants are set to their default initial values.

For example, consider the type Mailing_Address_Type (from Section 10.2.1) once again. The discriminant has a default initial value of True. Thus the declaration

```
Next_Address : Mailing_Address_Type;
```

causes the discriminant Next_Address.US_Address to be initialized to True. Next_Address begins with State_Part and Zip_Code_Part components but no Country_Part component. The discriminant constraint in the declaration

```
Next_Foreign_Address :
   Mailing_Address_Type (US_Address => False);
```

sets the value of Next_Foreign_Address to False. Next_Foreign_Address has a Country_Part component but no State_Part or Zip_Code_Part components.

10.3.2 Constrained and Unconstrained Records

When a discriminant constraint appears in a variable declaration, the variable is said to be *constrained*. This means that the discriminant values, and thus the structure of the variable, are frozen for the life of the variable. When a variable in a record type with discriminants is declared without a discriminant constraint, the variable is said to be *unconstrained*. The discriminants begin with their default initial values but may assume new values during the life of the variable. Because of the rules listed in Section 10.3, unconstrained variables can only be declared in a record type whose discriminants have default initial values.

For example, the type Varying_String_Type declared in Section 10.2.2 has no default initial value for its discriminants. Therefore, a declaration such as

```
s : Varying_String_Type;
```

is illegal. A `Varying_String_Type` object must be declared with a discriminant constraint, as in

```
s : Varying_String_Type (Maximum_Length => 80);
```

which forces `s` to always have the same discriminant value.

In contrast, the declaration of `Mailing_Address_Type` in Section 10.2.1 specifies a default initial value of `True` for it discriminant. Thus all the following declarations are legal:

```
Next_Address : Mailing_Address_Type;

Next_Domestic_Address :
   Mailing_Address_Type (US_Address => True);

Next_Foreign_Address :
   Mailing_Address_Type (US_Address => False);
```

The record `Next_Address` begins with a `US_Address` component of `True`, but later it can take on values with `US_Address` components of `False`. The record `Next_Domestic_Address` begins with and retains a `US_Address` component of `True`. The record `Next_Foreign_Address` begins with and retains a `US_Address` component of `False`. The assignment statement

```
Next_Address := Next_Foreign_Address;
```

always succeeds. The assignment statement

```
Next_Foreign_Address := Next_Address;
```

succeeds if executed while `Next_Address` has a `US_Address` component of `False`, but it causes an error if executed while `Next_Address` has a `US_Address` component of `True`.

Changing the discriminants of an unconstrained variable may cause certain components of the variable to come into existence, vanish, grow, shrink, or change their internal structure. Thus it is typically not meaningful to change the value of a variable's discriminant without providing new values for other components as well. An assignment statement that attempts to change the value of a discriminant by itself, such as

```
Next_Address.US_Address := False;
```

is illegal. A subprogram call in which a discriminant is used as an actual parameter and in which the parameter mode is `IN OUT` or `OUT` is also illegal. The only way to change the discriminants of an unconstrained variable is to replace the entire record with the value of another record of the same type. This other record provides new values for the discriminants along with values for other components that are appropriate for those discriminant values.

If an unconstrained record has a component declared in a variant part, a consistency check is performed whenever that component is updated or given a new value. The discriminant controlling that variant part is examined to make sure that the current form of the record includes the variant containing the component. For example, a Mailing_Address_Type record has a Country_Part component only when the discriminant US_Address is False. Therefore, the statements

```
Next_Address.Country_Part := "United Kingdom        ";
```

and

```
Basic_IO.Put (Next_Address.Country_Part);
```

succeed if executed when Next_Address.US_Address has the value False and cause an error if executed when Next_Address.US_Address has the value True. Together with the rule that forbids changing discriminant parts by themselves, this check ensures that the current structure of the variable is accurately reflected by the values of the discriminants and that the variable is only used in a manner consistent with that structure.

(Pascal programmers should note that the Ada language provides no equivalent to the Pascal *free union*. Any Ada record with variants has a discriminant indicating which variant is currently "active"; only record components in the currently active variant may be manipulated; and the discriminant cannot be changed without changing the entire record. Thus Ada variant parts do not provide a way to view the same storage as if it belonged to two different types. On the rare occasions that such a capability is necessary, it can be obtained using a low-level mechanism, *unchecked conversion,* that will be described in Chapter 20.)

With typical compilers, care must be taken in declaring an unconstrained record in which a discriminant determines the size of an array. Typically, compilers allocate enough storage for an unconstrained record to represent the largest record value in the type. In the case of declarations such as

```
TYPE Integer_List_Type IS ARRAY (Positive RANGE <>) OF Integer;
TYPE List_Type (Size : Natural := 100) IS
   RECORD
      Contents_Part : Integer_List_Type (1 .. Size);
   END RECORD;
List : List_Type;
```

List.Contents_Part is initially a 100-component array. However, List can, in theory, assume values in which the number of components in List.Contents_Part is Natural'Last. An attempt to allocate enough storage for such an array is likely to fail. If it is known that the maximum array length will, in fact, be smaller, a smaller subtype can be declared for the discriminant:

```
SUBTYPE List_Length_Subtype IS Integer RANGE 0 .. 500;
TYPE List_Type (Size : List_Length_Subtype := 100) IS
   RECORD
      Contents_Part : Integer_List_Type (1 .. Size);
   END RECORD;
List : List_Type;
```

The subtype of the discriminant has been changed in the declaration of `List_Type`. Now the unconstrained record `List` need be large enough only to accommodate an array of up to 500 components.

10.3.3 Subtypes of Record Types

Record types have subtypes. A subtype of a record type may consist of either all the records in the type or of all the records in the type that have particular discriminant values. Just as range constraints specify subtypes of numeric types and enumeration types and index constraints specify subtypes of array types, discriminant constraints specify subtypes of record types. Subtypes of record types can be given names:

```
SUBTYPE Domestic_Address_Subtype IS
   Mailing_Address_Type (US_Address => True);
SUBTYPE Foreign_Address_Subtype IS
   Mailing_Address_Type (US_Address => False);
```

Given these subtype declarations, the object declarations

```
Next_Domestic_Address :
   Mailing_Address_Type (US_Address => True);
```

and

```
Next_Domestic_Address : Domestic_Address_Subtype;
```

are equivalent. (The record type name followed by the discriminant constraint form a *subtype indication* in the sense of Section 6.2.2.) There are two ways to determine the subtype of a record value: either by examining the discriminant values directly, as in

```
IF Next_Address.US_Address THEN
   ...
END IF;
```

or by a membership test like

```
IF Next_Address IN Domestic_Address_Subtype THEN
   ...
END IF;
```

A subtype of a record type may be either *constrained* or *unconstrained.* A record type without discriminants is a constrained record subtype. A record type with discriminants is an unconstrained record subtype. A subtype consisting of records with particular discriminant values is a constrained record subtype. Thus, given the declarations

```
TYPE Complex_Type IS
   RECORD
      Real_Part, Imaginary_Part : Float;
   END RECORD;

TYPE Varying_String_Type (Maximum_Length : Natural) IS
   RECORD
      Current_Length_Part : Natural:= 0;
      Contents_Part       : String (1 .. Maximum_Length);
   END RECORD;

SUBTYPE String_Of_80_Subtype IS
   Varying_String_Type (Maximum_Length => 80);
```

`Complex_Type` and `String_Of_80_Subtype` are constrained record subtypes. `Varying_String_Type` is an unconstrained record subtype. The only kind of record subtype to which a discriminant constraint can be applied is an unconstrained subtype, and the resulting subtype indication always names a constrained array subtype.

(The terms *constrained* and *unconstrained* are used in two different senses in this chapter, for objects and for subtypes. A record subtype is unconstrained if it includes records with different discriminant values; otherwise it is constrained. An object in a record type is unconstrained if it is declared as belonging to an unconstrained record subtype; otherwise it is constrained. A constrained record variable either has no discriminants or discriminants that always keep the same value. An unconstrained record variable can contain different discriminant values at different times.

Like record types, array types can have either constrained or unconstrained subtypes. An unconstrained array subtype consists of arrays with different index bounds, while a constrained array subtype consists of arrays that all have the same index bounds. Since every object in an unconstrained array subtype must be declared with an index constraint, however, there is no such thing as an unconstrained array *object*. The bounds of any array object are fixed for the life of the object.)

10.4 DYNAMICALLY ALLOCATED RECORDS WITH DISCRIMINANTS

A record with discriminants can be dynamically allocated, but the allocated record is always constrained. That is, its discriminant values can never change. Hence the allocated record always has the same components; if any of these components have index constraints, they always have the same index constraints, for the life of the allocated object.

10.4.1 Allocators for Records with Discriminants

There are three different forms of allocators that can be used to allocate a record with discriminants:

NEW *typemark*

NEW *typemark* ' (*expression*)

NEW *typemark discriminant-constraint*

(We have not seen the third form until now.)

The first form is prohibited unless the discriminants have default initial values. It specifies that a new record is to be allocated and discriminants are to be given their default initial values, but no initial values are to be specified for other record components. Unlike a declared variable whose initial discriminant values are the default values, the allocated variable keeps its initial discriminant values for life. Given the declarations

```
TYPE Mailing_Address_Type (US_Address : Boolean := True) IS
   RECORD
      Name_Part, Street_Part : String (1 .. 30);
      City_Part              : String (1 .. 20);
      CASE US_Address IS
         WHEN True =>
            State_Part    : State_Type;
            Zip_Code_Part : Integer RANGE 0 .. 99999;
         WHEN False =>
            Country_Part : String (1 .. 20);
      END CASE;
   END RECORD;

TYPE Mailing_Address_Pointer_Type IS
   ACCESS Mailing_Address_Type;

Mailing_Address_Pointer : Mailing_Address_Pointer_Type;
```

the statement

```
Mailing_Address_Pointer := NEW Mailing_Address_Pointer_Type;
```

allocates a record with a US_Address component permanently set to True and uninitialized Name_Part, Street_Part, City_Part, State_Part, and Zip_Code_Part components.

Even given the declarations

```
TYPE Varying_String_Type (Maximum_Length : Natural) IS
   RECORD
      Current_Length_Part : Natural := 0;
      Contents_Part       : String (1 .. Maximum_Length);
   END RECORD;
```

```
TYPE String_Of_80_Pointer_Type IS
   ACCESS Varying_String_Type (Maximum_Length => 80);
String_Pointer : String_Of_80_Pointer_Type;
```

the statement

```
String_Pointer := NEW Varying_String_Type;
```

is illegal, because the discriminant of `Varying_String_Type` does not have a default initial value. It does not matter that the allocator appears in a context where only a particular discriminant would be acceptable.

In the second form of the allocator, the expression must belong to the designated record type. A record belonging to the same subtype as the expression is allocated and given the same value as the expression. The discriminant values of the allocated record are frozen for the life of the record, but other component values may later change. The statement

```
Mailing_Address_Pointer :=
   NEW Mailing_Address_Type'
      ((US_Address    => False,
        Name_Part     => "Winston Churchill                   ",
        Street_Part   => "10 Downing Street                   ",
        City_Part     => "London              ",
        Country_Part  => "United Kingdom      "));
```

allocates a new record with the value specified by the record aggregate. The assignment

```
Mailing_Address_Pointer.Name_Part :=
   "Clement Attlee                  ";
```

is legal, but the assignment

```
Mailing_Address.ALL  :=
   (US_Address     => True,
    Name_Part      => "Franklin Roosevelt                   ",
    Street_Part    => "1600 Pennsylvania Avenue N.W.        ",
    City_Part      => "Washington          ",
    State_Part     => DC,
    Zip_Code_Part  => 20500);
```

—which attempts to change the discriminant of the allocated record—would cause an error. In the assignment statement

```
Mailing_Address_Pointer :=
   NEW Mailing_Address_Type'
      ((US_Address    => False,
        Name_Part     => "Winston Churchill                   ",
        Street_Part   => "10 Downing Street                   ",
        City_Part     => "London              ",
        Country_Part  => "United Kingdom      "));
```

the inner parentheses are part of the record aggregate. As in allocators for arrays, the double parentheses may be replaced by single parentheses when the initial value is specified by an aggregate:

```
Mailing_Address_Pointer :=
   NEW Mailing_Address_Type'
      (US_Address    => False,
       Name_Part     => "Winston Churchill              ",
       Street_Part   => "10 Downing Street              ",
       City_Part     => "London               ",
       Country_Part  => "United Kingdom       ");
```

In the third form of allocator, the typemark must name an unconstrained record type. Like the first form of allocator, the third form specifies the initial values of the discriminants but not the other components. The initial values of the discriminants are specified by the discriminant constraint rather than by default initial values, so the third form is allowed whether or not the discriminants have default initial values. Here is an example:

```
Mailing_Address_Pointer :=
   NEW Mailing_Address_Type (US_Address => False);
```

10.4.2 Discriminant Constraints for Access Types

As explained in Section 5.5, an index constraint can be applied not only to an unconstrained array subtype, but to an access subtype designating values in an unconstrained array subtype. Together, the name of the access subtype and the index constraint specify the subset of access values that point to allocated arrays with particular bounds.

The situation is analogous for discriminant constraints. A discriminant constraint can be applied to an access type designating an unconstrained record type. Together, the name of the access type and the discriminant constraint specify the subset of access values that point to allocated records with particular discriminant values:

```
TYPE Mailing_Address_Pointer_Type IS
   ACCESS Mailing_Address_Type;
SUBTYPE Domestic_Address_Pointer_Type IS
   Mailing_Address_Pointer_Type (US_Address => True);
```

The values in `Mailing_Address_Pointer_Type` are access values pointing to `Mailing_Address_Type` records. `Domestic_Address_Pointer_Subtype` consists of the subset of those values that point to `Mailing_Address_Type` records with `US_Address` components of `True`. (In contrast, the declaration

```
TYPE Domestic_Address_Pointer_Type IS
   ACCESS Mailing_Address_Type (US_Address => True);
```

would have created a base access type consisting entirely of pointers to `Mailing_Address_Type` records with `US_Address` components of `True`.)

A discriminant constraint can be applied to an access type only if the access type designates an unconstrained record type. The subtype indication specifies an access subtype designating a constrained record subtype. An access subtype designating an unconstrained array or record subtype is called an *unconstrained access subtype.* (An access subtype designating any other subtype is called a *constrained access subtype.*)

10.5 SUBPROGRAM PARAMETERS WITH DISCRIMINANTS

Subprogram parameters can belong to unconstrained record subtypes. On a given call, the formal parameters assume the subtypes of the corresponding actual parameters. The subtype of a parameter can be determined either by examining the values of its discriminants or by a membership test. These forms of examination are allowed even for a parameter of mode OUT, although it is not permitted to examine the *ordinary* record components of an OUT parameter.

For example, the following procedure copies a Varying_String_Type value from one parameter to another with a possibly different physical size. The procedure truncates the value if the logical size of the source exceeds the physical size of the target.

```
PROCEDURE Copy_String
   (From : IN Varying_String_Type;
    To   : OUT Varying_String_Type) IS
BEGIN
   IF From.Current_Length_Part <= To.Maximum_Length THEN
      To.Current_Length_Part := From.Current_Length_Part;
      To.Contents_Part (1 .. To.Current_Length_Part) :=
         From.Contents_Part (1 .. From.Current_Length_Part);
   ELSE
      To.Current_Length_Part := To.Maximum_Length;
      To.Contents_Part (1 .. To.Maximum_Length) :=
         From.Contents_Part (1 .. To.Maximum_Length);
   END IF;
END Copy_String;
```

The procedure body can refer to To.Maximum_Length, even though To is of mode OUT, because Maximum_Length is a discriminant. It would not have been legal to examine To.Current_Length_Part or To.Contents_Part. It is illegal to assign a new value to To.Maximum_Length, regardless of the parameter mode, because it is never legal to assign a new value to a discriminant by itself.

Like an assignment statement, a subprogram call may replace a record by one with different discriminant values if and only if the record is unconstrained. From the subprogram writer's point of view, if an OUT or IN OUT parameter belongs to a record type with discriminants, it is illegal to update the parameter unless at least one of two conditions holds:

1. The new value has the same discriminant values as the original value of the actual parameter.
2. The actual parameter is unconstrained.

Condition 1 can be checked simply by examining the discriminants of the formal parameter. To check condition 2, a subprogram writer can use the attribute `X'Constrained`. Suppose `X` is a value in a record type with discriminants. `X'Constrained` names the value `True` (of type `Boolean`) if `X` is a constrained object. Otherwise, `X'Constrained` names the value `False`. It is permissible to examine the `'Constrained` attribute of an `OUT` parameter. A formal parameter of mode `OUT` or `IN OUT` is constrained if and only if the corresponding actual parameter is constrained. A formal parameter of mode `IN` is always constrained, since a parameter of mode `IN` cannot be modified in any way.

10.6 DETAILS

10.6.1 Full Form of a Discriminant Constraint

Like the list of actual parameters in a subprogram call, a discriminant constraint may be given in named notation, positional notation, or a mixture. Until now, we have shown only the named form, which is almost always the most readable. The general form of a discriminant constraint is

`(` *discriminant association* `,` ~~~ `,` *discriminant association* `)`

Each discriminant association may be either a named association of the form

discriminant name | ~~~ | *discriminant name* `=>` *expression*

or a positional association consisting only of an expression. Given the declarations

```
TYPE Matrix_Type IS
   ARRAY
      (Positive RANGE <>,
       Positive RANGE <>,
       Positive RANGE <>)
      OF Float;

TYPE Space_Grid_Type
   (Width, Height, Depth : Integer := 1) IS

   RECORD
      Grid_Part :
         Matrix_Type (1 .. Height, 1 .. Width, 1 .. Depth);
   END RECORD;
```

the following declarations are equivalent:

```
Grid :
   Space_Grid_Type (Height => 10, Width => 20, Depth => 10);
Grid : Space_Grid_Type (10, 20, 10);
Grid : Space_Grid_Type (10, Depth => 10, Width => 20);
Grid : Space_Grid_Type (Depth | Height => 10, Width => 20);
```

As in subprogram calls, any positional associations must come first, and no positional associations are allowed once a named association is given. Named associations may be listed in any order. There are two important differences between discriminant constraints and subprogram calls. First, individual discriminants may not be defaulted. A discriminant constraint may be omitted entirely if the discriminants have default initial values; however, if a discriminant constraint appears, it must specify a value for every discriminant of the record type. Second, discriminants to receive the same value may be specified in the same discriminant association, with their names separated by the | symbol. (This is only allowed if all the discriminants listed are of the same type. A single integer literal may not be used to specify the values of discriminants in different integer types, for example.)

10.6.2 Position of Discriminants Within Records

Since discriminants are record components, they are listed along with ordinary components in record aggregates. (See Section 8.1.5.) In a positional record aggregate, the discriminants are listed first, in the order of their discriminant specifications. Given the declaration

```
TYPE Varying_String_Type (Maximum_Length : Natural) IS
   RECORD
      Current_Length_Part : Natural := 0;
      Contents_Part       : String (1 .. Maximum_Length);
   END RECORD;
```

for example, the positional aggregate

```
(10, 5, "Hello     ")
```

is equivalent to the named aggregate

```
(Maximum_Length      => 10,
 Current_Length_Part => 5,
 Contents_Part       => "Hello     ")
```

10.6.3 When Expressions Are Evaluated

This section is concerned with the times at which three different kinds of expressions are evaluated: the expressions for discriminant components in record aggregates, the default initial value expressions in discriminant specifications, and the expressions in discriminant constraints.

When a record type has a variant part, an aggregate for the record type must contain a static expression (see Section 8.3.5) for the discriminant that determines the current variant. For example, given the declarations

```
TYPE Mailing_Address_Type (US_Address : Boolean := True) IS
   RECORD
      Name_Part, Street_Part : String (1 .. 30);
      City_Part              : String (1 .. 20);
      CASE US_Address IS
         WHEN True =>
            State_Part    : State_Type;
            Zip_Code_Part : Integer RANGE 0 .. 99999;
         WHEN False =>
            Country_Part : String (1 .. 20);
      END CASE;
   END RECORD;
Current_Name, Current_Street  : String (1 .. 30);
Current_City, Current_Country : String (1 .. 20);
```

the aggregate

```
(US_Address =>
   Current_Country = "United States       "
 Name_Part    => Current_Name,
 Street_Part  => Current_Street,
 City_Part    => Current_City,
 Country_Part => Current_Country)
```

is illegal. There is no way for the compiler to determine whether the `Country_Part` value really belongs in the record aggregate (rather than `State_Part` and `Zip_Code_Part` values) since the expression

```
Current_Country = "United States       "
```

giving the discriminant value cannot be evaluated until the program starts running. In contrast, the aggregate

```
(US_Address   => False,
 Name_Part    => Current_Name,
 Street_Part  => Current_Street,
 City_Part    => Current_City,
 Country_Part => Current_Country)
```

is legal, because the expression `False` is static. An aggregate may contain a nonstatic expression for a discriminant if the discriminant does not determine the currently active variant. For example, given the declarations

```
TYPE Varying_String_Type (Maximum_Length : Natural) IS
   RECORD
      Current_Length_Part : Natural := 0;
      Contents_Part       : String (1 .. Maximum_Length);
   END RECORD;
Number_Of_Blanks : Natural;
```

the following is a legal `Varying_String_Type` aggregate, even though the expression `Number_Of_Blanks` is not static:

```
(Maximum_Length      => Number_Of_Blanks,
 Current_Length_Part => Number_Of_Blanks,
 Contents_Part       => (1 .. Number_Of_Blanks => ' '))
```

The default initial value expression in a discriminant specification is not evaluated when the record-type declaration is elaborated. Rather, it is evaluated when a record of the corresponding type is created and no values are given for the record's discriminants in an initial value for the record or in a discriminant constraint. A record may be created as the result of elaborating an object declaration or evaluating an allocator, either for the record itself or for some object containing the record. The expression is reevaluated for each such record created, and different evaluations may yield different values. When two or more discriminants are declared in the same discriminant specification, the default initial value expression is reevaluated once for each of these discriminants.

The expressions in a discriminant constraint are evaluated when the declaration containing the constraint is elaborated. For example, given the declarations

```
Buffer_Size : Positive;
SUBTYPE Buffer_Subtype IS
   Varying_String_Type (Maximum_Length => Buffer_Size);
```

the value of `Buffer_Size` at the time the subtype declaration is elaborated determines the value of `Maximum_Length` for all records in `Buffer_Subtype`. This value stays the same even if the value of `Buffer_Size` later changes. In a discriminant association with more than one discriminant name, the expression is evaluated once for each named discriminant. For example, in the discriminant constraint

```
Grid :
   Space_Grid_Type (Depth | Height => f (x), Width => g (x));
```

the function `f` is called two times.

10.7 SUMMARY

A record type can be declared with special components called *discriminants*. Besides acting as record components that occur before any of the other components in the record, discriminants act as "parameters" for objects in the type. Values for discriminants can be specified in a *discriminant constraint* as part of an object declaration, and the values of the discriminants can determine the structure of the object.

A record type with discriminants is declared as follows:

```
TYPE identifier ( discriminant specification ; ~~~; discriminant specification ) IS
   RECORD

      ......................
      : component declaration :
      :       ~~~             :
      : component declaration :
      ......................

      ............
      : variant part :
      ............

   END RECORD ;
```

The form of a discriminant specification is:

```
identifier , ~~~ , identifier : typemark   ............
                                           : := expression :  ;
                                           ............
```

The typemark in a discriminant specification must name a subtype of an integer or enumeration type. The optional expression following it gives a *default initial value* for the discriminants being declared. Default initial values must be specified either for all of a record type's discriminants or for none of them.

The form of a variant part is:

```
CASE identifier IS
   WHEN choice list =>
      component list
      ~~~

   WHEN choice list =>
      component list

   WHEN OTHERS =>
      component list

END CASE;
```

Each component list may itself consist of zero or more ordinary record-component declarations optionally followed by a single, nested variant part. An empty component list has the form

```
NULL;
```

The variant part specifies record components that exist only in records for which the discriminants have particular values. The identifier following the word CASE in the variant part must be one of the record type's discriminants. The choice lists in a variant part have the same form as the choice lists in a CASE statement. Given a value for the discriminant, the components declared in the corresponding arm of the CASE structure are part of the record, and components declared in other arms of the CASE structure are not. An error results from any attempt to examine or modify a record component which, according to the current discriminant values, is not currently part of the record. All components of a record must have distinct names, even if they are in different variants.

Within the record type declaration, discriminants may be used in only four ways:

1. Following the word CASE in a variant part, to determine which record components are currently part of the record.
2. In an index constraint of a record-component declaration, following the type-mark of an unconstrained array subtype. The value of the discriminant determines how many array components are contained in the record component.
3. In a discriminant constraint of a record-component declaration, when the record component itself belongs to a record type with discriminants. This allows discriminants of the outer record to determine the discriminant values of the inner record.
4. As the default initial value in a record-component declaration (for an ordinary record component, not another discriminant).

The discriminant must form the entire index bound, discriminant value, or default initial value; it may not be part of a larger expression.

The form of a discriminant constraint is

(*discriminant association* , ~~~ , *discriminant association*)

where each discriminant association is either a named association of the form

discriminant name | ~~~ | *discriminant name* => *expression*

or a positional association of the form

expression

All positional associations must come before all named associations in the discriminant constraint. Named associations may be listed in any order. Discriminants consisting entirely of named associations are the most informative to a reader of the program.

If a record type has discriminants and the discriminants do not have default initial values, a discriminant constraint must follow the name of the type in variable declarations. Furthermore, if the record type is used as a component type in another array-type or record-type declaration, a discriminant constraint must be provided in that type declaration. If the record type with discriminants does have default initial values, a discriminant constraint is still allowed in each of these contexts, but it is not required. Similarly, a discriminant constraint is allowed but not required in the declaration of a constant belonging to a record type with discriminants.

These rules guarantee that the initial value of a discriminant is always well defined. If a discriminant constraint is specified, it supplies the initial discriminant values. Otherwise, in a constant declaration, the initial value of the constant supplies the initial discriminant values. In any other case, the default initial value expressions in the record-type declaration are evaluated to obtain initial values of the discriminants.

When a discriminant constraint appears in a record-type variable declaration, the variable is *constrained*. This means that the values of its discriminants must remain fixed for the life of the variable. If no discriminant constraint appears, the variable is *unconstrained*. In this case, the initial values of the discriminants are given by the default initial value expressions (which must exist for the discriminant constraint to be omitted), but the discriminants can assume different values later. A discriminant may not be changed by itself, either by assignment to the discriminant as a record component or by using the discriminant as an OUT or IN OUT parameter. Rather, an entire record value with different discriminant values can be placed in an unconstrained record variable. This rule makes it impossible to produce a record whose discriminants are inconsistent with the values of the other record components. See Figure 10.2.

A discriminant constraint specifies a subtype of a record type. This subtype is a subset of the record type consisting of all records that have the discriminant values specified in the constraint. Subtypes of record types can be given names by subtype declarations. Membership of a record in a subtype can be determined either by direct examination of the discriminant values or by a membership test. A subtype of a record type is *unconstrained* if it contains records with different discriminant values; otherwise it is *constrained*. (In particular, record types without discriminants are constrained subtypes.) A discriminant constraint is applied to an unconstrained record subtype to obtain a constrained record subtype.

A record with discriminants can be dynamically allocated by an allocator of one of the following forms:

NEW *typemark*

NEW *typemark* ' (*expression*)

NEW *typemark discriminant-constraint*

The first form is only allowed when the record-type declaration specifies default initial values. The second form specifies an initial value for all components of the dynamically allocated record. When this initial value is specified by an aggregate, the parentheses in the allocator and the parentheses around the aggregate may be combined into a single set of parentheses. The third form is allowed when the typemark names an unconstrained record subtype. The discriminants of a dynamically allocated record can never change. That is, all dynamically allocated records are constrained.

If an access subtype designates an unconstrained record subtype, it is called an *unconstrained access subtype*. A discriminant constraint may be applied to such an access subtype to obtain a *constrained* access subtype. The constrained access

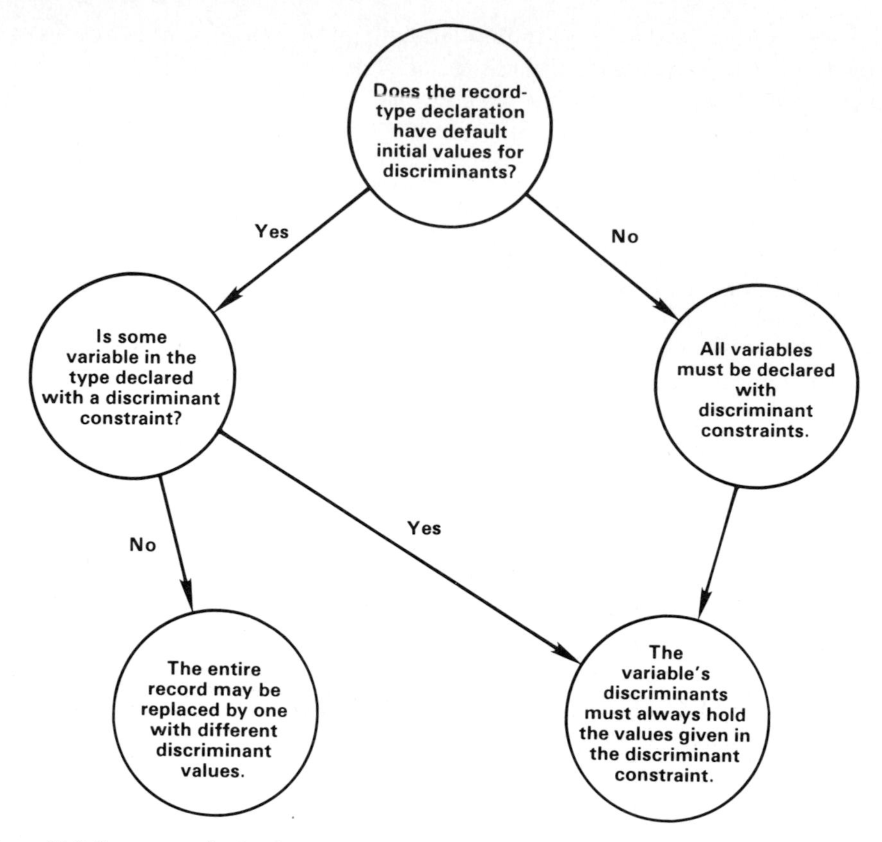

Figure 10.2 Summary of rules for record types with discriminants. If a record-type declaration has default initial values for discriminants, variables in the type may be declared with or without discriminant constraints. If there are no default initial values in the record-type declaration, all variables in the type must be declared with discriminant constraints. If a variable is declared with a discriminant constraint, the discriminant values remain fixed for the life of the variable. If there is no discriminant constraint, the discriminant values can be changed by replacing the entire record at once with one having different discriminant values.

subtype consists of only those access values pointing to records with the discriminant values specified in the constraint.

Figure 6.2 summarized rules for applying constraints to subtypes to obtain new subtypes. Now that we have considered subtypes of record types and subtypes of access types designating record types, we can complete the table. Figure 10.3 is an updated table, including new rows for these subtypes and a new column for discriminant constraints.

Subprogram parameters can belong to unconstrained record types. The formal parameters inherit the discriminants of the actual parameters, so the discriminant values may be different on different calls. The discriminants of a subprogram parameter may be examined, either directly or through a membership test, even if the parameter is of mode `OUT`. The formal parameter is unconstrained if and only if the actual parameter is unconstrained. If `X` is a formal parameter of mode `OUT` or

Kind of subtype named by typemark	Range constraint	Floating-point accuracy constraint	Fixed-point accuracy constraint	Index constraint	Discriminant constraint
integer subtype	integer subtype	constraint not allowed	constraint not allowed	constraint not allowed	constraint not allowed
floating-point subtype	floating-point subtype	floating-point subtype	constraint not allowed	constraint not allowed	constraint not allowed
fixed-point subtype	fixed-point subtype	constraint not allowed	fixed-point subtype	constraint not allowed	constraint not allowed
enumeration subtype	enumeration subtype	constraint not allowed	constraint not allowed	constraint not allowed	constraint not allowed
constrained subtype of an array type	constraint not allowed	constraint not allowed	constraint not allowed	constraint not allowed	constraint not allowed
unconstrained subtype of an array type	constraint not allowed	constraint not allowed	constraint not allowed	constrained subtype of an array type	constraint not allowed
constrained subtype of a record type	constraint not allowed	constraint not allowed	constraint not allowed	constraint not allowed	constraint not allowed
unconstrained subtype of a record type	constraint not allowed	constraint not allowed	constraint not allowed	constraint not allowed	constrained subtype of a record type
access subtype designating an unconstrained array subtype	constraint not allowed	constraint not allowed	constraint not allowed	access subtype designating a constrained array subtype	constraint not allowed
access subtype designating an unconstrained record type	constraint not allowed	constraint not allowed	constraint not allowed	constraint not allowed	access subtype designating a constrained record subtype
any other access subtype	constraint not allowed	constraint not allowed	constraint not allowed	constraint not allowed	constraint not allowed

Figure 10.3 Complete rules for using constraints. A subtype indication consists of a typemark optionally followed by a constraint. The allowable constraints depend on the kind of subtype named by the typemark. The typemark and constraint taken together name a new subtype of the kind indicated in the table. The figure is identical to Figure 6.2 except that rows have been added for subtypes of record types and of access values designating subtypes, and a column has been added for discriminant constraints.

`IN OUT`, the attribute `X'Constrained` may be examined to determine whether or not it is permitted to copy a record with different discriminant values into the parameter.

EXERCISES

10.1 Rewrite the declaration of `Command_Type` in Section 10.2.1 with a single variant part, bearing in mind that record components in different variants must have different names.

10.2 Declare a type for representing square matrices of `Float` values with index values of subtype `Positive`. (A square matrix is a two-dimensional array having the same number of index values in each dimension.) The type should have one discriminant indicating the number of rows (and columns) in the matrix. It should be impossible to represent a matrix that is not square.

10.3 Revise the `Reverse_Lines` program of Section 5.4.4 so that it no longer makes any assumptions about the number of lines in the input file. (*Hint:* Use the linked list approach of the `Reverse_Integers` program in Section 5.4.5, but have each list cell contain a string instead of an integer. Give the type for list cells a discriminant. This discriminant will indicate the length of the string stored in a given cell.)

10.4 Declare a record type for representing the contents of a square on a checkerboard (along with any other types needed to declare the record type). A square is either empty or nonempty. A nonempty square contains a checker that is either red or black and either is or is not a king.

10.5 An electronic thermometer provides temperature readings in the range -30.0 to 130.0, accurate to within one-half of a degree. The thermometer also has a self-test mechanism to determine whether the reported temperature reading is valid. Thus thermometer data includes a flag indicating whether the reading is valid and, if the reading is valid, the value of the reading. There is no meaningful value associated with an invalid reading. Declare a type for thermometer data.

10.6 Given the type for thermometer data declared in the previous exercise, declare an unconstrained array type for lists of thermometer data items. Write a function that takes such a list and returns the "average data" in the list as a thermometer data value. If at least half of the items in the list are valid readings, the "average data" is a valid reading equal to the mean of the valid readings in the list. If the majority of the items in the list are invalid readings, the "average data" is itself an invalid reading.

CHAPTER

ELEVEN

PACKAGES

Large programs are often difficult to understand and perilous to modify because of the many ways in which different parts of the program interact. Often a simple change to one part of a large program will affect many different parts of the program in surprising and disconcerting ways. The sheer size of a program makes it impossible to understand the relationship of each part of the program to all the other parts.

This problem can be controlled by dividing a program into *modules.* Each module consists of a part of the program responsible for a narrow part of the program's behavior. Well-designed modules are concerned with very specific aspects of the program and have simple, well-documented *interfaces.* This means that it is easy to understand a module in near-isolation from other modules and easy to understand the ways in which the modules interact with each other. As a result, it is easier to determine the parts of a program that have to be changed to modify the program's behavior in a certain way. More significantly, it is safer to modify those parts of the program without affecting other aspects of the program's behavior in unexpected ways.

This program design philosophy, called *modular programming,* can be used with any programming language. However, the Ada language is one of the few languages designed specifically to support modular programming. In the Ada language, modules are called *packages,* and they are part of the language.

A package is a collection of entities providing a set of related "facilities" to a program. These facilities may include new types, subprograms, and groups of data objects, among other things. Different facilities are placed in the same package because they are closely related to each other in purpose or implementation. Like subprograms, packages are *program units*—that is, components out of which larger programs are built. Unlike subprograms, packages do not exist primarily to be executed. Rather, they exist primarily for the facilities they provide to be used.

11.1 PACKAGE SPECIFICATIONS AND PACKAGE BODIES

This section describes the parts that make up a package and the purposes of those parts. Our objective is to consider general principles. Detailed rules, syntax, and examples are given in following sections.

One of the most difficult problems in understanding a module is determining which parts of the module form the *interface* with other modules. Typically, only a small part of a module interacts directly with other parts of a program. The rest of the module exists only to *implement* the services provided through the interface. A programmer trying to *understand* a module *M* need not be concerned with every line of every module that interacts with *M*. He need only be concerned with interfaces of those modules, if he can distinguish the interfaces from their implementations. A programmer who wishes to *change* a module without adversely affecting other modules must carefully consider any changes he makes to the module's interface. However, parts of the module that do not form part of the module's interface may be changed with impunity, as long as their effect on the interface is well understood. Thus it is important to programmers changing a module to understand which parts of the module form its interface.

The structure of an Ada package clearly reflects this vital distinction between a module's interface and its implementation. An Ada package is divided into two parts—the *package specification,* which describes the interface of the package, and the *package body,* which describes the implementation of that interface. The package specification lists the facilities that the package provides to the rest of the program and how those facilities may be used. The package body contains the package's innards, the mechanisms that make these facilities behave as they do.

The package specification describes the types, subprograms, variables, and other facilities declared inside the package and intended for use outside the package. Types declared in the package specification may be used by other parts of the program in object and subprogram declarations, for instance. A subprogram declared in the package specification may be called by other parts of the program. A variable declared in the package specification may be examined and modified by other parts of the program.

When a package provides a subprogram for use by other parts of the program, only a *subprogram declaration* appears in the package specification; the full subprogram body is given inside the package body. The subprogram declaration, which was introduced in Section 9.4 as a mechanism allowing the declaration of mutually recursive subprograms, contains all the information preceding the word `IS` in a subprogram body. This includes the name of the subprogram, the names and subtypes of its formal parameters, and, in the case of functions, the subtype of the result. For example, the subprogram declaration for the subprogram

```
FUNCTION Maximum (I1, I2 : Integer) RETURN Integer IS
BEGIN
   IF I1 > I2 THEN
      RETURN I1;
   ELSE
      RETURN I2;
   END IF;
END Maximum;
```

reads as follows:

```
FUNCTION Maximum (I1, I2 : Integer) RETURN Integer;
```

The subprogram declaration provides all the information necessary to write or identify a syntactically correct call on the subprogram. (This includes names of formal parameters, since they may be used in named parameter associations.) The rest of the subprogram body describes how the subprogram goes about doing its job. These details are irrelevant to users of the subprogram, as long as the users understand what a call on the subprogram is supposed to accomplish. If the declarative part or statements of a subprogram are changed so that the subprogram accomplishes the same thing in a different way, the users of a subprogram are unaffected. Thus the subprogram declaration is part of the package's interface, but the rest of the subprogram body is part of the package's implementation. That is why the subprogram declaration goes in the package specification and the subprogram body goes in the package body.

Besides the bodies of subprograms declared in the package specification, the package body may define facilities used by those subprogram bodies but not meant for use by other parts of the program. The facilities may include (among other things) additional variable, type, and subprogram declarations. These facilities are part of the implementation of the package and are not relevant to parts of the program outside the package.

Packages make large programs more manageable by breaking them up into smaller pieces, each playing a specific role, and by rigorously specifying the limited ways in which these pieces may interact. This has the effect of limiting the amount of program text you have to be concerned with when trying to understand some part of the program. When writing a part of a program that uses a package written by somebody else, you do not have to understand that package's body, only the intended use of each facility described in the package's specification. When modifying a package that is used by other parts of a large program, you can forget about the rest of the program as long as you modify only the package body and not the package specification and do not change the external behavior of the facilities described in the package specification.

11.2 THE SYNTAX OF PACKAGES

A package specification and the corresponding package body are two physically separate entities. The term *package* refers to the package specification and package body together. A package specification may be written as follows:

```
PACKAGE identifier IS
    basic declaration
        ~~~
    basic declaration
END identifier ;
```

The identifier at the end must match the identifier at the top. Basic declarations include variable, constant, named number, type, subtype, and procedure declarations, but not procedure bodies. A package body may be written as follows:

```
PACKAGE BODY identifier IS
    declarative part
.................................
: BEGIN                         :
:   sequence of initialization statements :
.................................
END identifier ;
```

Except for the first line and the fact that the sequence of statements is optional, this is the same as the form of the subprogram bodies we have seen so far. Again, the identifier at the top and the identifier at the bottom are identical.

The declarative part of a package body has the same form as the declarative part of a subprogram body. Basic declarations (e.g., variable, constant, named number, type, and subtype declarations) come first, and later declarations (e.g., subprogram bodies) come afterward. Subprogram declarations may appear with either group of declarations.

Since the primary purpose of a subprogram is to execute, we tend to think of the statements in a subprogram body as being the substantive part of the body and the declarations as providing only supporting information. In a package body, precisely the opposite is true. The primary purpose of a package body is to provide facilities that are specified in a declarative part. These include subprograms, as well as variables, types, and other entities used by those subprograms. The sequence of statements in the package body, if it is present, is executed only once—at the time the package comes into existence. (Section 11.3 will describe precisely when this happens.) Its purpose is typically to initialize the variables in the package body. Thus the substantive part of a package body is its declarative part, and the sequence of statements plays only a supporting role.

Variables declared in either the package specification or package body remain in existence for the lifetime of the package. In particular, they retain their values between calls on the subprograms provided by the package. Since variables declared in a subprogram body do not retain their values from call to call, a package body surrounding the subprogram body is an appropriate place to put variables whose values must remain unchanged between calls on a subprogram.

Here is an example of a package, consisting of a package specification and a package body:

```
PACKAGE Fibonacci_Package IS
   SUBTYPE Argument_Subtype IS Integer RANGE 0 .. 20;
   FUNCTION Fibonacci
      (n : Argument_Subtype) RETURN Positive;
END Fibonacci_Package;

PACKAGE BODY Fibonacci_Package IS
   Table : ARRAY (Argument_Subtype) OF Positive;
   FUNCTION Fibonacci
      (n : Argument_Subtype) RETURN Positive IS
   BEGIN
      RETURN Table (n);
   END Fibonacci;
BEGIN
   Table (0) := 1;
   Table (1) := 1;
   FOR i IN 2 .. Argument_Subtype'Last LOOP
      Table (i) := Table (i-2) + Table (i-1);
   END LOOP;
END Fibonacci_Package;
```

The *Fibonacci series* is a series whose first two elements are one and whose subsequent elements are the sums of the two preceding elements. The facilities provided by the package `Fibonacci_Package` are a subtype of type `Integer` consisting of the values from zero to twenty and a function `Fibonacci` that, given a parameter n in this subtype, returns the nth element of the Fibonacci series. By convention, the elements of the Fibonacci series are numbered starting with zero.

It is easy to write a loop that, given the value n, computes the nth element of the Fibonacci series by repeated addition. In a program requiring many Fibonacci values to be computed, however, this would be an inefficient approach, especially since computation of values occurring late in the series would involve recomputation of values occurring early in the series. `Fibonacci_Package` implements the function `Fibonacci` by setting up a table holding elements zero through twenty of the Fibonacci series and then having each call on the function simply look up the appropriate value in the table. The table is filled in element by element by the initialization statements in the package body, which are executed only when the package first comes into existence. The array `Table` remains in existence between calls on the function `Fibonacci` and retains its value for the lifetime of `Fibonacci_Package`. The array `Table` could also have been initialized by an aggregate initial value in its declaration, but this would have required a tedious and error-prone manual computation by the programmer. Since the initialization statements of the package are only executed once, it makes more sense to let the computer fill in the table. (The variable `Table` belongs to an anonymous array type.)

A variable, constant, named number, type, subtype, or subprogram declared in the package specification of the form

```
PACKAGE identifier IS
   basic declaration
      ~~~
   basic declaration
END identifier ;
```

may be referred to later in the package specification and throughout the package body by the identifier naming it. It may also be referred to from outside the package by an expanded name consisting of the name of the package, a period, and the identifier naming the declared entity. Thus the entities declared in a package specification are available to other parts of the program containing the package.

In the `Fibonacci_Package` example, we see that `Argument_Subtype`, declared in the package specification, is referred to later in the package specification (in the parameter specification of the function declaration for `Fibonacci`) and again in the package body (in the declaration of `Table` and the iteration scheme of the `FOR` loop). The subtype declared in the package specification may be referred to outside of the package by the expanded name

```
Fibonacci_Package.Argument_Subtype
```

Similarly, the function declared in the package specification may be called from outside the package by referring to its expanded name, as in the call

```
Fibonacci_Package.Fibonacci (n)
```

A variable, constant, named number, type, or subtype declared in the package *body* may be referred to later in the package body by the identifier naming it. It may not be referred to in any way outside of the package, so it is strictly part of the package's implementation rather than its interface. A subprogram whose body appears inside a package body may be called from outside the package if and only if the corresponding subprogram declaration is given in the package specification. When it is declared in the package specification, the subprogram may be called from outside the package body by referring to its expanded name. When it is not declared in the package specification, the subprogram may only be called from one of the other subprogram bodies appearing in the package body.

In the `Fibonacci` example, the variable `Table` cannot be referred to outside the package body. This variable, the statements to initialize `Table`, and the `Fibonacci` function body are all part of the implementation of the package, not its interface. They are irrelevant to other parts of the program using Fibonacci_Package. It is possible to reimplement the function Fibonacci in the obvious but inefficient way (executing a loop each time the function is called) by leaving the package specification unchanged and rewriting the package body. The change will be invisible to the rest of the program (except in terms of the execution speed of the function).

11.3 THE PLACEMENT AND LIFETIME OF A PACKAGE

So far, we have discussed the structure of a package, but we have not discussed where a package goes. Neither have we said anything about when a package comes into existence and when it ceases to exist. These issues are related. There are several different places a package can fit in a program, and the lifetime of the package depends on the place chosen.

The package specification and package body can each be compiled as separate compilation units. This is the way that packages are most commonly used in large programs, because it is most conducive to partitioning a program into modules. Besides being forms of compilation units, however, package specifications and package bodies are both forms of declarations. A package body is a later declaration, while a package specification can be used either as a basic declaration or a later declaration. Consequently, they can be placed in the declarative part of a block statement or a subprogram body. Moreover, a package can be nested inside another package in either of two ways. First, the inner specification can occur inside the outer specification as a basic declaration while the inner body occurs inside the declarative part of the outer body as a later declaration:

```
PACKAGE Outer_Package IS
   ...
   PACKAGE Inner_Package IS
      ...
   END Inner_Package;
   ...
END Outer_Package;

PACKAGE BODY Outer_Package IS
   ...
   PACKAGE BODY Inner_Package IS
      ...
   BEGIN -- Inner_Package
      ...
   END Inner_Package;
   ...
BEGIN -- Outer_Package
   ...
END Outer_Package;
```

Second, the inner specification and inner body can both occur as declarations in the declarative part of the outer body:

```
PACKAGE Outer_Package IS
    ...
END Outer_Package;

PACKAGE BODY Outer_Package IS
    ...
    PACKAGE Inner_Package IS
       ...
    END Inner_Package;
    ...
    PACKAGE BODY Inner_Package IS
       ...
    BEGIN -- Inner_Package
       ...
    END Inner_Package;
    ...
BEGIN -- Outer_Package
    ...
END Outer_Package;
```

We shall discuss all these possibilities in greater detail after we have considered the lifetime of a package.

A package comes into existence when its specification and body are elaborated. Any statements in the package body are executed when the package body is elaborated. Independently compiled packages and packages in declarative parts are elaborated at different times.

When the specification and body are independent compilation units, they are elaborated before execution of the main program. This means that all sequences of initialization statements in independently compiled packages are actually executed before the statements of the main program! Independently compiled packages remain in existence for the entire program.

When a package specification and body occur as declarations in the declarative part of a block statement or subprogram body, they are elaborated in turn along with the other declarations in that declarative part. These declarations remain in effect until the block statement or subprogram is finished. Then the package ceases to exist. If the block statement or subprogram body is executed again later, its declarations are elaborated once again, and this creates a new incarnation of the package. The variables inside the new incarnation of the package do not have the values last held by the previous incarnation; if there is a sequence of initialization statements in the package body, it is reexecuted to initialize the variables of the new incarnation. Finally, if a package is nested inside another package, the inner package comes into existence when the outer package is being elaborated, and ceases to exist when the outer package ceases to exist. Thus the lifetime of the inner package is essentially the same as that of the outer package and depends on where the outer package is placed.

If a separately compiled package is to be used by another compilation unit in the program, that compilation unit generally must begin with a *context clause* naming the package. In its simplest form, a context clause consists of a single `WITH` *clause* of the following form:

`WITH` *compilation unit name* `,` ~~~ `,` *compilation unit name* `;`

For example, the compilation unit `Basic_IO`, which has been used in most of the programs you have seen until now, is a separately compiled package. That is why every compilation unit that uses the package `Basic_IO` begins `WITH Basic_IO;`.

(The facilities provided by the package `Basic_IO` are described by the following package specification:

```
WITH IO_Exceptions;
PACKAGE Basic_IO IS
   PROCEDURE Get (Item : OUT Integer);
   PROCEDURE Get (Item : OUT Character);
   PROCEDURE Get (Item : OUT String);
   PROCEDURE Put (Item : IN Integer);
   PROCEDURE Put (Item : IN Character);
   PROCEDURE Put (Item : IN String);
   PROCEDURE Get_Line
      (Item : OUT String; Last : OUT Natural);
   PROCEDURE New_Line;
   PROCEDURE New_Page;
   FUNCTION End_Of_File RETURN Boolean;

   Device_Error  : EXCEPTION RENAMES IO_Exceptions.Device_Error;
   End_Error     : EXCEPTION RENAMES IO_Exceptions.End_Error;
   Data_Error    : EXCEPTION RENAMES IO_Exceptions.Data_Error;

END Basic_IO;
```

These facilities may be referred to in other compilation units by the following expanded names:

```
Basic_IO.Get
Basic_IO.Put
Basic_IO.Get_Line
Basic_IO.New_Line
Basic_IO.New_Page
Basic_IO.End_of_File
Basic_IO.Device_Error
Basic_IO.End_Error
Basic_IO.Data_Error
```

`Basic_IO.Get` and `Basic_IO.Put` are overloaded so that they may be invoked with parameters of various types.)

When the package specification and package body are placed in the declarative part of a block statement or subprogram body, the package specification must come first and the package body follows later in the same declarative part, after all the basic declarations. The facilities provided by the package cannot be used outside of the block statement or subprogram body in which the package is declared. The placement of packages inside a block statement or subprogram body is extremely rare.

Finally, let us consider the two different ways (depicted earlier) to nest one package inside another. The first is used when the outer package provides the inner package as a facility for use by the rest of the program. Then the description of the facilities provided by the outer package should include a description of the facilities provided by the inner package. Thus the inner package's specification is placed as a basic declaration in the outer package's specification. However, the implementation of the inner package constitutes the implementation of one of the facilities provided by the outer package. Thus the inner package's body is placed among the later declarations in the declarative part of the outer package's body. The second form of package nesting is used when the inner package is used only to help implement the outer package, so that the inner package is of no concern to the rest of the program. Since both the specification and body of the inner package are describing aspects of the implementation of the outer package, both are placed in the declarative part of the outer package's body. The facilities of the inner package may not be used outside of the outer package.

As an example of the first form of package nesting, consider a program to control an alarm system. The system must monitor temperature, humidity, and power supply voltage and indicate abnormal conditions by lighting appropriate indicator lights and sounding an alarm. The alarm may sound different sirens to indicate different levels of urgency.

Part of the program is concerned with performing computations, such as determining the acceptable level of humidity for a given temperature or determining whether the voltage levels recorded over the last five seconds are fluctuating dangerously. Another part of the program may be concerned with maintaining a disk file logging the conditions observed at different times. Finally, there is a part of the program to communicate with the hardware components of the system. This involves actions like sending cryptic control codes to esoteric device addresses at carefully determined intervals. If the portions of the program performing the communications function are interspersed with the portions of the program performing the other functions, the program will be terribly hard to understand.

The program's complexity can be controlled by placing the hardware interface portion of the program in one package, `Hardware_Interface_Package`. This package provides subprograms that allow communication with the hardware on an abstract level, in terms of the logical function of each device. The other portions of the program can call these subprograms to communicate with the hardware without being concerned with internal codes, data formats, timing requirements, and so forth. Programmers writing the other parts of the system do not have to know anything about Hardware_Interface_Package except how to call the subprograms described in the package specification. Conversely, the Hardware_Interface_Package body can be *written* by an expert in the hardware interface who knows nothing about the rest of the program. The subprograms described in the Hardware_Interface_Package specification each call for a basic hardware function to be performed, and the expert need only implement these basic functions in terms of the low-level codes with which he is familiar. Thus the only common ground between the part of the program concerned with the hardware and the rest of the program is the Hardware_Interface_Package specification.

Because of the package's size, it may make sense to distribute the facilities of Hardware_Interface_Package among three *subpackages,* one concerned with each of the three general hardware functions—reading sensors, controlling warning lights, and controlling the alarm. Each of the subprograms provided by Hardware_Interface_Package is delegated to one of these three subpackages. Thus Hardware_Interface_Package directly provides three facilities:

a subpackage named Sensor_Package
a subpackage named Warning_Light_Package
a subpackage named Alarm_Package

The specification of Hardware_Interface_Package describes these three facilities by describing the facilities provided in turn by each subpackage:

```
PACKAGE Hardware_Interface_Package IS

   PACKAGE Sensor_Package IS
      TYPE Temperature_Type IS DELTA 0.1 RANGE 0.0 .. 100.0;
      TYPE Humidity_Type IS DELTA 0.5 RANGE 0.0 .. 100.0;
      TYPE Voltage_Type IS DELTA 0.01 RANGE 0.0 .. 150.0;

      FUNCTION Thermometer_Reading RETURN Temperature_Type;
      FUNCTION Hygrometer_Reading RETURN Humidity_Type;
      FUNCTION Voltmeter_Reading RETURN Voltage_Type;

   END Sensor_Package;

   PACKAGE Warning_Light_Package IS

      TYPE Light_Type IS
         (High_Temperature_Light, Low_Temperature_Light,
          High_Humidity_Light, Low_Voltage_Light,
          Unsteady_Voltage_Light, All_Okay_Light);

      PROCEDURE Turn_On (Light : IN Light_Type);
      PROCEDURE Turn_Off (Light : IN Light_Type);

   END Warning_Light_Package;
```

```
   PACKAGE Alarm_Package IS
      TYPE Siren_Type IS
         (Warning_Siren, Problem_Siren, Critical_Siren);
      PROCEDURE Sound_Alarm (Problem_Level : IN Siren_Type);
      PROCEDURE Deactivate_Alarm;
   END Alarm_Package;

END Hardware_Interface_Package;
```

For each package whose specification occurs in the specification of `Hardware_Interface_Package`, the corresponding package body must occur in the body of `Hardware_Interface_Package`. These package bodies describe the implementation of the facilities (types and subprograms) provided by the facilities (subpackages) provided by `Hardware_Interface_Package`. In this indirect sense, the subpackage bodies describe the implementation of the facilities provided by `Hardware_Interface_Package` itself. The body of the outer package `Hardware_Interface_Package` might take the following form:

```
PACKAGE BODY Hardware_Interface_Package IS

   [declarations used by all three of the package bodies below]

   PACKAGE BODY Sensor_Package IS
      [declarations used by the three subprogram bodies below]
      FUNCTION Thermometer_Reading RETURN Temperature_Type IS
         ...
      END Thermometer_Reading;
      FUNCTION Hygrometer_Reading RETURN Humidity_Type IS
         ...
      END Hygrometer_Reading;
      FUNCTION Voltmeter_Reading RETURN Voltage_Type IS
         ...
      END Voltmeter_Reading;
   END Sensor_Package;

   PACKAGE Warning_Light_Package IS
      [declarations used by the two subprogram bodies below]
      PROCEDURE Turn_On (Light : IN Light_Type) IS
         ...
      END Turn_On;
      PROCEDURE Turn_Off (Light : IN Light_Type) IS
         ...
      END Turn_Off;
   END Warning_Light_Package;
```

```
   PACKAGE Alarm_Package IS
      [declarations used by the two subprogram bodies below]
      PROCEDURE Sound_Alarm
         (Problem_Level : IN Siren_Type) IS
         ...
      END Sound_Alarm;
      PROCEDURE Deactivate_Alarm IS
         ...
      END Deactivate_Alarm;
   END Alarm_Package;

END Hardware_Interface_Package;
```

Since `Sensor_Package` is one of the three facilities provided by the outer package `Hardware_Interface_Package`, it may be referred to within `Hardware_Interface_Package` by the name `Sensor_Package`, and everywhere else by the name

```
Hardware_Interface_Package.Sensor_Package
```

Thus the function `Thermometer_Reading` may be referred to outside of `Hardware_Interface_Package` by the name

```
Hardware_Interface_Package.Sensor_Package.Thermometer_Reading
```

(Within the specification or body of `Hardware_Interface_Package`, the function may be referred to simply as

```
Sensor_Package.Thermometer_Reading
```

and within the specification or body of `Sensor_Package` it may be referred to simply as `Thermometer_Reading`.)

As an example of the second form of package nesting, consider a billing system with an independently compiled package responsible for inserting, deleting, and modifying customer name, address, and phone number information about each account. The package provides three procedures, each of which initiates a dialogue with the console operator to make the appropriate change to the customer data base. The procedures to modify or delete an existing account take the account number as an input parameter. The procedure to add a new account provides the new account number as an output parameter. The package specification is as follows:

```
PACKAGE Account_Data_Package IS

   TYPE Account_Number_Type IS
      RANGE 111_11_111 .. 999_99_999;

   PROCEDURE Add_Account
      (Account : OUT Account_Number_Type);

   PROCEDURE Modify_Account
      (Account : IN Account_Number_Type);

   PROCEDURE Delete_Account
      (Account : IN Account_Number_Type);

END Account_Data_Package;
```

Calls on `Add_Account` are to assign account numbers in sequence. This requires declaring somewhere within the package body a variable holding the next account number to be assigned. The variable cannot be declared in the body of `Add_Account` because it then would not retain its value from one call on `Add_Account` to another. However, if it is declared directly in the declarative part of the `Account_Data_Package` body (which is likely to be fairly large), it will not be clear which parts of the package body actually modify the variable. In fact, someone modifying the program at a later date might inadvertently cause some part of the package body other than the body of `Add_Account` to modify the variable. An appropriate solution is to place the variable in the body of a subpackage, so that its value can only be obtained by a procedure declared in the specification of the subpackage:

```
PACKAGE BODY Account_Data_Package IS

   [other declarations needed to implement Account_Data_Package]

   PACKAGE Next_Account_Number_Package IS
      PROCEDURE Get_Next_Account_Number
         (Account_Number : OUT Account_Number_Type);

   END Next_Account_Number_Package;

   PACKAGE BODY Next_Account_Number_Package IS
      Counter : Account_Number_Type := Account_Number_Type'First;
      PROCEDURE Get_Next_Account_Number
         (Account_Number : OUT Account_Number_Type) IS
      BEGIN
         Account_Number := Counter;
         Counter := Counter + 1;
      END Get_Next_Account_Number;
   END Next_Account_Number_Package;
```

```
      PROCEDURE Add_Account
         (Account : OUT Account_Number_Type) IS
         New_Account_Number : Account_Number_Type;
         ...
      BEGIN
         ...
         Next_Account_Number_Package.Get_Next_Account_Number
            (New_Account_Number);
         ...
         Account := New_Account_Number;
      END Add_Account;

      PROCEDURE Modify_Account
         (Account : IN Account_Number_Type) IS
         ...
      END Modify_Account;

      PROCEDURE Delete_Account
         (Account : IN Account_Number_Type) IS
         ...
      END Delete_Account;
   END Account_Data_Package;
```

Next_Account_Number_Package cannot be referred to outside the body of Account_Data_Package. A programmer using Account_Data_Package when writing some other part of the billing system need not be aware of the internal subpackage Next_Account_Number_Package, but only of those aspects of the outer package Account_Data_Package described in the specification of Account_Data_Package.

The use of packages (e.g., Next_Account_Number_Package) to enclose a set of variables (e.g., Counter) and a set of subprograms (e.g., the procedure Get_Next_Account_Number) using those variables is very common. This style of programming gives the package writer complete control over the ways in which the variables are used, because the variables are directly accessible only to the subprograms whose bodies appear in the package body. Other parts of the program use the variables only indirectly, by calling the subprograms declared in the package specification. Because the variables retain their values between calls on these subprograms, the entire package can be viewed as a single data object, and the subprograms declared in the package specification can be viewed as the complete set of operations on that object.

11.4 FRACTIONS REVISITED

Section 9.6 presented a declaration for the type Fraction_Type and a set of function definitions overloading the arithmetic operators to work on values of type

Fraction_Type. It makes sense to put this type declaration and the declarations of these functions in a package. The package specification would read as follows:

```
PACKAGE Fraction_Package IS

 TYPE Fraction_Type IS
    RECORD
       Numerator_Part   : Integer;
       Denominator_Part : Positive;
    END RECORD;

 FUNCTION "+" (Right : Fraction_Type) RETURN Fraction_Type;

 FUNCTION "-" (Right : Fraction_Type) RETURN Fraction_Type;

 FUNCTION "+"
    (Left, Right : Fraction_Type) RETURN Fraction_Type;

 FUNCTION "-"
    (Left, Right : Fraction_Type) RETURN Fraction_Type;

 FUNCTION "*"
    (Left, Right : Fraction_Type) RETURN Fraction_Type;

 FUNCTION "/"
    (Left, Right : Fraction_Type) RETURN Fraction_Type;
    --This function assumes that
    -- Right.Numerator_Part /= 0. It will not work
    -- correctly when this is not the case.

 FUNCTION "**"
    (Left : Fraction_Type; Right : Integer)
    RETURN Fraction_Type;

 FUNCTION "ABS"
    (Right : Fraction_Type) RETURN Fraction_Type;

 FUNCTION "/"
    (Left, Right: Integer) RETURN Fraction_Type;
    -- This function assumes that Right /= 0.
    -- It will not work correctly when Right = 0.

END Fraction_Package;
```

The bodies of these functions are placed in the body of Fraction_Package. In addition, the bodies of subprograms written for use by the functions above, but not meant to be called from outside the package, are placed in the Fraction_Package body. The procedure Reduce, which reduces a Fraction_Type value to lowest terms, is such a subprogram. The procedure Reduce, in turn, calls a function Greatest_Common_Divisor to compute the greatest common divisor of the numerator and denominator using Euclid's algorithm. This function's body is also placed in the package body, so Reduce can call it.

Except for the bodies of Reduce and Greatest_Common_Divisor, the subprogram bodies in the following package body are taken directly from Section 9.6:

```
PACKAGE BODY Fraction_Package IS

   FUNCTION Greatest_Common_Divisor
      (a : Natural; b : Positive) RETURN Positive IS
      x     : Natural := a;
      y     : Positive := b;
      Old_y : Positive;
   BEGIN
      -- Since x=a and y=b, GCD(x,y)=GCD(a,b)
      WHILE x /= 0 LOOP
         -- GCD(x,y)=GCD(a,b) at this point.
         Old_y := y;
         y := x;
         x := Old_y MOD x;
         --Since all common divisors of x and y are
         --  divisors of y and y MOD x, GCD(x,y) still
         --  equals GCD(a,b).
      END LOOP;
      --GCD(a,b) = GCD(x,y) = GCD(0,y) = y, since all
      --  numbers are divisors of 0, and y itself is
      --  the greatest divisor of y.
      RETURN y;
   END Greatest_Common_Divisor;

   PROCEDURE Reduce (f : IN OUT Fraction_Type) IS
      GCD :
         Positive :=
            Greatest_Common_Divisor
               (ABS f.Numerator, f.Denominator);
   BEGIN
      f.Numerator := f.Numerator / GCD;
      f.Denominator := f.Denominator / GCD;
   END Reduce;

   FUNCTION "+"
      (Right: Fraction_Type) RETURN Fraction_Type IS
   BEGIN
      RETURN Right;
   END "+";
```

```
FUNCTION "-"
   (Right: Fraction_Type) RETURN Fraction_Type IS
BEGIN
   RETURN
     Fraction_Type'
        (Numerator_Part   => -Right.Numerator_Part,
         Denominator_Part => Right.Denominator_Part);
END "-";

FUNCTION "+"
   (Left, Right: Fraction_Type) RETURN Fraction_Type IS
   Result : Fraction_Type;
BEGIN
   Result.Numerator_Part :=
      Left.Numerator_Part * Right.Denominator_Part +
      Right.Numerator_Part * Left.Denominator_Part;
   Result.Denominator_Part :=
      Left.Denominator_Part * Right.Denominator_Part;
   Reduce (Result);
   RETURN Result;
END "+";

FUNCTION "-"
   (Left, Right: Fraction_Type) RETURN Fraction_Type IS
   Result : Fraction_Type;
BEGIN
   Result.Numerator_Part :=
      Left.Numerator_Part * Right.Denominator_Part -
      Right.Numerator_Part * Left.Denominator_Part;
   Result.Denominator_Part :=
      Left.Denominator_Part * Right.Denominator_Part;
   Reduce (Result);
   RETURN Result;
END "-";

FUNCTION "*"
   (Left, Right: Fraction_Type) RETURN Fraction_Type IS
   Result : Fraction_Type;
BEGIN
   Result.Numerator_Part :=
      Left.Numerator_Part * Right.Numerator_Part;
   Result.Denominator_Part :=
      Left.Denominator_Part * Right.Denominator_Part;
```

```
   Reduce (Result);
   RETURN Result;
END "*";


FUNCTION "/"
   (Left, Right: Fraction_Type) RETURN Fraction_Type IS
   -- This function assumes that
   --    Right.Numerator_Part /= 0. It will not work
   --    correctly when this is not the case.
   Result_Numerator, Result_Denominator  : Integer;
   Result                                : Fraction_Type;

BEGIN
   Result_Numerator :=
      Left.Numerator_Part * Right.Denominator_Part;
   Result_Denominator :=
      Left.Denominator_Part * Right.Numerator_Part;
   IF Result_Denominator > 0 THEN
      Result :=
         Fraction_Type'
            (Numerator_Part    => Result_Numerator,
             Denominator_Part  => Result_Denominator);
   ELSE
      Result :=
         Fraction_Type'
            (Numerator_Part    => -Result_Numerator,
             Denominator_Part  => -Result_Denominator);

   END IF;
   Reduce (Result);
   RETURN Result;
END "/";


FUNCTION "**"
   (Left: Fraction_Type; Right: Integer)
   RETURN Fraction_Type IS
BEGIN
   RETURN
      Fraction_Type'
         (Numerator_Part =>
            Left.Numerator_Part ** Right,
          Denominator_Part =>
            Left.Denominator_Part ** Right);
END "**";
```

```
   FUNCTION "ABS"
      (Right: Fraction_Type) RETURN Fraction_Type IS
   BEGIN
      RETURN
         Fraction_Type'
            (Numerator_Part   => ABS Right.Numerator_Part,
             Denominator_Part => Right.Denominator_Part);
   END "ABS";

   FUNCTION "/"
      (Left, Right: Integer) RETURN Fraction_Type IS
      -- This function assumes that Right /= 0.
      -- It will not work correctly when Right = 0.
      Result : Fraction_Type;
   BEGIN
      IF Right > 0 THEN
         Result :=
            Fraction_Type'
               (Numerator_Part   => Left,
                Denominator_Part => Right);
      ELSE
         Result :=
            Fraction_Type'
               (Numerator_Part   => -Left,
                Denominator_Part => -Right);
      END IF;
      Reduce (Result);
      RETURN Result;
   END "/";

END Fraction_Package;
```

This package gathers the definition of `Fraction_Type` and the operations on that type into one module. The subprograms `Greatest_Common_Divisor` and `Reduce`, which are used only to implement the arithmetic operations for fractions, are placed in the package body but not declared in the package specification. Thus they are inaccessible to the rest of the program. This clarifies the role of these subprograms in the full program. It also preserves the apparent simplicity of `Fraction_Package`, as seen by the rest of the program.

The package is written without any assumptions about how it will be used (except that the right operand of `/` will not be zero), and implements a set of generally applicable functions. This makes it a logical candidate for reuse in other programs. It is because the structure of a package so clearly delineates the package's interface that it is easy to plug it into other programs and achieve the desired results.

11.5 USE CLAUSES

There is an apparent problem with the package Fraction_Package presented in Section 11.4. The intent is clearly to provide a set of functions overloading the predefined arithmetic operators, so that, for example, the expression A*B will compute the product of Fraction_Type values A and B. Unfortunately, the function "*" declared in the Fraction_Package specification is known outside the package not by the name "*", but by the expanded name Fraction_Package."*". The syntax of the Ada language does not permit an expression such as

```
A Fraction_Package."*" B        --ILLEGAL SYNTAX!
```

so another compilation unit beginning WITH Fraction_Package; can only call the fraction multiplication function using the traditional function call notation:

```
Fraction_Package."*"(A,B)
```

This defeats the whole point of overloading the predefined operators, which is to provide a natural mathematical notation for operations on fractions.

This problem can be solved with a USE *clause* in the compilation units using Fraction_Package. A USE clause names one or more packages and stipulates that, in the part of the program to which the USE clause applies, the entities declared in the specifications of the named packages may be referred to without using expanded names. For example, the USE clause

```
USE Fraction_Package;
```

allows the functions declared in the Fraction_Package specification to be known by the names "+", "*", and so forth. This means that they can be invoked by expressions such as A+B and A*B, where A and B are of type Fraction_Type. Similarly, the USE clause

```
USE Hardware_Interface_Package.Sensor_Package;
```

allows the function

```
Hardware_Interface_Package.Sensor_Package.Thermometer_Reading
```

of Section 11.3 to be referred to by the name Thermometer_Reading. A USE clause does not affect which entities a given part of the program *may* refer to; it only allows a more succinct way of referring to certain entities that could have been referred to, in the absence of the USE clause, by expanded names.

The general form of a USE clause is as follows:

USE *package name* , ~~~ , *package name*;

A USE clause may be placed in either of two places. First, it may be used as either a basic declaration or a later declaration. Second, any number of USE clauses may follow a WITH clause in the context clause at the top of a compilation unit. A context clause may, in fact, contain any number of WITH clauses, each followed by zero or more USE clauses. A USE clause appearing in a declarative part applies to the portion of the declarative part below it and to any sequence of statements to which the declarative part applies. A USE clause appearing in a context clause applies to the entire program unit following the context clause.

It is important not to confuse WITH clauses and USE clauses. A WITH clause can only occur in the context clause at the top of a compilation unit, and it specifies that the compilation unit will avail itself of the facilities provided by one or more other compilation units. A USE clause may occur in a context clause, a declarative part, or a package specification, and it specifies that, in a certain part of the program, facilities provided by certain packages (independently compiled or not) may be referred to in a more succinct way than they could have been referred to otherwise.

Unfortunately, the words WITH and USE can lead to confusion, especially for those familiar with Pascal. In the Ada language, you write a WITH clause to indicate that one compilation unit is going to *use* some other compilation unit! You write a USE clause to indicate that names of the form *X.Y* are going to be abbreviated by the name *Y*, a function performed in Pascal by the **with** statement! The Ada terminology can be rationalized and remembered as follows: A WITH clause indicates that a compilation unit can only be understood along *with* the interfaces of certain other compilation units to which it refers. A USE clause indicates that certain packages' facilities will be referred to by more succinct names, making those facilities easy to *use*.

Until now, we have been using expanded names like Basic_IO.Put and Basic_IO.New_Line for the facilities provided by the package Basic_IO, as in the following program:

```
WITH Basic_IO;
PROCEDURE Copy_Input IS
   Line        : String (1 .. 80);
   Line_Length : Integer RANGE 1 .. 80;
BEGIN
   WHILE NOT Basic_IO.End_Of_File LOOP
      Basic_IO.Get_Line ( Line, Line_Length );
      Basic_IO.Put ( Line (1 .. Line_Length) );
      Basic_IO.New_Line;
   END LOOP;
END Copy_Input;
```

By adding a USE clause for Basic_IO to the context clause in this program, we can be less verbose:

```
WITH Basic_IO; USE Basic_IO;
PROCEDURE Copy_Input IS
   Line        : String (1 .. 80);
   Line_Length : Integer RANGE 1 .. 80;

BEGIN
   WHILE NOT End_Of_File LOOP
      Get_Line ( Line, Line_Length );
      Put ( Line (1 .. Line_Length) );
      New_Line;
   END LOOP;
END Copy_Input;
```

This is the approach we shall take in the remainder of this book.

In the case of the program above, the same effect could have been achieved by placing the USE clause in the declarative part of Copy_Input:

```
WITH Basic_IO;
PROCEDURE Copy_Input IS
   Line        : String (1 .. 80);
   Line_Length : Integer RANGE 1 .. 80;

   USE Basic_IO;

BEGIN
   WHILE NOT End_Of_File LOOP
      Get_Line ( Line, Line_Length );
      Put ( Line (1 .. Line_Length) );
      New_Line;
   END LOOP;
END Copy_Input;
```

However, this is not always the case. Consider the following separately compiled function:

```
WITH Fraction_Package; USE Fraction_Package;
FUNCTION Fraction_Average
   (a, b: Fraction_Type) RETURN Fraction_Type IS
BEGIN
   RETURN (a + b) * (1 / 2);
END Fraction_Average;
```

If the USE clause were placed in the declarative part of the function instead of the context specification, it would not apply to the function header, so the parameter subtype name and result subtype name would have to be changed from Fraction_Type to Fraction_Package.Fraction_Type :

```
WITH Fraction_Package;
FUNCTION Fraction_Average
   (a, b: Fraction_Package.Fraction_Type)
   RETURN Fraction_Package.Fraction_Type IS
   USE Fraction_Package;
BEGIN
   RETURN (a + b) * (1 / 2);
END Fraction_Average;
```

A USE clause naming some package does not apply to an entity declared in that package's specification if the entity's name, by itself, would clash with some other name. For example, consider yet another version of Copy_Input:

```
WITH Basic_IO;
PROCEDURE Copy_Input IS
   New_Line    : String (1 .. 80);
   Line_Length : Integer RANGE 1 .. 80;
   USE Basic_IO;
BEGIN
   WHILE NOT End_Of_File LOOP
      Get_Line ( New_Line, Line_Length );
      Put ( New_Line (1 .. Line_Length) );
      Basic_IO.New_Line;
   END LOOP;
END Copy_Input;
```

Because the name of the variable Line has been changed to New_Line, the USE clause still applies to Basic_IO.End_Of_File, Basic_IO.Get_Line, and Basic_IO.Put, but not to Basic_IO.New_Line. Basic_IO.New_Line must be referred to by its expanded name despite the USE clause. Similarly, if two packages provide entities whose names, by themselves, would clash, and USE clauses for both packages are given in the same place, the USE clauses do not apply to those two entities. Given the package specifications

```
PACKAGE One IS
   Alpha, Beta : Integer;
END One;
PACKAGE Two IS
   Beta, Gamma : Integer;
END Two;
```

the USE clause USE One, Two; does not apply to either One.Beta or Two.Beta. Given the USE clause, the most succinct names possible for the variables in these packages are Alpha, One.Beta, Two.Beta, and Gamma.

In applying this rule, two names are considered to clash if they are the same name and cannot be interpreted as naming distinct overloaded subprograms or enumeration literals. To be interpreted as overloaded, subprograms or enumeration literals must have different parameter and result type profiles (see Section 9.5). Suppose a subprogram (e.g., a function named f) is provided by a package and that another subprogram may be referred to by the same name at the point where a USE clause is given for the package:

```
FUNCTION f (...) RETURN ... IS
   ...
END f;
PACKAGE p IS
   ...
   FUNCTION f (...) RETURN ... ;
   ...
END p;
USE p;
```

If these subprograms have different parameter and result type profiles, then the USE clause applies to the subprogram provided by the package (p.f in this case), causing the subprograms to be overloaded. If the two subprograms have the same parameter and result type profile, their names clash and the USE clause does not apply to the subprogram provided by the package.

For example, the USE clause

```
USE Fraction_Package;
```

causes the versions of "+", "-", "*", "/", "**", and "ABS" defined in Fraction_Package to overload the predefined versions of these operators; however, if Fraction_Package were also to provide a version of "+" taking two parameters of type Integer and returning a result of type Integer, that subprogram would clash with one of the predefined versions of "/", so the USE clause would not apply to the version defined in the package. The version defined in Fraction_Package would have to be referred to as Fraction_Package."+".

USE clauses should be used with restraint. They can make it harder to understand the part of the program containing the USE clauses. This is because USE clauses, especially when applied to several separately compiled packages, allow part of a program to refer to a large set of names without providing any clue as to what the names mean or where they came from. For example, in a compilation unit beginning with the context specification

```
WITH Package_1, Package_2, Package_3;
USE Package_1, Package_2, Package_3;
```

a name X, declared nowhere in that compilation unit, could refer to an entity declared by Package_1, Package_2, or Package_3. In order to understand the compilation unit containing the USE clause, it may be necessary to examine each of these packages in search for a declaration of the entity X. However, an expanded name like Package_1.X unquestionably refers to the entity X provided in

Package_1; someone reading the program knows exactly where to go to find further details about this entity.

USE clauses are appropriate for packages overloading operators or for any other package providing primitive entities whose purposes are obvious from their names. Basic_IO is such a package because the names of its entities—Get, Put, and so forth—clearly define their purpose. As we shall see in Chapter 17, an Ada program may use many packages providing analogous input/output services, all of which bear the same standard names. A standard mathematical package providing subprograms named Square_Root, Sine, Cosine, and so forth is another appropriate candidate for a USE clause. If USE clauses are applied to more specialized packages, any time saved when a program is being typed will be lost many times over when the program is reviewed, debugged, and maintained.

11.6 RENAMING DECLARATIONS

A *renaming declaration* is a declaration that does not bring a new entity into existence, but provides another name for an existing entity. Renaming declarations can provide many of the benefits of USE clauses without their drawbacks. This is because a renaming declaration can provide an identifier to rename an entity that could otherwise only be referred to by an expanded name. Renaming declarations can be used to provide new names for variables, constants, subprograms, packages, and exceptions. (Renaming declarations for exceptions will be covered in Chapter 15.)

For example, suppose that one of the entities provided by a package Video_Display_Package is a constant named Characters_Per_Line, of type Integer. Then a compilation unit using Video_Display_Package may include the declaration

```
Characters_Per_Line :
   Integer RENAMES
      Video_Display_Package.Characters_Per_Line;
```

This establishes the identifier Characters_Per_Line as an alternative name for the object Video_Display_Package.Characters_Per_Line. This renaming declaration has an effect superficially similar to that of the USE clause USE Video_Display_Package;. However, the renaming declaration applies only to the one name Characters_Per_Line, not to every name provided by Video_Display_Package. Furthermore, the compilation unit containing the renaming declaration retains important information about the meaning and source of the name Characters_Per_Line. The renaming declaration indicates both that it names an object of type Integer and that the object it names was declared under the same name in Video_Display_Package. Usually, a compilation unit using a package will be easier to understand if it contains a renaming declaration for each of the package's facilities that it actually uses than if it has a USE clause applying to all the package's facilities at once.

The renaming declaration

```
PROCEDURE Add_Account (Account : OUT Account_Number_Type)
   RENAMES Account_Data_Package.Add_Account;
```

establishes the identifier `Add_Account` as another name for the procedure `Account_Data_Package.Add_Account`. The renaming declaration

```
PACKAGE Sensor_Package RENAMES
   Hardware_Interface_Package.Sensor_Package;
```

establishes the identifier `Sensor_Package` as another name for the nested package `Hardware_Interface_Package.Sensor_Package`.

There are no renaming declarations for types, subtypes, or named numbers, but there are other ways to achieve the same effect. A subtype declaration without a constraint, such as

```
SUBTYPE Account_Number_Type IS
   Account_Data_Package.Account_Number_Type;
```

can be used to establish a new name for an existing subtype (or type). (In fact, this declaration should precede the renaming declaration above for `Add_Account` in order to make the parameter specification in that renaming declaration legal.) A number declaration such as

```
Seconds_To_Refresh:
   CONSTANT := Video_Display_Package.Seconds_To_Refresh;
```

can be used to establish a new name for an existing named number.

The examples above all show how renaming declarations, subtype declarations, and constant declarations can be used to abbreviate an expanded name of the form *x*.*y* by the identifier *y*. However, the new name established by one of these declarations need not bear any relationship to the previously existing name. The following declarations are all legal:

```
Video_Display_Line_Length :
   Integer RENAMES
      Video_Display_Package.Characters_Per_Line;
FUNCTION Build_Fraction
   (Left, Right: Integer) RETURN Fraction_Type
   RENAMES Fraction_Package."/";
PACKAGE Sensor_Interface_Package RENAMES
   Hardware_Interface_Package.Sensor_Package;
SUBTYPE Account_Type IS
   Account_Data_Package.Account_Number_Type;
Display_Refresh_Time :
   CONSTANT := Video_Display_Package.Seconds_To_Refresh;
```

The intent of each of these declarations is to rename one of the facilities provided by a package with a name that is more meaningful in the context in which the declaration appears.

Renaming declarations are quite powerful and have many uses besides shortening the names of facilities provided by packages. The remainder of this section gives the detailed rules for renaming objects, subprograms, and packages. As we cover each variety of renaming declaration, we shall consider some of its uses.

A renaming declaration for a variable or constant has the following form:

identifier **:** *typemark* **RENAMES** *object name* **;**

The object name may be a complex name, involving indexed components, selected components, or slices, for example. The subtype named by the typemark must have the same base type as the object being renamed. Constraints associated with this typemark are ignored, since the declaration is just providing another name for an existing object that already has its own constraints. For example, given the declarations

```
SUBTYPE Digit_Subtype IS Integer RANGE 0 .. 9;
X : Integer RANGE 1 .. 100;
Y : Digit_Subtype RENAMES X;
```

`Y` becomes another name for the variable `X`. The renaming declaration is legal because the base type of `Digit_Subtype` is the type of `X`. However, `Y` may be assigned any value from one to 100; the range of `Digit_Subtype` is irrelevant. To avoid confusion, it is wise to name the same subtype in the renaming declaration as in the original declaration of the object being renamed.

Subscripts, slice bounds, and access values appearing in the object name are evaluated when the renaming declaration is elaborated. For example, if `A` is an array with components of type `Integer` and the declaration

```
Next_Value : Integer RENAMES A (I);
```

is elaborated while `I` has the value four, `Next_Value` continues to name the component `A (4)` even if the value of `I` later changes. Block statements containing renaming declarations for slices, components, or allocated objects can often unclutter part of a program, enhancing readability. For example, consider the following declarations:

```
TYPE Point_Type IS
   RECORD
      X_Coordinate, Y_Coordinate, Z_Coordinate : Float;
   END RECORD;
```

```
TYPE Point_List_Cell_Type;
TYPE Point_List_Type IS ACCESS Point_List_Cell_Type;
TYPE Point_List_Cell_Type IS
   RECORD
      Point_Part : Point_Type;
      Link_Part  : Point_List_Type;
   END RECORD;
Curve, Next_Cell : Point_List_Type;
Scale_Factor     : Float;
```

A `Point_Type` value represents a point in three-dimensional space. A `Point_List_Type` value represents a set of such points. The following statements multiply each coordinate of each point in `Curve` by the value in `Scale_Factor`:

```
Next_Cell := Curve;
WHILE Next_Cell /= NULL LOOP
   Next_Cell.Point_Part.X_Coordinate :=
      Scale_Factor * Next_Cell.Point_Part.X_Coordinate;
   Next_Cell.Point_Part.Y_Coordinate :=
      Scale_Factor * Next_Cell.Point_Part.Y_Coordinate;
   Next_Cell.Point_Part.Z_Coordinate :=
      Scale_Factor * Next_Cell.Point_Part.Z_Coordinate;
   Next_Cell := Next_Cell.Link_Part;
END LOOP;
```

The following statements do the same thing more succinctly:

```
Next_Cell := Curve;
WHILE Next_Cell /= NULL LOOP
   DECLARE
      P : Point_Type RENAMES Next_Cell.Point_Part;
   BEGIN
      P.X_Coordinate := Scale_Factor * P.X_Coordinate;
      P.Y_Coordinate := Scale_Factor * P.Y_Coordinate;
      P.Z_Coordinate := Scale_Factor * P.Z_Coordinate;
   END;
   Next_Cell := Next_Cell.Link_Part;
END LOOP;
```

This formulation emphasizes that each iteration of the loop performs a particular operation for some point `P`. In understanding that operation, it is irrelevant that the point resides in the `Point_Part` component of a `Point_List_Cell_Type` record, or that that record is designated by the access value in `Next_Cell`.

Pascal programmers will recognize this use of block statements and renaming declarations as similar to the use of the **with** statement in Pascal. However, the Ada mechanism is more flexible because it can provide succinct names for the components of more than one record of the same type. Furthermore, statements inside the block statement are free to change the values of variables occurring in renaming declarations, since this does not change the identity of the renamed variables.

The form of a renaming declaration for a procedure is as follows:

```
PROCEDURE identifier
   [ ( parameter specification ; ~~~ ; parameter specification ) ]
   RENAMES procedure name ;
```

(Parameter specifications were described in Section 9.1.) If there is more than one procedure with the given name, the number and types of parameters given in the renaming declaration determine which overloaded version is renamed. The renaming declaration is illegal if there is not exactly one procedure with the given name and the appropriate parameter and result type profile.

The form of a renaming declaration for a function is similar:

```
FUNCTION designator
   [ ( parameter specification ; ~~~ ; parameter specification ) ]
   RETURN typemark
   RENAMES function name ;
```

The *designator* is either an identifier or a string literal containing an operator symbol. The function name following the word `RENAMES` may also contain such a string literal. If there is more than one function with the given name, the overloaded version having the same parameter and result type profile is the one that is renamed. Again, the renaming declaration is illegal if there is not exactly one such subprogram.

Subprograms may be renamed to resolve overloading. For example, given the context clause

```
WITH Fraction_Package; USE Fraction_Package;
```

the expression `(3/4)/(10/2)` is illegal in a context requiring a `Fraction_Type` value, because there are two possible interpretations. (As explained at the end of Section 9.6, the parenthesized division operators may be either the predefined division operator for type `Integer` or the one that takes two `Integer` values and returns a `Fraction_Type` value. The division operator in the middle may take either two `Fraction_Type` values or two `Integer` values, returning a value in either case.) However, the declaration

```
FUNCTION Build_Fraction
   (Numerator, Denominator : Integer) RETURN Fraction_Type
   RENAMES Fraction_Package."/";
```

provides a name that uniquely identifies the version of / taking two Integer values and returning a Fraction_Type value. The following two expressions are both legal in a context requiring a value of type Fraction_Type and correspond to the two possible interpretations of the expression (3/4)/(10/2):

```
Build_Fraction ( 3/4, 10/2 )
Build_Fraction (3, 4) / Build_Fraction (10, 2)
```

Renaming declarations for subprograms may provide new names for the formal parameters. For the sake of consistency with the predefined versions of /, the two versions of / defined in Fraction_Package had a first parameter named Left and a second parameter named Right. The renaming declaration used the names Numerator and Denominator instead, because the named parameter associations in the function call

```
Build_Fraction ( Numerator => 3, Denominator => 4)
```

are more helpful to a program reader than the named associations in the call

```
Build_Fraction ( Left => 3, Right => 4)
```

would be.

A renaming declaration for a subprogram can provide default expressions for parameters of mode IN that differ from those given in the original subprogram. Different expressions can be provided, expressions can be provided where there were none in the original subprogram, or expressions can be omitted where they were present in the original subprogram. The default expressions given in the original subprogram apply when the subprogram is called using its original name; those given in the renaming declaration apply when the subprogram is called under the name given in the renaming declaration. For example, the declaration of Build_Fraction could have been written as follows:

```
FUNCTION Build_Fraction
   (Numerator : Integer; Denominator: Integer := 1)
   RETURN Fraction_Type
   RENAMES Fraction_Package."/";
```

Then a call like Build_Fraction (3) would be legal and would have the apparent effect of converting a value of type Integer to the equivalent value of type `Fraction_Type`. The expression `Fraction_Package."/" (3)` would continue to be illegal.

The form of a renaming declaration for a package is as follows:

PACKAGE *identifier* RENAMES *package name* ;

It simply declares an occurrence of the identifier to be equivalent to an occurrence of the package name. This form of a renaming declaration is primarily useful when the package name is itself an expanded name.

11.7 DERIVED SUBPROGRAMS

Chapter 3 defined a data type as consisting of a set of values plus a set of *operations* on those values. A derived type is a copy of its parent type. That is why (as Section 6.4 explained) a derived type inherits certain operations from its parent type. Given the declarations

```
TYPE Motor_Setting_Type IS (Off, Low, Medium, High);
TYPE Switch_Setting_Type IS NEW Motor_Setting_Type;
```

for example, the derived type `Switch_Setting_Type` inherits the predefined operations of its parent type `Motor_Setting_Type`. These predefined operations include the `'Succ`, `'Pred`, `'First`, `'Last`, `'Pos`, and `'Val` attributes.

When a package provides a type and a set of subprograms, the subprograms can usually be viewed as operations on that type. For example, the functions provided by `Fraction_Package` are operations on `Fraction_Type`. If the parent type in a derived-type declaration is provided by a package, the derived type inherits the operations on the parent type that are provided by that package. The inherited subprograms are called *derived subprograms.*

For a subprogram to be inherited when some type is derived from type *t,* the subprogram must meet two conditions. First, both the subprogram and type *t* must be declared in the same package specification. Second, the subprogram must have at least one parameter or a function result of type *t*. All of the functions provided by `Fraction_Package` in Section 11.4 meet both these conditions for type `Fraction_Type`. Therefore, the derived type declaration

```
TYPE Distance_Type IS NEW Fraction_Package.Fraction_Type;
```

causes `Distance_Type` to inherit all of the operations of `Fraction_Type`.

A derived subprogram works just like the subprogram from which it was derived, except that it has parameters or function results of the derived type instead of the parent type. The effect is as if the following subprograms were declared just after the declaration of Distance_Type:

```
FUNCTION "-" (Right : Distance_Type) RETURN Distance_Type;
FUNCTION "+"
   (Left, Right : Distance_Type) RETURN Distance_Type;
FUNCTION "-"
   (Left, Right : Distance_Type) RETURN Distance_Type;
FUNCTION "*"
   (Left, Right : Distance_Type) RETURN Distance_Type;
FUNCTION "/"
   (Left, Right : Distance_Type) RETURN Distance_Type;
FUNCTION "**"
   (Left : Distance_Type; Right : Integer)
   RETURN Distance_Type;
FUNCTION "ABS"
   (Right : Distance_Type) RETURN Distance_Type;
FUNCTION "/"
   (Left, Right: Integer) RETURN Distance_Type;
```

(These subprogram declarations are identical to those in the Fraction_Package specification, except that each occurrence of Fraction_Type has been replaced by Distance_Type.)

The behavior of a derived subprogram is defined in terms of the type conversion (see Section 8.1.7) between a derived type and its parent type. When a derived *procedure* is called, any IN or IN OUT parameters belonging to the derived type are converted to the parent type and the original subprogram is called. Upon completion of the original subprogram, any IN OUT or OUT parameters of the parent type are converted back to the derived type and copied back to the actual parameters. When a derived *function* is called, any parameters belonging to the derived type are converted to the parent type and the original function is called. If the result of the original function belongs to the parent type, it is converted to the derived type at the end of the function call.

Because the derived subprograms are, in effect, declared just after the derived-type declaration, they cannot be named by expanded names that include the original package name. Given the declarations

```
a, b, c : Distance_Type;
```

the assignment statement

```
a := Fraction_Package."+" (b, c);
```

is illegal. Fraction_Package."+" is the name of a function declared in

Fraction_Package and taking Fraction_Type parameters. To call the version of "+" taking Distance_Type parameters, we write

```
a := "+" (b, c);
```

or simply

```
a := b + c;
```

Because this version of "+" is, in effect, declared just after the derived-type declaration and not in Fraction_Package, no USE clause is necessary.

11.8 PACKAGES WITHOUT BODIES

A package specification need not be accompanied by a package body. A package consisting only of a specification may be appropriate when the specification contains type, subtype, object, or named number declarations, but no subprogram declarations. For example, if the type declarations

```
TYPE Vector_Type IS ARRAY (Positive RANGE <>) OF Float;
TYPE Matrix_Type IS
   ARRAY (Positive RANGE <>, Positive RANGE <>) OF Float;
```

are to be used throughout many different compilation units in a program, it may make sense to write a package consisting only of the following specification:

```
PACKAGE Basic_Type_Declarations IS
   TYPE Vector_Type IS ARRAY (Positive RANGE <>) OF Float;
   TYPE Matrix_Type IS
      ARRAY (Positive RANGE <>, Positive RANGE <>) OF Float;
END Basic_Type_Declarations;
```

Then the types Vector_Type and Matrix_Type would be available to every compilation unit beginning with the context clause

```
WITH Basic_Type_Declarations;
```

(In practice the type declarations might be more numerous or more complex.) The package has no package body because there is nothing to implement; the facilities provided by the package are simply the type declarations given in the package specification.

A package without a body can also be used to make a series of constants available to any compilation unit using the package. Here is an example of such a package:

```
PACKAGE Earth_Orbit_Data IS
   Sea_Level_Gravity              : CONSTANT := 9.78049;
   G                              : CONSTANT := 6.673E-11;
   Mass_Of_Earth                  : CONSTANT := 5.975E24;
   Mean_Radius_Of_Earth           : CONSTANT := 6.371E6;
   Equatorial_Radius_Of_Earth : CONSTANT := 6.378E6;

   -- Sea_Level_Gravity is acceleration due to gravity at
   --   sea level at the equator, in meters per second per
   --   second.
   -- G is the universal gravitational constant, in
   --   newtons * meters**2 / kilograms**2.
   -- Mass_Of_Earth is in kilograms.
   -- Mean_Radius_Of_Earth is in meters.
   -- Equatorial_Radius_Of_Earth is in meters.

END Earth_Orbit_Data;
```

This package is a likely candidate for inclusion in a public file. It can be used by any compilation unit that must refer to the physical constants it specifies.

A package without a body might also have a specification consisting only of variable declarations. These variables could be updated and examined by any compilation unit mentioning the package in a context clause. Such a package would play a role very similar to the role played by a named `COMMON` block in FORTRAN—it would provide a pool of data that could be manipulated by any program unit naming that pool. The major difference is that the Ada language would not allow different program units to view a variable in the pool as belonging to different types.

However, this approach does not make good use of the capabilities of packages. A common pool of data, freely accessible by several compilation units, makes a program hard to understand. It is hard to keep track of which program units manipulate which variables in which ways or to convince oneself that a certain property always holds for a given set of variables. A superior approach, taking advantage of the Ada language's advances over FORTRAN, is to enclose the variables in a package body and to allow manipulation of the variables only through the execution of subprograms declared in the package specification. This restricts the ways in which other parts of the program can use the variables. If you can ascertain that some relationship holds among certain variables after the package body is elaborated (and thus after any sequence of initialization statements has been executed) and that each subprogram declared in the package specification keeps this relationship true if it was true before the subprogram was executed, then you know that the relationship holds between calls on the subprograms declared in the package specification. (If any of these subprograms can be called from within the package body—that is, if it is recursive or if it is called directly or indirectly by one of the other subprograms declared in the specification—then it is also necessary to ascertain that the relationship holds at each point the subprogram is called from within the package body.)

A package body may be omitted only in limited circumstances. Whenever a package specification contains a subprogram declaration, there must be a corresponding package body containing the subprogram's body. When a package specification contains a nested package specification and the inner package specification requires a package body, then the outer specification must be accompanied by a body containing the inner package's body.

11.9 PREDEFINED PACKAGES

There are six predefined packages that must be provided by every implementation of the Ada language. Their names are:

```
ASCII
Calendar
IO_Exceptions
Low_Level_IO
System
Text_IO
```

In addition, there is a package named `Machine_Code` that an implementation may or may not provide.

The package `ASCII` provides constant declarations for 79 values of type `Character` corresponding to characters that are not printable or might not be available on all data-entry equipment. The package `Calendar` provides facilities for manipulating information about times and dates and for determining the current time and date. The package `IO_Exceptions` provides facilities for dealing with errors that arise from input and output operations. The package `Low_Level_IO` provides facilities for direct control of input and output devices. The package `System` provides type declarations and constant declarations describing characteristics of the computer on which the program will run. The package `Text_IO` provides facilities for performing input and output with files viewed as streams of characters. The optional package `Machine_Code` provides type declarations needed to specify the exact set of machine-language instructions to be executed by a particular procedure.

A compilation unit using any of these packages, with the exception of package `ASCII`, must begin with a context specification that includes a `WITH` clause for that package. The package `ASCII`, however, is assumed to be available to all compilation units automatically, like the predefined types `Integer` and `Float`. No context clause is necessary to use the facilities provided by this package (nor is a `WITH ASCII;` clause permitted).

Packages `IO_Exceptions` and `Text_IO` are described in Chapter 17, along with two related *generic packages* named `Direct_IO` and `Sequential_IO`. (Generic packages are described in Chapter 16.) The packages `Low_Level_IO`, `System`, and `Machine_Code` are described in Chapter 20. The package `Calendar` is described in Chapter 12. The remainder of this section is devoted to a discussion of the package `ASCII`.

The only values of type `Character` that may be named by character literals are the 94 printing ASCII characters and the space character. The remaining 33 ASCII characters are *control characters.* Although they do not correspond to any enumeration literal, they are bona fide values of type `Character`. The control characters are commonly known by standard two-letter or three-letter abbreviations indicating their usual functions (e.g., BEL for the character that causes a terminal to ring a bell or beep, CR for the carriage return character, or ESC for the escape character).

The constants in package `ASCII` allow these values of type `Character` to be referred to by mnemonic names like `ASCII.BEL`, `ASCII.CR`, and `ASCII.ESC`, rather than in terms of their ASCII codes (as in `Character'Val(7)`, `Character'Val(13)`, and `Character'Val(27)`). This avoids the need to memorize ASCII codes, is less error-prone, and leads to more readable programs. In addition to constants for the control characters, the package `ASCII` contains constants for certain printing ASCII characters that might be impossible to enter or read on certain terminals, or that do not appear correctly on certain printers. For example, there are constants named `ASCII.L_Bracket` and `ASCII.R_Bracket`, which correspond to the characters `'['` and `']'` respectively. There are also constants named `LC_a`, `LC_b`, and so forth, corresponding to the lower-case alphabet. Given these constants, a program written entirely in upper-case letters and a few standard special characters can manipulate lower-case data. The limitations of the programmer's equipment need not affect the behavior of a program intended to run on more sophisticated equipment.

The only facilities provided by package `ASCII` are these constants. That is, the package specification consists entirely of constant declarations. Therefore the package has no body.

Figure 11.1 lists the 79 constants declared in package `ASCII`, along with their values and the corresponding ASCII codes. Values corresponding to printing characters are given as character literals; values corresponding to control characters are given in terms of their standard two-letter and three-letter abbreviations. The control characters with ASCII codes one through 26 can be entered on many terminals by simultaneously depressing the *control* key and one of the keys *a* through *z*, respectively, so they are identified by control key as well as by abbreviation. (For example, ↑A denotes "control-A," the character entered by simultaneously depressing the control key and the *a* key.)

Only the printing characters may be included in string literals. The constants in package `ASCII`, together with the catenation operator `&`, may be used to specify strings containing nonprinting characters. For example, the string

```
"The symbol O" & ASCII.BS & "/ denotes the empty set."
```

contains the character `BS` (control-H) between the `'O'` and the `'/'`. (The `BS` stands for *backspace.* On many printing terminals, the backspace character causes the typing element to back up one position, so that the `'/'` will be printed on top of the `'O'`.)

ASCII Code	Character	Constant name	ASCII Code	Character	Constant Name
000	NUL	NUL	063	'?'	Query
001	SOH (↑A)	SOH	064	'@'	At_Sign
002	STX (↑B)	STX	091	'['	L_Bracket
003	ETX (↑C)	ETX	092	'\'	Back_Slash
004	EOT (↑D)	EOT	093	']'	R_Bracket
005	ENQ (↑E)	ENQ	094	'^'	Circumflex
006	ACK (↑F)	ACK	095	'_'	Underline
007	BEL (↑G)	BEL	096	'`'	Grave
008	BS (↑H)	BS	097	'a'	LC_a
009	HT (↑I)	HT	098	'b'	LC_b
010	LF (↑J)	LF	099	'c'	LC_c
011	VT (↑K)	VT	100	'd'	LC_d
012	FF (↑L)	FF	101	'e'	LC_e
013	CR (↑M)	CR	102	'f'	LC_f
014	SO (↑N)	SO	103	'g'	LC_g
015	SI (↑O)	SI	104	'h'	LC_h
016	DLE (↑P)	DLE	105	'i'	LC_i
017	DC1 (↑Q)	DC1	106	'j'	LC_j
018	DC2 (↑R)	DC2	107	'k'	LC_k
019	DC3 (↑S)	DC3	108	'l'	LC_l
020	DC4 (↑T)	DC4	109	'm'	LC_m
021	NAK (↑U)	NAK	110	'n'	LC_n
022	SYN (↑V)	SYN	111	'o'	LC_o
023	ETB (↑W)	ETB	112	'p'	LC_p
024	CAN (↑X)	CAN	113	'q'	LC_q
025	EM (↑Y)	EM	114	'r'	LC_r
026	SUB (↑Z)	SUB	115	's'	LC_s
027	ESC	ESC	116	't'	LC_t
028	FS	FS	117	'u'	LC_u
029	GS	GS	118	'v'	LC_v
030	RS	RS	119	'w'	LC_w
031	US	US	120	'x'	LC_x
033	'!'	Exclam	121	'y'	LC_y
034	'"'	Quotation	122	'z'	LC_z
035	'#'	Sharp	123	'{'	L_Brace
036	'$'	Dollar	124	'|'	Bar
037	'%'	Percent	125	'{'	R_Brace
038	'&'	Ampersand	126	'~'	Tilde
058	':'	Colon	127	DEL	DEL
059	';'	Semicolon			

Figure 11.1 The constants declared in package **ASCII**. The first column gives ASCII codes (in base ten). The second column lists character literals for printing characters and mnemonic abbreviations for nonprinting characters. The notations ↑A, ↑B, and so forth specify that the corresponding characters can typically be entered from keyboards as control-A, control-B, and so forth. The third column gives the names of the constants declared in package **ASCII**.

11.10 SUMMARY

Large programs can be made easier to understand by dividing them into *modules* that can be understood individually. A module has an *interface* with the other parts of a program and an *implementation.* When trying to understand one module of a program, it may be necessary to examine the interface of another module, but not its implementation.

In the Ada language, a module is known as a *package.* A package consists of a *package specification* describing the package's interface and, in most cases, a *package body* describing the implementation of that interface. A package specification may be written as follows:

```
PACKAGE identifier IS
    basic declaration
        ~~~
    basic declaration
END identifier ;
```

The basic declarations include declarations of types and variables provided by the package. They also include subprogram declarations for subprograms called from outside the package. A package body may be written as follows:

```
PACKAGE BODY identifier IS
    declarative part
.....................................
: BEGIN                             :
:     sequence of initialization statements :
.....................................
END identifier ;
```

The declarative part of the package body must contain a subprogram body corresponding to each subprogram declaration in the package specification. In addition, it may contain other declarations of facilities used only by those subprogram bodies. These may include types, variables, and "internal subprograms" that are never directly called from outside the package. The optional sequence of initialization statements in the package body is executed once, at the time the package comes into existence. A package that provides only types, subtypes, objects, and named numbers—but no subprograms—need not have a package body.

An entity declared in a package specification of the form above may be referred to later in the package specification and throughout the package body by the identifier naming it. It may be referred to outside of the package by an *expanded name* of the form

```
package-name . identifier
```

An entity declared in the package body may be declared later in the package body by the identifier naming it; it may not be referred to in any way outside of the package.

Typically, a package specification and package body are compiled separately (as two distinct compilation units). A compilation unit using the facilities of a separately compiled package begins with a *context clause* containing a `WITH` clause of the form

> `WITH` *compilation unit name* `,` ~~~ `,` *compilation unit name* `;`

A separately compiled package comes into existence before execution of the main program and exists for the duration of the program. Any initialization statements in the body of a separately compiled package are executed before the main program starts.

However, package specifications and package bodies can also be used as declarations. Specifically, a package specification may occur in the declarative part of a block statement, a subprogram body, or the body of another package, followed later (somewhere after the last object, named number, type, or subtype declaration) by the corresponding package body. The package comes into existence when the declarative part is entered. The package ceases to exist upon departure from the outer block statement or subprogram, or when the outer package ceases to exist. Finally, a package specification may occur in the *specification* of an outer package, with the inner package's body occurring in the declarative part of the outer package's body. In this case, the inner package is one of the facilities provided by the outer package. The inner package comes into existence when the outer package is elaborated and ceases to exist when the outer package ceases to exist.

A `USE` *clause* of the form

> `USE` *package name* `,` ~~~ `,` *package name* `;`

allows entities provided by the listed packages to be named by identifiers (e.g., `Put`) rather than expanded names (e.g., `Basic_IO.Put`). The context clause at the beginning of a compilation unit may consist of any number of `WITH` clauses, each followed by any number of `USE` clauses. A `USE` clause may also appear anywhere within a declarative part.

Sometimes a `USE` clause does not apply to every entity provided by a package. It does not apply to entities whose names clash with other names that can be used at that point. Similarly, in the case of `USE` clauses for two or more packages providing entities with names that clash, the `USE` clause does not apply to any of the clashing entities. Two names clash if they are the same, unless they are the names of subprograms or enumerations literals with different parameter and result type profiles. In that case, the names do not clash because the entities they name are overloaded.

`USE` clauses can make a program hard to understand by allowing a compilation to refer to a large set of names that are not declared in the compilation unit. In the absence of an expanded name, there is no indication of where the entity is declared.

Except when packages provide overloaded versions of operators or subprograms with familiar names like Get and Put, it is preferable to use a *renaming declaration.* We have seen four forms of renaming declarations, for objects, procedures, functions, and packages:

> *identifier* : *typemark* RENAMES *object name* ;
>
> PROCEDURE *identifier*
> [(*parameter specification* ; ~~~ ; *parameter specification*)]
> RENAMES *procedure name* ;
>
> FUNCTION *designator*
> [(*parameter specification* ; ~~~ ; *parameter specification*)]
> RETURN *typemark*
> RENAMES *function name* ;
>
> PACKAGE *identifier* RENAMES *package name* ;

The effect of a USE clause is obtained (for a single entity rather than for all entities provided by a package) when the old name is an expanded name and the new name is the identifier following the period in the expanded name. However, a renaming declaration may be used with any name, to provide a more meaningful or more succinct name. A renaming declaration for a subprogram can provide new formal parameter names and new sets of default parameter values.

When the parent type in a derived-type declaration is a type provided by a package, the derived type inherits the operations on that type provided by the package. These operations consist of every subprogram provided by the package that has at least one parameter or a function result of the parent type. The inherited versions, called *derived subprograms,* work by converting values from the derived type to the parent type, calling the corresponding subprograms for the parent type, and then converting values from the parent type back to the derived type. Derived subprograms are implicitly declared just after the derived-type declaration. Thus we do not refer to the package that provided the operations on the parent type when we name the derived subprograms.

Several separately compiled packages are predefined in the Ada language. One of these, the package ASCII, provides constant declarations giving mnemonic names to certain values of type Character. Unlike the other predefined packages, the package ASCII is available automatically, without using a WITH clause.

EXERCISES

11.1 Write the specification and body of a package providing facilities for generating and using word frequency counts. The package should provide the following facilities:

a subtype named Word_Subtype consisting of ten-character strings

a procedure named Count_Word such that the call Count_Word (W), where W is of subtype Word_Subtype, causes an occurrence of the word in W to be counted a procedure named `Report_Frequency` such that the call

```
Report_Frequency (Rank, Word, Frequency)
```

reads the value of `Rank`—an integer between one and 100 inclusive—sets `Word` to a `Word_Subtype` value indicating the `Rank`th most frequently occurring word, and sets `Frequency` to a `Float` value in the range 0.0 to 1.0 indicating the proportion of occurrences counted so far that are occurrences of that word. You may assume that there are no more than 100 distinct words. A call on `Report_Frequency` with a rank less than or equal to 100 but greater than the number of distinct words encountered so far should cause `Word` to be set to blanks and `Frequency` to be set to 0.0.

11.2 Write a main program to use the package developed in Exercise 11.1. The program should assume that the standard input file contains text consisting of words separated by spaces. There are no more than 100 *unique* words, although the same word may occur many times. No word is more than ten characters long. The output should be a list of words in order of frequency, with the most frequent words listed first, and a percentage (i.e., a number between zero and 100) indicating the proportion of all word occurrences in the text that are occurrences of that word. The output should contain one line for each unique word.

11.3 The Ada language's predefined exponentiation operator requires the right operand of the exponentiation operator to be of type `Integer`. However, `"**"` can be overloaded with a function accepting a right operand of type `Float`. Mathematically, the value of a positive number raised to a fractional power is defined by the formula *x**y = exp(y*ln(x))*, where *ln* is the natural logarithm function and *exp* is the inverse function, the *exponential function.* The following package provides subprograms that compute the exponential and natural logarithm functions using Taylor series:

```
PACKAGE Taylor_Series_Package IS

   SUBTYPE Positive_Float IS
      Float RANGE Float'Small .. Float'Large;

   FUNCTION Ln (x : Positive_Float) RETURN Float;
   FUNCTION Exp (x : Float) RETURN Float;

END Taylor_Series_Package;


PACKAGE BODY Taylor_Series_Package IS

   e : Float; -- the base for natural logarithms
              -- (Initialized when package is elaborated.)

   FUNCTION Ln (x : Positive_Float) RETURN Float IS

      Characteristic, i : Integer := 0;
      Mantissa          : Float := 0.0;
      Argument          : Float := x;
      Term              : Float := -1.0;

   BEGIN -- Ln

      -- Get Argument in the interval (0, 2):

      WHILE Argument > 2.0 LOOP
         Argument := Argument / e;
         Characteristic := Characteristic + 1;
      END LOOP;

      -- Subtract 1 and compute Taylor series:

      Argument := Argument - 1.0;

      LOOP
         i := i + 1;
         Term := Term * (-Argument / Float (i));
         Mantissa := Mantissa + Term;
         EXIT WHEN Term/Mantissa < Float'Epsilon;
      END LOOP;

      RETURN Float (Characteristic) + Mantissa;

   END Ln;
```

```
    FUNCTION Exp (x : Float) RETURN Float IS

       Sum  : Float := 0.0;
       Term : Float := 1.0;
       i    : Integer := 0;

    BEGIN -- Exp

       LOOP
          Sum := Sum + Term;
          EXIT WHEN Term/Sum < Float'Epsilon;
          i := i + 1;
          Term := Term * x / Float (i);
       END LOOP;

       RETURN Sum;

    END Exp;

 BEGIN -- Taylor_Series_Package

    e := Exp (1.0);

 END Taylor_Series_Package;
```

Overload `"**"` to take left and right operands of type `Float`, *nesting* the package `Taylor_Series_Package` *inside* the `"**"` function body. You may write ellipses (...) in place of the declarations and statements inside `Ln` and `Exp`, and you may ignore the danger of the left operand not being positive.

11.4 Write a package named `Exponential_Package` providing the following two overloaded versions of `"**"`:

```
FUNCTION "**" (Left, Right : Float) RETURN Float;

FUNCTION "**"
   (Left : Positive; Right : Float) RETURN Float;
```

Implement these functions by *nesting* `Taylor_Series_Package`, described in Exercise 11.3, *inside* `Exponential_Package`. Again, you may write ellipses (...) in place of the declarations and statements of `Ln` and `Exp`. For the version taking two parameters of type `Float`, you may ignore the danger of the left operand not being positive.

11.5 Exercise 11.3 describes the package `Taylor_Series_Package` and the use of its functions to raise positive numbers to fractional exponents. Overload `"**"` with a version taking a left operand of the subtype `Positive_Float` declared in the `Taylor_Series_Package` specification, and a right operand of type `Float`, assuming that `Taylor_Series_Package` has been *separately compiled*.

11.6 Write a package `Vector_Package` providing two subpackages, `Plane_Vector_Package` and `Space_Vector_Package`. Each subpackage should provide a record type named `Vector_Type` with components of type `Float`. There should be two components in `Plane_Vector_Package.Vector_Type` and three components in `Space_Vector_Package.Vector_Type`. Besides the type `Vector_Type`, each subpackage should provide a version of `"+"` taking two `Vector_Type` parameters and computing a component-by-component `Vector_Type` sum, as well as a version of `"*"` taking a left operand of type `Float` and a right operand of type `Vector_Type` and computing a product of type `Vector_Type` by multiplying each component of the right operand by the left operand.

11.7 The following three compilation units are a package specification, a package body, and a main program utilizing the package. What is the output of the main program?

```
PACKAGE Powers_Of_2_Package IS

   SUBTYPE Exponent_Subtype IS Integer RANGE 0 .. 10;

   FUNCTION Power_Of_2
      (n : Exponent_Subtype) RETURN Integer;

END Powers_Of_2_Package;
```

```
---------------------------------------
WITH Basic_IO; USE Basic_IO;

PACKAGE BODY Powers_Of_2_Package IS

   Table : ARRAY (0 .. 10) OF Integer;

   FUNCTION Power_Of_2
      (n : Exponent_Subtype) RETURN Integer IS

   BEGIN -- Power_Of_2

      RETURN Table (n);

   END Power_Of_2;

BEGIN -- Powers_Of_2_Package

   Table (0) := 1;

   FOR i IN 1 .. 10 LOOP
      Table (i) := 2 * Table (i-1);
   END LOOP;

   Put ("Table is filled.");
   New_Line;

END Powers_Of_2_Package;
---------------------------------------

WITH Powers_Of_2_Package, Basic_IO;
USE Basic_IO;

PROCEDURE Print_Powers IS

BEGIN

   FOR i IN REVERSE 1 .. 10 LOOP
      Put ( Powers_Of_2_Package.Power_Of_2 (i) );
   END LOOP;

END Print_Powers;
```

11.8 Consider the following declarations:

```
TYPE Time_Request_Type IS
   RECORD
      Minutes_Part : Natural;
      Seconds_Part : Integer RANGE 0 .. 59;
   END RECORD;

TYPE Batch_Job_Type IS
   RECORD
      Job_Name_Part : String (1 .. 8);
      Time_Part     : Time_Request_Type;
   END RECORD;

TYPE Batch_Job_Array_Type IS
   ARRAY (0 .. 255) OF Batch_Job_Type;

TYPE Batch_Queue_Type IS
   RECORD
      Front_Position_Part,
         Back_Position_Part : Integer RANGE 0 .. 255;
      Job_Array_Part        : Batch_Job_Array_Type;
   END RECORD;

Queue         : Batch_Queue_Type;
Shortest_Job  : Batch_Job_Type;
Next_Position : Integer RANGE 0 .. 255;
```

Rewrite the following statements more succinctly using a block statement containing one or more renaming declarations:

```
Shortest_Job :=
   Queue.Job_Array_Part(Queue.Front_Position_Part);

Next_Position := Queue.Front_Position_Part;

WHILE Next_Position /= Queue.Back_Position_Part LOOP

   IF Next_Position = 255 THEN
      Next_Position := 0;
   ELSE
      Next_Position := Next_Position + 1;
   END IF;

   IF Queue.Job_Array_Part(Next_Position).
         Time_Part.Minutes_Part <
      Shortest_Job.Time_Part.Minutes_Part THEN

      Shortest_Job := Queue.Job_Array_Part(Next_Position);

   ELSIF Queue.Job_Array_Part(Next_Position).
            Time_Part.Minutes_Part =
         Shortest_Job.Time_Part.Minutes_Part AND
         Queue.Job_Array_Part(Next_Position).
            Time_Part.Seconds_Part <
         Shortest_Job.Time_Part.Seconds_Part THEN

      Shortest_Job := Queue.Job_Array_Part(Next_Position);

   END IF;

END LOOP;
```

11.9 Suppose you were writing a program using a package with the following specification:

```
PACKAGE Stack_Package IS

   TYPE Integer_Array_Type IS ARRAY (1 .. 100) OF Integer;

   TYPE Stack_Type IS
      RECORD
         Top      : Integer RANGE 0 .. 100;
         Elements : Integer_Array_Type;
      END RECORD;

   FUNCTION Empty_Stack RETURN Stack_Type;

   PROCEDURE Push
      (Element : IN Integer; Stack : IN OUT Stack_Type);

   PROCEDURE Pop
      (Element : OUT Integer; Stack : IN OUT Stack_Type);

END Stack_Package;
```

Write a renaming declaration for the `Push` procedure that will allow it to be called with only the second parameter when the intended value of the first parameter is zero.

11.10 Write a package providing the type declarations for a linked list of elements of type `Integer`, but no operations for the types declared.

11.11 Write a package providing an enumeration type containing one value for each month of the year and a table giving the number of days in each month, assuming the year is not a leap year.

11.12 Write a program that reads in integers and keeps track of the sum of the numbers read in so far, until the sum exceeds 100. When the sum exceeds 100, the program should cause the terminal to display the message

```
100 exceeded.
```

and beep. Assume that the terminal beeps whenever it is asked to "display" the ASCII control character `BEL`.

CHAPTER

TWELVE

PRIVATE AND LIMITED PRIVATE TYPES

12.1 ABSTRACT DATA TYPES VERSUS INTERNAL REPRESENTATIONS

Section 3.1 discussed the distinction between abstract data types and their internal representations. The package `Fraction_Package`, given in Section 11.4, illustrates this distinction. On an abstract level, the package provides a data type whose values are exact representations of fractions and whose operations are the arithmetic operations declared in the package specification. But the data type `Fraction_Type` can also be viewed simply as a record type with two components—one of type `Integer`, named `Numerator_Part`, and one of subtype `Positive`, named `Denominator_Part`. The functions declared in the `Fraction_Package` specification provide convenient mechanisms for manipulating these record values, but they are not the only operations available. It is also possible to examine a component of the record, to assign a value to a component of the record, or to describe a value of type `Fraction_Type` with a record aggregate.

The abstract view is more consistent with the intent of the package writer. Operations referring to the components of the record do not always have a meaning in terms of the abstraction that the package writer is trying to provide—exact fractional values. More seriously, the correct functioning of the data type depends on its values not being manipulated in unanticipated ways.

If `A` and `B` are `Fraction_Type` objects, the expression `A = B` is true if and only if `A.Numerator_Part = B.Numerator_Part` and `A.Denominator_Part = B.Denominator_Part`. If `A` has the value `(3, 4)` and `B` has the value `(6, 8)`, then the expression `A = B` is false. This is inconsistent with the abstract view of `Fraction_Type` values. To avoid this discrepancy, the package writer deals only with fractions reduced to lowest terms (i.e., such that the numerator and denominator have no common factors larger than one). This ensures that each representable fractional value has a *unique* representation. The function bodies for binary "+", binary "-", "*", and both versions of "/" call the procedure Reduce (which is internal to the Fraction_Package body) to reduce their results to lowest terms. The function bodies for unary "+", unary "-", "**", and "ABS" do not call Reduce. These functions are written in such a way that if their Fraction_Type parameters are reduced, the results will be reduced without further action. Thus correct functioning of Fraction_Package depends on the assumption that the *parameters* to unary "+", unary "-", "**", and "ABS" are always reduced.

As long as users of the package produce Fraction_Type values exclusively by calling the package's functions, and not by building Fraction_Type values directly out of record components, this assumption will remain valid. All fractions *produced* by these functions are reduced when their parameters are reduced. However, the Fraction_Package writer has little control over how the facilities provided by Fraction_Package, as defined in Section 11.4, will be used.

The Ada language provides a mechanism for asserting such control. Fraction_Type can be declared as a *private type*. This means that, except inside Fraction_Package, the internal representation of Fraction_Type values is considered "hidden." Programmers using Fraction_Package are not prevented from *looking at* the Fraction_Package source listing to learn what the internal representation is, but they will be unable to *make use of* that knowledge when using Fraction_Package.

Specifically, if Fraction_Type is declared to be a private type, then objects of type Fraction_Type may be declared outside of Fraction_Package, the functions provided by Fraction_Package may be called to compute new Fraction_Type values, Fraction_Type values may be assigned to Fraction_Type variables, and Fraction_Type values may be compared for equality and inequality. However, outside the package, values may not be assigned to components of Fraction_Type variables, and Fraction_Type values may not be specified by record aggregates. Within Fraction_Package, Fraction_Type values may be manipulated as records to implement the functions provided by the package.

Besides giving the package writer more control over the way in which values are manipulated (for example, allowing the Fraction_Package writer to assume that all Fraction_Type parameters to the Fraction_Package functions are reduced), private types simplify the interface of the package for its users. When a package provides a private type, users of that type need not be concerned with its internal representation. All they have to know about the type is the abstract behavior of the operations provided by the package for manipulating values belonging to the private type.

Furthermore, private types give the package writer the freedom to change the implementation of the type, provided that the operations for manipulating the type continue to manifest the same external behavior. For example, consider a package providing a private type for complex numbers and a set of subprograms for manipulating values belonging to that type. The package writer can change the internal representation of complex numbers from rectangular coordinates to polar coordinates, provided that the bodies of the subprograms provided by the package are changed accordingly. Since users of the package were permitted to manipulate complex numbers only in terms of the operations provided by the package and not in terms of the internal representation, no part of the program outside the package can possibly be affected by the change (except perhaps in terms of execution speed).

A private type behaves very much like a predefined type. Internally, values of type `Integer` are generally implemented in terms of a sequence of bits viewed as a binary numeral. There are several possible schemes for representing negative numbers. As a user of type `Integer`, you are unconcerned with these details. All you care about is that the operations defined for the type—addition, subtraction, the attributes `Integer'First` and `Integer'Last`, and so forth—all work as expected. Similarly, when you use a package providing a private type and operations for manipulating that type, you are not concerned with the internal representation of the type, but with the operations provided for that type and the external behavior of those operations.

12.2 DECLARATION OF PRIVATE TYPES

Section 11.2 described the simplest form of package specification. A more complete description is as follows:

```
PACKAGE identifier IS

      basic declaration
           ~~~
      basic declaration
.....................
: PRIVATE           :
:                   :
:     basic declaration :
:          ~~~      :
:     basic declaration :
.....................
END identifier ;
```

The optional part of the package specification consisting of the word `PRIVATE` and the basic declarations following it is called the *private part* of the package specification. The basic declarations above the word `PRIVATE` form the *visible part* of the package specification. Until now we have been using package specifications having only visible parts.

A private type can be declared only in a package specification. A declaration of the form

```
TYPE identifier IS PRIVATE ;
```

in the visible part of the package specification declares the given identifier to be the name of a private type. This declaration must be accompanied by an ordinary type declaration for the same type in the private part of the package specification.

The specification of Fraction_Package given in Section 11.4 could be rewritten as follows to make Fraction_Type a private type:

```
PACKAGE Fraction_Package IS
   TYPE Fraction_Type IS PRIVATE;
   FUNCTION "+" (Right : Fraction_Type) RETURN Fraction_Type;
   FUNCTION "-" (Right : Fraction_Type) RETURN Fraction_Type;
   FUNCTION "+"
      (Left, Right : Fraction_Type) RETURN Fraction_Type;
   FUNCTION "-"
      (Left, Right : Fraction_Type) RETURN Fraction_Type;
   FUNCTION "*"
      (Left, Right : Fraction_Type) RETURN Fraction_Type;
   FUNCTION "/"
      (Left, Right : Fraction_Type) RETURN Fraction_Type;
      -- This function assumes that
      --    Right.Numerator_Part /= 0. It will not work
      --    correctly when this is not the case.
   FUNCTION "**"
      (Left : Fraction_Type; Right : Integer)
      RETURN Fraction_Type;
   FUNCTION "ABS"
      (Right : Fraction_Type) RETURN Fraction_Type;
   FUNCTION "/" (Left, Right : Integer) RETURN Fraction_Type;
      -- This function assumes that Right /= 0.
      -- It will not work correctly when Right = 0.
PRIVATE
   TYPE Fraction_Type IS
      RECORD
         Numerator_Part   : Integer;
         Denominator_Part : Positive;
      END RECORD;
END Fraction_Package;
```

The package body could remain unchanged.

Chapter 11 stated that a package specification describes the facilities provided by the package and the package body describes the implementation of those facilities. Now that you have seen package specifications with private parts, this statement must be amended slightly. The *visible part* of a package specification describes the facilities provided by the package; the private part of the specification and the package body together describe the implementation of those facilities. In the case of Fraction_Package, the visible part of the package specification conveys that Fraction_Package provides a private type named Fraction_Type and nine functions for manipulating Fraction_Type values. The private part of the package specification describes the internal representation of Fraction_Type values, and the package body describes the algorithms manipulating that representation.

The private part of the specification may contain declarations other than full declarations for the private types declared in the visible part. Consider the package below, providing a type for lists of up to ten String values and operations to create an empty list, add a string of any length to the list, and print out the list. The Add_String operation has no effect when it is called with a list already containing ten elements. The Print_String_List operation prints the strings one per line, with special lines marking the start and end of the list.

```
PACKAGE String_List_Package IS
   TYPE String_List_Type IS PRIVATE;
   FUNCTION Empty_String_List RETURN String_List_Type;
   PROCEDURE Add_String
      (New_String  : IN String;
       String_List : IN OUT String_List_Type);
   PROCEDURE Print_String_List
      (String_List : IN String_List_Type);
PRIVATE
   TYPE String_Pointer_Type IS ACCESS String;
   TYPE String_Pointer_Array_Type IS
      ARRAY (1 .. 10) OF String_Pointer_Type;
   TYPE String_List_Type IS
      RECORD
         Size_Part  : Integer RANGE 0 .. 10;
         Array_Part : String_Pointer_Array_Type;
      END RECORD;
END String_List_Package;

-- -- -- -- -- -- -- -- -- -- -- -- -- -- -- --

WITH Basic_IO; USE Basic_IO;

PACKAGE BODY String_List_Package IS

   FUNCTION Empty_String_List RETURN String_List_Type IS
   BEGIN
      RETURN
         (Size_Part  => 0,
          Array_Part =>
            (String_Pointer_Array_Type'Range => NULL) );
   END Empty_String_List;
```

```
   PROCEDURE Add_String
      (New_String  : IN String;
       String_List : IN OUT String_List_Type) IS
   BEGIN
      IF String_List.Size_Part < 10 THEN
         String_List.Size_Part :=
            String_List.Size_Part + 1;
         String_List.Array_Part(String_List.Size_Part) :=
            NEW String'(New_String);
      END IF;
   END Add_String;


   PROCEDURE Print_String_List
      (String_List : IN String_List_Type) IS
   BEGIN
      Put ("-- Start of list --");
      New_Line;
      FOR i IN 1 .. String_List.Size_Part LOOP
         Put (String_List.Array_Part (i).ALL);
         New_Line;
      END LOOP;
      Put ("-- End of list --");
      New_Line;
   END Print_String_List;

END String_List_Package;
```

The types `String_Pointer_Type` and `String_Pointer_Array_Type` are declared as part of the implementation of `String_List_Type` and are not meant to be provided to the outside world. Thus it would be inappropriate to declare them in the visible part of the package specification. Nonetheless, `String_Pointer_Array_Type` must be declared before the full declaration of `String_List_Type`, because it is referred to in that declaration; similarly, `String_Pointer_Type` must be declared before `String_Pointer_Array_Type`. Therefore, all three types are declared in the private part of the package specification.

Entities declared only in the private part of a package specification may be referred to later in the private part and throughout the package body, but not outside of the package. `String_Pointer_Type` is referred to later in the private part, in the declaration of `String_Pointer_Array_Type`. `String_Pointer_Array_Type` is referred to later in the private part (in the full declaration of `String_List_Type`) and also in the package body (in the `Empty_String_List` function body). Neither `String_Pointer_Type` nor `String_Pointer_Array_Type` may be referred to outside of `String_List_Package`. `String_List_Type` may be referred to outside of String_List_Package, but only by virtue of its declaration as a private type in the visible part of the package specification, not because of its declaration as a record type in the private part of the specification. The two components of the record type, Size_Part and Array_Part, are declared in the private part of the specification (by the record-type declaration for String_List_Type). These components are referred to many places in the String_List_Package body but may not be referred to outside String_List_Package.

Logically, it seems that the private part of the package specification should be part of the package body. Like the package body, the private part of the specification describes the implementation of facilities declared in the visible part of the specification—in this case the internal structure of a private type. Like the package body, the private part of the specification contains declarations that may be referred to throughout the rest of the package but not outside the package. In fact, any basic declaration in a package body may be moved to the private part of the package specification without changing the meaning of the program.

The only reason that the private part of a package specification exists is to allow a part of the program using the package to be compiled after the package specification has been compiled but before the package body has been compiled. If the package specification contains a private-type declaration, the part of the program using the package may contain a declaration of an object belonging to that private type. In general, a compiler could not be expected to translate uses of that object into efficient machine instructions if it did not have access to the size of the object. The full declaration of the private type in the private part of the package specification provides the information necessary to compile efficient translations of uses of the package's private types.

As a matter of style, the only declarations that you should place in the private part of the package specification rather than the package body are those that the rules of the Ada language *require* you to place there. These include the full declarations of private types and any declarations that must precede these full declarations (e.g., the declarations of String_Pointer_Type and String_Pointer_Array_Type that had to precede the full declaration of String_List_Type). To the greatest extent possible, the division between the package specification and the package body should reflect the division between the interface of the package and its implementation. Furthermore, for reasons that will be explained in Chapter 13, making a change to a package specification generally necessitates more recompilation than a change to a package body. (Roughly speaking, this is because a change to a package body is clearly an internal change that does not affect other parts of the program.) The more information that is placed in the package body rather than the package specification, the less likely it is that the package specification will need to be changed.

When a package writer declares a type private, he deprives the package user of the ability to manipulate objects in the type in any way other than by the operations provided by the package. Therefore, the package writer must be sure to provide a complete set of operations sufficient for any reasonable use of the private type. In particular, these must include operations to initialize or create objects belonging to the private type. Were it not for the second version of "/" provided by Fraction_Package (taking two Integer operands and producing a Fraction_Type result), there would be no way for a user of the package to create values of the private type Fraction_Type, and thus nothing to which to apply the other operations! Similarly, were String_List_Package not to provide the function Empty_String_List, there would be no way for a user of the package to create an empty list of strings to which Add_String could be applied.

In fact, Fraction_Package is still missing certain important operations. Because a user of Fraction_Package cannot refer to the Numerator_Part and Denominator_Part components of a Fraction_Type value, he has no way to determine whether one Fraction_Type value is greater or less than another. The relational operators ought to be overloaded with versions taking Fraction_Type parameters and providing this information. Furthermore, there is no way to make use of a Fraction_Type result once it has been computed. The output procedure Put should be overloaded to take a Fraction_Type parameter and print its value, perhaps in the form

numerator / denominator

Finally, there should be a function, say Fraction_To_Float, to convert a Fraction_Type value to its approximation in type Float. This allows computed Fraction_Type values to be used in conjunction with other arithmetic values that an Ada program can compute. The provision of these additional operations is left as an exercise at the end of this chapter.

12.3 THE PREDEFINED PACKAGE Calendar

As another example of a package providing a private type and a complete set of operations for manipulating values in that type, we shall now consider one of the predefined packages introduced in Section 11.9—the package Calendar. This package provides a private type named Time and subprograms for manipulating values of type Time and type Duration. Duration is a predefined fixed-point type that measures seconds. It was described in Section 7.8.

To understand the facilities provided by this package, you must understand the difference between the data abstraction provided by type Duration and that provided by type Time. To understand this distinction, you must realize that the word *time* is used in two different senses in the English language. The question "What time is it?" is answered by naming a particular moment, a point on a time line. The question "How much time does it take to print a page?" is answered by naming an amount of time, the distance between two points on a time line. Values of type Calendar.Time name points on a time line. Values of type Duration name the amount of time between two points on a time line.

```
PACKAGE Calendar IS
   TYPE Time IS PRIVATE;

   SUBTYPE Year_Number  IS Integer RANGE 1901 .. 2099;
   SUBTYPE Month_Number IS Integer RANGE 1 .. 12;
   SUBTYPE Day_Number   IS Integer RANGE 1 .. 31;
   SUBTYPE Day_Duration IS Duration RANGE 0.0 .. 86_400.0;

   FUNCTION Clock RETURN Time;

   FUNCTION Year (Date : Time) RETURN Year_Number;
   FUNCTION Month (Date : Time) RETURN Month_Number;
   FUNCTION Day (Date : Time) RETURN Day_Number;
   FUNCTION Seconds (Date : Time) RETURN Day_Duration;

   PROCEDURE Split
      (Date    : IN Time;
       Year    : OUT Year_Number;
       Month   : OUT Month_Number;
       Day     : OUT Day_Number;
       Seconds : OUT Day_Duration);

   FUNCTION Time_Of
      (Year    : Year_Number;
       Month   : Month_Number;
       Day     : Day_Number;
       Seconds : Day_Duration := 0.0)
      RETURN Time;

   FUNCTION "+" (Left: Time; Right: Duration) RETURN Time;
   FUNCTION "+" (Left: Duration; Right: Time) RETURN Time;
   FUNCTION "-" (Left: Time; Right: Duration) RETURN Time;
   FUNCTION "-" (Left: Time; Right: Time) RETURN Duration;

   FUNCTION "<" (Left, Right: Time) RETURN Boolean;
   FUNCTION "<=" (Left, Right: Time) RETURN Boolean;
   FUNCTION ">" (Left, Right: Time) RETURN Boolean;
   FUNCTION ">=" (Left, Right: Time) RETURN Boolean;

   Time_Error : EXCEPTION;
PRIVATE

   -- ???

END Calendar;
```

This specification has a comment with question marks in place of the actual private part because the private part will differ from one Ada compiler to another. All Ada compilers are required to provide the same facilities, described in the visible part of the specification, but each is entitled to its own representation for values of type `Time` (specified in the private part of the package specification) and its own algorithms (given in the package body) to implement the subprograms declared in the visible part of the package specification.

Regardless of how values of type `Time` are represented internally, a point on a time line can be described abstractly in terms of a particular date and an amount of time since the stroke of midnight at which that date began. The date, in turn, can be described in terms of a year, a month, and a day of the month. The amount of time since midnight is a distance between two points on a time line, so it can be described by a value of type `Duration`. The procedure `Split` takes an `IN` parameter of type `Time` and sets its `OUT` parameters to the year, month, day of the month, and amount of time since midnight describing that `Time` value. The function `Time_Of` does just the opposite, taking a year, month, day of the month, and amount of time since midnight and returning the corresponding value of type `Time`.

Examining the subtypes of the parameters to `Split` and `Time_Of` and the declarations of those subtypes near the top of the package specification, we see that values of type `Time` are only meant to represent moments in the years 1901 to 2099, inclusive. Within this range of years, a year is a leap year if and only if it is evenly divisible by four. (Years divisible by 100 are not leap years unless they are also divisible by 400, so 2000 is a leap year, but 1900 and 2100 are not.) Month numbers are always in the range one to twelve. Days of the month are always in the range one to 31 and—although the package specification does not indicate this—always bounded by the number of days in the month with which they are associated. For example, the function call

```
Calendar.Time_Of (1983, 2, 29)
```

is incorrect because February 1983 had fewer than 29 days. The time since midnight, measured in seconds, must be in the range zero to 86,400—the number of seconds in 24 hours. (The predefined type `Duration` is required to include at least the range -86,400 to 86,400, but an implementation may provide a larger range. The subtype `Calendar.Day_Duration` has the same range for all implementations.)

The functions `Year`, `Month`, `Day`, and `Seconds` each take a single parameter of type `Time` and return the corresponding part of the description of that `Time` value. Strictly speaking, it was not necessary for the package `Calendar` to provide both the procedure `Split` and the set of functions `Year`, `Month`, `Day`, and `Seconds`. It is easy for a user of the package to implement either the procedure in terms of the set of functions or the set of functions in terms of the procedure. Both are provided as a convenience to the package user.

The parameterless function `Clock` returns the value of type `Time` naming the moment at which the function was invoked. In other words, a call on this function answers the question "What time is it now?" The function may return a different value each time it is called.

The two versions of `"+"` defined in the package `Calendar` both take one parameter of type `Time` (a moment, or a point on a time line) and one of type `Duration` (an amount of time, or the distance between two points on a time line). They both compute the moment occurring a specified amount of time after some other moment. The computed moment is a value of type `Time`. The first version of `"-"` subtracts a value of type `Duration` from a value of type `Time` to compute the moment that occurred a specified amount of time prior to some other moment. The computed moment is again a value of type `Time`. The second version of `"-"`

subtracts two values of type Time to obtain the amount of time between two specified moments. This amount of time between two moments is a value of type Duration.

The versions of "<", "<=", ">", and ">=" provided by package Calendar take two parameters of type Time and return a Boolean result based on which parameter corresponds to an earlier moment. Like the functions Year, Month, Day, and Seconds, these relational operators could have been defined by the user of the package in terms of the procedure Split. They too are provided only as a convenience. For example, a function Less_Than, behaving exactly like Calendar."<", could have been defined outside the package as follows:

```
WITH Calendar;
FUNCTION Less_Than
   (Left, Right : Calendar.Time) RETURN Boolean IS
   Left_Year, Right_Year         : Calendar.Year_Number;
   Left_Month, Right_Month       : Calendar.Month_Number;
   Left_Day, Right_Day           : Calendar.Day_Number;
   Left_Seconds, Right_Seconds : Calendar.Day_Duration;
BEGIN
   Calendar.Split
      (Left,
       Year    => Left_Year,
       Month   => Left_Month,
       Day     => Left_Day,
       Seconds => Left_Seconds);
   Calendar.Split
      (Right,
       Year    => Right_Year,
       Month   => Right_Month,
       Day     => Right_Day,
       Seconds => Right_Seconds);
   IF Left_Year /= Right_Year THEN
      RETURN Left_Year < Right_Year;
   ELSIF Left_Month /= Right_Month THEN
      RETURN Left_Month < Right_Month;
   ELSIF Left_Day /= Right_Day THEN
      RETURN Left_Day < Right_Day;
   ELSE
      RETURN Left_Seconds < Right_Seconds;
   END IF;
END Less_Than;
```

Note the WITH clause WITH Calendar; at the beginning of the compilation unit. Even though package Calendar is predefined in all implementations of the Ada language, it cannot be used without this WITH clause. This is the case for all the predefined packages except the package ASCII.

The last declaration in the visible part of the package specification declares

`Time_Error` to be an *exception.* This is a mechanism for reporting a call on one of the package's subprograms with improper parameter values, as in the call

```
Calendar.Time_Of (1983, 2, 29)
```

Exceptions are described in Chapter 15.

The following procedure uses the package `Calendar` to print out a message giving the date and time in the form

month / *day* / *year hours* : *minutes* : *seconds*

The message is not followed by the start of a new line, so it may be used as part of a larger message.

```
WITH Calendar, Basic_IO;
USE Basic_IO;

PROCEDURE Print_Date_And_Time IS

   Seconds_Per_Minute : CONSTANT := 60;
   Seconds_Per_Hour   : CONSTANT := 3600;

   Current_Year             : Calendar.Year_Number;
   Current_Month            : Calendar.Month_Number;
   Current_Day              : Calendar.Day_Number;
   Seconds_Since_Midnight : Integer RANGE 0 .. 86_400;
   Seconds_This_Hour        : Integer RANGE 0 .. 3599;
   Current_Hours            : Integer RANGE 0 .. 24;
   Current_Minutes,
      Current_Seconds       : Integer RANGE 0 .. 59;
   Abbreviated_Year         : Integer RANGE 0 .. 99;

BEGIN

   -- Obtain current date and time:

   Calendar.Split
     ( Calendar.Clock,
       Year    => Current_Year,
       Month   => Current_Month,
       Day     => Current_Day,
       Seconds => Calendar.Day_Duration
                    (Seconds_Since_Midnight) );

   -- Print date

   Put (Current_Month);
   Put ("/");
   Put (Current_Day);
   Put ("/");
   Abbreviated_Year := Current_Year MOD 100;
      -- just last two digits
   IF Abbreviated_Year < 10 THEN
      Put ("0");  -- Make sure year field has two digits.
   END IF;
   Put (Abbreviated_Year);

   Put (" ");
```

```
      -- Decompose current time into hours, seconds,
      --   and minutes using integer division:
      Current_Hours :=
         Seconds_Since_Midnight / Seconds_Per_Hour;
      Seconds_This_Hour :=
         Seconds_Since_Midnight MOD Seconds_Per_Hour;
      Current_Minutes :=
         Seconds_This_Hour / Seconds_Per_Minute;
      Current_Seconds :=
         Seconds_This_Hour MOD Seconds_Per_Minute;
      -- Print time:
      Put (Current_Hours);
      Put (":");
      IF Current_Minutes < 10 THEN
         Put ("0");  -- Make sure minutes field has two digits.
      END IF;
      Put (Current_Minutes);
      Put (":");
      IF Current_Seconds < 10 THEN
         Put ("0"); -- Make sure seconds field has two digits.
      END IF;
      Put (Current_Seconds);
   END Print_Date_And_Time;
```

Because we are only interested in the time to the nearest second, `Seconds_Per_Midnight` is declared to be of type `Integer`. This allows use of the `MOD` operator and integer division with truncation to decompose the current time of day into hours, minutes, and seconds. Because the parameter of procedure `Calendar.Split` returning the seconds since midnight is of subtype `Calendar.Day_Duration`, the variable `Seconds_Per_Midnight` is enclosed in a type conversion in the actual parameter. As explained in Section 9.3, a type conversion may be used for an `OUT` actual parameter, in which case it really denotes the inverse type conversion. In this case, the value of subtype `Calendar.Day_Duration` placed in the fourth parameter of `Split` is "unconverted" back to the type of `Seconds_Since_Midnight`—type `Integer`.

This inverse type conversion, like any conversion of a fixed-point or floating-point value to an integer type, rounds to the nearest whole number. This causes the procedure to behave in an interesting (and appropriate) way if it is invoked within a half-second of midnight. Within a half-second before midnight, a `Day_Duration` value like 86399.56 will be rounded to 86400, and the time will be printed as `24:00:00`, with the old date; within a half-second after midnight, a `Day_Duration` value like 0.45 will be rounded to zero, and the time will be printed as `0:00:00`, with the new date.

12.4 DEFERRED CONSTANTS

Often it is desirable for a package providing a private type to also provide constants belonging to that private type. For example, Fraction_Package could have provided Fraction_Type constants named Zero and One, having the values

```
(Numerator_Part => 0, Denominator_Part => 1)
```

and

```
(Numerator_Part => 1, Denominator_Part => 1)
```

respectively. This would make it possible to refer to these frequently used values outside the package without invoking the second "/" function to compute 0/1 and 1/1. Similarly, String_List_Package could have provided a constant named Empty_String_List rather than a parameterless function of that name. Then each reference to Empty_String_List would not cause a subprogram to be invoked. More importantly, it would be clear to a reader of the package specification that each reference to Empty_String_List has the same value.

Unfortunately, there is a complication. A constant declaration must specify the value of the constant. Usually, this is most easily done in terms of the underlying structure of the constant, as in the following declaration:

```
Empty_String_List :
   CONSTANT String_List_Type :=
      (Size_Part => 0,
       Array_Part =>
         (String_Pointer_Array_Type'Range => NULL) );
```

However, if the constant is to be used outside the package, it must be declared in the visible part of the package specification. It would be inappropriate to refer to the underlying structure of a private type in the visible part. In fact, it is illegal to do so before the full declaration in the private part that establishes that underlying structure.

To get around this problem, the Ada language provides a mechanism known as a *deferred constant*. A deferred constant is declared by a special form of constant declaration that does not specify the value of the constant. This special form is only allowed in the visible part of a package specification. An ordinary declaration for the same constant, including the constant's value, must follow in the private part of the package specification. A deferred constant must belong to a private type declared in the same package. The deferred-constant declaration occurs at some point after the private-type declaration in the visible part, and the ordinary constant declaration occurs at some point after the corresponding full type declaration in the private part.

Here is what the revised `Fraction_Package` specification would look like if it provided `Fraction_Type` constants `Zero` and `One`:

```
PACKAGE Fraction_Package IS
   TYPE Fraction_Type IS PRIVATE;
   Zero, One : CONSTANT Fraction_Type;  -- Deferred constants

   FUNCTION "+" (Right : Fraction_Type) RETURN Fraction_Type;

   FUNCTION "-" (Right : Fraction_Type) RETURN Fraction_Type;

   FUNCTION "+"
      (Left, Right : Fraction_Type) RETURN Fraction_Type;

   FUNCTION "-"
      (Left, Right : Fraction_Type) RETURN Fraction_Type;

   FUNCTION "*"
      (Left, Right : Fraction_Type) RETURN Fraction_Type;

   FUNCTION "/"
      (Left, Right : Fraction_Type) RETURN Fraction_Type;

   FUNCTION "**"
      (Left : Fraction_Type; Right : Integer)
      RETURN Fraction_Type;

   FUNCTION "ABS"
      (Right : Fraction_Type) RETURN Fraction_Type;

   FUNCTION "/" (Left, Right : Integer) RETURN Fraction_Type;

PRIVATE
   TYPE Fraction_Type IS
      RECORD
         Numerator_Part   : Integer;
         Denominator_Part : Positive;
      END RECORD;

   -- Ordinary constant declarations for deferred constants:

   Zero :
      CONSTANT Fraction_Type :=
         (Numerator_Part => 0, Denominator_Part => 1);

   One :
      CONSTANT Fraction_Type :=
         (Numerator_Part => 1, Denominator_Part => 1);

END Fraction_Package;
```

Here is what the specification of `String_List_Package` would look like if the `Empty_String_List` were a constant rather than a parameterless function:

```
PACKAGE String_List_Package IS

   TYPE String_List_Type IS PRIVATE;

   Empty_String_List : CONSTANT String_List_Type;
      -- Deferred constant

   PROCEDURE Add_String
      (New_String  : IN String;
       String_List : IN OUT String_List_Type);

   PROCEDURE Print_String_List
      (String_List : IN String_List_Type);

PRIVATE

   TYPE String_Pointer_Type IS ACCESS String;

   TYPE String_Pointer_Array_Type IS
      ARRAY (1 .. 10) OF String_Pointer_Type;

   TYPE String_List_Type IS
      RECORD
         Size_Part  : Integer RANGE 0 .. 10;
         Array_Part : String_Pointer_Array_Type;
      END RECORD;

   Empty_String_List :
      CONSTANT String_List_Type :=
         (Size_Part => 0,
          Array_Part =>
            (String_Pointer_Array_Type'Range => NULL) );

      -- Ordinary constant declaration

END String_List_Package;
```

12.5 A PRIVATE TYPE FOR SETS OF INTEGERS

This section provides another illustration of a private type. At the end of the section we shall point out two subtle problems with this private type. Section 12.6 describes a mechanism for solving these problems.

The package that follows provides a private type named `Integer_Set_Type`, whose values are sets of integers. Operations include inserting an integer in a set, testing whether an integer is a member of a set, and computing the union and intersection of two sets. There is also a constant equal to the empty set. The package specification is as follows:

```
PACKAGE Integer_Set_Package IS

   TYPE Integer_Set_Type IS PRIVATE;

   Empty_Set : CONSTANT Integer_Set_Type;

   PROCEDURE Insert_Member
      (New_Member : IN Integer;
       Into_Set   : IN OUT Integer_Set_Type);
```

```
      FUNCTION Member_Of
         (Item : Integer; Set : Integer_Set_Type)
         RETURN Boolean;
      FUNCTION Union
         (Set_1, Set_2 : Integer_Set_Type)
         RETURN Integer_Set_Type;
      FUNCTION Intersection
         (Set_1, Set_2 : Integer_Set_Type)
         RETURN Integer_Set_Type;
   PRIVATE
      TYPE Integer_Set_Cell_Type IS
         RECORD
            Member_Part    : Integer;
            Next_Cell_Part : Integer_Set_Type;
         END RECORD;
      TYPE Integer_Set_Type IS ACCESS Integer_Set_Cell_Type;
      Empty_Set :
         CONSTANT Integer_Set_Type :=
            NEW Integer_Set_Cell_Type'(0, NULL);
   END Integer_Set_Package;
```

The private part of the specification reveals that `Integer_Set_Type` values are represented as linked lists of `Integer` values, but this is irrelevant to the user of the package. Furthermore, each linked list begins with a dummy *header cell* whose `Member_Part` component contains an arbitrary value and whose `Next_Cell_Part` component designates the first cell containing an actual member of the set (if there are any). This explains the internal representation of the constant `Empty_Set` as a list consisting of only a dummy header cell. The `Member_Part` component of the dummy header cell contains the arbitrary value zero, and the `Next_Cell_Part` component contains the value `NULL`, indicating that there are no members in the set. The dummy header cell makes it easy to insert new cells because insertion at the beginning of the list (i.e., just after the dummy header cell) need not be handled specially. Any new cell to be inserted in the list will always be inserted just after some cell already in the list.

The declaration of the `Next_Cell_Part` component of `List_Cell_Type` can refer to `Integer_Set_Type`, because `Integer_Set_Type` has already been declared—as a private type—earlier in the package specification. Thus no incomplete type declaration is necessary. In general, a recursive type can be declared without an incomplete type declaration if and only if it is a private type. Alternatively, if an incomplete type declaration is given in the private part of the package specification, the corresponding full type declaration can be deferred until the package body:

```
   PACKAGE Integer_Set_Package IS
      TYPE Integer_Set_Type IS PRIVATE;
      ...
   PRIVATE
      TYPE Integer_Set_Cell_Type;
      TYPE Integer_Set_Type IS ACCESS Integer_Set_Cell_Type;
```

```
   ...
END Integer_Set_Package;

PACKAGE BODY Integer_Set_Package IS
   ...
   TYPE Integer_Set_Cell_Type IS
      RECORD
         Member_Part    : Integer;
         Next_Cell_Part : Integer_Set_Type;
      END RECORD;
   ...
END Integer_Set_Package;
```

This approach avoids the need to recompile the `Integer_Set_Package` specification (and all parts of the program that refer to it) if the definition of `Integer_Set_Cell_Type` later changes. However, it scatters the type declarations used to implement `Integer_Set_Type` over a larger portion of the program. This makes it harder for a reader to learn how sets of integers are represented.

The `Integer_Set_Package` body contains an internal procedure named `Insert_At_End`, called by the functions `Union` and `Intersection`. `Insert_At_End` inserts a new cell containing a specified `Integer` value at the end of a linked list. The procedure takes two parameters. The first gives the `Integer` value to be inserted. The second parameter designates the last cell on the list (the dummy header cell in the case of an empty list). The second parameter is updated by the procedure to designate the new last cell once that cell is added to the list. The package body is as follows:

```
PACKAGE BODY Integer_Set_Package IS

   PROCEDURE Insert_At_End
      (Member    : IN Integer;
       Last_Cell : IN OUT Integer_Set_Type) IS
   BEGIN
      Last_Cell.Next_Cell_Part :=
         NEW Integer_Set_Cell_Type'(Member, NULL);
      Last_Cell := Last_Cell.Next_Cell_Part;
   END Insert_At_End;

   PROCEDURE Insert_Member
      (New_Member : IN Integer;
       Into_Set   : IN OUT Integer_Set_Type) IS
      Previous_Cell : Integer_Set_Type := Into_Set;
      Current_Cell :
         Integer_Set_Type := Previous_Cell.Next_Cell_Part;
```

```
BEGIN
   WHILE Current_Cell /= NULL AND THEN
         Current_Cell.Member_Part < New_Member LOOP
      Previous_Cell := Current_Cell;
      Current_Cell := Current_Cell.Next_Cell_Part;
   END LOOP;
   IF Current_Cell = NULL OR ELSE
        Current_Cell.Member_Part > New_Member THEN
      Previous_Cell.Next_Cell_Part :=
      NEW Integer_Set_Cell_Type'
         (New_Member, Current_Cell);
   END IF;
   -- Otherwise, Current_Cell.Member_Part = New_Member,
   --    so the integer to be inserted is already
   --    in the set.
END Insert_Member;


FUNCTION Member_Of
   (Item : Integer; Set : Integer_Set_Type)
   RETURN Boolean IS
   Current_Cell :
      Integer_Set_Type := Set.Next_Cell_Part;
BEGIN
   WHILE Current_Cell /= NULL AND THEN
         Current_Cell.Member_Part < Item LOOP
      Current_Cell := Current_Cell.Next_Cell_Part;
   END LOOP;
   RETURN
      Current_Cell /= NULL AND THEN
         Current_Cell.Member_Part = Item;
END Member_Of;


FUNCTION Union
   (Set_1, Set_2 : Integer_Set_Type)
   RETURN Integer_Set_Type IS
   Remaining_Set_1_Members :
      Integer_Set_Type := Set_1.Next_Cell_Part;
   Remaining_Set_2_Members :
      Integer_Set_Type := Set_2.Next_Cell_Part;
   Remaining_Members : Integer_Set_Type;
   First_Result_Cell :
      Integer_Set_Type :=
         NEW Integer_Set_Cell_Type'(0, NULL);
   Last_Result_Cell :
      Integer_Set_Type := First_Result_Cell;
```

```
BEGIN
  WHILE Remaining_Set_1_Members /= NULL AND
        Remaining_Set_2_Members /= NULL LOOP
     DECLARE
        Next_Set_1_Member :
           Integer RENAMES
              Remaining_Set_1_Members.Member_Part;
        Next_Set_2_Member :
           Integer RENAMES
              Remaining_Set_2_Members.Member_Part;
     BEGIN
        IF Next_Set_1_Member < Next_Set_2_Member THEN
           Insert_At_End
              (Next_Set_1_Member, Last_Result_Cell);
           Remaining_Set_1_Members :=
              Remaining_Set_1_Members.Next_Cell_Part;
        ELSIF Next_Set_2_Member < Next_Set_1_Member THEN
           Insert_At_End
              (Next_Set_2_Member, Last_Result_Cell);
           Remaining_Set_2_Members :=
              Remaining_Set_2_Members.Next_Cell_Part;
        ELSE    -- Same value belongs to both sets.
           Insert_At_End
              (Next_Set_1_Member, Last_Result_Cell);
           Remaining_Set_1_Members :=
              Remaining_Set_1_Members.Next_Cell_Part;
           Remaining_Set_2_Members :=
              Remaining_Set_2_Members.Next_Cell_Part;
        END IF;
     END;
  END LOOP;
  IF Remaining_Set_1_Members = NULL THEN
     Remaining_Members := Remaining_Set_2_Members;
  ELSE
     Remaining_Members := Remaining_Set_1_Members;
  END IF;
  WHILE Remaining_Members /= NULL LOOP
     Insert_At_End
        (Remaining_Members.Member_Part,
         Last_Result_Cell);
     Remaining_Members :=
        Remaining_Members.Next_Cell_Part;
  END LOOP;
  RETURN First_Result_Cell;
END Union;
```

```
      FUNCTION Intersection
         (Set_1, Set_2 : Integer_Set_Type)
         RETURN Integer_Set_Type IS
         Remaining_Set_1_Members :
            Integer_Set_Type := Set_1.Next_Cell_Part;
         Remaining_Set_2_Members :
            Integer_Set_Type := Set_2.Next_Cell_Part;
         First_Result_Cell :
            Integer_Set_Type :=
               NEW Integer_Set_Cell_Type'(0, NULL);
         Last_Result_Cell :
            Integer_Set_Type := First_Result_Cell;
      BEGIN
         WHILE Remaining_Set_1_Members /= NULL AND
               Remaining_Set_2_Members /= NULL LOOP
            DECLARE
               Next_Set_1_Member :
                  Integer RENAMES
                     Remaining_Set_1_Members.Member_Part;
               Next_Set_2_Member :
                  Integer RENAMES
                     Remaining_Set_2_Members.Member_Part;
            BEGIN
               IF Next_Set_1_Member < Next_Set_2_Member THEN
                  Remaining_Set_1_Members :=
                     Remaining_Set_1_Members.Next_Cell_Part;
               ELSIF Next_Set_2_Member < Next_Set_1_Member THEN
                  Remaining_Set_2_Members :=
                     Remaining_Set_2_Members.Next_Cell_Part;
               ELSE   -- Value belongs to both sets.
                  Insert_At_End
                     (Next_Set_1_Member, Last_Result_Cell);
                  Remaining_Set_1_Members :=
                     Remaining_Set_1_Members.Next_Cell_Part;
                  Remaining_Set_2_Members :=
                     Remaining_Set_2_Members.Next_Cell_Part;
               END IF;
            END;
         END LOOP;
         RETURN First_Result_Cell;
      END Intersection;

   END Integer_Set_Package;
```

The package's subprograms maintain all Integer values in a linked list in ascending order (except for the arbitrary value in the dummy header cell). This allows the subprograms to be implemented more efficiently. Insert_Member should have no effect if the member to be inserted is already a member of the set. Because the list is kept in ascending order, Insert_Member need not examine every cell in the list to check for this condition, only the cells containing values less than or equal to the parameter New_Member. (Note the use of a short-circuit control form in the Insert_Member procedure body to avoid referring to Current_Cell.Member_Part when Current_Cell is null.) Similarly, Member_Of need not check every list cell in search for the value Item. Once a value greater than Item is encountered, the value Item cannot be in the list. (The body of Member_Of contains a short-circuit control form analogous to the one in the body of Insert_Member.) The implementations of Union and Intersection are similar to each other. Both work essentially by merging the two sorted lists passed to them as parameters, producing a new sorted list. Union makes sure that values occurring in both parameter lists are placed in the result list only once; Intersection makes sure that only values occurring in both parameter lists are placed in the result list. (As soon as one list is exhausted, Union places all remaining values in the other list on the result list. Intersection ignores all values remaining on the other list and returns.) Because two sorted lists are being merged, it is easy to spot values occurring in both lists.

The subprograms in the Integer_Set_Package body cannot be expected to work correctly unless they are given parameters in ascending order and each parameter contains a dummy header node. Fortunately, given Integer_Set_Type parameters satisfying these conditions, the subprograms produce Integer_Set_Type results that also satisfy these conditions. Since Integer_Set_Type is a private type, values of this type can only be produced by the subprograms provided by Integer_Set_Package. Consequently, malformed lists cannot arise.

Despite this, there are two problems with this type. First, consider the following sequence of statements, assuming that S1 and S2 are Integer_Set_Type variables:

```
S1 := Integer_Set_Package.Empty_Set;           -- S1 = {}
Integer_Set_Package.Insert_Member (1, S1); -- S1 = {1}
Integer_Set_Package.Insert_Member (3, S1); -- S1 = {1,3}
S2 := S1;                                      -- S2 = {1,3}
Integer_Set_Package.Insert_Member (2, S1); -- S1 = {1,2,3}
```

From an abstract point of view, we would expect these operations to leave the set {1, 3} in S2 and {1, 2, 3} in S1. However, careful examination of the implementation of Integer_Set_Package reveals that this is not so. Because Integer_Set_Type is implemented as an access type (a fact supposedly irrelevant to a user of the Integer_Set_Package), the assignment statement

```
S2 := S1;
```

assigns to S2 the access value designating *the same dummy header cell designated by* S1. Thus the final call on Insert_Member, which adds a cell to the linked list headed by S1's dummy header cell, also has the effect of changing the value of S2!

Moreover, assuming once again that S1 and S2 are Integer_Set_Type variables, consider the following expression:

```
Integer_Set_Package.Union (S1, S2) =
   Integer_Set_Package.Union (S1, S2)
```

From an abstract point of view, this expression should obviously be true. However, the implementation of Integer_Set_Type as an access type again complicates matters. Access values designating distinct allocated variables are unequal, regardless of the contents of those variables. Each call on Union allocates a new dummy header cell, and the value eventually returned by the function call is an access value designating that cell. Thus the two calls on Union with identical parameters produce unequal results. The expression is false!

To solve these problems, the Integer_Set_Package writer needs even more control over the use of the package than the control obtained by a private-type declaration. A user of the package must be prevented from assigning access values representing Integer_Set_Type values and from comparing two such values for equality. This additional measure of control can be obtained by declaring Integer_Set_Type to be *limited* private, as described in the next section.

12.6 LIMITED PRIVATE TYPES

Outside the package in which a private type is declared, objects in that type may be manipulated through the subprograms provided by the package. In addition, they may be compared using the = and /= operators, and an expression belonging to a private type may be assigned to a variable belonging to that type. However, objects in a private type may not be manipulated outside the package in terms of their internal representation.

A package writer can gain even more control over the use of a private type by making it *limited.* A limited type is one for which assignment is forbidden and the operators = and /= may not be used unless = is explicitly overloaded. Limited types arise in five ways:

1. A private type may be declared to be *limited private.*
2. *Task types,* discussed in Chapter 18, are always limited.
3. If the component type of an array type is limited, then the array type is also limited.
4. If at least one component in a record type belongs to a limited type, then the record type is also limited.
5. A derived type is limited if the type from which it is derived is limited.

This section is primarily concerned with the first way of creating a limited type, by declaring it to be limited private.

The rules for creating a limited private type are identical to those for creating any private type, except that the private-type declaration includes the word LIMITED:

```
TYPE identifier IS LIMITED PRIVATE ;
```

As in the case of ordinary private types, this declaration must occur within the visible part of a package specification, and a full declaration for the type must follow in the private part of the package specification. The restrictions associated with a limited type apply outside the package; assignment and tests for equality and inequality are permitted inside the package body, as part of the implementation of the type's operations.

Although the relational operator = may not be overloaded for ordinary types, it may be overloaded with versions taking two parameters in the same *limited* type and returning a value of type Boolean. The relational operator /= may never be overloaded by a function named "/=", but overloading = for some limited type *implicitly* overloads /= with a version taking parameters of that same type and returning the opposite result. Thus the expressions x /= y and NOT (x = y) are always equivalent, even when = has been overloaded.

The problems with Integer_Set_Package noted at the end of Section 12.5 can be eliminated by making Integer_Set_Type limited private. The operator = can be overloaded with a version comparing not the access values designating list cells, but the contents of the list cells. To make up for the absence of Integer_Set_Type assignment, we can provide a procedure Copy_Set taking two Integer_Set_Type parameters, such that the call

```
Integer_Set_Package.Copy_Set (From => S1, To => S2);
```

places a freshly allocated *copy* of the list designated by S1 into the variable S2. Later operations changing the list designated by S1 have no effect upon the copy. From an abstract point of view, the operator = tests whether two Integer_Set_Type values have the same members, and Copy_Set places the *value* of an Integer_Set_Type expression in an Integer_Set_Type variable.

There is one further complication. The declaration of "=" in the specification of Integer_Set_Package applies throughout the package specification and the package body. As previously written, the subprogram bodies in the Integer_Set_Package body applied the predefined versions of = and /= to Integer_Set_Type values to test whether access values were equal to NULL. These uses of = and /= will now cause the new version of = to be invoked, producing incorrect results. The problem is that we want to use = and /= in their literal sense (to compare access values) inside the package and in their abstract sense (to compare sets) outside the package. A solution is to define two different types corresponding to these two different views of the linked-list value. We can define linked lists in terms of a type, say List_Cell_Pointer_Type, that is only declared within the private part of the package specification, and we can define Integer_Set_Type as a derived type, derived from List_Cell_Pointer_Type. Since the programmer-defined version of "=" applies only to Integer_Set_Type operands, the = operator applied to `List_Cell_Pointer_Type` operands will still compare access values. (The usual rules for overloading resolution are used to determine the meaning of a particular occurrence of the = operator based on the types of the operands. See Section 9.5.)

The revised package specification is then as follows:

```
PACKAGE Integer_Set_Package IS

   TYPE Integer_Set_Type IS LIMITED PRIVATE;

   Empty_Set : CONSTANT Integer_Set_Type;

   PROCEDURE Insert_Member
      (New_Member : IN Integer;
       Into_Set : IN OUT Integer_Set_Type);

   FUNCTION Member_Of
      (Item : Integer; Set : Integer_Set_Type)
      RETURN Boolean;

   FUNCTION "="
      (Left, Right : Integer_Set_Type) RETURN Boolean;

   FUNCTION Union
      (Set_1, Set_2 : Integer_Set_Type)
      RETURN Integer_Set_Type;

   FUNCTION Intersection
      (Set_1, Set_2 : Integer_Set_Type)
      RETURN Integer_Set_Type;

   PROCEDURE Copy_Set
      (From : IN Integer_Set_Type;
       To   : OUT Integer_Set_Type);

PRIVATE

   -- Definition of the internal type
        List_Cell_Pointer_Type:

   TYPE Integer_Set_Cell_Type;

   TYPE List_Cell_Pointer_Type IS
      ACCESS Integer_Set_Cell_Type;

   TYPE Integer_Set_Cell_Type IS
      RECORD
         Member_Part    : Integer;
         Next_Cell_Part : List_Cell_Pointer_Type;
      END RECORD;

   -- Definition  of the limited private type
   --    Integer_Set_Type:

   TYPE Integer_Set_Type IS NEW List_Cell_Pointer_Type;

   --Full declaration of the deferred constant Empty_Set:

   Empty_Set :
      CONSTANT Integer_Set_Type :=
         NEW Integer_Set_Cell_Type'(0, NULL);

END Integer_Set_Package;
```

List_Cell_Pointer_Type is declared for the first time in the private part of the package specification, so its recursive definition requires an incomplete type declaration. Both List_Cell_Pointer_Type values and Integer_Set_Values are access values designating Integer_Set_Cell_Type values, so the allocator

```
NEW Integer_Set_Cell_Type'(0, NULL)
```

could be interpreted as a value of either access type. In the full constant declaration for Empty_Set, an Integer_Set_Type value is expected in the context where the allocator occurs, so the allocator is interpreted as one producing Integer_Set_Type values.

The following function body overloading = is added to the body of Integer_Set_Package:

```
FUNCTION "="
   (Left, Right : Integer_Set_Type)
   RETURN Boolean IS
   Current_Left_Cell:
      List_Cell_Pointer_Type := Left.Next_Cell_Part;
   Current_Right_Cell:
      List_Cell_Pointer_Type := Right.Next_Cell_Part;
BEGIN
   LOOP
      IF Current_Left_Cell = NULL THEN
         RETURN Current_Right_Cell = NULL;
      ELSIF Current_Right_Cell = NULL THEN
         RETURN False;
      ELSIF Current_Left_Cell.Member_Part /=
               Current_Right_Cell.Member_Part THEN
         RETURN False;
      END IF;
      Current_Left_Cell :=
         Current_Left_Cell.Next_Cell_Part;
      Current_Right_Cell :=
         Current_Right_Cell.Next_Cell_Part;
   END LOOP;
END "=";
```

This algorithm traverses the two lists in parallel, comparing the contents of corresponding list cells. The result False is returned as soon as a mismatch is found. Otherwise, if one of the lists runs out of cells to compare, the result True is returned if the other list has also run out of elements (indicating that the lists were the same length and all corresponding cells contained equal values). The result False is returned if the other list has not run out of elements (indicating that it contains values not contained in the first list). Because Current_Left_Cell and Current_Right_Cell are of List_Cell_Pointer_Type, the expressions testing whether these variables are equal to NULL refer to the version of "=" comparing access values. Had these variables belonged to Integer_Set_Type instead, the = operators in these expressions would have denoted recursive calls on the version of "=" comparing set contents!

The following procedure body is also added to the Integer_Set_Package body:

```
PROCEDURE Copy_Set
   (From : IN Integer_Set_Type;
    To   : OUT Integer_Set_Type) IS
   Remaining_Members:
      List_Cell_Pointer_Type := From.Next_Cell_Part;
   Last_Result_Cell:
      Integer_Set_Type :=
         NEW Integer_Set_Cell_Type'(0, NULL);
BEGIN
   To := Last_Result_Cell;
   WHILE Remaining_Members /= NULL LOOP
      Insert_At_End
         (Remaining_Members.Member_Part,
          Last_Result_Cell);
      Remaining_Members := Remaining_Members.Next_Cell_Part;
   END LOOP;
END Copy_Set;
```

The allocator used to initialize Last_Result_Cell allocates a new dummy header cell, and each call on Insert_At_End (defined in the Integer_Set_Package body in Section 12.5) allocates another new cell, producing a list not sharing cells with any previously existing list, but containing the same Integer values, cell for cell, as the list From.

The other subprogram bodies in the Integer_Set_Package body must be revised to reflect that Next_Cell_Part components now belong to List_Cell_Pointer_Type rather than Integer_Set_Type. For the most part, this only requires changing certain Integer_Set_Type variable declarations to List_Cell_Pointer_Type variable declarations. Because Integer_Set_Type is derived from List_Cell_Pointer_Type, conversions between these two types are possible. However, such conversions are not always needed. Many of the rewritten subprograms turn out to contain declarations that resemble the following, taken from the Copy_Set procedure body:

```
Remaining_Members:
   List_Cell_Pointer_Type := From.Next_Cell_Part;
```

From is an Integer_Set_Type parameter designating a dummy header cell of type List_Cell_Type. The Next_Cell_Part component of the designated cell is of List_Cell_Pointer_Type. Thus a List_Cell_Pointer_Type value is computed from an Integer_Set_Type parameter by component selection rather than by type conversion. Details of revising the subprograms in the Integer_Set_Package body are left as an exercise.

The prohibition of "assignment" for limited types (outside the packages providing the types) bans not only assignment statements, but several other operations that involve copying a value:

Object declarations for limited types may not contain initial values. (Hence constants of limited types can only be declared within packages providing limited private types.)

Record-type declarations may not contain default initial values for components belonging to limited private types.

Procedure parameters of mode OUT may not belong to limited types.

An allocator creating an allocated variable belonging to a limited type may not specify an initial value for the allocated variable.

An expression of a limited type may not appear in a record or array aggregate. (In fact, aggregates may not be used to describe any value in a limited type. Since a record type with a limited component is itself limited, aggregates may not even be used to describe variants in the record type that do not include a limited component.)

Arrays belonging to a limited type may not be catenated.

These restrictions, like the restrictions on assignment statements and the operators = and /=, do not apply within a package defining a limited private type. For example, the procedure Copy_Set provided by Integer_Set_Package has an OUT parameter belonging to the limited private type Integer_Set_Type.

There is no restriction on defining a subprogram with an IN or IN OUT parameter of a limited type. Although the symbol := may not be used in assignment statements, object declarations, or record-type component declarations involving limited types, it may be used to specify a default initial value for a limited IN parameter. A function may return a result of a limited type. Outside a package defining the limited private type, a call on such a function can only appear as an actual parameter of another subprogram call, as in the following procedure call statement:

```
Integer_Set_Package.Copy_Set
   (From => Integer_Set_Package.Union (S1, S2),
    To   => S3);
```

Despite some complicating details, the basic idea behind limited types is straightforward. Limited types are types for which language-defined copying and comparison operations are not permitted. A limited type is appropriate when an operation on a value can affect the state of something indirectly referenced by that value; when two values should be deemed equal even if their underlying representations are different; when it is desirable to control the initial values of all objects in a type; and when it is necessary to "trap" each copying operation to perform a special action each time a value in a type is copied. The remainder of this section describes these situations in greater detail.

The Insert_Member procedure of Integer_Set_Package is an example of an operation on a value that can affect the state of some entity (a linked list) indirectly referenced by that value. Assignment of such values can lead to two values indirectly referencing the same entity, so that an operation on one of the values affects properties of the other value. Similarly, values passed to input and output operations, identifying a file to be operated on, indirectly reference the file. Assignment of such values could cause the state of a file identified by one such value to change as a result of writing to or reading from a file identified by another such value. Therefore, as we shall see in Chapter 17, the predefined packages for performing file input and output define the types for such values to be limited private. Similarly, as we shall see in Chapter 18, variables may hold values referring to concurrently executing tasks. If assignment of such values were permitted, an operation affecting the state of a task referred to by one such variable could affect the state of the task referred to by another such variable. Therefore, types whose values refer to tasks are always limited types.

Another reason for making Integer_Set_Type limited was that two Integer_Set_Type values should be deemed equal even if they are distinct access values denoting two lists with the same contents. There are other circumstances as well in which the predefined equality operator does not correspond to the programmer's abstract notion of equality. Often, data structures contain components indicating which other components contain meaningful data and which should be considered empty. The predefined equality operator will report two values unequal even when their meaningful components are identical but their "empty" components are not. You will see an example of such a data structure in Section 12.7.

A type can be made limited private to control the initial value of all objects in the type. If the type is implemented as a record type, default initial values can be specified for its components. Since a user of the package providing the limited private type cannot specify his own initial value for a variable in that type, the default initial values will always apply. (It is sometimes useful to define a one-component record type just so that a default component value can be used in this way.) By completely controlling the initial values in a type, a package writer can have the type's values include a flag indicating whether or not each variable has been passed to a specified initialization subprogram. Then the package writer can check that a variable of some type Account_Type has been passed to the subprogram Establish_Account before it is used in any other operations, or that a file variable is passed to the Open subprogram before it is used in a call on some other input or output subprogram.

On occasion, a package providing a limited private type may provide a copy operation that does everything ordinary assignment does but performs additional actions as well. Since there is no other way to copy values in the type outside the package, the action is guaranteed to be performed every time the value is copied.

This action may be to generate an *audit trail* documenting the history of data manipulations involving the limited private type. Such an audit trail is useful in enforcing security or accounting regulations by showing how information was made available to different parts of a program. It can also be used as a "trace" in debugging a program. In programs carefully controlling the use of storage for allocated variables, it is sometimes useful to maintain *reference counts* indicating the number of distinct access objects designating each allocated variable. When a particular allocated variable's reference count reaches zero, storage for that variable may be reused for another allocation. Maintaining a reference count requires the ability to intercept access value assignments. The operation copying the access value in variable `A` into variable `B` must decrement the reference count of the allocated variable formerly designated by `B` and increment the reference count of the allocated variable designated by `A`.

Sometimes, the abstract notions of copying and comparison make sense for a particular type, but the predefined copying and comparison operations do not have the desired behavior. In such cases, it is wise to overload `"="` and to provide an abstract copying operation, such as `Copy_Set`, to the users of a limited private type. In other cases, as with files and tasks, the notions of copying and comparison are alien to the abstraction being implemented, and these operations should not be provided. For these types, each variable can be thought of as an entity to be manipulated in its own right, rather than as a container holding an entity to be manipulated.

12.7 PRIVATE TYPES WITH DISCRIMINANTS

As Chapter 10 explained, record types may have "parameters" called discriminants. A private type may also have discriminants. The private-type declaration then takes one of the following forms:

```
TYPE identifier
    ( discriminant specification ; ~~~ ; discriminant specification ) IS
    PRIVATE ;

TYPE identifier
    ( discriminant specification ; ~~~ ; discriminant specification ) IS
    LIMITED PRIVATE ;
```

(Discriminant specifications were described in Section 10.2.) The corresponding full type declaration in the private part of the package specification must be for a record type with discriminants. (In fact, this is the only case in which the full declaration of a private type may be a declaration of a type with discriminants.) The discriminant specifications in the full type declaration must match those in in the private-type declaration.

The rules for using a private type with discriminants are the same as for a record type with discriminants. Default discriminant values must either be present in all discriminant specifications for the type or absent from all of them. If they are absent, each variable declaration for the type must contain a discriminant constraint, and only values with the same discriminants as in the constraint may be assigned to the variable. If default values are present in the discriminant specification, unconstrained variables may be declared. It is illegal to assign values to the discriminants of such variables directly, but their discriminants may be changed by an assignment to the entire variable. Each possible combination of discriminant values constitutes a subtype of the private type.

A private type with discriminants is not "as private" as an ordinary private type. The discriminants, specified in the private-type declaration in the visible part of a package specification, become part of the package's interface. Thus the type class of a private type with discriminants is not private; the type can only be implemented as a record type. In fact, selected components may be used outside the package to refer to the discriminants of a value in the type (but not to any other components of the value). Discriminant values may also be ascertained outside the package by a membership test checking whether a value in the private type belongs to a particular subtype of that type.

Below is a package providing a private type with discriminants. The type, first introduced in Section 10.2.2, is named `Varying_String_Type`, and its values are character strings of varying length. `Varying_String_Type` has one discriminant, specifying the length of the largest string that may be held in a particular variable. Thus the declaration

```
s: Varying_String_Type (132);
```

is equivalent to the following PL/I declaration:

```
DECLARE S: CHARACTER VARYING (132);
```

It is equivalent to the following declaration in the UCSD version of Pascal:

```
s: string [132]
```

A `Varying_String_Type` variable may contain strings of different lengths at different times, provided that this maximum length is not exceeded. Initially, a `Varying_String_Type` variable contains a string of length zero.

The following operations on `Varying_String_Type` are provided by the package:

The function `Varying_String` converts a value of type `String` to a `Varying_String_Type` value. For example, `Varying_String ("Hello")` returns a `Varying_String_Type` value with a length of five, containing the characters `'H'`, `'e'`, `'l'`, `'l'`, `'o'`.

The function `Length` returns the current length of its `Varying_String_Type` parameter.

The operator & may be used to catenate two Varying_String_Type operands to produce a Varying_String_Type result. The length of the result is the sum of the lengths of the operands.

The operators = and /= may be used to determine whether two Varying_String_Type values are equivalent.

The function Slice may be used to extract consecutive characters from a Varying_String_Type value, producing a Varying_String_Type result. If VS is of Varying_String_Type and M and N are of subtype Natural, Slice (VS, M, N) is generally the slice consisting of characters M through N of VS. If M is less than one, one is used as a lower bound instead of M. If N is greater than the current length of VS, the current length is used as an upper bound instead of N. If the lower bound is greater than the upper bound, the empty string is returned.

The procedure Get may be used to read all the remaining characters on a line into its Varying_String_Type parameter, up to the maximum length of the actual parameter.

The procedure Put may be used to write a Varying_String_Type value.

The procedure Copy_String may be used to copy a Varying_String_Type value into a Varying_String_Type variable. Specifically, the procedure call Copy_String (From, To) copies the contents of From into To, truncating From if its current length exceeds the maximum length of To.

Varying_String_Type is limited for two reasons. First, it should be possible to copy the abstract contents of a variable of subtype Varying_String_Type (*i*) into a variable of subtype Varying_String_Type (*j*), even when *i* /= *j*. (The discriminant reflects the maximum length of the variable, not its abstract current length.) Ordinary assignment cannot perform such copying. Furthermore, depending on the underlying representation of Varying_String_Type values, ordinary assignment between two Varying_String_Type variables with the same maximum length could move considerably more data than necessary in some cases. Second, it should be possible for the contents of two Varying_String_Type variables to be deemed equal even when they have different discriminants. (From an abstract point of view, the discriminant of a Varying_String_Type variable is a property of the container, not its contents.)

The package specification is as follows:

```
PACKAGE Varying_String_Package IS

   TYPE Varying_String_Type
      (Maximum_Length : Natural) IS
      LIMITED PRIVATE;

   FUNCTION Varying_String
      (s : String) RETURN Varying_String_Type;

   FUNCTION Length
      (Varying_String : Varying_String_Type)
      RETURN Natural;
```

```
      FUNCTION "&"
         (Left, Right : Varying_String_Type)
         RETURN Varying_String_Type;
      FUNCTION "="
         (Left, Right : Varying_String_Type)
         RETURN Boolean;
      FUNCTION Slice
         (Full_String : Varying_String_Type;
          Lower_Bound, Upper_Bound : Natural)
         RETURN Varying_String_Type;
      PROCEDURE Get (Item : OUT Varying_String_Type);
      PROCEDURE Put (Item : IN Varying_String_Type);
      PROCEDURE Copy_String
         (From : IN Varying_String_Type;
          To   : OUT Varying_String_Type);
   PRIVATE
      TYPE Varying_String_Type (Maximum_Length : Natural) IS
         RECORD
            Current_Length_Part : Natural := 0;
            Contents_Part : String (1 .. Maximum_Length);
         END RECORD;
   END Varying_String_Package;
```

As indicated in the private part of this package specification, a `Varying_String_Type` value is represented as a record having two components besides the discriminant `Maximum_Length`. `Contents_Part` is a string whose upper bound is given by `Maximum_Length`. `Current_Length_Part` is a number indicating how many of the components of this string should currently be considered part of the varying-length string. Thus the slice

```
   V.Contents_Part (1 .. V.Current_Length_Part)
```

contains the current *abstract* contents of the `Varying_String_Type` variable `V`; the remaining components of `V.Contents_Part` should be considered meaningless. (This is another reason that the predefined version of = is inappropriate. It would consider two `Varying_String_Type` values unequal even if they differed only in their "meaningless" parts.) Because the discriminant has no default value, every `Varying_String_Type` variable must be declared with a discriminant constraint. The physical length of the variable is thus fixed for the lifetime of the variable. However, the *abstract* length of the string held by a given variable may change with each call on `Copy_String`, as long as the physical length is not exceeded. This is consistent with varying-length string variables in PL/I and UCSD Pascal. The initial value for the `Current_Length_Part` record component causes a `Varying_String_Type` object to initially hold a string of length zero. (Because `Varying_String_Type` is limited, this initial value cannot be overridden by an initial value in the object declaration.)

Here is the body of the package:

```
WITH Basic_IO;

PACKAGE BODY Varying_String_Package IS

   FUNCTION Varying_String
      (s : String) RETURN Varying_String_Type IS

   BEGIN
      RETURN
         Varying_String_Type'
            (Maximum_Length | Current_Length_Part =>
               s'Length,
             Contents_Part => s);

   END Varying_String;


   FUNCTION Length
      (Varying_String : Varying_String_Type)
      RETURN Natural IS

   BEGIN
      RETURN Varying_String.Current_Length_Part;

   END Length;


   FUNCTION "&"
      (Left, Right: Varying_String_Type)
      RETURN Varying_String_Type IS

      Left_Length:
         Natural RENAMES Left.Current_Length_Part;

      Right_Length:
         Natural RENAMES Right.Current_Length_Part;

      Result_Length:
         CONSTANT Natural := Left_Length + Right_Length;

      Result: Varying_String_Type (Result_Length);

   BEGIN
      Result.Contents_Part (1 .. Left_Length) :=
         Left.Contents_Part (1 .. Left_Length);

      Result.Contents_Part
         (Left_Length + 1 .. Result_Length) :=
         Right.Contents_Part (1 .. Right_Length);

      Result.Current_Length_Part := Result_Length;

      RETURN Result;

   END "&";
```

```
  FUNCTION "="
     (Left, Right: Varying_String_Type)
     RETURN Boolean IS
  BEGIN

     RETURN
        Left.Contents_Part (1 .. Left.Current_Length_Part) =
        Right.Contents_Part (1 .. Right.Current_Length_Part);
  END "=";

  FUNCTION Slice
     (Full_String                : Varying_String_Type;
      Lower_Bound, Upper_Bound : Natural)
     RETURN Varying_String_Type IS

     Actual_Lower_Bound : Natural := Lower_Bound;
     Actual_Upper_Bound : Natural := Upper_Bound;
     Result_Length      : Natural;
  BEGIN

     IF Actual_Lower_Bound < 1 THEN
        Actual_Lower_Bound := 1;
     END IF;

     IF Actual_Upper_Bound >
           Full_String.Current_Length_Part THEN
        Actual_Upper_Bound :=
           Full_String.Current_Length_Part;
     END IF;

     Result_Length :=
        Actual_Upper_Bound - Actual_Lower_Bound + 1;

     IF Result_Length <= 0 THEN
        RETURN
           Varying_String_Type'
              (Maximum_Length      => 0,
               Current_Length_Part => 0,
               Contents_Part       => "");
     ELSE
        RETURN
           Varying_String_Type'
              (Maximum_Length | Current_Length_Part =>
                 Result_Length,
               Contents_Part =>
                 Full_String.Contents_Part
                    ( Actual_Lower_Bound ..
                      Actual_Upper_Bound ) );
     END IF;
  END Slice;

  PROCEDURE Get (Item : OUT Varying_String_Type) IS
  BEGIN

     Basic_IO.Get_Line
        (Item.Contents_Part, Item.Current_Length_Part);
  END Get;
```

```
    PROCEDURE Put (Item : IN Varying_String_Type) IS
    BEGIN
       Basic_IO.Put
          ( Item.Contents_Part
             (1 .. Item.Current_Length_Part) );
    END Put;

    PROCEDURE Copy_String
       (From : IN Varying_String_Type;
        To   : OUT Varying_String_Type) IS
    BEGIN
       IF From.Current_Length_Part > To.Maximum_Length THEN
          To.Contents_Part :=
             From.Contents_Part (1 .. To.Maximum_Length);
          To.Current_Length_Part := To.Maximum_Length;
       ELSE
          To.Contents_Part (1 .. From.Current_Length_Part):=
             From.Contents_Part
                (1 .. From.Current_Length_Part);
          To.Current_Length_Part :=
             From.Current_Length_Part;
       END IF;
    END Copy_String;

 END Varying_String_Package;
```

(In this package body we have omitted a `USE` clause for `Basic_IO` because the use of that package's facilities is minimal and localized.)

Each of the `Varying_String_Package` functions returning a `Varying_String_Type` result returns a record whose physical length (reflected by the discriminant `Maximum_Length`) is equal to its abstract length (reflected by the component `Current_Length_Part`). In fact, the maximum length of a function result is almost irrelevant. When the call on the function itself appears as a `Varying_String_Type` parameter in a call on one of the subprograms `Length`, `"&"`, `"="`, `Slice`, or `Put`, or as the `From` parameter in a call on `Copy_String`, the value of the function result's `Maximum_Length` component is ignored. (See the bodies of each of these subprograms.) Because `Varying_String_Type` is limited, the only other use that can be made of a `Varying_String_Type` function result outside `Varying_String_Package` is in expressions such as:

```
Slice (v, 1, n).Maximum_Length
Slice (v, 1, n) IN Varying_String_Type (10)
```

Such expressions are not likely to arise in practice, because there are more direct ways to compute their values.

12.8 SUMMARY

An abstract data type consists of a set of values plus a set of operations on those values. Packages providing private types reflect this principle. A private type provided by some package can only be manipulated using the operations provided by the package. As far as the compiler is concerned, the internal structure of a private type is unknown outside of the package defining it, and any references to that structure outside the package are illegal.

A private type is provided by a package with a specification of the following form:

```
PACKAGE identifier IS
    basic declaration
        ~~~
    basic declaration
....................
: PRIVATE          :
:   basic declaration :
:       ~~~        :
:   basic declaration :
....................
END identifier ;
```

The basic declarations preceding the word **PRIVATE** constitute the *visible part* of the package, and the basic declarations following it constitute the *private part*. A declaration of the form

```
TYPE identifier IS PRIVATE ;
```

may appear in the visible part provided that an ordinary type declaration with the same identifier appears in the private part. The declaration in the visible part declares that the identifier is the name of a private type, that is, a type whose structure cannot be referred to outside the package. The visible part may also include *deferred-constant declarations* for constants in the private type—that is, constant declarations without initial values—provided that ordinary constant declarations for the same constants appear in the private part. Besides the ordinary type declaration giving the structure of the private type and the ordinary constant declaration corresponding to a deferred-constant declaration, the private part may contain other declarations used in these declarations. Entities declared only in the private part of the package specification cannot be referred to outside of the package.

The visible part may also contain a declaration of the form

```
TYPE identifier IS LIMITED PRIVATE ;
```

indicating that the private type being declared is also *limited.* Assignment statements are forbidden for values in a limited type, as are the following value-copying operations:

initial values in object declarations
default initial values in record-component declarations (for components of a limited type)
procedures with OUT parameters in a limited type
allocators
aggregates
catenation

There are no predefined versions of = and /= for values in a limited type, but the function "=" may be overloaded with a version taking two operands in the same limited type and returning a value of type Boolean. This automatically overloads the operator /= to return the opposite result, but the programmer cannot overload "/=" explicitly. An array or record type with a limited component type is itself a limited type.

It is appropriate to make a type limited private if operations on a value of the type affect some entity indirectly referenced by that value. For example, private types implemented as access types should be made limited if operations on a value in the type may alter the object pointed by that type. Otherwise, assignment could lead to unexpected sharing, so that an operation on one object affects a supposedly independent object. A private type should also be declared limited if it contains physically different representations for the same abstract value. Because objects in a limited type cannot be declared with initial values, you can make a type limited private to ensure that each value in the type has some particular initial value. A limited private type can also be used to make sure that all copying of values in the type is performed by a special copying routine written by the programmer.

The predefined package Calendar, whose specification is shown in Section 12.3, provides a private type named Time and operations for manipulating those values. A value of type Time identifies a moment from the beginning of the year 1901 to the end of the year 2099 to within a fraction of a second. A WITH clause for Calendar is needed to use the package.

EXERCISES

12.1 Exercise 9.6 required the declaration of a type to represent complex numbers and the overloading of certain arithmetic operations to handle complex numbers. Solve this problem with a package providing a private type for complex numbers. You may assume that the function Square_Root is provided by another, already written, package named Math_Package.

12.2 A *priority queue* is a type with three operations—the creation of an empty priority queue, the insertion of a value into the queue, and the extraction of the "highest priority" value from the queue. Write a package providing a private type for a priority queue holding up to ten Integer values, assuming that a smaller integer has higher priority for extraction than a larger integer. That is, the extraction operation should extract the lowest `Integer` value contained in the priority queue. The insertion operation should have no effect when the queue already has ten values in it.

12.3 Modify the version of `Fraction_Package` given in Section 12.2 to provide functions `"<"`, `">"`, `"<="`, and `">="` for comparing `Fraction_Type` values, a procedure `Put` for displaying `Fraction_Type` values, and a function `Fraction_To_Float` for converting `Fraction_Type` values to type `Float`.

12.4 Write a subprogram taking a `String` parameter `Message` and printing `Message` if and only if it is the last day of the month. (Use the package `Calendar`, and declare a table giving the number of days in each month. Don't forget to account for leap years.)

12.5 Fill in the private part of the `Calendar` package specification assuming each of the following representations of the type `Time`:

(*a*) as a record type with components for the year, the month number, the day of the month, and the (possibly fractional) number of seconds since midnight

(*b*) as a record type with components for the number of whole days since the beginning of 1901 and the fraction of the current day that has elapsed so far (for example, 0.5 for 12:00 noon and 0.75 for 6:00 p.m.)

In addition, give subprogram bodies for `Split` and `Time_Of` corresponding to each representation.

12.6 Rewrite the subprogram bodies `Insert_At_End`, `Insert_Member`, and `Intersection`, found in the `Integer_Set_Package` body in Section 12.5, to reflect the revised specification for the package given in Section 12.6. (In the revised specification, `Integer_Set_Type` is a limited private type implemented as a derived type.)

12.7 Augment `Varying_String_Package`, given in Section 12.7, with versions of `"&"` taking one `Varying_String_Type` parameter and one parameter of type `Character` or type `String`, returning a `Varying_String_Type` result.

12.8 Overloading `"="` for `Integer_Set_Type` in Section 12.6 led to complications requiring the use of a derived type. Overloading `"="` for `Varying_String_Type` in Section 12.7 did not. What was the difference?

12.9 Use `Integer_Set_Package` to solve the following problem: Print out all numbers less than or equal to 1,000 that are

(*a*) multiples of 2

(*b*) multiples of 3

(*c*) multiples of 5

(*d*) multiples of 6

(*e*) multiples of 30

(*f*) multiples of 2, 5, or both

First construct a set containing the multiples of 2, a set containing the multiples of 3, and a set containing the multiples of 5. (These sets contain the numbers to be printed in answer to (*a*), (*b*), and (*c*) respectively.) Then take unions and intersections of these sets to construct the sets needed to answer (*d*), (*e*), and (*f*). To print the numbers in a set, use a `FOR` loop that tests each number from 1 to 1,000 for membership in the set and prints only those numbers that belong to the set.

CHAPTER

THIRTEEN

SEPARATE COMPILATION

Separate compilation means breaking a program into several parts and submitting these parts to a compiler one at a time. A programming language for writing very large programs must include some provision for separate compilation. Separate compilation makes it possible to change one part of a program without recompiling it in its entirety; allows parts of a program being developed by different programmers to be kept in independent files; and allows the program to be written, checked for syntactic errors, and tested piece by piece. Most languages deal with separate compilation of program components as an afterthought, but separate compilation was one of the main considerations behind the design of the Ada language. Consequently, the language's facilities for separate compilation are distinctive.

With a language requiring a program to be compiled all at once, a change to even a small part of a program requires that the compiler process every statement anew. In a large program, recompilation can consume large amounts of computer time and keep programmers idle. This makes both initial program development and later program modifications more difficult. If the language allows a large program to be broken up into separate compilation units, however, only one or a few small compilation units need be recompiled to incorporate small changes. Furthermore, a program component used in many programs can be compiled once and incorporated in object module form rather than incorporated in source module form and recompiled every time it is used.

Large programs are typically developed by teams of many programmers. Without separate compilation, all of these programmers modify the same compilation unit. This creates logistic difficulties. Each programmer must wait his turn for access to the common source code, or special measures must be taken to ensure that each programmer is modifying the most recent version of the source code and not overwriting someone else's changes when he saves his own.

Separate compilation allows individual parts of a program to be compiled as soon as they are written. Without separate compilation, an entire program must be written before any part of it is tested. Then the entire program must be tested at once. With separate compilation, a program can be built incrementally, with each part compiled and perhaps even tested as soon as it is written. This affords a concrete measure of progress toward completion of a programming project.

In many languages, separate compilation units are also used to divide a program into modules that can be considered in isolation. This is not a major reason for separate compilation in the Ada language, however. In the Ada language, the term *module* usually refers to a package rather than a compilation unit. It is certainly possible and often appropriate to compile a package separately, but it is also possible to write a compilation unit containing several packages or a package spread over several compilation units.

In most languages, separate compilation means the ability to compile several program components independently and then to combine the results with a linkage editor. If one compilation unit calls a subprogram in another compilation unit by the wrong name, this will not be detected until the linkage editor is invoked. If it calls the subprogram using the wrong number of parameters, or parameters of the wrong type, the error may not manifest itself until the program is run.

In the Ada language, different parts of a program may be compiled *separately* but not *independently* of each other. An Ada compiler retains certain information about the source programs it compiles, even after they are compiled. It uses this information to perform the same consistency checks between separately compiled parts of a program that it performs between different parts of a single compilation unit. This allows the early discovery of errors that might otherwise not be detected until the separately compiled parts of a large program were combined.

A common source of error in projects using many compilation units is failure to recompile a program whose object code is no longer valid. A change to one compilation unit (e.g., the addition of a parameter to a subprogram called by other compilation units), may render other, previously correct compilation units inconsistent. The Ada language has rules defining when a change to one compilation unit potentially requires recompilation of another compilation unit. An Ada implementation must enforce this recompilation, thus removing another source of insidious program errors.

13.1 PROGRAM LIBRARIES

The *program library* is the mechanism by which an Ada compiler retains information about previously compiled compilation units. When an Ada compiler is invoked, it not only translates a source program into an object program, it also adds information about the source program to the program library. When a compilation unit *A* makes use of facilities provided by another compilation unit *B, A* may not be compiled until information about *B* has been placed in the program library. When *A* is compiled, the Ada compiler consults the information about *B* in the program library to check that *A*'s use of *B*'s facilities is consistent with the declaration of those facilities. Thus an Ada compilation typically both reads and updates the program library while producing an object program. As you see, compilation units cannot be submitted to an Ada compiler in an arbitrary order. We shall discuss this issue in detail in Section 13.4.

The term *program library* is easily misunderstood because it is commonly used in a sense different from its sense in the Ada language. An Ada program library is not a library *of* programs, but a library for *a* program, where a program is a collection of compilation units. A program library in the Ada language sense need not contain object code, but it must contain information about declarations in previously compiled units. This information is used to check that compilation units compiled later are consistent with these declarations. (Some Ada implementations have combined the two senses of *program library,* and provide program libraries that contain both object code and information about declarations. In this book, when we refer to a program library, we are only concerned with the fact that it contains information about declarations in previously compiled units.)

13.2 COMPILATION UNITS AND COMPILATIONS

A *compilation unit* may be a context clause followed by any of the following:

a subprogram declaration
a subprogram body
a package specification
a package body

There are other kinds of compilation units as well, that will be explained in Section 13.3, Chapter 16, and Chapter 18.

A *compilation* is a sequence of zero or more compilation units submitted to the compiler at once. These compilation units may be interleaved with certain pragmas, including the `List` and `Page` pragmas described in Section 2.1 and certain low-level pragmas that will be described in Chapter 20. It is possible for a compilation to consist only of pragmas and no program text. Compiling a compilation consisting of several compilation units has the same effect as compiling each of those compilation units in turn. For example, a compilation consisting of a package specification and the corresponding package body calls for the separate compilation of the specification followed by separate compilation of the body.

When one compilation unit uses facilities provided by another compilation unit, it must contain a context clause mentioning the other compilation unit in a `WITH` clause. (As explained in Section 11.5, a context clause consists of zero or more `WITH` clauses, each followed by zero or more `USE` clauses.) If compilation unit with a `WITH` clause mentioning a subprogram may contain calls on that subprogram. If a compilation unit has a `WITH` clause mentioning a package, then the compilation unit may contain uses of entities declared in the visible part of that package's specification, as well as a USE clause for the package.

A context clause on a subprogram declaration applies implicitly to two compilation units—the subprogram declaration and the corresponding subprogram body. That is, if a subprogram declaration has a context clause listing other compilation units, facilities provided by those units may be referred to both in the subprogram declaration and the subprogram body. Similarly, a context clause on a package specification applies implicitly to two compilation units—the package specification and the package body. An explicit context clause on a subprogram body or a package body applies only to that compilation unit.

The compilation below consists of six compilation units: the Matrix_Package package specification, the Matrix_Package package body, the Matrix_IO_Package specification, the Matrix_IO_Package body, the Invert_Matrix procedure body, and the Print_Inverse procedure body. Print_Inverse is the main program. It reads an integer n and then reads n^2 real literals to fill an n by n matrix with Float values. Then it computes and prints the inverse of the matrix. The main program does all of its work by calling other subprograms. Input and output of matrix values is performed by the procedures Get_Matrix and Put_Matrix provided by Matrix_IO_Package. Matrix_IO_Package, in turn, uses Type_Float_IO_Package, not included in this compilation. Type_Float_IO_Package provides two subprograms: a version of Get that reads real literals from the input file and interprets them as values of type Float and a version of Put that prints a type Float value in a fixed-width scientific notation format. The procedure Invert_Matrix performs the actual matrix inversion by Gaussian elimination, using the Add_Row_Multiple, Exchange_Rows, and Multiply_Row procedures provided by Matrix_Package. (If you are unfamiliar with linear algebra, you may not understand how Invert_Matrix works. Don't worry—our discussion of separate compilation does not depend on this.)

```
-- Compilation unit 1:

PACKAGE Matrix_Package IS
   TYPE Matrix_Type IS
      ARRAY (Positive RANGE <>, Positive RANGE <>)
         OF Float;
   PROCEDURE Add_Row_Multiple
      (Matrix                 : IN OUT Matrix_Type;
       Multiple               : IN Float;
       Times_Row, Add_To_Row  : IN Positive);
   PROCEDURE Exchange_Rows
      (Matrix       : IN OUT Matrix_Type;
       Row_1, Row_2 : IN Positive);
   PROCEDURE Multiply_Row
      (Matrix   : IN OUT Matrix_Type;
       Multiple : IN Float;
       Row      : IN Positive);
END Matrix_Package;
```

```
-- Compilation unit 2:

PACKAGE BODY Matrix_Package IS

   PROCEDURE Add_Row_Multiple
      (Matrix                 : IN OUT Matrix_Type;
       Multiple               : IN Float;
       Times_Row, Add_To_Row : IN Positive) IS
   BEGIN
      FOR Column IN Matrix'Range(2) LOOP
         Matrix (Add_To_Row, Column) :=
            Matrix (Add_To_Row, Column) +
            Multiple * Matrix (Times_Row, Column);
      END LOOP;
   END Add_Row_Multiple;

   PROCEDURE Exchange_Rows
      (Matrix        : IN OUT Matrix_Type;
       Row_1, Row_2 : IN Positive) IS
      Old_Row_1_Element: Float;
   BEGIN
      FOR Column IN Matrix'Range(2) LOOP
         Old_Row_1_Element := Matrix (Row_1, Column);
         Matrix (Row_1, Column) := Matrix (Row_2, Column);
         Matrix (Row_2, Column) := Old_Row_1_Element;
      END LOOP;
   END Exchange_Rows;

   PROCEDURE Multiply_Row
      (Matrix   : IN OUT Matrix_Type;
       Multiple : IN Float;
       Row      : IN Positive) IS
   BEGIN
      FOR Column IN Matrix'Range(2) LOOP
         Matrix (Row, Column) :=
            Multiple * Matrix (Row, Column);
      END LOOP;
   END Multiply_Row;

END Matrix Package;

-- Compilation unit 3:

WITH Matrix_Package;

PACKAGE Matrix_IO_Package IS

   PROCEDURE Get_Matrix
      (Matrix : OUT Matrix_Package.Matrix_Type);
   PROCEDURE Put_Matrix
      (Matrix: IN Matrix_Package.Matrix_Type);
END Matrix_IO_Package;
```

```
-- Compilation unit 4:

WITH Type_Float_IO_Package, Basic_IO;

PACKAGE BODY Matrix_IO_Package IS

   PROCEDURE Get_Matrix
      (Matrix : OUT Matrix_Package.Matrix_Type) IS
   BEGIN
      FOR Row IN Matrix'Range(1) LOOP
         FOR Column IN Matrix'Range(2) LOOP
            Type_Float_IO_Package.Get (Matrix (Row, Column));
         END LOOP;
      END LOOP;
   END Get_Matrix;

   PROCEDURE Put_Matrix
      (Matrix: IN Matrix_Package.Matrix_Type) IS
   BEGIN
      FOR Row IN Matrix'Range(1) LOOP
         FOR Column IN Matrix'Range(2) LOOP
            Type_Float_IO_Package.Put (Matrix (Row, Column));
            Basic_IO.Put (" ");
         END LOOP;
         Basic_IO.New_Line;
      END LOOP;
   END Put_Matrix;
END Matrix_IO_Package;

-- Compilation unit 5:

WITH Matrix_Package;

PROCEDURE Invert_Matrix
   (Matrix   : IN OUT Matrix_Package.Matrix_Type;
    Singular : OUT Boolean) IS
   Inverse :
      Matrix_Package.Matrix_Type
         (Matrix'Range(1), Matrix'Range(2));
   Pivot_Row :
      Integer RANGE Matrix'First(1) .. Matrix'Last(1) + 1;
   Pivot_Factor, Multiple : Float;
```

```
BEGIN
    -- Initialize Inverse to the identity matrix:

    FOR Row IN Inverse'Range(1) LOOP
       FOR Column IN Inverse'Range(2) LOOP
          IF Row = Column THEN
             Inverse (Row, Column) := 1.0;
          ELSE
             Inverse (Row, Column) := 0.0;
          END IF;
       END LOOP;
    END LOOP;

    -- Apply identical row operations to Matrix and Inverse
    --   until Matrix is either discovered to be singular or
    --   transformed into the identity matrix:

    FOR i IN Matrix'Range(2) LOOP

    -- Search for a non-zero element in column i of
    --   Matrix, at or below row i:

    Pivot_Row := i;

    WHILE Pivot_Row <= Matrix'Last(1) AND THEN
          Matrix (Pivot_Row, i) = 0.0 LOOP

         Pivot_Row := Pivot_Row + 1;

    END LOOP;

    -- If no non-zero element found, Matrix is singular:

    IF Pivot_Row > Matrix'Last(1) THEN
       Singular := True;
       RETURN;
    END IF;

    -- Exchange rows if necessary to place non-zero
    --   element in Matrix (i, i):

    IF Pivot_Row /= i THEN
       Matrix_Package.Exchange_Rows (Matrix, , Pivot_Row);
       Matrix_Package.Exchange_Rows (Inverse, , Pivot_Row);
    END IF;

    -- Multiply each element in row i by the same
    --   value, so that Matrix (i, i) 1.0:

    Pivot_Factor := 1.0 / Matrix (i, i);
    Matrix_Package.Multiply_Row (Matrix, Pivot_Factor, i);
    Matrix_Package.Multiply_Row (Inverse, Pivot_Factor, i);
```

```
            -- Add multiples of row i to each other row so that
            --   Matrix (i, i) becomes the only non-zero element
            --   in column i of Matrix:
            FOR j IN Matrix'Range(1) LOOP
               IF j /= i THEN
                  Multiple := -Matrix (j, i);
                  Matrix_Package.Add_Row_Multiple
                     (Matrix,
                      Multiple,
                      Times_Row  => i,
                      Add_To_Row => j);
                  Matrix_Package.Add_Row_Multiple
                     (Inverse,
                      Multiple,
                      Times_Row  => i,
                      Add_To_Row => j);
               END IF;
            END LOOP;
         END LOOP;
         -- Now Matrix is equal to the identity matrix.
         -- If T is the linear transformation corresponding to
         --   the sequence of row operations applied to both
         --   matrices, M is the original value of Matrix and I
         --   is the identity matrix, then Matrix = TM = I (so
         --   that T is the inverse of M) and Inverse = TI = T.
         --   Therefore Inverse holds the inverse of M.
         Matrix := Inverse;
         Singular := False;
      END Invert_Matrix;


      -- Compilation unit 6:

      WITH Matrix_Package, Matrix_IO_Package, Invert_Matrix,
           Basic_IO;
      USE Basic_IO;

      PROCEDURE Print_Inverse IS
         Matrix_Size: Positive;
      BEGIN
         Put ("Enter size of matrix to be inverted.");
         New_Line;
         Get (Matrix_Size);
         DECLARE
            Matrix:
               Matrix_Package.Matrix_Type
                  (1 .. Matrix_Size, 1 .. Matrix_Size);
            Singular: Boolean;
```

```
    BEGIN

        Put ("Enter ");
        Put (Matrix_Size ** 2);
        Put (" elements, scanning the matrix row-by-row.");

        Matrix_IO_Package.Get_Matrix (Matrix);

        Invert_Matrix (Matrix, Singular);

        IF Singular THEN
           Put ("The matrix is singular.");
           New_Line;
        ELSE
           Matrix_IO_Package.Put_Matrix (Matrix);
        END IF;

    END;

  END Print_Inverse;
```

(The purpose of the block statement in `Print_Inverse` is to contain the declaration of `Matrix`. The index constraint in that declaration refers to `Matrix_Size`, which is set by the statement preceding the block statement. This is one way to declare an array whose bounds are determined during program execution. Another way is to declare an access type whose values designate values in the relevant array type. Then the array is created by evaluation of an allocator once the bounds have been determined.)

The `WITH` clause on the `Matrix_IO_Package` specification allows the use of facilities provided by `Matrix_Package` (namely the type `Matrix_Type`) in both the specification and body of `Matrix_IO_Package`. The `WITH` clause of the `Matrix_IO_Package` body, in contrast, affects only that body. It allows the use of facilities provided by `Type_Float_IO_Package` (`Get` and `Put` for type `Float`) and facilities provided by `Basic_IO` (`Put` for type `String` and `New_Line`) within the `Matrix_IO_Package` body. The `WITH` clause on the separately compiled procedure `Invert_Matrix` allows the use of facilities provided by `Matrix_Package` (type `Matrix_Type` and procedures `Add_Row_Multiple`, `Exchange_Rows`, and `Multiply_Row`) within the `Invert_Matrix` procedure body. Finally, the `WITH` clause on `Print_Inverse` allows the use of facilities provided by `Matrix_Package` (type `Matrix_Type`), facilities provided by `Matrix_IO_Package` (procedures `Get_Matrix` and `Put_Matrix`), the procedure `Invert_Matrix`, and facilities provided by the package `Basic_IO` (procedures `Put`, `Get`, and `New_Line`).

`WITH` clauses only apply directly to the units on which they appear and, in the case of package specifications and subprogram declarations, to the corresponding bodies. They do not apply indirectly. For instance, despite the fact that `Print_Inverse` has a `WITH` clause for `Matrix_IO_Package` and `Matrix_IO_Package` has a `WITH` clause for `Matrix_Package`, `Print_Inverse` needs its own `WITH` clause for `Matrix_Package` because it refers to the type `Matrix_Package.Matrix_Type`.

Similarly, a WITH clause is not necessary for a compilation unit that is used *only* indirectly. For example, Print_Inverse does not use Type_Float_IO_Package directly, so it need not mention Type_Float_IO_Package in a WITH clause. It does not matter that Print_Inverse uses Matrix_IO_Package directly and Matrix_IO_Package uses Type_Float_IO_Package directly. When we consider Print_Inverse, Matrix_IO_Package's use of Type_Float_IO_Package is just an aspect of Matrix_IO_Package's implementation, not its interface, and is therefore irrelevant.

The above example did not include any subprogram declarations as compilation units. Normally, as with Invert_Matrix and Print_Inverse above, a subprogram can be compiled without compiling a corresponding subprogram declaration. However, as will be explained more fully in Section 13.4, a compilation unit calling a separately compiled subprogram cannot be compiled until *either* the declaration of that subprogram has been compiled *or* the body has been compiled. A separately compiled subprogram declaration allows compilation units calling a subprogram to be compiled before that subprogram's body is written.

For example, the compilation below is illegal because the compilation unit Letters_In_String comes before the function named in its WITH clause:

```
WITH Is_A_Letter;  -- Illegal at this point!

FUNCTION Letters_In_String (s : String) RETURN Natural IS
   Count : Natural := 0;
BEGIN
   FOR i IN s'Range LOOP
      IF Is_A_Letter ( s(i) ) THEN
         Count := Count + 1;
      END IF;
   END LOOP;
   RETURN Count;
END Letters_In_String;


FUNCTION Is_A_Letter (c : Character) RETURN Boolean IS
BEGIN
   RETURN c IN 'A' .. 'Z' OR c IN 'a' .. 'z';
END Is_A_Letter;
```

The compilation can be made legal by inserting a function declaration for Is_A_Letter before the Letters_In_String function body:

```
FUNCTION Is_A_Letter (c : Character) RETURN Boolean;


WITH Is_A_Letter; -- Now legal.
FUNCTION Letters_In_String (s : String) RETURN Natural IS
   Count : Natural := 0;
BEGIN
   FOR i IN s'Range LOOP
      IF Is_A_Letter ( s(i) ) THEN
         Count := Count + 1;
      END IF;
   END LOOP;
   RETURN Count;
END Letters_In_String;


FUNCTION Is_A_Letter (c : Character) RETURN Boolean IS
BEGIN
   RETURN c IN 'A' .. 'Z' OR c IN 'a' .. 'z';
END Is_A_Letter;
```

The function declaration for `Is_A_Letter` is a separate one-line compilation unit!

There are several reasons for doing this. Two reasons, top-down program development and independent development of program components, will be discussed in Section 13.4.1. Another reason for presenting a calling subprogram before a subprogram it calls is mutual recursion. When separately compiled subprogram bodies contain calls on each other, there is no choice but to present a call on some subprogram before we have presented its body. This is permissible as long as we have already presented its declaration. This use of subprogram declarations to allow separately compiled mutually recursive subprograms is similar to the use of subprogram declarations explained in Section 9.4, to allow mutually recursive subprograms within a declarative part.

Sometimes it is even useful to compile a subprogram declaration immediately followed by the corresponding subprogram body. This can reduce the number of compilation units that must be recompiled when part of a program is changed, by allowing the interface of a subprogram to remain untouched while its implementation is changed. This use of subprogram declarations will be explained in Section 13.4.

A separately compiled package specification or subprogram declaration is called a *library unit* because its compilation places information in the program library. This information is referenced when compiling the corresponding body and when compiling any other unit naming the library unit in a WITH clause. A package body is not a library unit; it is a *secondary unit.* Except in circumstances to be described in Section 13.3, the compilation of a secondary unit does not produce information needed by other compilations. A subprogram body is a secondary unit if it is compiled after a corresponding subprogram declaration; otherwise, it is a library unit.

Library units may not overload other library units. That is, each library subprogram must have a distinct name. Furthermore, the names of library functions must be identifiers, not string literals containing operator symbols (as described in Section 9.6).

13.3 SUBUNITS

Deeply nested program structures can make programs difficult to follow. Especially in large programs, it is hard for a reader to keep track of the points at which nested constructs begin and end. Indenting program lines to reflect depth of nesting can clarify the nesting structure on a particular page of a listing, but once nested structures grow to span several pages, indentation becomes less apparent to the eye. Furthermore, the high level of indentation at deeply nested parts of a program leaves little room on a line for program text, so statements and expressions tend to be split across several lines, making them harder to read. Certain practices, such as use of global variables and declaration of the same name at different levels of nesting, can make heavily nested programs especially difficult to understand.

Nonetheless, there are legitimate uses for nesting. Well-designed programs tend to be largely hierarchical, with many subprograms called by only one other subprogram. A program can be made to reflect this treelike structure if all subprograms called only by a subprogram P are nested inside P. Since the Ada language's rules allow a subprogram nested in another subprogram's body to be called only from somewhere within that body, nesting makes it easier for a reader to determine where an inner subprogram is used. A reader need not be concerned with subprograms nested inside P when trying to understand parts of the program outside P, provided that he understands the behavior P presents to the outside world. In addition, there is a circumstance in which the Ada language requires nesting: When a subprogram is declared in a package specification, the subprogram body must be nested in the corresponding package body.

At first glance, nesting and separate compilation seem mutually exclusive. When one unit of a program is nested inside another, the inner unit must be preceded and followed by parts of the outer unit. However, the Ada language distinguishes between logical nesting relationships and physical placement of program units.

When an inner subprogram or package body occurs directly in the declarative part of another compilation unit, the body may be replaced within that declarative part by a *body stub* and compiled separately as a *subunit.* Although the inner unit is thus physically removed from the outer unit, the meaning of the program is precisely the same as if the subunit occurred at the place of the body stub.

The form of a subprogram body stub is as follows:

subprogram specification **IS SEPARATE ;**

(Recall that a subprogram specification is a subprogram declaration without the terminating semicolon. Equivalently, it is the part of a subprogram body preceding the word **IS**.) Like a library function, a subunit that is a function must be named by an identifier, not a string literal containing an operator symbol. The form of a package body stub is as follows:

PACKAGE BODY *identifier* **IS SEPARATE ;**

A program unit containing a body stub is called the *parent* of the corresponding subunit. A subunit begins with an optional context clause, followed by a **SEPARATE** *clause* of the form

SEPARATE (*parent unit name* **)**

followed by an ordinary subprogram body or package body. If a context clause is given, it applies only to the subunit. The **SEPARATE** clause is not followed by a semicolon. The subprogram body or package body may refer to entities declared in the parent unit precisely as if it were physically located where the body stub appears. However, a subunit is a compilation unit in its own right. Like package bodies and subprogram bodies that are not library units, subunits are considered secondary units.

Two restrictions apply to the use of subunits. The first is that a body stub is allowed only in the declarative part of another compilation unit (which might or might not itself be a subunit). For example, the following is forbidden:

```
PROCEDURE Outer IS
   PROCEDURE Middle IS
      PROCEDURE Inner IS SEPARATE;
         -- ILLEGAL PLACEMENT OF A BODY STUB INSIDE A
         --  PHYSICALLY NESTED UNIT!
      ...
   BEGIN  -- Middle
      ...
   END Middle;
   ...
BEGIN - Outer
   ...
END Outer;
```

The only way to make Inner a subunit is to make Middle a subunit also:

```
PROCEDURE Outer IS
   PROCEDURE Middle IS SEPARATE;
   ...
BEGIN -- Outer
   ...
END Outer;
-- -- -- -- -- -- -- -- -- -- --
SEPARATE (Outer)
PROCEDURE Middle IS
   PROCEDURE Inner IS SEPARATE;
      -- Now body stub is at the top level
      --    of a compilation unit
   ...
BEGIN -- Middle
   ...
END Middle;
```

The second restriction is that functions overloading operator symbols may not be written as subunits. Thus the body stub

```
FUNCTION "+"
   (Left, Right : Fraction_Type) RETURN Fraction_Type
   IS SEPARATE;
   -- ILLEGAL BODY STUB FOR A FUNCTION NAMED BY AN
   --   OPERATOR SYMBOL!
```

is disallowed.

As an example, consider the package Varying_String_Package presented in Section 12.7. The body of that package can be split into a parent unit and six subunits:

```
-- Compilation unit 1:

PACKAGE BODY Varying_String_Package IS

 FUNCTION Varying_String
    (s : String) RETURN Varying_String_Type
    IS SEPARATE;
 FUNCTION Length
    (Varying_String : Varying_String_Type) RETURN Natural
    IS SEPARATE;
```

```
   FUNCTION Slice
      (Full_String : Varying_String_Type;
       Lower_Bound, Upper_Bound : Natural)
      RETURN Varying_String_Type
      IS SEPARATE;

   PROCEDURE Get (Item : OUT Varying_String_Type)
      IS SEPARATE;

   PROCEDURE Put (Item : IN Varying_String_Type)
      IS SEPARATE;

   PROCEDURE Copy_String
      (From : IN Varying_String_Type;
       To   : OUT Varying_String_Type)
      IS SEPARATE;


   FUNCTION "&"
      (Left, Right : Varying_String_Type)
      RETURN Varying_String_Type IS

      Left_Length :
         Natural RENAMES Left.Current_Length_Part;
      Right_Length :
         Natural RENAMES Right.Current_Length_Part;
      Result_Length :
         CONSTANT Natural := Left_Length + Right_Length;
      Result : Varying_String_Type (Result_Length);

   BEGIN

      Result.Contents_Part (1 .. Left_Length) :=
         Left.Contents_Part (1 .. Left_Length);

      Result.Contents_Part
         (Left_Length + 1 .. Result_Length) :=
         Right.Contents_Part (1 .. Right_Length);

      Result.Current_Length_Part := Result_Length;

      RETURN Result;

   END "&";


   FUNCTION "="
      (Left, Right : Varying_String_Type) RETURN Boolean IS

   BEGIN

      RETURN
         Left.Contents_Part (1 .. Left.Current_Length_Part) =
         Right.Contents_Part (1 .. Right.Current_Length_Part);

   END "=";

END Varying_String_Package;
```

```
-- Compilation unit 2:

SEPARATE (Varying_String_Package)

FUNCTION Varying_String
   (s : String) RETURN Varying_String_Type IS

BEGIN

   RETURN
      Varying_String_Type'
         (Maximum_Length | Current_Length_Part => s'Length,
          Contents_Part => s);

END Varying_String;


-- Compilation unit 3:

SEPARATE (Varying_String_Package)

FUNCTION Length
   (Varying_String : Varying_String_Type) RETURN Natural IS

BEGIN

   RETURN Varying_String.Current_Length_Part;

END Length;


-- Compilation unit 4:

SEPARATE (Varying_String_Package)

FUNCTION Slice
   (Full_String                : Varying_String_Type;
    Lower_Bound, Upper_Bound : Natural)
   RETURN Varying_String_Type IS

   Actual_Lower_Bound : Natural := Lower_Bound;
   Actual_Upper_Bound : Natural := Upper_Bound;
   Result_Length      : Natural;

BEGIN

   IF Actual_Lower_Bound < 1 THEN
      Actual_Lower_Bound := 1;
   END IF;

   IF Actual_Upper_Bound >
         Full_String.Current_Length_Part THEN

      Actual_Upper_Bound :=
         Full_String.Current_Length_Part;

   END IF;
```

```
   Result_Length :=
      Actual_Upper_Bound - Actual_Lower_Bound + 1;
   IF Result_Length <= 0 THEN
      RETURN
         Varying_String_Type'
            (Maximum_Length      => 0,
             Current_Length_Part => 0,
             Contents_Part       => "");
   ELSE
      RETURN
         Varying_String_Type'
            (Maximum_Length | Current_Length_Part =>
               Result_Length,
             Contents_Part =>
               Full_String.Contents_Part
                  ( Actual_Lower_Bound ..
                    Actual_Upper_Bound ) );
   END IF;
END Slice;

-- Compilation unit 5:
WITH Basic_IO;
SEPARATE (Varying_String_Package)
PROCEDURE Get (Item : OUT Varying_String_Type) IS
BEGIN
   Basic_IO.Get_Line
      (Item.Contents_Part, Item.Current_Length_Part);
END Get;

-- Compilation unit 6:
WITH Basic_IO;
SEPARATE (Varying_String_Package)
PROCEDURE Put (Item : IN Varying_String_Type) IS
BEGIN
   Basic_IO.Put
      ( Item.Contents_Part
         (1 .. Item.Current_Length_Part) );
END Put;
```

```
-- Compilation unit 7:
SEPARATE (Varying_String_Package)
PROCEDURE Copy_String
   (From : IN Varying_String_Type;
    To   : OUT Varying_String_Type) IS
BEGIN
   IF From.Current_Length_Part > To.Maximum_Length THEN
      To.Contents_Part :=
         From.Contents_Part (1 .. To.Maximum_Length);
      To.Current_Length_Part := To.Maximum_Length;
   ELSE
      To.Contents_Part (1 .. From.Current_Length_Part) :=
         From.Contents_Part (1 .. From.Current_Length_Part);
      To.Current_Length_Part := From.Current_Length_Part;
   END IF;
END Copy_String;
```

We have kept the bodies for `"="` and `"&"` in the package body because functions overloading operators may not be written as subunits. The other six subprogram bodies nested inside the package body have been replaced by subprogram body stubs. These subprogram bodies follow as subunits, each beginning with a `SEPARATE` clause referring back to the parent unit `Varying_String_Package`. The context clause

```
WITH Basic_IO;
```

has been removed from the package body and placed instead on the two subunits, `Get` and `Put`, that actually use `Basic_IO`. It also would have been possible to leave some of the subprogram bodies inside the package body and break off the remaining ones into subunits. Although the subunits in the previous compilation are listed in the same order as the corresponding body stubs, this is not necessary—the subunits can be compiled in any order after the parent unit.

Subunits themselves may have subunits. For example, the subunit `Slice` in the compilation could be broken into two compilation units as follows:

```
-- Compilation unit 4a:

SEPARATE (Varying_String_Package)
FUNCTION Slice
   (Full_String                : Varying_String_Type;
    Lower_Bound, Upper_Bound : Natural)
   RETURN Varying_String_Type IS

   Actual_Lower_Bound, Actual_Upper_Bound : Natural;
   Result_Length                          : Natural;
```

```
PROCEDURE Determine_Actual_Bounds
    (Nominal_Lower_Bound, Nominal_Upper_Bound : IN Natural;
     Actual_Lower_Bound, Actual_Upper_Bound    : OUT Natural)
    IS SEPARATE;
   BEGIN
      Determine_Actual_Bounds
         (Lower_Bound,
          Upper_Bound,
          Actual_Lower_Bound,
          Actual_Upper_Bound);

      Result_Length :=
         Actual_Upper_Bound - Actual_Lower_Bound + 1;

      IF Result_Length <= 0 THEN

         RETURN
            Varying_String_Type'
               (Maximum_Length      => 0,
                Current_Length_Part => 0,
                Contents_Part       => "");

      ELSE

         RETURN
            Varying_String_Type'
               (Maximum_Length | Current_Length_Part =>
                  Result_Length,
                Contents_Part =>
                  Full_String.Contents_Part
                     ( Actual_Lower_Bound ..
                       Actual_Upper_Bound ) );

      END IF;

   END Slice;

   -- Compilation unit 4b:

   SEPARATE (Varying_String_Package.Slice)
PROCEDURE Determine_Actual_Bounds
   (Nominal_Lower_Bound, Nominal_Upper_Bound  : IN Natural;
    Actual_Lower_Bound, Actual_Upper_Bound    : OUT Natural) IS

 BEGIN

      IF Actual_Lower_Bound < 1 THEN
         Actual_Lower_Bound := 1;
      ELSE
         Actual Lower_Bound := Nominal_Lower_Bound;
      END IF;
      IF Actual_Upper_Bound >
            Full_String.Current_Length_Part THEN

         Actual_Upper_Bound :=
            Full_String.Current_Length_Part;
      ELSE

         Actual_Upper_Bound := Nominal_Upper_Bound;
      END IF;
   END Determine_Actual_Bounds;
```

Determine_Actual_Bounds refers to Full_String as a global variable. This is not an advisable programming practice—it would have been preferable to pass Full_String as a parameter—but it demonstrates that the subunit is logically nested inside the declarative part of Slice and can be written exactly as if it were physically located at the site of the body stub. The SEPARATE clause contains the expanded name Varying_String_Package.Slice rather than the simple name Slice.

Whenever the program unit directly surrounding the body stub is not the body of a library unit, the subunit's SEPARATE clause must contain such an expanded name. The expanded name must include the name of every logically surrounding unit, starting at the outermost level with the body of a library unit. Since a body stub is only allowed at the top level of a compilation unit, every identifier in this expanded name is always the name of a compilation unit.

Subunits provide several benefits. They make it easy to break large program units into several pieces possibly maintained in different files or by different programmers, even if the program is deeply nested. Furthermore, they can contribute to program readability in a number of ways.

First, subunits clarify where in a large program a particular subprogram or package is used. The fact that a subunit is logically nested within another unit limits the places where the subunit is available for use. Furthermore, a subunit's SEPARATE clause explicitly documents which part of the program uses it. Library units do not contain analogous cross-reference information specifying which compilation units name them in WITH clauses.

When a large program unit like the Varying_String_Package body contains a WITH clause for a compilation unit like Basic_IO used in only a few places, those places can be broken off into subunits, and the WITH clause can be placed on the subunits instead. This makes it easier to understand which compilation units are used where. As we shall see in Section 13.4, it also limits the amount of program text that must be recompiled when the compilation unit named in the WITH clause is changed.

Subunits can make it easier to format programs in a way that makes them more readable. A physically nested program unit should be indented one level deeper than the unit that surrounds it. Consequently, deeply nested statements may begin halfway across the line. If the nested subunit is broken off into a separately compiled subunit, indentation can begin back at the left margin, providing longer lines on which to format declarations and statements.

Finally, when one subprogram body is nested inside another, the inner subprogram body must occur after all the variable declarations in the outer subprogram. Thus the inner subprogram physically separates the outer subprogram's variable declarations from the outer subprogram's statements using those variables. When there are several levels of subprogram nesting, it can be difficult to scan back from a statement to find the corresponding variable declarations, because declarations in the inner subprograms are found first. One must count beginnings and ends of intervening procedure bodies to ascertain that a declaration, once it is found, is at the same level of nesting as the statement. Subunits reduce the distance between the variable declarations and corresponding statements. When a nested subprogram body is replaced by a body stub, there are no confusing inner declarations that intervene between a statement and the declarations that apply to that statement.

Use of global variables, which is a bad programming practice to begin with, is especially pernicious in subunits. A subunit using a global variable contains no declaration of the variable and no hint of how the variable is used elsewhere. This information can be found only in other compilation units, possibly in other files. Worse yet, if a subunit modifies a global variable, the parent unit contains no clue that one of the variables declared there may be modified mysteriously by a subprogram call not even naming that variable. If a global variable must be used in a subunit, it is essential that both the subunit and the parent unit contain extensive comments explaining the use of the variable. Still, it is preferable to replace the global variable in the subunit by a new parameter, as described in Section 9.8.1.

It was stated earlier that compilation of a library unit places information in a program library, but compilation of a secondary unit generally does not. However, when a secondary unit contains one or more body stubs, its compilation places information in the program library that is used when compiling the corresponding subunits. This is necessary because the subunits must be compiled as if they were physically surrounded by their parent unit, with access to the parent unit's declarations.

13.4 ORDER OF COMPILATION

The use of a program library to enforce consistency among separate compilation units necessitates restrictions on the order in which units are compiled. A unit whose compilation adds certain information to the program library must be compiled before a unit whose compilation requires that information. There are three straightforward rules:

1. A library unit must be compiled before the corresponding body. Specifically, a package specification must be compiled before the corresponding package body, and a subprogram declaration, if it is compiled at all, must be compiled before the corresponding subprogram body.
2. A library unit must be compiled before any compilation unit naming that library unit in a `WITH` clause.
3. A parent unit must be compiled before any of its subunits.

Compilation units may be compiled in any order consistent with these rules. A program is illegal if there is no order obeying these rules. (For example, a program is illegal if two separately compiled package specifications each name the other in a `WITH` clause, because by Rule 2 each must then be compiled before the other.)

The restrictions on the order in which compilation units are submitted to the compiler are independent of the way the compilation units are grouped into compilations. If two compilation units that must be compiled in a given order are part of the same compilation, the rules determine which compilation unit must occur earlier in the compilation. If the compilation units are part of different compilations, the rules determine which compilation must be submitted to the compiler first.

Let us consider the matrix multiplication example of Section 13.2. By Rule 1, the Matrix_Package specification must be compiled before the Matrix_Package body. The Matrix_IO_Package specification begins with a WITH clause for Matrix_Package, so by Rule 2 the Matrix_Package specification must be compiled before the Matrix_IO_Package specification. However, the Matrix_Package *body* may be compiled either before or after the Matrix_IO_Package specification. WITH clauses refer to library units, and only the package specification, not its corresponding body, is a library unit. By Rule 1, the Matrix_IO_Package body must be compiled after the Matrix_IO_Package specification. Furthermore, by Rule 2, the Matrix_IO_Package body must be compiled after the specifications of the two packages named in its WITH clause, Type_Float_IO_Package, and Basic_IO. The separately compiled procedure Invert_Matrix has a WITH clause naming Matrix_Package, so the Matrix_Package specification must be compiled before Invert_Matrix by Rule 2. Finally, the procedure Print_Inverse has a WITH clause naming Matrix_Package, Matrix_IO_Package, Invert_Matrix, and Basic_IO. By Rule 2, the Matrix_IO_Package and Basic_IO specifications (both library units) must be compiled before Print_Inverse. Since the Invert_Matrix procedure body is compiled without a procedure declaration for Invert_Matrix having been compiled earlier, the procedure body acts as a library unit. Therefore, the Invert_Matrix procedure body must be compiled before the Print_Inverse procedure body. There are two reasons why the Matrix_Package specification must be compiled before Print_Inverse. The first reason is by direct application of Rule 2. The second reason is that the Matrix_Package specification must be compiled before the Matrix_IO_Package specification and the Invert_Matrix procedure body (as explained previously); and those two units, in turn, must be compiled before Print_Inverse (again, as explained previously). Either of these two reasons would have been sufficient to determine that the Matrix_Package specification must be compiled before Print_Inverse.

The restrictions are summarized in Figure 13.1. Assuming that Type_Float_IO_Package and Basic_IO have been compiled earlier, the remaining six compilation units could be compiled in any of the following orders:

Matrix_Package specification, Invert_Matrix, Matrix_IO_Package specification, Matrix_IO_Package body, Print_Inverse, with the Matrix_Package body compiled any time after the Matrix_Package specification (five possible orders).

Matrix_Package specification, Matrix_IO_Package specification, Invert_Matrix, Matrix_IO_Package body, Print_Inverse, with the Matrix_Package body compiled any time after the Matrix_Package specification (five possible orders).

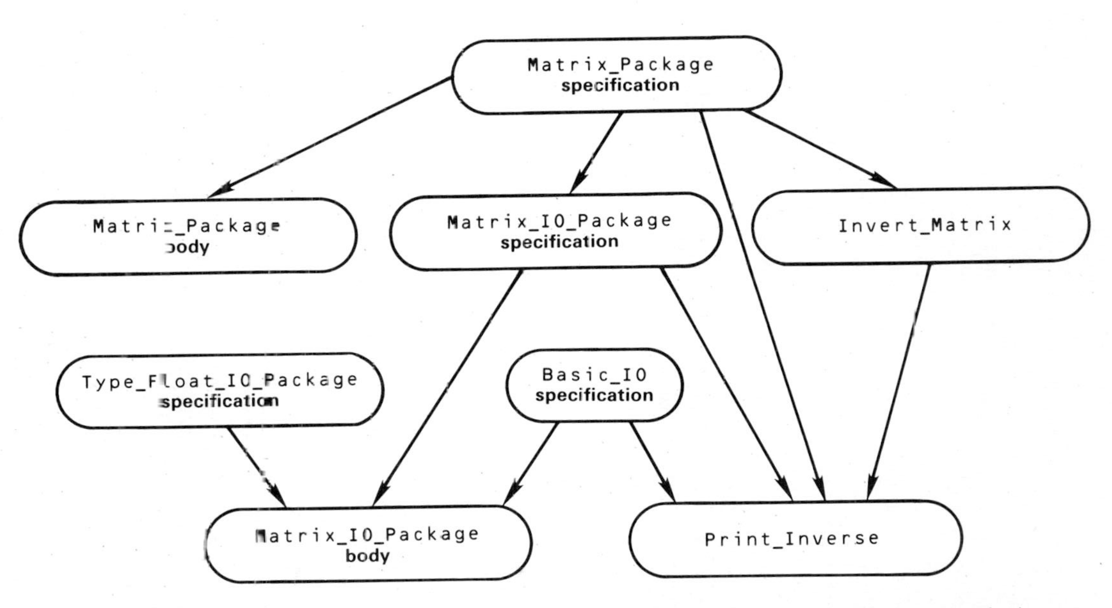

Figure 13.1 Restrictions on compilation order for the compilation units of the matrix multiplication example. An arrow from one compilation unit to another means that the compilation unit from which the arrow emanates must be compiled before the compilation unit to which the arrow points.

Matrix_Package specification, Matrix_IO_Package specification, Matrix_IO_Package body, Invert_Matrix, Print_Inverse, with the Matrix_Package body compiled any time after the Matrix_Package specification (five possible orders).

In all, there are fifteen possible orders in which the six compilation units could legally have been compiled.

The matrix inversion example did not illustrate Rule 3. However, the Varying_String_Package example of Section 13.3 does. By Rule 1, the Varying_String_Package specification must be compiled before the Varying_String_Package body. By Rule 3, the six subunits of the package body—the subprograms Varying_String, Length, Slice, Get, Put, and Copy_String—must be compiled after the package body. They may be compiled in any order once the package body has been compiled, with one restriction: both Get and Put have context clauses naming Basic_IO, so by Rule 2 both of these subunits must be compiled some time after the Basic_IO specification. (Put another way, Basic_IO can be compiled any time before the compilation of Get and Put. This may be before the Varying_String_Package specification or between two of the subunits, for example.) If the Determine_Actual_Bounds subunit is broken out of Slice as described in Section 13.3, it may be compiled any time after Slice has been compiled. Figure 13.2 summarizes these restrictions.

13.4.1 Top-Down Development and Independent Development

Perhaps the most significant aspect of the compilation order rules is that once a subprogram declaration or package specification has been compiled, other compilation units using the subprogram or package can be compiled before the corresponding subprogram or package body. This has important implications for program development methodology. It supports both *top-down development* of programs and *independent development* of different parts of large programs.

Top-down development is the design of a program in terms of hypothetical abstract operations and data types that make the problem easy to solve. Once the problem has been solved in terms of these hypothetical powerful abstractions—and only then—we turn to the problem of implementing the abstractions. To do this, we may hypothesize the existence of yet another level of abstract operations and data types. This process is repeated, with the hypothetical operations becoming more specific and less powerful each time, until problems are easily solved directly in terms of actual Ada operations and types. This repetitive process is called *stepwise refinement,* because each time we implement one of the abstractions we are refining our description of the overall solution, filling in details about how various high-level goals are achieved. Top-down problem solution prevents a programmer from becoming mired in detail too early and limits the amount of complexity the programmer must deal with at any given time.

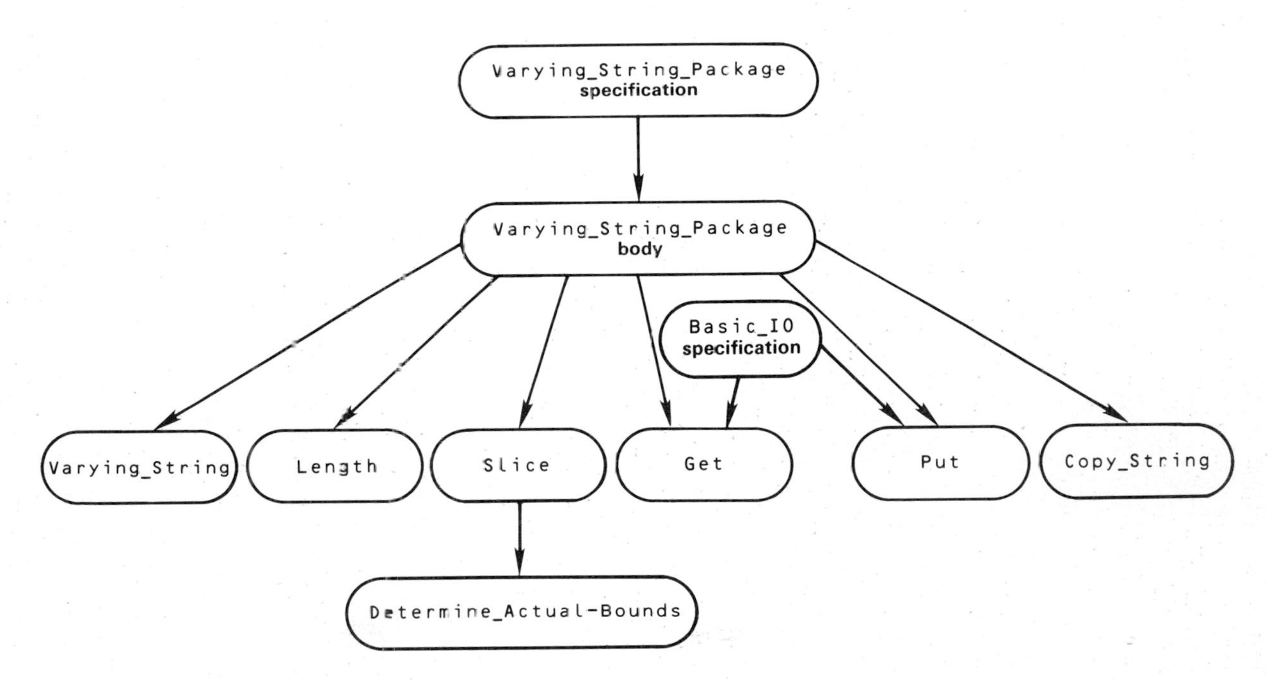

Figure 13.2 Restrictions on compilation order for the Varying_String_Package specification, body and subunits. The meaning of the arrows is as in Figure 13.1.

Separate compilation can facilitate top-down development. Once the need for certain abstractions has been identified, the abstractions can be described by subprogram declarations and package specifications, and these library units can be compiled. The library units represent promises to implement the abstractions later. Given these promises, an Ada compiler will accept compilation units that use the abstractions described by the library units. Thus the problem can be solved in terms of abstract operations and data types before these abstractions are implemented. The abstractions are ultimately implemented by writing and compiling the bodies corresponding to the library units. If necessary, we may first compile still other library units describing abstractions to be used in writing those bodies.

(This is an ideal scenario. In reality, some thought must be given to the implementation of abstractions before they are used, in order to be sure that the implementation is feasible. Furthermore, if a package providing a private type is used to implement a data abstraction, the rules of the Ada language require the internal representation of the data type to be determined before the abstraction is compiled, so that the private part of the package specification may be written.)

In a large programming project, it must be possible for programmers to work on different parts of a program simultaneously and independently of each other. Before they can do this, they must agree on an interface by which those parts of the program communicate. If one programmer is to implement a subprogram or package to be used by the other, compilation of the subprogram declaration or package specification constitutes determination of the interface. Development of the body implementing the interface and the compilation unit using the facilities to be implemented can then proceed independently. Either can be compiled once the library unit specifying the interface has been compiled. These compilations check that both the body and the compilation unit using the facilities are consistent with the previously compiled interface. This, in turn, guarantees that the body and the compilation unit using the facilities are consistent with each other.

Subunits are also conducive to top-down development and independent development. For top-down development, body stubs are written in place of bodies implementing hypothesized abstractions. The abstractions are implemented later by writing and compiling subunits corresponding to the body stubs. For independent development, a compilation unit containing body stubs is written and compiled first, and the corresponding subunits are then developed and compiled independently, possibly in parallel.

13.4.2 Recompilation

When we state that one particular compilation unit must be compiled before another, what we really mean is that the *latest version* of that compilation unit must be compiled before the *latest version* of the other. Consequently, the rules governing compilation order also require compilation units to be *recompiled* in certain circumstances. Specifically, if the rules given at the beginning of Section 13.4 require some compilation unit *A* to be compiled before some other compilation unit *B,* then if *A* is successfully recompiled, *B* also must be recompiled.

If the rules require *A* to be compiled before *B*, then the compilation of *A* places information in the program library that is examined during compilation of *B*. This information is used both to check that *B* is consistent with *A* and to properly translate into machine language *B*'s use of *A*'s facilities. Recompilation of *A* makes this information obsolete. The compilation of *B*, which established that *B* was consistent with the original version of *A*, must be repeated to establish that *B* is consistent with the new version of *A*. Even if *B*'s source text is still consistent with *A*, the change to *A* may render the original machine-language translation of *B* incorrect. For example, if *A* is a package specification containing a data type declaration and *B* contains declarations of objects belonging to that data type, then a change to the type declaration in *A* may require that a different amount of storage be used to represent the objects declared in *B*.

Sometimes a change made to one compilation unit does not really affect the compilation units compiled after it. For example, addition of a new subprogram declaration to a package specification requires modification of the package body to include a new subprogram body, but it is not obvious why compilation units referring to the package in a `WITH` clause should have to be recompiled. Such compilation units cannot be rendered inconsistent by the change, nor are their machine-language translations affected. In such cases, a sophisticated compiler may be able to determine that nothing of significance has changed and limit the actions taken during recompilation accordingly. The programmer is still required to request recompilation, but the compiler may fulfill that request by doing little or nothing.

Recompilation of one compilation unit may require recompilation of a second compilation unit, and that in turn may require recompilation of a third. Care must be taken when designing a program so that small changes will not set off chain reactions leading to recompilation of a major portion of the program. Fortunately, there are simple guidelines, consistent with good program design, that will minimize the necessity for recompilation.

The guidelines are based on the following observations:

Recompilation of a library unit requires recompilation of the corresponding body, if any, recompilation of all subunits logically contained in the body, and recompilation of all compilation units naming the library in a `WITH` clause. If these compilation units with `WITH` clauses are themselves library units, their recompilations generate further recompilation requirements in the same way.

Recompilation of a body requires recompilation only of those subunits logically contained in the body (directly or indirectly).

Recompilation of a subunit requires recompilation only of those subunits it itself logically contains.

In short, recompilation of a library unit tends to require much other recompilation; recompilation of a secondary unit tends not to, unless that secondary unit logically contains many subunits. Furthermore, recompilation requirements are propagated through a system by `WITH` clauses. Our goals should be to minimize the number of subunits logically nested inside program units that are likely to change, to minimize the need for recompilation of library units, and to minimize the amount of program text to which `WITH` clauses apply.

We stated earlier that logical nesting of program units can be used to reflect program hierarchy. This hierarchy may be several levels deep. The higher levels of the hierarchy represent major decisions in the design of the program, and the lower levels represent more minor decisions. A fundamental tenet of top-down program design is that design decisions should be postponed as long as possible. If this principle is followed, decision changes will be more likely to occur lower in the hierarchy, where they will entail less recompilation. The major decisions should be carefully considered, and an effort should be made to adhere to those decisions, because recompilation of a unit high in the hierarchy will be very expensive.

Declarations should be placed in package bodies rather than package specifications whenever possible. In particular, declarations not required for the definition of private types or deferred constants should be placed in the package body rather than the private part of the package specification. Except for declarations that must go in the private part, declarations that are used only to implement the package should be placed in the package body. The greater the number of declarations that are placed in the package body rather than the package specification, the less the chance that a change to a declaration will be a change to the package specification (a library unit).

When a subprogram body is separately compiled without a separately compiled subprogram declaration, the subprogram body acts as a library unit. Any change to the declarations or statements of the subprogram body will necessitate recompilation of this library unit. However, if a subprogram declaration is separately compiled, the declaration rather than the body is the library unit. Changes to the subprogram that do not require changes to the parameters or the result subtype then lead to recompilation of the subprogram body, but not of the corresponding library unit. Therefore, separately compiled subprograms should have separately compiled declarations if it is anticipated that the declarations or statements of the subprogram might change while the subprogram declaration remains intact. This is especially important if many other compilation units are directly or indirectly dependent on the subprogram.

A `WITH` clause should be placed on a package body rather than a package specification if it is only actually needed within the package body. Then recompilation of a unit named in the `WITH` clause will not require recompilation of the package specification (a library unit), only the package body. Similarly, a `WITH` clause should be placed on a subprogram body rather than a subprogram declaration unless a compilation unit named in the `WITH` clause is needed to write the declaration. (This is another reason for compiling subprogram declarations separately.) A `WITH` clause naming several compilation units can be split into two `WITH` clauses to facilitate these transformations.

Furthermore, if a `WITH` clause on a body is actually needed only in a small part of the body, that part of the body should be broken off into a subunit, and the `WITH` clause should be moved from the parent unit to the subunit. Then recompilation of the unit named in the WITH clause necessitates recompilation only of the subunit, not the entire parent unit. This is especially beneficial if the parent unit already contains other subunits, because it avoids recompilation of these other subunits.

13.5 ORDER OF ELABORATION

Before execution of a main program, all compilation units directly or indirectly used by the main program are elaborated. Initialization statements in the bodies of library packages are executed as the package bodies are elaborated. Depending on the compiler, these compilation units may be elaborated in any order that would have been a legal compilation order according to the rules given in Section 13.4, with one additional restriction: A library unit named in the WITH clause of a subunit is guaranteed to be elaborated not only before the subunit, but before the parent unit as well.

Occasionally, the elaboration of one compilation unit directly or indirectly uses the facilities of another compilation unit. This can happen if an expression in a package declaration includes a function call, if an expression in the declarative part of a package body contains a function call, or if the initialization statements in a package body contain a function or procedure call. The following compilation illustrates the first of these possibilities:

```
PACKAGE Precomputed_Sine_Package IS
   TYPE Integer_Degree_Type IS RANGE 0 .. 90;
   FUNCTION Precomputed_Sine
      (Angle : Integer_Degree_Type) RETURN Float;
END Precomputed_Sine_Package;


WITH Precomputed_Sine_Package;
PACKAGE Runway_Data_Package IS
   ...
   Runway_4_Sine :
      CONSTANT Float :=
         Precomputed_Sine_Package.Precomputed_Sine (40);
   ...
END Runway_Data_Package;


WITH Sine;

PACKAGE BODY Precomputed_Sine_Package IS

   Sine_Table : ARRAY (Integer_Degree_Type) OF Float;
```

```
      FUNCTION Precomputed_Sine
         (Angle : Integer_Degree_Type) RETURN Float IS
      BEGIN -- Precomputed_Sine function
         RETURN Sine_Table (Angle);
      END Precomputed_Sine;

   BEGIN -- Precomputed_Sine_Package initialization
      FOR d IN Integer_Degree_Type LOOP
         Sine_Table (d) := Sine (Float (d));
      END LOOP;
   END Precomputed_Sine_Package;
```

Elaboration of the `Runway_Data_Package` specification uses a facility provided by `Precomputed_Sine_Package`.

It is an error to call a subprogram before its body has been elaborated or to call a subprogram provided by a package before the package body has been elaborated. Therefore, when the elaboration of one compilation unit directly or indirectly uses the facilities of another compilation unit, the body of the second compilation unit must be elaborated first. In the previous example, the body of `Precomputed_Sine_Package` must be elaborated (and the table used by the `Precomputed_Sine` function initialized) before the `Runway_Data_Package` specification is elaborated (causing `Precomputed_Sine` to be called).

Because the `Runway_Data_Package` specification begins with a `WITH` clause for `Precomputed_Sine_Package`, the `Precomputed_Sine_Package` specification must be elaborated before the `Runway_Data_Package` specification. However, according to the elaboration order rules, `Precomputed_Sine_Package` body can be elaborated before or after the `Runway_Data_Package` specification. When such a situation arises, it is the programmer's responsibility to indicate that a particular body must be elaborated before some other compilation unit. This is done by placing the following pragma immediately after the context clause of the other compilation unit:

`PRAGMA Elaborate (` *identifier* `,` ~~~ `,` *identifier* `) ;`

Each identifier names a library unit, and the pragma specifies that the *bodies* of those units must be elaborated before the compilation unit in which the pragma appears. In this case, we rewrite the `Runway_Data_Package` specification as follows:

```
WITH Precomputed_Sine_Package;
PRAGMA Elaborate (Precomputed_Sine_Package);
PACKAGE Runway_Data_Package IS
   ...
   Runway_4_Sine :
      CONSTANT Float :=
         Precomputed_Sine_Package.Precomputed_Sine (40);
   ...
END Runway_Data_Package;
```

This specifies that the Precomputed_Sine_Package *body* must be elaborated before the Runway_Data_Package specification.

13.6 SUMMARY

Ada programs can be compiled in separate pieces called *compilation units*. This limits the amount of program text that must be recompiled when the program changes, allows team members to work independently on different compilation units, and allows a large object program to be built a piece at a time. Separate compilation is indispensable to the development of very large programs.

Ada compilation units are compiled *separately*, but not *independently*. Consistency checks are performed between different compilation units. An Ada implementation demands recompilation of a unit when a change to another unit renders the previous compilation obsolete. An Ada compiler, besides producing object code, places information about the unit it is compiling in a *program library*. Later, when compiling another unit, the compiler may retrieve this information to check for consistency between the two units.

Ada's compilation units include subprogram declarations, subprogram bodies, package specifications, package bodies, and subunits, among others. Subprogram declarations and package specifications are called *library units*. Package bodies and subunits are called *secondary units*. A subprogram body is a secondary unit if a declaration for that subprogram was compiled earlier; otherwise the subprogram body is a library unit. All library subprograms for a given compilation must have distinct names, and library functions may not overload operators. Each compilation unit begins with a (possibly empty) context clause. Compilation units may be combined to form a *compilation*, which is simply a sequence of compilation units and pragmas submitted to the compiler together.

A *subunit* is a body that is *logically* nested inside the declarative part of another compilation unit but is *physically* a separate compilation unit. Within the other unit, called the *parent unit*, the nested body is replaced by a *body stub* with a form such as:

> *subprogram specification* IS SEPARATE ;
>
> PACKAGE BODY *identifier* IS SEPARATE ;

The subunit itself consists of a possibly empty context clause, a SEPARATE *clause* of the form

> SEPARATE (*parent unit name*)

and the body. Functions that are subunits may not overload operators.

A context clause for a given unit contains zero or more WITH clauses listing the other compilation units to which the given unit refers. Each WITH clause may itself be followed by zero or more USE clauses. A WITH clause on a package specification or subprogram declaration makes the listed compilation units available both in that library unit and in the corresponding body. A **WITH** clause on a package body, subprogram body, or subunit makes the listed compilation units available only in the unit containing the **WITH** clause. If compilation unit *A* has a **WITH** clause for compilation unit *B* and compilation unit *B* has a **WITH** clause for compilation unit *C*, then *A* may or may not have a **WITH** clause for *C*. *A* must have its own **WITH** clause for *C* if it directly refers to facilities provided by *C*; otherwise, *A* need not have a **WITH** clause for *C*.

Compilation units (whether part of the same compilation or different compilations) may only be compiled in certain orders. The following three rules guarantee that information required for consistency checks is already in the program library when it is needed:

1. A library unit must be compiled before the corresponding body. Specifically, a package specification must be compiled before the corresponding package body, and a subprogram declaration, if it is compiled at all, must be compiled before the corresponding subprogram body.
2. A library unit must be compiled before any compilation unit naming that library unit in a **WITH** clause.
3. A parent unit must be compiled before any of its subunits.

Once a subprogram declaration or package specification has been compiled, the subprogram or package body and another unit using the subprogram or package can be compiled in any order. This facilitates independent implementation of a module and its "client modules" once the module's interface has been established. It also facilitates top-down programming, in which a unit's interface is established to provide an abstraction, the abstraction is used in implementing a high-level unit, and the abstraction is implemented later.

Whenever the three compilation-order rules require one unit to be compiled before another, recompilation of the first unit makes it necessary to recompile the second unit. Careful planning is required to design a program in which small changes will not necessitate recompilation of many units. Following the guidelines below will minimize the need for recompilation:

A program should have a hierarchical structure, with design decisions incorporated as low in the hierarchy as possible. More stable design decisions should be incorporated higher in the hierarchy than decisions that are likely candidates for change.

Declarations that can be placed in either a package specification or a package body should be placed in the package body.

Separately compiled subprograms should have separately compiled declarations, especially if the subprogram's interface is less likely to change than its body.

A **WITH** clause should be placed on a subprogram or package body rather than on a subprogram declaration or package specification if it is for a unit that is referred to only in the body.

If a **WITH** clause is needed only for a small part of a body, that part of the body should be broken off as a subunit, and the **WITH** clause should be moved to the subunit.

All the compilation units directly or indirectly used by a main program are elaborated before the main program begins execution. The compiler may choose the order in which these units are to be elaborated, provided that it is an order in which the units could legally have been compiled and provided that any unit named in a **WITH** clause for a subunit is elaborated before the parent unit. Sometimes a programmer must assert more control over the order of elaboration to ensure that a subprogram or package is not used before its body is elaborated. The pragma

```
PRAGMA Elaborate ( identifier , ~~~ , identifier ) ;
```

may be placed just after the context clause of a compilation unit to specify that, before the compilation unit is elaborated, the bodies of the library units named by the identifiers must be elaborated.

EXERCISES

13.1 Describe problems you have encountered combining separately compiled components of programs written in other languages. Would these problems have arisen if you had been using the Ada language? Why or why not?

13.2 Consider the following sequence of compilation units:

```
PACKAGE Unit_Alpha IS
  ...
END Unit_Alpha;
----------------------

WITH Unit_Alpha;
PROCEDURE Unit_Beta IS
  ...
END Unit_Beta;
----------------------

WITH Unit_Beta;
PACKAGE Unit_Gamma IS
  ...
END Unit_Gamma;
----------------------

WITH Unit_Alpha;
PACKAGE BODY Unit_Gamma IS
   PROCEDURE Unit_Delta IS SEPARATE;
  ...
END Unit_Gamma;
----------------------

SEPARATE (Unit_Gamma)
PROCEDURE Unit_Delta IS
  ...
END Unit_Delta;
```

In which compilation units is `Unit_Alpha` available for use? In which compilation units is `Unit_Beta` available for use?

13.3 Which of the compilation units in the previous problem are library units, and which are secondary units?

13.4 Section 13.2 presented a compilation culminating in the main subprogram Print_Inverse. Use separately compiled subprogram declarations to rewrite this in top-down order. You may abbreviate everything between the first IS and the last END in subprogram bodies, package specifications, and package bodies by ellipses ("...").

13.5 Write a compilation containing the procedures Process_Expression_List, Process_Expression, Process_Term, and Process_Factor of Section 9.4 as *library units*. You may replace the declarations and statements of each subprogram by ellipses.

13.6 Write a compilation containing the procedures Process_Expression, Process_Term, and Process_Factor of Section 9.4 *as subunits* of Process_Expression_List. You may replace the declarations and statements of each subprogram by ellipses.

13.7 You are given an input file of thirty-column lines. Each line corresponds to a one-way airline connection from one city to another. The city of origin is named in columns 1 through 15, and the destination city is named in columns 16 through 30. The connections are not listed in any particular order. There may be up to 100 cities named in all. You are to write a program producing two cross-references. The first cross-reference lists cities of origin in alphabetical order and, indented under each city of origin, lists the destinations that can be reached directly from that city in alphabetical order. The second cross-reference lists destination cities in alphabetical order and, indented under each destination city, lists the cities from which that destination can be reached in alphabetical order.

Your solution should be a single compilation, divided into compilation units as you see fit, with or without subunits. Your program should include at least the following components:

A package City_Name_Package providing only a subtype City_Name_Subtype and a type City_Name_List_Type. City_Name_Subtype is a subtype of type String with the index constraint (1 .. 15). City_Name_List_Type is a record type with two components: an integer giving the length of the list and an array of 100 City_Name_Subtype components giving the members of the list.

A procedure Sort_City_Name_List that puts the City_Name_List_Type value passed to it in alphabetical order.

A package City_Number_Package providing an integer type City_Number_Type with values from one to 100 and two subprograms. Internally, this package maintains a one-to-one correspondence between City_Name_Subtype values and City_Number_Type values. The function City_Number takes a City_Name_Subtype value and returns the corresponding City_Number_Type value, assigning a new one if the city name has not been encountered before. The procedure Obtain_Alphabetized_List, implemented by calling Sort_City_Name_List, sets its parameter to an alphabetized city name list containing all the cities with which City_Number has been called.

A package Connection_Package providing two subprograms and maintaining a record of connections between cities. The procedure Record_Connection takes two City_Name_Subtype values and establishes a connection between the two cities. The function Connection_Exists takes two City_Name_Subtype values and returns a Boolean value indicating whether there is a connection from the first city specified to the second. Internally, connection data can be modelled by a two-dimensional array of Boolean components, indexed in each dimension by City_Number_Type values.

A procedure Process_Input_Data that reads the input file and makes appropriate calls on Connection_Package.Record_Connection.

A procedure List_By_Origin that takes a complete alphabetized city name list as a parameter and produces the first cross-reference listing.

A procedure List_By_Destination that takes a complete alphabetized city name list as a parameter and produces the second cross-reference listing.

The main procedure. This procedure simply calls each of the procedures Process_Input_Data, City_Number_Package.Obtain_Alphabetized_List, List_By_Origin, and List_By_Destination in turn.

13.8 Consider the following legal compilation order for the compilation units of the matrix inversion program:

1. `Matrix_Package` specification
2. `Matrix_Package` body
3. `Matrix_IO_Package` specification
4. `Invert_Matrix`
5. `Matrix_IO_Package` body
6. `Print_Inverse`

Assuming that `Type_Float_IO_Package` had not been previously compiled, insert the specification of `Type_Float_IO_Package` in this list in every way possible.

13.9 Draw a diagram similar to Figures 13.1 and 13.2 indicating the compilation order restrictions on the following eleven compilation units:

```
PACKAGE Package_1 IS
   ...
END Package_1;

PACKAGE Package_2 IS
   ...
END Package_2;

WITH Package_1;
PACKAGE BODY Package_2 IS
   ...
END Package_2;

WITH Package_1;
PACKAGE Package_3 IS
   ...
END Package_3;

WITH Package_1;
PROCEDURE Procedure_1 ( ... ) IS
   ...
END Procedure_1;

PROCEDURE Procedure_2 ( ... );

WITH Package_2;
PROCEDURE Procedure_2 ( ... ) IS
   ...
END Procedure_2;

PROCEDURE Procedure_3 IS
   FUNCTION Function_1 ( ... ) RETURN ... IS SEPARATE;
   FUNCTION Function_2 ( ... ) RETURN ... IS SEPARATE;
   FUNCTION Function_3 ( ... ) RETURN ... IS SEPARATE;
   ...
BEGIN
   ...
END Procedure_3;

WITH Procedure_1, Procedure_2;
SEPARATE (Procedure_3)
FUNCTION Function_1 ( ... ) RETURN ... IS
   ...
END Function_1;
```

```
WITH Procedure_2;
SEPARATE (Procedure_3)
FUNCTION Function_2 ( ... ) RETURN ... IS
   ...
END Function_2;

WITH Package_3;
SEPARATE (Procedure_3)
FUNCTION Function_3 ( ... ) RETURN ... IS
   ...
END Function_3;
```

13.10 Which of the compilation units in Exercise 13.9 would have to be recompiled after recompilation of

(*a*) the `Package_1` specification?
(*b*) the `Package_2` body?
(*c*) the `Package_3` specification?
(*d*) the `Procedure_1` body?
(*e*) the `Procedure_2` body?
(*f*) the `Function_1` body?

CHAPTER

FOURTEEN

SCOPE AND VISIBILITY

The purpose of this chapter is not to introduce new Ada language features, but to formalize certain rules that have been presented only informally until now. These rules concern where in a program you can refer to declared names and how the Ada language associates each occurrence of an identifier with a particular declaration. By now you should have an intuitive understanding of these issues, and that will make it easy to learn the specific rules. Knowing the rules, in turn, will help you avoid confusion and answer difficult questions.

The formalism presented here is not the same as that presented in the reference manual giving the standard definition of the Ada language. Chapter 8 of the *Ada Language Reference Manual* provides a concise and mathematically elegant definition of these rules, but one that is not intuitive from a programmer's point of view. Furthermore, the standard rules refer to features of the language—principally generic units and tasks—that we have not yet covered. We provide a longer set of rules, but one that should make it easier for a programmer to find answers to specific practical questions. Because we are using a different formalism, there may be subtle differences between the rules presented here and those presented in the *Ada Language Reference Manual.* Any such differences should occur only in very unusual circumstances not likely to arise in most programs. In such circumstances, of course, it is the rules in the *Ada Language Reference Manual* that apply.

A declaration in a program may have an effect in certain parts of the program but not in others. For example, a variable declared in the declarative part of a subprogram body may have an effect any place in the subprogram after its declaration, but it never has any effect outside the subprogram. The part of the program in which a declaration has an effect is called the *scope of the declaration.*

Although scope is defined in terms of declarations, it is sometimes more convenient to talk about the *scope of an entity,* such as a parameter or a type, introduced by a declaration. The scope of such an entity is therefore defined to be identical to the scope of the declaration introducing the entity. For example, the scope of a variable *declaration* in a subprogram body extends from the declaration to the end of the subprogram, and so does the scope of the *variable* being declared.

Within the scope of a declaration associating a certain identifier with a certain entity, there may be places where the identifier does not refer to that entity. Consider the following program, which adds up the ASCII codes of all the characters in the standard input file and prints their sum, assuming that no line in the input file contains more than 132 characters:

```
WITH Basic_IO; USE Basic_IO;
PROCEDURE Sum_ASCII_Codes IS
   Sum    : Natural := 0;
   Length : Natural;
   Line   : String (1 .. 132);

   FUNCTION Line_Sum (Line : IN String) RETURN Natural IS
      Result : Natural := 0;
   BEGIN  -- Line_Sum
      FOR i IN Line'Range LOOP
         Result := Result + Character'Pos ( Line(i) );
      END LOOP;
      RETURN Result;
   END Line_Sum;

BEGIN  -- Sum_ASCII_Codes
   WHILE NOT End_Of_File LOOP
      Get_Line (Line, Length);
      Sum := Sum + Line_Sum (Line => Line (1 .. Length));
   END LOOP;

   Put (Sum);
   New_Line;

END Sum_ASCII_Codes;
```

Of particular interest is the function call on `Line_Sum`:

```
Line_Sum (Line => Line (1 .. Length))
```

This call states that the value of the *formal parameter* `Line` is given by a slice of the *variable* `Line` declared just before the `Line_Sum` function body. Although the function call occurs within the scope of the variable, the first occurrence of the identifier `Line` inside the function call does not refer to the variable, but to the formal parameter. A declaration is defined to be *visible* at those places in its scope where an occurrence of the identifier may refer to the entity introduced by the declaration. For example, the declaration of `Line` as a variable is visible from just after the declaration to the end of `Sum_ASCII_Codes`, except within the `Line_Sum` function body and in the part of the `Line_Sum` function call between the left parenthesis and the `=>` symbol. As with the scope rules, we say that an *entity* is visible at those places where its *declaration* is visible. For example, the variable `Line` is visible at the same places as its declaration.

All questions about where an identifier may occur and what its meaning is at a given point in a program can be answered in terms of these two fundamental concepts—scope and visibility. Section 14.1 gives the rules determining the scope of a declaration. Section 14.2 gives the rules determining where within its scope a declaration is visible. There are no special rules for separately compiled subunits. The scope and visibility rules for a separately compiled subunit are precisely the same as if the subunit were actually nested at the place where its body stub appears.

14.1 SCOPE RULES

Subprogram bodies, package bodies, and block statements may all have declarative parts consisting of zero or more declarations. The scope of each such declaration extends from the beginning of the declaration to the end of the subprogram body, package body, or block statement. For example, in `Sum_ASCII_Codes`, the scope of the declaration of `Length` extends from the beginning of the declaration to the end of the `Sum_ASCII_Codes` procedure body; the declaration of `Result` extends from the beginning of that declaration to the end of the `Line_Sum` function body.

From now on, we shall call a subprogram body, package body, or block statement the *enclosing frame* of each declaration occurring in its declarative part. Thus the `Sum_ASCII_Codes` procedure body is the enclosing frame of the declarations of variables `Sum`, `Line`, and `Length`; the `Line_Sum` function body is the enclosing frame of the declaration of `Result`. The scope rule stated above can be restated as follows:

Scope Rule 1:

The scope of a declaration in a declarative part extends from the beginning of that declaration to the end of its enclosing frame.

As explained in Section 9.4, mutual recursion sometimes makes it necessary to include a *subprogram declaration* (containing the information that precedes the word `IS` in a subprogram body) in a declarative part. A subprogram declaration occurring in a declarative part obeys Scope Rule 1 just like any other declaration. It has a scope extending from the beginning of the declaration to the end of its enclosing frame.

When a declarative part contains a subprogram body but not a corresponding subprogram declaration, the body itself acts as a declaration of the subprogram, and it has the same scope that it would have had if the subprogram body had been a *bona fide* subprogram declaration instead. That is, the scope of a subprogram body acting as a subprogram declaration extends from the beginning of the subprogram body to the end of its enclosing frame. Again, we are just applying Scope Rule 1. The `Line_Sum` function body acts as a function declaration occurring in the declarative part of `Sum_ASCII_Codes`. The scope of this pseudo-declaration extends from its beginning (i.e., the beginning of the function body) to the end of its enclosing frame (i.e., the end of the `Sum_ASCII_Codes` procedure body).

A package specification occurring in a declarative part is considered to be one of declarative part's declarations. Therefore, Scope Rule 1 applies to package specifications. In the package below, the Account_Number_Package specification is one of the declarations in the declarative part of the Account_Package body. Therefore, the scope of the Account_Number_Package specification extends from the beginning of the Account_Number_Package specification to the end of the Account_Package body. Because a package is declared by its package specification, the *scope of a package* is the same as the scope of its package specification.

```
PACKAGE Account_Package IS

   TYPE Account_Type IS PRIVATE;

   PROCEDURE Start_New_Account
      (Opening_Balance : IN Integer := 0;
       New_Account     : OUT Account_Type);

   PROCEDURE Change_Balance
      (Account : IN OUT Account_Type; Change : IN Integer) IS

   PROCEDURE Report_Account_Status
      (Account         : IN Account_Type;
       Account_Number  : OUT Positive;
       Account_Balance : OUT Integer);

PRIVATE

   TYPE Account_Type IS
      RECORD
         Account_Number_Part : Positive;
         Balance_Part        : Integer;
      END RECORD;

END Account_Package;


PACKAGE BODY Account_Package IS


   PACKAGE Account_Number_Package IS

      PROCEDURE Get_Next_Account_Number
         (Account_Number : OUT Positive);

   END Account_Number_Package;


   PACKAGE BODY Account_Number_Package IS

      Counter: Natural := 0;

      PROCEDURE Get_Next_Account_Number
         (Account_Number : OUT Positive) IS

      BEGIN

         Counter := Counter + 1;
         Account_Number := Counter;

      END Get_Next_Account_Number;

   END Account_Number_Package;
```

```
      PROCEDURE Start_New_Account
         (Opening_Balance : IN Integer := 0;
          New_Account     : OUT Account_Type) IS

         Next_Account_Number : Positive;

      BEGIN

         Account_Number_Package.Get_Next_Account_Number
            (Next_Account_Number);

         New_Account :=
            (Account_Number_Part => Next_Account_Number,
             Balance_Part        => Opening_Balance);

      END Start_New_Account;


      PROCEDURE Change_Balance
          (Account : IN OUT Account_Type; Change : IN Integer) IS

      BEGIN
         Account.Balance_Part :=
            Account.Balance_Part + Change;
      END Change_Balance;


      PROCEDURE Report_Account_Status
         (Account         : IN Account_Type;
          Account_Number  : OUT Positive;
          Account_Balance : OUT Integer) IS

      BEGIN

         Account_Number := Account.Account_Number_Part;
         Account_Balance := Account.Balance_Part;

      END Report_Account_Status;

   END Account_Package;
```

Certain declarations introduce several identifiers at once—the name of the *principal entity* being declared and the names of *auxiliary* entities that "come along with" the principal entity. The principal entity declared by a record-type declaration is the record type itself, and the auxiliary entities are the record components. The principal entity declared by an enumeration-type declaration is the enumeration type itself, and the auxiliary entities are the type's enumeration literals. The principal entity declared by a subprogram declaration, or by a subprogram body acting as a subprogram declaration, is the subprogram itself; the auxiliary entities are formal parameters, which can be used outside the subprogram in subprogram calls with named parameter associations. The principal entity, and usually the only entity, declared by a private-type declaration is the private type itself, but if the private type has discriminants then the discriminants are auxiliary entities declared by the same declaration. Perhaps most importantly, the primary entity declared by a package specification is the package itself, and the auxiliary entities are the entities declared in the visible part of the package specification for use outside the package.

Each of these declarations declaring a principal entity shall be called a *principal declaration*. The part of a principal declaration declaring a particular auxiliary entity shall be called an *auxiliary declaration*. Record-component declarations, discriminant specifications, enumeration literals listed in an enumeration-type declaration, formal parameter specifications, and all declarations listed in the visible part of a package specification are auxiliary declarations.

In the procedure `Sum_ASCII_Codes`, the scope of the formal parameter `Line` begins with the parameter specification of `Line_Sum` and includes the rest of the scope of that function, in other words, the rest of the `Sum_ASCII_Codes` procedure body. The formal parameter `Line` may appear in a named parameter association anywhere within this scope. The scopes of other auxiliary entities work in the same way:

Scope Rule 2:

The scope of an auxiliary declaration starts at the beginning of the auxiliary declaration and includes the rest of the scope of the enclosing principal declaration.

Most of the time, the enclosing principal declaration occurs in a declarative part, so its scope is given by Scope Rule 1. Then the scope of the auxiliary declaration starts at the beginning of the auxiliary declaration and extends to the end of the enclosing frame of the enclosing principal declaration. For example, when a record-type declaration occurs in the declarative part of a subprogram body, the scope of each of its component declarations starts at the beginning of that component declaration and extends to the end of the subprogram body. (The subprogram body is the enclosing frame of the record-type declaration, and the record-type declaration is the principal declaration enclosing the auxiliary component declaration.)

The scope of the enclosing principal declaration is not given by Scope Rule 1 when the principal declaration is a separately compiled subprogram or package. Scope Rule 1 gives the scope of an entity declared in a declarative part. A separate rule is needed for entities whose declarations are compilation units:

Scope Rule 3:

The scope of a separately compiled package specification or subprogram declaration includes (a) that package or subprogram declaration itself, (b) the corresponding package body or subprogram body, and (c) any other compilation unit listing that package or subprogram in a `WITH` clause.

Let us assume that there is another compilation unit named `Main_Program` beginning with the context specification `WITH Account_Package;`. By Scope Rule 3, the scope of the `Account_Package` specification includes the `Account_Package` specification itself, the `Account_Package` body, and the compilation unit Main_Program. Since the Change_Balance procedure declaration is an auxiliary declaration of the package specification, its scope includes the portion of the Account_Package specification from the beginning of the procedure declaration to the end of the package specification, all of the Account_Package body, and all of Main_Program. The parameter specification for Change is, in turn, an auxiliary declaration of the Change_Balance procedure declaration. By Scope Rule 2, the scope of a parameter specification starts at the beginning of the parameter specification and includes the rest of the scope of Change_Balance. Specifically, the scope of the parameter specification includes the remaining part of the procedure declaration, the part of the Account_Package specification following the declaration of Change_Balance, the Account_Package body, and the compilation unit Main_Program.

Scope Rule 2 covers declarations in the visible part of a package specification, but not the private part. A separate rule is needed for the private part:

Scope Rule 4:

The scope of a declaration in the private part of a package specification extends from the beginning of that declaration to the end of the package specification and also includes the entire package body.

When an entity such as a private type or constant is declared in both the visible part and the private part of a package specification, the *scope of the entity* means the scope of the declaration in the visible part. In the case of a private type with discriminants, the discriminants are declared by the discriminant specifications in the visible part.

A loop parameter is implicitly declared by the iteration scheme of a FOR loop. This implicit declaration applies only within the loop itself. Thus we have the following rule:

Scope Rule 5:

The scope of the implicit declaration of a loop parameter extends from the appearance of the loop parameter in the iteration scheme of a FOR loop to the end of the LOOP statement.

Finally, a variation on Scope Rule 1 is needed to define the scope of a block name, loop name, or statement label. First, we extend the definition of *enclosing frame* to apply to statements as well as to declarations. Thus a subprogram body, package body, or block statement is considered the enclosing frame of each statement in its sequence of statements. The rule is as follows:

Scope Rule 6:

The scope of a block name, loop name, or statement label is the entire sequence of statements of the enclosing frame.

14.2 VISIBILITY RULES

The scope of a declaration does not tell us everything we want to know about occurrences of declared identifiers. For example, in `Sum_ASCII_Codes`, the scope of the variable `Line` and the formal parameter `Line` overlap. The scope of the formal parameter `Line` extends from the beginning of the parameter specification in the `Line_Sum` function body to the end of the `Sum_ASCII_Codes` procedure body, and this is also part of the scope of the variable `Line`. It is the visibility rules that tell us that all occurrences of the identifier `Line` in the `Line_Sum` function body refer to the parameter; that all occurrences of that identifier in the `Sum_ASCII_Codes` sequence of statements, except to the left of the `=>` symbol in the named parameter association, refer to the variable; and that the occurrence to the left of the `=>` refers to the formal parameter.

A declaration for a given identifier is *visible* at those places in the program where an occurrence of the identifier could correspond to that declaration. A declaration can only be visible at certain places within its scope. Section 14.2.3 gives the rules determining where within its scope a declaration is visible. The visibility rules, together with the rules for resolving overloading, uniquely determine the meaning of an identifier occurring at a particular place in a program.

We must deal with some preliminaries before we get to the actual rules. Section 14.2.1 addresses the relationship between the visibility rules and the rules for resolving overloading. Section 14.2.2 addresses the effect of nesting a declaration inside the scope of another declaration for the same identifier.

14.2.1 Visibility and Overloading

In the absence of overloading, the visibility rules determine a unique meaning for an occurrence of an identifier. If the identifier is overloaded, the visibility rules may determine several possible meanings as versions of overloaded subprograms or enumeration literals. The rules of overloading resolution are then applied to determine which of the meanings allowed by the visibility rules is the correct meaning.

Specifically, two declarations for the same identifier are *mutually exclusive according to the visibility rules* unless the declarations are as subprograms or enumeration literals and the declarations have different parameter and result type profiles. (Parameter and result type profiles were defined in Section 9.5.) When these conditions hold, the visibility rules classify both declarations as giving possible meanings for the identifier, and the overloading resolution rules select one of these meanings.

(Declarations that are mutually exclusive according to the visibility rules are called *homographs* of each other. In its ordinary English sense, a homograph is a word with two unrelated meanings. For example, the word *saw* is a homograph because it is both the name of a tool and the past tense of *see*. In the Ada language, two declarations are homographs of each other if they are different declarations with the same identifier and, in the case of subprograms and enumeration literals, the same parameter and result type profiles.)

14.2.2 Nesting and Hiding

The Ada language provides several ways to nest one declaration inside the scope of another declaration for the same identifier. A declarative part may contain subprogram bodies or package bodies with their own declarative parts, and the sequence of statements associated with a declarative part may contain a block statement with its own declarative part and sequence of statements. Nesting may be several levels deep. The inner declaration's enclosing frame may be directly or indirectly surrounded by the outer declaration's enclosing frame.

When one declaration is nested inside the scope of another declaration for the same identifier and the two declarations are mutually exclusive according to the visibility rules, the inner declaration *hides* the outer one. This means that within the scope of the inner declaration, except in certain specific contexts to be described later, an occurrence of the identifier refers to the meaning given by the inner declaration. When one declaration is nested inside the scope of another declaration for the same identifier and the two declarations are *not* mutually exclusive according to the visibility rules, the two declarations must be for subprograms or enumeration literals with different parameter and result type profiles. Then the inner declaration *overloads* the outer declaration throughout the scope of the inner declaration.

The following artificial program illustrates these rules:

```
PROCEDURE Main IS

   Score   : Integer;
   Inverse : Float;

   FUNCTION One_More (x : Integer) RETURN Integer IS
   BEGIN
      RETURN x + 1;
   END One_More;

   FUNCTION Mean (x, y : Float) RETURN Float IS
   BEGIN
      RETURN (x + y) / 2.0;
   END Mean;

   FUNCTION Abs_Sum (x, y : Integer) RETURN Integer IS
   BEGIN
      RETURN ABS (x + y);
   END Abs_Sum;

BEGIN -- Main

   Block:
      DECLARE

         Score    : Float;
         One_More : Integer;

         FUNCTION Inverse (x : Float) RETURN Float IS
         BEGIN
            RETURN 1.0 / x;
         END Inverse;
```

```
            FUNCTION Mean (x, y, z : Float) RETURN Float IS
            BEGIN
               RETURN (x + y + z) / 3.0;
            END Mean;

            FUNCTION Abs_Sum (m, n : Integer) RETURN Integer IS
            BEGIN
               RETURN ABS m + ABS n;
            END Abs_Sum;
         BEGIN -- Block
            NULL; -- Point 1
         END Block;
      -- Point 2
   END Main;
```

The sequence of statements for this program consists of one block statement, whose own sequence of statements consists of one `NULL` statement. This program does nothing but illustrate the rules for nested scopes. Comments in the program designate one point as Point 1 and another as Point 2. Point 1 is within the scope of each declaration in the main program's declarative part and also within the scope of each declaration in the block statement's declarative part. The identifiers `Score`, `Inverse`, `One_More`, `Mean`, and `Abs_Sum` are each declared in both the main program's declarative part and the block statement's declarative part. Point 2 is within the scope only of the declarations in the main program's declarative part.

The inner and outer declarations of `Score` are mutually exclusive according to the visibility rules, so the inner declaration hides the outer one within the block statement. The same applies to the inner and outer declarations of `Inverse` and the inner and outer declarations of `One_More`. The inner and outer declarations of `Mean` are for functions with different numbers of parameters, so they are not mutually exclusive according to the visibility rules; within the block statement, the two versions of `Mean` are overloaded. In contrast, the inner and outer declarations of `Abs_Sum` are for two different functions with the same parameter and result type profile, so they are mutually exclusive (even though they have different formal parameter names); the inner declaration of `Abs_Sum` hides the outer one within the block statement.

Consequently, occurrences of the identifiers `Score`, `Inverse`, `One_More`, and `Abs_Sum` refer to the inner declarations at Point 1, except in certain specific contexts. Occurrences of these identifiers refer to the outer declarations at Point 2. A call on `Mean` refers to the outer version at Point 2. It may refer to either version at Point 1, depending on the number of formal parameters.

The hiding rules of the Ada language are similar to those of PL/I and Pascal, with the notable difference of allowing overloading. There is another difference as well. The Ada language provides a mechanism for overriding hiding and letting the programmer refer to the outer meaning of an identifier within the scope of the inner declaration. That mechanism is the *expanded name.*

We have already seen another use of expanded names—to refer outside of a package to entities declared in that package's visible part. If *p* is the name of the package and *e* is the name of the entity, then the entity may be referred to outside the package by the expanded name *p.e*. The other use of expanded names is quite different. If *e* is the name of some declared entity and *f* is the name of the declaration's enclosing frame (either a subprogram body, a package body, or a named block statement), then the entity may be referred to *within that enclosing frame* by the expanded name *f.e*, even where the name *e*, occurring by itself, would be hidden by an inner declaration.

The expanded names `Main.Score`, `Main.Inverse`, `Main.One_More`, and `Main.Abs_Sum` can be used at Point 1 to name the entities declared in the declarative part of `Main`. It is also possible to refer to `Main.Mean` there, but this is unnecessary since the outer declaration of `Mean` is not hidden by the inner one. (However, if the third parameter of the inner version of `Mean` were given a default value, then a call on `Mean` with two actual parameters could be a call on either version of `Mean`. The overloading resolution rules would be unable to identify uniquely the version being called. The expanded name `Main.Mean` could be used to uniquely identify the outer version and avoid the need to resolve overloading.) It is also possible to use the expanded names `Block.Score`, `Block.Inverse`, `Block.One_More`, `Block.Abs_Sum`, and `Block.Mean` at Point 1 to refer to the entities declared in the block statement. The first four of these expanded names have precisely the same meanings at Point 1 as the simple names `Score`, `Inverse`, `One_More`, and `Abs_Sum`, respectively. In contrast to the simple name `Mean`, which can name either of two overloaded functions at Point 1, the expanded name `Block.Mean` uniquely identifies the inner version (and makes it unnecessary to resolve overloading).

An expanded name beginning with the name of a subprogram can be used within the subprogram body to name not only entities declared in the declarative part of a subprogram body, but also the subprogram's formal parameters. An expanded name beginning with a package name can be used within the package to name not only entities declared in the declarative part of a package body, but also entities declared in either the visible part or the private part of the package specification. Within a named `FOR` loop, an expanded name beginning with the name of the loop can be used to name the loop parameter. Unless *f* is the name of a package and *e* is the name of an entity declared in the visible part of that package, an expanded name of the form *f.e* can only occur somewhere *inside* a construct named *f*.

In practice, hiding should generally be avoided because it is confusing to the program reader. It is especially confusing when a program refers to a hidden outer entity in an inner scope. A programmer does not lose any expressive power by choosing new names for inner declarations. In programs that are free of hiding, of course, there is no need for the kind of expanded names we have just discussed.

14.2.3 Direct Visibility and Visibility by Selection

We now come to the rules determining where a declaration is visible. These rules determine the meaning of an identifier occurring at a particular point in a program. If only one declaration of the identifier is visible at that point, the meaning of the identifier is given by that declaration; if more than onc declaration of the identifier is visible at that point, the declarations must be for overloaded subprograms or enumeration literals, and the meaning of the identifier is that determined by resolving the overloading.

In some cases, declarations are *directly visible* throughout certain portions of a program. In other cases, declarations can be made *visible by selection* when they appear in certain specific contexts. A declaration can only be visible, either directly or by selection, within its scope. The first seven rules that follow stipulate when various kinds of declarations are directly visible; the next five describe the contexts in which certain kinds of entities are visible by selection; the last rule, given in Section 14.2.4, describes how USE clauses make certain declarations directly visible instead of visible by selection.

Visibility Rule 1:

A declaration in a declarative part is directly visible from the end of the declaration to the end of its enclosing frame, except where it is hidden by an inner declaration.

A declaration in a declarative part may be for a variable, constant, named number, type, or subtype, for example. It may also be a subprogram declaration, a subprogram body acting as a subprogram declaration, or a package specification declaring a package. Visibility Rule 1 explains why, when a declaration occurs in some declarative part, the declared identifier may usually be used in the remaining portion of the declarative part and in the corresponding sequence of statements to refer to the declared entity. It explains, for example, why the occurrences of the identifier `Result` in the assignment and `RETURN` statements of `Line_Sum` refer to the variable declared in the `Line_Sum` function body's declarative part.

Even though Scope Rule 1 stipulated that the *scope* of a declaration in a declarative part starts at the *beginning* of a declaration, Visibility Rule 1 states that the declaration is not *visible* until just *after* its declaration. It follows, for example, that the second of the following two declarations is not legal:

```
TYPE Integer_List_Type IS ARRAY (1 .. 10) OF Integer;
Counts : Integer_List_Type := (Counts'Range => 0);
   -- ILLEGAL REFERENCE TO Counts!
```

Because the identifier `Counts` is not visible until the end of the declaration, it cannot be used in the initial value part of the declaration. The declaration can be made legal by replacing `Counts'Range` with `Integer_List_Type'Range`, for example.

Enumeration literals appearing in an enumeration-type declaration are treated as if they were declarations in their own right appearing in the same context as the enumeration-type declaration. Thus the literals of an enumeration type declared in a declarative part may be used, except where hidden, throughout the rest of the declarative part and throughout the corresponding sequence of statements, just like the name of the enumeration type.

The following rule determines where subprogram formal parameters are directly visible:

Visibility Rule 2:

A parameter specification in a subprogram declaration (or, in the absence of a subprogram declaration, in a subprogram body) is directly visible throughout the subprogram's body, except where it is hidden by an inner declaration.

Visibility Rule 2 explains why the identifier `Line` may be used in the `Line_Sum` function body to refer to the formal parameter `Line`. (Even though the scope of the outer declaration for the variable `Line` includes all of the `Line_Sum` function body, the outer declaration is hidden in this part of its scope by the parameter specification declaring `Line` as a formal parameter. Therefore, Visibility Rule 1 does not apply to the variable `Line` within the `Line_Sum` function body.)

The following rule determines where declarations in a package specification are directly visible:

Visibility Rule 3:

A declaration in either the visible part or the private part of a package specification is directly visible from the end of the declaration to the end of the package specification and also throughout the package body, except where hidden by an inner declaration.

Visibility Rule 3 explains why the identifier `Account_Type`, declared in the `Account_Package` specification, may be referred to in the remainder of the specification and throughout the `Account_Package` body. It does *not* explain why the declared type may be referred to outside the package by the name `Account_Package.Account_Type`; that is explained by Visibility Rule 8. When an enumeration type is declared in a package specification, the visibility of its literals within the package is determined by Visibility Rule 3.

The following rule is required so that discriminants may be referred to in the declaration of other record components.

Visibility Rule 4:

A discriminant specification occurring in a record-type declaration is directly visible from just after the discriminant specification to the end of the record-type declaration.

A library unit acts as a declaration of a separately compiled program component. The direct visibility of this declaration is given by the following rule:

Visibility Rule 5:

A separately compiled package specification or subprogram declaration (or, in the absence of a separate subprogram declaration, a subprogram body acting as a declaration) is directly visible throughout any compilation unit naming that subprogram or package in a `WITH` clause, except where it is hidden by an inner declaration.

Visibility Rule 5 determines the visibility of the name of the separately compiled unit itself. It does not determine, for example, the visibility of declarations *provided by* a separately compiled package specification. (Visibility Rules 8 and 13 do that.) It is Visibility Rule 5 that allows us to call a separately compiled subprogram after we have named it in a `WITH` clause. It is Visibility Rule 5 that allows us to name a separately compiled package in a `USE` clause or to the *left* of the period in an expanded name after we have named it in a `WITH` clause.

The last two rules for direct visibility deal with implicit declarations that are not covered by any of the previous rules:

Visibility Rule 6:

A loop parameter is directly visible throughout its loop, except where hidden by an inner declaration.

Visibility Rule 7:

A block name, loop name, or statement label is directly visible throughout the sequence of statements of the enclosing frame, except where it is hidden by an inner declaration.

Visibility Rule 7 is misleading. It states that *in theory* a block name or loop name could be referred to anywhere in the sequence of statements of the frame enclosing the block or loop. In fact, the Ada language provides no opportunity to refer to such a name except within the block or loop itself.

The rules for direct visibility all describe a portion of a program in which a declaration is directly visible unless it is hidden. The rules for visibility by selection, given below, deal with individual occurrences of identifiers in specific contexts. A declaration which would otherwise be directly visible is hidden in a context where another declaration for the same identifier is visible by selection. In other words, the rules for visibility by selection override the rules for direct visibility given above.

Visibility Rule 8:

A declaration in the visible part of a package specification is visible by selection just after the dot in an expanded name of the form *p*.__, where *p* is a name denoting the package.

Visibility Rule 8 explains why the name `Account_Type` may appear in the context

```
Count_Package.Account_Type
```

and the name `Start_New_Account` may appear in the context

```
Account_Package.Start_New_Account
```

(The specification of `Account_Package` is given in Section 14.1.)

Visibility Rule 9:

A parameter specification is visible by selection just before the => symbol in a named parameter association of a call on the corresponding subprogram.

Visibility Rule 9 explains why a formal parameter name may appear in a named subprogram call. For example, the formal parameter `New_Account` is visible by selection in the subprogram call

```
Start_New_Account (New_Account => Cash_Account);
```

(Despite its name, visibility *by selection* occurs not only in selected components, but in other contexts as well.)

Visibility Rule 10:

A record-component declaration is visible by selection just after the period in a selected name of the form *r*.__, where *r* is a value or object belonging to the corresponding record type. It is also visible by selection in the component list of a record aggregate (see Section 8.1.5).

Given the record-type declaration

```
TYPE Account_Type IS
   RECORD
      Account_Number_Part : Positive;
      Balance_Part        : Integer;
   END RECORD;
```

and a variable `Account` of type `Account_Type`, for example, the record component name `Balance_Part` is visible by selection in the selected component

```
Account.Balance_Part
```

and in the record aggregate

```
(Account_Number_Part => New_Account_Number,
 Balance_Part        => New_Balance)
```

A discriminant acts both as an ordinary record component and as a "formal parameter" of a type. Thus the visibility rule for discriminant specifications combines elements of Visibility Rule 9 and Visibility Rule 10:

Visibility Rule 11:

A discriminant specification is visible by selection at the same places as a component declaration for an ordinary record component, and also just before the => symbol in a discriminant constraint applied to the corresponding record type.

Finally, we need a rule to cover the use of expanded names introduced in Section 14.2.2, to override hiding.

Visibility Rule 12:

Any declaration occurring in the declarative part of a subprogram body, package body, or named block statement, in the formal parameter list of a subprogram declaration or body, or in the visible or private part of a package specification is visible by selection just after the dot in an expanded name of the form *n*.__ **occurring** *inside* **the subprogram, package, or block statement, where** *n* **names the subprogram, package, or block statement. Similarly, the implicit declaration of the loop parameter of a named FOR loop is visible by selection just after the dot in an expanded name of the form** *n*.__ **occurring** *inside* **the FOR loop, where** *n* **is the name of the FOR loop.**

14.2.4 The Effect of USE Clauses

We need one more visibility rule to explain the effect of USE clauses. A USE clause makes certain entities directly visible which would otherwise only be visible by selection. That is, an entity which otherwise could only be referred to by the name *p*.e can be referred to simply as *e*. The entities made directly visible by a USE clause are declared in the specifications of the packages named in the USE clause.

The part of a program in which a USE clause has an effect is called the *scope of the* USE *clause*. The scope of a USE clause occurring in a declarative part extends from just after the USE clause to the end of the enclosing frame. The scope of a USE clause occurring in a package specification extends from just after the USE clause to the end of the specification and also throughout the package body. The scope of a USE clause appearing in a context clause of a compilation unit extends from just after the USE clause to the end of the compilation unit; if the compilation unit is a subprogram declaration or package specification, the scope of the USE clause also includes the separately compiled body.

Visibility Rule 13:

A declaration in the visible part of a package specification is directly visible within the scope of a USE clause naming the package except at places where one of the following conditions holds:

(a) There is another declaration for the same identifier that is already directly visible and would be hidden if the declaration in the package specification were made directly visible.

(b) The place is in the scope of a `USE` clause naming some other package whose visible part has another declaration of the same identifier, and the two declarations are mutually exclusive according to the visibility rules.

Informally, condition (a) states that `USE` clauses never override local declarations, and condition (b) states that when two `USE` clauses clash over a given identifier, neither `USE` clause applies to that identifier. If subprograms to be made directly visible by two `USE` clauses can be overloaded, the `USE` clauses are not considered to clash over the name of those subprograms.

14.3 THE PACKAGE `Standard`

There is one predefined package that was not included in the list of predefined packages in Section 11.9, the package `Standard`. `Standard` is an imaginary package whose body is presumed to surround every compilation unit as it is compiled. The `Standard` package specification contains, among other things, all the declarations of predefined types and subtypes and their operations. For example, the predefined types `Integer` and `Float`, the predefined subtypes `Natural` and `Positive`, and the predefined type `String` are all declared in `Standard`. The predefined versions of `"+"` and `"-"` taking two `Integer` operands and returning an `Integer` result are also declared in `Standard`.

This formulation allows the scope and visibility rules to be applied to the predefined identifiers. A compilation unit is presumed to be nested inside the `Standard` package body. Thus each compilation unit is within the scope of each predefined declaration. Furthermore, each predefined declaration is directly visible throughout each compilation unit, except where it is hidden by an inner declaration. Any declaration in a compilation unit, including the compilation unit itself, is an "inner declaration" in this sense.

A program may contain its own declaration for the identifier `Integer` (although this is obviously a reprehensible programming practice). This declaration hides the outer—that is, the predefined—declaration of the type `Integer`. The function declaration

```
FUNCTION "+" (Left, Right : Integer) RETURN Integer;
```

hides one of the predefined meanings of the + operator, while the function declaration

```
FUNCTION "+" (Left : Integer; Right : Float) RETURN Float;
```

overloads the predefined meanings. (These declarations of `"+"` must occur *inside* some other compilation unit, since library functions may not overload operators.)

A hidden predefined declaration can still be referred to by an expanded name beginning with the name of the enclosing program unit directly containing the hidden declaration—that is, with the name `Standard`. Thus (unless the name `Standard` itself has been redeclared), the expanded name `Standard.Integer` refers to the predefined type `Integer`, even where the simple name `Integer` has been hidden by another declaration; if `A` and `B` belong to this predefined type, the function call `Standard."+" (A, B)` applies the predefined version of `Integer` addition to `A` and `B`, even if that version of `"+"` has been hidden.

Formally, the effect of a `WITH` clause is to add previously compiled library units to the `Standard` package body, before the place at which the current compilation unit occurs. Previously compiled units are placed in `Standard` in an order consistent with their own `WITH` clauses. Given this model, Scope Rule 3 and Visibility Rule 5 are unnecessary. The scope and visibility of separate compilation units follow directly from the other scope and visibility rules.

The package `ASCII` is not a library package, but nested in the `Standard` package specification. This is why a `WITH` clause for `ASCII` is neither required nor legal. The other predefined packages discussed in Section 11.9 are library packages in their own right. Thus a compilation unit using one of those packages must name it in a `WITH` clause.

14.4 SUMMARY

The *scope* of a declaration is the part of a program's text in which the entity introduced by a declaration may be considered to exist. A declaration is *visible* at those places in its scope where an occurrence of the declared identifier may refer to the entity introduced by the declaration. Scope and visibility rules tell us where an identifier may occur and what its meaning is at a given point in a program.

The following six rules determine the scope of the kinds of declarations we have seen so far. By the *enclosing frame* of a declaration or statement, we mean the subprogram body, package body, or block statement enclosing it. By an *auxiliary declaration,* we mean a record-component declaration inside a record-type declaration, the enumeration literals within an enumeration-type declaration, the formal parameter specifications in a subprogram declaration, the discriminant specifications in the declaration of a private type with discriminants, and any declaration in the visible part of a package. We call the surrounding record-component declaration, enumeration-type declaration, subprogram declaration, private-type declaration, or package specification the *principal declaration.*

1. The scope of a declaration in a declarative part extends from the beginning of that declaration to the end of its enclosing frame.
2. The scope of an auxiliary declaration starts at the beginning of the auxiliary declaration and includes the rest of the scope of the enclosing principal declaration.
3. The scope of a separately compiled package specification or subprogram declaration includes (*a*) that package or subprogram declaration itself, (*b*) the

corresponding package body or subprogram body, and (*c*) any other compilation unit listing that package or subprogram in a `WITH` clause.
4. The scope of a declaration in the private part of a package specification extends from the beginning of that declaration to the end of the package specification and also includes the entire package body.
5. The scope of the implicit declaration of a loop parameter extends from the appearance of the loop parameter in the iteration scheme of a `FOR` loop to the end of the `LOOP` statement.
6. The scope of a block name, loop name, or statement label is the entire sequence of statements of the enclosing frame.

The visibility rules determine a set of possible meanings for a given identifier at a given point in a program. Two declarations of the same identifier are *mutually exclusive according to the visibility rules* unless they are declarations of subprograms or enumeration literals that overload each other. Thus the visibility rules always determine either a unique meaning for an identifier or a set of overloaded meanings, one of which is selected by resolving overloading. When the scope of one declaration is nested inside the scope of another declaration for the same identifier and the two declarations are mutually exclusive according to the visibility rules, the inner declaration *hides* the outer one within the scope of the inner declaration. If the two declarations are not mutually exclusive, the two declarations are overloaded within the scope of the inner declaration. (Only subprograms and enumeration literals may be overloaded, and only if they have different parameter and result type profiles.)

The following thirteen rules determine the visibility of the declarations we have seen so far:

1. A declaration in a declarative part is directly visible from the end of the declaration to the end of its enclosing frame, except where it is hidden by an inner declaration.
2. A parameter specification in a subprogram declaration (or, in the absence of a subprogram declaration, in a subprogram body) is directly visible throughout the subprogram's body, except where it is hidden by an inner declaration.
3. A declaration in either the visible part or the private part of a package specification is directly visible from the end of the declaration to the end of the package specification and also throughout the package body, except where hidden by an inner declaration.
4. A discriminant specification occurring in a record-type declaration is directly visible from just after the discriminant specification to the end of the record-type declaration.
5. A separately compiled package specification or subprogram declaration (or, in the absence of a separate subprogram declaration, a subprogram body acting as a declaration) is directly visible throughout any compilation unit naming that subprogram or package in a `WITH` clause, except where it is hidden by an inner declaration.

6. A loop parameter is directly visible throughout its loop, except where hidden by an inner declaration.
7. A block name, loop name, or statement label is directly visible throughout the sequence of statements of the enclosing frame, except where it is hidden by an inner declaration.
8. A declaration in the visible part of a package specification is visible by selection just after the dot in an expanded name of the form *p*.__, where *p* is a name denoting the package.
9. A parameter specification is visible by selection just before the => symbol in a named parameter association of a call on the corresponding subprogram.
10. A record-component declaration is visible by selection just after the period in a selected name of the form *r*.__, where *r* is a value or object belonging to the corresponding record type. It is also visible by selection in the component list of a record aggregate.
11. A discriminant specification is visible by selection at the same places as a component declaration for an ordinary record component, and also just before the => symbol in a discriminant constraint applied to the corresponding record type.
12. Any declaration occurring in the declarative part of a subprogram body, package body, or named block statement, in the formal parameter list of a subprogram declaration or body, or in the visible or private part of a package specification is directly visible just after the dot in an expanded name of the form *n*.__ occurring *inside* the subprogram, package, or block statement, where *n* names the subprogram, package, or block statement. Similarly, the implicit declaration of the loop parameter of a named FOR loop is directly visible just after the dot in an expanded name of the form *n*.__ occurring *inside* the FOR loop, where *n* is the name of the FOR loop.
13. A declaration in the visible part of a package specification is directly visible within the scope of a USE clause naming the package except at places where one of the following conditions holds:
    (a) There is another declaration for the same identifier that is already directly visible and would be hidden if the declaration in the package specification were made directly visible.
    (b) The place is in the scope of a USE clause naming some other package whose visible part has another declaration of the same identifier, and the two declarations are not both for subprograms or enumeration literals.

There is an imaginary package named Standard that includes declarations of predefined types, operations on those types, predefined subtypes, and the package ASCII, among other things. A compiler treats each compilation unit as if it were nested in the body of package Standard while being compiled. Compilation units named in WITH clauses of the unit being compiled are considered to occur earlier in the Standard package body. A predefined entity can be named even where it is hidden by an expanded name beginning with the package name Standard.

EXERCISES

14.1 The following questions concern the program Process_Expression_List given at the end of Section 9.4. For each question, state which scope and visibility rules, if any, provide the answer.

(*a*) What is the scope of the variable Next_Character, declared in the first declaration of the main program?

(*b*) Point out an occurrence of the identifier Next_Character that refers to this declaration.

(*c*) The first statement of the procedure Process_Factor contains the identifier Next_Character. To what declaration does this occurrence of the identifier occur?

(*d*) What is the scope of the procedure Process_Expression?

(*e*) What is the scope of the procedure Process_Term?

(*f*) The procedure Next_Term has a formal parameter named Next_Character. What is the scope of this parameter?

(*g*) Point out an occurrence of the identifier Next_Character referring to the formal parameter described in (*f*).

(*h*) How could the procedure Process_Expression be changed to make the formal parameter described in (*f*) visible by selection?

(*i*) What is the scope of the procedure Get?

(*j*) Where is the procedure Get directly visible?

(*k*) Where is the procedure Get visible by selection?

(*l*) How could the procedure Get be made directly visible within the procedure Process_Factor, but not elsewhere?

14.2 The following questions concern the package String_List_Package given in Section 12.2. For each question, state which scope and visibility rules, if any, provide the answer.

(*a*) What is the scope of the procedure Put?

(*b*) Where is the procedure Put directly visible?

(*c*) In a program consisting of String_List_Package and a main procedure beginning WITH String_List_Package;, what is the scope of String_List_Type? Where within that scope is String_List_Type directly visible?

(*d*) At places in its scope where it is not directly visible, in what contexts can String_List_Type be made visible by selection?

(*e*) In the program described in (*c*), what is the scope of String_Pointer_Type, and where is String_Pointer_Type directly visible?

(*f*) In the program described in (*c*), what is the scope of the record component Size_Part, and where is Size_Part directly visible?

(*g*) Point out all places in the String_List_Package body where the record component Array_Part is visible by selection.

14.3 Consider the following package:

```
PACKAGE Search_Matrix_Package IS

   TYPE Matrix_Type IS
      ARRAY (Positive RANGE <>, Positive RANGE <>)
         OF Integer;

   PROCEDURE Search_Matrix
      (Matrix      : IN Matrix_Type;
       Element     : IN Integer;
       Row, Column : OUT Natural);

END Search_Matrix_Package;

PACKAGE BODY Search_Matrix_Package IS

   PROCEDURE Search_Matrix
      (Matrix      : IN Matrix_Type;
       Element     : IN Integer;
       Row, Column : OUT Natural) IS
```

```
   BEGIN

      Row := 0;
      Column := 0;

      Row_Loop:
         FOR i IN Matrix'Range(1) LOOP
            Column_Loop:
               FOR i IN Matrix'Range(2) LOOP
                  IF Matrix (Row_Loop.i, i) = Element THEN
                     Row := Row_Loop.i;
                     Column := Column_Loop.i;
                     EXIT Row_Loop;
                  END IF;
               END LOOP Column_Loop;
         END LOOP Row_Loop;

   END Search_Matrix;

END Search_Matrix_Package;
```

As you answer each of the questions below, indicate which scope and visibility rules provide the answer.

(*a*) What is the scope of each loop parameter?

(*b*) Where is each loop parameter directly visible, where is each loop parameter hidden, and where is each loop parameter visible by selection?

(*c*) What is the scope of each loop name?

(*d*) Where is each loop name directly visible?

(*e*) In a program consisting of `Search_Matrix_Package` and a main procedure beginning `WITH Search_Matrix_Package;`, what is the scope of the declaration of `Matrix_Type`?

(*f*) In the program described in (*e*), what is the scope of the formal parameter `Element`?

(*g*) In the program described in (*e*), where is the formal parameter `Element` directly visible? Where can it be made visible by selection?

(*h*) How would the answer to (*g*) be affected if the main procedure were given a `USE` clause for `Search_Matrix_Package`?

14.4 Consider the following nested block statements:

```
DECLARE
   TYPE a IS (b, c, d);
BEGIN
   DECLARE
      TYPE d IS (c, b, a);
   BEGIN
      --*--
   END;
END;
```

At the point of the comment "--*--", which declarations are directly visible, which are hidden, and which are overloaded?

CHAPTER

FIFTEEN

EXCEPTIONS

The Ada language is designed for systems in which very high reliability is imperative. To be considered reliable, a program must function sensibly even when presented with malformed input data, unusually high or low numbers, or a hardware malfunction. Obviously, great care must be taken to avoid errors in the program itself, but the program must also be designed to account for the possibility of such errors. Truly reliable programs monitor themselves and take some appropriate action when a computation is discovered to be in an unexpected state. Even when there is no safe way to continue execution after such a discovery has been made, the program can, for example, inform an operator that it has failed and then terminate in an orderly way.

The Ada language provides a mechanism for dealing with unexpected situations. Such situations are known as *exceptions*. The act of announcing that an exception has occurred is called *raising* the exception. Responding to this announcement is called *handling* the exception.

Some exceptions are predefined by the language and raised automatically when certain improper actions are attempted. For example, an attempt to divide by zero causes the predefined exception `Numeric_Error` to be raised; an attempt to use an out-of-bounds array index causes the predefined exception `Constraint_Error` to be raised. The predefined exceptions are described in detail in Section 15.3. In addition, a programmer can define exceptions of his own and cause them to be raised when certain conditions are detected. For example, a programmer could write a function that takes an array of `Float` values and returns the average of its components but raises a programmer-defined exception `Empty_Array_Error` when called with a null array.

15.1 HANDLING EXCEPTIONS

The program

```
WITH Basic_IO; USE Basic_IO;
PROCEDURE Perform_Integer_Division IS
   Dividend, Divisor, Number_Of_Cases : Integer;
BEGIN
   Put ("How many cases?");
   New_Line;
   Get (Number_Of_Cases);
   FOR i IN 1 .. Number_Of_Cases LOOP
      Put ("Enter dividend and divisor.");
      New_Line;
      Get (Dividend);
      Get (Divisor);
      Put ("The quotient is ");
      Put (Dividend / Divisor);
      Put (" and the remainder is ");
      Put (Dividend REM Divisor);
      Put (".");
      New_Line;
   END LOOP;
END Perform_Integer_Division;
```

reads successive pairs of integers and prints their integer quotient and remainder. If, at some point, zero is entered for `Divisor`, the attempt to divide by zero will be caught. The exception `Numeric_Error` will be raised and the program will stop.

To make programs more reliable and resilient, we can *handle* an exception rather than letting it terminate the program. The version below prints a message when an attempt is made to divide by zero, then it keeps on running:

```
WITH Basic_IO; USE Basic_IO;
PROCEDURE Perform_Integer_Division IS
   Dividend, Divisor, Quotient : Integer;
   Number_Of_Cases             : Integer;
BEGIN
   Put ("How many cases?");
   New_Line;
   Get (Number_Of_Cases);
   FOR i IN 1 .. Number_Of_Cases LOOP
      Put ("Enter dividend and divisor.");
      New_Line;
      Get (Dividend);
      Get (Divisor);
```

```
      BEGIN
         Quotient := Dividend / Divisor;
         Put ("The quotient is ");
         Put (Quotient);
         Put (" and the remainder is ");
         Put (Dividend REM Divisor);
         Put (".");
      EXCEPTION
         WHEN Numeric_Error =>
            Put
               ("The quotient and remainder are " &
                "undefined when the divisor is zero.");
      END;
      New_Line;
   END LOOP;
END Perform_Integer_Division;
```

Subprogram bodies, block statements, and package bodies are known collectively as *frames.* A frame may have a sequence of statements and a list of handlers associated with those statements. When an exception is raised within a frame's sequence of statements (the usual case), the frame's handlers determine how the exception is handled, as described in Section 15.1.1. However, an exception may also be raised in the declarative part preceding a frame or within one of the frame's handlers. Then different rules apply, described in Sections 15.1.2 and 15.1.3, respectively.

15.1.1 Exceptions in Sequences of Statements

The sequence of statements in a subprogram body, block statement, or package body may be followed by a list of exception handlers specifying actions to be taken if an exception is raised within that sequence of statements. Different handlers may be specified for different exceptions. When one of the statements in the sequence causes an exception to be raised, the remainder of the statement sequence is *abandoned,* and the handler for that exception, if one is present, is executed *instead* of the remainder of the sequence. This completes the execution of the subprogram, block statement, or package initialization. If there is no handler for the exception, as in the first example in this chapter, the remainder of the sequence is abandoned anyway, and the exception is *propagated* to a higher level of control. A subprogram propagates an exception, for example, by re-raising the exception at the point from which the subprogram was invoked. An unhandled exception in the main program halts the program. Propagation of exceptions is described in detail in Section 15.2.

Until now, we have not seen the full form of a subprogram body, package body, or block statement, including the exception handlers. The full form of a subprogram body is as follows:

```
subprogram specification IS
    declarative part
BEGIN
    sequence of statements
..................
: EXCEPTION     :
:     handler   :
:         ~~~   :
:     handler   :
..................
END : subprogram name : ;
```

The form of a handler is

```
WHEN exception name | ~~~ | exception name =>
    sequence of statements
```

except that the last handler in the list may be of the following form:

```
WHEN OTHERS =>
    sequence of statements
```

An exception may only be named once in the list of handlers. The sequence of statements following a particular exception specifies the actions to be taken when that exception is raised. The **WHEN OTHERS** handler, if present, applies to any exception not named earlier in the list of handlers. It is permissible for the **WHEN OTHERS** handler to be the only handler, in which case it applies to any exception.

The full form of a package body is as follows:

```
PACKAGE BODY package name IS
    declarative part
.........................................
: BEGIN                                 :
:     sequence of initialization statements :
: ..................                    :
: : EXCEPTION     :                     :
: :     handler   :                     :
: :         ~~~   :                     :
: :     handler   :                     :
: ..................                    :
.........................................
END : package name : ;
```

The list of handlers has the same form and meaning as in a subprogram body. It may appear only if the package body contains a sequence of initialization statements.

The handlers apply only to exceptions arising during execution of the initialization statements, not to exceptions arising during execution of subprogram bodies given in the declarative part of the package body. Of course, the subprogram bodies in the declarative part may have their own exception handlers.

(The careful reader may notice that, in the full form of a subprogram or package body, the name following the word **END** is not actually required. It may be omitted in any subprogram or package body, whether or not the body contains exception handlers. We have not mentioned this earlier because it is never a good idea to omit the name. We mention it now, when giving the full form of the bodies, only because you may see the name omitted in programs written by others.)

The full form of a block statement is as follows:

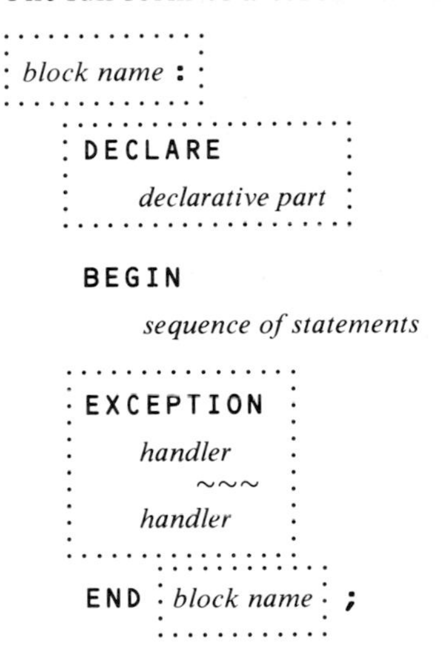

Notice that both the declarative part (along with the opening word **DECLARE**) and the sequence of handlers (along with the opening word **EXCEPTION**) are optional. (The block name must be given at both the top and the bottom of the block statement or be omitted from both places.) Block statements of the form

```
BEGIN

EXCEPTION
   ...
END;
```

are used to specify handlers that apply to only part of the surrounding sequence of statements.

(Since both the **DECLARE** part and the **EXCEPTION** part of a block statement are optional, a block statement of the form

```
BEGIN
   sequence of statements
END;
```

is legal. However, it is completely useless. In PL/I and Pascal, constructs like this are used to group several statements into a single statement, so they may appear in a context where only a single statement is allowed. There are no such contexts in the Ada language, which allows a sequence of statements wherever it allows a single statement.)

Although a sequence of statements raising an exception is abandoned as soon as an exception occurs, block statements can be used to limit the extent of this abandonment. Execution of a handler in the block statement completes execution of the *block statement*. Normal execution resumes in the sequence of statements *containing* the block statement, at the point just after the block statement. Control stays within the outer sequence of statements. This is the most important use of block statements in the Ada language.

Let us consider an example. A production program requiring numeric input should not generally assume that the input file contains only correctly formed numbers. A program can respond to invalid input by handling the exception `Basic_IO.Data_Error`, which is raised by a call on `Basic_IO.Get` with an `Integer` parameter when the next nonblank character in the standard input file is not a digit. In a batch program, it might suffice to terminate with an informative error message when invalid data is detected:

```
WITH Basic_IO; USE Basic_IO;
PROCEDURE Process_Offline IS
   x          : Integer;
   Items_Read : Natural := 0;
   ...
BEGIN
   ...
   Get (x);
   Items_Read := Items_Read + 1;
   ...
EXCEPTION
   WHEN Data_Error =>
      Put ("Invalid numeric input following input item #");
      Put (Items_Read);
      New_Line;
      Put ("EXECUTION TERMINATED");
      New_Line;
END Process_Offline;
```

(Like any other qualified name for an entity provided by `Basic_IO`, the exception name `Basic_IO.Data_Error` may be abbreviated as `Data_Error` because of the `USE` clause.) In an interactive program, a more appropriate response than terminating the program would be to ask the user to reenter the input. Since we do not want to abandon the sequence of statements of the main program when

Data_Error is raised, we must enclose any statement that might raise Data_Error in a block statement that handles that exception:

```
WITH Basic_IO; USE Basic_IO;
PROCEDURE Process_Online IS
   x                   : Integer;
   Well_Formed_Number : Boolean;
   ...
BEGIN
   ...
   Put ("Please enter a number between 1 and 10.");
   New_Line;
   LOOP
      BEGIN
         Get (x);
         Well_Formed_Number := True;
      EXCEPTION
         WHEN Data_Error =>
            Well_Formed_Number := False;
      END;
      EXIT WHEN Well_Formed_Number AND THEN x IN 1 .. 10;
      IF Well_Formed_Number THEN
         Put ("That is not between 1 and 10.");
      ELSE
         Put ("That is not a number.");
      END IF;
      Put (" Please re-enter.");
      New_Line;
   END LOOP;
   ...
END Process_Online;
```

When the call on Get obtains a valid number, the next statement sets Well_Formed_Number to True. When the call on Get raises Data_Error because of nonnumeric input data, the sequence of statements inside the block statement is abandoned before True is assigned, and the handler sets Well_Formed_Number to False. This completes execution of the block statement, so the EXIT and IF statements are executed next, and control remains inside the loop. The block statement always terminates with a number read into x and Well_Formed_Number set to True, or with Well_Formed_Number set to False because no number could be read into x. The raising of the exception is always confined to the block statement.

Any action legal in a particular sequence of statements is also legal in the handlers following those statements. For example, all the declarations available throughout the sequence of statements are available in the handler. A handler occurring in a subprogram body may contain a RETURN statement. In fact, a handler corresponding to the outermost sequence of statements in a function body *must* contain a **RETURN** statement if it is to complete the execution of the function body with a result value. However, a **GOTO** statement in a handler cannot transfer control back into the sequence of statements in which the exception was raised. The only way to keep control in that sequence of statements after handling the exception is by enclosing in a block any statement that might raise an exception and handling the exception within the block.

15.1.2 Exceptions Raised by Declarations

Exceptions can be raised by declarations as well as by statements. For example, an exception may be raised by evaluation of the expression giving an object's initial value. The entire declaration is then treated as though it raised the exception.

In general, there may be a declarative part, a sequence of statements, and a list of handlers corresponding to a frame. The list of handlers applies only to the sequence of statements, not to the declarative part. If an exception is raised by a declaration, it is immediately propagated out of the frame in which the exception occurred, whether or not that frame has a handler for the exception. This is because a frame's handlers may refer to entities whose declarations have not yet been elaborated at the time the exception occurs. Only once the declarative part is completely elaborated can the handlers be considered executable.

15.1.3 Exceptions Raised in Handlers

A sequence of handlers does not apply to itself. If a handler raises a new exception while trying to handle an old one, the new exception is immediately propagated out of the frame. Thus there is no danger of entering a loop in which a handler repeatedly reinvokes itself by raising the exception it was meant to handle. (Of course, if a handler contains a block statement, an exception raised inside the block statement may be handled in the block statement and never raised in the outermost sequence of statements of the handler itself.) As we shall see in Section 15.5, it is sometimes appropriate to handle one exception by intentionally raising and propagating another exception.

15.2 PROPAGATION OF EXCEPTIONS

When an exception is raised within the sequence of statements of the frame and not handled by one of the frame's handlers, the frame is abandoned and the exception is *propagated.* Similarly, exceptions raised in a frame's declarative part or handlers are propagated. This section describes precisely what propagation means.

15.2.1 Propagation from Subprogram Bodies

In the case of a subprogram body, propagation means that the exception is re-raised at the point at which the subprogram was called, as if the subprogram call itself had caused the exception directly. In the case of a procedure, the procedure call statement is considered to have raised the exception. A function call may occur as part of an expression in either a declaration or a statement. That declaration or statement is considered to have raised the exception.

Once the exception is propagated to the calling subprogram, it may be handled by a handler that applies there or it may be propagated yet another level. If an exception continues to be propagated from called subprograms to calling subprograms without being handled, it will eventually be raised in the main program. When an exception is raised in the main program and not handled there, execution of the main program is aborted.

15.2.2 Propagation from Block Statements

Propagation of an exception raised but not handled inside a block statement means that the exception is re-raised in the sequence of statements containing the block statement. In effect, the block statement, taken as a single statement, is considered to have raised the exception. For example, the interactive program presented earlier can be revised as follows:

```
WITH Basic_IO; USE Basic_IO;
PROCEDURE Process_Online IS
   x                  : Integer;
   Well_Formed_Number : Boolean;
   ...
BEGIN
   ...
   Put ("Please enter a number between 1 and 10.");
   New_Line;
   LOOP
      BEGIN
         Get (x);
         Well_Formed_Number := True;
      EXCEPTION
         WHEN Data_Error =>
            Well_Formed_Number := False;
      END;
      EXIT WHEN Well_Formed_Number AND THEN x IN 1 .. 10;
      IF Well_Formed_Number THEN
         Put ("That is not between 1 and 10.");
      ELSE
         Put ("That is not a number.");
      END IF;
      Put (" Please re-enter.");
      New_Line;
   END LOOP;
```

```
   ...
EXCEPTION
   WHEN OTHERS =>
      Put
         ("***** SORRY, PROGRAM TERMINATING DUE TO " &
          "INTERNAL MALFUNCTION.");
END Process_OnLine;
```

This version accounts for the possibility that some other, unanticipated exception might arise somewhere in the program. If an unanticipated exception is raised outside of the block statement, control is immediately transferred to the handler that prints an apologetic message, after which the program terminates. If an exception other than `Data_Error` is raised inside the block statement, then the exception will be propagated, since there is no handler for it inside the block statement. In this case, propagation means that the block statement itself will raise the exception in the main program's sequence of statements, and the main program's handler will be invoked as before.

15.2.3 Propagation from Packages

Packages may occur in a declarative part or as separately compiled library packages. (A package whose body is a subunit falls into the first category since the body logically occurs at the place of the body stub in some declarative part.) When a package specification or package body is a declaration, propagation of an exception causes the exception to be re-raised by the package specification or body itself (viewed as a declaration) in some declarative part. Library packages are elaborated once, before execution of the main program. There is no place to handle an exception propagated by the elaboration of a library package, so propagation is treated as a fatal error in initializing the program. All further execution is abandoned.

15.3 PREDEFINED EXCEPTIONS

In earlier chapters, we stated that attempts to perform certain actions "cause an error" without being precise about just what this means. In fact, an attempt to perform an action that is disallowed by the rules of the Ada language causes one of the predefined exceptions of the language to be raised. This exception may be handled in the same manner as any other exception. Thus it is possible to recover from an error and continue execution if there is a sensible way to do so. Alternatively, it is possible to perform appropriate clean-up actions while propagating the exception back to the main program. If no handlers are supplied for predefined exceptions, an execution error will cause the exception to be propagated back through one or more frames, ultimately causing the main program to be abandoned.

The predefined exceptions are named `Constraint_Error`, `Numeric_Error`, `Program_Error`, `Storage_Error`, and `Tasking_Error`. (Other predefined exceptions, which arise only in input/output operations, will be discussed in Chapter 17.) The exception Tasking_Error is raised in multitask programs, and will be discussed in Chapter 19. This section discusses the circumstances in which the remaining four predefined exceptions are raised.

Constraint_Error is the most general of the predefined exceptions. There are many circumstances in which it can be raised, most of which correspond to an attempt to violate a range constraint, an index constraint, or a discriminant constraint. Specifically, Constraint_Error is raised by each of the following errors:

an assignment statement in which the value of the expression does not lie within the subtype of the variable being assigned to (or, in the case of an array assignment, in which the array expression and the array being assigned to do not have the same number of components in each dimension, thus making it impossible to perform the implicit subtype conversion described in Section 7.1)

a subprogram call in which the value of an actual parameter of mode **IN** or **IN OUT** is not in the subtype of the corresponding formal parameter

an attempt to return from a procedure while a formal parameter of mode **IN OUT** or **OUT** contains a value not in the subtype of the corresponding actual parameter

a **RETURN** statement with an expression whose value does not lie within the result subtype of the function

an attempt to apply the operator ** to a negative right operand if the left operand belongs to an integer type

an attempt to apply one of the operators **AND**, **OR**, or **XOR** to one-dimensional arrays of different lengths

an application of the operator & resulting in an array with more components than there are values in the array's index type

an indexed component with a subscript out of bounds

a selected component naming a component in a variant that is not present in the record according to the current values of the record's discriminants

a name referring to the variable designated by a particular access value when that access value is null

an application of one of the functions T'Pred, T'Succ, T'Val, or T'Value (where T is some discrete type) to a value for which the function is not defined

an array or record aggregate in which a specified component value does not belong to the subtype of that component

a qualified expression in which the value of the expression is not in the subtype specified by the typemark

a type conversion in which the converted value of the expression is not in the subtype specified by the typemark

an allocator with an initial value that is not in the subtype specified by the typemark

an object declaration in which the initial value is not in the subtype of the object

a range constraint applied to a subtype that does not include both bounds of the range

a fixed-point or floating-point accuracy constraint applied to a subtype with less precision than that indicated by the constraint

`Numeric_Error` is raised by a predefined arithmetic operation that cannot produce a correct result (or, in the case of fixed-point or floating-point types, a sufficiently precise approximation of a correct result). The operations `/`, `MOD`, and `REM` for integer types raise `Numeric_Error` when their right operands are zero. `Numeric_Error` is also raised by use of a numeric literal as a value in some type whose range does not include the value of the literal. For example, if `Integer'Last` is 32,767 and `x` is of type `Integer`, the expression

```
x + 32_768
```

may raise `Numeric_Error` when an attempt is made to use `32_768` as a value of type `Integer`. (Technically, the exception is raised by the implicit conversion of the literal from type *universal_integer*—see Section 8.3.6—to type `Integer`.)

An arithmetic operation *overflows* when its mathematical result does not lie in the range of the result type. In the evaluation of an arithmetic expression, an intermediate result that overflows *may* raise `Numeric_Error`, but it is not guaranteed to do so. There are several reasons for this:

An implementation may choose not to raise `Numeric_Error` in an expression whose ultimate result can be determined without actually performing the overflowing operation. For example, an implementation may choose to optimize the expression

```
b /= 0 AND a/b > c
```

by evaluating it as if it were written

```
b /= 0 AND THEN a/b > c
```

Then a value of zero for *b* would not raise `Numeric_Error`. However, this optimization is up to the individual compiler. A programmer is guaranteed of avoiding the exception only by writing the short-circuit control form.

As explained in Section 8.3.8, a type declared as

```
TYPE t IS RANGE a .. b;
```

really declares *t* to be a *subtype* of some anonymous base type whose range may *include* the range *a* `..` *b*. For `Numeric_Error` to be raised, it is not enough for the subtype range *a* `..` *b* to be exceeded; the wider base type range

```
t'Base'First .. t'Base'Last
```

must be exceeded. This depends on the base type that the compiler selects for *t*.

Some compilers may avoid `Numeric_Error` by using a type with even a larger range than the base type to evaluate arithmetic expressions. For example, a compiler that represents values of type `Integer` in a word of memory may use two words to hold the result of a multiplication. This might avoid overflow in an expression like `a * b / c`.

Certain Ada compilers may completely ignore overflow for particular fixed-point or floating-point types if the machine running the program makes overflow difficult to detect. (This is not permitted for integer types.) For any fixed-point or floating-point type `T`, the attribute `T'Machine_Overflows` has the Boolean value `True` if the implementation of the Ada language detects overflow for that type and has the value `False` otherwise. If `X` is a variable in some type for which this attribute is false, the expression `X / 0.0` might not raise `Numeric_Error`.

Because of the many compiler-dependent aspects of when `Numeric_Error` will be raised, it is often difficult to ascertain whether an out-of-range numeric result will lead to `Numeric_Error`, `Constraint_Error`, or no exception at all. Given the declarations

```
TYPE Hour_Type IS RANGE 0 .. 23;
Hour : Hour_Type;
```

and assuming that `Hour = 23`, the assignment statement

```
Hour := 10 * Hour;
```

could raise `Numeric_Error` if the base type chosen by the compiler for `Hour_Type` has the range `-128 .. 127`. If the base type has a wider range, say `-32_768 .. 32_767`, the product 230 will be computed without an exception, but `Constraint_Error` will be raised upon the attempt to place this value in `Hour`. The assignment statement

```
Hour := (Hour + 1) MOD 24;
```

could raise `Numeric_Error` if executed with `Hour` equal to 23, but only in the unlikely event that the compiler chooses a base type for `Hour_Type` whose last value is 23. More likely, no exception will be raised. (In particular, this statement is incapable of raising `Constraint_Error`.)

Typically, handlers for `Numeric_Error` should also be invoked when `Constraint_Error` is raised:

```
BEGIN
   Hour := 10 * Hour;
   In_Range := True;
EXCEPTION
   WHEN Numeric_Error | Constraint_Error =>
      In_Range := False;
END;
```

Otherwise, proper handling of an out-of-bounds numeric result will depend on internal choices made by the compiler. This will make the program hard to understand and maintain. Furthermore, the program may behave incorrectly when moved to a different machine or even when compiled with a new release of the original compiler.

Program_Error is raised in a variety of circumstances when a program is improperly formed. There are many rules of program formation whose violation cannot always be detected until a program is executed. For example, the following function may or may not finish by executing a RETURN statement, depending on the input data:

```
WITH Basic_IO; USE Basic_IO;
FUNCTION Percentage RETURN Float IS
   n : Integer;
BEGIN
   Get (n);
   IF n IN 0 .. 100 THEN
      RETURN Float(n) / 100.0;
   END IF;
END Percentage;
```

A function raises Program_Error if it finishes without executing a RETURN statement.

Program_Error is also raised by a call upon a subprogram before its subprogram body has been elaborated. Consider the following illegal version of the Fraction_Package specification:

```
PACKAGE Fraction_Package IS
   TYPE Fraction_Type IS PRIVATE;
   ...
   FUNCTION "/" (Left, Right: Integer) RETURN Fraction_Type;
   Zero: CONSTANT Fraction_Type := 0 / 1;
                                       -- Incorrect call on "/"
PRIVATE
   ...
END Fraction_Package;
```

(The declaration of Zero as a deferred constant, with the initial value given in the private part as a record aggregate, has been replaced by an ordinary constant declaration.)

When Fraction_Package is elaborated, the declarations in the package specification will be elaborated first, followed by the declarations in the package body, all in the order in which they appear. The declaration of the constant Zero contains a call on a version of "/" taking two Integer operands and returning a

Fraction_Type result. Elaboration of the constant declaration requires this function to be called. At the time the declaration of Zero is elaborated, the declaration of "/" has been elaborated but the body of "/" has not been. Therefore, the call on "/" in the declaration of Zero raises Program_Error.

(This situation should not be confused with the following, which is perfectly legitimate:

```
PROCEDURE Main IS

   ...

   PROCEDURE Procedure_2;

   PROCEDURE Procedure_1 IS
      ...
   BEGIN
      ...
      Procedure_2; -- Call on procedure whose body follows.
      ...
   END Procedure_1;

   PROCEDURE Procedure_2 IS
      ...
   BEGIN
      ...
   END Procedure_2;

BEGIN -- Main

   ...
   Procedure_1;
   ...

END Main;
```

The body of Procedure_1 contains a call on Procedure_2; and the body of Procedure_2 does not appear until later, but this is not an error. The difference is that the call on Procedure_2 is not executed when the body of Procedure_1 is elaborated; the call is executed later, when Procedure_1 is actually called. Thus the subprogram bodies can be elaborated in the order shown without any subprogram being called before its body is elaborated.)

There are some rules of the Ada language that are considered difficult to enforce, and a compiler is not required to enforce them. For example, a program is incorrect if its outcome depends on which operand of an operator is evaluated first or whether arrays are copied when they are passed as parameters. An Ada implementation that undertakes to enforce such a rule raises Program_Error when it discovers a violation.

Storage_Error is raised when a program runs out of storage. In particular, this exception is raised by evaluation of an allocator when there is insufficient storage for a new allocated variable. (A compiler may use different pools of storage for different access types, so that an allocator for one type may be evaluated normally at the same time that an allocator for another type raises Storage_Error.) Storage_Error can be raised by a subprogram call if many subprograms are still in progress when a new one is called. Unbounded recursion—that is, a recursive subprogram that does not eventually lead to a simple case in which no recursion is necessary—usually manifests itself in this way. Storage_Error can also be raised by elaboration of a declaration—for instance, the declaration of an array too large to be accommodated in the available storage.

15.4 PROGRAMMER-DEFINED EXCEPTIONS

Just as programmers can, in effect, extend the Ada language by declaring their own types and operations, so programmers can extend the language by declaring their own exceptions and causing them to be raised in appropriate circumstances. For example, the following package provides a function named Square_Root and a programmer-defined exception named Imaginary_Root_Error. The function returns the square root of its parameter (using Newton's method) when the parameter is nonnegative but raises Imaginary_Root_Error when the parameter is negative.

```
PACKAGE Square_Root_Package IS
   FUNCTION Square_Root (Square : Float) RETURN Float;
   Imaginary_Root_Error : EXCEPTION;
END Square_Root_Package;

PACKAGE BODY Square_Root_Package IS
   FUNCTION Square_Root (Square : Float) RETURN Float IS
      Guess                : Float := Square / 2.0;
      Previous_Proximity : Float := ABS (Square - Guess**2);
      Proximity            : Float;
   BEGIN
      IF Square >= 0.0 THEN
         LOOP
            Guess := (Guess + Square / Guess) / 2.0;
            Proximity := ABS (Square - Guess**2);
            EXIT WHEN Proximity >= Previous_Proximity;
            Previous_Proximity := Proximity;
         END LOOP;
         RETURN Guess;
      ELSE
         RAISE Imaginary_Root_Error;
      END IF;
   END Square_Root;
END Square_Root_Package;
```

Exception declarations establish identifiers as names of exceptions. The form of an exception declaration is as follows:

identifier **,** ~~~ **,** *identifier* **: EXCEPTION ;**

This declaration may appear anywhere type, subtype, object, and named number declarations may appear. Exceptions are typically declared in package specifications, so that they may be provided along with the subprograms that raise them. However, exception declarations are also allowed in the declarative parts of subprogram bodies, package bodies, and block statements.

In addition, an exception may be declared by a renaming declaration of the following form:

identifier **: EXCEPTION RENAMES** *exception name* **;**

For example, if the specification of a package named `Queue_Package` contains the declaration

```
Full_Queue_Error : EXCEPTION;
```

then a subprogram starting with a `WITH` clause for `Queue_Package` could contain the following declaration:

```
Full_Queue_Error :
   EXCEPTION RENAMES Queue_Package.Full_Queue_Error;
```

This would allow the exception to be referred to in the subprogram by the simple name `Full_Queue_Error` rather than the expanded name `Queue_Package.Full_Queue_Error`.

An exception name may be used in `RAISE` *statements*. The usual form of a `RAISE` statement is as follows:

RAISE *exception name* **;**

Such a statement may appear in any sequence of statements and causes the named exception to be raised. Predefined exceptions may be raised either automatically, when an illegal operation is attempted, or explicitly, by a `RAISE` statement. Exceptions declared by the programmer can only be raised explicitly, by `RAISE` statements. (As we shall explain shortly, it is generally not a good idea to raise a predefined exception explicitly, even though the language rules allow it.)

An exception propagated by a subprogram appears to the caller to be raised directly by the subprogram call. This is fitting, given the role of subprograms in writing abstract programs. A procedure call statement can be viewed as an abstract description of an action. Just as an assignment statement either copies a value into a variable or raises an exception if it cannot (because the value is not in the variable's subtype), so a subprogram call performs a certain action or raises an exception if it cannot. A function call can be viewed as an invocation of a programmer-defined operator. Just as the expression P / Q evaluates to the quotient of P and Q or raises an exception if the quotient is undefined for the current values of P and Q, so the expression

```
Square_Root_Package.Square_Root (Q)
```

evaluates to the square root of Q or raises an exception if the square root is undefined for the current value of Q. In fact, overloaded versions of operators, defined by the programmer, can (and should) be made to behave just as the predefined versions, yielding a result value when given sensible operands and raising an exception when given improper operands.

Sections 9.6, 11.4, and 12.2 presented functions for manipulating Fraction_Type values, exact representations of rational numbers. There were two versions of "/" returning Fraction_Type values, one computing the quotient of two Fraction_Type operands, and the other computing the rational quotient of two Integer operands. Both of these functions were written under the assumption that the right operand was not equal to zero. A more appropriate approach is to declare a new exception, say Zero_Denominator_Error, in the specification of the package Fraction_Package providing both versions of "/". The two division operators should raise this exception when given right operands of zero:

```
PACKAGE Fraction_Package IS
   TYPE Fraction_Type IS PRIVATE;
   Zero_Denominator_Error : EXCEPTION;
   FUNCTION "+" (Right : Fraction_Type) RETURN Fraction_Type;
   FUNCTION "-" (Right : Fraction_Type) RETURN Fraction_Type;
   FUNCTION "+"
      (Left, Right : Fraction_Type) RETURN Fraction_Type;
   FUNCTION "-"
      (Left, Right : Fraction_Type) RETURN Fraction_Type;
   FUNCTION "*"
      (Left, Right : Fraction_Type) RETURN Fraction_Type;
   FUNCTION "/"
      (Left, Right : Fraction_Type) RETURN Fraction_Type;
      -- Raises Zero_Denominator_Error when
      --    Right.Numerator_Part = 0.
   FUNCTION "**"
      (Left : Fraction_Type; Right : Integer)
      RETURN Fraction_Type;
   FUNCTION "ABS"
      (Right : Fraction_Type) RETURN Fraction_Type;
   FUNCTION "/" (Left, Right : Integer) RETURN Fraction_Type;
      -- Raises Zero_Denominator_Error when Right = 0.
```

```
PRIVATE
   TYPE Fraction_Type IS
      RECORD
         Numerator_Part   : Integer;
         Denominator_Part : Positive;
      END RECORD;
END Fraction_Package;
```

The body of the version of "/" taking two Integer operands, for example, would look like this:

```
FUNCTION "/"
   (Left, Right: Integer) RETURN Fraction_Type IS
   Result : Fraction_Type;
BEGIN
   IF Right = 0 THEN
      RAISE Zero_Denominator_Error;
   ELSE
      IF Right > 0 THEN
         Result :=
            Fraction_Type'
               (Numerator_Part   => Left,
                Denominator_Part => Right);
      ELSE -- Right < 0
         Result :=
            Fraction_Type'
               (Numerator_Part   => - Left,
                Denominator_Part => - Right);
      END IF;
      Reduce (Result);
      RETURN Result;
   END IF;
END "/";
```

Evaluation of a Fraction_Type expression of the form *P / Q* always computes a quotient or raises Zero_Denominator_Error. This exception is part of the interface of Fraction_Package. Its name and the comments in the package specification make its meaning clear.

Like exceptions declared by a programmer, the predefined exceptions can be raised intentionally with RAISE statements. However, this is not a wise practice. The predefined exceptions—especially Constraint_Error—are very broadly defined and can easily be raised for reasons other than those anticipated when a handler was written. Rather than adding still other meanings to these exceptions by raising them explicitly when the program detects certain conditions, one should do just the opposite: declare new exceptions to differentiate among the many possible causes of the predefined exceptions. When a predefined exception may be raised in a narrow context where its meaning is unmistakable, the context should be enclosed in a block statement and the exception handled immediately. It might be handled simply by raising another exception, declared by the programmer, that specifically describes the presumed cause of the predefined exception.

For example, the following package implements stacks as linked lists:

```
PACKAGE Stack_Package IS

   TYPE Stack_Type IS LIMITED PRIVATE;

   PROCEDURE Push
      (Item : IN Integer; Onto : IN OUT Stack_Type);
      -- Raises Stack_Overflow_Error when storage is
      --     exhausted.

   PROCEDURE Pop
      (Item : OUT Integer; Off_Of : IN OUT Stack_Type);
      -- Raises Stack_Underflow_Error when called with an
      --     empty stack.

   FUNCTION Stack_Size (Stack : Stack_Type) RETURN Natural;

   Stack_Underflow_Error, Stack_Overflow_Error : EXCEPTION;

PRIVATE

   TYPE Stack_Cell_Type;

   TYPE Cell_List_Type IS ACCESS Stack_Cell_Type;

   TYPE Stack_Cell_Type IS
      RECORD
         Item_Part      : Integer;
         Next_Cell_Part : Cell_List_Type;
      END RECORD;

   TYPE Stack_Type IS
      RECORD
         Size_Part : Natural := 0;
         List_Part : Cell_List_Type;
      END RECORD;

END Stack_Package;


PACKAGE BODY Stack_Package IS

   PROCEDURE Push
      (Item : IN Integer; Onto : IN OUT Stack_Type) IS
   BEGIN

      BEGIN
         Onto.List_Part :=
            NEW Stack_Cell_Type'
               (Item_Part      => Item,
                Next_Cell_Part => Onto.List_Part);
      EXCEPTION
         WHEN Storage_Error =>
            RAISE Stack_Overflow_Error;
      END;

      Onto.Size_Part := Onto.Size_Part + 1;

   END Push;
```

```
      PROCEDURE Pop
         (Item : OUT Integer; Off_Of : IN OUT Stack_Type) IS
      BEGIN
         IF Off_Of.List_Part = NULL THEN
            RAISE Stack_Underflow_Error;
         ELSE
            Item := Off_Of.List_Part.Item_Part;
            Off_Of.List_Part := Off_Of.List_Part.Next_Cell_Part;
            Off_Of.Size_Part := Off_Of.Size_Part - 1;
         END IF;
      END Pop;

      FUNCTION Stack_Size
         (Stack : Stack_Type) RETURN Natural IS
      BEGIN
         RETURN Stack.Size_Part;
      END Stack_Size;

   END Stack_Package;
```

In the body of `Push`, if the allocator in the statement

```
   Onto.List_Part :=
      NEW Stack_Cell_Type'
         (Item_Part      => Item,
          Next_Cell_Part => Onto.List_Part);
```

raises `Storage_Error`, the block propagates `Stack_Overflow_Error`. This allows a user of the package to handle the error with a handler for `Stack_Overflow_Error` rather than a handler for `Storage_Error`. `Stack_Overflow_Error` can only indicate insufficient storage to push another item onto a stack. In contrast, `Storage_Error` can indicate the failure of an allocator, unbounded recursion, or some other problem.

It is common for handlers to raise exceptions intentionally with `RAISE` statements. When an exception is deemed symptomatic of a fatal error, the proper response often is to have the program terminate gracefully, leaving the surrounding environment in a well-defined state and providing useful diagnostic information. Handlers of the following form are typical:

```
   WHEN Exception_X =>
      Clean_Up;
      RAISE Exception_X;
```

The procedure `Clean_Up` may perform such actions as releasing resources, saving data in files, closing files, recording trace information useful in debugging, turning off devices, lighting fault indicator lamps, and so forth. Assuming that this handler occurs in a subprogram *S*, the effect of the `RAISE` statement is to propagate `Exception_X` to the calling subprogram even though the exception was partly handled in *S*. Handlers such as this can propagate an exception back through several levels of subprogram calls, performing appropriate clean-up actions at each level, until the exception is propagated out of the main program to terminate execution.

There is a special notation for re-raising exceptions. In the sequence of statements of a handler—and nowhere else—a RAISE statement of the form

```
RAISE;
```

(without an exception name) is allowed. It means that whatever exception brought control to the handler should be re-raised and thus immediately propagated. For example, the handler above could also have been written as follows:

```
WHEN Exception_X =>
   Clean_Up;
   RAISE;
```

However, this form of RAISE statement is most useful in handlers that apply to more than one exception, such as these:

```
WHEN Constraint_Error | Numeric_Error =>
   Put ("Numbers were too large in procedure P.");
   New_Line;
   RAISE;
WHEN OTHERS =>
   Put ("An unanticipated error occurred in procedure P.");
   New_Line;
   RAISE;
```

15.5 THE Suppress PRAGMA

In theory, for each statement, expression, or declaration that can raise a predefined exception, a check must be performed to determine whether the exception should be raised. In practice, a clever compiler can determine that many of these checks may be safely omitted. As a simple example, the assignment `A := B;`, where `A` and `B` are declared to belong to the same subtype and `B` has an initial value, cannot possibly raise `Constraint_Error`. The value of `B` always belongs to the subtype of `A`, so there is no need to check it.

Nonetheless, a compiler may continue to generate checks that a programmer knows are unnecessary, and these checks may make a critical difference in the running time of a program. For example, the package below provides a binary search program in which the indexed component `Table (Midpoint)` is always guaranteed to be valid and in which the assignments to `Lower_Bound` and `Upper_Bound` are guaranteed to obey those variables' range constraints. Nonetheless, even a good optimizing compiler is unlikely to perform the sophisticated reasoning necessary to reach this conclusion. In a case like this, the programmer may use the pragma Suppress to give the compiler permission to omit certain specific checks. The compiler may or may not take advantage of this permission.

```
PACKAGE Search_Package IS
   SUBTYPE Name_Subtype IS String (1 .. 10);
   TYPE Name_List_Type IS
      ARRAY (Positive RANGE <>) OF Name_Subtype;
   FUNCTION Position_Of_Name
      (Name  :  Name_Subtype; Table : Name_List_Type)
      RETURN Natural;
      --  Table is assumed to be in ascending order.
      --
      --  Return zero if Name does not occur in Table.
      --  Otherwise, return the index at which it occurs.
END Search_Package;

PACKAGE BODY Search_Package IS
   FUNCTION Position_Of_Name
      (Name : Name_Subtype; Table : Name_List_Type)
      RETURN Natural IS
      Lower_Bound : Integer RANGE Table'Range := Table'First;
      Upper_Bound : Integer RANGE Table'Range := Table'Last;
      Midpoint    : Integer RANGE Table'Range;
   BEGIN
      LOOP
         IF Upper_Bound < Lower_Bound THEN
            RETURN 0;
         END IF;
         Midpoint := (Lower_Bound + Upper_Bound) / 2;
            -- Integer division
         IF Table (Midpoint) = Name THEN
            RETURN Midpoint;
         END IF;
         IF Name < Table (Midpoint) THEN
            Upper_Bound := Midpoint - 1;
         ELSE
            Lower_Bound := Midpoint + 1;
         END IF;
      END LOOP;
   END Position_Of_Name;
END Search_Package;
```

The Suppress pragma does not advise the compiler to *ignore* certain improper situations but to *assume* that they will not occur. Improper situations cannot simply be ignored because they may leave a computation in an inconsistent or unpredictable state. Use of the `Suppress` pragma constitutes a promise by the programmer that certain improper situations will not arise. If this promise is not kept, the program is not a correct Ada program (although this may be undetectable) and the program's subsequent behavior may be arbitrary.

Because the `Suppress` pragma is so dangerous, it should not be used routinely. Several conditions should be met first:

A programmer should not even consider using the `Suppress` pragma until he has a program that runs correctly but too slowly. The pragma should not appear in programs that have not been thoroughly tested. Furthermore, the programmer should not presume that the program will run too slowly before he has had a chance to see it run.

The pragma should not be applied indiscriminately. Given that a performance problem really exists, the programmer should use a software metering tool to determine where the program is spending most of its time. (Such a tool ought to be a part of any Ada Program Support Environment.) Typically, a program spends most of its time executing a very small portion of the code, such as a loop nested in one or more outer loops. Improving the performance of this small part of the program usually drastically improves the performance of the entire program.

Once the programmer has identified the critical portion of the program slowing his computation down, he should explore alternative means of improving its efficiency before giving up error checking. Sometimes, careful reprogramming of the critical portion of the program is all that is needed.

If the programmer concludes that he must use the `Suppress` pragma, he should confine its effects as much as possible. The small portion of the program he is trying to speed up should be enclosed in a block statement, and the pragma should be placed in its declarative part. The statements in the block should be scrutinized especially carefully to verify that they cannot give rise to exceptional situations.

In general, there may be several different kinds of checks resulting in a given predefined exception. The `Suppress` pragma specifies not which exceptions need not be checked for, but which specific kinds of checks may be omitted. For instance, the pragma may give a compiler permission not to check for violation of a discriminant constraint, while still requiring it to check for other potential causes of `Constraint_Error`. There are nine identifiers that have special meanings within the `Suppress` pragma as names of checks: `Access_Check`, `Discriminant_Check`, `Division_Check`, `Elaboration_Check`, `Index_Check`, `Length_Check`, `Overflow_Check`, `Range_Check`, and `Storage_Check`.

`Access_Check`, `Discriminant_Check`, `Index_Check`, `Length_Check`, and `Range_Check` are all checks performed to determine whether `Constraint_Error` should be raised. `Access_Check` is the check performed when referring to the variable designated by an access value to determine whether the access value is null. `Discriminant_Check` actually refers to two checks:

the check performed to determine whether a value with discriminants violates a discriminant constraint applicable to the context in which it is used
the check performed to determine whether a selected component of some record with variants exists, given the record's current discriminant values

Index_Check actually refers to three checks:

the check performed to determine whether an array value has the bounds required by some index constraint
the check performed to determine whether an index in an indexed component is in bounds
the check performed to determine whether the bounds in a slice of an array are consistent with the bounds of the array. (The bounds of the slice must lie within the bounds of the array unless the slice is null.)

Length_Check is the check that two arrays, or an array and an array subtype, have the same number of index values in each dimension. (This check is performed when copying an array value to a variable or parameter, when returning an array value from a function, when converting an array value to another array type, and when applying one of the operators **AND**, **OR**, and **XOR** to two one-dimensional arrays with Boolean components.) Range_Check actually refers to four checks:

the check to determine whether a scalar value violates a range constraint applicable to the context in which it occurs
the check that a range constraint following a typemark specifies a subset of the subtype named by the typemark
the check that an index value in a named array aggregate belongs to the appropriate index subtype
a check that generic units (described in Chapter 16) are used properly

Division_Check and Overflow_Check are both checks performed to determine whether Numeric_Error should be raised. Division_Check is the check that the right operand of one of the operators /, **REM**, and **MOD** is not zero. Overflow_Check is the check that the result of a numeric operation lies within the range of the result type. (The interpretation of a numeric literal as a value of a particular type is considered to be a numeric operation in this sense.)

Elaboration_Check is the check performed to determine whether Program_Error should be raised because a program unit has been invoked before its body has been elaborated. Storage_Check is the check performed to determine whether Storage_Error should be raised because a program does not have enough storage for a particular purpose.

The Suppress pragma has two forms:

```
PRAGMA Suppress ( check name ) ;

PRAGMA Suppress ( check name, [ On => ] entity name ) ;
```

In the second form, omitting the symbols On => does not affect the meaning of the pragma. The first form gives blanket permission to omit the named check. The second form gives permission to omit the check only when it involves the object, type, or program unit named by the entity name. The entity name may be an object name or a type name for the checks associated with Constraint_Error (with a type name meaning that the check should be suppressed for all objects in the type), the name of a numeric type for the checks associated with Numeric_Error, the name of a program unit for Elaboration_Check, and the name of a program unit or access type for Storage_Check.

The Suppress pragma may go in the declarative part of some frame or in a package specification. When it occurs in a declarative part, the pragma applies to the part of the program from the pragma to the end of the frame. When it occurs in a package specification, the pragma must include an entity name and the entity named must be one declared earlier in the package specification. The pragma then applies from the point at which it occurs through the rest of the scope of the named entity. This includes the rest of the package specification, the rest of the corresponding package body (if there is one) and, if the entity is declared in the visible part of the package specification, the scope of the package itself.

We conclude with an example of the use of the Suppress pragma. Suppose x, y, and z are variables in the subtype Float RANGE 0.0 .. 1.0, and an inner loop in a program contains the following statement:

```
IF x > 0 THEN
   z := (x ** 2 + y ** 2) / (x + y) ** 2;
END IF;
```

Suppose further that the program has been thoroughly tested and appears to work correctly, but the programmer is dissatisfied with its execution speed. The programmer has determined through the use of a metering tool that the program is spending a significant portion of its time in this inner loop. The program may be checking that none of the arithmetic operations in this statement overflow, that the right operand of / is not zero, and that the quotient lies within the declared subtype of z. In fact, mathematical analysis reveals that none of these checks is necessary. At least part of this analysis is too sophisticated for any realistic optimizing compiler. Not seeing any other way to speed up the inner loop, the programmer can inform the compiler that the checks may be omitted by rewriting the statement as follows:

```
DECLARE
   PRAGMA Suppress (Overflow_Check);
   PRAGMA Suppress (Division_Check);
   PRAGMA Suppress (Range_Check);
BEGIN
   IF x > 0 THEN
      z := (x ** 2 + y ** 2) / (x + y) ** 2;
   END IF;
END;
```

The block statement confines the effect of the pragmas to the one statement in which it is clearly safe to omit the checks. The pragmas could also have been written either as

```
PRAGMA Suppress (Overflow_Check, On => Float);
PRAGMA Suppress (Division_Check, On => Float);
PRAGMA Suppress (Range_Check, On => z);
```

or, equivalently, as

```
PRAGMA Suppress (Overflow_Check, Float);
PRAGMA Suppress (Division_Check, Float);
PRAGMA Suppress (Range_Check, z);
```

but this is unnecessary. The block statement so effectively restricts the effect of the pragmas that the only instances of `Overflow_Check` or `Division_Check` they may affect are on the type `Float`, and the only instance of `Range_Check` they may affect is on the variable `z`.

15.6 A COMPARISON WITH PL/I CONDITIONS*

PL/I has a mechanism that is at least superficially similar to the Ada language's exception-handling mechanism. PL/I's *conditions* play a role analogous to the Ada language's exceptions. As with exceptions, some conditions are built into the language, and others may be defined by the programmer. Just as an Ada program may raise an exception, so a PL/I program may raise a condition. Built-in conditions are raised automatically when certain circumstances arise. In addition, both built-in and programmer-defined conditions may be raised explicitly.

However, this is where the similarity ends. There are major differences in the way exceptions and conditions are handled. These differences include the way that a response is associated with an exception or condition occurring in a particular place and the way that a computation is continued after such a response. The purpose of this section is relieve those familiar with PL/I conditions of any preconceptions that will confuse their understanding of Ada exceptions.

For each predefined PL/I condition there is a standard system response. A new response may be associated with a condition by the execution of an `ON` *statement* specifying a block of statements to be executed if the condition is raised. (This block is called an `ON`-*unit*.) `ON` statements are ordinary executable statements that may occur at several places in a sequence of statements, even in an `IF` statement. Thus different `ON`-units may apply to a given statement at different times, and the `ON`-unit applicable at a given time may depend on input data. As a PL/I subprogram or

*This section is optional. In particular, it should be skipped by readers unfamiliar with the "conditions" and "`ON`-units" of PL/I.

block is entered, it inherits the current ON-units of the place from which it was entered. Thus the ON-unit in effect for a given condition when a subprogram is entered depends on the ON statements executed by its caller before the subprogram was called.

In contrast, Ada exception handlers are permanently associated with sequences of statements when the handler appears in the same frame as the statements. It is easy to determine by cursory examination of a single frame whether an exception raised in a particular statement will be handled within that frame or propagated. If it will be handled, it is just as easy to identify the handler that will be executed. It is still possible to associate different handlers with different parts of a sequence of statements by enclosing those parts in block statements.

When a PL/I condition is raised and execution of an ON-unit begins, the ON-unit remains the current ON-unit for that condition. Thus, if the condition is raised again during execution of the ON-unit, another invocation of the same ON-unit begins. This can easily lead to an unusual form of nonterminating recursion, with the ON-unit repeatedly initiating new invocations of itself. To avoid this, it is often necessary to begin an ON-unit for a particular condition with an ON statement establishing a new current ON-unit for the condition.

The rules associating fixed exception handlers with fixed regions of text guarantee that this problem cannot arise in the Ada language. An exception handler can never apply to itself. If an exception is raised during execution of a handler, control is propagated out of the frame containing the handler.

In PL/I, the raising of a condition is viewed as a momentary interruption of the normal flow of control. After the ON-unit corresponding to a condition is executed, execution normally resumes at about the place it was interrupted by the raising of the condition. (The exact continuation point depends on the condition that was raised. In some cases, execution is resumed at the point just after the statement that raised the condition. In other cases, execution is resumed precisely at the point where the condition was raised, possibly in the middle of a statement. Finally, some conditions are meant to be handled by ON-units that repair the problem that raised the condition. After an ON-unit for one of these conditions is executed, the program backs up and retries the operation that failed.) However, an ON-unit may contain a GOTO statement that transfers control out of the ON-unit and resumes execution at some other point. In certain circumstances, this is the only appropriate way to resume execution because resumption at the place the condition was raised would have undefined results.

When an exception is raised in a sequence of Ada statements, that sequence of statements is abandoned, never resumed. Control is passed to a handler if there is one; otherwise, it is passed to an invoking program unit according to the rules for propagation. Execution of a handler is followed by whatever would have followed normal completion of the frame. A GOTO statement in a handler cannot transfer control back into the sequence of statements that raised the exception.

Part of the reason for this difference in the way computations are resumed is that Ada exceptions are intended to be raised in abnormal situations, while PL/I conditions may be raised routinely. For example, there are PL/I conditions raised whenever output to a file is about to start a new page or when a program is about to complete execution. Another condition (intended primarily for debugging) is raised whenever specified variables are modified or specified statements are about to be executed. The end of a PL/I input file can *only* be detected by a condition raised by an input statement when no input data remains. PL/I conditions provide a way to intercept execution of the program at critical points and then continue. Ada exceptions provide a way to react to a problem by executing an alternative sequence of statements.

There are over twenty conditions built into PL/I, considerably more specific than the five exceptions predefined in the Ada language. Moreover, PL/I provides a number of built-in functions that may be called in an ON-unit to narrow down the cause of the condition even further. There are also functions returning the improper data values that cause certain conditions to be raised, and there are means for an ON-unit to replace this improper data with new values specified in the ON-unit. A PL/I programmer must realize that in an Ada exception handler he has significantly less information about the cause of the exception and significantly less control over where execution will be resumed and with what values.

15.7 GUIDELINES FOR THE USE OF EXCEPTIONS

Learning the rules for declaring, raising, propagating, and handling exceptions is one matter; learning to use exceptions properly is another. Inappropriate use of exceptions can actually make a program's behavior less predictable and less reliable and make the program harder to understand. This section offers some guidelines on using exceptions properly.

Exceptions should not be used to specify "normal" computations. For example, given the declarations

```
TYPE Day_Type IS
   (Sunday, Monday, Tuesday, Wednesday, Thursday, Friday,
    Saturday);
Day: Day_Type;
```

the statement

```
BEGIN
   Day := Day_Type'Succ (Day);
EXCEPTION
   WHEN Constraint_Error =>
      Day := Sunday;
END;
```

advances Day to the next day of the week by using an exception handler to cover the case where Day = Saturday (so that evaluation of Day_Type'Succ (Day) raises Constraint_Error). The following formulation expresses the computation more simply and directly:

```
IF Day = Saturday THEN
   Day := Sunday;
ELSE
   Day := Day_Type'Succ (Day);
END IF;
```

It decomposes the problem into two distinct cases and shows how the problem is solved in each case. The flow of control is represented explicitly and corresponds to the textual structure of the program.

In contrast, consider the problem of responding to a multiplication that overflows. If `a`, `b`, and `c` all belong to the subtype `Float RANGE 1.0 .. Float'Last`, the following statements set `c` to `a * b`, approximating the product by the value `Float'Last` in the unusual case that the multiplication overflows:

```
IF a > Float'Last / b THEN
   c := Float'Last;
ELSE
   c := a * b;
END IF;
```

Assuming that `Float'Machine_Overflows` is true, this can also be programmed with an exception handler, as follows:

```
BEGIN
   c := a * b;
EXCEPTION
   WHEN Numeric_Error | Constraint_Error =>
      c := Float'Last;
END;
```

In this case, the formulation using a handler is more direct, easier to understand, and probably considerably more efficient.

The difference is that the handler for advancing from `Saturday` to `Sunday` is invoked to process data that arise predictably during the normal course of processing, while the handler for multiplying `a` and `b` is invoked in response to a situation that is not normally expected to arise. The first handler obscures the normal processing involved in determining the next day of the week. The second handler separates the description of the aberrant case from the description of normal processing, making the normal processing easier to understand.

Of course, the distinction between a case arising in normal processing and a deviation from normal processing is a subjective one. However, it is often possible to arrive at a consensus. Many informal software requirements are actually written by describing the normal rules that must be followed and then listing "exceptions" to these rules that apply in special circumstances. Except in the case of out-of-range numeric results, it is usually easy to avoid raising `Constraint_Error` by testing for some condition before executing a statement that might raise that exception. However, such tests are difficult to write for `Numeric_Error` and `Storage_Error`.

There is rarely a simple abstract description, in terms of the problem a program is to solve, of the input data that will cause these exceptions to be raised. For that reason, the raising of `Numeric_Error` or `Storage_Error` tends to be perceived as an aberrant situation.

Sometimes, within a limited context, it is possible to infer the reason that an exception was raised and to take appropriate corrective action. `Numeric_Error` might be handled by using the highest or lowest value in a type as the value of an arithmetic operation, as in the multiplication above. Alternatively, it might be handled by raising a programmer-declared exception signifying that certain specific values were too high or low. `Storage_Error` raised by an allocator might be handled by determining which already-allocated variables can be reused and making arrangements to reuse them.

However, the appropriate response to an exception is not always this clear. As Section 15.3 explained, the predefined exceptions are broadly defined and may be raised for reasons other than those that occur to a programmer when he writes a handler. Thus contexts in which a predefined exception might be raised for a known reason should be enclosed in a small block statement that handles the exception either directly or by raising a more specific programmer-declared exception.

Moreover, wise program designs recognize that programmers are fallible, and they anticipate that an exception might be raised for an unforeseen reason. A `WHEN OTHERS` handler can handle all exceptions not explicitly considered by earlier handlers. (An exception *e* that is anticipated but that is simply to be propagated when it is raised can be handled by a handler of the form

```
WHEN e => RAISE;
```

so that it is not handled by the `WHEN OTHERS` handler.) The most appropriate action for the `WHEN OTHERS` handler is to perform any necessary clean-up actions and then raise a special exception whose meaning is "Something has gone wrong, but it's not clear what." (If there is another subprogram higher up in the calling hierarchy that can make sense out of the original exception, then the exception is not unforeseen, and the program design should explicitly call on the lower-level subprogram to raise a more specific exception.)

Thus we have considered two cases. When we are certain of the cause of an exception, we can either take direct action to correct the problem or we can pass on the responsibility to a calling program by raising a new exception uniquely identifying the cause of the problem. When we are uncertain of the cause of an exception, we can only give up, cleaning up after ourselves and informing the calling program that some unanticipated exception has occurred. It would be wrong to do any more. Handling an exception by guessing at its cause might give us a false sense that a program was more reliable, but in fact the program would be less reliable and less predictable.

Some programs process successive fragments of input data independently, producing the output corresponding to one fragment before reading the next fragment. If an unanticipated exception arises during the processing of one fragment, an appropriate message can be produced and the program can continue with the next fragment. For example, suppose we have a hypothetical function Simplification_Of that takes a mathematical formula as a string of up to 132 characters and returns a simplification of the formula as a 132-character string. (For example, the formula "(a+b)*(a-b)+b**2" might be simplified to "a**2".) We want to write a program that will read a sequence of formulas given one formula per line and write a corresponding sequence of simplified formulas. The main program can be structured as follows:

```
WITH Basic_IO; USE Basic_IO;

PROCEDURE Simplify_Formulas IS

   SUBTYPE Formula_Subtype IS String (1 .. 132);
   Input_Line, Simplified_Formula : Formula_Subtype;
   Line_Length                    : Integer RANGE 0 .. 132;

   FUNCTION Simplification_Of
      (Formula : String) RETURN Formula_Subtype
      IS SEPARATE;

BEGIN

   WHILE NOT End_Of_File LOOP

      Get_Line (Input_Line, Line_Length);

      BEGIN
         Simplified_Formula :=
            Simplification_Of
               ( Input_Line (1 .. Line_Length) );
         Put (Simplified_Formula);
         New_Line;
      EXCEPTION
         WHEN OTHERS =>
            Put
               ("***** UNABLE TO SIMPLIFY THE FOLLOWING " &
                "FORMULA DUE TO INTERNAL PROGRAM " &
                "MALFUNCTION:");
            New_Line;
            Put ( Input_Line (1 .. Line_Length) );
            New_Line;
      END;

   END LOOP;

END Simplify_Formulas;
```

(This program treats all exceptions propagated by Simplification_Of as unanticipated errors. If the function could be written to raise a special exception, for instance, Formula_Syntax_Error, when given an invalid input, we could rewrite the handlers of the main program as follows:

```
EXCEPTION
   WHEN Formula_Syntax_Error =>
      Put ("/**** INVALID SYNTAX FOR FORMULA:");
      New_Line;
      Put ( Input_Line (1 .. Line_Length) );
      New_Line;
   WHEN OTHERS =>
      Put
         ("***** UNABLE TO SIMPLIFY THE FOLLOWING " &
          "FORMULA DUE TO INTERNAL PROGRAM " &
          "MALFUNCTION:");
      New_Line;
      Put ( Input_Line (1 .. Line_Length) );
      New_Line;
```

The exception `Formula_Syntax_Error` would have to be declared in the main program.)

More typically, recovery from an exception is more complex than this. An unexpected error arising in the middle of a computation may make all further processing impossible or unreliable. An interactive program could respond to this situation by giving its user the choice of terminating execution, restarting the computation with new data, or changing the state of the program in some more limited way and then retrying part of the computation. In a batch program with a predetermined input stream, the only sensible response might be to provide an informative error message and then terminate. A program that concedes defeat is always preferable to one that continues to produce output when there is no longer any basis for believing that the output is correct.

There is another approach to handling unanticipated errors that is appropriate when an extraordinarily high degree of reliability is more important than the cost of the software (for instance, on a manned space flight). This approach is to have one or more independently developed backup versions of each software component. When a software component "fails" by raising an unanticipated exception, it can be "replaced" by a "spare." That is, a backup version can be invoked, with the exception propagated only after all backup versions fail. Such a system has the greatest chance of survival if the primary and backup versions use entirely different algorithms.

For systems embedded in hardware, exceptions may signal either hardware or software failure. There are a number of possible responses to the exception. One not usually thought of by those who have dealt only with software is to retry the operation that raised the exception, in the hope that it was due to a transient hardware failure. Another possible response is to logically disconnect the malfunctioning hardware and connect a spare. Alternatively, if no spare is available, it might be possible to reconfigure the system to work in a degraded mode without the malfunctioning device. In this case, the handler would be responsible for the reconfiguration. (One example of this approach is informing the scheduler of an operating system to stop using one of the processors of a multiprocessor system.

Another example is informing the nodes on a communications network that one of the nodes is no longer able to receive or relay messages.)

In many cases, the most appropriate response for a subprogram encountering a problem is to report the problem to its caller. In languages other than the Ada language, this is typically done by providing each subprogram with an extra parameter, often called a status parameter. A subprogram sets its status parameter to one value upon normal completion of its job or to other values corresponding to various error situations. After one subprogram calls another, the calling subprogram checks the value that the called subprogram placed in the status parameter. If it is not the "normal completion" value, the calling subprogram immediately performs any appropriate "handling" actions, sets its own status parameter to a corresponding abnormal value, and returns.

In the Ada language, this error-reporting strategy is much easier to implement, because it is implicit in the exception-propagation mechanism. An Ada programmer can simply declare an exception for each abnormal status value and raise that exception instead of setting a status parameter and returning. More importantly, there is no need to check a status parameter after each subprogram call; a subprogram call raising an exception will automatically cause the calling subprogram's handler to be invoked in place of the remaining statements of the calling subprogram. This handler can re-raise an exception after performing any appropriate handling actions. If there are no handling or clean-up actions to be performed, the handler can be omitted, and the calling subprogram will automatically propagate the exception to its own caller. The removal of explicit status parameter checks after each subprogram call unclutters the calling subprogram and makes the normal course of processing clearer.

When writing a general-purpose software component to be used in many different programs, you have no control over how that component will be invoked. If subprograms are called in the wrong order or with incorrect parameter values, there may be no sensible result values. Along with the "normal" facilities, a general-purpose software component should provide one exception for each invalid way of using these facilities. Every subprogram call should have a precisely defined outcome—either normal completion with certain parameter values, result values, or effects upon the state of the system, or the raising of a particular exception.

The exceptions that may be raised by a reusable software component should be declared in the visible part of a package specification. Even if your primary purpose is to provide a single subprogram that may raise an exception (e.g., the function `Square_Root` at the beginning of Section 15.5), you should enclose the subprogram in a package (e.g., `Square_Root_Package`) and declare the subprogram and the exception in the package specification. Exceptions that may be raised are part of the interface of the facility you are providing. By declaring the exceptions in a package specification, you allow users of the package to name the exception in handlers. Were the exception to be declared in a subprogram or package body, it still could be propagated out of that body. However, outside of its scope, an exception cannot be named, so it can only be handled by a `WHEN OTHERS` handler. This greatly limits its usefulness.

The beginning of this section suggested that it is better to handle normally arising conditions with IF statements than by knowingly allowing exceptions to be raised and then handling those exceptions. A general-purpose package should afford its user the chance to follow this guideline. Specifically, if a package provides a subprogram that may raise an exception, it should also provide a mechanism for a programmer to determine, without actually raising the exception, whether a particular call on one of the package's subprograms *would* raise an exception. For example, a package providing operations on stacks, including a procedure Pop that raises an exception when called with an empty stack, should also provide a function that may be used to test whether a stack is empty before calling Pop.

The proper handling of exceptions, both anticipated and unanticipated, is a difficult matter that must be considered carefully in the initial high-level design of a program. The response of a system to exceptional conditions is an important aspect of the system's behavior. A system design is not complete if it does not address this issue. In particular, the design must account for all necessary clean-up actions and assign them to specific program components. It is better to confront the problem directly when designing the system than to sweep it under the rug and let programmers working on individual components haphazardly invent their own exception-handling schemes. Just as a system design specifies the way subprograms interact using parameters and function results, so it should specify the way they interact using exceptions.

Programmers writing individual components of a system should adhere to the exception-handling scheme specified in the system design. A component should never propagate an exception that the system design does not call for it to propagate. (However, a good design will allow any component to propagate a special exception reserved for unanticipated problems.) A programmer can rarely be certain that a subprogram meets this criterion unless it has a WHEN OTHERS handler to intercept unexpected exceptions.

Similarly, if the system design calls upon a subprogram to propagate a particular exception whenever it is encountered, the subprogram should not handle the exception without re-raising it. In fact, if propagating the exception is the only action to be performed when the exception is encountered, this should be reflected explicitly by a handler of the form

```
WHEN ... =>
   RAISE;
```

As indicated earlier, this prevents the exception from being intercepted by a WHEN OTHERS handler. Moreover, it documents for future maintenance programmers that the exception may be raised and propagated by the subprogram. (If an exception is raised by a low-level subprogram and handled by another subprogram several levels higher without being mentioned at the intermediate levels through which it is propagated, it will be very hard for a reader to understand the exception propagation scheme.) Even if the subprogram contains no WHEN OTHERS handler presently, a handler consisting only of a RAISE statement guards against the possibility that one might be introduced later, inadvertently handling an exception that should be propagated.

A programmer's use of exceptions is largely, but not completely, determined by the system design. It is acceptable for a component to declare, raise, and handle exceptions not specified as part of the system design, provided that all such exceptions are handled internally rather than propagated. Such exceptions are simply part of the component's implementation and are of no concern to other parts of the system.

15.8 SUMMARY

An attempt to perform an illegal action, such as to divide by zero or to use an invalid index value for an array component, causes an *exception* to be *raised. Exception handlers* can be supplied in block statements, subprogram bodies, and package bodies to specify what is to be done when an exception is raised.

The full form of a block statement, including exception handlers, is

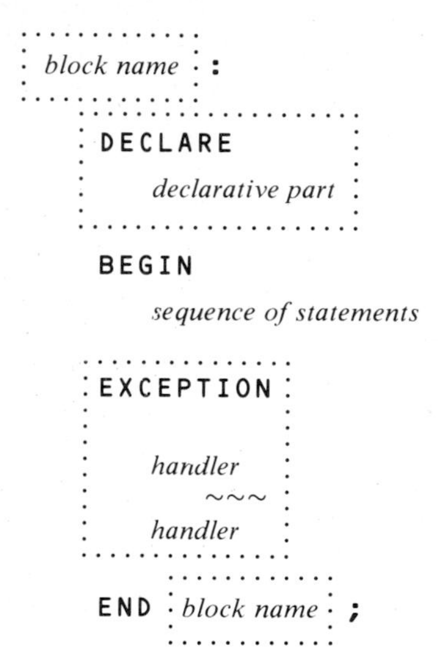

The form of a handler is

WHEN *exception name* | ~~~ | *exception name* =>
    sequence of statements

or, for the last handler in the list,

WHEN OTHERS =>
    sequence of statements

The full form of a subprogram body, including exception handlers, is

```
subprogram specification IS
    declarative part
BEGIN
    sequence of statements
.................
:EXCEPTION      :
:    handler    :
:        ~~~    :
:    handler    :
.................
      .....................
END : subprogram name : ;
      .....................
```

The full form of a package body, including exception handlers, is

```
PACKAGE BODY package name IS
    declarative part
......................................
:  BEGIN                              :
:      sequence of initialization statements :
: ...............                     :
: :EXCEPTION    :                     :
: :    handler  :                     :
: :       ~~~   :                     :
: :    handler  :                     :
: ...............                     :
......................................
      ..................
END : package name : ;
      ..................
```

Handlers may occur in a package body only if the package body contains initialization statements. The handlers apply only to the execution of those initialization statements during elaboration of the package body.

In each case, an exception arising during execution of the sequence of statements causes the sequence of statements to be *abandoned.* If there is a corresponding handler—that is, a handler naming the exception, or failing that, a **WHEN OTHERS** handler—that handler is executed *instead.* This completes the execution of the block statement or subprogram body, or the elaboration or the package body, in which the handler occurred. If there is no corresponding handler, the sequence of statements in which the exception occurred is again abandoned, but the exception is *propagated.* That is, the exception is re-raised at a higher level of control. An unhandled exception in the main program causes the main program to be abandoned.

Handlers apply to sequences of statements, not to declarative parts. An exception arising in the declarative part of a block statement, subprogram body, or package body causes execution of the block statement or subprogram body, or elaboration of the package body, to be abandoned immediately. The exception is propagated.

Similarly, handlers do not apply to themselves. An exception arising in a handler causes the block statement, subprogram body, or package body containing the handler to be abandoned, and the exception is propagated.

Propagation of an exception from a subprogram body causes the exception to be re-raised at the point from which the subprogram was called. Propagation of an exception from a block statement causes the block statement itself to re-raise the exception within the sequence of statements containing the block statement. Propagation of an exception from a package body occurring in a declarative part causes the package body (viewed as a declaration) to raise the exception within the declarative part. Propagation of an exception from a library package (i.e., a separately compiled package that is not a subunit), causes the main program to be abandoned.

The Ada language provides the following predefined exceptions:

`Constraint_Error` — This exception may be raised in a wide variety of circumstances, most of which correspond to the use of a value in a context where it would violate some subtype constraint. These include assignment of a value that would violate a variable's range constraint and the use of an out-of-bounds value as an array index, for example. `Constraint_Error` is also raised by an attempt to determine the allocated variable pointed to by a null access value.

`Numeric_Error` — This exception is raised by a numeric operation that cannot produce a correct result, either because the result is undefined (as in division by zero) or because the result of the operation overflows.

`Program_Error` — This exception is raised when execution of a program reveals that the program was improperly formed (for example, when a function attempts to complete without executing a **`RETURN`** statement).

`Storage_Error` — This exception is raised when a program runs out of storage, typically during evaluation of an allocator or a subprogram call at a deep level of recursion.

`Tasking_Error` — This exception is raised in multitask programs. It will be discussed in Chapter 19.

In addition, exceptions that can be raised by input and output operations will be described in Chapter 17. Whether or not a given expression raises `Numeric_Error` in a given situation depends on the implementation. Sometimes an out-of-range numeric result can lead to either `Numeric_Error` or `Constraint_Error`, and handlers should account for both possibilities.

A programmer can define his own exceptions with exception declarations of the form

identifier **,** ~~~ **,** *identifier* **: EXCEPTION ;**

Such declarations typically occur in package specifications, where their purpose is to declare exceptions that can be raised by the subprograms a package provides. However, they are also allowed within declarative parts. An existing exception can be declared with a new name by an exception declaration of the following form:

identifier **: EXCEPTION RENAMES** *exception name* **;**

A programmer-defined exception can be raised by a **RAISE** statement of the form

RAISE *exception name* **;**

(A predefined exception can also be raised in this way, but that is not good programming practice.) A raise statement of the form

RAISE ;

is allowed only within an exception handler. It specifies that whatever exception that caused the handler to be entered should be re-raised within the handler (and therefore propagated).

Raising of predefined exceptions requires that certain checks be performed during program execution. If a programmer

has a program that runs correctly, but too slowly,
has determined with metering tools that the program is spending most of its time in a particular, small region,
sees no other way to speed up that region of the program, and
is positive, after careful examination of the program, that certain conditions being checked for cannot possibly arise anyway,

he can advise the compiler to eliminate certain checks within that region. This is done with the `Suppress` pragma.

If the compiler takes this advice, it may greatly improve execution speed. However, if the conditions for which checks were suppressed do arise after all, the subsequent behavior of the program is unpredictable. Therefore the `Suppress` pragma is dangerous and should be used only as a last resort.

The Suppress pragma has two forms:

```
PRAGMA Suppress ( check name ) ;

PRAGMA Suppress ( check name, [On =>] entity name ) ;
```

The first form may occur only within a declarative part. It specifies that within the corresponding sequence of statements, the named check need not be performed. The second form indicates that the named check need not be performed for a particular object, type, or program unit. The second form is allowed not only within a declarative part, but also within a package specification, provided that the entity named is one declared earlier in the package specification. It states that checks may be omitted for all uses of the entity, inside or outside the package.

The check name may be one of the following:

Access_Check	(for Constraint_Error) Does a variable name contain a null access value?
Discriminant_Check	(for Constraint_Error) Is a discriminant constraint being violated? Does a selected component name some component of a variant that is not currently active?
Division_Check	(for Numeric_Error) Is the second operand of /, REM, or MOD zero?
Elaboration_Check	(for Program_Error) Is a program unit being invoked before it has been elaborated?
Index_Check	(for Constraint_Error) Is an index constraint being violated?
Length_Check	(for Constraint_Error) Do two arrays have incompatible lengths (for a copying operation or the application of a predefined logical operator)?
Overflow_Check	(for Constraint_Error) Does the result of a numeric operation lie outside the range of the result type?
Range_Check	(for Constraint_Error) Is a range constraint being violated? Is the range constraint following a typemark incompatible with the typemark? Are the index values in a named array aggregate invalid? Is a generic unit being used improperly?
Storage_Check	(for Storage_Error) Is there insufficient storage for a particular purpose?

Exception handlers should not be used to specify the handling of "normal" situations that are most straightforwardly detected with ordinary IF statements. Rather, exception handlers are appropriate for situations like overflow and depletion of storage, which cannot easily be predicted. When used properly, exceptions clearly separate normal processing from abnormal processing and simplify the description of the normal processing. In particular, exception propagation makes it simple to implement a strategy in which each subprogram reports its "completion status" to its caller.

Predefined exceptions can be raised at many places in a program for many different reasons. Sometimes, within a restricted context, it is possible to ascertain why a particular predefined exception has been raised. Such a context should be enclosed within a block statement in which the exception is handled either directly or by raising a programmer-defined exception that more precisely indicates the cause of the problem. For systems embedded in hardware, possible responses to an exception include retrying a hardware operation that failed, installing backup hardware, or reconfiguring the system to work in a degraded mode with only some of its hardware functioning.

A WHEN OTHERS handler can be used to capture any exception that arises for an unforeseen reason, such as a programming error. The handler can perform any necessary clean-up actions and then propagate a special programmer-defined exception meant to denote that an unanticipated exception has occurred. This exception can be propagated up the calling hierarchy, with appropriate clean-up actions performed at each level, so that the program can give up gracefully without making any unwarranted assumptions about the cause of the exception. Giving up may entail moving on to another independent piece of processing, terminating the program, or invoking a backup version, for example.

Reusable software components should be written so that each operation raises an exception if it cannot produce a meaningful result. The exceptions raised should be declared in the visible part of a package specification. Additional operations should be provided so that a user can tell without actually invoking an operation whether invocation of that operation would raise an exception.

The handling of exceptions is a difficult issue that must be addressed by a program design. Otherwise, the design cannot be considered complete. Programmers working on individual parts of a program must be careful to adhere to, and not to interfere with, the exception propagation and handling strategy specified in the design.

EXERCISES

15.1 Write a package Mean_Package providing three facilities: a one-dimensional unconstrained array type with components of type Float, a function Mean taking a parameter in this array type and returning the mean of the array components, and an exception Empty_Array_Error raised by Mean when its parameter is a null array.

15.2 Modify the complex numbers package written for Exercise 12.2 to provide an exception raised upon division by the complex number `0+0`*i*.

15.3 Section 13.2 gave a six-compilation-unit program for reading a matrix and printing its inverse. Modify the program as follows:

1. Declare the exception `Singular_Matrix` in the `Matrix_Package` specification.
2. Rewrite the procedure `Invert_Matrix` as a function `Inverse` that returns the inverse of its `Matrix_Type` parameter when the parameter is not singular, but raises the exception `Matrix_Package.Singular_Matrix` when the matrix is singular. (Singularity can be detected in the same way as in Section 13.2.)
3. Modify the main procedure `Print_Inverse` accordingly.

15.4 Design and implement a package providing a private or limited private type for queues of `Integer` values and operations for manipulating such queues. A queue is an object in which values (in this case of type `Integer`) can be inserted (enqueued) and extracted (dequeued). Values are always extracted in the order in which they are inserted. You should provide some limit on the capacity of the queue. It is an error to try to insert an item into a queue filled to capacity or to extract an item from an empty queue.

15.5 Assume there is a package `Engine_Package` providing an interface with a computer-controlled engine. Among the facilities provided by the package are parameterless procedures named `Start_Engine` and `Engage_Engine` and an exception named `Start_Failure`. `Start_Engine` triggers a sequence of actions that normally starts the engine. When this sequence of actions does not cause the engine to start, `Start_Engine` raises the exception `Start_Failure`. The procedure `Engage_Engine` triggers a sequence of actions that engages a running engine. Using `Engine_Package`, write a package providing a procedure `Start_And_Engage_Engine` and an exception `Unable_To_Start_Engine`. `Start_And_Engage_Engine` should call `Engine_Package.Start_Engine` up to five times, until the engine is started, and then call `Engine_Package.Engage_Engine`; or raise `Unable_To_Start_Engine` if the engine cannot be started in five attempts. Use the `DELAY` statement to ensure a delay of at least thirty seconds between each call on `Start_Engine`.

15.6 Give an informal proof that the statements of function `Search_Package.Position_Of_Name` (given in Section 15.4) cannot raise `Constraint_Error`. (Can the same be said of the declarations? Why or why not?) Insert `Suppress` pragmas to advise the compiler to omit unnecessary checks.

15.7 Rewrite the package `Stack_Package` of Section 15.5 to provide an additional function,

```
FUNCTION Stack_Space_Available RETURN Boolean;
```

that indicates whether a call on `Push` can be made without raising `Stack_Overflow_Error`. (*Hint:* Declare a `Cell_List_Type` variable in the package body that points to the cell that will be used on the *next* call to `Push`, or that equals `NULL` if no cell is available. During package initialization and after a cell is added to a stack during a call on `Push`, attempt to allocate another cell and set the variable accordingly.)

15.8 Suppose an aircraft navigation program has three procedures declared as follows:

```
PROCEDURE Get_Position_Version_1 (Position : OUT Position_Type);
PROCEDURE Get_Position_Version_2 (Position : OUT Position_Type);
PROCEDURE Get_Position_Version_3 (Position : OUT Position_Type);
```

All three procedures are designed to compute the same values, using different algorithms. Write a procedure that uses version 2 as a backup for version 1 and version 3 as a backup for version 2 to obtain a `Position_Type` value. Whenever version 1 or 2 raises any exception, its backup should be invoked. If all three versions raise exceptions, your procedure should propagate an exception named `Navigation_Failure`.

CHAPTER

SIXTEEN

GENERIC UNITS

One of the Ada language's goals is to facilitate the writing of general-purpose, reusable software components. *Generic units* make it possible to solve a set of similar but not identical problems with a single program unit. Generic units are *templates* from which several analogous subprograms and packages can be produced without duplication of effort.

16.1 TEMPLATES AND INSTANCES

Let us begin with an example, *symmetric matrices*. A matrix M is *symmetric* if, for all valid indices i and j, $M(i, j) = M(j, i)$. Such matrices might be used, for example, to store distances between pairs of points; the distance from point i to point j is identical to that from point j to point i. Rather than using a traditional two-dimensional array with 10,000 components for a 100-by-100 symmetric matrix, we can save space by storing only the lower left triangle of the array, corresponding to the 5,050 matrix elements for which the row index is greater than or equal to the column index. Because of the symmetry, the values in the upper right triangle of the matrix can be determined by examining the values in the lower left triangle.

The package below implements a private type called `Symmetric_Matrix_Type`, whose values are 100-by-100 symmetric matrices of integers. This type has two operations: The procedure call

```
Store (M, i, j, x)
```

simultaneously replaces the values that we think of as `M (i, j)` and `M (j, i)` by `x`. The function call

```
Component (M, i, j)
```

returns the value we think of as `M (i, j)`. The package specification is as follows:

```
PACKAGE Symmetric_Matrix_Package IS
   TYPE Symmetric_Matrix_Type IS PRIVATE;
   SUBTYPE Index_Subtype IS Integer RANGE 1 .. 100;
   PROCEDURE Store
      (Matrix      : IN OUT Symmetric_Matrix_Type;
       Row, Column : IN Index_Subtype;
       Value       : IN Integer);
   FUNCTION Component
      (Matrix      : Symmetric_Matrix_Type;
       Row, Column : Index_Subtype)
      RETURN Integer;
PRIVATE
   SUBTYPE Internal_Index_Subtype IS
      Integer RANGE 1 .. 5050;
   TYPE Symmetric_Matrix_Type IS
      ARRAY (Internal_Index_Subtype) OF Integer;
END Symmetric_Matrix_Package;
```

We implement a symmetric matrix by storing the values in the lower left triangle in a one-dimensional array. Within the one-dimensional array, the one component of the first row of the triangle is followed by the two components of the second row of the triangle, then the three components of the third row, and so forth, as shown in Figure 16.1. The indices of the one-dimensional array run from 1 to 5,050, and the index corresponding to row i, column j (where i is greater than or equal to j because our attention is confined to the lower left triangle) is given by the following formula:

$$\frac{i(i-1)}{2} + j$$

The package body describing this implementation is quite simple:

```
PACKAGE BODY Symmetric_Matrix_Package IS
   FUNCTION Component_Position
      (Row, Column: Index_Subtype)
      RETURN Internal_Index_Subtype IS
      Lower, Higher: Index_Subtype;
```

```
      BEGIN

         IF Row < Column THEN
            Lower := Row;
            Higher := Column;
         ELSE
            Lower := Column;
            Higher := Row;
         END IF;

         RETURN Higher * (Higher-1) / 2 + Lower;

      END Component_Position;

      PROCEDURE Store
         (Matrix      : IN OUT Symmetric_Matrix_Type;
          Row, Column : IN Index_Subtype;
          Value       : IN Integer) IS
      BEGIN
         Matrix ( Component_Position (Row, Column) ) := Value;
      END Store;

      FUNCTION Component
         (Matrix      : Symmetric_Matrix_Type;
          Row, Column : Index_Subtype)
         RETURN Integer IS
      BEGIN
         RETURN Matrix ( Component_Position (Row, Column) );
      END Component;

   END Symmetric_Matrix_Package;
```

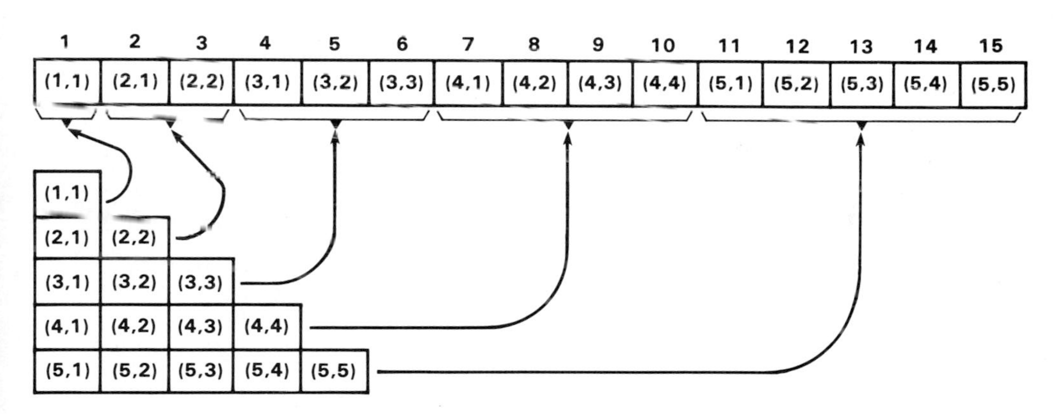

Figure 16.1 The first five rows of the lower triangle of a symmetric matrix. The rows have one, two, three, four, and five components, respectively. These components are stored in the first fifteen elements of a one-dimensional array, row by row. $(1+2+3+4+5=15.)$ The matrix component corresponding to the index values `(i, j)` is stored in component `i * (i - 1) / 2 + j` of the one-dimensional array.

Suppose, however, that the same program also uses 100-by-100 symmetric matrices of strings. A new type must be declared to represent such matrices. New subprograms must be provided. These subprograms will be analogous to those provided in `Symmetric_Matrix_Package`, but with different parameter and result types. The new type and subprograms can be provided by a second package identical to the first except for the type of the matrix components.

Not only is the writing of this near-copy a tedious task; it also makes the program harder to maintain. If the formula used in `Component_Position` were found to contain an error, for example, that error would have to be fixed in two places. Virtually duplicate programming would also be required for a package providing different-sized symmetric matrices with the same component type, for example 150-by-150 symmetric matrices of integers.

Redundant programming can be avoided by the use of *generic units.* There are two kinds of generic units—*generic subprograms* and *generic packages.* A generic unit is a *template* for a subprogram or package, with certain parts left blank. An *instance* of the template is a subprogram or package created by filling in the blanks. The process of creating an instance of a template by filling in its blanks is called *instantiation.*

Conceptually, a template for `Symmetric_Matrix_Package` would look like this:

```
PACKAGE [name of package] IS

   TYPE Symmetric_Matrix_Type IS PRIVATE;

   SUBTYPE Index_Subtype IS
      Integer RANGE 1 .. [number of rows and columns];

   PROCEDURE Store
      (Matrix      : IN OUT Symmetric_Matrix_Type;
       Row, Column : IN Index_Subtype;
       Value       : IN [type of components] );

   FUNCTION Component
      (Matrix      : Symmetric_Matrix_Type;
       Row, Column : Index_Subtype)
      RETURN [type of components];

PRIVATE

   SUBTYPE Internal_Index_Subtype IS
      Integer RANGE
         1 ..
              [number of rows and columns] *
                  ([number of rows and columns] + 1) / 2;

   TYPE Symmetric_Matrix_Type IS
      ARRAY (Internal_Index_Subtype) OF [type of components];

END [name of package];
```

```
PACKAGE BODY [name of package] IS
   FUNCTION Component_Position
      (Row, Column: Index_Subtype)
      RETURN Internal_Index_Subtype IS
      Lower, Higher: Index_Subtype;
   BEGIN
      IF Row < Column THEN
         Lower := Row;
         Higher := Column;
      ELSE
         Lower := Column;
         Higher := Row;
      END IF;
      RETURN Higher * (Higher-1) / 2 + Lower;
   END Component_Position;
   PROCEDURE Store
      (Matrix       : IN OUT Symmetric_Matrix_Type;
       Row, Column  : IN Index_Subtype;
       Value        : IN [type of components] ) IS
   BEGIN
      Matrix ( Component_Position (Row, Column) ) := Value;
   END Store;
   FUNCTION Component
      (Matrix      : Symmetric_Matrix_Type;
       Row, Column : Index_Subtype)
      RETURN [type of components] IS
   BEGIN
      RETURN Matrix ( Component_Position (Row, Column) );
   END Component;
END [name of package];
```

The bracketed items in this template represent blanks. The number 5050 in the declaration of Internal_Index_Subtype has been replaced by a formula for deriving the number of components in the lower left triangle of the matrix from the number of rows and columns, but otherwise this template corresponds exactly to Symmetric_Matrix_Package. An instance of this template can be obtained by replacing all occurrences of the blank *[name of package]* by the same identifier, all occurrences of the blank *[number of rows and columns]* by the same integer literal, and all occurrences of the blank *[type of components]* by the same typemark.

A generic template always implicitly contains a blank to be filled with the name of the instance. In addition, there may be explicit blanks for values, for variables, for subprograms, and for types and subtypes. Within the template, explicit blanks are specified by *generic formal parameters*. A generic instantiation specifies how an instance is to be created. Besides specifying a name for the instance, the generic instantiation may provide *generic actual parameters* specifying how the explicit blanks are to be filled in.

A generic template consists of two parts: the *generic declaration* and the *generic body*. The form of a generic declaration is

```
GENERIC
   ..................................
   : generic formal parameter declaration :
   :        ~~~                        :
   : generic formal parameter declaration :
   ..................................
unit declaration
```

where the unit declaration is either a subprogram declaration or a package specification. Section 16.2 explains the many forms of generic formal parameter declarations. A generic body has the same form as an ordinary subprogram body or package body.

Here is a generic package for symmetric matrices:

```
-- Generic package declaration:
GENERIC
   -- Generic formal parameter declarations:
   Matrix_Size : IN Positive;
   TYPE Component_Type IS PRIVATE;
PACKAGE Symmetric_Matrix_Package_Template IS
   TYPE Symmetric_Matrix_Type IS PRIVATE;
   SUBTYPE Index_Subtype IS Integer RANGE 1 .. Matrix_Size;
   PROCEDURE Store
      (Matrix        : IN OUT Symmetric_Matrix_Type;
       Row, Column : IN Index_Subtype;
       Value         : IN Component_Type);
   FUNCTION Component
      (Matrix        : Symmetric_Matrix_Type;
       Row, Column : Index_Subtype)
      RETURN Component_Type;
PRIVATE
   SUBTYPE Internal_Index_Subtype IS
      Integer RANGE 1 .. Matrix_Size * (Matrix_Size+1) / 2;
   TYPE Symmetric_Matrix_Type IS
      ARRAY (Internal_Index_Subtype) OF Component_Type;
END Symmetric_Matrix_Package_Template;
```

```
-- Generic package body:

PACKAGE BODY Symmetric_Matrix_Package_Template IS

   FUNCTION Component_Position
      (Row, Column : Index_Subtype)
      RETURN Internal_Index_Subtype IS

      Lower, Higher : Index_Subtype;

   BEGIN

      IF Row < Column THEN
         Lower := Row;
         Higher := Column;
      ELSE
         Lower := Column;
         Higher := Row;
      END IF;

      RETURN Higher * (Higher-1) / 2 + Lower;

   END Component_Position;

   PROCEDURE Store
      (Matrix       : IN OUT Symmetric_Matrix_Type;
       Row, Column : IN Index_Subtype;
       Value        : IN Component_Type) IS
   BEGIN
      Matrix ( Component_Position (Row, Column) ) := Value;
   END Store;

   FUNCTION Component
      (Matrix      : Symmetric_Matrix_Type;
       Row, Column : Index_Subtype)
      RETURN Component_Type IS
   BEGIN
      RETURN Matrix ( Component_Position (Row, Column) );
   END Component;

END Symmetric_Matrix_Package_Template;
```

The line

```
Matrix_Size : IN Positive;
```

is a generic formal parameter declaration. It specifies that the identifier `Matrix_Size` acts as a blank for a value of subtype `Positive` within the generic package. The line

```
TYPE Component_Type IS PRIVATE;
```

is also a generic formal parameter declaration. It specifies that the identifier Component_Type acts as a blank for the name of a nonlimited type within the generic package. (As we shall see in Section 16.2, this blank does not have to be filled in with the name of a private type.) Finally, the generic package name Symmetric_Matrix_Package_Template acts as a blank for the name of a package created as an instance of the generic package. Thus this generic package is a direct expression of the template given earlier.

Here is an instantiation of Symmetric_Matrix_Package_Template:

```
PACKAGE Mileage_Table_Package IS
   NEW Symmetric_Matrix_Package_Template
      (Matrix_Size    => 25,
       Component_Type => Float);
```

It declares a package named Mileage_Table_Package. This package is an instance of the generic package, with the generic formal parameters Matrix_Size and Component_Type replaced by the value 25 and the type Float, respectively.

At first, generic instantiation seems to be a form of "macro expansion," in which the text of the instantiation is replaced by a copy of the template with the blanks filled in. However, this model is not quite accurate. A generic unit is actually compiled—either separately or as part of an enclosing compilation unit—before it is used in an instantiation. When compiling a generic unit, a compiler checks that the unit is internally consistent. Depending on the compiler, compilation of a generic unit may produce machine code that is general enough to work for a wide variety of generic parameters, or it may save a copy of the source module. (In the first case, an assignment statement might be translated into a machine-language loop to move some number of bytes, where the number is stored in a "control block" and depends on the size of a type passed as a generic parameter. Compilation of a generic instantiation might have the effect of filling in a control block containing this number. In the second case, a generic instantiation would be implemented by retrieving the copy of the source module, making appropriate textual substitutions, and compiling the resulting program text.) The external behavior of generic units is independent of the underlying implementation, so a programmer does not have to know how his compiler implements generic units.

Here is an example of a generic subprogram:

```
-- Generic subprogram declaration:

GENERIC

   -- Generic formal parameter declaration:
   TYPE Discrete_Type IS ( <> );

FUNCTION Cyclic_Successor_Template
   (x : Discrete_Type) RETURN Discrete_Type;
```

```
-- Generic subprogram body:

FUNCTION Cyclic_Successor_Template
   (x : Discrete_Type) RETURN Discrete_Type IS

BEGIN
   IF x = Discrete_Type'Last THEN
      RETURN Discrete_Type'First;
   ELSE
      RETURN Discrete_Type'Succ (x);
   END IF;

END Cyclic_Successor_Template;
```

The line

```
TYPE Discrete_Type IS ( <> );
```

is a generic formal parameter declaration. It specifies that the identifier `Discrete_Type` acts as a blank for the name of an enumeration or integer subtype within the generic function. In addition, the template name `Cyclic_Successor_Template` acts as a blank for the name of a function created as an instance of this generic function. Each instance of this generic function is a one-parameter function that treats the discrete subtype as a cycle in which the last value is followed by the first; the function returns the value following its parameter in this cycle.

Unlike an ordinary subprogram, a generic subprogram must always consist of both a declaration and a body. The declaration begins with the word `GENERIC`, possibly followed by generic formal parameters. The body is an ordinary subprogram body. The following is illegal:

```
-- ILLEGAL generic function!
-- Generic declaration and generic body cannot be combined:

GENERIC

   TYPE Discrete_Type IS ( <> );

FUNCTION Cyclic_Successor_Template
   (x: Discrete_Type) RETURN Discrete_Type IS

BEGIN

   IF x Discrete_Type'Last THEN
      RETURN Discrete_Type'First;
   ELSE
      RETURN Discrete_Type'Succ (x);
   END IF;

END Cyclic_Successor_Template;
```

In contrast, a generic package is permitted to consist only of a generic declaration, without a generic body. An instance of such a generic package is a package consisting only of a package specification with no package body.

A generic package is not really a package, but a template for a package. Thus it is illegal outside of a generic package to refer to entities declared in the visible part of the generic package declaration. For example, the following expanded name would be illegal outside of the generic unit Symmetric_Matrix_Package_Template:

```
Symmetric_Matrix_Package_Template.Symmetric_Matrix_Type
```

Similarly, a USE clause naming Symmetric_Matrix_Package_Template would be illegal in any context.

In contrast, an instance of a generic package is equivalent in all respects to an ordinary package. Given the previous instantiation of Mileage_Table_Package, the expanded name

```
Mileage_Table_Package.Symmetric_Matrix_Type
```

is a legal expanded name referring to a type provided by that instance. Given the USE clause

```
USE Mileage_Table_Package;
```

this type could be referred to simply as Symmetric_Matrix_Type.

Generic subprograms work the same way. Cyclic_Successor_Template is not a function, but a template for a function. It may not be called; however, it may be instantiated. Each instance is a bona fide function. For example, given the declaration

```
TYPE Day_Type IS
   (Sunday, Monday, Tuesday, Wednesday, Thursday, Friday,
    Saturday);
```

the generic instantiation

```
FUNCTION Day_After IS
   NEW Cyclic_Successor_Template
      (Discrete_Type => Day_Type);
```

makes Day_After the name of an instance of Cyclic_Successor_Template. You may write a call on the function Day_After.

An instantiation of a generic package may take the following form:

```
PACKAGE identifier IS
   NEW template name
      ...............................................................
      : ( generic formal parameter => generic actual parameter ,   :
      :      ~~~,                                                   :
      :   generic formal parameter => generic actual parameter )   :  ;
      ...............................................................
```

(Other forms will be given in Section 16.3.) The identifier becomes the name of the instance, and the generic formal parameters in the template are replaced by the corresponding generic actual parameters in the instance.

Similarly, instantiations of generic procedures and generic functions may be written as follows:

```
PROCEDURE identifier IS
   NEW template name
      ( generic formal parameter => generic actual parameter ,
          ~~~,
        generic formal parameter => generic actual parameter ) ;
```

```
FUNCTION designator IS
   NEW template name
      ( generic formal parameter => generic actual parameter ,
          ~~~,
        generic formal parameter => generic actual parameter ) ;
```

A designator is either an identifier (such as `Day_After`) or a string literal containing an operator symbol (such as `"*"` or `"ABS"`). Again, the identifier or operator symbol becomes the name of the instance, and the generic formal parameters in the template are replaced by the corresponding generic actual parameters in the instance.

Different instances of generic subprograms may be given the same name, causing the instances to be overloaded, if the instances have different parameter and result type profiles (see Section 9.5). A generic function instantiation with an operator symbol defines the instance to be a new overloaded version of the operator. The number of function parameters must be appropriate for that operator (either one or two).

Consider the following declarations of integer types:

```
TYPE Conventional_Hour_Type IS RANGE 1 .. 12;
TYPE Military_Hour_Type IS RANGE 0 .. 23;
```

The following instantiations of `Cyclic_Successor_Template` are permitted (in addition to the instantiation of `Day_After`):

```
FUNCTION Hour_After IS
   NEW Cyclic_Successor_Template
      (Discrete_Type => Conventional_Hour_Type);

FUNCTION Hour_After IS
   NEW Cyclic_Successor_Template
      (Discrete_Type => Military_Hour_Type);
```

These instantiations create two overloaded functions named `Hour_After`, one with a parameter and result of `Conventional_Hour_Type` and one with a parameter and result of `Military_Hour_Type`.

A generic unit may be placed in the declarative part of a block statement, subprogram body, or package body. The generic declaration must occur first, and the generic body must follow later in the same declarative part. A generic unit may also be one of the facilities provided by a package. Then the generic declaration—which describes both the interface for instantiating the template and the interface for using the resulting instance—goes in the package specification, and the generic body goes in the package body. It is possible to write generic packages providing generic packages.

Most often, however, generic units are separately compiled. The generic declaration and generic body are two distinct compilation units. Nonetheless, an Ada compiler is permitted to require that these two compilation units be part of the same compilation, that is, that they be submitted to the compiler together. Similarly, a compiler may require that any subunits of the generic body be part of the same compilation. You should check your compiler's reference manual to see if your compiler imposes these restrictions.

Separately compiled generic declarations are library units, and the corresponding generic bodies are secondary units. (See Section 13.2.) A compilation unit containing an instantiation of a generic unit must name the generic unit in a `WITH` clause. Regardless of whether the generic declaration and generic body are submitted in the same compilation, the generic declaration must be compiled first. Instantiations of a generic unit may be compiled any time after the generic unit has been compiled, even before the generic body has been compiled. Recompilation of the generic declaration requires recompilation of the generic body and of any compilation unit naming the generic unit in a `WITH` clause.

An instantiation is allowed anywhere a subprogram declaration or package specification is allowed. Thus an instantiation may occur in the declarative part of a block statement, subprogram body, or package body, or in a package specification. Furthermore, a generic instantiation may be separately compiled. The resulting instance is, in essence, a separately compiled subprogram or package. It may be used by other compilation units that have `WITH` clauses naming the instance. For example, after the compilation unit

```
WITH Symmetric_Matrix_Package_Template;
PACKAGE Mileage_Table_Package IS
   NEW Symmetric_Matrix_Package_Template
      (Matrix_Size    => 25,
       Component_Type => Float);
```

is compiled, another compilation beginning `WITH Mileage_Table_Package;` may refer to the facilities provided by the instance `Mileage_Table_Package`.

16.2 GENERIC FORMAL PARAMETERS

There are three classes of generic formal parameters. *Generic formal objects* are blanks standing for values or for variables. *Generic formal subprograms* are blanks standing for procedures with specified parameter types or functions with specified procedure and result types. *Generic formal types* are blanks standing for types or subtypes. Generic formal parameter declarations have a distinct form for each class of generic formal parameter. In addition, there are variations within each class. All the forms are discussed in this section.

A generic formal parameter may be defined in terms of another generic formal parameter declared earlier. Generic formal parameter declarations are, in effect, processed in sequence when the generic unit is instantiated. All occurrences of a generic formal parameter within the generic unit are replaced by the corresponding generic actual parameter as the parameter declaration is processed. This includes occurrences of the generic formal parameter in subsequent declarations of other generic formal parameters. The order of processing is critical—a generic formal parameter declaration may refer to another generic formal parameter declared earlier, but not to one declared later.

16.2.1 Generic Formal Objects

There are two kinds of generic formal objects—*generic formal constants* and *generic formal variables.* A generic formal constant stands for a fixed value. A generic formal variable stands for some variable outside the generic unit whose value may change during the lifetime of the instance.

Generic formal object declarations look very much like subprogram parameter specifications. A generic formal constant declaration may be written as follows:

identifier **,** ~~~ **,** *identifier* **: IN** *typemark* **;**

The form of a generic formal variable is similar:

identifier **,** ~~~ **,** *identifier* **: IN OUT** *typemark* **;**

A generic formal constant can be thought of as a generic formal object of mode **IN**, and a generic formal variable can be thought of as a generic formal object of mode **IN OUT**. There are no generic formal objects of mode **OUT**. (As with subprogram parameters, the parameter mode can be omitted, in which case the mode **IN** is assumed. However, it is a good idea to specify the mode explicitly to emphasize that the generic formal parameter stands for a value rather than a variable.)

As with subprogram parameters, a generic actual parameter corresponding to a generic formal parameter of mode **IN** may be any expression of the appropriate type. This expression is evaluated at the time of the generic instantiation and remains fixed for the life of the instance. Within the generic unit, a generic formal constant may be used as an ordinary constant. Its value may be examined but not altered. The generic formal parameter `Matrix_Size` of `Symmetric_Matrix_Package_Template` is an example of a generic formal constant.

A generic actual parameter corresponding to a generic formal parameter of mode **IN OUT** must be a variable of the appropriate type. That is, it must be an object declared in a variable declaration, an allocated variable, a subprogram formal parameter of mode **IN OUT**, or a component of a variable. Within the generic unit, a generic formal variable may be used as an ordinary variable of the type specified by the generic formal variable declaration. Its value may be examined or modified.

The notion of copying a subprogram parameter into a formal parameter of mode IN OUT at the start of a subprogram invocation and then copying it back at the end does not extend to generic formal variables. Rather, the generic formal variable exists for the life of the instance as another name for the variable acting as a generic actual parameter. This variable can be changed from within the generic unit by modifying the generic formal parameter or from outside the generic unit by modifying the generic actual parameter.

The generic actual parameter corresponding to a generic formal variable must be a variable whose scope includes the point of the generic instantiation. The effect of the instantiation is equivalent to making a copy of the generic template within that scope and replacing all references to the generic formal variable by references to the generic actual parameter as a global variable. Since instantiation of a generic unit with generic formal variables has the effect of creating subprograms or packages that refer to global variables, the resulting instances suffer from the drawbacks described in Section 9.8.1 of ordinary subprograms containing global variables.

The following example illustrates both generic formal constants and generic formal variables. However, for the reasons just described, it does not constitute good programming practice:

```
GENERIC
   Variable           : IN OUT Integer;
   Limit, Reset_Value : IN Integer;
PROCEDURE Reset_Integer_Template;


PROCEDURE Reset_Integer_Template IS
BEGIN
   IF Variable > Limit THEN
      Variable := Reset_Value;
   END IF;
END Reset_Integer_Template;
```

Assume some declarative part contains the declarations

```
A : Integer;
B : Integer := 10;
C : Integer := 0;
PROCEDURE Reset_A IS
   NEW Reset_Integer_Template
      (Variable => A, Limit => B, Reset_Value => C);
```

and the accompanying sequence of statements contains calls on the instance Reset_A as well as other statements modifying the value of A. Each call on Reset_A checks whether the current value of A is greater than ten and resets A to zero when this is the case. Because Limit and Reset_Value are generic formal constants, the *values* ten and zero are always used, even if the values of B and C change after the instantiation. Because `Variable` is a generic formal variable, it is always the latest value of `A` that is examined and replaced.

(It would have been preferable to delete the first generic parameter and make `Variable` an ordinary subprogram parameter instead:

```
GENERIC
   Limit, Reset_Value : IN Integer;
PROCEDURE Reset_Integer_Template (Variable : IN OUT Integer);

PROCEDURE Reset_Integer_Template
   (Variable : IN OUT Integer) IS
BEGIN
   IF Variable > Limit THEN
      Variable := Reset_Value;
   END IF;
END Reset_Integer_Template;
```

Then an instantiation might look like this:

```
PROCEDURE Reset IS
   NEW Reset_Integer_Template
      (Limit => B, Reset_Value => C);
```

The call

```
Reset (A);
```

would explicitly name the variable that it examines and sometimes modifies.)

16.2.2 Generic Formal Subprograms

A generic formal subprogram is a "blank" corresponding to a subprogram. It may be either a *generic formal procedure* or a *generic formal function*. A generic formal subprogram declaration consists of a subprogram specification preceded by the word `WITH`. Within the generic unit, the generic formal subprogram may be called in accordance with this subprogram specification. In an instantiation, the generic actual parameter corresponding to the generic formal subprogram may be the name of any subprogram that has the same parameter and result type profile and the same parameter modes. (If the subprogram specification is for a function with no parameters and a result in some enumeration type, the generic actual parameter can be an enumeration literal of that type.) Since each call within the generic unit is in accordance with the subprogram specification and the generic actual parameter has a matching subprogram specification, each call is guaranteed to be in accordance with the specification of the subprogram used as a generic actual parameter.

The subprogram name used as a generic actual parameter may be an overloaded name, possibly an operator symbol. However, for the instantiation to be legal, there must be only one version with a matching parameter and result type profile. It is this version that is used as the generic actual parameter.

The following is an example of a generic function whose single generic parameter is a generic formal function. (Remember, a *generic function* is a template for a function. A *generic formal function* is a generic formal parameter that appears in a template as a blank standing for a function.)

```
GENERIC
   WITH FUNCTION Term (Index: Integer) RETURN Float;
FUNCTION Sum_Template (From, To: Integer) RETURN Float;

FUNCTION Sum_Template (From, To: Integer) RETURN Float IS
   Sum: Float := 0.0;
BEGIN
   FOR i IN From .. To LOOP
      Sum := Sum + Term (i);
   END LOOP;
   RETURN Sum;
END Sum_Template;
```

The line

```
WITH FUNCTION Term (Index: Integer) RETURN Float;
```

is a generic formal parameter declaration declaring `Term` to be a generic formal function. Within the generic unit, `Term` serves as a blank for a function taking one parameter whose base type is `Integer` and returning a result whose base type is `Float`. `Sum_Template` can be instantiated with any such function specified as a generic actual parameter. The resulting instance is an ordinary function taking two parameters, `From` and `To`, and returning the sum

$$\sum_{i=\mathrm{From}}^{\mathrm{To}} \mathrm{Term}\ (i)$$

For example, the following function is a possible generic actual parameter:

```
FUNCTION Square (n : Integer) RETURN Float IS
BEGIN
   RETURN Float (n ** 2);
END Square;
```

The instantiation

```
FUNCTION Sum_Of_Squares IS
   NEW Sum_Template (Term => Square);
```

yields an instance such that the call

```
Sum_Of_Squares (From => A, To => B)
```

(where `A` and `B` are of type `Integer`) returns the `Float` value equal to

```
A**2 + (A+1)**2 + (A+2)**2 + ... + B**2.
```

The next example is based on the following package:

```
PACKAGE Integer_List_Package IS
   TYPE Integer_List_Type IS
      ARRAY (Positive RANGE <>) OF Integer;
END Integer_List_Package;
```

Given a generic actual parameter specifying what it means to "process an `Integer` variable," an instance of the following generic procedure takes a subprogram parameter of type `Integer_List_Type` and "processes" each element of the list:

```
WITH Integer_List_Package; USE Integer_List_Package;
GENERIC
   WITH PROCEDURE Process_Element (n : IN OUT Integer);
PROCEDURE Process_Integer_List_Template
   (Integer_List : IN OUT Integer_List_Type);

PROCEDURE Process_Integer_List_Template
   (Integer_List : IN OUT Integer_List_Type) IS
BEGIN
   FOR i IN Integer_List'Range LOOP
      Process_Element ( Integer_List (i) );
   END LOOP;
END Process_Integer_List_Template;
```

Here are two procedures that can be used as generic actual parameters:

```
WITH Basic_IO; USE Basic_IO;
PROCEDURE Put_And_Skip (n: IN OUT Integer) IS
BEGIN
   Put (n);
   New_Line;
END Put_And_Skip;
```

```
PROCEDURE Increment (x: IN OUT Integer) IS
BEGIN
   x := x + 1;
END Increment;
```

(If you were to examine Put_And_Skip out of context, it would not be clear why its formal parameter was of mode IN OUT rather than of mode IN. However, only a procedure with an Integer parameter of mode IN OUT can be used as a generic actual parameter to Process_Integer_List_Template.)

Here are instantiations using these procedures as generic actual parameters:

```
PROCEDURE Put_Components IS
   NEW Process_Integer_List_Template
      (Process_Element => Put_And_Skip);
PROCEDURE Increment_Array IS
   NEW Process_Integer_List_Template
      (Process_Element => Increment);
```

The procedure Put_Components takes an Integer_List_Type parameter and prints each element of the list on a separate line of the standard output file. The procedure Increment_Array takes an Integer_List_Type parameter and increments each component of the array.

The following package provides a generic function analogous to the generic procedure Process_Integer_List_Template:

```
PACKAGE List_Function_Package IS
   TYPE Integer_List_Type IS
      ARRAY (Positive RANGE <>) OF Integer;
   List_Length_Error : EXCEPTION;
   GENERIC
      WITH FUNCTION f (Left, Right : Integer) RETURN Integer;
   FUNCTION List_Function_Template
      (Left, Right : Integer_List_Type)
      RETURN Integer_List_Type;
END List_Function_Package;

PACKAGE BODY List_Function_Package IS
   FUNCTION List_Function_Template
      (Left, Right : Integer_List_Type)
      RETURN Integer_List_Type IS
      Index_Offset :
         CONSTANT Integer := Right'First - Left'First;
      Result : Integer_List_Type (Left'Range);
```

```
      BEGIN
         IF Left'Length /= Right'Length THEN
            RAISE List_Length_Error;
         ELSE
            FOR i IN Left'Range LOOP
               Result (i) :=
                  f ( Left (i), Right (i + Index_Offset) );
            END LOOP;
            RETURN Result;
         END IF;
      END List_Function_Template;
   END List_Function_Package;
```

Now consider the following instantiations:

```
   FUNCTION "+" IS
      NEW List_Function_Package.List_Function_Template
         (f => "+");
   FUNCTION "*" IS
      NEW List_Function_Package.List_Function_Template
         (f => "*");
```

Because the generic formal function declaration for `f` specifies a function taking two `Integer` parameters and returning an `Integer` result, the generic actual parameters `"+"` and `"*"` (appearing after the `=>`) refer to the predefined addition and multiplication operators for type `Integer`. Because the instance names (following the word `FUNCTION`) are operator symbols, these instantiations create new overloaded versions of the `+` and `*` operators, taking two `Integer_List_Type` operands and returning an `Integer_List_Type` result.

The new version of `+` takes two equal-length lists and returns a list of the same length, in which each element is the sum of the corresponding elements of the operands. Similarly, the new version of `*` takes two equal-length lists and returns a list of the same length in which each element is the product of the corresponding elements of the operands. The generic function is modeled after the Boolean array versions of `AND`, `OR`, and `XOR`, which allow operands with different lower bounds as long as their lengths are the same. (This is the purpose of the constant `Index_Offset` in the generic body.) As with the array versions of the logical operators, the bounds of the result are those of the left operand.

16.2.3 Generic Formal Types

Generic formal types are "blanks" that stand for types or subtypes. An identifier declared to be a generic formal type may be used within the generic unit as a typemark. For example, it may appear in a qualified expression or in the declaration of an object or another type. A generic actual parameter corresponding to a generic formal type may be any subtype (including a full base type). Within the generic unit, however, each generic formal type is treated as though it were a distinct full type.

There are several forms of generic-formal-type declarations. Each form looks roughly like a type declaration for a different class of types, such as the class of integer types, the class of access types, and the class of limited private types. The type class of a generic-formal-type declaration determines both the ways in which the generic formal type may be used inside the generic unit and the subtypes that may be used as generic actual parameters.

There is a set of operations associated with each class of types. For example, the operations on integer types include arithmetic operations and the `'Succ` attribute; operations on array types include slices and the `'Length` attribute. When a generic formal type is declared to belong to a certain class of types, it must be used within the generic unit as a type belonging to that class. That is, the only predefined operations that may be applied to the generic formal type within the generic unit are those associated with the declared class of types. The corresponding generic actual parameter in an instantiation must be some subtype providing at least the predefined operations assumed to be available within the generic unit.

The actual parameter corresponding to a generic formal type need not be a static subtype. Therefore, a generic formal type is not considered a static subtype. This means, for example, that attributes of a generic formal type are not static expressions. (See Section 8.3.5 for a complete discussion of static expressions and static subtypes.)

16.2.3.1 Generic formal parameters for numeric types. There are three kinds of generic formal parameters that correspond to numeric types—*generic formal integer types, generic formal floating-point types,* and *generic formal fixed-point types.* A generic formal integer type is declared as follows:

```
TYPE identifier IS RANGE <> ;
```

This is the general form of an integer-type declaration, but with the actual range replaced by the "box" `<>`. (The connotation of the box is that the information one would normally expect at that place will be provided later.) The declaration of a generic formal floating-point type looks like a floating-point type declaration with no range and with the number of digits of precision replaced by a box:

```
TYPE identifier IS DIGITS <> ;
```

The declaration of a generic formal fixed-point type looks like a fixed-point type declaration with the range deleted and with the size of the delta replaced by a box:

```
TYPE identifier IS DELTA <> ;
```

Within a generic unit, a generic formal integer type may be used as an ordinary integer type. For example, it may be used as an index type in an array-type declaration, and values in the type may be described by integer literals. A generic formal floating-point type may be used within the generic unit as an ordinary floating-point type. For example, an expression of the type may be used as the left operand to a predefined version of `"**"`. A generic formal fixed-point type may be used within the generic unit as an ordinary fixed-point type. For example, it can be used to form a `'Delta` attribute, and values in the type can be multiplied by values of type `Integer`.

In a generic instantiation, the corresponding actual parameter must be a subtype whose base type is of the appropriate class—the class of integer types, the class of floating-point types, or the class of fixed-point types. This guarantees that the generic actual parameter has all the operations that are permitted for the corresponding generic formal type.

Suppose we are to write a function that takes a `String` parameter containing the digits of a hexadecimal numeral and returns the corresponding numeric value. Our first inclination might be to have the function return a result of type `Integer`. However, the need could arise in the future to have a similar function returning a value in some other integer type, such as `Long_Integer`. (The wider the range of the result type, the longer the hexadecimal numerals that can be accepted as input.) With just a little more effort, we can write a generic solution that can be instantiated with an actual parameter specifying the integer subtype to be used for function results.

There are two reasons for which the function could fail to produce a valid result. First, the input might not be a well-formed hexadecimal numeral. Second, the input might be a well-formed hexadecimal numeral, but with a value too large to be represented in the result subtype. When writing the function, we should also provide exceptions corresponding to each of these possibilities. Thus we should write a generic package rather than a generic function.

The generic package declaration takes the following form:

```
GENERIC
   TYPE Result_Type IS RANGE <>;
PACKAGE Hexadecimal_Numeral_Package_Template IS
   FUNCTION Hexadecimal_Numeral_Value
      (Numeral : String) RETURN Result_Type;
   Invalid_Digit_Error, Result_Size_Error : EXCEPTION;
END Hexadecimal_Numeral_Package_Template;
```

Within the generic package declaration, the generic formal integer type `Result_Type` is used as the result type of a function.

The algorithm for computing the numeric value of a hexadecimal numeral is adapted from the program `Hexadecimal_To_Decimal` given in Section 8.1.4. The package body is as follows:

```
PACKAGE BODY Hexadecimal_Numeral_Package_Template IS
   FUNCTION Hexadecimal_Numeral_Value
      (Numeral : String) RETURN Result_Type IS

      Digit_Character : Character;
      Digit_Value     : Result_Type RANGE 0 .. 15;
      Result          : Result_Type := 0;

      Zero_Position      : CONSTANT := Character'Pos('0');
      Capital_A_Position : CONSTANT := Character'Pos('A');
      Small_a_Position   : CONSTANT := Character'Pos('a');

   BEGIN

      FOR i IN Numeral'Range LOOP

         Digit_Character := Numeral (i);

         CASE Digit_Character IS

            WHEN '0' .. '9' =>
               Digit_Value :=
                  Character'Pos (Digit_Character) -
                  Zero_Position;

            WHEN 'A' .. 'F' =>
               Digit_Value :=
                  Character'Pos (Digit_Character) -
                  Capital_A_Position +
                  10;

            WHEN 'a' .. 'f' =>
               Digit_Value :=
                  Character'Pos (Digit_Character) -
                  Small_a_Position +
                  10;

            WHEN OTHERS =>
               RAISE Invalid_Digit_Error;

         END CASE;

         BEGIN
            Result := 16 * Result + Digit_Value;
         EXCEPTION
            WHEN Numeric_Error | Constraint_Error =>
               RAISE Result_Size_Error;
         END;

      END LOOP;

      RETURN Result;

   END Hexadecimal_Numeral_Value;

END Hexadecimal_Numeral_Package_Template;
```

Within the generic package body, `Result_Type` is used in three variable declarations. One of these declarations contains an integer range constraint and another contains an initial value specified by an integer literal. Expressions in integer types are assigned to, multiplied by, and added to these variables. For these reasons, the generic formal type `Result_Type` must be a generic formal integer type, and the corresponding generic actual parameter must be a subtype of an integer type. (The assignment statement

```
Result := 16 * Result + Digit_Value;
```

may raise `Numeric_Error` when the value of the expression

```
16 * Result + Digit_Value;
```

exceeds the highest value in the base type of `Result_Type`. The statement raises `Constraint_Error` when the value of the expression can be computed, but the value cannot be stored in `Result` because it exceeds the range of the subtype `Result_Type`. The block statement ensures that `Constraint_Error` and `Numeric_Error` are interpreted as symptoms of `Result_Size_Error` only within this one statement.)

16.2.3.2 Generic formal discrete types. Often it is desirable to write a generic unit that can perform some function for any discrete type. (A discrete type is either an enumeration type or an integer type.) To pass a discrete subtype as a generic parameter, we use a *generic formal discrete type.* The form of a generic-formal-discrete-type declaration is:

```
TYPE identifier IS ( <> );
```

This looks like an enumeration-type declaration with the list of enumeration literals left unspecified (as indicated by the "box" `<>`). Within the generic unit, the generic formal discrete type may be used as an ordinary discrete type. For example, it may be used as an array index, and it has attributes such as `'Succ`, `'Pred`, `'Val`, and `'Pos`.

The corresponding actual parameter in a generic instantiation may be any subtype that has all the properties a generic formal discrete type is assumed to have within the generic unit. Thus the generic actual parameter may be a subtype of an enumeration type or of an integer type. It does not matter that integer subtypes have other, arithmetic, operations as well.

An instance of the following generic package provides a type for sets whose elements belong to some discrete type, operations on those sets, and a type used for describing a set as a list of elements:

```
GENERIC
   TYPE Element_Type IS ( <> );
PACKAGE Discrete_Set_Package_Template IS
   TYPE Set_Type IS PRIVATE;
   FUNCTION Union
      (Set_1, Set_2 : Set_Type) RETURN Set_Type;
```

```
      FUNCTION Intersection
         (Set_1, Set_2 : Set_Type) RETURN Set_Type;
      FUNCTION Complement (Set : Set_Type) RETURN Set_Type;
      FUNCTION Belongs_To
         (Element : Element_Type; Set : Set_Type)
         RETURN Boolean;
      TYPE Element_List_Type IS
         ARRAY (Positive RANGE <>) OF Element_Type;
      FUNCTION Set_Of
         (Element_List : Element_List_Type) RETURN Set_Type;
   PRIVATE
      TYPE Set_Type IS ARRAY (Element_Type) OF Boolean;
   END Discrete_Set_Package_Template;
```

Internally, a set of values in some discrete type is represented as an array indexed by values in that type. Array component $a(x)$ is true if and only if x is an element of the set represented by a. The purpose of the function `Set_Of` is to take an `Element_List_Type` array aggregate listing the elements of a set and to return the representation of that set as a `Set_Type` value.

Given the subtype declaration

```
   SUBTYPE Digit_Subtype IS Integer RANGE 0 .. 9;
```

the instantiation

```
   PACKAGE Digit_Set_Package IS
      NEW Discrete_Set_Package_Template
         (Element_Type => Digit_Subtype);
```

provides a package for sets of values in the range `0 .. 9`. If *s* is a variable in `Digit_Set_Package.Set_Type`, for example, the function call

```
   Digit_Set_Package.Intersection
      (s, Digit_Set_Package.Set_Of ((0, 2, 4, 6, 8)) );
```

returns the `Set_Type` value containing the even elements of *s*. The call on `Set_Of` has a single parameter, which is a five-component aggregate of type `Digit_Set_Package.Element_List_Type`. The instantiation

```
   PACKAGE Character_Set_Package IS
      NEW Discrete_Set_Package_Template
         (Element_Type => Character);
```

produces a package for sets of elements in a nonnumeric discrete type.

`Discrete_Set_Package_Template` provides an Ada programmer with set types similar to those found in Pascal. The main difference is that in Pascal one writes a type definition like

```
CharSet = set of Char;
```

instead of the generic instantiation above. (Pascal also uses operators such as + and * rather than identifiers such as `Union` and `Intersection` to denote set operations, a feature that easily could have been incorporated in the Ada generic package by operator overloading.) Once a generic package like `Discrete_Set_Package_Template` is placed in a library, an Ada programmer can create set types with discrete elements almost as easily as a Pascal programmer.

The generic package body uses the versions of the logical operators **AND**, **OR**, and **NOT** that apply component-by-component to one-dimensional arrays of Boolean values (described in Section 8.2.8). When applied to arrays representing sets, these versions of **AND**, **OR**, and **NOT** correspond directly to `Intersection`, `Union`, and `Complement`, respectively:

```
PACKAGE BODY Discrete_Set_Package_Template IS

   FUNCTION Union
      (Set_1, Set_2 : Set_Type) RETURN Set_Type IS
   BEGIN
      RETURN Set_1 OR Set_2;
   END Union;

   FUNCTION Intersection
      (Set_1, Set_2 : Set_Type) RETURN Set_Type IS
   BEGIN
      RETURN Set_1 AND Set_2;
   END Intersection;

   FUNCTION Complement (Set : Set_Type) RETURN Set_Type IS
   BEGIN
      RETURN NOT Set;
   END Complement;

   FUNCTION Belongs_To
      (Element : Element_Type; Set : Set_Type)
      RETURN Boolean IS
   BEGIN
      RETURN Set (Element); -- array component
   END Belongs_To;
```

```
   FUNCTION Set_Of
      (Element_List : Element_List_Type) RETURN Set_Type IS
      Result : Set_Type := (Element_Type => False);
   BEGIN
      FOR e IN Element_List'Range LOOP
         Result ( Element_List (e) ) := True;
      END LOOP;
      RETURN Result;
   END Set_Of;

END Discrete_Set_Package_Template;
```

16.2.3.3 Generic formal array types. There are many operations on arrays that make sense for a large class of component types. These include sorting an array, performing some operation for each element of an array, and transposing a square two-dimensional array, to name just a few. General-purpose array manipulation algorithms can be written using generic units with *generic formal array types.*

There are two kinds of generic formal array types—one standing for an unconstrained array subtype and one standing for a constrained array subtype. A declaration for an unconstrained generic formal array type looks much like an ordinary unconstrained array-type declaration:

```
TYPE identifier IS
   ARRAY ( typemark RANGE <> , ~~~ , typemark RANGE <> )
      OF typemark ;
```

The only difference is that the specification of the component subtype must not include a constraint. A constrained generic-formal-array-type declaration has the following form:

```
TYPE identifier IS
   ARRAY ( typemark , ~~~ , typemark ) OF typemark ;
```

This looks like a constrained array-type declaration. However, the discrete ranges specifying index bounds and the subtype indication specifying the component subtype must all be typemarks.

The typemarks used to specify the index subtypes may themselves be generic formal discrete types or generic formal integer types declared *earlier* in the same generic unit. The typemark used to specify the component subtype may be a generic formal type declared earlier in the same generic unit. However, any typemark visible at the point of the generic declaration may be used in the generic formal array-type declaration, including names of predefined types and subtypes. Typically, a generic unit applicable to a wide class of array subtypes will have generic parameters for the index subtypes, a generic parameter for the component subtype, and a generic parameter for the array subtype itself.

An instance of the following generic procedure sorts a one-dimensional array using an insertion sort. The subtype of the array components and the (unconstrained) subtype of the array are passed as generic parameters. The predefined subtype `Positive` is used as the index subtype of the generic formal array type.

```
GENERIC
   TYPE Component_Type IS ( <> );
   TYPE Array_Type IS
      ARRAY (Positive RANGE <>) OF Component_Type;
PROCEDURE Sort_Template (a : IN OUT Array_Type);
```

Given the declaration

```
TYPE Integer_List_Type IS
   ARRAY (Positive RANGE <>) OF Integer;
```

We could instantiate this generic procedure as follows:

```
PROCEDURE Sort_Integers IS
   NEW Sort_Template
      (Component_Type => Integer,
       Array_Type     => Integer_List_Type);
```

In an instantiation, a generic actual parameter corresponding to a generic formal array type must be an array subtype *S* that matches the generic formal array type in the following senses:

If the generic formal array type is unconstrained, *S* must be unconstrained; if the generic formal array type is constrained, *S* must be constrained.

S must have the same number of dimensions as the generic formal array type.

In each dimension, the index subtype of *S* must have the same base type as in the corresponding dimension of the generic formal array type. If *S* and the generic formal array type are constrained, the bounds in corresponding dimensions must be identical.

The component *subtype* of *S* must be the same as the component subtype of the generic formal array type. That is, if the component subtype of the generic formal array type has a constraint, the component subtype of *S* must have the same constraint. If the component subtype of the generic formal array type is an unconstrained type with discriminants, the component subtype of *S* must also be an unconstrained type with discriminants.

If the generic formal array type is declared in terms of earlier generic formal parameters, the corresponding generic actual parameters are substituted for them to determine whether these conditions hold. For example, to determine that the previous instantiation given for Sort_Template is legal, we replace the generic formal parameter Component_Type in the declaration

```
TYPE Array_Type IS
   ARRAY (Positive RANGE <>) OF Component_Type;
```

by the corresponding actual parameter Integer:

```
TYPE Array_Type IS
   ARRAY (Positive RANGE <>) OF Integer;
```

We then observe that both Integer_List_Type and Array_Type are unconstrained; both have one dimension; both have index subtypes that are subtypes of type Integer; and both have components of subtype Integer.

Within a generic unit, an unconstrained generic formal array type may be used as an ordinary unconstrained array type. In particular, all declarations of variables in that type must have index constraints. Operations only available for one-dimensional array types, such as slices, are available for the generic formal array type if and only if the generic formal array type is one-dimensional. Other operations may or may not be available for the generic formal array type depending on the type of its components. For example, the operators <, >, >=, and <= may be applied to two one-dimensional arrays with discrete components (as described in Section 8.2.7); the operators AND, OR, and NOT may be applied to two one-dimensional arrays with Boolean components (as described in Section 8.2.8). Assignment and comparison for equality are *not* available for the generic formal array type if its component type is limited, since types with limited components are themselves limited. (See Section 12.6.)

A constrained generic formal array type may be used within a generic unit in essentially the same ways as an unconstrained one. The main difference is that an index constraint must *not* be specified for individual objects belonging to the type. Another difference is that the 'First, 'Last, 'Range, and 'Length attribute designators may be applied to the name of the formal type itself as well as to the names of objects in the type.

Here is the generic body for Sort_Template. The algorithm is the same one used for the insertion sort main program of Section 8.2.8.

```
PROCEDURE Sort_Template (a : IN OUT Array_Type) IS
   New_Item : Component_Type;
   Candidate_Position :
      Integer RANGE a'First - 1 .. a'Last - 1;
BEGIN
   FOR Next IN a'First + 1 .. a'Last LOOP
      -- a (1 .. Next-1) is already sorted.
      New_Item := a (Next);
```

```
         -- Set Candidate_Position to position after which
         --   New_Item should be inserted:

         Candidate_Position := Next - 1;

         WHILE Candidate_Position >= a'First AND THEN
                  a (Candidate_Position) > New_Item LOOP

            Candidate_Position := Candidate_Position - 1;

         END LOOP;

         -- Slide other elements to the right to make room,
         --   then insert New_Item at that position:

         a (Candidate_Position+2 .. Next) :=
            a (Candidate_Position+1 .. Next-1);

         a (Candidate_Position+1) := New_Item;

         -- Now a (1 .. Next) is sorted.

      END LOOP;

   END Sort_Template;
```

Indexed components, slices, array attributes, and catenation occur within the generic unit. We have made `Component_Type` a generic formal discrete type because the comparison operators >, >=, <, and <= are available for such types. However, the sorting program can be made much more general, as will be shown later in Section 16.5.

An instance of the following generic formal function takes an array as a parameter and returns a Boolean value indicating whether or not the array is already sorted in ascending order, assuming once again that the array components belong to a discrete type:

```
   GENERIC

      TYPE Index_Type IS ( <> );
      TYPE Component_Type IS ( <> );
      TYPE Array_Type IS
         ARRAY (Index_Type RANGE <>) OF Component_Type;

   FUNCTION Is_Sorted_Template (a : Array_Type) RETURN Boolean;


   FUNCTION Is_Sorted_Template
      (a : Array_Type) RETURN Boolean IS

   BEGIN

      FOR i IN a'First .. Index_Type'Pred (a'Last) LOOP
         IF a (i) > a (Index_Type'Succ (i)) THEN
            RETURN False;
         END IF;
      END LOOP;

      RETURN True;

   END Is_Sorted_Template;
```

In this case, the index type is also specified by a generic parameter. Generic formal discrete types and generic formal integer types are the only kinds of generic formal parameters that may be used as index types in generic-formal-array-type declarations. Of these, generic formal discrete types allow a wider range of instantiations. However, we are required to phrase the algorithm in terms of operations like `Index_Type'Pred` and `Index_Type'Succ` rather than subtraction or addition of one.

The following generic function has both an unconstrained and a constrained generic formal array type. An instance of the generic function takes a sequence of values in some discrete type and a translation table specifying a "translation" for each value of the discrete type, and returns a translated sequence with each component replaced by its translation. The type for sequences is unconstrained, allowing sequences of any length to be translated. The type for translation tables is constrained, requiring one component to be present for each value in the discrete type.

```
GENERIC

   TYPE Discrete_Type IS ( <> );
   TYPE Translation_Table_Type IS
      ARRAY (Discrete_Type) OF Discrete_Type;
   TYPE Sequence_Type IS
      ARRAY (Positive RANGE <>) OF Discrete_Type;

FUNCTION Translate_Template
   (Original          : Sequence_Type;
    Translation_Table : Translation_Table_Type)
   RETURN Sequence_Type;


FUNCTION Translate_Template
   (Original          : Sequence_Type;
    Translation_Table : Translation_Table_Type)
   RETURN Sequence_Type IS

   Result : Sequence_Type (Original'Range);

BEGIN

   FOR i IN Original'Range LOOP
      Result (i) := Translation_Table ( Original (i) );
   END LOOP;

   RETURN Result;

END Translate_Template;
```

Given the constrained array-type declaration

```
TYPE Character_Table_Type IS
   ARRAY (Character) OF Character;
```

Translate_Template can be instantiated as follows:

```
FUNCTION Translate_String IS
   NEW Translate_Template
      (Discrete_Type           => Character,
       Translation_Table_Type => Character_Table_Type,
       Sequence_Type           => String);
```

16.2.3.4 Generic formal access types. A generic formal access type is declared as follows:

TYPE *identifier* IS ACCESS *typemark* ;

This is the form of an access-type declaration, except that a constraint may not be used to specify the designated subtype. Usually, the designated subtype is a generic formal type declared earlier in the same generic unit. (The language rules do not require this, but there is not much point in writing a generic unit for manipulating, for instance, all access types for which the designated type is Integer.)

Within a generic unit, the generic formal access type may be used as an ordinary access type. For example, values in the type may be created by allocators and used with the selector .ALL to name the variables they designate. The literal NULL may be used as a value of the generic formal access type.

Suppose a generic formal access type designates values in subtype *t*. In a generic instantiation, the corresponding actual parameter must be a subtype of an access type designating values in subtype *t*. Here is an example:

```
GENERIC
   TYPE Whole_Number_Type IS RANGE <>;
   TYPE Whole_Number_Pointer_Type IS
      ACCESS Whole_Number_Type;
   WITH
      FUNCTION Operator
         (Left, Right : Whole_Number_Type)
         RETURN Whole_Number_Type;
FUNCTION Indirect_Operator_Template
   (Left, Right : Whole_Number_Pointer_Type)
   RETURN Whole_Number_Pointer_Type;
```

In this case, the second generic actual parameter in an instantiation must be an access subtype designating values in the subtype passed as the first generic actual parameter.

Uses for generic formal access types are rare. However, the predefined generic procedure Unchecked_Deallocation has a generic formal access type. Unchecked_Deallocation is described in Section 16.6.

16.2.3.5 Generic formal private types. So far, there has been an intuitively obvious correspondence between the form of a generic-formal-type declaration and the class of types that may be used as corresponding generic actual parameters. In the case of generic formal private types, the correspondence is less intuitive. However, it is based on the same two principles:

1. Within its generic unit, a generic formal type may be used only as a type of the class suggested by the generic-formal-type declaration. This determines the set of operations that may be assumed to be available for the generic formal type.
2. In a generic instantiation, the corresponding generic actual parameter may be any subtype for which all those operations are available.

(For example, the form of a generic-formal-discrete-type declaration is suggestive of an enumeration-type declaration. Within its generic unit, a generic formal discrete type may only be used in the same ways as an enumeration type. Since all the operations defined for enumeration types are also defined for integer types, a subtype of either an integer type or an enumeration type may be used as the corresponding generic actual parameter.)

The form of a generic-formal-private-type declaration is

TYPE *identifier* IS PRIVATE ;

This has the same form as a private-type declaration in a package specification, but a different meaning. It follows from the first principle that a generic formal type may only be used within its generic unit as a private type. The only operations available for private types are certain operations available for all types (e.g., the ability to call subprograms with parameters of that type), plus assignment and comparison for equality. Since all these operations are available for any nonlimited subtype, it follows from the second principle that any nonlimited subtype may be used as a generic actual parameter. Thus generic formal private types are quite general.

A *generic formal limited private type* is even more general. Its declaration has the following form:

TYPE *identifier* IS LIMITED PRIVATE ;

Within the generic unit, the generic formal limited private type may only be used as a limited private type. Not even assignment and tests for equality are available. In fact, the only operations that may be assumed available are those operations defined for all types. Thus *any* subtype may be used as a corresponding generic actual parameter.

The operation of exchanging the values in two variables arises frequently in many programs. Thus it would be convenient to have a generic exchange procedure, with the type of the exchanged values specified by a generic parameter. The procedure must contain assignment statements for values of the generic formal type. This rules out the use of a generic formal *limited* private type.

Here is the generic exchange procedure:

```
GENERIC
   TYPE Exchanged_Type IS PRIVATE;
PROCEDURE Exchange_Template
   (First, Second : IN OUT Exchanged_Type);


PROCEDURE Exchange_Template
   (First, Second : IN OUT Exchanged_Type) IS
   Old_First : CONSTANT Exchanged_Type := First;
BEGIN
   First := Second;
   Second := Old_First;
END Exchange_Template;
```

Here are some overloaded instantiations:

```
PROCEDURE Exchange IS
   NEW Exchange_Template (Exchanged_Type => Integer);
PROCEDURE Exchange IS
   NEW Exchange_Template (Exchanged_Type => Float);
PROCEDURE Exchange IS
   NEW Exchange_Template (Exchanged_Type => Fraction_Type);
```

Given a function *f* taking a parameter in some type `Argument_Type` and returning a result in some type `Result_Type`, many programs require a function that will take an array of values in `Argument_Type` and apply *f* to each component to obtain an array of values in `Result_Type`. Each instance of the following generic unit is such a function:

```
GENERIC
   TYPE Argument_Type IS LIMITED PRIVATE;
   TYPE Argument_List_Type IS
      ARRAY (Positive RANGE <>) OF Argument_Type;
   TYPE Result_Type IS PRIVATE;
   TYPE Result_List_Type IS
      ARRAY (Positive RANGE <>) OF Result_Type;
   WITH
      FUNCTION Argument_Image
         (Argument : Argument_Type) RETURN Result_Type;
FUNCTION List_Image_Template
   (Argument_List : Argument_List_Type)
   RETURN Result_List_Type;
```

```
FUNCTION List_Image_Template
   (Argument_List : Argument_List_Type)
   RETURN Result_List_Type IS

   Result_List : Result_List_Type (Argument_List'Range);

BEGIN

   FOR i IN Argument_List'Range LOOP
      Result_List (i) := Argument_Image (Argument_List (i));
   END LOOP;

   RETURN Result_List;

END List_Image_Template;
```

Argument_Type is used within the generic unit only as the component type of Argument_List_Type and the parameter type of Argument_Image. Both of these uses are available for any type, so Argument_Type can be made a generic formal limited private type. Result_Type is used as the component type of Result_List_Type and as the result type of Argument_Image, but a Result_Type value is also used in the assignment statement inside the generic body. Therefore, Result_Type can be made a generic formal private type, but not limited private. In an instantiation, any subtype may be used as the first generic actual parameter and any subtype except a limited subtype may be used as the third generic actual parameter.

The following declarations are based on the package Integer_Set_Package given in Section 12.6. Integer_Set_Package provides a limited private type Integer_Set_Type and operations on that type such as Insert_Member and Member_Of.

```
TYPE Set_List_Type IS
   ARRAY (Positive RANGE <>) OF
      Integer_Set_Package.Integer_Set_Type;

TYPE Boolean_List_Type IS
   ARRAY (Positive RANGE <>) OF Boolean;

FUNCTION Contains_Zero
   (Set : Integer_Set_Package.Integer_Set_Type)
   RETURN Boolean IS
BEGIN
   RETURN Integer_Set_Package.Member_Of (0, Set);
END Contains_Zero;
```

Given these declarations, we can write the following instantiation:

```
FUNCTION Zero_Flag_List IS
   NEW List_Image_Template
      (Argument_Type =>
         Integer_Set_Package.Integer_Set_Type,
       Argument_List_Type => Set_List_Type,
       Result_Type        => Boolean,
       Result_List_Type   => Boolean_List_Type,
       Argument_Image     => Contains_Zero);
```

If L is a four-component `Set_List_Type` value containing the sets {0, 1, 2}, {1, 2, 3}, {2, 4, 6}, and {0, 5, 10}, then `Zero_Flag_List (L)` returns the four-component `Boolean_List_Type` value `(True, False, False, True)`. Because `Integer_Set_Type` is limited, it is allowed as the first generic actual parameter but would not be allowed as the third. `Boolean` is allowed as the third generic actual parameter even though it is not a private type, because the generic actual parameter corresponding to a generic formal private type may be any nonlimited subtype. In fact, given the declaration

```
TYPE Integer_List_Type IS
   ARRAY (Positive RANGE <>) OF Integer;
```

the following instantiation is also allowed:

```
FUNCTION Successor_List IS
   NEW List_Image_Template
      (Argument_Type      => Integer,
       Argument_List_Type => Integer_List_Type,
       Result_Type        => Integer,
       Result_List_Type   => Integer_List_Type,
       Argument_Image     => Integer'Succ);
```

The function call

```
Successor_List ( (1, 1, 2, 3, 5, 8, 13) )
```

returns the `Integer_List_Type` result `(2, 2, 3, 4, 6, 9, 14)`.

There are two points worth noting here. First, the same subtype may be used as the generic actual parameter for two different generic formal types. (Since the generic unit is compiled independently of any instantiation, the two generic formal types must still be treated as distinct types within the generic unit.) Second, attributes that are functions with parameters and results in specific types may be used as generic actual parameters corresponding to generic formal functions with the same parameter and result types. The `'Pred`, `'Succ`, `'Image`, and `'Value` attributes of a discrete type can be used in this way. The `'Val` attribute, which accepts parameters of any integer type, and the `'Pos` attribute, whose result is of type *universal_integer* (see Section 8.3.6), cannot be passed as generic actual parameters.

16.2.3.6 Generic formal types with discriminants. Record types and private types may have discriminants. So may generic formal private and limited private types. A generic formal private type with discriminants is declared as follows:

```
TYPE identifier
   ( generic discriminant specification ,
       ~~~ ,
     generic discriminant specification ) IS
   PRIVATE ;
```

The form for a generic formal limited private type with discriminants is analogous:

```
TYPE identifier
    ( generic discriminant specification ,
        ~~~ ,
      generic discriminant specification ) IS
    LIMITED PRIVATE ;
```

The form of a generic discriminant specification is the same as for an ordinary discriminant specification, except that default initial values may not be specified:

```
identifier , ~~~ , identifier : typemark ;
```

Typically, the typemark in a generic discriminant specification names a generic formal discrete type or a generic formal integer type declared earlier; however, it can name any discrete subtype.

A generic formal type with discriminants has the same operations available within the generic unit as the corresponding kind of generic formal type without discriminants, plus certain operations associated with discriminants. These include the ability to name the discriminants in selected components, the ability to use the membership tests `IN` and `NOT IN` to check whether a given value in the type obeys a particular discriminant constraint, the ability to write discriminant constraints, and the ability to use the `'Constrained` attribute described in Section 10.3. All object declarations for the generic formal type with discriminants must include discriminant constraints, since the generic formal type does not have default initial values.

The actual parameter corresponding to a generic formal private or limited private type with discriminants must be an unconstrained subtype that has corresponding discriminants. This means that the subtype and the generic formal type must have the same number of discriminants, and corresponding discriminants must have the same base type. In addition, the actual parameter corresponding to a generic formal *private* type with discriminants must be a nonlimited subtype. The actual parameter's discriminants may have defaults even though the generic formal type's discriminants do not.

These restrictions on the subtype used as a generic actual parameter guarantee that all the operations permitted for the generic formal type—including operations on discriminants—are defined for that subtype. However, a subtype with discriminants may also be used as a generic actual parameter corresponding to a generic formal type *without* discriminants. All this means is that the generic unit cannot make any use of the discriminants.

16.2.3.7 Generic formal parameters for arbitrary numeric types. Many of the same operations are available for generic formal integer types, generic formal floating-point types, and generic formal fixed-point types. These include the arithmetic operations (with variations in the allowed operand and result types and the meaning of division) and numeric literals (integer literals for integer types and real literals for floating-point and fixed-point types), among others. Nonetheless, there is no such thing as a "generic formal numeric type" for which all these operations are available and for which any numeric subtype may be used as a generic actual parameter. Rather, a generic algorithm applicable to any numeric type must be written with the numeric type represented by a generic formal private type and with any numeric type operations used in the algorithm passed as generic parameters.

As an example, let us revisit the generic function `Sum_Template` given in Section 16.2.2. That generic function was written to sum terms of type `Float`; but, in fact, summation of indexed terms is a meaningful operation for any numeric type. To make `Sum_Template` usable for any numeric type, we add a generic formal private type, such as `Numeric_Type`, and insert it in place of all occurrences of the typemark `Float` within the generic unit. We add a generic formal constant `Zero`, of type `Numeric_Type`, and insert it in place of the occurrence of the real literal `0.0` as a value of type `Float`. Finally, we add a generic formal function `"+"` with operands and results of type `Numeric_Type`. Within the function body, the `+` operator that originally denoted predefined addition for type `Float` now denotes a call on this generic formal function. Through this process we identify and isolate those numeric operations actually exploited in writing `Sum_Template`. The result is as follows:

```
GENERIC
   TYPE Numeric_Type IS PRIVATE;
   Zero : IN Numeric_Type;
   WITH
      FUNCTION "+"
         (Left, Right : Numeric_Type) RETURN Numeric_Type;
   WITH FUNCTION Term (Index : Integer) RETURN Numeric_Type;
FUNCTION Sum_Template
   (From, To : Integer) RETURN Numeric_Type;


FUNCTION Sum_Template
   (From, To : Integer) RETURN Numeric_Type IS
   Sum : Numeric_Type := Zero;
BEGIN
   FOR i IN From .. To LOOP
      Sum := Sum + Term (i);
   END LOOP;
   RETURN Sum;
END Sum_Template;
```

To create a function for summing the elements of an array of `Integer` values, we could write

```
Integer_Array : ARRAY (1 .. 100) OF Integer;

FUNCTION Integer_Array_Component
   (i : Integer) RETURN Integer IS
BEGIN
   RETURN Integer_Array (i);
END Integer_Array_Component;

FUNCTION Integer_Array_Element_Sum IS
   NEW Sum_Template
      (Numeric_Type => Integer,
       Zero         => 0,
       "+"          => "+",
       Term         => Integer_Array_Component);
```

To do the same for an array of `Float` values, we could write

```
Float_Array : ARRAY (1 .. 100) OF Float;

FUNCTION Float_Array_Component
   (i : Integer) RETURN Float IS
BEGIN
   RETURN Float_Array (i);
END Float_Array_Component;

FUNCTION Float_Array_Element_Sum IS
   NEW Sum_Template
      (Numeric_Type => Float,
       Zero         => 0.0,
       "+"          => "+",
       Term         => Float_Array_Component);
```

In the first instantiation, the generic actual parameter `0` is used as a value of type `Integer`, and the generic actual parameter `"+"` stands for the predefined addition operator for type `Integer` (since this is the only version of `"+"` whose parameter and result type profile matches that of the generic formal function). In the second instantiation, the generic actual parameter `0.0` is used as a value of type `Float`, and the generic actual parameter `"+"` stands for predefined addition operator for type `Float` (for the same reason as before). Similar instantiations are possible for fixed-point types. It is typical for the generic actual parameters corresponding to arithmetic operators to have the same names as the generic formal parameters with which they are associated. A convenient shorthand that can be used in such situations will be given in Section 16.4.

16.3 GENERIC INSTANTIATIONS

There are various forms for generic actual parameters corresponding to the different kinds of generic formal parameters. The generic actual parameter corresponding to a generic formal constant may be any expression of the appropriate type. The generic actual parameter corresponding to a generic formal variable may be the name of a variable of the appropriate type. The generic actual parameter corresponding to a generic formal subprogram may be the name of an appropriate subprogram, an attribute that is a function with appropriate parameter and result types, or an enumeration literal viewed as a function without parameters. The generic actual parameter corresponding to a generic formal type may be a typemark naming any appropriate subtype. When used as a generic actual parameter, a typemark may not be followed by a constraint.

Like actual parameters in a subprogram call, the generic actual parameters in a generic instantiation may be given in either named or positional notation. Until now, we have only shown generic parameters in named notation, as in this instantiation:

```
FUNCTION Float_Array_Element_Sum IS
   NEW Sum_Template
      (Numeric_Type => Float,
       Zero         => 0.0,
       "+"          => "+",
       Term         => Float_Array_Component);
```

In named notation, a generic actual parameter appearing to the right of a `=>` corresponds to the generic formal parameter appearing to the left of that `=>`. Although we have always listed generic actual parameters in the order of their declaration, in fact, named generic parameters can be listed in any order. The following instantiation is equivalent to the one above:

```
FUNCTION Float_Array_Element_Sum IS
   NEW Sum_Template
      (Term         => Float_Array_Component,
       Numeric_Type => Float,
       "+"          => "+",
       Zero         => 0.0);
```

In positional notation, generic actual parameters appear by themselves in the order in which the corresponding formal parameters were declared. There is only one way to write the previous instantiation in positional notation:

```
FUNCTION Float_Array_Element_Sum IS
   NEW Sum_Template
      (Float, 0.0, "+", Float_Array_Component);
```

This instantiation tells us that the generic actual parameters corresponding to the first, second, third, and fourth generic formal parameters are `Float`, `0.0`, `"+"`, and `Float_Array_Component`, respectively, but it does not tell us the names of the generic formal parameters. We must examine the generic declaration to determine the names. Thus positional notation tends to be less helpful to someone reading and trying to understand an instantiation.

Like record aggregates, subprogram calls, and discriminant constraints, a generic instantiation may contain a mixture of named and positional notation. The parameters in positional notation must be given first, in the appropriate positions. The parameters in named notation may then follow in any order. Here is one way of writing the same instantiation in mixed notation:

```
FUNCTION Float_Array_Element_Sum IS
   NEW Sum_Template
      (Float,
       Term => Float_Array_Component,
       "+"  => "+",
       Zero => 0.0);
```

There is one further parallel between the two kinds of actual parameters. A subprogram formal parameter of mode **IN** may be given a default value. This makes it possible to call the subprogram without specifying the corresponding actual parameter. As we shall see in the next section, defaults may also be specified for certain kinds of generic formal parameters. When a default is specified for a generic formal parameter, the corresponding generic actual parameter may be omitted from instantiation. As with subprogram calls, any generic actual parameter following the position of the omitted generic actual parameter must be written using named notation.

16.4 DEFAULTS FOR GENERIC PARAMETERS

Defaults may be specified for generic formal constants and generic formal subprograms, but not for generic formal variables or generic formal types. A default specifies what the generic formal parameter stands for when the corresponding actual parameter is omitted from a generic instantiation.

A generic-formal-constant declaration with a default has the following form:

identifier **,** ~~~**,** *identifier* **: IN** *typemark* **:=** *expression* **;**

At the time of the generic instantiation, the expression is evaluated once for each of the generic parameters that it applies to for which no generic actual parameter is specified. As with any generic-formal-constant declaration, the word **IN** may be omitted, but there is no good reason to omit it.

For example, `Symmetric_Matrix_Package_Template`, presented in Section 16.1, had a generic formal constant `Matrix_Size`. This generic formal constant could be given a default value of 100:

```
GENERIC
   Matrix_Size : IN Positive := 100;
   TYPE Component_Type IS PRIVATE;
PACKAGE Symmetric_Matrix_Package_Template IS
   ...
PRIVATE
   ...
END Symmetric_Matrix_Package_Template;
```

Then the generic instantiation

```
PACKAGE Connection_Table_Package IS
   NEW Symmetric_Table_Package (Component_Type => Boolean);
```

would be equivalent to

```
PACKAGE Connection_Table_Package IS
   NEW Symmetric_Table_Package
      (Matrix_Size => 100, Component_Type => Boolean);
```

Of course, different values for `Matrix_Size` could still be stipulated by instantiations specifying both generic actual parameters.

There are two ways to declare generic formal subprograms with defaults. The first is with a subprogram declaration of the following form:

`WITH` *subprogram specification* `IS` *name of default subprogram* `;`

The named subprogram must be one that is visible at the place of the generic formal subprogram declaration, has the same parameter and result type profile as the subprogram specification, and has the same parameter modes as the subprogram specification. (There may be several overloaded versions of the subprogram visible at the place of the generic-formal-subprogram declaration, but the visibility rules guarantee that only one of them can possibly have the same parameter and result type profile.) The subprogram named as a default may be any of the following:

a predefined subprogram
an explicitly declared subprogram whose scope includes the generic unit
another generic formal subprogram declared earlier
an enumeration literal (viewed as a function with no parameters and a result in the corresponding enumeration type)
the attribute *d*`'Succ`, *d*`'Pred`, *d*`'Value`, or *d*`'Image` of a discrete subtype *d*

Consider the following generic declaration:

```
GENERIC
   TYPE Data_Type IS PRIVATE;
   Default_Data   : IN Data_Type;
   Table_Capacity : IN Positive := 100;
   WITH
      FUNCTION Equivalent_Strings
         (String_1, String_2 : String) RETURN Boolean
      IS "=";
PACKAGE String_Lookup_Package_Template IS
   PROCEDURE Store (Key : IN String; Data : IN Data_Type);
   FUNCTION Current_Value (Key : String) RETURN Data_Type;
   Table_Overflow : EXCEPTION;
END String_Lookup_Package_Template;
```

An instance of this package hides a table of data in which each table entry is identified by a string. Operations provided by the package are to store data in the table and to look up data stored in the table. (Any string for which no explicit data has been stored is assumed to have an implicit entry in which the value `Default_Data` is stored.) Two strings, *s1* and *s2*, for which `Equivalent_Strings (`*s1*`,` *s2*`)` is true are considered to be equivalent and thus to identify the same table entry.

One possible actual parameter corresponding to the generic formal function `Equivalent_Strings` is a function that tests whether two strings are equal when trailing blanks are disregarded. Another is a function that tests whether two strings are equal when all lower-case letters are replaced by their upper-case equivalents. In the first case, the strings `"alpha"` and `"alpha  "` would identify the same table entry; in the second case, `"alpha"`, `"Alpha"`, and `"ALPHA"` would identify the same table entry.

If the generic actual parameter corresponding to `Equivalent_Strings` were omitted, the default would be used. This is the predefined version of `"="` taking two `String` operands and returning a Boolean result. (This version of `"="` is visible at the point of the declaration of `Equivalent_Strings` because it is declared in the package `Standard`, whose scope includes every compilation unit.) If *s1* and *s2* are strings, the expression *s1* = *s2* is true if and only if *s1* and *s2* contain exactly the same sequences of characters. Thus the default policy, if no actual parameter for `Equivalent_Strings` is specified, is for each distinct string to identify a different table entry.

The second way to declare a generic formal subprogram with a default is with a subprogram declaration of the following form:

`WITH` *subprogram specification* `IS <> ;`

The box indicates that the default is a subprogram or enumeration literal directly visible at the place of the generic *instantiation* that has the same name, parameter and result type profile, and parameter modes as the generic formal subprogram. The subprogram name may be either an identifier or a string literal containing an operator symbol. (There may be several overloaded subprograms with that name directly visible at the point of the instantiation, but only one with a matching parameter and result type profile.) If there is no matching subprogram directly visible at the point of the generic instantiation, the corresponding actual parameter may not be omitted from the instantiation.

This form of default is most useful with operator symbols that have meanings for several different types. In particular, the last subsection of Section 16.2.3 explained that a generic unit for arbitrary numeric types could be written with a generic formal private type standing for the numeric type and with the required constants and arithmetic operators specified by generic parameters. The generic formal functions for the operators can be given defaults using the <> notation. Then, when the generic unit is instantiated with a numeric type, that type's version of each operator becomes the default, and the corresponding generic actual parameter need not be specified.

The declaration of the generic function `Sum_Template` given in Section 16.2.3 can be rewritten as follows:

```
GENERIC
   TYPE Numeric_Type IS PRIVATE;
   Zero : IN Numeric_Type;
   WITH
      FUNCTION "+"
         (Left, Right : Numeric_Type) RETURN Numeric_Type
      IS <>;
   WITH FUNCTION Term (Index : Integer) RETURN Numeric_Type;
FUNCTION Sum_Template
   (From, To : Integer) RETURN Numeric_Type;
```

Then the actual parameter corresponding to the generic formal function `"+"` can be omitted from an instantiation if the actual parameter corresponding to `Numeric_Type` has a version of `"+"` with two operands and a result of that type. This version of `"+"` is used by default for the generic formal function `"+"`. Thus the instantiation

```
FUNCTION Integer_Array_Element_Sum IS
   NEW Sum_Template
      (Numeric_Type => Integer,
       Zero         => 0,
       "+"          => "+",
       Term         => Integer_Array_Component);
```

can be written equivalently as follows:

```
FUNCTION Integer_Array_Element_Sum IS
   NEW Sum_Template
      (Numeric_Type => Integer,
       Zero         => 0,
       Term         => Integer_Array_Component);
```

16.5 GENERALIZATION

When you decide to write a generic package or subprogram rather than an ordinary package or subprogram, you are thinking in terms of the future. Rather than solving only the problem at hand, you are developing a solution that may be applicable to other problems as well. Of course, this requires extra effort.

Much of this effort is to recognize the problem at hand as a special case of some more general problem. You choose to view certain aspects of the problem at hand as part of the more general problem and the remaining aspects of the problem at hand as the distinguishing characteristics of this special case. Then you can write a generic solution for the more general problem, in which the distinguishing characteristics of the special case are specified by generic parameters.

A case in point is the package `Integer_Set_Package` presented in Chapter 12. That package provides a limited private type for sets of `Integer` values, with sets represented internally as linked lists. We could have recognized the problem of providing sets of `Integer` values as a special case of the more general problem of providing sets of values in *some* nonlimited type. That is, we could have chosen to view the required operations on sets as defining the more general problem and the fact that the set elements belong to type `Integer` as a distinguishing characteristic of this special case. This view would have lead us to write a generic set package, with a generic formal private type used as the type of the set elements:

```
GENERIC
   TYPE Element_Type IS PRIVATE;
PACKAGE Set_Package_Template IS
   ...
END Set_Package_Template;
```

Even after a more general problem is identified, extra effort may be required to write a generic solution. This is because you cannot take advantage of all the properties of the problem at hand—only those properties defined to be part of the more general problem. Properties that apply only to the special case must be ignored if the solution is to be applicable to other special cases that do not share those properties. Often this means that the general solution cannot be as efficient as a solution using properties of the special case.

Unlike Integer_Set_Package, a generic set package accommodating elements of any nonlimited type cannot keep its linked lists in ascending order, because there may be no order defined for values in the element type. In comparing set elements with the operators < and >, Integer_Set_Package uses a property that we have now defined to be a property of the special case rather than property of the more general problem. We can implement sets as linked lists without keeping the lists sorted, but it is more complicated and considerably less efficient. Operations to insert a new element (if it is not already present) or to test for set membership will, on the average, take twice as long. (This is because they will have to scan the entire list rather than stopping as soon as a sufficiently high element is encountered.) Union or Intersection of two lists with n elements each will take an amount of time proportional to n^2 rather than an amount of time proportional to n. (Rather than traversing two lists of elements one time, we must compare each element of one list with each element of the other.)

There are many ways to divide the defining characteristics of a problem into the characteristics defining a more general problem and the characteristics distinguishing a special case of the more general problem. There is no one right way to make the division. By viewing more of the characteristics as defining a special case and fewer as defining the more general problem, you make your solution more widely applicable. You also make your solution more difficult to write; and you make it less likely to be as efficient as a more specialized solution. Sometimes it is worthwhile to narrow the range of problems to which a solution is applicable, so that you can exploit certain properties shared by some but not all of the problems.

Rather than choosing the implementation of sets as the general problem, we can choose the implementation of sets *whose elements can be ordered.* The special case is then distinguished by the selection of the element type Integer not from among all nonlimited types, but from among all types whose values can be ordered. This leads to a generic set package such as:

```
GENERIC
   TYPE Element_Type IS PRIVATE;
   WITH
      FUNCTION "<"
         (Left, Right : Element_Type) RETURN Boolean
      IS <>;
PACKAGE Set_Package_Template IS
   ...
END Set_Package_Template;
```

The generic formal function "<" is used to keep lists in sorted order, so that the efficient implementation used for Integer_Set_Package can be used in the generic package as well. (We could just as easily have provided ">" rather than "<" as a generic parameter. Either relation can be defined in terms of the other within the generic package.) The resulting solution is slightly less general than the one originally envisioned but may be more useful.

Indeed, whenever a more general solution is significantly harder to program or less efficient than the solution to the special case, it is difficult to justify pursuing the more general solution. Any such justification must be based on evidence that the added generality will in fact be exploited. The eventual use of general-purpose software components is rarely predictable.

Now we shall consider another example, sorting an array of `Integer` values using an insertion sort. There are several ways to view this as a special case of a more general problem. We can define the general problem to be sorting an array of values in *some* integer type, or, as in Section 16.2.3, sorting an array of values in some discrete type:

```
GENERIC
   TYPE Component_Type IS ( <> );
   TYPE Array_Type IS
      ARRAY (Positive RANGE <>) OF Component_Type;
PROCEDURE Sort_Template (a : IN OUT Array_Type);
```

This more general view is possible because the only properties of integer types used in the insertion sort algorithm are the availability of the > operator and the availability of assignment.

However, this insight allows us to be even more general. We can choose the more general problem to be sorting an array in any type for which the > operator and assignment are available. Then the generic declaration becomes:

```
GENERIC
   TYPE Component_Type IS PRIVATE;
   TYPE Array_Type IS
      ARRAY (Positive RANGE <>) OF Component_Type;
   WITH
      FUNCTION ">"
         (Left, Right : Component_Type) RETURN Boolean
      IS <>;
PROCEDURE Sort_Template (a : IN OUT Array_Type);
```

No change to the generic body is necessary. Without realizing it, we had already written an algorithm capable of solving a more general problem!

It is worthwhile to consider the wide variety of problems that can be viewed as special cases of this general problem. As before, `Sort_Template` can be instantiated with any discrete subtype corresponding to `Component_Type`. It is not even necessary to specify the third generic actual parameter in such instantiations, because of the default for the generic formal function `">"`. In fact, the third generic actual parameter can also be omitted for instantiations in which `Component_Type` corresponds to a floating-point subtype, a fixed-point subtype, or a one-dimensional array subtype with discrete components, such as `String (1 .. 80)`.

Furthermore, the function ">" can be overloaded for types for which it is not predefined. Consider the following example:

```
TYPE Customer_Record_Type IS
   RECORD
      Name_Part           : String (1 .. 30);
      Street_Address_Part : String (1 .. 40);
      City_Part           : String (1 .. 20);
      Zip_Code_Part       : Integer RANGE 00000 .. 99999;
   END RECORD;

TYPE Customer_List_Type
   IS ARRAY (Positive RANGE <>) OF Customer_Record_Type;

FUNCTION ">"
   (Left, Right : Customer_Record_Type) RETURN Boolean IS
BEGIN
   RETURN Left.Name_Part > Right.Name_Part;
END ">";
```

Record types do not have predefined versions of ">", but this function provides a version of ">" such that one `Customer_Record_Type` value is considered greater than another if its `Name_Part` component is greater (according to the version of ">" predefined for type `String`). Thus the instantiation

```
PROCEDURE Sort_By_Name IS
   NEW Sort_Template
      (Component_Type => Customer_Record_Type,
       Array_Type     => Customer_List_Type);
```

rearranges `Customer_List_Type` arrays so that the `Name_Part` components of the `Customer_Record_Type` values are in ascending order.

We can also define a function to compare `Customer_Record_Type` values according to their `Zip_Code_Part` components:

```
FUNCTION Has_Higher_Zip_Code_Than
   (Record_1, Record_2 : Customer_Record_Type)
   RETURN Boolean IS
BEGIN
   RETURN Record_1.Zip_Code_Part > Record_2.Zip_Code_Part;
END Has_Higher_Zip_Code_Than;
```

Then the following instance sorts `Customer_Record_Type` values under the assumption that one `Customer_Record_Type` value is greater than another if its `Zip_Code_Part` component is greater:

```
PROCEDURE Sort_By_Zip_Code IS
   NEW Sort_Template
      (Component_Type => Customer_Record_Type,
       Array_Type     => Customer_List_Type,
       ">"            => Has_Higher_Zip_Code_Than);
```

Thus a call on `Sort_By_Zip_Code` rearranges the records of a `Customer_List_Type` array in order of increasing `Zip_Code_Part` components.

Finally, consider the following declarations:

```
TYPE Integer_List_Type IS
   ARRAY (Positive RANGE <>) OF Integer;
PROCEDURE Sort_Descending IS
   NEW Sort_Template
      (Component_Type => Integer,
       Array_Type     => Integer_List_Type,
       ">"            => "<");
```

In this instantiation, the generic actual parameter corresponding to the generic formal function `">"` (*greater than*) is the version of `"<"` (*less than*) predefined for type `Integer`. Within the generic body, an expression of the form $x > y$ comparing two array components is true—indicating that x should come later than y in the sorted array, precisely when x is numerically *less* than y. Thus `Sort_Descending` places an array of `Integer` values in descending order.

This instantiation is rather confusing. As we discover how generally applicable `Sort_Template` is, it becomes evident that the name `">"` does not fully reflect the role of the generic formal function. A more appropriate name would be `Belongs_Later_Than`. Given this name, the instantiations above could be rewritten as follows:

```
PROCEDURE Sort_By_Name IS
   NEW Sort_Template
      (Component_Type     => Customer_Record_Type,
       Array_Type         => Customer_List_Type
       Belongs_Later_Than => ">");
   -- X belongs later than Y in the sorted array when X > Y.
PROCEDURE Sort_By_Zip_Code IS
   NEW Sort_Template
      (Component_Type     => Customer_Record_Type,
       Array_Type         => Customer_List_Type,
       Belongs_Later_Than => Has_Higher_Zip_Code_Than);
   -- X belongs later than Y in the sorted array when X has
   --   a higher zip code than Y.
PROCEDURE Sort_Descending IS
   NEW Sort_Template
      (Component_Type     => Integer,
       Array_Type         => Integer_List_Type,
       Belongs_Later_Than => "<");
   -- X belongs later than Y in the sorted array when X < Y.
```

Within the generic body, the expression

```
a (Candidate_Position) > New_Item
```

must be rewritten as

```
Belongs_Later_Than (a (Candidate_Position), New_Item)
```

However, the generic instantiations using the new name are easier to understand.

There is another way to generalize Sort_Template. That is to allow any discrete subtype—rather than just Positive—to be specified by a generic parameter and used as the index type of Array_Type. However, this is not as useful as it sounds. Some arrays are used to establish an *association* between specific index values and component values. Other arrays are used to hold *lists* in which the order of the components may be important, but in which there is no intrinsic relationship between an index value and the value of the component it indexes. Enumeration types are generally used as index values only for the first kind of array, but sorting is generally a meaningful operation only for the second kind of array.

If we were to pursue this generalization anyway, we would have to rewrite the generic body, replacing operations such as adding one or subtracting one by applications of the 'Succ and 'Pred attributes of the index type. However, this would not be enough. The algorithm used in Section 16.2.3.3 sometimes decreases the variable Candidate_Position to the value just below the first index position of the array to be sorted. In an array with index *subtype* Positive, the index *type* of the array—Integer—always includes values less than the first index of the array. However, if the index subtype is made a generic formal type, an instance of Sort_Template can be called with an array whose first index position has no predecessor. One of the exercises given at the end of this chapter is to solve this problem.

16.6 PREDEFINED GENERIC UNITS

There are four predefined generic units that are provided by every implementation of the Ada language. They are generic packages named Sequential_IO and Direct_IO, a generic function named Unchecked_Conversion, and a generic procedure named Unchecked_Deallocation. These are all library units. In addition, the predefined library package Text_IO *provides* generic packages named Integer_IO, Float_IO, Fixed_IO, and Enumeration_IO.

The generic packages Sequential_IO and Direct_IO and the package Text_IO, all of which provide advanced file manipulation, input, and output operations, are described in Chapter 17. The generic function Unchecked_Conversion, used in low-level programming, is discussed in Chapter 20. The remainder of this section describes the generic procedure Unchecked_Deallocation.

Programmers often picture allocators dipping into an inexhaustible pool of storage to create allocated variables. For many programs, this view is appropriate, because the amount of storage the programs allocate is minuscule compared to the amount of storage available. However, other programs allocate so many variables that they force us to confront the finiteness of storage. Unless special measures are taken, these programs may raise Storage_Error when allocation is attempted.

Sometimes, a program can determine that it will have no further use for some variable that it has allocated. It can then *deallocate* the variable. When an allocated variable is deallocated, it ceases to exist. The storage used by that variable then can be reused to allocate new variables.

Allocated variables in PL/I programs are deallocated by executing a FREE statement. Allocated variables in Pascal programs are deallocated by calling the standard procedure Dispose. In the Ada language, allocated variables are deallocated by calling an instance of the generic procedure Unchecked_Deallocation.

Unchecked_Deallocation should not be used routinely. As we shall see, it can lead to subtle but devastating errors. If storage for allocated variables is plentiful, there is no point in complicating the program to keep track of which allocated variables are no longer needed. Furthermore, in certain implementations of the Ada language, deallocation sometimes occurs automatically when an allocated variable is no longer pointed to by any other variable. In most implementations, storage for allocated variables is released upon departure from the scope of the corresponding access-type declaration.

When a programmer must control deallocation himself, Unchecked_Deallocation is instantiated for each access type whose values may designate variables to be deallocated. The generic declaration for Unchecked_Deallocation is as follows:

```
GENERIC
   TYPE Object IS LIMITED PRIVATE;
   TYPE Name IS ACCESS Object;
PROCEDURE Unchecked_Deallocation (x : IN OUT Name);
```

There are two generic parameters, the first giving the type of the variables to be deallocated and the second giving the access type whose values may designate those variables. A call on an instance of Unchecked_Deallocation takes one parameter, which is a variable in the access type. The allocated variable designated by the parameter is deallocated, and the parameter is set to NULL. (The instance may also be called with a variable already containing the value NULL, in which case the call has no effect.)

As an example, consider the procedure Copy_Set given in Section 12.6. This procedure is provided by Integer_Set_Package, which represents sets of Integer values as linked lists. Each call on Copy_Set allocates new list cells. So, in fact, do the functions Union and Intersection. It is quite conceivable that a program making heavy use of Integer_Set_Package could run out of storage.

Once Copy_Set copies a list into some variable, the cells on the list *formerly* held by that variable never will be used again. In fact, it will no longer even be possible for the program to name those cells, since there will be no object designating the first cell of the list. Thus Copy_Set can be modified to deallocate the cells in a variable's list before replacing the list. This will greatly reduce the number of list cells allocated at any one time.

In this modified version of the Integer_Set_Package body, Copy_Set does not deallocate the dummy list cell at the beginning of the list, but reuses it for the new list. Copy_Set deallocates all other cells on the list being replaced.

```
WITH Unchecked_Deallocation;
PACKAGE BODY Integer_Set_Package IS

   ...

   PROCEDURE Deallocate_Cell IS
      NEW Unchecked_Deallocation
         (Object => Integer_Set_Cell_Type,
          Name   => List_Cell_Pointer_Type);

   PROCEDURE Copy_Set
      (From : IN Integer_Set_Type;
       To   : IN OUT Integer_Set_Type) IS

      Cells_To_Deallocate:
         List_Cell_Pointer_Type := To.Next_Cell_Part;

      Cells_To_Copy:
         List_Cell_Pointer_Type := From.Next_Cell_Part;

      Last_Result_Cell : Integer_Set_Type := To;
      Old_Cell         : List_Cell_Pointer_Type;

   BEGIN

      WHILE Cells_To_Deallocate /= NULL LOOP

         Old_Cell := Cells_To_Deallocate;
         Cells_To_Deallocate :=
            Cells_To_Deallocate.Next_Cell_Part;
         Deallocate_Cell (Old_Cell);

      END LOOP;

      WHILE Cells_To_Copy /= NULL LOOP

         Insert_At_End
            (Cells_To_Copy.Member_Part,
             Last_Result_Cell);

         Cells_To_Copy := Cells_To_Copy.Next_Cell_Part;

      END LOOP;

   END Copy_Set;

   ...

END Integer_Set_Package;
```

The library generic procedure Unchecked_Deallocation is named in a WITH clause so that it can be instantiated within the Integer_Set_Package body. The instance is named Deallocate_Cell, and it takes a parameter of type List_Cell_Pointer_Type. (The mode of the Copy_Set parameter To is changed from OUT to IN OUT, since the revised procedure must examine its old value.)

Deallocation must be used with care. Deallocating the variable designated by some access value *A* allows the variable's storage to be used for other purposes.

From that point on, *A* is no longer a meaningful access value, because the variable *A*.ALL no longer exists. If you try to examine the contents of *A*.ALL, you may find all or part of some newly allocated variable. If you try to modify the contents of *A*.ALL, you may inadvertently modify some supposedly separate variable allocated later. You might even replace a value representing an address to which the program will later try to branch. In short, making any use of the access value *A*, once the variable it designates has been deallocated, can have unpredictable and possibly disastrous results.

The reason that an instance of Unchecked_Deallocation sets its parameter to NULL is to destroy the old contents of that variable—a now meaningless access value. This affords some protection against inadvertent use of an access value designating a deallocated variable. However, the protection is incomplete, because there may be other variables containing the same access value. Consider the following example:

```
WITH Basic_IO, Unchecked_Deallocation; USE Basic_IO;
PROCEDURE Deallocation_Error_Example IS
   TYPE Integer_Pointer_Type IS ACCESS Integer;
   PROCEDURE Deallocate_Integer IS
      NEW Unchecked_Deallocation
         (Object => Integer, Name => Integer_Pointer_Type);
   a, b, c : Integer_Pointer_Type;
BEGIN
   a := NEW Integer;
   b := a;
   b.ALL := 100;
   Deallocate_Integer (a);
   -- The variable designated by a and b no longer exists.
   -- a = NULL.
   -- b holds its original (and now meaningless) value.
   c := NEW Integer'(200);
   b.ALL := b.ALL + 1; -- Erroneous since b.ALL
                       -- has been deallocated!
   Put (b.ALL); -- Unpredictable results
   New_Line;
   Put (c.ALL); -- Unpredictable results
   New_Line;
END Deallocation_Error_Example;
```

The first three assignment statements set a and b to designate the same allocated variable and place the value 100 in that allocated variable. The call on Deallocate_Integer deallocates that allocated variable and sets a to NULL. This prevents use of the name a.ALL to refer to the now deallocated variable. However, the call on Deallocate_Integer does not change the contents of b.

Thus b contains a meaningless access value, one that is not NULL yet does not designate any allocated variable. The allocator in the next statement might reuse all or part of the storage originally used by b.ALL. (Then again, it might not. It all depends on the Ada implementation and the sequence of allocations and deallocations that have occurred until now.) The initial value of 200 for c.ALL may overwrite all or part of what used to be b.ALL. The assignment statement incrementing b.ALL is erroneous. There is no way of knowing what value is computed by the expression b.ALL + 1, and the attempt to modify b.ALL *may* change all or part of the value in c.ALL.

When Unchecked_Deallocation is not used, meaningless access values cannot arise. This is because all objects in an access type have a default initial value of NULL, other access values are created only by allocators, and an access value designating an allocated variable never stops designating that variable. There are ways for compilers to check for the illegal use of deallocated variables (such as the references to b.ALL in the previous program), but they are expensive in terms of both time and storage space. Since the whole purpose of deallocation is to make better use of storage space, the rules of the Ada language do not require that this check be performed. That is why the generic procedure has the name Unchecked_Deallocation. When you deallocate variables, you do so at your own risk. If you make a mistake, the mistake may not be caught; but the results may be disastrous just the same.

For this reason, Unchecked_Deallocation should be used only when the programmer can be certain that there are no other objects containing access values that designate the variable to be deallocated. For example, because Integer_Set_Type is limited private, Integer_Set_Package has complete control over the copying of Integer_Set_Type values. If we examine each of the subprograms provided by Integer_Set_Package, we find that all Integer_Set_Type values that are returned and all Integer_Set_Type parameters that are set are new lists containing only cells that did not exist before the subprogram call. When we replace the list passed to Copy_Set through the parameter To, we can be certain that there is no longer any way for the user of the package to get to any of the cells on that list. Therefore it is safe to deallocate each cell on the list

16.7 SUMMARY

A generic unit is a *template* for a package, procedure, or function. It is a package, procedure, or function in which certain items are "left blank." A *generic instantiation* fills in the blanks to produce an *instance* of the template. This instance can be used as an ordinary package, procedure, or function.

General-purpose reusable program components can be written as generic units. A single generic unit can be instantiated in different ways to solve different problems. The differences between the problems are reflected by the way the blanks are filled in. There is no need for redundant programming of the same algorithms using different types, for example. Maintenance is simplified by having a single generic program unit instead of several almost identical copies.

Within a generic unit, a "blank" is represented by a *generic formal parameter.* This is an identifier that stands for one of the following:

a value of a specified subtype
a variable of a specified subtype
a subprogram with a specified parameter and result type profile and specified
  parameter modes
a type for which certain operations are defined

A generic unit consists of a *generic declaration* and a *generic body*. The form of a generic declaration is

```
GENERIC
   ................................
   : generic formal parameter declaration :
   :         ~~~                          :
   : generic formal parameter declaration :
   ................................
unit declaration
```

where the unit declaration is either a package specification, a procedure declaration, or a function declaration. A generic body is an ordinary package, procedure, or function body, except that it may refer to generic formal parameters.

A generic unit may occur in three different contexts:

in a declarative part, with the generic declaration occurring first and the generic
  body occurring later in the same declarative part
provided by a package, with the generic declaration occurring in the package
  specification and the generic body occurring in the corresponding package
  body
separately compiled, with the generic declaration as a library unit and the generic
  body as the corresponding secondary unit.

When the generic declaration and generic body are not part of the same compilation unit, some implementations may require that the compilation unit containing the generic declaration and the compilation unit containing the generic body be submitted to the compiler together, along with any subunits of the generic body.

A generic instantiation takes one of the following forms:

```
PROCEDURE identifier IS
   NEW generic procedure name
      ..............................
      : ( generic actual parameter list ) : ;
      ..............................
FUNCTION designator IS
   NEW generic function name
      ..............................
      : ( generic actual parameter list ) : ;
      ..............................
```

```
PACKAGE identifier IS
    NEW generic package name
        [ ( generic actual parameter list ) ] ;
```

(A designator is either an identifier or a string literal containing an operator symbol.) The generic actual parameter list may be named, positional, or mixed. A generic unit may be instantiated in a package specification, in a declarative part, or as a separate compilation unit. The generic instantiation must occur after the generic declaration, but it may occur before the generic body.

There are three kinds of generic formal parameters—generic formal objects, generic formal subprograms, and generic formal types. Each kind of generic formal parameter is distinguished by three characteristics: the way it is declared, the ways in which it may be used within the generic formal unit, and the kinds of generic actual parameters that may correspond to it.

A generic formal object may be either a generic formal constant or a generic formal variable. A generic formal constant declaration can take the following form:

```
identifier , ~~~ , identifier : IN typemark [ := default ] ;
```

The default is an expression of the type specified by the typemark. The generic formal constant may be used within the generic unit as a constant of that type. Any expression of that type may be used as the corresponding generic actual parameter. A generic formal variable declaration has the following form:

```
identifier , ~~~ , identifier : IN OUT typemark ;
```

It may be used within the generic unit as a variable of the type indicated by the typemark, and the corresponding generic actual parameter may be any variable of that type. The value of the variable can be changed from both inside and outside the generic formal subprogram.

There are two kinds of generic formal subprograms—generic formal procedures and generic formal functions. In either case, the form of the generic formal parameter declaration is as follows:

```
WITH subprogram specification [ IS default ] ;
```

The default may take one of two forms:

the name of a subprogram that is visible at the point of the generic unit and that has the same parameter and result type profile and parameter modes as the subprogram specification

the symbol <>, specifying that a subprogram visible at the point of the generic instantiation with the same name, parameter and result type profile, and parameter modes should be used as the default

Within the generic unit, a generic formal subprogram may be used as a subprogram with the given subprogram specification. The corresponding generic actual parameter may be a subprogram, enumeration literal, or attribute with the appropriate parameter and result type profile and parameter modes.

There are several kinds of generic formal types:

1. A generic formal integer type has a declaration of the form

```
TYPE identifier IS RANGE <> ;
```

and is used within the generic unit as an integer type. The corresponding generic actual parameter may be any subtype of an integer type.

2. A generic formal floating-point type has a declaration of the form

```
TYPE identifier IS DIGITS <> ;
```

and is used within the generic unit as a floating-point type. The corresponding generic actual parameter may be any subtype of a floating-point type.

3. A generic formal fixed-point type has a declaration of the form

```
TYPE identifier IS DELTA <> ;
```

and is used within the generic unit as a fixed-point type. The corresponding generic actual parameter may be any subtype of a fixed-point type.

4. A generic formal discrete type has a declaration of the form

```
TYPE identifier IS ( <> ) ;
```

and is used within the generic unit as an enumeration type. The corresponding generic actual parameter may be a subtype of any discrete type (i.e., any subtype of an integer type or any subtype of an enumeration type).

5. A generic formal unconstrained array type has a declaration of the following form:

```
TYPE identifier IS
    ARRAY ( typemark RANGE <> , ~~~ , typemark RANGE <> )
        OF typemark ;
```

It may be used within the generic unit as an unconstrained array type with the specified index subtypes and component subtype. The corresponding generic actual parameter must be an unconstrained array subtype with the same number of dimensions, the same base types for corresponding index subtypes, and the same component subtype.

6. A generic formal constrained array type has a declaration of the following form:

```
TYPE identifier IS
    ARRAY ( typemark , ~~~ , typemark ) OF typemark ;
```

It may be used within the generic unit as a constrained array type with the specified index subtypes and component subtype. The corresponding generic actual parameter must be an unconstrained array subtype with the same number of dimensions, the same index subtypes, and the same component subtype.

7. A generic formal access type has a declaration of the form

```
TYPE identifier IS ACCESS typemark ;
```

and may be used within the generic unit as an access type designating allocated variables of the subtype *s* specified by the typemark. The corresponding generic actual parameter may be any subtype of an access type designating allocated variables of subtype *s*.

8. A generic formal (nonlimited) private type can be declared as follows:

```
TYPE identifier IS PRIVATE ;
```

It may be used within the generic unit as a private type. The corresponding generic actual parameter may be any subtype of a nonlimited type. A generic formal private type can also be declared with discriminants:

```
TYPE identifier
    ( generic discriminant specification ,
        ~~~ ,
      generic discriminant specification ) IS
    PRIVATE ;
```

In this case, it can be used within the generic unit as a private type having discriminants with the specified names and subtypes. The corresponding generic actual parameter must be an unconstrained subtype of a nonlimited type with the same number of discriminants and the same base types for discriminants.

9. A generic formal limited private type can be declared as follows:

```
TYPE identifier IS LIMITED PRIVATE ;
```

It may only be used within the generic unit as a limited private type, but any subtype whatsoever may be used as the corresponding generic actual parameter. A generic formal limited private type can also be declared with discriminants:

```
TYPE identifier
   ( generic discriminant specification ,
      ~~~ ,
     generic discriminant specification ) IS
   LIMITED PRIVATE ;
```

In this case, it can be used within the generic unit as a limited private type having discriminants with the specified names and subtypes. The corresponding generic actual parameter must be an unconstrained subtype of a type with the same number of discriminants and the same base types for discriminants.

Different operations are assumed to be available within a generic unit for different kinds of generic formal types. In each case, the corresponding generic actual parameter may be any subtype for which all these operations are defined. Thus there is a tradeoff between flexibility in writing a generic unit and flexibility in instantiating it. A generic formal type for which more operations are defined can be used in more ways within the generic unit. A generic formal type for which fewer operations are defined can be matched by a larger class of generic actual parameters.

Figure 16.2 shows the relationships of the different kinds of generic formal types. Each type class in this diagram has all the operations of the type classes to which it is connected above, plus some additional operations. For a generic formal parameter of a given class, a subtype in any of the classes below it may be used as a generic actual parameter. The higher a class of types in this diagram, the more kinds of generic actual parameters that match it. The lower a class of types in this diagram, the greater the number of operations available for it within a generic unit.

Among the generic units predefined by the Ada language is the generic procedure `Unchecked_Deallocation`. An instance of this generic unit can be called to deallocate an allocated variable. Deallocation can be extremely dangerous and should be used with caution.

EXERCISES

16.1 `List_Function_Package` (given in Section 16.2.2) provides an exception `List_Length_Error` and a generic function `List_Function_Template` whose instances may raise this exception. Redesign this program unit so that each instantiation creates a function that raises a *different* exception when called with parameters of unequal length.

16.2 Rewrite the program `Hexadecimal_To_Decimal` given in Section 8.1.4 using an instantiation of the generic package `Hexadecimal_Numeral_Package_Template` given in Section 16.2.3.7.

16.3 Redesign `Symmetric_Matrix_Package_Template` (given in Section 16.1) so that an instantiation does not specify the number of rows and columns, but a single discrete subtype that will be used to index both rows and columns of the symmetric matrix. For example, given the declaration

```
TYPE Note_Type IS
   (Do_Note, Re_Note, Me_Note, Fa_Note, Sol_Note, La_Note, Ti_Note);
```

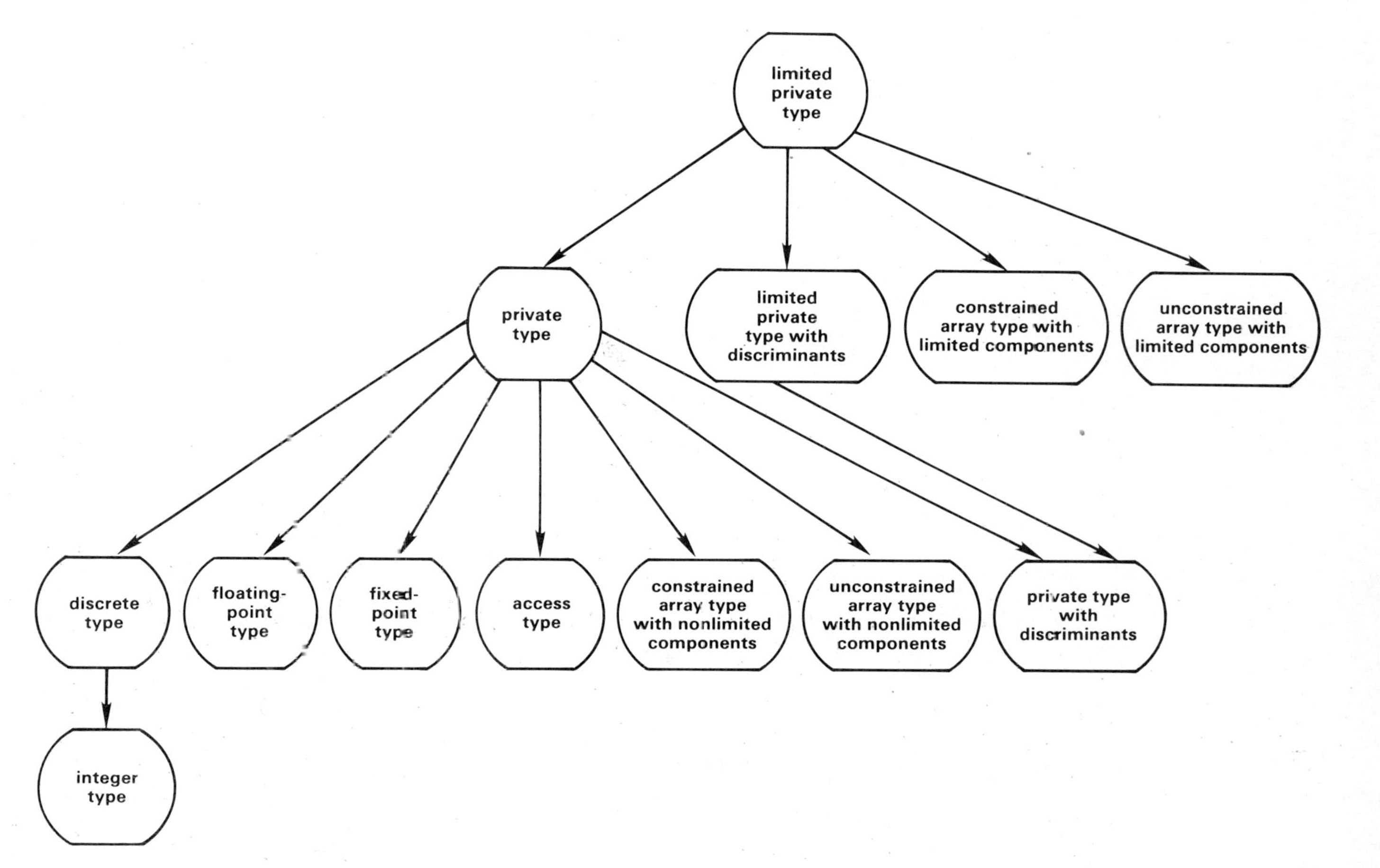

Figure 16.2 Relationships among the various kinds of generic formal types. Type classes are arranged hierarchically according to the operations associated with each class. This hierarchy determines allowable uses of a generic formal type within the generic unit and allowable generic actual parameters in an instantiation, as explained in the text.

an instantiation like

```
PACKAGE Harmony_Table_Package IS
   NEW Symmetric_Matrix_Package_Template_2
      (Index_Type      => Note_Type,
       Component_Type => Boolean);
```

would provide symmetric matrices of Boolean values with rows and columns indexed by `Note_Type` values. The function call

```
Harmony_Table_Package.Component (Harmony_Table, Do_Note, So_Note)
```

might return the value `True`, for example.

16.4 Extend `Generic_Set_Package_Template`, presented in Section 16.2.3.2, so that an instance also provides a (nested) generic procedure `Process_Set_Template`. An instance of `Process_Set_Template` applies some operation to all elements of a set. The operation, a procedure with one `IN` parameter of the discrete type, is specified by a generic parameter of `Process_Set_Template`. An instance of `Process_Set_Template` is a procedure taking a single parameter in the type for sets. The instance applies the operation specified as a generic parameter to each element of this set. For example, given the separately compiled instantiation

```
PACKAGE Character_Set_Package IS
   NEW Discrete_Set_Package (Element_Type => Character);
```

it should be possible to write the following instantiation:

```
WITH Character_Set_Package, Text_IO;
PROCEDURE Put_Elements IS
   NEW Character_Set_Package.Process_Set_Template
      (Process_One_Element => Text_IO.Put);
```

The call `Put_Elements (`*S*`)`, where *S* is of type `Character_Set_Package.Set_Type`, prints each element of the set *S* (by calling `Text_IO.Put` with each character of the set in turn).

16.5 Write a generic procedure `Process_Each_Element_Template`. An instance of this procedure should take a single `IN OUT` parameter belonging to an unconstrained one-dimensional array type and "process" each component of the array. The nature of the array and the meaning of "processing" a component of the array should be specified by generic parameters. Be as general as possible.

16.6 In the instantiation of `Translate_Template` in Section 16.2.3.3, why does the generic actual parameter `String` match the generic formal array type `Sequence_Type`?

16.7 Rewrite the declaration and body of `Sort_Template` given in Section 16.2.3.3 so that both the index type for `Array_Type` and the comparison function `">"` are specified by generic parameters. In the `WHILE` loop decreasing the variable `Candidate_Position`, be sure to account for the possibility that an instance will be called with an array whose first index value is the first value of the index type. (*Hint:* Rewrite the body so that, at each point in the computation, `Candidate_Position` holds the successor of the value it would hold at the same point in the original version. Adjust all references to `Candidate_Position` accordingly.)

16.8 Generalize the generic function `Translate_Template` given in Section 16.2.3.3 to allow components of one type to be translated to components in a *different* type. Be as general as you can without changing the underlying algorithm.

16.9 Write a generic package whose instances provide a private type for vectors and a set of operations on that type. Each value in the type may be thought of as a sequence of values in some floating-point type. All sequences in the type have the same number of values. The floating-point type and the number of values should be specified by generic parameters. The operations include a version of `"+"` that adds two vectors to produce a vector result, a version of `"*"` that multiplies a floating-point value (of the type used to build vectors) by a vector to produce a vector result, and a version of `"*"` that takes the "dot product" of two vectors and produces a result in the floating-point type. These operations are defined as follows, where $<x_1, ..., x_n>$ denotes a vector consisting of n floating-point values:

$$<x_1 , ..., x_n> + <y_1 , ..., y_n> = <x_1 + y_1 , ..., x_n + y_n>$$

$$x * <y_1 , ..., y_n > = <x*y_1 , ..., x*y_n>$$

$$<x_1 , ..., x_n> * <y_1 , ..., y_n> = <x_1 , ..., x_n> + <y_1 , ..., y_n$$

There also should be a function named `Unit_Vector` which takes a value d between one and the number of floating-point values in a vector and returns a vector whose d^{th} floating-point value is 1.0 and whose other floating-point values are 0.0.

16.10 Enclose the generic vector package developed in the previous exercise in an ordinary package. This package should provide both the generic vector package and an exception named `Instantiation_Error`. The exception should be raised by any *instantiation* of the generic vector package with a floating-point subtype that does not include the values 0.0 and 1.0. (*Hint:* When a generic package is instantiated, the specification and body of the instance are elaborated. Any exception raised by this elaboration is propagated to the point of the generic instantiation. Any statements inside a package body are executed at the time the package is elaborated.)

16.11 Write the body for the generic function `Indirect_Operator_Template` given in Section 16.2.3.4.

16.12 Generalize `Indirect_Operator_Template` (given in Section 16.2.3.4) to work with any type rather than just an integer type. Given an access value designating x and an access value designating y, an instance of this generic function should return an access value designating a variable containing `f (x, y)`.

16.13 Show how you could instantiate the second version of `Set_Package_Template` described in Section 16.5 (the version with a generic formal function `"<"`) to obtain a package for sets of complex numbers. Assume that a complex number is implemented as a record type having two components of type `Float`, named `Real_Part` and `Imaginary_Part`.

CHAPTER

SEVENTEEN

PREDEFINED INPUT AND OUTPUT

There are no input and output *statements* in the Ada language. Instead there is a collection of subprograms, types, subtypes, and exceptions used for file manipulation, input, and output. These facilities are provided by general purpose packages that are specified in the Ada language (and can, in theory, be implemented in the language). Once you have learned enough about the framework of the language, learning about input and output is just like learning to use any other general-purpose package. The definition of the Ada language includes the specification of packages providing standard input and output facilities, but a programmer can also define his own input and output facilities.

In fact, that is exactly what we did in earlier chapters. Until now, all input and output operations you have seen have been operations provided by the package `Basic_IO`. `Basic_IO` is not part of the Ada language, but is a package written specifically for this book. All implementations of the Ada language include four predefined library units that provide considerably more sophisticated and flexible input and output operations than those provided by `Basic_IO`. These units are the packages `IO_Exceptions` and `Text_IO` and the generic packages `Sequential_IO` and `Direct_IO`. The capabilities provided by `Basic_IO` are a small subset of those provided by `Text_IO`.

The exact behavior of input, output, and file manipulation operations is heavily dependent on the environment in which an Ada program is run. The Ada language definition specifies the standard input and output facilities in detail but with enough flexibility to allow reasonable variations from one implementation to another. These variations include, among others, the allowed forms of a file name, the descriptive information that can be specified when creating a new file, the availability of certain operations such as deleting a file from within a program, and the effect of certain actions such as completing a program without closing an open file. Whenever we get to a feature that may work differently in different implementations, we shall explain possible variations. Your implementation's reference manual should explain how that implementation behaves in such situations.

17.1 BASIC CONCEPTS

Before we consider the Ada language's input/output features, we must consider the language's model of files. The Ada language provides two views of files, one from outside the program (in which the program receives data from or sends data to some other part of the environment) and one from inside the program (in which certain sources or destinations of data play certain roles in an algorithm). Section 17.1.1 addresses these two views. Files may be manipulated either as sequences of actual values or as streams of characters describing values, as explained in Section 17.1.2. Section 17.1.3 describes how data in a file may be processed either from the beginning of the file to the end or in some order determined by the program. Finally, Section 17.1.4 discusses the direction in which data flows between a file and a program.

17.1.1 External and Internal Files

Until now, we have only obtained input data from the *standard input file* (typically a terminal keyboard or a card reader) and sent output data to the *standard output file* (typically terminal output or a line printer). Of course, there are many other possible sources of input data and destinations for output data. These include disk files, magnetic tapes, and telecommunications links, for example. The various sources and destinations of data are called *external files.*

In contrast, a program reads data from and writes data to *internal files.* Internal files are *logical* sources or destinations of data playing particular roles in a program. A billing program, for example, might have six internal files, used for the following purposes:

reading new transactions (charges and payments)
reading old balances
writing new balances
writing bills
reporting overdue accounts
reporting errors in input data

Before the program reads data from or writes data to an internal file, it associates that internal file with some external file. This is called *opening* the internal file. The associations of internal files with external files may change from one run of the program to another or even during a single run. For the billing program, the external file associated with the new-balance internal file during one run might be associated with the old-balance internal file during the next run.

Some implementations may allow a number of internal files to be simultaneously associated with the same external file. Other implementations may forbid this. The meaning of associating several internal files with the same external file depends on the implementation.

Sometimes, when the meaning is clear, we use the term *file* to mean *internal file.*

17.1.2 Stream-Oriented and Record-Oriented Input/Output

Until now, we have only used *stream-oriented* input and output. In stream-oriented input and output, files are viewed as streams of characters. A stream-oriented input operation reads a sequence of characters, interprets them as the representation of some value (say a sequence of digits as the representation of an integer value), and delivers that value to the program. A stream-oriented output operation takes a value from the program and writes a sequence of characters representing that value.

The Ada language also provides *record-oriented* input and output, in which a file is viewed as a sequence of values all of the same type. Typically, these values are represented in the file in the same internal format as in a running program. Unlike stream-oriented output, record-oriented output is not easily read by a human. Its primary role is to serve as a source for later record-oriented input, perhaps by a different program.

17.1.3 Sequential and Direct Access

There are two ways of manipulating files, known as *sequential access* and *direct access*. Sequential access means that the contents of a file are processed in order. Data are read from the beginning of an input file or written to the end of an output file. Direct access means that a file is viewed as a set of *elements* identified by consecutive integers. Any element of the file may be read or written at any time by specifying the integer that identifies it. In essence, the file acts as a one-dimensional array. Of course, it is possible to read from or write to elements of a direct-access file consecutively, starting with the first element and ending with the last. In fact, the Ada language makes it quite easy to do this. (Direct access sometimes is called *random access*. When direct access elements are processed in order, it sometimes is called *indexed sequential access*. However, neither of these terms is standard Ada terminology.)

Stream-oriented input and output are inherently sequential. Characters may only be read from the beginning of an input stream or written to the end of an output stream. Record-oriented input and output may be either sequential or direct.

17.1.4 File Modes

Information can be transferred either from a file to a program or from a program to a file. The allowable operations for an internal file depend on the file's *mode*. File modes are much like parameter modes: a file mode of *in* means that the program may read data from the file; a file mode of *out* means that the program may write data to the file; and a file mode of *in-out* means that the program may both read data from and write data to the file.

The file mode *in-out* is only allowed for direct-access files. Sequential devices that both send and receive data, like a terminal or a telecommunications link, are treated as two separate files, one of mode *in* (e.g., a terminal keyboard) and one of mode *out* (e.g., a terminal display).

	Sequential Access	Direct Access
Stream Oriented	in out	X
Record Oriented	in out	in in-out out

Figure 17.1 Allowable combinations of stream versus record orientation, sequential versus direct access, and file mode.

Every open file has a current mode. The mode of an internal file is first specified when the program associates the internal file with some external file. In addition, the mode sometimes can be changed by "resetting" the file, that is, backing up to the beginning of the file.

17.1.5 Summary

The allowable combinations of stream and record orientation, access method, and file mode are summarized in Figure 17.1.

17.2 AN OVERVIEW OF THE INPUT/OUTPUT PACKAGES

This section describes the roles of the package `Text_IO`, the generic packages `Sequential_IO` and `Direct_IO`, and the package `IO_Exceptions`. We briefly sketch the facilities provided by each package and how the packages relate to each other, concluding with a quick description of the exceptions that can be raised by these packages' operations. Further details follow in Sections 17.4, 17.5, and 17.6.

Facilities for stream-oriented input/output are provided by the predefined library package `Text_IO`. This package provides a limited private type named `File_Type`, whose values are internal files. It also provides operations on `File_Type`, along with other types used in these operations. One of these is a type for file modes, defined as follows:

```
TYPE File_Mode IS (In_File, Out_File);
```

Among the operations provided are operations to deal with external files and operations concerned with the formatting of input and output streams (e.g., operations to skip to a specified page, line, or column).

Most importantly, Text_IO provides overloaded versions of procedures named Get and Put for performing stream input and output, respectively. Versions of Get and Put for data of type Character and type String are provided directly by Text_IO. Versions for data of other scalar types are provided by four generic packages declared *within* the Text_IO package specification. The generic package Integer_IO is instantiated by specifying an integer type as an actual parameter; the generic package Float_IO by specifying a floating-point type; the generic package Fixed_IO by specifying a fixed-point type; and the generic package Enumeration_IO by specifying an enumeration type. In each case, the instance provides versions of Get and Put for the subtype specified as a generic actual parameter.

Facilities for record-oriented sequential input/output are provided by instances of the predefined library generic package Sequential_IO. In record-oriented input/output, each file is viewed as a sequence of values of the same type, called the *element type* of the file. Sequential_IO is instantiated with a subtype of any nonlimited type to produce a package for reading and writing files with that element type. Like Text_IO, each instance of Sequential_IO provides a limited private type named File_Type whose values are internal files and an enumeration type named File_Mode whose values are In_File and Out_File. Each instance also provides operations for dealing with external files and for performing sequential input and output.

Facilities for direct-access input/output are provided by instances of the predefined library generic package Direct_IO. Like Sequential_IO, Direct_IO is instantiated with a subtype of any nonlimited type to produce a package for manipulating files with that element type. Like Text_IO and instances of Sequential_IO, each instance of Direct_IO provides a limited private type named File_Type, whose values are internal files. An instance of Direct_IO also provides a type for file modes, but in this case the definition allows for files of mode *in-out:*

```
TYPE File_Mode IS (In_File, Inout_File, Out_File);
```

(Note that the identifier Inout_File contains only one underscore.) Instances of Direct_IO provide operations for dealing with external files and operations for performing direct-access input and output.

In summary, stream-oriented input/output facilities are provided by the ordinary package Text_IO, record-oriented sequential input/output is provided by instances of the generic package Sequential_IO, and direct-access input/output is provided by instances of the generic package Direct_IO. Text_IO provides, among other things, four generic packages that can be instantiated to provide stream-oriented input/output operations for types other than Character and String. (See Figure 17.2.)

Text_IO, instances of Sequential_IO, and instances of Direct_IO provide many similar facilities, including a limited private type File_Type for internal files and an enumeration type File_Mode for file modes. The subprograms dealing

```
PACKAGE Text_IO IS
  TYPE File_Type IS LIMITED PRIVATE;
  TYPE File_Mode IS (In_File, Out_File);
  ...
  [operations on external files]
  [Get and Put for characters]
  [Get and Put for strings]
  [formatting operations]

  GENERIC
    TYPE Num IS RANGE <>;
  PACKAGE Integer_IO IS
    ...
    [Get and Put for integer literals]
  END Integer_IO;

  GENERIC
    TYPE Num IS DIGITS <>;
  PACKAGE Float_IO IS
    ...
    [Get and Put for real literals]
  END Float_IO;

  GENERIC
    Type Num IS DELTA <>;
  PACKAGE Fixed_IO IS
    [Get and Put for real literals]
  END Fixed_IO;

  GENERIC
    TYPE Enum IS (<>);
  PACKAGE Enumeration_IO IS
    [Get and Put for enumeration literals]
  END Enumeration_IO;

END Text_IO;
```

```
GENERIC
  TYPE Element_Type IS PRIVATE;
PACKAGE Sequential_IO IS
  TYPE File_Type IS LIMITED PRIVATE;
  TYPE File_Mode IS (In_File, Out_File);
  ...
  [operations on external files]
  [operations for sequential input and output of
   Element_Type values]

END Sequential_IO;
```

```
GENERIC
  TYPE Element_Type IS PRIVATE;
PACKAGE Direct_IO IS
  TYPE File_Type IS LIMITED PRIVATE;
  TYPE File_Mode is
    (In_File, Inout_File, Out_File);
  ...
  [operations on external files]
  [operations for direct input and output of
   Element_Type values]

END Direct_IO;
```

Figure 17.2 Three predefined library packages providing input, output, and file manipulation facilities. `Text_IO` is an ordinary library package providing (among other things) four generic packages. `Sequential_IO` and `Direct_IO` are generic library packages. Each of these three units contains renaming declarations for exceptions declared in a fourth unit not shown here, an ordinary library package named `IO_Exceptions`.

with external files are identical in each case. Nonetheless, *the facilities provided by these packages are distinct entities.* Text_IO, each instance of Sequential_IO, and each instance of Direct_IO all provide *different* limited private types named File_Type, *different* enumeration types named File_Mode, and *different* (although identically named and similarly behaved) subprograms for dealing with external files.

Text_IO, instances of Sequential_IO, and instances of Direct_IO also provide exceptions that may be raised by their operations. However, *they all provide the same exceptions.* There is a fourth predefined library unit, an ordinary package named IO_Exceptions:

```
PACKAGE IO_Exceptions IS
   Status_Error : EXCEPTION;
   Mode_Error   : EXCEPTION;
   Name_Error   : EXCEPTION;
   Use_Error    : EXCEPTION;
   Device_Error : EXCEPTION;
   End_Error    : EXCEPTION;
   Data_Error   : EXCEPTION;
   Layout_Error : EXCEPTION;
END IO_Exceptions;
```

The Text_IO package specification and the Sequential_IO and Direct_IO generic declarations each begin with the context clause

```
WITH IO_Exceptions;
```

and contain the following seven renaming declarations:

```
Status_Error : EXCEPTION RENAMES IO_Exceptions.Status_Error;
Mode_Error   : EXCEPTION RENAMES IO_Exceptions.Mode_Error;
Name_Error   : EXCEPTION RENAMES IO_Exceptions.Name_Error;
Use_Error    : EXCEPTION RENAMES IO_Exceptions.Use_Error;
Device_Error : EXCEPTION RENAMES IO_Exceptions.Device_Error;
End_Error    : EXCEPTION RENAMES IO_Exceptions.End_Error;
Data_Error   : EXCEPTION RENAMES IO_Exceptions.Data_Error;
```

In addition, the Text_IO package specification has a renaming declaration for Layout_Error.

Because these renaming declarations occur in a package specification and in templates for package specifications, the exceptions declared in IO_Exceptions are also available directly to users of Text_IO, users of instances of Sequential_IO, and users of instances of Direct_IO. For example, suppose we have written the following instantiations:

```
PACKAGE Sequential_Integer_IO IS NEW Sequential_IO (Integer);
PACKAGE Direct_Integer_IO IS NEW Direct_IO (Integer);
```

Then Text_IO.Use_Error, Sequential_Integer_IO.Use_Error, and Direct_Integer_IO.Use_Error are different names for the same exception—the one originally declared as IO_Exceptions.Use_Error. A handler for Text_IO.Use_Error, for example, will be invoked if Use_Error is raised by an operation of Text_IO, Sequential_Integer_IO, or Direct_Integer_IO. In contrast, the types Text_IO.File_Type, Sequential_Integer_IO.File_Type, and Direct_Integer_IO.File_Type are three distinct types.

The eight exceptions declared in IO_Exceptions are raised in the following circumstances:

Status_Error:	an attempt to use an internal file that has not been associated with an external file (i.e., has not been *opened*); or to open an internal file that is already open
Mode_Error:	an attempt to perform an input operation on a file of mode *out* or an output operation on a file of mode *in*
Name_Error:	an attempt to associate an internal file with an external file if an invalid external file name is specified
Use_Error:	an attempt to perform some input/output operation on an external file for which the implementation does not allow that operation
Device_Error:	a problem with the hardware, software, or media providing input/output services
End_Error:	an attempt to read past the end of an input file
Data_Error:	input data that is not of the expected form
Layout_Error:	invalid Text_IO formatting operations

17.3 MANIPULATING EXTERNAL FILES

External files are manipulated by nine subprograms—procedures named Create, Open, Close, Delete, and Reset and functions named Mode, Name, Form, and Is_Open. Actually, there are several distinct versions of these subprograms, provided by Text_IO, by each instance of Sequential_IO, and by each instance of

Direct_IO. Because all the versions of a given subprogram have essentially the same behavior, however, we can give one description of each subprogram. Sections 17.3.1 through 17.3.4 concentrate on the normal behavior of the nine subprograms, and Section 17.3.5 describes the exceptions they can raise.

Any package providing versions of these nine subprograms also provides types named File_Type and File_Mode. Some of the nine subprograms have parameters or results of these types. In what follows, when we refer to File_Type or File_Mode, we mean the type by that name provided by the same package as the subprogram version we are considering. For example, the procedure Text_IO.Create has parameters of type Text_IO.File_Type and Text_IO.File_Mode, among others.

17.3.1 Opening Files

The procedures Create and Open both open internal files, associating them with external files. Create establishes a new external file and associates an internal file with it, while Open associates an internal file with an existing external file. The version of Create provided by Text_IO and instances of Sequential_IO is declared as follows:

```
PROCEDURE Create
   (File : IN OUT File_Type;
    Mode : IN File_Mode := Out_File;
    Name : IN String := "";
    Form : IN String := "");
```

The version provided by instances of Direct_IO is declared in the same way except for the default initial value of the Mode parameter:

```
PROCEDURE Create
   (File : IN OUT File_Type;
    Mode : IN File_Mode := Inout_File;
    Name : IN String := "";
    Form : IN String := "");
```

The procedure Open is always declared as follows:

```
PROCEDURE Open
   (File : IN OUT File_Type;
    Mode : IN File_Mode;
    Name : IN String;
    Form : IN String := "");
```

In each case, the strings Name and Form together describe an external file. The string Name identifies the external file, and the string Form describes certain characteristics of the external file. The internal file passed as parameter File is associated with this external file—thus opening the internal file—and the current mode of the internal file is set to that given by Mode. In the case of Create, Name and Form describe a new external file to be created; in the case of Open, Name and Form describe an existing file.

Both the allowable contents of Name and the characteristics described by Form depend on the implementation and the file mode. In particular, certain names may be reserved for devices such as a card reader or line printer. The name reserved for a card reader would not be allowed for direct-access files or for files of mode Out_File. If Create is called with an empty string ("") for Name, it specifies that the external file is to be a temporary file (i.e., a file that will not be used again after the program finishes).

Depending on the values of parameters Name and Mode, different implementations might use the parameter Form to specify characteristics like the following, for example:

the device providing the external file
the density and label of a tape file
baud rate, number of bits per character, number of start and stop bits, and parity for a communications link
the amount of space initially to be allocated for a disk file
whether the operating system is to restrict permission to read or write the external file
a password required to read and/or write the external file

An empty string for the parameter Form indicates that implementation-defined defaults are to be used.

When called with the name of a nonexistent file, Open does not create the file. Rather, it raises the exception Name_Error. The following block statement opens an existing file for output or creates and opens a new file with the specified name if none already exists:

```
BEGIN
   Open (File, Out_File, Name, Form);
EXCEPTION
   WHEN Name_Error =>
      Create (File, Out_File, Name, Form);
END;
```

17.3.2 Closing Files

Opening an internal file establishes an association between the internal file and some external file; closing an internal file removes that association. There are two procedures for closing files. The procedure Close simply breaks the association between an internal file and an external file. The procedure Delete breaks the association and then deletes the external file. Each procedure is passed a single internal file as a parameter:

```
PROCEDURE Close (File : IN OUT File_Type);
PROCEDURE Delete (File : IN OUT File_Type);
```

The Ada language does not define what happens to an external file upon completion of a program, but certain implementations may lose all trace of a file that was written but not closed by the program. (Unlike Pascal, the Ada language does not automatically close files at the end of a program.) Furthermore, some implementations may prevent other users from using an external file between the time the file is opened and the time the file is closed. For these reasons, it is a good idea for a program to close all files that it opens.

17.3.3 Resetting Files

Resetting a file means going back to the beginning of the file, possibly changing the file mode, and allowing reading and writing operations to resume from the beginning of the file. It is equivalent to closing and then reopening the file. The most common reason for resetting a file is to read a file that was written earlier in the program.

`Text_IO`, instances of `Sequential_IO`, and instances of `Direct_IO` each provide two overloaded procedures named `Reset`—one to specify a new file mode and one to reset a file without changing its file mode:

```
PROCEDURE Reset
   (File : IN OUT File_Type; Mode : IN File_Mode);
PROCEDURE Reset (File : IN OUT File_Type);
```

Not all resetting operations are meaningful for all external files. For instance, in typical implementations, a program cannot reset a file associated with a terminal, card reader, printer, or communications link. Neither is every file mode meaningful for every external file. The external files for which resetting is meaningful, and the allowable modes for each external file, are determined by the implementation.

17.3.4 Determining the Status of Files

The procedures `Create`, `Open`, `Close`, `Delete`, and `Reset` control certain characteristics of files: whether a file is open, the name of the external file associated with an open internal file, the form describing that external file, and the mode of an open internal file. Four functions, named `Is_Open`, `Name`, `Form`, and `Mode`, return this information when called with an internal file. The functions are declared as follows:

```
FUNCTION Is_Open (File : File_Type) RETURN Boolean;
FUNCTION Name (File : File_Type) RETURN String;
FUNCTION Form (File : File_Type) RETURN String;
FUNCTION Mode (File : File_Type) RETURN File_Mode;
```

7.3.5 Exceptions

Not all calls on the subprograms described above produce meaningful results. Certain calls raise one of the exceptions `Name_Error`, `Status_Error`, or `Use_Error`. (These three exceptions are among the eight declared in `IO_Exceptions` and renamed in `Text_IO`, `Sequential_IO`, and `Direct_IO`.)

`Name_Error` is raised by `Create` or `Open` if the `Name` parameter is invalid. In the case of `Create`, `Name_Error` is raised if `Name` is an improperly structured string (according to the implementation's rules for file names). In the case of `Open`, `Name_Error` is raised if `Name` is an improperly structured string or (as explained in Section 17.3.1) if the structure is proper but the string does not name an existing file.

`Status_Error` is raised when operations meaningful only for an open file are applied to a closed file, or vice versa. Specifically, `Status_Error` is raised when `Close`, `Delete`, `Reset`, `Mode`, `Name`, or `Form` is called with a closed internal file; or when `Open` or `Create` is called with an internal file that is already open. (`Status_Error` is *not* raised by a call on `Open` or `Create` specifying an *external* file that is already associated with some internal file. As explained in Section 17.1.1, some implementations may allow this. Implementations that do not allow it will raise `Use_Error`, described in the next paragraph, rather than `Status_Error`.) The function `Is_Open` cannot raise `Status_Error`. In fact, calls on `Is_Open` can be used to avoid raising this exception.

`Use_Error` is raised for operations that cannot be performed for a given external file. The circumstances under which `Use_Error` is raised depend on the implementation. `Create` raises `Use_Error` when the parameter `Name` contains a valid file name, but it is impossible to create a new file with the specified name, mode, and form. For example, the string `Form` may have an invalid structure or a valid structure that is incompatible with the specified external file and file mode; or a file with the same name may already exist, and the implementation may prohibit creation of a new file with the same name. Similarly, `Open` raises `Use_Error` when the parameter `Name` names an existing external file, but it is impossible to open that file with the specified mode and form. For example, the named external file may be a device (i.e., a card reader) for which certain file modes are inappropriate; again, `Form` may contain an improperly structured string or one that is incompatible with the specified external file and file mode. `Delete` raises `Use_Error` if the implementation does not allow deletion of the external file associated with the specified internal file. For example, the external file may be a device, or it may be a disk file that the operating system has protected against deletion. `Reset` raises `Use_Error` if, as explained in Section 17.3.3, the specified internal file is associated with an external file for which resetting is not appropriate or for which the specified mode is not appropriate.

17.3.6 An Example: Merge Sort

Merge sorting is a sorting technique amenable to files that can only be accessed sequentially (e.g., magnetic tape files). Because it entails creating and making several passes through temporary files, merge sorting offers good examples of external file manipulation. We shall present the highest level of a generic merge sort procedure now to illustrate external file manipulation; we shall present lower levels in Section 17.5 to illustrate sequential input and output.

Merge sorting involves repeated passes in which two input files are read and two output files are written. At the beginning of the nth pass, the input files can be thought of as divided into sorted "segments" each containing 2^{n-1} items in ascending order. Repeatedly, the front segment of one input file is merged with the front segment of the other input file to form a new sorted segment of size 2^n. The new output segments are alternately written to one output file, then the other. At the end of the pass, the role of the input files and output files is reversed, and the process is repeated with input segments twice as large. On the first pass, a single file, viewed as a sequence of one-item segments, plays the role of both input files. On the last pass, two input files, each containing a single sorted segment, are merged to form one sorted segment on one file.

We shall write a generic procedure taking two generic parameters: the type of the file contents to be sorted and the function "<" indicating when one item should be placed in front of another. An instance of the generic procedure is called with two procedure parameters. These parameters are strings giving the names of the input and output files. The generic declaration is as follows:

```
GENERIC
   TYPE Item_Type IS PRIVATE;
   WITH
      FUNCTION "<" (Left, Right : Item_Type) RETURN Boolean
      IS <>;
PROCEDURE Merge_Sort_Template
   (Input_File_Name, Output_File_Name : IN String);
```

Here is the corresponding generic procedure body:

```
WITH Sequential_IO, Swap_Template;
PROCEDURE Merge_Sort_Template
   (Input_File_Name, Output_File_Name : IN String) IS
   PACKAGE Item_IO IS NEW Sequential_IO (Item_Type);
   USE Item_IO;
   TYPE File_Pointer_Type IS ACCESS File_Type;
   Input_File,
      Output_File,
      Source_1,
      Source_2,
      Destination_1,
      Destination_2 : File_Pointer_Type := NEW File_Type;
   Segments_Formed, Segment_Size : Positive;
   Scratch_Tape_Form:
      CONSTANT String :=
         "DEVICE=TAPE(9),DENSITY=1600,VOLUME=SCRATCH";
         -- Implementation-dependent
   PROCEDURE Swap_File_Pointers IS
      NEW Swap_Template (File_Pointer_Type);
```

```
   PROCEDURE Merge_Segments
      (Source_1,
         Source_2,
         Destination_1,
         Destination_2          : IN File_Pointer_Type;
       Input_Segment_Size       : IN Positive;
       Output_Segment_Count     : OUT Positive)
      IS SEPARATE;  -- To be given in section 17.5

BEGIN

   Open (Input_File.ALL, In_File, Input_File_Name);
   Create (Source_1.ALL, Form => Scratch_Tape_Form);
   Create (Source_2.ALL, Form => Scratch_Tape_Form);

   -- First pass:
   --   Use Input_File for both sources, placing merged
   --   segments of size 2 on files Source_1.ALL and
   --   Source_2.ALL

   Merge_Segments
      (Source_1              => Input_File,
       Source_2              => Input_File,
       Destination_1         => Source_1,
       Destination_2         => Source_2,
       Input_Segment_Size    => 1,
       Output_Segment_Count  => Segments_Formed);

   Segment_Size := 2;
   Close (Input_File.ALL);
   Reset (Source_1.ALL, In_File);
   Reset (Source_2.ALL, In_File);
   Create (Destination_1.ALL, Form => Scratch_Tape_Form);
   Create (Destination_2.ALL, Form => Scratch_Tape_Form);

   -- Intermediate passes:
   --   On each pass, merge segments from Source_1.ALL and
   --   Source_2.ALL, placing merged segments in
   --   Destination_1.ALL and Destination_2.ALL, then
   --   exchange roles of source and destination files for
   --   next pass.

   WHILE Segments_Formed > 2 LOOP

      Merge_Segments
         (Source_1,
          Source_2,
          Destination_1,
          Destination_2,
          Segment_Size,
          Segments_Formed);

      Segment_Size := 2 * Segment_Size;
      Swap_File_Pointers (Source_1, Destination_1);
      Swap_File_Pointers (Source_2, Destination_2);
      Reset (Source_1.ALL, In_File);
      Reset (Source_2.ALL, In_File);
      Reset (Destination_1.ALL, Out_File);
      Reset (Destination_2.ALL, Out_File);

   END LOOP;
```

```
         Delete (Destination_1.ALL);
         Delete (Destination_2.ALL);
         Create (Output_File.ALL, Name => Output_File_Name);

         -- Final pass:
         --   Merge the segment in Source_1.ALL and the segment
         --   in Source_2.ALL into a single segment in
         --   Output_File.ALL

         Merge_Segments
            (Source_1,
             Source_2,
             Destination_1         => Output_File,
             Destination_2         => NULL,
             Input_Segment_Size    => Segment_Size,
             Output_Segment_Count  => Segments_Formed);

         Delete (Source_1.ALL);
         Delete (Source_2.ALL);
         Close (Output_File.ALL);

      END Merge_Sort_Template;
```

The behavior of this program is illustrated in Figure 17.3.

Within the generic body, the generic *formal* parameter `Item_Type` is used as the generic *actual* parameter in an instantiation of `Sequential_IO`. The resulting instance is named `Item_IO`. In a merge sort, different files take turns playing certain roles, and it is convenient to have variables indicating which file is currently playing each role. Because `Item_IO.File_Type` is limited, objects in that type cannot be copied. Therefore, we declare an access type `File_Pointer_Type` whose values point to objects of type `Item_IO.File_Type`. `File_Pointer_Type` values can be copied. To make it easy to exchange `File_Pointer_Type` values, we instantiate a generic procedure `Swap_Template`. An instance of this generic procedure exchanges the values of its two `IN OUT` parameters.

The subunit `Merge_Segments`, which does all the work during one pass of the merge sort, will be presented in Section 17.5. The first and second parameters point to the input files for that pass, the third and fourth parameters point to the output files for that pass, the fifth parameter indicates the size of the sorted segments in the input files, and the sixth parameter is set to the total number of sorted segments written to both output files.

There are six `File_Pointer_Type` variables declared in the `Merge_Sort_Template` body, with the initial value given by the expression

```
NEW File_Type
```

This allocator is evaluated once for each variable, so six unopened internal file objects are allocated. The call on `Open` with parameter `Input_File.ALL` opens the internal file *pointed to* by the `File_Pointer_Type` value `Input_File`. The other calls on `Open`, `Create`, `Reset`, and `Close` are similar. The calls on `Create` use the string constant `Scratch_Tape_Mode` for the `Mode` parameter. *This is a hypothetical string* that an implementation *might* use to specify that the file

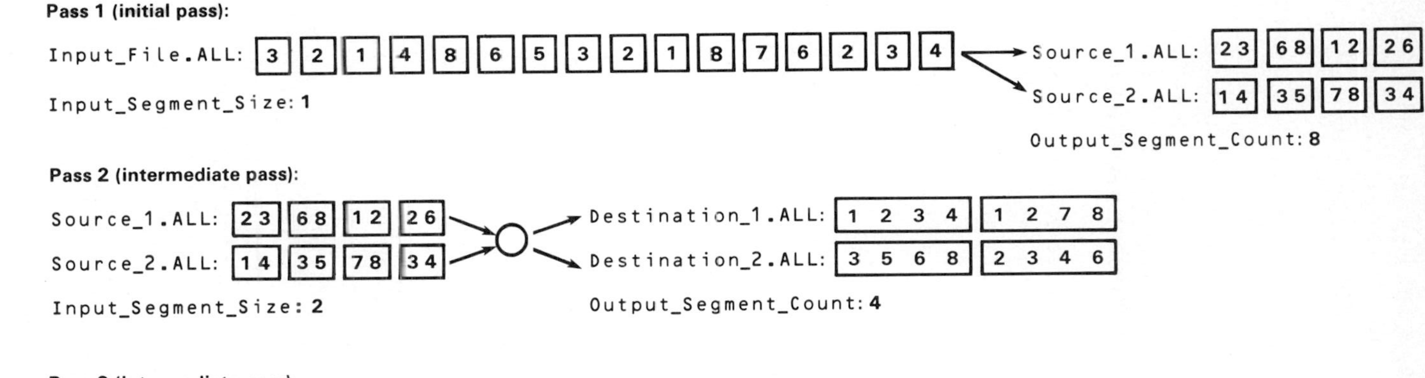

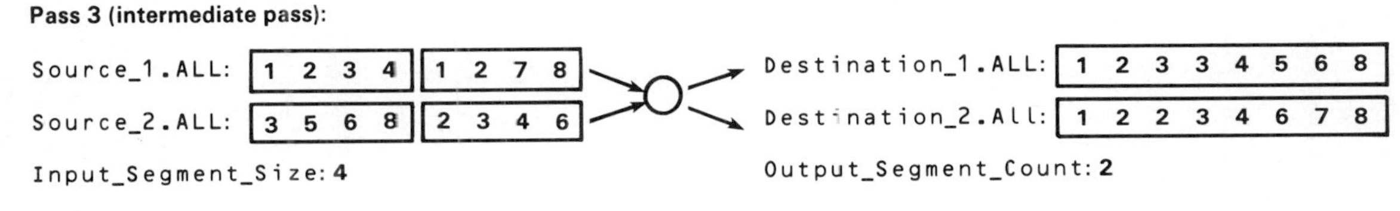

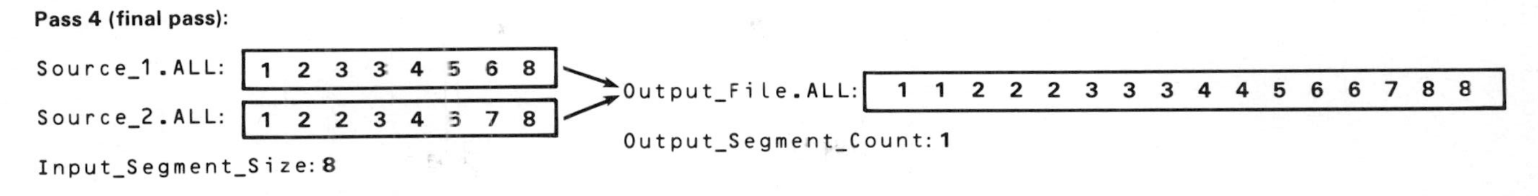

Figure 17.3 Illustrative execution of an instance of `Merge_Sort_Template`. Four passes are performed to sort a file of sixteen integers. The sorted segments at each stage are enclosed in boxes.

is to be created by writing a library scratch tape with nine tracks and 1,600 bits per inch. Because the calls on Create do not specify file names, unnamed temporary files are created. These files are used during the various passes of the merge sort and eventually discarded by calls on Delete.

The first call on Merge_Segments uses the same actual parameter, Input_File, in the first two parameter positions. Because the segment size is specified as one, Merge_Segments will alternately read one value from the file pointed to by its first parameter and one value from the file pointed to by its second parameter. Since these are the same file, the effect of the first pass is to split the contents of one completely unsorted file among two files each containing sorted segments of length two.

After the first pass is complete, the program prepares for the loop that performs all the intermediate passes. The segment size is set to two, the size of the segments that have just been written to Source_1.ALL and Source_2.ALL. The original input file, which is no longer needed at this point, is closed. Source_1.ALL and Source_2.ALL, which were opened with mode Out_File (the default mode for the version of Create provided by instances of Sequential_IO), are now reset to mode In_File. This will enable the next pass to begin *reading* from the beginning of these files. Finally, the two temporary files that will serve as the output files for the next pass are created.

The decision to close the original input file before opening these two temporary files is deliberate. It means that the program will never have more than four files open at once. This could be very important if the input file and the output file were also tape files and the system running the program had few tape drives. For the same reason, two of the temporary files will later be closed before the final output file is opened.

The WHILE loop repeatedly calls Merge_Segments, doubles Segment_Size to reflect the size of the newly created output segments, and exchanges the values in the source and destination file-pointer variables. At this point, Source_1 and Source_2 point to the files that were just written to and will be read from on the next pass; Destination_1 and Destination_2 point to the files that were just read from and may be written to on the next pass (unless the WHILE loop terminates first). Four calls on Reset reverse the modes of each file and allow the next pass to process each file from the beginning.

The WHILE loop terminates after a pass that writes only two sorted segments, one to each output file. The next pass will merge these two segments into one sorted segment on the first output file, leaving the second output file untouched. This one sorted segment will be the desired output, consisting of all the items in the original input arranged in order. Therefore, before the final call on Merge_Segments, we delete the two temporary files that would have been used as the destination files. Having freed two tape drives, we now open the external file designated to hold the final output; we pass a pointer to the corresponding internal file as the first output file pointer to Merge_Segments. Since this pass will not write anything to the second output file, we pass NULL as the second output file pointer. After the final pass is complete, we close all remaining open files.

17.4 STREAM-ORIENTED INPUT AND OUTPUT

The package `Text_IO` provides input and output facilities for files containing data in a form easily read or written by a human. Files of type `Text_IO.File_Type` consist of streams of characters to be interpreted as individual characters, numeric literals, or enumeration literals. The primary operations provided by `Text_IO` are the procedures `Get` and `Put`. There are many different versions of these two procedures, most of which will be described in Section 17.4.2. Generally speaking, `Get` reads a stream of characters from a file of mode `In_File`, interprets the characters as the representation of a value in some type, and places that value in an *out* parameter; `Put` takes a value given as an *in* parameter, builds a sequence of characters representing that value, and writes those characters to a file of mode `Out_File`. As we shall see in Section 17.4.4, there are also versions of `Get` and `Put` that work with `String` values instead of files.

All these operations can raise exceptions. The most obvious cause of exceptions is improperly formed input, but there are others as well. The exceptions that can be raised by `Text_IO`'s input and output operations are described in Section 17.4.5. Until then, we shall describe only how each subprogram behaves when it returns normally.

Any compilation unit directly using the facilities of `Text_IO` must have a `WITH` clause naming that package. Among the facilities provided by `Text_IO` are versions of the external file manipulation subprograms that were described in Section 17.3. Throughout Section 17.4, whenever we refer to the types `File_Type` and `File_Mode`, we shall mean `Text_IO.File_Type` and `Text_IO.File_Mode`.

17.4.1 Columns, Lines, and Pages

A stream-oriented file is viewed as a sequence of *pages* followed by a *file terminator*. Each page consists of a sequence of *lines* followed by a *page terminator*. Each line consists of a sequence of characters followed by a *line terminator*. This structure is depicted in Figure 17.4. Every page terminator is immediately preceded by a line terminator, and the file terminator is always immediately preceded by a page terminator. A programmer can make a page of a file correspond to a page of printed output or to a screen of terminal output, but nothing in the specification of `Text_IO` requires this. Logically, a page is just a group of consecutive lines in an input file or output file.

It is possible to set a *maximum line length* and a *maximum page length* for an output file. After the maximum number of characters have been written in a line, a line terminator is automatically written to the output file. After the maximum number of lines have been written in a page, a page terminator is automatically written to the output file. It is also possible to insert a line terminator or page terminator explicitly at any point in a line or page. A "maximum line length" of zero is used to indicate that the line length is unbounded. Then new lines are started only when explicitly requested. Similarly, a "maximum page length" of zero indicates that there is no limit on the number of lines in a page, and new pages are started only

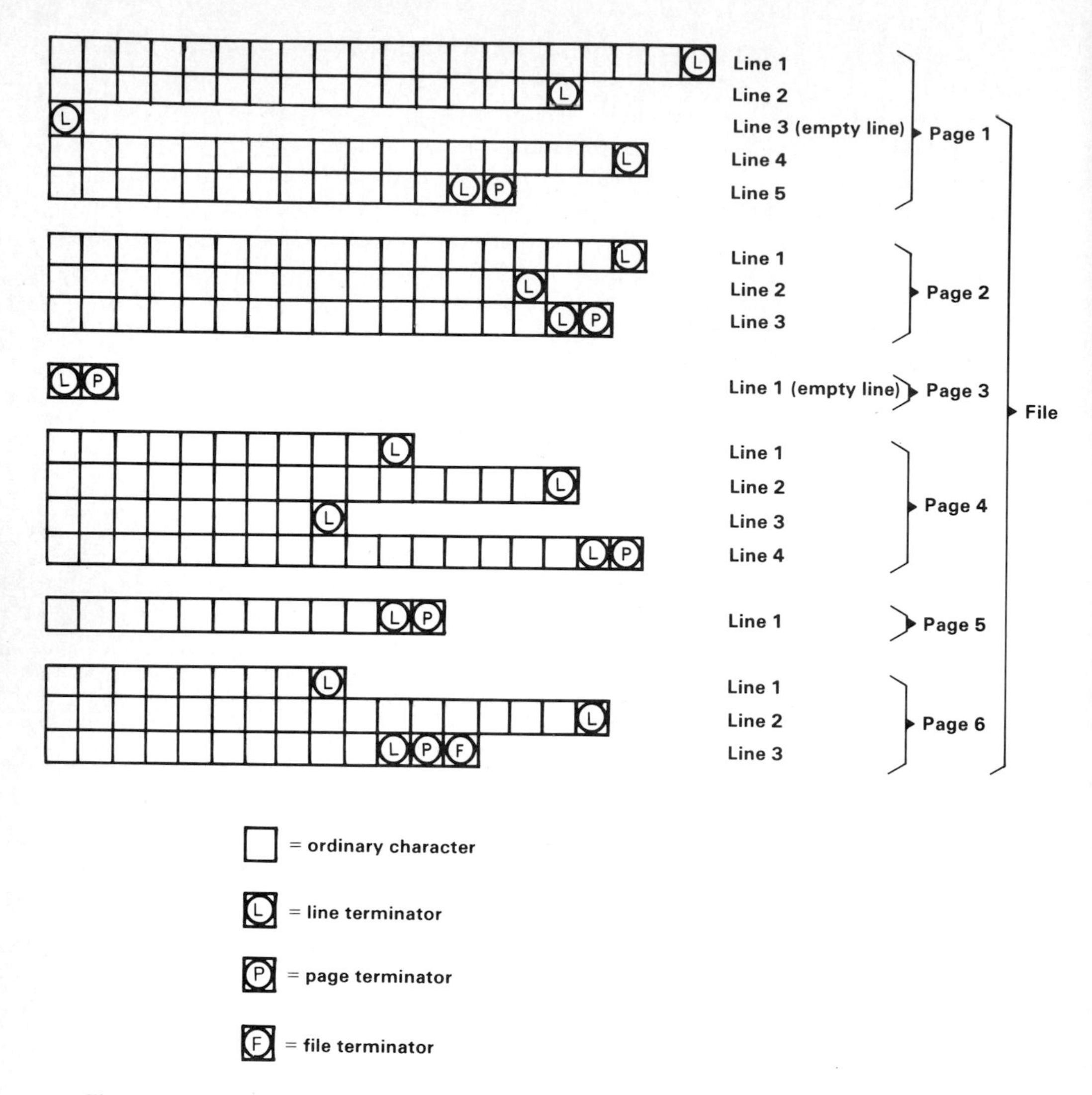

Figure 17.4 Division of a file into pages, lines, and characters. Each line consists of zero or more characters with a line terminator. Each page consists of one or more such lines and ends with a page terminator. A file consists of one or more such pages and ends with a file terminator. Terminators are not data, but they can be viewed as special markers occurring before and after data characters.

by explicit request. Terminators for the current line, the current page, and the file are automatically written as needed when a file is closed.

The characters within a line, the lines within a page, and the pages within a file are all numbered, starting with one. `Text_IO` provides an integer type named `Count`, with a range from zero to some implementation-defined maximum, whose values are character, line, and page numbers. The package also provides a subtype of Count named Positive_Count, extending from one to the last value of type Count. Any time that a stream-oriented file is open, the position at which the next input or output operation will take place can be uniquely described in terms of a *current page number*, a *current line number* within the page, and a *current column number* within the line. Text_IO provides functions that return the current page number, current line number, and current column number. They are named Page, Line, and Col, respectively, and are declared as follows:

```
FUNCTION Page (File : IN File_Type) RETURN Positive_Count;
FUNCTION Line (File : IN File_Type) RETURN Positive_Count;
FUNCTION Col (File : IN File_Type) RETURN Positive_Count;
```

17.4.1.1 Columns, lines, and pages in output files. The following procedures are used to control the line and page structure of an output file:

```
PROCEDURE Set_Line_Length
   (File : IN File_Type; To : IN Count);
PROCEDURE Set_Page_Length
   (File : IN File_Type; To : IN Count);
PROCEDURE New_Line
   (File : IN File_Type; Spacing : IN Positive_Count := 1);
PROCEDURE New_Page (File : IN File_Type);
PROCEDURE Set_Col
   (File : IN File_Type; To : IN Positive_Count);
PROCEDURE Set_Line
   (File : IN File_Type; To : IN Positive_Count);
```

Set_Line_Length and Set_Page_Length are used to set the maximum line and page lengths. When a stream-oriented input file is opened or reset, the current line and page lengths are automatically set to zero, meaning that the number of characters in a line and the number of lines in a page are unbounded. Text_IO provides a constant of type Count named Unbounded, whose value is zero. This allows you to write procedure calls such as

```
Set_Line_Length (File => f, To => Unbounded);
```

and

```
Set_Page_Length (File => f, To => Unbounded);
```

Text_IO also provides functions to report the current maximum line length and maximum page length:

```
FUNCTION Line_Length (File : IN File_Type) RETURN Count;
FUNCTION Page_Length (File : IN File_Type) RETURN Count;
```

`New_Line` inserts `Spacing` line terminators in the specified output file and also inserts a page terminator following any line terminator that fills a page with the maximum number of lines. When called with a `Spacing` parameter of one (or with the `Spacing` parameter omitted), this has the effect of advancing the position for the next output operation to column one of the next line. When called with a `Spacing` parameter of *n*, where *n* is greater than one, this has the effect of leaving *n*-1 blank lines and advancing the position for the next output operation to column one of the first line following these blank lines.

If a line terminator has just been written to the specified output file, `New_Page` inserts a page terminator in that file; otherwise, it inserts a line terminator followed by a page terminator. This has the effect of advancing the position for the next output operation to column one of line one of the next page. If `New_Page` is called at the very top of the page, this leaves one empty line in the page and starts a new page.

`Set_Col` advances the position for the next output operation in the specified output file to the specified column. If the current position is after the specified column, `Set_Col` first inserts a line terminator to advance to column one of the next line. (If this line terminator fills the current page with the maximum number of lines, it is followed by a page terminator.) Once on the appropriate line, positioned at or before the desired column, `Set_Col` advances to the desired column by writing zero or more spaces to the output file.

`Set_Line` is analogous to `Set_Col`. It advances the position for the next output operation in the specified output file to the specified line. If the current line number is after that specified by the parameter `To`, `Set_Line` first inserts a page terminator to advance to line one of the next page. Once on the appropriate page, `Set_Line` advances to the desired line by inserting as many line terminators as are necessary (possibly zero).

The following program copies the characters in the input file `IN.TXT` character for character to the output file `OUT.TXT`, in such a way that each page of the output file has 66 lines and all characters are placed in columns one through eighty of lines four through 63 of each page. The procedure call

```
Get (Input_File, Next_Character);
```

places the next character of the internal file `Input_File` into the `Character` variable `Next_Character`, ignoring any line or page terminators occurring between characters. The function call

```
End_Of_File (Input_File)
```

returns `True` if the last character in `Input_File` has been read; otherwise, it returns `False`. The procedure call

```
Put (Output_File, Next_Character);
```

sends the value in `Next_Character` to the internal file `Output_File`, generating a line terminator before the character if the maximum line length is exceeded.

```
WITH Text_IO; USE Text_IO;
PROCEDURE Reformat IS

   Input_File, Output_File : File_Type;
   Next_Character          : Character;

BEGIN

   Open (Input_File, In_File, "IN.TXT");
   Create (Output_File, Out_File, "OUT.TXT");

   IF NOT End_Of_File (Input_File) THEN

      Set_Line_Length (Input_File, 80);
      Set_Line (Output_File, 4);

      Page_Loop:
         LOOP
           Set_Line (Output_File, 4);
              -- Start new page and write empty lines for
              --   lines 1-3.

           Character_Loop:
              LOOP

                 Get (Input_File, Next_Character);

                 Put (Output_File, Next_Character);
                    -- Automatically advances to next line
                    --   if previous character was written
                    --   in column 80.

                 EXIT Page_Loop
                    WHEN End_Of_File (Input_File);

                 EXIT Character_Loop
                    WHEN Line (Output_File) = 64;

              END LOOP Character_Loop;

           New_Line (Output_File, 3);
              -- Write line terminators for empty lines
              --   64, 65, 66

         END LOOP Page_Loop;

      IF Line (Output_File) /= 67 THEN
         New_Line ( Output_File, 67 - Line (Output_File) );
      END IF;

   END IF;

   Close (Input_File);
   Close (Output_File);

END Reformat;
```

The outer IF statement handles an empty input file as a special case. The call on Set_Line_Length sets a maximum line length of eighty for Output_File. This causes a new line to be started automatically after every eightieth character is written.

The loop Page_Loop starts with a call on Set_Line. The first time through the loop, this call is executed while the current output line number is one. It causes three line terminators to be written, creating three empty lines. On subsequent iterations of Page_Loop, the call is executed while the current output line is 67. This causes a page terminator to be written (immediately after the line terminator for line 66), followed by three line terminators (for lines one through three of the new page).

The inner loop Character_Loop is executed once for each character. After the eightieth character is written on line 63, the output file will automatically advance to line 64. The last statement in Character_Loop exits the loop when this condition occurs. Then, at the bottom of Page_Loop, the call on New_Line writes three page terminators, creating empty lines numbered 64, 65, and 66 and advancing the current line number to 67. The check for the end of the input file is made before the check for a full page so that a new output page is not started when no input data remains. (The outer IF statement ensures that we are not at the end of the input file before the first call on Get.)

Finally, after exiting Page_Loop, we call New_Line to write as many line terminators as necessary to fill the last page with 66 lines. The IF statement surrounding the call is necessary because the subtype of the second parameter to New_Line is Positive_Count. Since Positive_Count'First is one, a call on New_Line with a second parameter of zero would raise Constraint_Error.

17.4.1.2 Columns, lines, and pages in input files. Just as there are procedures to control the line and page structure of an output file, so there are ways to traverse the line and page structure of an input file. There are procedures named Skip_Line and Skip_Page that perform functions for input files analogous to those performed by New_Line and New_Page for output files. The procedures Set_Col and Set_Line work for input files as well as for output files. Finally, there are functions to report whether the current position in the input file is at the end of a line, page, or file.

The declarations of Skip_Line and Skip_Page are as follows:

```
PROCEDURE Skip_Line
   (File : IN File_Type; Spacing : IN Positive_Count := 1);
PROCEDURE Skip_Page (File : IN File_Type);
```

These procedures are used to skip over data in the input stream. Skip_Line advances past Spacing line terminators. If the last of these line terminators is followed by a page terminator, Skip_Line also advances past that. Skip_Page advances past the next page terminator. The effect of the call Skip_Line (n) is to advance to the beginning of the nth following line, or, if the current input position was already in the nth line from the end of the file, to the file terminator. (The Spacing parameter can be omitted if the desired spacing is one. This advances the input position to the beginning of the next line, or from the last line in the file to the file terminator.) The effect of calling Skip_Page is to advance to the beginning of the next page in the input file or to the file terminator if the current input position was already in the last page of the file.

The declarations of Set_Col and Set_Line were given in the previous subsection. When called with an input file, Set_Col advances the current input position of the file until the current position is in the column specified by the parameter To. Sometimes this can be done simply by advancing to a point later in the same line. At other times, it is necessary to advance past one or more line terminators, until a line is found with a sufficient number of columns. The behavior of Set_Line when called with an input file is analogous. It advances to the beginning of the next line whose line number equals To. This may entail skipping past one or more pages until a page with a sufficient number of lines is found. Set_Col and Set_Line can only go forward in the file, never backward.

The following three functions return Boolean values indicating whether the current position in the specified input file is at the end of a line, a page, or a file:

```
FUNCTION End_Of_Line (File : IN File_Type) RETURN Boolean;
FUNCTION End_Of_Page (File : IN File_Type) RETURN Boolean;
FUNCTION End_Of_File (File : IN File_Type) RETURN Boolean;
```

End_Of_Line, End_Of_Page, and End_Of_File all return True just after the last character in a file has been read (so that the input file is positioned at the file terminator). End_Of_Page and End_Of_Line also return True just after the last character in a page has been read (so that the input file is positioned at a line terminator that is followed by a page terminator). Finally, End_Of_Line also returns True just after the last character in a line has been read (so that the input file is positioned at a line terminator). End_Of_Line normally returns False just after a call on Skip_Line, because Skip_Line advances just *past* a line terminator (and any page terminator that immediately follows it). End_Of_Page normally returns False just after a call on Skip_Page because Skip_Page advances just past a page terminator. (However, a call on Skip_Line that advances to an empty line leaves End_Of_Line returning True, and a call on Skip_Page that advances to an empty page leaves End_Of_Page returning True.) It is never possible for End_Of_Page to be true while End_Of_Line is false, because a page terminator is always preceded by a line terminator, and every operation that advances past the last line terminator of a page also advances past the page terminator.

The following program copies the file IN.TXT to the file OUT.TXT, preserving the line and page structure found in the input file:

```
WITH Text_IO; USE Text_IO;
   PROCEDURE Copy_File IS

      Input_File, Output_File : File_Type;
      Next_Character          : Character;

BEGIN

   Open (Input_File, In_File, "IN.TXT");
   Create (Output_File, Out_File, "OUT.TXT");

   WHILE NOT End_Of_File (Input_File) LOOP

      -- Copy next page:
      WHILE NOT End_Of_Page (Input_File) LOOP
         -- Copy next line:
         WHILE NOT End_Of_Line (Input_File) LOOP
            Get (Input_File, Next_Character);
            Put (Output_File, Next_Character);
         END LOOP;
         New_Line (Output_File); -- Default spacing of 1
      END LOOP;

      New_Page;

   END LOOP;

   Close (Input_File);
   Close (Output_File);

END Copy_File;
```

17.4.1.3 Control characters in stream-oriented files. Logically, line, page, and file terminators are not part of the stream of characters forming a file; they are special marks that logically occur between two characters in the stream. Nonetheless, an implementation may use sequences of control characters (ASCII codes 0 through 31 and 127) as terminators. (For example, an implementation might use `ASCII.LF`, `ASCII.CR`, `ASCII.CR & ASCII.LF`, or `ASCII.LF & ASCII.CR` for a line terminator, `ASCII.FF` for a page terminator, and `ASCII.NUL`, `ASCII.EOT`, or `ASCII.SUB` as a file terminator. (See Figure 11.1.) Some implementations may use a single control character to represent the combination of a line terminator followed immediately by a page terminator.) In such an implementation, a control character occurring as part of an input file may be interpreted as a terminator upon input; and a control character explicitly written to an output file may be indistinguishable from a terminator in the output file.

Hence you should be very careful searching for control characters in an input file or writing control characters to an output file. In some implementations, for example, writing `ASCII.FF` to the output file is equivalent to calling `New_Page`; for these implementations, the only way to detect the character `ASCII.FF` in an input file may be to check for `End_Of_Page` becoming true. Such considerations are irrelevant in the many programs that manipulate input and output streams consisting entirely of printable characters. If you are manipulating input and output streams containing control characters, however, it is important to consult your implementation's reference manual to determine exactly how control characters are treated.

17.4.2 Versions of Get and Put

`Text_IO` directly provides versions of `Get` and `Put` for reading and writing values of types `Character` and `String`. There are versions declared as follows:

```
PROCEDURE Get (File : IN File_Type; Item : OUT Character);
PROCEDURE Get (File : IN File_Type; Item : OUT String);

PROCEDURE Put (File : IN File_Type; Item : IN Character);
PROCEDURE Put (File : IN File_Type; Item : IN String);
```

(The first version of `Get` and the first version of `Put` were used in the `Reformat` and `Copy_File` programs of Section 17.4.1.)

The first version of `Get` takes the next character from the input stream and places it in the parameter `Item`. The second version takes the next `Item'Length` characters from the input stream and places them in successive components of the parameter `Item`. (For the second version, it is the length of the `String` variable used as an actual parameter that determines the number of characters read.) Both versions pass and ignore any line or page terminators encountered in the input stream. Thus, given the declaration

```
s : String (1 .. 8);
```

and an input file positioned just before the two lines

```
ABCD
EFGHI
```

the call `Get (s)` places the string `"ABCDEFGH"` in `s`. It is completely equivalent to the loop

```
FOR i IN s'Range LOOP
   Get ( s (i) );
END LOOP;
```

in which the actual parameter to `Get` is of type `Character`.

`Put`, when called with a parameter of type `Character`, first inserts a line terminator if the current line is full, then inserts a page terminator if this line terminator causes the current page to become full, then places the value of the parameter in the output stream. A call on `Put` with a parameter `Item` of type `String` is equivalent to the following loop:

```
FOR i IN Item'Range LOOP
   Put ( Item (i) );
END LOOP;
```

The contents of the string may be split across lines if the current line becomes full or across pages if the current page becomes full.

These versions of `Get` and `Put` treat a file not as a stream of character literals or string literals, but simply as a stream of characters. An apostrophe or quotation mark encountered by `Get` is treated just as any other character in the input stream is treated. Similarly, `Put` copies characters directly from `Item` to the output stream, but does not surround the characters with apostrophes or quotation marks.

`Text_IO` also provides two procedures named `Get_Line` and `Put_Line` that are convenient for performing line-oriented input and output of strings. They are declared as follows:

```
PROCEDURE Get_Line
   (File : IN File_Type;
    Item : OUT String;
    Last : OUT Natural);
PROCEDURE Put_Line (File : IN File_Type; Item : IN String);
```

`Get_Line` reads characters from the specified input file into successive components of `Item` until either `Item` is full or the end of the line is reached (or both). If the end of the line is reached, `Get_Line` then advances past the line terminator, to the beginning of the next line (or to the file terminator). The line terminator itself does not appear in `Item`. `Last` is set to the index of the last component of `Item` into which a character is read, or to `Item'First - 1` if no characters are read. When `Item'First = 1`, as is usually the case, this means that `Last` is set to the number of characters read. In any event, the slice `Item (Item'First .. Last)` always ends up containing precisely the characters that were read in.

A call on `Put_Line` simply writes the characters in `Item` to the specified output file, followed by a line terminator. If this line terminator causes the current page to become filled, the line terminator is followed by a page terminator. A call on `Put_Line` is equivalent to a call on `Put` followed by a call on `New_Line` with a spacing of one.

The following program reads text from the input file `WORD.TXT`, recognizing each period as the end of a sentence, and copies the text to the output file `SENTENCE.TXT`, one sentence per line:

```
WITH Text_IO; USE Text_IO;
PROCEDURE Put_Sentences IS
   Input_File, Output_File : File_Type;
   c                       : Character;
```

```
BEGIN

   Open (Input_File, In_File, "WORD.TXT");
   Create (Output_File, Out_File, "SENTENCE.TXT");

   WHILE NOT End_Of_File (Input_File) LOOP
      Get (Input_File, c);
      IF c = '.' THEN
         Put_Line (Output_File, ".");
      ELSE
         Put (Output_File, c);
      END IF;
   END LOOP;

   Close (Input_File);
   Close (Output_File);

END Put_Sentences;
```

(The second parameter to `Put_Line` is of type `String`, while the second parameter to `Put` is of type `Character`.)

`Text_IO` also provides four generic packages for input and output of values in scalar types. The generic package `Text_IO.Integer_IO` can be instantiated with any integer subtype; the generic package `Text_IO.Float_IO` can be instantiated with any floating-point subtype; the generic package `Text_IO.Fixed_IO` can be instantiated with any fixed-point subtype; and the package `Enumeration_IO` can be instantiated with any *discrete* subtype. (`Text_IO.Enumeration_IO` is intended to be used only with enumeration types. There is no way to declare a generic formal type for which an enumeration subtype is allowed as a generic actual parameter but an integer subtype is not.) The names `Integer_IO` and `Float_IO` refer to the *class* of integer types and the *class* of floating-point types, not to the individual predefined types `Integer` and `Float`.

Among the facilities provided by instances of these four generic packages are versions of `Get`. Each version has an `OUT` parameter named `Item` belonging to the type named in the generic instantiation. A call on `Get` first advances past spaces, tab characters (`ASCII.HT`), and terminators. It then interprets the next characters in the input stream as forming a numeric literal, a plus or minus sign followed by a numeric literal, or an enumeration literal, and places the corresponding value in `Item`. In the case of `Integer_IO`, `Float_IO`, and `Fixed_IO`, `Get` has a parameter named `Width` that can be used to specify the number of characters that will be read unless a line terminator is encountered first. A value of zero for this parameter specifies that `Get` is to read as many characters as can be interpreted as part of a numeric literal; but that the first character or terminator that cannot be so interpreted should remain unread.

Instances of the four generic packages also provide versions of `Put`. Each version has an `IN` parameter `Item` belonging to the type named in the generic instantiation. A call on `Put` writes a sequence of characters representing the value of `Item` as a numeric literal, a minus sign followed by a numeric literal, or an enumeration literal.

There are additional parameters to Put that can be used to specify the width of the field to be output. Spaces are inserted before a numeric value or after an enumeration literal if the value itself does not fill the field. If the field is too small to contain the characters representing the value, the parameters specifying the width of the field are ignored and Put uses as many characters as it needs to represent the value. Specifying a field width of zero guarantees that Put will output precisely as many characters as are necessary to represent the value. Before writing a literal to the output stream, these versions of Put check whether the current line still has enough room for all the characters in the literal. If not, a new line (and possibly a new page) is started before *any* characters are sent. Literals are never split across lines.

Numeric literals in the input stream may be preceded by a plus sign, a minus sign, or no sign at all. They may contain leading zeroes, underscores, and exponents. Similarly, an exponent may include a plus sign, a minus sign (in the case of a real literal), or no sign at all, and it may contain leading zeroes. The *E* preceding the exponent may be upper case or lower case. Literals may be ordinary decimal literals or numeric literals written in some other base, as described in Section 8.3.2. Thus the following combinations are all valid input for versions of Get provided by instances of Integer_IO:

```
1000      +1000      -1000      1_000      +1_000      -1_000
01000     10E2       +10e2      10E+2      10E02       010E+02
16#2E8#  +16#2e8#  -16#2E8#  16#02_E8#  8#175#E+01  16#2E8#e0
```

The following combinations are all valid input for versions of Get provided by Float_IO and Fixed_IO:

```
1000.0       +1000.0           -1000.0       1_000.0       -1_000.0
001_000.0    10.0E2            +10.0E+2      10_000.0e-1   -10.0E02
16#2e8.0#    16#2E_80.0#E-1    -16#2e8.0#    8#17.5#e+02   16#2e8#E0
```

Output is not so flexible. Versions of Put for numeric types never write plus signs before literals (although a plus sign can always be written as a character rather than as part of a number). Leading zeroes and underscores are never written. Versions of Put provided by instances of Integer_IO have a parameter specifying the base in which a number is to be written, but the versions provided by instances of Float_IO and Fixed_IO always write decimal literals. Versions provided by instances of Float_IO and Fixed_IO have a parameter controlling whether a literal is written with or without an exponent, but versions provided by instances of Integer_IO never write exponents. Letters appearing in the output—either the extended digits *A* through *F* or the *E* before an exponent—are always written in upper case. Every exponent is preceded either by a plus sign or a minus sign. When an exponent appears, the most significant digit is written to the left of the decimal point and all other digits are written to the right of the decimal point.

A program using one of the four generic packages always starts with a WITH clause for Text_IO (since that is the library unit providing the four generic packages). Typically, this is followed by a USE clause for Text_IO. The program itself must contain an instantiation of any generic package to be used. Typically, the instantiation is followed by a USE clause for the instance:

```
WITH Text_IO; USE Text_IO;
PROCEDURE [program name] IS
    ...
    PACKAGE [instance name] IS
        NEW [generic package name] ( [typemark] );
    USE [instance name];
    ...
BEGIN
    ...
END [program name];
```

The USE clauses allow both the versions of Get and Put provided directly by Text_IO (for type Character and type String) and the versions provided by the instance of the generic package to be identified by the simple names Get and Put. The rules for resolving overloading determine which versions are called.

A program can use more than one of the generic packages, and intersperse calls on different versions of Put and Get. The following program reads a file REALS.DAT, containing some integer literal *n* in the range 1 .. 1000 followed by *n* real literals in the range 0.0 .. 1000.0. Each real literal is rounded to the nearest whole number, and the corresponding integer literal is written on a separate line of the output file WHOLES.DAT. A closing message is written at the end of the file.

```
WITH Text_IO; USE Text_IO;
PROCEDURE Round IS
   TYPE Real_Type IS DELTA 1.0 RANGE 0.0 .. 1000.0;
   TYPE Whole_Type IS RANGE 0 .. 1000;
   PACKAGE Real_Type_IO IS NEW Fixed IO (Real_Type);
   PACKAGE Whole_Type_IO IS NEW Integer_IO (Whole_Type);
   USE Real_Type_IO, Whole_Type_IO;
   Input_File, Output_File : File_Type;
   Number Of_Literals      : Whole_Type;
   Next_Literal            : Real_Type;
BEGIN
   Open (Input_File, In_File, "REALS.DAT");
   Create (Output_File, Out_File, "WHOLES.DAT");
   Get (Input_File, Number_Of_Literals);
   FOR i IN 1 .. Number_Of_Literals LOOP
      Get (Input_File, Next_Literal);
      Put (Output_File, Whole_Type (Next_Literal) );
      New_Line (Output_File);
   END LOOP;
```

```
      Put (Output_File, "-- end of output --");
      Close (Input_File);
      Close (Output_File);
   END Round;
```

There are additional types and subtypes declared within the specification of Text_IO and used in the generic package declarations of Integer_IO, Float_IO, Fixed_IO, and Enumeration_IO. There is a subtype of Integer named Field, whose values are used to specify widths of fields. The subtype includes values ranging from zero to some value defined by the implementation. The subtype Number_Base, declared

```
   SUBTYPE Number_Base IS Integer RANGE 2 .. 16;
```

is used to specify the base for output of an integer literal. The enumeration type Type_Set, declared

```
   TYPE Type_Set IS (Lower_Case, Upper_Case);
```

is used to specify whether lower-case or upper-case letters should be used in the output of an enumeration literal.

17.4.2.1 Get and Put for integer types. The generic package declaration for Integer_IO has the following form:

```
   GENERIC
      TYPE Num IS RANGE <>;
   PACKAGE Integer_IO IS
      Default_Width : Field := Num'Width;
      Default_Base  : Number_Base := 10;
      PROCEDURE Get
         (File  : IN File_Type;
          Item  : OUT Num;
          Width : IN Field := 0);
      PROCEDURE Put
         (File  : IN File_Type;
          Item  : IN Num;
          Width : IN Field := Default_Width;
          Base  : IN Number_Base := Default_Base);
      -- ... [other versions of Get and Put]
   END Integer_IO;
```

We shall cover the other versions of Get and Put in sections 17.4.3 and 17.4.4.

When the Width parameter of Get is zero, Get reads past any spaces, tabs, and terminators at the front of the input stream, and then reads as many characters as can be interpreted as part of an integer literal (optionally preceded by a plus or minus sign). The next character in the input stream that cannot be interpreted as part of the literal, or the line terminator if the literal occurs at the end of a line, is left in the input stream to be found by the next input operation. A call on `Get` with a `Width` parameter of zero is appropriate when the input stream is a sequence of integer literals optionally preceded by plus or minus signs and separated by one or more spaces or tabs. Even if the exact position of each literal within the input stream is unknown, a call on `Get` with a `Width` of zero advances to the next number and reads it. Since the `Width` parameter has a default value of zero, `Get` acts this way when the `Width` parameter is not specified in a call. For example, the following function sums the values in the file named by its parameter `File_Name` and returns the sum:

```
WITH Text_IO; USE Text_IO;
FUNCTION File_Sum (File_Name : String) RETURN Integer IS
   PACKAGE Type_Integer_IO IS NEW Integer_IO (Integer);
   USE Type_Integer_IO;
   Input_File : File_Type;
   Next_Item  : Integer;
   Sum        : Integer := 0;
BEGIN
   Open (Input_File, In_File, File_Name);
   WHILE NOT End_Of_File (Input_File) LOOP
      Get (Input_File, Next_Item); -- Width defaults to 0.
      Sum := Sum + Next_Item;
   END LOOP;
   Close (Input_File);
   RETURN Sum;
END File_Sum;
```

This function would work with a file containing the following text, for example, assuming that the 9 is the last character in the last line of the file:

```
   12    34    -523                   67      22
 -1083          28374     27   -73   645                    9
```

If there are spaces, tabs, or empty lines following the 9, however, the program will not work correctly. After the 9 is read, the call on `End_Of_File` at the top of the loop will return `False`. The program will call `Get` one more time, attempting to read another number. This call will advance past the file terminator without finding a number and raise an exception. (One of the exercises at the end of the chapter is to solve this problem.)

When `Get` is called with a nonzero value *w* for `Width` and at least *w* characters remain in the current line, exactly *w* characters are read. Otherwise, all the remaining characters on the line are read, but **Get** does not advance past the line terminator. The characters read should include at least one digit. The characters may include spaces and tabs before the number (with each counting as one of the *w* characters), but not after the number. (Unlike FORTRAN and PL/I input operations, **Get** does not treat a field containing only spaces as if it contained a zero.) A nonzero value for **Width** is useful when a number is known to occupy certain columns in the input file, particularly if the last character of one number might be followed immediately by the first character of another number. For example, suppose each line of an input file **POPUVOTE.DAT** has data formatted as follows:

Columns 1-2	: State abbreviation
Columns 3-5	: Electoral votes allocated to state
Column 6	: Blank
Columns 7-14	: Popular votes cast for Democratic candidate
Columns 15-22	: Popular votes cast for Republican candidate

The following package provides a function that reads this file to determine the winner of a presidential election. (Whichever candidate receives more popular votes in a state wins all of that state's electoral votes, and whoever wins a majority of the electoral votes wins the election. Assume there are only two candidates and that neither wins a state's electoral votes in case of a tie in that state's popular vote.)

```
PACKAGE Election_Package IS

   TYPE Party_Type IS (Democratic, Republican);
   FUNCTION Winner RETURN Party_Type;

   No_Winner : EXCEPTION;
      -- Raised by Winner when neither candidate has won a
      --   majority of the electoral votes.

END Election_Package;


WITH Text_IO; USE Text_IO;

PACKAGE BODY Election_Package IS

   FUNCTION Winner RETURN Party_Type IS

      TYPE Popular_Vote_Type IS RANGE 0 .. 20_000_000;

      PACKAGE Popular_Vote_IO IS
         NEW Integer_IO (Popular_Vote_Type);

      PACKAGE Type_Integer_IO IS NEW Integer_IO (Integer);

      USE Popular_Vote_IO, Type_Integer_IO;

      Election_File : File_Type;

      Democratic_Electoral_Vote,
         Republican_Electoral_Vote,
         Total_Electoral_Vote          : Natural := 0;

      State_Electoral_Vote, Majority : Natural;

      Democratic_Popular_Vote,
         Republican_Popular_Vote      : Popular_Vote_Type;
```

```
      BEGIN
         Open (Election_File, In_File, "POPUVOTE.DAT");
         WHILE NOT End_Of_File (Election_File) LOOP
            Set_Col (Election_File, 3);
            Get (Election_File, State_Electoral_Vote);
            Set_Col (Election_File, 7);
            Get (Election_File, Democratic_Popular_Vote, 8);
            Get (Election_File, Republican_Popular_Vote, 8);
            IF Democratic_Popular_Vote >
                  Republican_Popular_Vote THEN
               Democratic_Electoral_Vote :=
                  Democratic_Electoral_Vote +
                  State_Electoral_Vote;
            ELSIF Republican_Popular_Vote >
                     Democratic_Popular_Vote THEN
               Republican_Electoral_Vote :=
                  Republican_Electoral_Vote +
                  State_Electoral_Vote;
            END IF;
            -- In case of a popular vote tie, the
            --  electoral votes go to neither candidate,
            --  but still figure in the computation of the
            --  electoral vote majority.
            Total_Electoral_Vote :=
               Total_Electoral_Vote + State_Electoral_Vote;
            Skip_Line (Election_File);
               -- Default of 1 means advance to start of
               --  next line, or to the file terminator.
            END LOOP;
         Close (Election_File);
         Majority := Total_Electoral_Vote / 2 + 1;
         IF Democratic_Electoral_Vote >= Majority THEN
            RETURN Democratic;
         ELSIF Republican_Electoral_Vote >= Majority THEN
            RETURN Republican;
         ELSE
            RAISE No_Winner;
         END IF;
      END Winner;
   END Election_Package;
```

A separate integer type is used for popular votes because a state's popular vote count could easily exceed a compiler's range for type Integer. We use type Integer for counting electoral votes because it is reasonable to assume that a compiler's type Integer will include the number 538, which is the highest electoral vote count possible. We instantiate Integer_IO once for Popular_Vote_Type and once for type Integer.

The first call on Set_Col advances to column three. Since the number in columns three through five is followed by a blank in column six, it is not necessary to specify a width for the call on Get that reads State_Electoral_Votes. The second call on Set_Col advances to column seven. Since columns seven through 22 may all contain digits, a call on Get without a Width parameter at this point could interpret all sixteen columns as forming one number. The Width parameter to Get ensures that only eight columns are read, beginning with the current column. The third call on Get reads through column 22, but does not advance past the terminator of the current line. The call on Skip_Line advances past the line terminator and any page terminator that immediately follows it. This brings us to the beginning of the next line, if there is a next line, or to the file terminator, if the line just processed was the last one. Thus, at the top of the loop, End_Of_File is guaranteed to return True if all input lines have been processed.

The Width parameter of Put specifies the *minimum* number of spaces that will be taken up by the output. If the value to be written will not fit in the specified number of columns, Put uses as many columns as are needed; otherwise, leading spaces are written if necessary so that the value appears at the right end of a field of the specified width. Thus a value of zero for Width causes the value to be written using exactly the number of columns needed to hold the value. A value of Width large enough for any value that will be printed is useful in causing numbers to appear in columns with their rightmost digits aligned.

The Base parameter of Put allows a value in an integer type to be written as a nondecimal literal, like 8#173# or 16#7B#. A value of ten for Base causes the value to be written in conventional nonbased form, such as 123 rather than 10#123#. The following program prints the number sixteen in every base from two to sixteen:

```
WITH Text_IO; USE Text_IO;
PROCEDURE Print_16 IS
   PACKAGE Type_Integer_IO IS NEW Integer_IO (Integer);
   USE Type_Integer_IO;
   Output_File : File_Type;
BEGIN
   Create (Output_File, Name => "SIXTEEN.DAT");
   FOR b IN 2 .. 16 LOOP
      Put (Output_File, Item => 16, Base => b);
      New_Line (Output_File);
   END LOOP;
   Close (Output_File);
END Print_16;
```

This program places the following text in the file SIXTEEN.DAT:

```
2#10000#
   3#121#
   4#100#
    5#31#
    6#24#
    7#22#
    8#20#
    9#17#
       16
   11#15#
   12#14#
   13#13#
   14#12#
   15#11#
   16#10#
```

The column in which the rightmost character of each number appears is the default value of the `Width` parameter.

Each instance of `Integer_IO` provides two variables named `Default_Width` and `Default_Base`. Since these variables are declared in the generic package declaration, they may be named and updated from outside the package. These variables are used as the default values for parameters `Width` and `Base` of `Put`. The default expression for a subprogram parameter is reevaluated each time a default value is needed. Therefore, changing the value of one of these variables during the execution of a program changes the default parameter values that will be used on subsequent calls on `Put`.

For example, the program `Print_16` just given can be rewritten as follows:

```
WITH Text_IO; USE Text_IO;
PROCEDURE Print_16 IS
   PACKAGE Type_Integer_IO IS NEW Integer_IO (Integer);
   USE Type_Integer_IO;
   Output_File : File_Type;
BEGIN
   Create (Output_File, Name => "SIXTEEN.DAT");
   FOR b IN 2 .. 16 LOOP
      Default_Base := b;
      Put (Output_File, 16);
      New_Line (Output_File);
   END LOOP;
   Close (Output_File);
END Print_16;
```

The line

```
Put (Output_File, 16, Base => b);
```

has been replaced by the two lines

```
Default_Base := b;
Put (Output_File, 16);
```

The call on Put no longer specifies the value of Base, so the default value—the current value of Default_Base—is used each time Put is called. However, the value of Default_Base is updated just before each call on Put, so the ultimate effect is the same. (The original formulation is stylistically preferable because the specification of the base to be used by Put is straightforward and explicit.)

The initial value of Default_Base is ten. Thus, if the Base parameter is never specified in calls on Put and the value of Default_Base is never changed, all integer literals will be written as decimal literals. This is the desired behavior of Put in the vast majority of programs.

The initial value of Default_Width is Num'Width. The 'Width attribute is defined for any integer or enumeration subtype. Its value is the width of the largest field required to hold character representations of values in the subtype. The character representation of an integer is assumed to start with either a space (for positive numbers or zero) or a minus sign (for negative numbers), followed by a decimal integer literal written without an exponent, underscores, or leading zeroes. (This is the sequence of characters returned by the 'Image attribute.) Thus, given the declarations

```
SUBTYPE Subtype_1 IS Integer RANGE 0 .. 9;
SUBTYPE Subtype_2 IS Integer RANGE -9 .. 9;
SUBTYPE Subtype_3 IS Integer RANGE 0 .. 10;
SUBTYPE Subtype_4 IS Integer RANGE -10 .. 100;
```

Subtype_1'Width and Subtype_2'Width both equal two, Subtype_3'Width equals three, and Subtype_4'Width equals four.

The initial value of Default_Width, then, gives the Width parameter of Put a default width large enough to accommodate any value in the integer type with which Integer_IO has been instantiated. This is appropriate for producing columns of aligned numbers. However, a default of zero is more appropriate if numbers are to be embedded in lines of text without any extraneous spaces. If this kind of output is desired throughout a program, the program should set Default_Width to zero before any calls on Put. Then the default behavior of Put if no width is specified will be to write precisely the number of characters required to represent the value being written. For example, the sequence of statements

```
Default_Width := 0;
Put (Output_File, "The disk contains ");
Put (Output_File, Byte_Count);
Put (Output_File, " bytes of data in ");
Put (Output_File, File_Count);
Put_Line (Output_File, " files.");
```

can be used to produce output of the following form:

```
The disk contains 32485 bytes of data in 14 files.
```

Without the initial assignment of zero to `Default_Width`, the line would have appeared something like this:

```
The disk contains          32485 bytes of data in          14 files.
```

The program below reads in a file of lines containing test scores between zero and 100 in columns 28 through thirty and prints out a report on the number of times each test score was found. Different integer types are used for test scores and counts, so `Integer_IO` must be instantiated twice. The test scores and the numbers of occurrences are listed in two columns. The input comes from a file named `SCORES.DAT`, and the report goes to a file named `DISTRIB.DAT`. After reading the input file and before writing the output file, the program computes the maximum number of times any one test score appeared and adjusts the default width for writing numbers of occurrences to the width required for this maximum value. This causes the two columns to appear as close together as possible.

```
WITH Text_IO; USE Text_IO;
PROCEDURE Print_Score_Distribution IS
   TYPE Score_Type IS RANGE 0 .. 100;
   Distribution:
      ARRAY (Score_Type) OF Natural :=
         (Score_Type => 0);
   Score                     : Score_Type;
   Maximum                   : Natural;
   Input_File, Output_File : File_Type;
   PACKAGE Score_Type_IO IS NEW Integer_IO (Score_Type);
   PACKAGE Natural_IO IS NEW Integer_IO (Natural);
   USE Score_Type_IO, Natural_IO;
BEGIN
   Open (Input_File, In_File, "SCORES.DAT");
   WHILE NOT End_Of_File (Input_File) LOOP
      Set_Col (Input_File, 28);
      Get (Input_File, Score);
      Distribution (Score) := Distribution (Score) + 1;
   END LOOP;
   Close (Input_File);
   Maximum := 0;
   FOR s IN Score_Type LOOP
      IF Distribution (s) > Maximum THEN
         Maximum := Distribution (s);
      END IF;
   END LOOP;
```

```
      Natural_IO.Default_Width :=
         Natural'Image(Maximum) ' Length - 1;
      -------------------------------------------------------
      -- Natural'Image(Maximum) is the string consisting
      --    of a blank followed by the digits of Maximum.
      --    Taking the 'Length attribute of this string
      --    and subtracting 1 (for the blank) gives the
      --    number of columns required to hold the
      --    largest component of Distribution.
      -------------------------------------------------------

   Create (Output_File, Out_File, "DISTRIB.DAT");
   FOR s IN Score_Type LOOP
      Put (Output_File, s); -- Score_Type_IO.Put
      Put (Output_File, ' '); -- Text_IO.Put
      Put (Output_File, Distribution (s)); --Natural_IO.Put
      New_Line (Output_File);
   END LOOP;
   Close (Output_File);
END Print_Score_Distribution;
```

`Score_Type_IO` and `Natural_IO` provide their own versions of `Get` and `Put` and their own variables named `Default_Width` and `Default_Base`. An instance's own `Default_Width` and `Default_Base` affect only the versions of `Put` provided by that instance. Thus the assignment to `Natural_IO.Default_Width` does not affect the width of the output from the first call on `Put`, only the third call. (Since only subprograms and enumeration literals can be overloaded, the `USE` clause for `Score_Type_IO` and `Natural_IO` does not apply to the variables `Default_Width` and `Default_Base`. `Natural_IO.Default_Width` can only be referred to by its expanded name.)

17.4.2.2 `Get` and `Put` for floating-point types. Just as instances of `Integer_IO` provide versions of `Get` and `Put` for integer types, so instances of `Float_IO` provide versions of `Get` and `Put` for floating-point types. The generic declaration of `Float_IO` is:

```
GENERIC
   TYPE Num IS DIGITS <>;
PACKAGE Float_IO IS
   Default_Fore : Field := 2;
   Default_Aft  : Field := Num'Digits - 1;
   Default_Exp  : Field := 3;
   PROCEDURE Get
      (File  : IN File_Type;
       Item  : OUT Num;
       Width : IN Field := 0);
```

```
    PROCEDURE Put
        (File : IN File_Type;
         Item : IN Num;
         Fore : IN Field := Default_Fore;
         Aft  : IN Field := Default_Aft;
         Exp  : IN Field := Default_Exp);

    -- ... [other versions of Get and Put]

END Float_IO;
```

(Sections 17.4.3 and 17.4.4 describe the other versions of `Get` and `Put`.)

Versions of `Get` provided by instances of `Float_IO` work in the same way as versions provided by instances of `Integer_IO`. When the value of the `Width` parameter is zero, `Get` advances past any spaces, tabs, and terminators at the front of the input stream and then reads as many characters as can be interpreted as part of a real literal optionally preceded by a plus or minus sign. When `Width` has some value *w* greater than zero and at least *w* characters remain in the current line, exactly *w* characters are read, possibly including leading spaces and tabs. If fewer than *w* characters remain in the current line, only the characters remaining in the line are read. In each case, the characters read should consist of zero or more blanks, tabs, and terminators, possibly a plus or minus sign, and a valid real literal. The default value for `Width` is zero.

Versions of `Put` supplied by instances of `Float_IO` differ from those provided by instances of `Integer_IO` in two ways. First, there is no `Base` parameter. Real literals are always written in ordinary decimal notation. Second, the number of characters written is controlled not by a single parameter `Width`, but by three parameters named `Fore`, `Aft`, and `Exp`. `Fore` affects the number of characters written before the decimal point. `Aft` determines the number of characters written after the decimal point but before any exponent part. `Exp` determines whether an exponent part will appear and affects its length.

When `Exp` is zero, no exponent part is written. The output consists of possible leading spaces, a possible minus sign, one or more digits, a decimal point, and one or more digits. `Fore` gives the *minimum* number of characters that will be written before the decimal point, possibly including leading spaces and a minus sign. If the number being written requires more than `Fore` characters before the decimal point, the value of `Fore` is ignored, and `Put` writes as many characters before the decimal point as are required. Thus a value of zero for `Fore` always results in exactly the required number of characters appearing before the decimal point. A value for `Aft` greater than zero gives the exact number of digits that appear after the decimal point. This does not depend on the magnitude of the number being written. (A value of zero for `Aft` causes one digit to appear after the decimal point, since the syntax of real literals requires at least one digit to appear there.) The number is *rounded* to `Aft` places after the decimal point, not truncated. Thus

```
Put (Output_File, 6.66, Fore => 1, Aft => 1, Exp => 0);
```

writes 6.7 to Output_File, not 6.6. If the number to be written were 6.65, rounding could occur in either direction, depending on the implementation.

Here are some examples of Put called with a value of zero for Exp. The symbol "*b*" is used to represent a blank written by the call on Put.

```
Put (Output_File, 12.3456, Fore => 4, Aft => 3 , Exp => 0);
   -- Writes  bb12.346
Put (Output_File, -12.3456, Fore => 4, Aft => 3, Exp => 0);
   -- Writes b-12.346
Put (Output_File, 12.3456, Fore => 4, Aft => 1, Exp => 0);
   -- Writes bb12.3
Put (Output_File, 12.3456, Fore => 2, Aft => 3, Exp => 0);
   -- Writes 12.346
Put (Output_File, -12.3456, Fore => 2, Aft => 3, Exp => 0);
   -- Writes -12.346
Put (Output_File, -12.3456, Fore => 2, Aft => 1, Exp => 0);
   -- Writes -12.3
Put (Output_File, 12.3456, Fore => 0, Aft => 3, Exp => 0);
   -- Writes 12.346
Put (Output_File, -12.3456, Fore => 0, Aft => 3, Exp => 0);
   -- Writes -12.346
```

Columns with decimal points aligned can be created by specifying a value for Fore large enough to accommodate any value that will appear. A value of zero for Fore is appropriate when a real literal is to appear in a line of printed text without any extraneous spaces.

When the value of Exp is greater than zero, a floating-point value is written in conventional scientific notation. The value of the exponent is adjusted so that one significant digit appears before the decimal point. This one digit may be preceded by a minus sign. The value of Fore again specifies the minimum number of characters, possibly including leading spaces and possibly including a minus sign, that will be written before the decimal point. However, this only affects the number of spaces that will appear to the left of the possible minus sign, the single digit, and the decimal point. Aft is interpreted as before to specify the number of digits that appear after the decimal point but before the letter *E* of the exponent. Exp gives the minimum number of characters that will appear in the exponent after the letter *E*. This does not include the *E* itself, but it does include either a plus or minus sign and the digits of the exponent. These digits include as many leading zeroes as are necessary to fill out the specified number of characters. If the exponent cannot fit in the specified number of characters, Put ignores the value of Exp and uses as many characters as it requires. The value 0.0 is always written with a single zero before the decimal point (possibly preceded by spaces) and an exponent of zero.

Here are some examples:

```
Put (Output_File, 12.3456, Fore => 3, Aft => 4, Exp => 2);
   -- Writes bb1.2346E+1
```

```
Put (Output_File, 12.3456, Fore => 3, Aft => 4, Exp => 2);
   -- Writes bb1.2346E+1
Put (Output_File, 0.123456, Fore => 3, Aft => 4, Exp => 2);
   -- Writes bb1.2346E-1
Put (Output_File, 12.3456, Fore => 3, Aft => 4, Exp => 4);
   -- Writes bb1.2346E+001
Put (Output_File, -12.3456, Fore => 3, Aft => 4, Exp => 3);
   -- Writes b-1.2346E+01
Put (Output_File, 12.3456, Fore => 2, Aft => 1, Exp => 3);
   -- Writes b1.2E+01
Put (Output_File, 12.3456, Fore => 1, Aft => 4, Exp => 1);
   -- Writes 1.2346E+1
Put (Output_File, 12.3456E99, Fore => 1, Aft => 4, Exp => 1);
   -- Writes 1.2346E+100
Put (Output_File, 12.3456E99, Fore => 2, Aft => 4, Exp => 1);
   -- Writes b1.2346E+100
Put (Output_File, -12.3456E99, Fore => 0, Aft => 3, Exp => 1);
   -- Writes -1.235E+100
```

Each instance of `Float_IO` provides three variables named `Default_Fore`, `Default_Aft`, and `Default_Exp`. The values of these variables give the default values used for `Fore`, `Aft`, or `Exp`, respectively, if one or more of these values is not specified in a call on `Put`. The defaults used can be changed by assigning new values to these variables. The initial values are two for `Default_Fore`, `Num'Digits - 1` for `Default_Aft`, and three for `Default_Exp`. (`Num'Digits` is the number of digits of precision declared for the subtype corresponding to the generic formal type `Num`.) These values specify a format consisting of the following parts:

a space or a minus sign
one digit
a decimal point
enough other digits to write the number to the precision of the subtype with which `Float_IO` has been instantiated
the letter `E`
a plus or minus sign for the exponent
two or more digits giving the value of the exponent

For example, consider the following program:

```
WITH Text_IO; USE Text_IO;
PROCEDURE Print_Powers_Of_Negative_16 IS
   TYPE Power_Type IS DIGITS 4;
   PACKAGE Power_Type_IO IS NEW Float_IO (Power_Type);
   USE Power_Type_IO;
   Output_File : File_Type;
```

```
BEGIN
   Open (Output_File, Out_File, "LPT:");
   FOR i IN 0 .. 10 LOOP
      Put (Output_File, (-16.0) ** i);
      New_Line (Output_File);
   END LOOP;
   Close (Output_File);
END Print_Powers_Of_Negative_16;
```

Calls on `Put` use the standard defaults of two for `Fore`, three for `Aft` (since `Power_Type'Digits` is four), and three for `Exp`. The following output is produced (where each *b* represents a blank):

```
b1.000E+00
-1.600E+01
b2.560E+02
-4.096E+03
b6.554E+04
-1.049E+06
b1.678E+07
-2.684E+08
b4.295E+09
-6.872E+10
b1.100E+12
```

17.4.2.3 `Get` and `Put` for fixed-point types. Instances of the generic package `Fixed_IO` provide versions of `Get` and `Put` for values in fixed-point types. `Fixed_IO` is almost identical in form and behavior to `Float_IO`:

```
GENERIC
   TYPE Num IS DELTA <>;
PACKAGE Fixed_IO IS
   Default_Fore : Field := Num'Fore;
   Default_Aft  : Field := Num'Aft;
   Default_Exp  : Field := 0;
   PROCEDURE Get
      (File  : IN File_Type;
       Item  : OUT Num;
       Width : IN Field := 0);
   PROCEDURE Put
      (File : IN File_Type;
       Item : IN Num;
       Fore : IN Field := Default_Fore;
       Aft  : IN Field := Default_Aft;
       Exp  : IN Field := Default_Exp);
   -- ... [other versions of Get and Put]
END Fixed_IO;
```

The `Width` parameter of `Get` and the `Fore`, `Aft`, and `Exp` parameters of `Put` have exactly the same meaning as in `Float_IO`. The only difference between the two generic packages is in the initial values of the variables `Default_Fore`, `Default_Aft`, and `Default_Exp`.

In `Fixed_IO`, the initial values of `Default_Fore` and `Default_Aft` are defined in terms of two attributes of fixed-point types, the `'Fore` and `'Aft` attributes. Suppose *T* is a fixed-point subtype with a declared range of *a* `..` *b* and a declared delta of *d*. Then *T*`'Fore` is the number of characters required before the decimal point to represent each number in the range *a* `..` *b* without an exponent, assuming that the first digit is preceded by either a space (for positive numbers) or a minus sign (for negative numbers). *T*`'Aft` is the number of digits after the decimal point required to represent each value to a precision of at least *d*. This is the number of digits appearing after the decimal point in *d*, assuming that *d* is written as a real literal without an exponent and without trailing zeroes. (Thus, because of the syntax of a real literal, *T*`'Aft` is always at least one.) For example, consider the following fixed-point type and subtype declarations:

```
TYPE Sine_Value_Type IS DELTA 0.0005 RANGE -1.0 .. 1.0;
   -- Sine_Value_Type'Fore = 2
   -- Sine_Value_Type'Aft = 4
TYPE Mileage_Type IS DELTA 5.0 RANGE 0.0 .. 30_000.0;
   -- Mileage_Type'Fore = 6
   -- Mileage_Type'Aft = 1
SUBTYPE Sine_Estimate_Subtype IS
   Sine_Value_Type DELTA 0.1;
      -- Sine_Estimate_Subtype'Fore = 2
      -- Sine_Estimate_Subtype'Aft = 1
SUBTYPE Low_Mileage_Subtype IS
   Mileage_Type RANGE 0.0 .. 500.0;
      -- Low_Mileage_Subtype'Fore = 4
      -- Low_Mileage_Subtype'Aft = 1
```

The initial values of `Default_Fore`, `Default_Aft`, and `Default_Exp` are `Num'Fore`, `Num'Aft`, and zero, respectively. These values specify a format without an exponent; with the number of spaces before the exponent just sufficient to accommodate the range of the subtype corresponding to `Num` (assuming each positive number is preceded by a space), and with the number of spaces after the exponent just sufficient to represent values to the precision specified for the subtype corresponding to `Num`.

For example, consider the following program, which reads in lines of data, each containing five values, and prints the average of the values in each line:

```
WITH Text_IO; USE Text_IO;
PROCEDURE Print_Average_Readings IS
   TYPE Sum_Type IS DELTA 0.025 RANGE -25.0 .. 25.0;
   SUBTYPE Data_Subtype IS Sum_Type RANGE -5.0 .. 5.0;
   PACKAGE Data_Subtype_IO IS NEW Fixed_IO (Data_Subtype);
   USE Data_Subtype_IO;
   Reading                   : Data_Subtype;
   Sum                       : Sum_Type;
   Input_File, Output_File : File_Type;
```

```
   BEGIN
      Open (Input_File, In_File, "READINGS.RAW");
      Create (Output_File, Out_File, "READINGS.AVG");
      WHILE NOT End_Of_File (Input_File) LOOP
         Sum := 0.0;
         FOR i IN 1 .. 5 LOOP
            Get (Input_File, Reading);
            Sum := Sum + Reading;
         END LOOP;
         Skip_Line (Input_File);
         Put (Output_File, Sum / 5);
         New_Line (Output_File);
      END LOOP;
      Close (Input_File);
      Close (Output_File);
   END Print_Average_Readings;
```

The output file produced by this program might look like this (where *b* again represents a blank):

```
b4.875
-3.500
b2.225
b0.000
-5.000
b2.350
b0.025
-0.050
```

(The input data is expected to be in the range `-5.0 .. 5.0`. We declare a base type `Sum_Type` able to hold the sum of any five values in this range.)

17.4.2.4 `Get` and `Put` for enumeration types. Instances of `Enumeration_IO` provide versions of `Get` and `Put` for enumeration types. The versions of `Get` read, and the versions of `Put` write, characters that form enumeration literals. The enumeration literals may include both identifiers like `Sunday` and character literals like `'X'`. `Enumeration_IO` is declared as follows:

```
GENERIC
   TYPE Enum IS ( <> );
PACKAGE Enumeration_IO IS
   Default_Width   : Field := 0;
   Default_Setting : Type_Set := Upper_Case;
   PROCEDURE Get (File : IN File_Type; Item : OUT Enum);
   PROCEDURE Put
     (File  : IN File_Type;
      Item  : IN Enum;
      Width : IN Field := Default_Width;
      Set   : IN Type_Set := Default_Setting);
   -- ... [other versions of Get and Put]
END Enumeration_IO;
```

(Type_Set is an enumeration type declared directly in Text_IO having two values—Lower_Case and Upper_Case.)

A call on Get skips past spaces, tabs, line terminators, and page terminators and then reads as many characters as can be interpreted as an identifier or a character literal. The identifier or character literal found should be an enumeration literal of the subtype corresponding to the generic formal type Enum. In a stream-oriented input file, as in an Ada program, upper case and lower case are considered equivalent in an identifier, but distinct in a character literal.

In a call on Put, the Width parameter gives the minimum number of characters that will be used to write the enumeration literal. If there are not enough characters in the enumeration literal itself, spaces are written *after* the enumeration literal to fill out the field. If the enumeration literal consists of more characters than specified by Width, the value of Width is ignored and all the characters forming the enumeration literal are written.

If the value of Set is Lower_Case, enumeration literals that are identifiers are written entirely in lower case; if the value of Set is Upper_Case, they are written entirely in upper case. There is no way to specify that identifiers are to be written in mixed case—for example, with only the first letter capitalized. The value of Set does not affect the printing of character literals: The call

```
Put (Output_File, 'b', Set => Upper_Case);
```

writes the literal 'b', not 'B'.

Versions of Put for enumeration types are extremely useful in debugging programs, because they allow you to trace program values and have them appear the same way in the output as they appear in your program. In particular, the predefined type Boolean is an enumeration type, so the instantiation

```
PACKAGE Boolean_IO IS NEW Enumeration_IO (Boolean);
```

creates a version of Put that writes the identifiers TRUE and FALSE.

Besides versions of Get and Put, an instance of Enumeration_IO provides two variables named Default_Width and Default_Setting. The current values of these variables are used as the default values of Width and Set, respectively, in calls on Put that do not specify these parameters. The initial value of Default_Setting is Upper_Case. The initial value of Default_Width is zero, so that a call on Put without a Width parameter writes exactly the number of characters forming the appropriate enumeration literal. The following program illustrates these defaults:

```
WITH Text_IO; USE Text_IO;
PROCEDURE Print_Day_Positions IS

   TYPE Day_Type IS
      (Sunday, Monday, Tuesday, Wednesday, Thursday,
       Friday, Saturday);
```

```
      PACKAGE Day_Type_IO IS NEW Enumeration_IO (Day_Type);
      PACKAGE Type_Integer_IO IS NEW Integer_IO (Integer);
      USE Day_Type_IO, Type_Integer_IO;

      Output_File : File_Type;
   BEGIN
      Open (Output_File, Out_File, "LPT:");
      FOR d IN Day_Type LOOP
         Put (Output_File, "The position number of ");
         Put (Output_File, d);
         Put (Output_File, " is ");
         Put (Output_File, Day_Type'Pos (d), 1);
         New_Line (Output_File);
      END LOOP;
      Close (Output_File);
   END Print_Day_Positions;
```

The output of the program is as follows:

```
The position number of SUNDAY is 0
The position number of MONDAY is 1
The position number of TUESDAY is 2
The position number of WEDNESDAY is 3
The position number of THURSDAY is 4
The position number of FRIDAY is 5
The position number of SATURDAY is 6
```

A value of `Width` large enough for the longest enumeration literal in a type is useful for making enumeration literals appear in columns with the leftmost characters aligned; the trailing spaces after shorter enumeration literals allow subsequent items on the same line to also be aligned in columns. For example, if the assignment

```
Day_Type_IO.Default_Width := Day_Type'Width;
```

were inserted just before the loop in `Print_Day_Positions` (making the default width nine because that is the number of characters required to write `Wednesday`), the output would look like this:

```
The position number of SUNDAY    is 0
The position number of MONDAY    is 1
The position number of TUESDAY   is 2
The position number of WEDNESDAY is 3
The position number of THURSDAY  is 4
The position number of FRIDAY    is 5
The position number of SATURDAY  is 6
```

Because the predefined type `Character` is an enumeration type, `Enumeration_IO` can be instantiated as follows:

```
PACKAGE Character_Literal_IO IS
   NEW Enumeration_IO (Character);
```

The package `Text_IO` directly provides versions of `Get` and `Put` that have an `Item` parameter of type `Character`, but the versions provided by `Character_Literal_IO` behave differently. `Text_IO.Get` reads the next character in the input stream, even if it is a space or tab, and places that character in `Item`. `Character_Literal_IO.Get` skips past spaces and tabs, reads a *sequence* of characters forming a character literal—that is, an apostrophe, some other character, and another apostrophe—and places the character *named by the character literal* in `Item`. `Text_IO.Get` gives the program complete control over how many characters are read and how they are interpreted, but `Character_Literal_IO.Get` does not. Similarly, `Text_IO.Put`, called with an `Item` parameter of type `Character`, writes a single character. `Character_Literal_IO.Put` writes three characters forming a character literal.

Suppose the file `ABC.IN` contains the following three lines (with no spaces before any of the apostrophes):

```
'A'
'B'
'C'
```

The program below writes the lines

```
A
B
C
```

to `ABC.OUT`:

```
WITH Text_IO; USE Text_IO;
PROCEDURE Character_IO_Example IS

   PACKAGE Character_Literal_IO IS
      NEW Enumeration_IO (Character);

   Input_File, Output_File : File_Type;
   c                       : Character;

BEGIN

   Open (Input_File, In_File, "ABC.IN");
   Create (Output_File, Out_File, "ABC.OUT");

   FOR i IN 1 .. 3 LOOP
      Character_Literal_IO.Get (Input_File, c);
      Text_IO.Put (Output_File, c);
      New_Line (Output_File);
   END LOOP;

   Close (Input_File);
   Close (Output_File);

END Character_IO_Example;
```

Were we to change the loop to read

```
FOR i IN 1 .. 3 LOOP
   Text_IO.Get (Input_File, c);
   Character_Literal_IO.Put (Output_File, c);
   New_Line (Output_File);
END LOOP;
```

(with `Text_IO` now used for input and `Character_Literal_IO` now used for output) then the output would be as follows:

```
'''
'A'
'''
```

(What is happening in each case?)

A common mistake in using character types—that is, enumeration types having one or more character literals—is to try to interpret characters in the input stream directly as values of the character type. There is no way to do this. For example, given the declaration

```
TYPE Roman_Digit_Type IS
   ('I', 'V', 'X', 'L', 'C', 'D', 'M');
```

you cannot treat an input stream like

```
MDMLXXXIV
```

as a sequence of `Roman_Digit_Type` values. The versions of `Get` provided directly by `Text_IO` only have Item parameters of type `Character` or type `String`. `Enumeration_IO` can be instantiated with any enumeration type; but if the enumeration literals are all character literals, the resulting versions of `Get` only recognize input items that begin and end with apostrophes, like `'I'`. (Remember, there is no inherent correspondence between the values `Roman_Digit_Type'('I')` and `Character'('I')`. They are two unrelated values that happen to be named by the same overloaded character literal.)

17.4.3 Standard and Default Files

Many programs performing stream-oriented input and output use one file as the principal source of input and one file as the principal recipient of output. Such programs can be written succinctly in the Ada language, without explicitly naming the principal input file and the principal output file each time they are used. Much of the time it is not even necessary to open and close these files explicitly. These short cuts are made possible by *standard* input and output files and *default* input and output files.

As a program using `Text_IO` begins execution, two internal files are already open. The *standard input file* is open with mode `In_File`, and the *standard output file* is open with mode `Out_File`. The association of these internal files with external files is determined outside the Ada program by the environment running the program. Typical associations for the standard input file are a terminal keyboard or a card reader. Typical associations for the standard output file are a terminal output device or a printer. Some environments allow other external files to be specified as the standard input and output files at the time an Ada program is invoked. Some environments even allow two Ada programs to be "piped" so that they can run together, with the standard output of one program connected to the standard input of the other. As the first program writes characters to its standard output file, the second program reads those characters from its standard input file.

To an Ada program, the standard input file is simply the principal source of input, and the standard output file is simply the principal recipient of output. The program need not be concerned with the origin of the input data or the disposition of the output data, which are determined outside the program. The association of the standard input and output files with external files is determined before an Ada program begins execution. This association remains fixed for the life of the program.

We have seen several subprograms for performing stream-oriented reading, writing, and positioning operations on internal files. In every case, the first parameter has been a `File_Type` value specifying the file to be operated on. Each of these subprograms is overloaded with a counterpart that is identical except that it has no `File_Type` parameter. These counterparts act upon an input file that has been designated the *default input file* or an output file that has been designated the *default output file*.

Initially, the standard input file is designated as the default input file and the standard output file is designated as the standard output file. Unlike the *standard* files, the *default* files can be changed at any time by calling the following procedures provided by `Text_IO`:

```
PROCEDURE Set_Input (File : IN File_Type);
PROCEDURE Set_Output (File : IN File_Type);
```

`Set_Input` takes an internal file opened with mode `In_File` and makes it the current default input file. `Set_Output` takes an internal file opened with mode `Out_File` and makes it the current default output file.

`Text_IO` provides two functions that return the standard input and output files as `File_Type` values:

```
FUNCTION Standard_Input RETURN File_Type;
FUNCTION Standard_Output RETURN File_Type;
```

Each of these functions returns the same value whenever it is called. Calls on these functions are useful for reestablishing the standard input or output file as the default file after the default has been changed. The following procedure calls accomplish this:

```
Set_Input (Standard_Input);
Set_Output (Standard_Output);
```

(The actual parameters in these procedure calls are themselves function calls without any parameters.)

There are also two functions that return the current *default* files as `File_Type` values:

```
FUNCTION Current_Input RETURN File_Type;
FUNCTION Current_Output RETURN File_Type;
```

Since the default input and output files may be changed by `Set_Input` and `Set_Output`, calls on these functions at different times may return different internal files.

Each of the subprograms described in Section 17.4.1 for dealing with columns, lines, and pages of a specified file has a version without a `File_Type` parameter. The following subprograms always use the default output file:

```
PROCEDURE Set_Line_Length (To : IN Count);
PROCEDURE Set_Page_Length (To : IN Count);
PROCEDURE New_Line (Spacing : IN Positive_Count := 1);
PROCEDURE New_Page;
FUNCTION Line_Length RETURN Count;
FUNCTION Page_Length RETURN Count;
```

The following subprograms always use the default input file:

```
PROCEDURE Skip_Line (Spacing : IN Positive_Count := 1);
PROCEDURE Skip_Page;
FUNCTION End_Of_Line RETURN Boolean;
FUNCTION End_Of_Page RETURN Boolean;
FUNCTION End_Of_File RETURN Boolean;
```

The functions `Page`, `Line`, and `Col` and the procedures `Set_Col` and `Set_Line` can be applied either to output files or input files. However, the versions without `File_Type` parameters always apply to the default *output* file. These versions are declared as follows:

```
FUNCTION Page RETURN Positive_Count;
FUNCTION Line RETURN Positive_Count;
FUNCTION Col RETURN Positive_Count;
PROCEDURE Set_Col (To : IN Positive_Count);
PROCEDURE Set_Line (To : IN Positive_Count);
```

Thus the procedure call `Set_Col (50)` is equivalent to the call `Set_Col (Current_Output, 50)`. To advance the input position of the default input file to column fifty, you must explicitly write `Set_Col (Current_Input, 50)`.

The procedures performing actual input and output, described in Section 17.4.2, also have versions without File_Type parameters. The following procedures are provided directly by Text_IO:

```
PROCEDURE Get (Item : OUT Character);
PROCEDURE Get (Item : OUT String);
PROCEDURE Put (Item : IN Character);
PROCEDURE Put (Item : IN String);
PROCEDURE Get_Line (Item : OUT String; Last : OUT Natural);
PROCEDURE Put_Line (Item : IN String);
```

Each instance of Integer_IO provides the following versions of Get and Put:

```
PROCEDURE Get (Item : OUT Num; Width : IN Field := 0);

PROCEDURE Put
   (Item  : IN Num;
    Width : IN Field := Default_Width;
    Base  : IN Number_Base := Default_Base);
```

Versions declared as follows are provided by each instance of Float_IO and each instance of Fixed_IO:

```
PROCEDURE Get (Item : OUT Num; Width : IN Field := 0);

PROCEDURE Put
   (Item : IN Num;
    Fore : IN Field := Default_Fore;
    Aft  : IN Field := Default_Aft;
    Exp  : IN Field := Default_Exp);
```

Finally, the following versions are provided by each instance of Enumeration_IO:

```
PROCEDURE Get (Item : OUT Enum);

PROCEDURE Put
   (Item  : IN Enum;
    Width : IN Field := Default_Width;
    Set   : IN Type_Set := Default_Setting);
```

Each of these versions of Get and Get_Line operates exactly like its counterpart in Section 17.4.2, except that it always uses the default input file. Each of these versions of Put and Put_Line operates exactly like its counterpart in Section 17.4.2, except that it always uses the default output file.

Each of the subprograms provided by Basic_IO was a specialized version of one of the subprograms provided either directly by Text_IO or by an instantiation of Integer_IO with the predefined type Integer. In each case, the File_Type parameter was omitted. Furthermore, the version of Put for type Integer did not have Width or Base parameters.

17.4.4 Output to and Input from Strings

A call on Get to read a numeric literal or an enumeration literal from a file does two things. First, it transfers characters from the file. Second, it *decodes* those characters, interpreting them as a literal and delivering the corresponding numeric or enumeration value. Similarly, a call on Put to write a numeric or enumeration literal to a file does two things. First, it *encodes* a specified value as a sequence of characters forming the corresponding literal. Second, it transfers the characters to the file.

Often, a program must perform this kind of decoding or encoding but has no need to transfer information from or to a file. Instances of Integer_IO, Float_IO, Fixed_IO, and Enumeration_IO provide special versions of Get and Put for this purpose. In these special versions of Get, the parameter specifying an input file is replaced by a parameter of type String acting as the source of the characters to be "read." In the special versions of Put, the parameter specifying an output file is replaced by a variable of type String that receives the characters to be "written."

The special versions of Get are declared in Integer_IO, Float_IO, and Fixed_IO as

```
PROCEDURE Get
   (From : IN String; Item : OUT Num; Last : OUT Positive);
```

and in Enumeration_IO as

```
PROCEDURE Get
   (From : IN String; Item : OUT Enum; Last : OUT Positive);
```

(The templates Integer_IO, Float_IO, and Fixed_IO all have generic formal types named Num, and Enumeration_IO has a generic formal type named Enum.) In each case, Get scans past blanks and tab characters in the string and then reads as many characters as can be interpreted as forming (depending on the version of Get) an integer literal optionally preceded by a plus or minus sign, a real literal optionally preceded by a plus or minus sign, an identifier, or a character literal. Item is set to the corresponding numeric or enumeration value, and Last is set to the index of the last character read.

Unlike the other versions of Put declared in Integer_IO, Float_IO, Fixed_IO, and Enumeration_IO, the versions obtaining input from a string do not have parameters like Width and Fore controlling the width of the field to be filled. Rather, the entire string is always filled. Numeric literals are always placed at the right end of the string, preceded by zero or more spaces, and enumeration literals are always placed at the left end of the string, followed by zero or more spaces. (If the literal does not fit in the string, the exception Layout_Error is raised.) One special version of Put is declared in Integer_IO as follows:

```
PROCEDURE Put
   (To   : OUT String;
    Item : IN Num;
    Base : IN Number_Base := Default_Base);
```

The meaning of Base is as described in Section 17.4.2.1. Special versions of Put are declared Float_IO and Fixed_IO as follows:

```
PROCEDURE Put
   (To   : OUT String;
    Item : IN Num;
    Aft  : IN Field := Default_Aft;
    Exp  : IN Field := Default_Exp);
```

The meaning of Aft and Exp are as described in Section 17.4.2.2. The following special version of Put is declared in Enumeration_IO:

```
PROCEDURE Put
   (To   : OUT String;
    Item : IN Enum;
    Set  : IN Type_Set := Default_Setting);
```

The meaning of Set is as described in Sction 17.4.2.4.

17.4.5 Exceptions

Most of the stream input/output operations described in Section 17.4 can raise exceptions. Some of these exceptions are due to the form or size of the data being manipulated, and they may be difficult to avoid. Other exceptions are indicative of programming errors and never arise in a correct program.

Most obviously, the versions of Get that attempt to interpret a sequence of characters as a literal (or as a sign followed by a literal) may encounter sequences of characters that are not of the required form. As soon as an unexpected character or terminator is encountered, Get raises Data_Error, and no further characters are read. The offending character or terminator remains unread and can be processed by a subsequent input operation if Data_Error is handled.

Versions of Get provided by instances of Integer_IO, Float_IO, and Fixed_IO also raise Data_Error if a well-formed numeric literal is found, but its value is not in the subtype corresponding to the generic formal type Num. Similarly, versions of Get provided by Enumeration_IO raise Data_Error if a legally formed identifier or character literal is found, but it is not one of the enumeration literals in the subtype corresponding to the generic formal type Enum. In each case, Get reads as many characters as are consistent with the *syntax* of the expected kind of literal. It is only after these characters are read that Get checks whether they correspond to a value in the appropriate subtype.

An input operation raises End_Error if it attempts to read the file terminator. Get, Get_Line, Skip_Line, Skip_Page, Set_Col, and Set_Line can do this. The special versions of Get obtaining input from a string raise End_Error if they attempt to read past the end of the string. End_Error can often be avoided by testing the value returned by End_Of_File before attempting an input operation, but this is not always sufficient. Get sometimes skips past spaces, line terminators, and page terminators in search of a literal; Set_Col skips past short lines in search of a line with the required number of columns; and Set_Line skips past short pages in search of a page with the required number of lines. Any of these searches may encounter the file terminator, in which case End_Error is raised even though End_Of_File returned False beforehand. Similarly, Skip_Line, called with a spacing greater than one, may attempt to read past the end of the file even if End_Of_File returned False beforehand.

For example, the following program reads integers from the standard input file and writes their sum to the standard output file. Invalid characters are reported on the standard output file and passed over. The standard input file is assumed to consist of a single page.

```
WITH Text_IO; USE Text_IO;
PROCEDURE Print_Sum IS
   PACKAGE Type_Integer_IO IS NEW Integer_IO (Integer);
   PACKAGE Count_IO IS NEW Integer_IO (Count);
      -- Provides Put for type Text_IO.Count, used to
      --    print line numbers.
   USE Type_Integer_IO, Count_IO;
   Sum          : Integer := 0;
   Next_Integer : Integer;
   c            : Character;
BEGIN
   WHILE NOT End_Of_File LOOP
      BEGIN
         Get (Next_Integer);
         Sum := Sum + Next_Integer;
      EXCEPTION
         WHEN Data_Error =>
            Put ("*****Illegal character on line ");
            Put (Line, Width => 0);
            Get (c); -- Read the offending character
            Put_Line (": '" & c & "'");
         WHEN End_Error =>
            Put_Line
               ("Trailing spaces or terminators ignored.");
            -- Now End_Of_File is true and loop will
            --    terminate.
      END;
   END LOOP;
   Put ("The sum is ");
   Put (Sum, Width => 0);
   Put_Line (".");
END Print_Sum;
```

Layout_Error is raised by an output operation that would overflow the capacity of the file or string receiving data. As explained in Section 17.4.1.1, maximum line and page lengths can be established for a stream-oriented output file by calls on Set_Line_Length and Set_Page_Length. These maximum lengths cause a new line to be started automatically when the current line is full and a new page to be started automatically when the current page is full. However, a literal is never split across lines. Normally, Put starts a new line before writing a literal if the literal would not fit in the remainder of the current line. However, if the literal would not even fit on the next line (because the length of the literal exceeds the maximum line length), Put raises Layout_Error. Similarly, calls on Set_Col and Set_Line to advance an output file to a specified column or line raise Layout_Error if they specify a column number greater than the maximum line length or a line number greater than the maximum page length. Finally, the special versions of Put that write to strings raise Layout_Error if the string is not large enough to contain the output that would be produced.

Column, line, and page numbers are values of the integer type Count provided by Text_IO. An input file, or an output file with no bounds on line and page lengths, may have more than Count'Last characters on a line, more than Count'Last lines on a page, or more than Count'Last pages in a file. However, the functions Col, Line, and Page described in Section 17.4.1 only return values of type Count (subtype Positive_Count). Layout_Error is raised by a call on Col, Line, or Page when the current column number, line number, or page number, respectively, is greater than Count'Last. If these functions are never called, the current column, line, or page number can get arbitrarily high without raising an exception.

An implementation may limit the allowable line and page lengths for certain external files. (For instance, an implementation might require line lengths of no more than 132 and page lengths of no more than 66 for internal files associated with a printer.) Use_Error is raised by a call on Set_Line_Length or Set_Page_Length that attempts to exceed such an implementation-imposed maximum.

Any input or output operation may raise Device_Error. Typically, this happens when using magnetic media or telecommunications. Depending on the implementation and the circumstances in which Device_Error is raised, data may remain available for subsequent input or it may be irretrievably lost. There is often no good way to recover from this exception, so typical handlers simply clean up and propagate an exception to a higher level.

Normally, Status_Error and Mode_Error are raised only as a result of programming errors. Status_Error is raised by an attempt to perform some operation (other than Open or Create) on an internal file that has not been opened. Mode_Error is raised by an attempt to perform an input operation on an internal file of mode Out_File or an output operation on an internal file of mode In_File. Skip_Line, Skip_Page, End_Of_Line, End_Of_Page, End_Of_File, Get, Get_Line, and Set_Input are input operations. Set_Line_Length, Set_Page_Length, Line_Length, Page_Length, New_Line, New_Page, Put, Put_Line, and Set_Output are output operations. Col, Line, Page, Set_Col, and Set_Line can be used in either mode.

17.5 SEQUENTIAL RECORD INPUT/OUTPUT

Sometimes a program stores data on a temporary file and then reads the file later. Sometimes a program writes a file that will be used only as an input file to another program. In either case, it is wasteful to encode values as streams of characters upon output and then decode the streams of characters upon input to retrieve the values. A more reasonable approach is to represent values in files in a way that is readily convertible to and from their representation inside variables. The library generic package `Sequential_IO` provides this capability. In typical implementations, precisely the same sequence of bits is used in files as in variables, so no conversion is needed at all.

A program using `Sequential_IO` must name it in a `WITH` clause. `Sequential_IO` may then be instantiated with any nonlimited subtype. Each instance of `Sequential_IO` provides a limited private type `File_Type`. `File_Type` values are internal files. These files contain sequences of values in the subtype used as a generic actual parameter. (For example, consider the instantiations

```
PACKAGE Sequential_Integer_IO IS
   NEW Sequential_IO (Integer);
PACKAGE Sequential_Float_IO IS NEW Sequential_IO (Float);
```

Given these instantiations, `Sequential_Integer_IO.File_Type` and `Sequential_Float_IO.File_Type` are two different types. The first consists of files containing `Integer` values, and the second consists of files containing `Float` values.) In addition, instances of `Sequential_IO` provide versions of the external file manipulation subprograms described in Section 17.3. Each instance provides versions that work with its own `File_Type`. (Each instance also provides its own type `File_Mode` with enumeration literals `In_File` and `Out_File`.)

Most importantly, an instance of `Sequential_IO` provides the following three subprograms, where `Element_Type` is the generic formal type (i.e., the type of each value in the files manipulated by the instance):

```
PROCEDURE Read
   (File : IN File_Type; Item : OUT Element_Type);
PROCEDURE Write
   (File : IN File_Type; Item : IN Element_Type);
FUNCTION End_Of_File (File : File_Type) RETURN Boolean;
```

These are the only subprograms for manipulating the contents of sequential record-oriented files. `Read` fetches the next value in the specified file and places it in `Item`, while `Write` adds the value of `Item` to the end of the specified file. `End_Of_File` indicates whether all values in an input file have been read.

Some implementations, but not all, raise `Data_Error` if the data obtained by a call on `Read` is not a valid representation of an `Element_Type` value. All implementations raise `End_Error` if `Read` is called after all values in a file have been read. Some implementations may impose a limit on the size of a sequential record-oriented file or may allow such a limit to be specified by the Form parameter of Open or Create. Such implementations raise Use_Error upon a call on Write that would exceed this limit. Mode_Error is raised by any call on Read or End_Of_File with a file of mode Out_File; and by any call on Write with a file of mode In_File.

The use of Sequential_IO is illustrated by the subunit Merge_Segments of the generic procedure Merge_Sort_Template given in Section 17.3:

```
SEPARATE (Merge_Sort_Template) -- See Section 17.3.6.
PROCEDURE Merge_Segments
   (Source_1,
      Source_2,
      Destination_1,
      Destination_2      : IN File_Pointer_Type;
   Input_Segment_Size    : IN Positive;
   Output_Segment_Count : OUT Positive) IS

   Current_Destination : File_Pointer_Type := Destination_1;
   Other_Destination   : File_Pointer_Type := Destination_2;
   Item                : Item_Type;
   Segments_Formed     : Natural := 0;

   PACKAGE Segment_Package IS

      PROCEDURE Initialize
         (Source_1, Source_2 : IN File_Pointer_Type;
          Segment_Size       : IN Positive);

      FUNCTION End_Of_Some_Segment RETURN Boolean;

      FUNCTION End_Of_Both_Files RETURN Boolean;

      PROCEDURE Extract_Smallest (Item : OUT Item_Type);

      PROCEDURE Flush_Nonempty_Segment
         (Destination : IN File_Type);

      -- Initialize must be called before the other
      --    subprograms whenever files are reset.

      -- Extract_Smallest may only be called when
      --    End_Of_Some_Segment is false, and
      --    Flush_Nonempty_Segment may only be called when
      --    End_Of_Some_Segment is true.

   END Segment_Package;

   USE Segment_Package;

   PACKAGE BODY Segment_Package IS SEPARATE;

BEGIN

   Initialize (Source_1, Source_2, Input_Segment_Size);

   WHILE NOT End_Of_Both_Files LOOP

      WHILE NOT End_Of_Some_Segment LOOP
         Extract_Smallest (Item);
         Write (Current_Destination.ALL, Item);
      END LOOP;
```

```
         Flush_Nonempty_Segment (Current_Destination.ALL);
         Segments_Formed := Segments_Formed + 1;
         Swap_File_Pointers
            (Current_Destination, Other_Destination);
      END LOOP;
      Output_Segment_Count := Segments_Formed;
   END Merge_Segments;
```

As explained in Section 17.3.6, `Merge_Segments` repeatedly takes the sorted segments at the front of each source file and merges them to form a sorted segment generally twice as large. The output segments are alternately directed to one destination file then the other. Minor complications arise because the number of items to be sorted is not always an exact power of two. The final input segment in a file may be less than the normal input length; this results in a final output segment less than the normal output length. The first source file may have one segment more than the second; the file with fewer segments is then treated as having an extra segment of length zero.

None of these special cases is explicitly addressed by `Merge_Segments`. The statements of this procedure are kept simple by hiding details of segment manipulation in the `Segment_Package` body. `Initialize` is called once at the beginning of each call on `Merge_Segments` to perform internal initialization. `End_Of_Some_Segment` returns a Boolean value indicating whether the end of a segment has been reached in one of the two input files (either because all `Input_Segment_Size` items have been removed from the segment or because the end of the file has been encountered). The name `End_Of_Both_Files` is self-explanatory. `Extract_Smallest`, called only when `End_Of_Some_Segment` is false, compares the next item in each segment, removes the smaller of these two values from its segment, and returns that value in `Item`. `Flush_Nonempty_Segment`, called as soon as the end of one input segment has been reached, copies all the remaining values in the other input segment to the end of the current output segment, then prepares for processing of the next pair of input segments. The file containing the current output segment is pointed to by the parameter of `Flush_Nonempty_Segment`.

The implementation of `Segment_Package` is as follows:

```
SEPARATE (Merge_Sort_Template. Merge_Segments)

PACKAGE BODY Segment_Package IS
   TYPE Boolean_Pair_Type IS ARRAY (1 .. 2) OF Boolean;
   At_End_Of_File, At_End_Of_Segment : Boolean_Pair_Type;
   Source_File_Pair : ARRAY (1 .. 2) OF File_Pointer_Type;
```

```
Remaining_Segment_Size : ARRAY (1 .. 2) OF Natural;
Next_Item              : ARRAY (1 .. 2) OF Item_Type;
Full_Segment_Size      : Natural;

-- Once Initialize has been called, the following
--    conditions always hold between subprogram calls:
--
-- For i in 1 .. 2, either At_End_Of_File (i) is true or
--    Next_Item (i) holds the next item from
--    Source_File_Pair (i).ALL that has not yet been
--    extracted.
-- For i in 1 .. 2, if At_End_Of_File (i) is true, then
--    so is At_End_Of_Segment (i).
-- At_End_Of_Segment (1) and At_End_Of_Segment (2) are
--    not both true unless At_End_Of_File (1) and
--    At_End_Of_File (2) are both true.


PROCEDURE Initialize
   (Source_1, Source_2 : IN File_Pointer_Type;
    Segment_Size       : IN Positive) IS

BEGIN

   Full_Segment_Size := Segment_Size;
   Source_File_Pair := (Source_1, Source_2);
   FOR i IN 1 .. 2 LOOP
      At_End_Of_File (i) :=
         Source_File_Pair (i) = NULL
         OR ELSE
         End_Of_File (Source_File_Pair(i).ALL);
      IF NOT At_End_Of_File (i) THEN
         Read (Source_File_Pair(i).ALL, Next_Item(i));
      END IF;
      At_End_Of_Segment (i) := At_End_Of_File (i);
      Remaining_Segment_Size (i) :=
         Full_Segment_Size;
   END LOOP;

END Initialize;


FUNCTION End_Of_Some_Segment RETURN Boolean IS

BEGIN

   RETURN At_End_Of_Segment /= (False, False);

END End_Of_Some_Segment;


FUNCTION End_Of_Both_Files RETURN Boolean IS

BEGIN

   RETURN At_End_Of_File = (True, True);

END End_Of_Both_Files;
```

```
PROCEDURE Extract_Smallest (Item : OUT Item_Type) IS
   Smaller : Integer RANGE 1 .. 2;
BEGIN
   -- Assume that we are at the end of neither segment
   --    (and therefore at the end of neither file).
   -- Identify file from which Item is to be taken:
   IF Next_Item (1) < Next_Item (2) THEN
      Smaller := 1;
   ELSE
      Smaller := 2;
   END IF;
   -- Advance the file and its current segment:
   DECLARE
      Selected_Item_Buffer :
         Item_Type RENAMES Next_Item (Smaller);
      Selected_File :
         File_Type RENAMES
            Source_File_Pair (Smaller).ALL;
      Selected_Segment_Size :
         Natural RENAMES
            Remaining_Segment_Size (Smaller);
   BEGIN
      Item := Selected_Item_Buffer;
      IF End_Of_File (Selected_File) THEN
         At_End_Of_File (Smaller) := True;
         At_End_Of_Segment (Smaller) := True;
      ELSE
         Read (Selected_File, Selected_Item_Buffer);
         Selected_Segment_Size :=
            Selected_Segment_Size - 1;
         IF Selected_Segment_Size = 0 THEN
            At_End_Of_Segment (Smaller) := True;
         END IF;
      END IF;
   END; -- block statement
END Extract_Smallest;


PROCEDURE Flush_Nonempty_Segment
   (Destination : IN File_Type) IS
   Nonempty_Segment : Integer RANGE 1 .. 2;
BEGIN
   -- We are at the end of one and only one segment.
   -- Identify nonempty segment:
   IF At_End_Of_Segment (1) THEN
      Nonempty_Segment := 2;
   ELSE
      Nonempty_Segment := 1;
   END IF;
```

```
      -- Copy remaining items in segment to Destination,
      --    leaving first item of next segment (if any) in
      --    Next_Item (Nonempty_Segment):
      DECLARE
         File_To_Flush :
            File_Type RENAMES
               Source_File_Pair(Nonempty_Segment).ALL;
         Item_Buffer :
            Item_Type RENAMES Next_Item (Nonempty_Segment);
         Remaining_Items :
            Integer RANGE 0 .. Full_Segment_Size :=
               Remaining_Segment_Size (Nonempty_Segment);
      BEGIN
         LOOP
            Write (Destination, Item_Buffer);
            Remaining_Items := Remaining_Items - 1;
            EXIT WHEN
               End_Of_File (File_To_Flush) OR
               Remaining_Items = 0;
            Read (File_To_Flush, Item_Buffer);
         END LOOP;
         IF End_Of_File (File_To_Flush) THEN
            At_End_Of_File (Nonempty_Segment) := True;
         ELSE
            Read (File_To_Flush, Item_Buffer);
         END IF;
      END; -- block statement

      -- Reset both segments:
      FOR i IN 1 .. 2 LOOP
         At_End_Of_Segment (i) := At_End_Of_File (i);
         Remaining_Segment_Size (i) := Full_Segment_Size;
      END LOOP;

   END Flush_Nonempty_Segment;

END Segment_Package;
```

All items in a given sequential file must be of the same type. This type can be a scalar type, an array type, or a record type. In particular, it can be a record type with discriminants. This allows different kinds of data to be stored in the same file. (However, some implementations may disallow instantiation of `Sequential_IO` with an unconstrained array subtype or an unconstrained record type whose discriminants do not have default initial values.)

For example, suppose a file is to contain a list of of those attending an organization's conference. Some of those attending are members of the organization, and others are not. The file should contain membership numbers for members and names and addresses for nonmembers. We might declare the following types:

```
TYPE Membership_Number_Type IS RANGE 1 .. 999_999;
TYPE Nonmember_Information_Type IS
   RECORD
      Name                             : String (1 .. 25);
      Address_Line_1, Address_Line_2 : String (1 .. 40);
   END RECORD;
```

It is impossible to intersperse calls writing `Membership_Number_Type` values with calls writing `Nonmember_Information_Type` values to the same internal file. A version of `Write` for `Membership_Number_Type` values must come from an instantiation like

```
PACKAGE Membership_Number_IO IS
   NEW Sequential_IO (Membership_Number_Type);
```

and a version for `Nonmember_Information_Type` values must come from an instantiation like

```
PACKAGE Nonmember_Information_IO IS
   NEW Sequential_IO (Nonmember_Information_Type);
```

But `Membership_Number_IO.Write` only writes to files of type

```
Membership_Number_IO.File_Type,
```

and `Nonmember_Information_IO.Write` only writes to files of type

```
Nonmember_Information_IO.File_Type.
```

A single file cannot belong to both of these types.

A solution is to declare a new record type with a variant for each kind of data to be written to the file:

```
TYPE Attender_Information_Type
   (Member : Boolean := True) IS
      RECORD
         CASE Member IS
            WHEN False =>
               Nonmember_Information_Part :
                  Nonmember_Information_Type;
            WHEN True =>
               Membership_Number_Part :
                  Membership_Number_Type;
         END CASE;
      END RECORD;
```

`Sequential_IO` can then be instantiated with this type:

```
TYPE Attender_Information_IO IS
   NEW Sequential_IO (Attender_Information_Type);
```

Files of type `Attender_Information_IO.File_Type` can contain information about both members and nonmembers.

The rules of the Ada language allow `Sequential_IO` to be instantiated with access types or with composite types having access-type components. However, this is dangerous and should be avoided. The effect of writing an access value and later reading it depends on the implementation. Usually, access values are represented internally as addresses of allocated variables, and a particular address ceases to have any significance once a program terminates. (Some implementations may even make room for further allocation by moving allocated variables during program execution, adjusting the representation of all access values accordingly.)

`Sequential_IO` can be instantiated with type `Character`. Like `Text_IO`, the resulting instance processes files containing sequences of characters. Unlike `Text_IO`, the instance does not try to interpret the contents of the file except as individual values of type `Character`. Furthermore, a sequential record-oriented file is not divided into pages and lines. Control characters interpreted as separators by certain implementations of `Text_IO` are interpreted as ordinary characters by the instance of `Sequential_IO`. In implementations using the same internal structure for a stream-oriented file as for a record-oriented file of characters, the instance of `Sequential_IO` can be used to write a program that treats control characters in the input file in the same way that it treats any other character.

17.6 DIRECT-ACCESS INPUT/OUTPUT

In sequential input and output, whether stream-oriented or record-oriented, data is always read from the beginning of the file and written to the end of the file. In direct-access input and output, any item in a file may be read, written, or overwritten at any time. The items in a file, or *file elements,* are numbered. Data can be read from or written to a particular file element identified by its position number, or *index*. Direct-access files are useful for applications such as data base manipulation.

Facilities for direct-access input and output are obtained by instantiating the library generic package `Direct_IO`. As with `Sequential_IO`, these is a single generic parameter, specifying the subtype of the data contained in a file element. The generic actual parameter may be any nonlimited subtype. (As with `Sequential_IO`, the generic actual parameter may be a record type with discriminants, allowing different kinds of data to be stored in different file elements. Again, an unconstrained array type or an unconstrained record subtype without default discriminant values may be forbidden by some implementations. Instantiation with an access type, or with a composite type having an access-type component, will have unpredictable effects in many implementations and should be avoided.)

Each instance of `Direct_IO` provides types named `File_Type`, `File_Mode`, and `Count`, along with versions of the external file manipulation routines described in Section 17.3. In this case, type `File_Mode` includes the value `Inout_File`. This is the default file mode if none is specified in a call on `Create`. The type `Count` is an integer type used for numbering and counting the elements in a file. Its lower bound is zero, and its upper bound depends on the implementation. File elements are numbered starting with one, and the value zero is only used in counting the number of elements in an empty file. An instance of Direct_IO provides a subtype Positive_Count consisting of every value of Count except for zero.

The following procedures allow data to be read from or written to a particular file element:

```
PROCEDURE Read
   (File : IN File_Type;
    Item : OUT Element_Type;
    From : IN Positive_Count);

PROCEDURE Write
   (File : IN File_Type;
    Item : IN Element_Type;
    To   : IN Positive_Count);
```

In each case, the third parameter identifies the file element. The type Element_Type is the generic formal parameter to Direct_IO.

For example, consider a package implementing a data base of inventory information. Each kind of item in the inventory is identified by an inventory number between one and 1,000. The data base stores a thirty-character description of each kind of item, as well as the current stock of each kind of item. The current stock may be negative, indicating that an item is back-ordered. The package is declared as follows:

```
PACKAGE Inventory_Package IS

   TYPE Inventory_Number_Type IS RANGE 1 .. 1000;

   FUNCTION Current_Stock
      (Inventory_Number : Inventory_Number_Type)
      RETURN Integer;

   PROCEDURE Update_Current_Stock
      (Inventory_Number : IN Inventory_Number_Type;
       Change           : IN Integer);

   PROCEDURE Print_Report
      (From, To : IN Inventory_Number_Type);

   PROCEDURE End_Processing;

   Stock_Size_Error : EXCEPTION;

END Inventory_Package;
```

The function Current_Stock returns the current stock of the item with the specified inventory number. Update_Current_Stock is called when an item is ordered or restocked. The current stock of the item with the specified item number is changed by the value of the parameter Change (which may be positive or negative). If the resulting stock is outside of type Integer, no change is made and Stock_Size_Error is raised. Print_Report writes a report of current stock for items with item numbers in the specified range (which may be empty). The report is written to the standard output file and includes the item number, description, and current stock of each item. For back-ordered items, the current stock is indicated by the message "Back-ordered (*n*)" where *n* is the number of back orders. A program using this package must call End_Processing when it is done using the package. Inventory_Package does not provide ways of creating the data base, adding new kinds of items, or specifying item descriptions. Rather, it assumes that a properly formed data base already exists.

The package is implemented by storing inventory data in the direct access file `"INVNTRY.DB"`. The description and current stock of the item with inventory number *i* are stored in the file element with index *i*. The package body is as follows:

```
WITH Direct_IO;
PACKAGE BODY Inventory_Package IS
   File_Name : CONSTANT String := "INVNTRY.DB";
   TYPE Inventory_Record_Type IS
      RECORD
         Description_Part   : String (1 .. 30);
         Current_Stock_Part : Integer;
      END RECORD;
   PACKAGE Inventory_Record_IO IS
      NEW Direct_IO (Inventory_Record_Type);
   USE Inventory_Record_IO;
   Data_Base : File_Type;

   FUNCTION Current_Stock
      (Inventory_Number : Inventory_Number_Type)
      RETURN Integer IS
      Index :
         CONSTANT Positive_Count :=
            Positive_Count (Inventory_Number);
      Item : Inventory_Record_Type;
   BEGIN
      Read (Data_Base, Item, Index);
      RETURN Item.Current_Stock_Part;
   END Current_Stock;

   PROCEDURE Update_Current_Stock
      (Inventory_Number : IN Inventory_Number_Type;
       Change           : IN Integer) IS
      Index :
         CONSTANT Positive_Count :=
            Positive_Count (Inventory_Number);
      Item : Inventory_Record_Type;
   BEGIN
      Read (Data_Base, Item, Index);
      BEGIN
         Item.Current_Stock_Part :=
            Item.Current_Stock_Part + Change;
      EXCEPTION
         WHEN Numeric_Error | Constraint_Error =>
            RAISE Stock_Size_Error;
      END;
      Write (Data_Base, Item, Index);
   END Update_Current_Stock;
```

```
      PROCEDURE Print_Report
         (From, To : IN Inventory_Number_Type)
         IS SEPARATE;

      PROCEDURE End_Processing IS
      BEGIN
         Close (Data_Base);
      END End_Processing;

   BEGIN -- package initialization

      Open (Data_Base, Inout_File, File_Name);

   END Inventory_Package;
```

(We shall return to the subunit `Print_Report` momentarily.) Note the need for type conversion between type `Count` (subtype `Positive_Count`) and `Inventory_Number_Type`.

Direct-access files can also be accessed sequentially. While it is possible to do this simply by calling `Read` or `Write` repeatedly with consecutive index values, there is a more convenient way. Each instance of `Direct_IO` maintains a *current index* for each file object. Furthermore, each instance provides versions of `Read` and `Write` that do not have index position parameters, but read from or write to the current index position:

```
   PROCEDURE Read
      (File : IN File_Type; Item : OUT Element_Type);
   PROCEDURE Write
      (File : IN File_Type; Item : IN Element_Type);
```

The current index is set to one when a file is opened or reset, and each call on `Read` or `Write` (either the two-parameter or three-parameter version) increments the current index by one after data has been transferred. Thus it is possible to step through a direct-access file sequentially simply by repeatedly calling the two-parameter version of `Read`.

Each instance of `Direct_IO` also provides a procedure `Set_Index` to set a file's current index to a specified value, and a function `Index` returning a file's current index:

```
   PROCEDURE Set_Index
      (File : IN File_Type; To : Positive_Count);
   FUNCTION Index (File : File_Type) RETURN Positive_Count;
```

Finally, there is a function `End_Of_File` that returns `True` if and only if the current index of a specified file exceeds the number of elements in the file:

```
FUNCTION End_Of_File (File : File_Type) RETURN Boolean;
```

Using these facilities for sequential access, we can implement the subunit `Print_Report` as follows:

```
WITH Text_IO; USE Text_IO;
SEPARATE (Inventory_Package)
PROCEDURE Print_Report
   (From, To : IN Inventory_Number_Type) IS
   SUBTYPE Count IS Inventory_Record_IO.Count;
      -- as opposed to Text_IO.Count
   PACKAGE Type_Integer_IO IS NEW Integer_IO (Integer);
   PACKAGE Count_IO IS NEW Integer_IO (Count);
   USE Type_Integer_IO, Count_IO;
   From_Count : CONSTANT Count := Count (From);
   To_Count   : CONSTANT Count := Count (To);
   Item       : Inventory_Record_Type;
BEGIN
   Set_Index (Data_Base, From_Count);
   FOR Inventory_Number IN From_Count .. To_Count LOOP
      Read (Data_Base, Item);
      Put (Inventory_Number, Width => 4);
      Set_Col (6);
      Put (Item.Description_Part);
      Set_Col (37);
      IF Item.Current_Stock_Part >= 0 THEN
         Put (Item.Current_Stock_Part);
      ELSE
         Put ( "Back-ordered (" );
         Put (- Item.Current_Stock_Part, Width => 0);
         Put ( ")" );
      END IF;
      New_Line;
   END LOOP;
END Print_Report;
```

An external file used for direct-access input and output has a *current size*. This is the index of the last element in the file. Each instance of `Direct_IO` provides a function returning the current size of the external file associated with a specified internal file:

```
FUNCTION Size (File : IN File_Type) RETURN Count;
```

The initial size of an external file after a call on `Create` depends on the implementation. Some implementations, for example, may give each file an initial size of zero and expand the file automatically when `Write` sends data to an index higher than the current size, up to some maximum size. Other implementations may allow a size to be specified by the `Form` parameter of `Create` (using some default size if no form is given) and not allow expansion beyond this initial size. Any call on `Write` that would exceed the maximum size of the external file (whether this maximum is the initial size of the file or some other value) raises `Use_Error`. Any attempt to read from an index greater than the size of the file raises `End_Error`. (It follows that the two-parameter version of `Read` raises `End_Error` precisely when `End_Of_File` would return `True` for the input file. This mimics the relationship between `Read` and `End_Of_File` in instances of `Sequential_IO`.) `Set_Index` may be called with a `Positive_Count` value greater than the size of the file. This will not raise an exception.

Every index value from one to the size of the file may be used as an index in a call on `Read`. However, the rules of the Ada language do not specify the effect of reading from a file element that has never been written to. Some implementations may initialize all file elements to a predictable value. In other implementations, the initial contents of a file element may be unpredictable. In some implementations, but not all, `Read` raises `Data_Error` if the contents of a file element cannot be interpreted as a value of the subtype specified in the instantiation of `Direct_IO`.

The other input/output exceptions are raised in instances of `Direct_IO` in the usual circumstances. `Status_Error` is raised by an attempt to call `Read`, `Write`, `Set_Index`, `Index`, `End_Of_File`, or `Size` with an internal file that has not been opened. `Mode_Error` is raised by a call on `Read` or `End_Of_File` with a file of mode `Out_File`; or by a call on `Write` with a file of mode `In_File`. The other operations are applicable to files of any mode, and all the operations are applicable to files of mode `Inout_File`.

17.7 SUMMARY

Input, output, and file manipulation are performed by using the predefined library package `Text_IO` and instances of the predefined library generic packages `Sequential_IO` and `Direct_IO`. `Text_IO` provides file management operations and operations to read and write data as streams of characters, in a form readable by humans. `Sequential_IO` can be instantiated with some nonlimited type *t1* to provide the following facilities:

a type *t2* for files containing *elements* of type *t1*
file management operations for files of type *t2*
operations for reading data of type *t1* from a file of type *t2*, from beginning to end
operations for writing data of type *t1* at the end of a file of type *t2*

Typical implementations of `Sequential_IO` represent file data in a binary form not easily read by humans but efficiently processed by the computer. An instance of `Direct_IO` provides facilities similar to those provided by an instance of `Sequential_IO`, plus operations to read or write any element of a file at random.

A physical source or destination for data, such as a card reader or a disk file, is called an *external file.* The logical entities from which an Ada program reads data or to which an Ada program writes data are called *internal files.* The same internal files may be associated with different external files at different times. Associating a specified external file with an internal file is called *opening* the file. An open file always has a current *file mode,* which is one of the following:

`In_File`, meaning that data are transferred from the external file to the program
`Out_File`, meaning that data are transferred from the program to the external file
for files provided by instances of `Direct_IO` only, `Inout_File`, meaning that data may be transferred in either direction

`Text_IO`, instances of `Sequential_IO`, and instances of `Direct_IO` all provide renaming declarations for exceptions provided by yet another package, `IO_Exceptions`. The renaming declarations create the appearance that the packages containing them provide the exceptions directly. The exceptions are as follows:

`Status_Error`: an attempt to use an internal file that has not been associated with an external file (i.e., has not been *opened*); or to open an internal file that is already open

`Mode_Error`: an attempt to perform an input operation on a file of mode *out* or an output operation on a file of mode *in*

`Name_Error`: an attempt to associate an internal file with an external file if an invalid external file name is specified

`Use_Error`: an attempt to perform some input/output operation on an external file for which the implementation does not allow that operation

`Device_Error`: a problem with the hardware, software, or media providing input/output services

`End_Error`: an attempt to read past the end of an input file

`Data_Error`: input data that are not of the expected form

`Layout_Error`: invalid `Text_IO` formatting operations

(A renaming declaration for `Layout_Error` is provided by `Text_IO` but not by instances of `Sequential_IO` and `Direct_IO`.)

`Text_IO` provides a limited private type named `File_Type` whose values are internal files. The following procedure provided by `Text_IO` creates a new external file and associates an internal file with it:

```
PROCEDURE Create
   (File : IN OUT File_Type;
    Mode : IN File_Mode := Out_File;
    Name : IN String := "";
    Form : IN String := "");
```

The following procedure associates an internal file with an *existing* external file:

```
PROCEDURE Open
   (File : IN OUT File_Type;
    Mode : IN File_Mode;
    Name : IN String;
    Form : IN String := "");
```

The procedure

```
PROCEDURE Close (File : IN OUT File_Type);
```

breaks the association between an external file and an internal file, or *closes* the file. The procedure

```
PROCEDURE Delete (File : IN OUT File_Type);
```

breaks the association and then removes the external file. The procedure

```
PROCEDURE Reset (File : IN OUT File_Type);
```

goes back to the beginning of the file and allows input or output operations to resume at the beginning of the file. The overloaded version

```
PROCEDURE Reset
   (File : IN OUT File_Type; Mode : IN File_Mode);
```

does the same thing, but allows a new file mode to be specified for the next pass through the file. The following functions return information indicating whether an internal file is open, the name and form with which it was opened, and the current file mode:

```
FUNCTION Is_Open (File : File_Type) RETURN Boolean;
FUNCTION Name (File : File_Type) RETURN String;
FUNCTION Form (File : File_Type) RETURN String;
FUNCTION Mode (File : File_Type) RETURN File_Mode;
```

Each operation on internal files provided by `Text_IO` has a version with a `File_Type` parameter and a version without a `File_Type` parameter. The version without a `File_Type` parameter operates on the current *default input file* or *default output file*. Initially, the *standard input file* is used as the default input file, and the *standard output file* is used as the default output file. The standard files are automatically open as a program begins execution and are associated with external files by some means outside of the program. The procedures

```
PROCEDURE Set_Input (File : IN File_Type);
PROCEDURE Set_Output (File : IN File_Type);
```

can be called to change the current default input and output files. The following functions return the current default input and output files as `File_Type` values:

```
FUNCTION Current_Input RETURN File_Type;
FUNCTION Current_Output RETURN File_Type;
```

The functions

```
FUNCTION Standard_Input RETURN File_Type;
FUNCTION Standard_Output RETURN File_Type;
```

return the standard input and output files as `File_Type` values.

A file manipulated by `Text_IO` is a sequence of one or more *pages,* followed by a *file terminator.* Each page is a sequence of one or more *lines,* followed by a *page terminator.* Each line is a sequence of zero or more characters, followed by a *line terminator.* The following functions return the current page, line, and column numbers for a given file:

```
FUNCTION Page (File : IN File_Type) RETURN Positive_Count;
FUNCTION Page RETURN Positive_Count;

FUNCTION Line (File : IN File_Type) RETURN Positive_Count;
FUNCTION Line RETURN Positive_Count;

FUNCTION Col (File : IN File_Type) RETURN Positive_Count;
FUNCTION Col RETURN Positive_Count;
```

The versions without `File_Type` parameters refer to the current default *output* file. The following procedures call for a file to be advanced to a column or line with a given number:

```
PROCEDURE Set_Col
   (File : IN File_Type; To : IN Positive_Count);

PROCEDURE Set_Col (To : IN Positive_Count);

PROCEDURE Set_Line
   (File : IN File_Type; To : IN Positive_Count);

PROCEDURE Set_Line (To : IN Positive_Count);
```

For input files, this may entail skipping lines until one with a sufficient number of columns is found or skipping pages until one with a sufficient number of lines is found. As with `Page`, `Line`, and `Col`, the versions without `File_Type` parameters act on the current default *output file.*

A program may set a *maximum line length* and a *maximum page length* for an output file. A new line is started automatically after the current line has been filled with the maximum number of characters, and a new page is started automatically after the current page has been filled with the maximum number of lines. A maximum line or page length of zero indicates that the corresponding length is unbounded and that a new line or page should be started only when it is explicitly requested. Text_IO provides a type Count whose values represent column, line, and page numbers. The following procedures set the maximum line and page length of an output file (possibly the default output file):

```
PROCEDURE Set_Line_Length
   (File : IN File_Type; To : IN Count);
PROCEDURE Set_Line_Length (To : IN Count);
PROCEDURE Set_Page_Length
   (File : IN File_Type; To : IN Count);
PROCEDURE Set_Page_Length (To : IN Count);
```

The following functions report these values:

```
FUNCTION Line_Length (File : IN File_Type) RETURN Count;
FUNCTION Line_Length RETURN Count;
FUNCTION Page_Length (File : IN File_Type) RETURN Count;
FUNCTION Page_Length RETURN Count;
```

The following procedures explicitly request that one or more new lines or a new page be started:

```
PROCEDURE New_Line
   (File : IN File_Type; Spacing : IN Positive_Count := 1);
PROCEDURE New_Line (Spacing : IN Positive_Count := 1);
PROCEDURE New_Page (File : IN File_Type);
PROCEDURE New_Page;
```

The following procedures advance past a specified number or lines or past the end of the current page in an input file (possibly the default input file):

```
PROCEDURE Skip_Line
   (File : IN File_Type; Spacing : IN Positive_Count := 1);
PROCEDURE Skip_Line (Spacing : IN Positive_Count := 1);
PROCEDURE Skip_Page (File : IN File_Type);
PROCEDURE Skip_Page;
```

The following functions report whether an input file is currently positioned at the end of a line, page, or file:

```
FUNCTION End_Of_Line (File : IN File_Type) RETURN Boolean;
FUNCTION End_Of_Line RETURN Boolean;

FUNCTION End_Of_Page (File : IN File_Type) RETURN Boolean;
FUNCTION End_Of_Page RETURN Boolean;

FUNCTION End_Of_File (File : IN File_Type) RETURN Boolean;
FUNCTION End_Of_File RETURN Boolean;
```

(End_Of_Line is true whenever End_Of_Page is true, but not vice versa. End_Of_Page is true whenever End_Of_File is true, but not vice versa.)

Text_IO provides the following versions of Get and Put for reading and writing values of type Character and type String:

```
PROCEDURE Get (File : IN File_Type; Item : OUT Character);
PROCEDURE Get (Item : OUT Character);

PROCEDURE Get (File : IN File_Type; Item : OUT String);
PROCEDURE Get (Item : OUT String);

PROCEDURE Put (File : IN File_Type; Item : IN Character);
PROCEDURE Put (Item : IN Character);

PROCEDURE Put (File : IN File_Type; Item : IN String);
PROCEDURE Put (Item : IN String);
```

The versions of Get for type String may read across several lines or pages until enough characters are read to fill the string. (Terminators encountered in the process do not become part of the string.) The characters written by the versions of Put for type String may be split across lines or pages if the maximum line or page length is exceeded. In addition, Text_IO provides the following procedures for line-oriented input and output of strings:

```
PROCEDURE Get_Line
   (File : IN File_Type;
    Item : OUT String;
    Last : OUT Natural);

PROCEDURE Get_Line (Item : OUT String; Last : OUT Natural);

PROCEDURE Put_Line (File : IN File_Type; Item : IN String);

PROCEDURE Put_Line (Item : IN String);
```

Get_Line reads characters until either the end of the line is encountered or the string corresponding to Item becomes full. Last is set to the index of the last component of Item that was filled, or to Item'First - 1 if no characters were read. Put_Line writes the specified characters to an output file, followed by a line terminator.

The following generic packages are declared inside the Text_IO package specification and provide for the input and output of numeric and enumeration values:

Integer_IO, which can be instantiated with any integer type to obtain a package providing versions of Get and Put for literals of that type

Float_IO, which can be instantiated with any floating-point type to obtain a package providing versions of Get and Put for literals of that type

Fixed_IO, which can be instantiated with any fixed-point type to obtain a package providing versions of Get and Put for literals of that type

Enumeration_IO, which can be instantiated with any enumeration type to obtain a package providing versions of Get and Put for literals of that type

Each instance provides a version of Get that reads past spaces, tab characters, and terminators and then interprets the next character as the beginning of the appropriate kind of literal, optionally preceded by a plus or minus sign in the case of numeric literals. The following versions are provided by an instance of Text_IO.Integer_IO, where Num is the generic formal integer type:

```
PROCEDURE Get
   (File  : IN File_Type;
    Item  : OUT Num;
    Width : IN Field := 0);

PROCEDURE Get (Item : OUT Num; Width : IN Field := 0);
```

(Field is a subtype of Integer provided by Text_IO, ranging from zero to some implementation-defined upper bound.) The following versions are provided by an instance of Text_IO.Float_IO, where Num is the generic formal floating-point type:

```
PROCEDURE Get
   (File  : IN File_Type;
    Item  : OUT Num;
    Width : IN Field := 0);

PROCEDURE Get (Item : OUT Num; Width : IN Field := 0);
```

Instances of Text_IO.Fixed_IO provide versions of Get declared just like those provided by instances of Text_IO.Float_IO, but where Num is the generic formal fixed-point type.

In each of these cases, the Width parameter can be used to specify the maximum number of characters to be read from the remainder of the current line. This is useful when input data occurs in fixed columns and different data items may occur in adjoining columns. A value of zero for Width specifies that as much of the current line as can be interpreted as a numeric literal optionally preceded by a sign should be so interpreted.

Instances of Integer_IO, Float_IO, and Fixed_IO also provide versions of Get that read characters from a string instead of from an input file:

```
PROCEDURE Get
   (From : IN String; Item : OUT Num; Last : OUT Positive);
```

These versions skip past blanks and tabs, recognize as much of the string as possible as a numeric literal optionally preceded by a plus or minus sign, and set Last to the index of the last character read.

The following versions of Get are provided by instances of Text_IO.Enumeration_IO, where Enum is the generic formal discrete type:

```
PROCEDURE Get (File : IN File_Type; Item : OUT Enum);

PROCEDURE Get (Item : OUT Enum);

PROCEDURE Get
   (From : IN String; Item : OUT Enum; Last : OUT Positive);
```

The version of Get reading an enumeration value from a string works just like its numeric counterparts.

Instances of the generic packages provided by Text_IO also provide versions of Put. All versions of Put for numeric and enumeration types start a new line before writing data if writing the data on the current line would cause the maximum length to be exceeded. (If the data itself contain more than the maximum number of characters, Layout_Error is raised.) There are also versions of Put that write a numeric or enumeration value to a string, or raise Layout_Error if the representation of the value will not fit in the string.

The following versions of Put are provided by instances of Text_IO.Integer_IO:

```
PROCEDURE Put
   (File  : IN File_Type;
    Item  : IN Num;
    Width : IN Field := Default_Width;
    Base  : IN Number_Base := Default_Base);

PROCEDURE Put
   (Item  : IN Num;
    Width : IN Field := Default_Width;
    Base  : IN Number_Base := Default_Base);

PROCEDURE Put
   (To   : OUT String;
    Item : IN Num;
    Base : IN Number_Base := Default_Base);
```

For the first two versions, the value of Width specifies the minimum number of characters that should be written, with spaces written before the numeric value if necessary. If the number of characters specified is less than the number required, the required number of characters are written. Thus a value of zero for Width causes Put to write exactly as many characters as are required. For the third version, the characters are preceded by as many blanks as necessary so that the numeric value appears at the right end of the string. For all three versions, the value of Base indicates whether the literal should be written as an ordinary decimal literal or as a based literal in some other base. (The subtype declaration

```
SUBTYPE Number_Base IS Integer RANGE 2 .. 16;
```

is found in the visible part of the Text_IO package specification.) Default_Width and Default_Base, used as default parameter values, are variables provided by each instance of Text_IO.Integer_IO. Default_Width is initially set to the minimum number of characters needed to represent each value in the generic formal type, with positive values preceded by a space. The initial value of Default_Base is ten.

The following versions of Put are provided by instances of Text_IO.Float_IO:

```
PROCEDURE Put
   (File : IN File_Type;
    Item : IN Num;
    Fore : IN Field := Default_Fore;
    Aft  : IN Field := Default_Aft;
    Exp  : IN Field := Default_Exp);
PROCEDURE Put
   (Item : IN Num;
    Fore : IN Field := Default_Fore;
    Aft  : IN Field := Default_Aft;
    Exp  : IN Field := Default_Exp);
PROCEDURE Put
   (To   : OUT String;
    Item : IN Num;
    Aft  : IN Field := Default_Aft;
    Exp  : IN Field := Default_Exp);
```

For the first two versions, Fore specifies the minimum number of characters to be written before the decimal point, with spaces inserted before the numeric value if necessary. If more than that many characters are required, the required number of characters are written, so that a value of zero causes exactly the required number of characters to be written. For the third version, enough blanks are written before the numeric value so that the numeric value appears at the right end of the string. For all three versions, Aft gives the number of digits to be written after the decimal point. A value of zero for Exp indicates that these digits are not followed by an exponent. If Exp has a value greater than zero, an exponent is chosen so that one digit appears before the decimal point; at least Exp characters, including a plus or minus sign and possibly leading zeroes, appear following the E introducing the exponent. If more than Exp characters are required to write the exponent, exactly the required number of characters are written. The variables Default_Fore, Default_Aft, and Default_Exp, used as default parameter values, are provided by each instance of Float_IO. The initial value of Default_Fore is two, the initial value of Default_Aft is one less than the number of significant digits specified in the floating-point type or subtype declaration for the subtype passed as an actual parameter, and the initial value of Default_Exp is three.

Identically declared versions of Put are provided by instances of Text_IO.Fixed_IO. However, the variables provided by instances of Fixed_IO have different initial values. The initial value of Default_Fore is the number of characters required before the decimal point to represent any value in the fixed-point subtype passed as a generic parameter, with no exponent and with positive values preceded by a space. The initial value of Default_Aft is the number of digits required after the decimal point to represent each value to within the delta of that subtype. The initial value of Default_Exp is zero.

The following versions of Put are provided by instances of Text_IO.Enumeration_IO:

```
PROCEDURE Put
   (File  : IN File_Type;
    Item  : IN Enum;
    Width : IN Field := Default_Width;
    Set   : IN Type_Set := Default_Setting);

PROCEDURE Put
   (Item  : IN Enum;
    Width : IN Field := Default_Width;
    Set   : IN Type_Set := Default_Setting);

PROCEDURE Put
   (To   : OUT String;
    Item : IN Enum;
    Set  : IN Type_Set := Default_Setting);
```

For the first two versions, the Width parameter specifies the minimum number of characters to be written, with extra spaces *following* the enumeration literal if necessary. If more characters are required, the required number of characters are written, so that a value of zero causes exactly the required number of characters to be written. For the third version, the enumeration literal is written starting at the first character of the string, and any remaining places at the right end of the string are filled with blanks. For all three versions, the value of Set determines whether identifier enumeration literals are written in upper case or lower case. (The enumeration-type declaration

```
TYPE Type_Set IS (Lower_Case, Upper_Case);
```

is found in the visible part of the Text_IO package specification.) The variables Default_Width and Default_Setting used as default parameter values are provided by each instance of Enumeration_IO. The initial value of Default_Width is zero, and the initial value of Default_Setting is Upper_Case.

The library generic package Sequential_IO is instantiated with a nonlimited subtype. The resulting instance provides facilities for manipulating files containing data of that subtype. Each instance provides its own type named File_Type; its own type named File_Mode; its own versions of the external file manipulation subprograms Create, Open, Close, Delete, Reset, Is_Open, Name, Form, and Mode; and its own versions of subprograms named Read, Write, and End_Of_File. The external file manipulation programs are declared exactly as the corresponding subprograms in Text_IO and behave in the same way. The other subprograms are declared as follows, where Element_Type is the generic formal type:

```
PROCEDURE Read
   (File : IN File_Type; Item : OUT Element_Type);
PROCEDURE Write
   (File : IN File_Type; Item : IN Element_Type);
FUNCTION End_Of_File (File : File_Type) RETURN Boolean;
```

A call on `Read` obtains the next data item in an input file, a call on `Write` places data at the end of an output file, and the function `End_Of_File` indicates whether all data in an input file has been read.

The library generic package `Direct_IO` is also instantiated with a nonlimited type. Like an instance of `Sequential_IO`, an instance of `Direct_IO` provides its own type named `File_Type`, its own type named `File_Mode`, its own versions of the external file manipulations subprograms `Create`, `Open`, `Close`, `Delete`, `Reset`, `Is_Open`, `Name`, `Form`, and `Mode`, and its own versions of subprograms named `Read`, `Write`, and `End_Of_File`. In this case, the type `File_Mode` has a value `Inout_File` in addition to the values `In_File` and `Out_File`. This value is used as the default file mode in a call on `Create`:

```
PROCEDURE Create
   (File : IN OUT File_Type;
    Mode : IN File_Mode := Inout_File;
    Name : IN String := "";
    Form : IN String := "");
```

Except for this, the external file manipulation subprograms provided by an instance of `Direct_IO` are identical to the external file manipulation subprograms provided by `Text_IO`. An instance of `Direct_IO` also provides an integer type named `Count`, whose first value is zero and whose last value is implementation-defined, and a subtype `Positive_Count` ranging from one to `Count'Last`. Values of subtype `Positive_Count` identify elements in a direct-access file.

The following procedures read from or write to a specific file element, indicated by the third parameter:

```
PROCEDURE Read
   (File : IN File_Type;
    Item : OUT Element_Type;
    From : IN Positive_Count);
PROCEDURE Write
   (File : IN File_Type;
    Item : IN Element_Type;
    To   : IN Positive_Count);
```

In addition, a *current index* is maintained for each open file, and versions of `Read` and `Write` declared as

```
PROCEDURE Read
   (File : IN File_Type; Item : OUT Element_Type);
PROCEDURE Write
   (File : IN File_Type; Item : IN Element_Type);
```

operate on the file element at the current index. The current index is set to one when a file is opened or reset, automatically incremented by a call on any version of `Read` or `Write`, and set explicitly by calls on the following procedure:

```
PROCEDURE Set_Index
   (File : IN File_Type; To : Positive_Count);
```

The following function returns a file's current index:

```
FUNCTION Index (File : File_Type) RETURN Positive_Count;
```

The function

```
FUNCTION End_Of_File (File : File_Type) RETURN Boolean;
```

returns `True` when the current index is higher than the number of elements in a file. The two-parameter versions of `Read` and `Write` and the function `End_Of_File` can be used to manipulate direct-access files as if they were sequential files. Finally, the following function returns the number of elements currently in a direct-access file:

```
FUNCTION Size (File : IN File_Type) RETURN Count;
```

EXERCISES

17.1 What does the following program do when one of the calls on `Get` raises `Text_IO.Data_Error`?

```
WITH Text_IO, Sequential_IO; USE Text_IO;

PROCEDURE Copy_Within_Limits IS

   PACKAGE Sequential_Integer_IO IS
      NEW Sequential_IO (Positive);

   PACKAGE Type_Integer_IO IS
      NEW Integer_IO (Integer);
   USE Sequential_Integer_IO, Type_Integer_IO;

   Lower_Limit, Higher_Limit, Item : Positive;

   Input_File, Output_File :
      Sequential_Integer_IO.File_Type;

BEGIN

   Get (Lower_Limit);
   Get (Higher_Limit);
   Open (Input_File, In_File, "NUMBERS.DAT");
   Create (Output_File, Out_File, "INRANGE.DAT");

   WHILE NOT End_Of_File (Input_File) LOOP
      Read (Input_File, Item);
      IF Item IN Lower_Limit .. Higher_Limit THEN
         Write (Output_File, Item);
      END IF;
   END LOOP;
```

```
      Close (Input_File);
      Close (Output_File);

   EXCEPTION

      WHEN Sequential_Integer_IO.Data_Error =>
         Put_Line ("Invalid input data.");

      WHEN OTHERS =>
         Put_Line ("Internal error. Execution terminated");

   END Copy_Within_Limits;
```

17.2 You are given an unsorted record-oriented sequential file containing items of type `Code_Type`. `Code_Type` is declared as follows:

```
   TYPE Code_Type IS ARRAY (1 .. 3) OF Integer RANGE 1 .. 5;
```

The following technique, known as *radix sorting,* will produce a file containing the same items in lexicographic order:

1. Read the input file, copying each `Code_Type` value read to one of five different files, depending on the value in the *third* component.
2. Read these five files in order (first the file containing only `1`'s in the third component, then the file containing only `2`'s in the third component, and so on). Copy each `Code_Type` value read to one of five other files, depending on the value in the *second* component. (Because of the order in which the five input files are read, the output file containing the items with a second component of `3`, for example, will have all items with a second component of `3` and a third component of `1` occurring before all items with a second component of `3` and a third component of `2`.)
3. Repeat step 2, using the files produced in step 3 as input and looking at the first component of each item instead of the second. (Now the output file containing the items with a first component of `3`, for example, will have all items sorted lexicographically according to the second and third components.)
4. Copy the five files produced by step 3 to the output file, in order (first the file containing only `1`'s in the first component, then the file containing only `2`'s in the first component, and so on.)

Implement this algorithm in the Ada language.

17.3 Rewrite the program `Round` (given in Section 17.4.2) without `USE` clauses. Write expanded names to identify the entities provided by `Text_IO`, by `Real_Type_IO`, and by `Whole_Type_IO`.

17.4 Fix the function `File_Sum` given in Section 17.4.2.1 so that it works even when the last integer literal in the input file is followed by spaces, tabs, or empty lines.

17.5 Write a program that reads an integer *n* from the standard input file and writes *n* lines of the following form on the standard output file:

```
   Two raised to the power 1  is 2.
   Two raised to the power 2  is 4.
   Two raised to the power 3  is 8.
   Two raised to the power 4  is 16.
   Two raised to the power 5  is 32.
   Two raised to the power 6  is 64.
   Two raised to the power 7  is 128.
   Two raised to the power 8  is 256.
   Two raised to the power 9  is 512.
   Two raised to the power 10 is 1024.
```

Be sure that no extraneous spaces appear in the output.

17.6 Modify the the program produced in the previous exercise to produce its output in the following form:

```
Two raised to the power  1 is    2.
Two raised to the power  2 is    4.
Two raised to the power  3 is    8.
Two raised to the power  4 is   16.
Two raised to the power  5 is   32.
Two raised to the power  6 is   64.
Two raised to the power  7 is  128.
Two raised to the power  8 is  256.
Two raised to the power  9 is  512.
Two raised to the power 10 is 1024.
```

The numbers in the last line should each be preceded by exactly one space, and the numbers in the previous lines should be aligned accordingly.

17.7 Consider the following declarations and instantiations:

```
TYPE Item_Count_Type IS RANGE 0 .. 5000;
TYPE Distance_Type IS DIGITS 5;
TYPE Degrees_Type IS DELTA 0.01 RANGE -50.0 .. 100.0;
TYPE Setting_Type IS (Low, Normal, High);

PACKAGE Item_Count_IO IS NEW Integer_IO (Item_Count_Type);
PACKAGE Distance_IO IS NEW Float_IO (Distance_Type);
PACKAGE Degrees_IO IS NEW Fixed_IO (Degrees_Type);
PACKAGE Setting_IO IS NEW Enumeration_IO (Setting_Type);
```

Indicate the output produced by each of the following calls on `Put`, assuming that the variables provided by `Item_Count_IO`, `Distance_IO`, `Degrees_IO`, and `Setting_IO` have not been changed. Indicate explicitly all spaces produced by the calls on `Put`.

```
(a) Item_Count_IO.Put (16);
(b) Item_Count_IO.Put (16, Width => 3);
(c) Item_Count_IO.Put (16, Width => 1);
(d) Item_Count_IO.Put (16, Base => 16);
(e) Item_Count_IO.Put (16, Width => 10, Base => 16);
(f) Distance_IO.Put (123.4567);
(g) Distance_IO.Put (123.4567, Fore => 5);
(h) Distance_IO.Put (123.4567, Aft => 3);
(i) Distance_IO.Put (123.4567, Exp => 2);
(j) Distance_IO.Put (123.4567, Exp => 0);
(k) Distance_IO.Put (123.4567, Fore => 5, Exp => 0);
(l) Degrees_IO.Put (50.0625);
(m) Degrees_IO.Put (50.0625, Fore => 5);
(n) Degrees_IO.Put (50.0625, Aft => 1);
(o) Degrees_IO.Put (50.0625, Exp => 4);
(p) Setting_IO.Put (High);
(q) Setting_IO.Put (High, Width => 3);
(r) Setting_IO.Put (High, Width => 10);
(s) Setting_IO.Put (High, Set => Upper_Case);
```

17.8 An input file contains lines of the following form:

Columns 1-20: Student name
Column 21: Student's year (1-4)
Column 22: Number of items graded (0-5)
Columns 23-25: Grade (if column 22 $\geq$ 1) for item #1 (0-100)
Columns 26-28: Grade (if column 22 $\geq$ 2) for item #2 (0-100)
Columns 29-31: Grade (if column 22 $\geq$ 3) for item #3 (0-100)
Columns 32-34: Grade (if column 22 $\geq$ 4) for item #4 (0-100)
Columns 35-37: Grade (if column 22 = 5) for item #5 (0-100)
Columns 40-80: Remarks

Write a program that reads this data from the file `CLASS.DAT` and writes a report of the following form to the standard output file:

Columns 27- 46: Student name
Columns 48- 56: Student's year (`FRESHMAN`, `SOPHOMORE`, `JUNIOR`, `SENIOR`)
Column 58: Number of items graded
Columns 60- 64: Average grade (in the form `99.99`)
Columns 67-107: Remarks

The output file should contain one line for each line in the input file, but no more than sixty lines per page. Each page should begin with a line giving the page number, followed by a blank line.

17.9 Write a package `Hexadecimal_Package` providing a function `Decimal_Equivalent` and an exception `Hexadecimal_Error`. The function should take a string containing a hexadecimal numeral as a parameter and return a string containing the corresponding decimal numeral (without leading spaces, leading zeroes, or underscores) as a result. The function should raise `Hexadecimal_Error` if the actual parameter is more than eight characters long or does not contain a valid hexadecimal numeral. Implement the function in such a way that almost all its work is performed by versions of `Get` and `Put` reading from and writing to strings.

17.10 Write a program that takes two sorted sequential record-oriented files of integers, `IN1.DAT` and `IN2.DAT`, and merges them to produce a new sorted file, `OUT.DAT`.

17.11 Rewrite the subunit `Print_Report` (given in Section 17.6) without `USE` clauses. Write expanded names to identify the entities provided by `Inventory_Record_IO`, by `Text_IO`, by `Type_Integer_IO`, and by `Count_IO`.

17.12 Write a program to create and load the data base used by `Inventory_Package` in Section 17.6. Assume that the data to be loaded is in a 1000-line text file `INVNTRY.DAT`, with each line containing an item description in columns one through thirty and an initial stock starting in column 31. Inventory numbers are to be assigned to items in order of appearance in this file.

CHAPTER

EIGHTEEN

INTRODUCTION TO TASKS

18.1 CONCURRENCY

The programs that we have seen up to this point specify a sequence of actions to be performed one after the other. In this chapter and the next, we consider programs that specify two or more sequences of actions to be performed *concurrently*. Each sequence of actions is performed by a *task*. The programs in earlier chapters each consist of a single task that executes the main procedure. In a program consisting of several tasks, each task performs actions in strict sequence but several tasks may be in progress at the same time. This chapter introduces the basic concepts and language features used in multitask programs. Chapter 19 explains the use of more advanced language features that provide flexible control over the way tasks interact.

Typically, a computer running a multitask program spends a little bit of time executing one task, switches its attention to other tasks, and eventually picks up where it left off on the original task. This is called *interleaved concurrency*. In environments with more than one processor, different processors may actually execute different tasks at the same time. This is called *overlapped concurrency*. The actual implementation of concurrency is hidden from the programmer. Just as a television picture tube displays individual lines in rapid sequence but *appears* to display an entire picture at once, so interleaved concurrency creates the *illusion* that all tasks in progress are running simultaneously. Regardless of how concurrency is actually achieved, a programmer can *imagine* that there is a separate processor running each task. Such an imaginary processor is called a *virtual processor*.

There are many reasons for writing multitask programs. The Ada language was designed for programs managing several concurrent activities—monitoring several sensors and controlling several motors, for example. Such programs are most easily written with one task managing each activity. Multitask programs are also useful for simulations. A simulation is a program that models some aspect of the real world, based on the assumption that entities in the real world behave according to certain rules. One task can be designed in accordance with the rules of each entity modeled. There are some problems that may not at first appear to involve concurrency, but that can be solved most simply by decomposing the solution into two or more concurrent activities producing and consuming streams of data. Such a problem will be presented in Section 18.4.2.

Another reason for writing multitask programs is to allow programs to finish more quickly. If concurrency is overlapped, a computation can be made to finish sooner by allowing parts that do not depend on each other to execute simultaneously on different processors. Even if concurrency is interleaved, decomposing a computation into tasks can allow work to proceed while one part of the computation is waiting for some external event such as the completion of an input operation.

Depending on how concurrency is implemented, different virtual processors may appear to execute at different, possibly varying speeds. Ordinarily, no assumptions can be made about the relative progress of one task with respect to another. We say that tasks are *asynchronous*. For tasks to work cooperatively, they must be able to *synchronize* on occasion. Synchronization forces two tasks to be at corresponding points, called *synchronization points,* at the same time. If one task arrives at its synchronization point before the other, it pauses until the other task catches up. Tasks synchronize and communicate through *rendezvous,* which are introduced in Section 18.3.

Sequences of statements in Ada programs are *reentrant*. This means that several tasks may execute the same sequence of statements at the same time. This is analogous to several people sharing the same instruction booklet while filling out their tax returns. The key to sharing the booklet is that each person follows its instructions by filling out his own copy of the tax return. If calculations were to be performed in the instruction booklet rather than on the tax returns, the booklet could not easily be shared. Similarly, different tasks executing the same statements can be given exclusive copies of the variables manipulated by those statements. For example, the statement `x := x + 1;` could be executed by several tasks each having its own copy of the variable `x`. None of these tasks need be affected by the others.

Concurrent programming is more difficult than sequential programming. There are many pitfalls for the unwary programmer. One danger is that a program may depend subtly on the relative speeds of different tasks. This happens, for example, when several tasks examine and then update a single variable. Another danger is *deadlock*. Deadlock arises when no task can proceed because each task is waiting for some action that can only be performed by another waiting task. Debugging a concurrent program can be agonizing because certain errors may depend on the timing of different tasks. The timing of tasks can vary from one execution of the program to another, so such errors might not be reproducible. The Ada features described in this chapter tend to make concurrent programming less difficult and less error-prone, but they are far from foolproof.

18.2 TASK OBJECTS AND TASK TYPES

We have already described a task as an entity that performs a sequence of actions. In the Ada language, each task corresponds to a data object, called a *task object*. Associated with each task object is a sequence of statements to be executed, a task to execute them, a set of variables for use only by this task, and an interface for synchronization and communication with other tasks.

Like other data objects, task objects belong to types, in this case *task types*. All the task objects in the same task type share certain characteristics:

Their tasks independently execute the same sequence of statements.
Their variables are described by the same declarations, although each task object has its own copy of these variables.
They have the same interface for communication with other tasks.

Task types are limited. That is, task objects cannot be copied or tested for equality. (Limited types were introduced in Section 12.6.) A task type can be used in the same way as any limited type. For example, if `Sensor_Handler_Type` is a task type, then the object declaration

```
Sensor_Handler_1, Sensor_Handler_2 : Sensor_Handler_Type;
```

declares `Sensor_Handler_1` and `Sensor_Handler_2` to be task objects. Task types can also be used to declare other types:

```
TYPE Sensor_Handler_List_Type IS
   ARRAY (1 .. 10) OF Sensor_Handler_Type;

TYPE Sensor_Handler_Pointer_Type IS
   ACCESS Sensor_Handler_Type;
```

`Sensor_Handler_Pointer_Type` values point to task objects created by allocators:

```
Active_Sensor :
   Sensor_Handler_Pointer_Type :=
      NEW Sensor_Handler_Type;
```

Each `Sensor_Handler_Type` object might be a task controlling a different temperature sensor, for example. All of these tasks asynchronously execute the same sensor interface routine, possibly for different sensors. Each maintains its own copy of the variables used by that routine (e.g., a variable containing the time at which the sensor should next be read). If there were ten sensors to be monitored, a `Sensor_Handler_List_Type` object could contain one component task for each sensor. These tasks could be named as indexed components of a `Sensor_Handler_List_Type` array. (As explained in Section 12.6, an array or record type is limited if it has a limited component type, so `Sensor_Handler_List_Type` is limited. In contrast,

Sensor_Handler_Pointer_Type is not limited. A pointer to some Sensor_Handler_Type object can be assigned to Active_Sensor, for example, and two Sensor_Handler_Pointer_Type values are equal if and only if they point to the same allocated task object.)

Like any other type, a task type has a set of operations associated with it. The principal operations on a task type involve communication and synchronization with the type's tasks. Task objects have *entries,* which are entities resembling procedures. One task can interact with another by *calling* one of the other task's entries in much the same way as it would call a procedure. Like procedures, entries have parameters, and each parameter is characterized by its name, its mode, its subtype, and possibly its default value. If Sensor_Handler_1 is a task object with entry Get_Temperature, then a call on this entry with actual parameter Reading is written as follows:

```
Sensor_Handler_1.Get_Temperature (Reading);
```

Task objects in the same task type have identical entries, with identical parameters. Thus the same operations (e.g., calling a Sensor_Handler_Type object's Get_Temperature entry) apply to all objects in the type. Section 18.3 explains entries and entry calls in greater detail.

Tasks types are not defined in the same way as other types. Two steps are required—a *task-type declaration* and a *task body.* The task-type declaration specifies the entries that may be called by other tasks. The task body contains the statements executed by tasks in the task type and the declarations of entities used in those statements. The task-type declaration and task body together are called a *task unit.*

The typical form of a task-type declaration is:

```
TASK TYPE identifier IS
    entry declaration
        ~~~
    entry declaration
END identifier ;
```

The identifier at the end of a task-type declaration must match the identifier at the beginning. Entry declarations are similar to procedure declarations, but the word PROCEDURE is replaced by the word ENTRY:

```
ENTRY identifier [ ( parameter specification ; ~~~ ; parameter specification ) ] ;
```

Parameter specifications of entries follow the same rules as those given in Section 9.1 for parameter specifications of procedures. Here is an example of a task-type declaration:

```
TASK TYPE Position_Type IS
   ENTRY Initialize (x, y : IN Float := 0.0);
   ENTRY Change
      (Delta_X, Delta_Y : IN Float;
       New_X, New_Y     : OUT Float);
END Position_Type;
```

There is a more succinct form of task-type declaration available for task types with no entries:

TASK TYPE *identifier* **;**

A task body looks like a subprogram body, except for the heading:

TASK BODY *identifier* **IS**

declarative part

BEGIN

sequence of statements

EXCEPTION

handler

~~~

handler

END *identifier* **;**

The identifier at the beginning of the task body and the identifier at the end must both be identical to the identifier given in the task-type declaration.

Some time after a task object is created—either by an object declaration or the evaluation of an allocator—the declarative part of the task body is elaborated and the sequence of statements is executed concurrently with other tasks. Any variables created during elaboration of the task body's declarative part belong to that task object alone. If another object in the same task type is created later, the declarative part is elaborated again and new variables are created for the new task according to the same declarations. The new task concurrently executes the same sequence of statements using its own copy of the variables.

A task body may contain statements that are not allowed elsewhere. We shall explain these statements later. Here is a task body corresponding to the declaration of `Position_Type`:
~~~

```
TASK BODY Position_Type IS
   Current_X, Current_Y : Float;

BEGIN
   ACCEPT Initialize (x, y : IN Float := 0.0) DO
      Current_X := x;
      Current_Y := y;
   END Initialize;

   LOOP

      SELECT

         ACCEPT Initialize (x, y : IN Float := 0.0) DO

            Current_X := x;
            Current_Y := y;

         END Initialize;

      OR

         ACCEPT Change
            (Delta_X, Delta_Y : IN Float;
             New_X, New_Y     : OUT Float) DO

            Current_X := Current_X + Delta_X;
            Current_Y := Current_Y + Delta_Y;
            New_X := Current_X;
            New_Y := Current_Y;

         END Change;

      OR

         TERMINATE;

      END SELECT;

   END LOOP;

END Position_Type;
```

Task-type declarations and task bodies can go in the declarative part of a subprogram body, package body, block statement, or outer task body. The task-type declaration must be given first. A task-type name may be used in other declarations any place after the task-type declaration, even before the body. Task-type declarations are basic declarations and task bodies are later declarations, so no basic declarations may follow the task body. (Basic declarations and later declarations were discussed in Section 9.1.) Here is one context in which the declaration and body of `Position_Type` might occur:

```
PROCEDURE Track_Aircraft IS
   TASK TYPE Position_Type IS
      ENTRY Initialize (x, y : IN Float := 0.0);
      ENTRY Change
         (Delta_X, Delta_Y : IN Float;
          New_X, New_Y     : OUT Float);
   END Position_Type;
   TYPE Position_Pointer_Type IS ACCESS Position_Type;
   Next_Position : Position_Type;
      ...
   TASK BODY Position_Type IS
      ...
   BEGIN
      ...
   END Position_Type;
BEGIN
   ...
END Track_Aircraft;
```

More typically, a task type is provided by a package. In this case, the task-type declaration goes in the package specification, and the task body goes in the package body:

```
PACKAGE Position_Task_Package IS
   TASK TYPE Position_Type IS
      ENTRY Initialize (x, y : IN Float := 0.0);
      ENTRY Change
         (Delta_X, Delta_Y : IN Float;
          New_X, New_Y     : OUT Float);
   END Position_Type;
END Position_Task_Package;

PACKAGE BODY Position_Task_Package IS
   TASK BODY Position_Type IS
      ...
   BEGIN
      ...
   END Position_Type;
END Position_Task_Package;
```

A limited private type may be declared in the private part of the package specification as a task type:

```
PACKAGE Position_Package IS

   TYPE Position_Type IS LIMITED PRIVATE;

   PROCEDURE Set_Position
      (Position : IN OUT Position_Type; x, y : IN Float);

   PROCEDURE Change_Position
      (Position           : IN OUT Position_Type;
       Delta_X, Delta_Y : IN Float;
       New_X, New_Y       : OUT Float);

PRIVATE

   TASK TYPE Position_Type IS
      ENTRY Initialize (x, y : IN Float := 0.0);
      ENTRY Change
         (Delta_X, Delta_Y : IN Float;
          New_X, New_Y       : OUT Float);
   END Position_Type;

END Position_Package;

PACKAGE BODY Position_Package IS

   TASK BODY Position_Type IS
      ...
   BEGIN
      ...
   END Position_Type;

   PROCEDURE Set_Position
      (Position : IN OUT Position_Type; x, y : IN Float) IS
   BEGIN
      Position.Initialize (x, y);
   END Set_Position;

   PROCEDURE Change_Position
      (Position           : IN OUT Position_Type;
       Delta_X, Delta_Y : IN Float;
       New_X, New_Y       : OUT Float) IS
   BEGIN
      Position.Change (Delta_X, Delta_Y, New_X, New_Y);
   END Change_Position;

END Position_Package;
```

In the private part of the Position_Package declaration, the task-type declaration plays the role of the full type declaration that must accompany any private or limited private-type declaration. Because the full type declaration is for a limited type—all task types are limited—the private-type declaration is required to be for a limited private type. From outside Position_Package, Position_Type is simply a limited private type with operations Set_Position and Change_Position. Looking inside Position_Package's private part and body, we see that Position_Type is implemented as a task type, and operations on a Position_Type object work by calling one of that object's entries. (Strictly speaking, the Position parameter of procedure Set_Position could have had mode IN. We use mode IN OUT anyway to convey the abstract view that a call on Set_Position changes the state of the Position_Type object passed to it.)

A task body occurring in the declarative part of a compilation unit may be replaced by a body stub of the form

```
TASK BODY identifier IS SEPARATE ;
```

and compiled separately as a subunit. (Body stubs and subunits were explained in Section 13.3.) The procedure Track_Aircraft given earlier could have been written in the following way:

```
-- Compilation unit 1:
PROCEDURE Track_Aircraft IS

   TASK TYPE Position_Type IS
      ENTRY Initialize (x, y : IN Float := 0.0);
      ENTRY Change
         (Delta_X, Delta_Y : IN Float;
          New_X, New_Y     : OUT Float);
   END Position_Type;

   TYPE Position_Pointer_Type IS ACCESS Position_Type;
   Next_Position : Position_Type;
      ...
   TASK BODY Position_Type IS SEPARATE;
BEGIN
   ...
END Track_Aircraft;

-- Compilation unit 2:
SEPARATE (Track_Aircraft)
TASK BODY Position_Type IS
   ...
BEGIN
   ...
END Position_Type;
```

Task units are one of the four kinds of *program units* in the Ada language. The others are subprograms, packages, and generic units. Each kind of program unit consists of two parts—a declaration (or specification) giving the external view of the program unit and a body giving the implementation. (See Figure 18.1.) In each case, the external view may appear in a declarative part, followed by the implementation later in the same declarative part. (The external view of a subprogram may be omitted in this context.) Alternatively, the external view may appear in a package specification, with the implementation appearing in a package body.

There is one major difference between task units and other kinds of program units. For the other kinds of task units, the external view and implementation may be separately compiled, with the external view becoming a library unit. Task-type declarations may *not* be compiled separately as library units. Task bodies may be compiled separately only as subunits. Similarly, there are no generic task units—only generic packages and subprograms.

The effect of a separately compiled task-type declaration and a corresponding separately compiled body can be achieved by enclosing the task-type declaration in a library package specification and the task body in the corresponding package body. The result is a package like `Position_Task_Package` on page 671, providing only a task type. The effect of a generic task unit can be achieved by enclosing a task unit in a generic package in the same way.

Section 4.2.6 presented a shorthand for one-of-a-kind arrays. One-of-a-kind task objects also arise frequently, so a similar shorthand exists for them. In the case of arrays, an object declaration like

```
Item_Pair : ARRAY (1 .. 2) OF Item_Type;
```

declares `Item_Pair` to be the only object in an *anonymous array type*. It is equivalent to the declarations

```
TYPE Item_Pair_Type IS ARRAY (1 .. 2) OF Item_Type;
Item_Pair : Item_Pair_Type;
```

assuming that the identifier `Item_Pair_Type` is not used elsewhere. In the case of tasks, a declaration like

```
TASK Joystick_Task IS
   ENTRY Get_Coordinates
      (Player : IN Player_ID_Type;
      (x, y   : OUT Coordinate_Type);
END Joystick_Task;
```

—in which the word `TASK` is not followed by the word `TYPE`—is equivalent to the two declarations

	SUBPROGRAMS	PACKAGES	GENERIC UNITS	TASK UNITS
EXTERNAL VIEW	subprogram declaration	package declaration	generic subprogram or generic package declaration	task-type declaration
IMPLEMENTATION	subprogram body	package body	subprogram or package body	task body

Figure 18.1 Comparison of task units and the other three kinds of program units—subprograms, packages, and generic units.

```
TASK TYPE Joystick_Task_Type IS
   ENTRY Get_Coordinates
      (Player : IN Player_ID_Type;
      (x, y   : OUT Coordinate_Type);
END Joystick_Task_Type;
Joystick_Task : Joystick_Task_Type;
```

assuming that the identifier `Joystick_Task_Type` is not used elsewhere. `Joystick_Task` belongs to an *anonymous task type* and is the only object in that type. A task object that belongs to an anonymous task type is sometimes called a *single task*. Its declaration is called a *task declaration*. The only syntactic difference between a task declaration and a task-type declaration is the absence of the word `TYPE`. Single task declarations occur in the same contexts as task-type declarations and must be accompanied by task bodies. There is a further shorthand for declaring a single task with no entries:

TASK *identifier* ;

(The task `Joystick_Task` is part of a simple video Ping-Pong game to which we will return in this chapter and the next to illustrate multitasking. Besides this task, which handles input from two joysticks, the program has a task type with two task objects, one to handle each racquet; a task to handle the Ping-Pong ball; and a task to manage the video display.)

18.3 ELEMENTARY RENDEZVOUS

A task can communicate with another task by *calling* another task's entry or by *accepting* a call on one of its own entries. When one task calls an entry of a second task and the second task accepts that call, a *rendezvous* takes place. Rendezvous are the principal means by which tasks communicate and synchronize. This section describes the simplest form of rendezvous. More flexible and powerful forms of rendezvous are described in Chapter 19.

As we have seen, a task calls an entry of another task by an entry call statement, which closely resembles a procedure call statement. Section 18.3.1 examines entry calls more closely. A task accepts an entry call by executing an ACCEPT statement. ACCEPT statements are described in Section 18.3.2.

When two people rendezvous, the first to arrive at the appointed place waits for the other. A simple rendezvous between two Ada tasks works in the same way. If one task calls an entry of a second task before the second task reaches an ACCEPT statement for that entry, the first task waits for the second task to reach such an ACCEPT statement. If a task reaches an ACCEPT statement for some entry before another task calls that entry, the task waits for the entry to be called. Once a task's entry has been called and the task has reached an ACCEPT statement for that entry, the ACCEPT statement is executed while the calling task waits. When execution of the ACCEPT statement is complete, the entry call is over and each task resumes independent asynchronous execution.

It is possible for several tasks to call the same entry before any of the calls is accepted. When this happens, the entry calls are *queued* and accepted on a first-come-first-served basis. While a call is queued, the task that issued that call waits at its entry call statement.

18.3.1 Entry Calls

The syntax of procedure calls was given in Section 9.3. Entry calls follow the same syntax, except that the name of a procedure is replaced by the name of an entry. The entry declarations in a task-type declaration specify names, modes, types, and possibly initial values for each of the entry's *formal parameters.* Like procedure calls, entry calls may be positional, named, or mixed. Actual parameters of mode IN OUT or OUT must be variables. Types of corresponding actual and formal parameters must match. An actual parameter may be omitted for a mode IN formal parameter with a default value expression.

Different objects in the same task type have entries denoted by the same identifier, but these entries are distinct entities. Therefore, an *entry name* includes both the name of a task object and an identifier denoting one of that task object's entries. Given the task-type declaration

```
TASK TYPE Racquet_Task_Type IS
   ENTRY Grant_ID (ID : IN Player_ID_Type);
   ENTRY Connect_Racquet;
   ENTRY Disconnect_Racquet;
   ENTRY Get_Racquet_Position (Position : OUT Game_Y_Type);
END Racquet_Task_Type;
```

all objects in Racquet_Task_Type will have entries denoted Grant_ID, Connect_Racquet, Disconnect_Racquet, and Get_Racquet_Position. Given the task-object declarations

```
Racquet_1, Racquet_2 : Racquet_Task_Type;
```

(declaring one task to handle each racquet in the Ping-Pong video game) the expanded name `Racquet_1.Grant_ID` names the `Grant_ID` entry of `Racquet_1`, and the expanded name `Racquet_2.Grant_ID` names the `Grant_ID` entry of `Racquet_2`. A call on the first of these entries might be written as follows:

```
Racquet_1.Grant_ID (ID => 1)
```

In general, if *t* is a declared task object with entry *e*, then outside of *t*'s own task body that entry can only be named by an expanded named of the form *t.e*. Similarly, if *a* is an access value pointing to an allocated task object, then the name *a.e* names entry *e* of task *a*`.ALL`. An entry call always specifies a particular task whose entry is to be called.

An entry may be renamed *as a procedure* by a renaming declaration of the form

```
PROCEDURE identifier [ ( parameter specification ; ~~~ ; parameter specification ) ]
   RENAMES entry name ;
```

For example, given the renaming declaration

```
PROCEDURE Get_Racquet_1_Position
   (Position_1 : OUT Game_Y_Type)
   RENAMES Racquet_1.Get_Racquet_Position ;
```

the procedure call

```
Get_Racquet_1_Position (Position_1 => p);
```

has the same effect as the entry call

```
Racquet_1.Get_Racquet_Position (Position => p);
```

The renaming declaration may specify new parameter names (as in this example) and new default values.

Procedure names created by renaming entries may overload other subprograms and enumeration literals. Similarly, a task type may have two entries denoted by the same identifier, provided that the entries have different parameter and result type profiles. In either case, overloading is resolved by the usual rules. (See Sections 9.5 and 9.8.3.)

18.3.2 ACCEPT Statements

An `ACCEPT` statement plays a role in an entry call similar to the role played by a procedure body in a procedure call. The crucial difference is that the `ACCEPT` statement occurs as part of the called task's sequence of statements and may only be executed when the called task gets to it. A task body may contain several ACCEPT statements for the same entry. The one executed during a given rendezvous is the one that the called task has reached.

18.3.2.1 ACCEPT statement parameters. The formal parameters specified in an entry declaration are also formal parameters of all ACCEPT statements for that entry. For example, consider the following single-task declaration:

```
TASK Joystick_Task IS
   ENTRY Get_Coordinates
      (Player : IN Player_ID_Type; x, y : OUT Coordinate_Type);
END Joystick_Task;
```

(This task handles the joysticks in the Ping-Pong video game. The hardware interface is such that a single input operation provides data from both sticks. A call on Joystick_Task.Get_Coordinates obtains x and y coordinates of a specified player's joystick. Player_ID_Type is an integer type ranging from one to two, and Coordinate_Type is a fixed-point type ranging from -1.0 to 1.0.) An ACCEPT statement in the Joystick_Task body might look like this:

```
ACCEPT Get_Coordinates
   (Player : IN Player_ID_Type;
    x, y   : OUT Coordinate_Type) DO
   x := Stick_Position_List (Player).X_Part;
   y := Stick_Position_List (Player).Y_Part;
END Get_Coordinates;
```

If this statement accepted the entry call

```
Joystick_Task.Get_Coordinates (1, x1, y1);
```

the following would occur:

The value one would be copied into the formal parameter Player.
The two assignment statements inside the ACCEPT statement would be executed.
The value left in the formal parameter x would be copied back into the actual parameter x1, and the value left in the formal parameter y would be copied back into the actual parameter y1.

The rendezvous would then be complete, and the calling task and Joystick_Task would go their separate ways.

18.3.2.2 The usual form of an ACCEPT statement. The usual form of the ACCEPT statement is as follows:

```
ACCEPT identifier
   ( parameter specification ; ~~~ ; parameter specification ) DO
   sequence of statements
END identifier ;
```

(Parameter specifications are described in Section 9.1.) The ACCEPT statement can only appear inside a task body, and the identifier following the word ACCEPT must denote one of the entries declared in the corresponding task-type declaration. The identifier following the word END must be identical.

From the point of view of a called task, a rendezvous consists of the execution of an ACCEPT statement. First, if the entry has any parameters of mode IN or IN OUT, the values of the corresponding actual parameters in the entry call are copied in to them. Second, the sequence of statements is executed. Third, if the entry has any parameters of mode IN OUT or OUT, their values are copied back into the actual parameters in the entry call.

Since the calling task is unable to proceed until execution of the ACCEPT statement is complete, the sequence of statements in the ACCEPT statement should be kept as short as possible. Any actions that could be performed just after the ACCEPT statement rather than inside it should be moved outside of the ACCEPT statement. For example, after delivering joystick positions in one call on Get_Coordinates, Joystick_Task might immediately call a procedure Read_Joysticks to obtain new data in preparation for the next call. The ACCEPT statement

```
ACCEPT Get_Coordinates
   (Player : IN Player_ID_Type;
    x, y   : OUT Coordinate_Type) DO
   x := Stick_Position_List (Player).X_Part;
   y := Stick_Position_List (Player).Y_Part;
   Read_Joysticks (Stick_Position_List);
END Get_Coordinates;
```

would be better written as follows:

```
ACCEPT Get_Coordinates
   (Player : IN Player_ID_Type;
    x, y   : OUT Coordinate_Type) DO
   x := Stick_Position_List (Player).X_Part;
   y := Stick_Position_List (Player).Y_Part;
END Get_Coordinates;
Read_Joysticks (Stick_Position_List);
```

The call on `Read_Joysticks` may trigger a long input operation entailing idle waiting. By ending the rendezvous before calling `Read_Joysticks`, we allow the calling task to move on while `Joystick_Task` waits for the input operation to finish.

18.3.2.3 `ACCEPT` statements without "bodies." Sometimes rendezvous are used simply to synchronize tasks, not to pass data between them. An `ACCEPT` statement can be used to force a task to wait at a certain point until some other task signals it by calling the corresponding entry. Alternatively, an entry call can be used to make a calling task wait at a certain point until another task accepts the entry call and allows the calling task to move on.

An `ACCEPT` statement of the form

```
ACCEPT identifier ;
```

can be used when a rendezvous is used only for synchronization. It is equivalent to an `ACCEPT` statement of the form

```
ACCEPT identifier DO
   NULL;
END identifier ;
```

The effect of executing such an `ACCEPT` statement is simply to allow the calling task and the called task to move on. For example, the following task repeatedly examines a button until it is found to be pressed and then accepts a call on its `Wait_For_Button_Press` entry:

```
TASK Button_Task IS
   ENTRY Wait_For_Button_Press;
END Button_Task;

TASK BODY Button_Task IS
   Pressed : Boolean;
BEGIN
   LOOP
      LOOP
         Read_Button (Pressed);
         EXIT WHEN Pressed;
         DELAY 0.5;
      END LOOP;
      ACCEPT Wait_For_Button_Press;
   END LOOP;
END Button_Task;
```

(It is assumed that the procedure Read_Button performs a low-level input operation to obtain the current status of the button, setting its parameter to True if the button was pressed and to False otherwise.) The entry call

```
Button_Task.Wait_For_Button_Press;
```

has the effect of making the calling task wait until the button has been pressed.

18.3.2.4 Restrictions on the placement of ACCEPT statements. An ACCEPT statement for a given task's entry may only occur within the sequence of statements of the corresponding task body *b*. It may not occur inside the body of a subprogram, package, or other task unit nested inside *b*. In other words, the only parts of a task's algorithm that can be broken off into subprograms are parts that do not contain ACCEPT statements.

18.4 PUTTING IT ALL TOGETHER

We shall now step back and look at the broader context in which rendezvous occur. We shall consider two large examples. The first is a simplified version of part of the Ping-Pong video game—a real-time application. The second is a text reformatting problem which, at first glance, seems not to call for a concurrent solution.

18.4.1 A Real-Time Example

First, let's consider simplified versions of the video game task units Racquet_Task_Type and Joystick_Task. Each Racquet_Task_Type task repeatedly calls Joystick_Task.Get_Coordinates to determine the current position of a racquet, based on the Y-coordinate of the corresponding joystick. The racquets are assumed to move along the ends of the table (i.e., vertically along the left and right edges of the screen), so the X-coordinates of the joysticks can be ignored. Upon determining the position of its racquet, a Racquet_Task_Type task calls Screen_Task.Erase_Racquet and Screen_Task.Display_Racquet to move the racquet to the appropriate place on the screen. Screen_Task is provided by the package Screen_Package. Joystick_Task is provided by the following package:

```
WITH Global_Types_Package;

PACKAGE Joystick_Package IS

        SUBTYPE Player_ID_Type IS
           Global_Types_Package.Player_ID_Type;

        TYPE Coordinate_Type IS DELTA 0.01 RANGE -1.0 .. 1.0;
```

```
      TASK Joystick_Task IS
         ENTRY Get_Coordinates
            (Player : IN Player_ID_Type;
             x, y   : OUT Coordinate_Type);
      END Joystick_Task;

   END Joystick_Package;
```

Screen_Task characterizes positions in terms of two fixed-point types named Game_X_Type and Game_Y_Type. The center of the table corresponds to Game_X_Type and Game_Y_Type values of 0.0. Game_X_Type, Game_Y_Type, and Player_ID_Type are provided by another library package, named Global_Types_Package.

Here is a package providing a simplified version of Racquet_Task_Type and an array of two Racquet_Task_Type objects:

```
WITH Global_Types_Package; USE Global_Types_Package;

PACKAGE Racquet_Package IS

   TASK TYPE Racquet_Task_Type IS
      ENTRY Grant_ID (ID : IN Player_ID_Type);
   END Racquet_Task_Type;

   Racquet_Task_List :
      ARRAY (Player_ID_Type) OF Racquet_Task_Type;

END Racquet_Package;
```

Tasks declared in a library package, such as Racquet_Task_List (1) and Racquet_Task_List (2), begin execution when the library package is elaborated, before the main program begins execution. (This will be explained further in Chapter 19.) The Grant_ID entry of Racquet_Task_Type is used to assign a specific racquet number to each task. It is called once for each task, as part of the Racquet_Package initialization:

```
PACKAGE BODY Racquet_Package IS
   TASK BODY Racquet_Task_Type IS SEPARATE;
BEGIN  -- Racquet_Package initialization
   FOR Player_ID IN Racquet_Task_List'Range LOOP
      Racquet_Task_List (Player_ID).Grant_ID (Player_ID);
   END LOOP;
END Racquet_Package;
```

This is a common pattern. Arrays of task objects are often used to perform similar processing for a number of real-world entities. A task object that is a component of an array cannot determine by itself its position in the array, and hence it cannot determine the real-world entity with which it is concerned. Therefore, it begins its work by accepting a call on a special initialization entry like `Grant_ID`. The program unit declaring the array executes a loop like that in the `Racquet_Package` body, calling the initialization entry of each array component with a parameter based on the component's position in the array. Here is the subunit for the simplified `Racquet_Task_Type` task body:

```
WITH Calendar, Joystick_Package, Screen_Package;
USE Calendar;
SEPARATE (Racquet_Package)
TASK BODY Racquet_Task_Type IS
   Update_Interval          : CONSTANT := 0.1;
   Next_Update_Time         : Time;
   My_ID                    : Player_ID_Type;
   Racquet_X                : Game_X_Type;
   Racquet_Y, Old_Racquet_Y : Game_Y_Type;
   Stick_X, Stick_Y : Joystick_Package.Coordinate_Type;

BEGIN
   ACCEPT Grant_ID (ID : IN Player_ID_Type) DO
      My_ID := ID;
   END Grant_ID;
   CASE My_ID IS
      WHEN 1 => Racquet_X := Game_X_Type'First;
      WHEN 2 => Racquet_X := Game_X_Type'Last;
   END CASE;
   Next_Update_Time := Clock;
   Joystick_Package.Joystick_Task.Get_Coordinates
      (My_ID, Stick_X, Stick_Y);
   Racquet_Y := Game_Y_Type (Game_Y_Type'Last * Stick_Y);
   Screen_Package.Screen_Task.Display_Racquet
      (Racquet_X, Racquet_Y);
   LOOP
      Next_Update_Time := Next_Update_Time + Update_Interval;
      Joystick_Package.Joystick_Task.Get_Coordinates
         (My_ID, Stick_X, Stick_Y);
      Old_Racquet_Y := Racquet_Y;
      Racquet_Y := Game_Y_Type (Game_Y_Type'Last * Stick_Y);
      Screen_Package.Screen_Task.Erase_Racquet
         (Racquet_X, Old_Racquet_Y);
      Screen_Package.Screen_Task.Display_Racquet
         (Racquet_X, Racquet_Y);
      DELAY Next_Update_Time - Clock;
   END LOOP;
END Racquet_Task_Type;
```

The entry call

```
Joystick_Package.Joystick_Task.Get_Coordinates
   (My_ID, Stick_X, Stick_Y);
```

sets Stick_X and Stick_Y to the X and Y coordinates of the joystick identified by My_ID. Stick_Y is a fixed-point value between -1.0 and 1.0. The fixed-point value Game_Y_Type'Last, the Y coordinate of the bottom of the screen, is the distance from the center of the screen to the top or bottom edge. Multiplying Stick_Y and Game_Y_Type'Last gives the screen Y coordinate proportional to the Y displacement of the joystick. (As required when multiplying two fixed-point values, we explicitly convert the product to the desired target type, in this case Game_Y_Type.)

The predefined package Calendar was described in Section 11.9. It plays a central role in real-time programs. Among the facilities Calendar provides are the type Time (whose values represent points on a time line); the parameterless function Clock, which returns the current time as a value of type Time; a version of "+" for adding a Duration value (a distance between points on a time line) to a Time value, obtaining a new Time value; and a version of "-" subtracting two Time values to obtain a Duration value.

Duration is a predefined fixed-point type declared in package Standard. It was described in Section 7.8. This type is used in DELAY statements. A DELAY statement causes the task executing it to remain inactive for *at least* the specified duration. The task becomes *eligible* to resume execution as soon as this amount of time has passed, but the processor may have other work to attend to before it can get back to the delayed task.

The loop in the Racquet_Task_Type body is repeated approximately every tenth of a second. Each time through the loop, the first statement sets Next_Update_Time to the scheduled time of the next repetition. The DELAY statement at the bottom of the loop subtracts the current time from Next_Update_Time to compute the amount of time remaining until the next scheduled iteration and delays the task for at least that duration. Sometimes the delay will be longer than that requested. However, since each delay is computed in terms of the *scheduled* time of the next repetition, an actual delay that is too long before one repetition will cause a correspondingly shorter delay to be requested before the next repetition. The inaccuracy of the DELAY statement may cause the loop starting time to "jitter" slightly, but it cannot get too far off track as long as the time between repetitions is sufficient for all the work the processor must do each time through the loop. In the long run, the loop will be executed an average of ten times a second.

Here is the body of Joystick_Package, including the task body for Joystick_Task:

```
PACKAGE BODY Joystick_Package IS

   TYPE Position_Type IS
      RECORD
         X_Part, Y_Part : Coordinate_Type;
      END RECORD;

   TYPE Position_List_Type IS
      ARRAY (Player_ID_Type) OF Position_Type;

   PROCEDURE Read_Joysticks
      (Position_List : OUT Position_List_Type)
      IS SEPARATE;

   TASK BODY Joystick_Task IS

      Stick_Position_List : Position_List_Type;

   BEGIN

      LOOP

         Read_Joysticks (Stick_Position_List);

         ACCEPT Get_Coordinates
            (Player : IN Player_ID_Type;
             x, y : OUT Coordinate_Type) DO

            x := Stick_Position_List (Player).X_Part;
            y := Stick_Position_List (Player).Y_Part;

         END Get_Coordinates;

      END LOOP;

   END Joystick_Task;

END Joystick_Package;
```

The subunit for `Read_Joysticks` is not shown here. As we saw earlier, `Racquet_Task_List (1)` and `Racquet_Task_List (2)` each call `Joystick_Task.Get_Coordinates` once for each repetition of the `Racquet_Task_Type` loop. Since each of these two tasks executes the loop an average of ten times a second, `Joystick_Task` will accept a call on `Get_Coordinates` an average of twenty times a second. Even though `Joystick_Task` never makes explicit reference to time, the `Get_Coordinates` rendezvous synchronize the task with the two racquet tasks and thus control the frequency with which the `Joystick_Task` loop is executed.

Here is a typical sequence of events, illustrated in Figure 18.2:

`Joystick_Task` calls `Read_Joysticks`, then waits at the `ACCEPT` statement for `Get_Coordinates`.

`Racquet_Task_List (1)` calls `Joystick_Task.Get_Coordinates`, and a rendezvous begins.

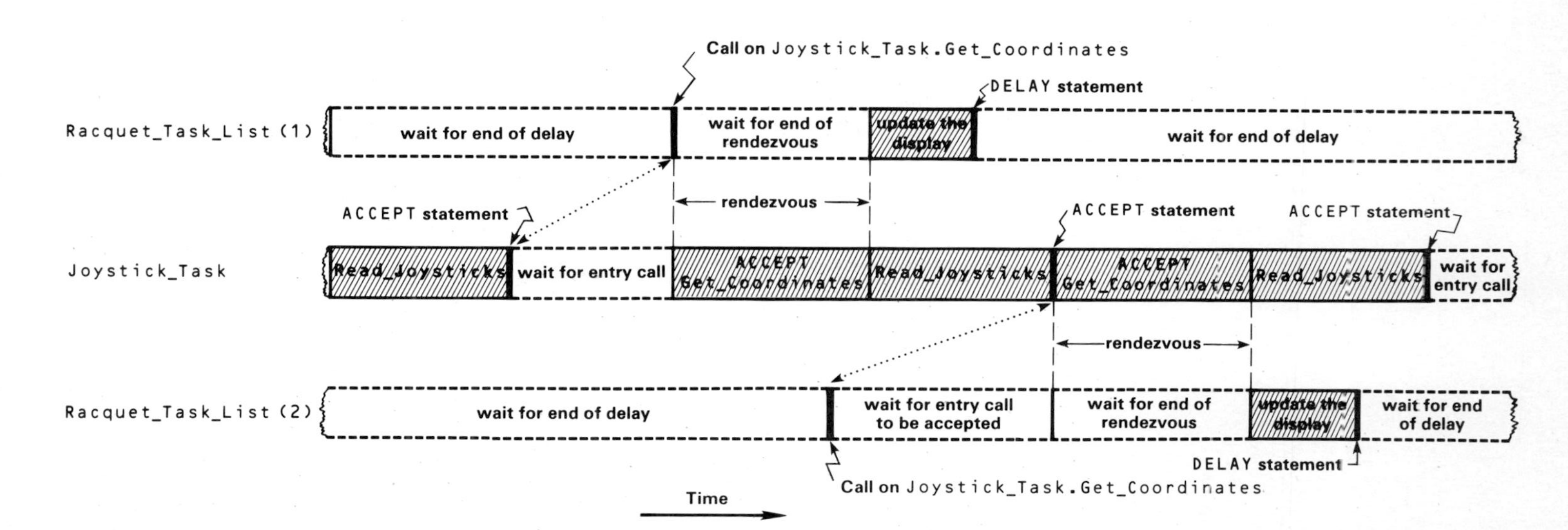

Figure 18.2 One possible sequence of events in the interaction of Joystick_Task, Raquet_Task_List (1), and Raquet_Task_List (2). A time line is shown for each task. Unshaded portions of a task's time line correspond to periods of time when a task is waiting for some action by another task before it can do anything else.

During the rendezvous, the task `Racquet_Task_List (2)` calls entry `Joystick_Task.Get_Coordinates` and waits for the call to be accepted.

`Racquet_Task_List (1)` and `Joystick_Task` complete the rendezvous. `Joystick_Task` begins another call on `Read_Joysticks`. `Racquet_Task_List (1)` updates the display and begins to execute its delay.

`Joystick_Task` completes the call on `Read_Joysticks` and accepts the waiting entry call from `Racquet_Task_List (2)`. Another rendezvous begins.

`Racquet_Task_List (2)` and `Joystick_Task` complete the rendezvous. `Joystick_Task` begins another call on `Read_Joysticks`. `Racquet_Task_List (2)` updates the display and begins to execute its delay.

`Joystick_Task` completes its call on `Read_Joysticks` and waits at the `ACCEPT` statement for `Get_Coordinates`.

Since the tasks are asynchronous, this is only one of many possible sequences of events.

18.4.2 A Concurrent Solution to a Sequential Problem

Tasks can be used to solve problems that are not inherently concurrent. Such problems are sometimes simplified by decomposing the problem into a series of simple *transformations* that take streams of input data and produce streams of output data. Each transformation involves an independent sequence of actions, so the transformations are most easily implemented as independent tasks. Streams of data are passed from one task to another by one task repeatedly calling an entry of the other.

For example, consider a primitive text reformatter. The reformatter's input is a stream of lines from the standard input file, each of arbitrary length up to 132 characters. Lines consist of words separated by arbitrary numbers of blanks, and an imaginary blank is assumed to exist between the last character of one line and the first character of the next. (That is, words do not continue across lines in the input file.) The input contains no control characters and no words more than 65 characters long. The reformatter's output is a stream of lines written to the standard output file containing the same sequence of words. Each output line starts in column one and contains as many words as possible without going past column 65. Consecutive words on a line are separated by one space.

This problem is simplified by decomposing it into three transformations, as shown in Figure 18.3. The first transformation takes the stream of input lines and transforms it into a stream of characters. The characters are those found in the input file, but with a space inserted at each line boundary. The control character `ASCII.NUL` is appended to the stream to mark its end. The second transformation takes this stream of characters, oblivious to where the input line boundaries were, scans past sequences of consecutive blanks to find words, and produces an output stream of words. The end of the stream of words is marked by a word of length zero.

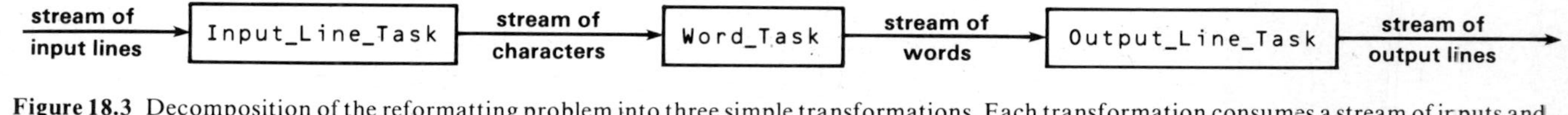

Figure 18.3 Decomposition of the reformatting problem into three simple transformations. Each transformation consumes a stream of inputs and produces a closely related stream of outputs.

The third transformation takes this sequence of words, oblivious to how they were extracted from the stream of characters, and uses them to assemble output lines.

The main program to solve this problem looks like this:

```
PROCEDURE Reformat IS
   TASK Input_Line_Task;

   TASK Word_Task IS
      ENTRY Deliver_Character (c : IN Character);
   END Word_Task;

   TASK Output_Line_Task IS
      ENTRY Deliver_Word (Word : IN String);
   END Output_Line_Task;

   TASK BODY Input_Line_Task IS SEPARATE;
   TASK BODY Word_Task IS SEPARATE;
   TASK BODY Output_Line_Task IS SEPARATE;

BEGIN

   NULL;

END Reformat;
```

`Input_Line_Task` performs the first transformation, `Word_Task` the second, and `Output_Line_Task` the third. `Input_Line_Task` passes a stream of characters to `Word_Task` by successive calls on its `Deliver_Character` entry. `Word_Task` passes a stream of words to `Output_Line_Task` by successive calls on its `Deliver_Word` entry.

As Chapter 19 will explain, the three tasks, because they are declared inside `Reformat`, begin executing their sequences of statements at the same time that `Reformat` begins executing its sequence of statements. The procedure `Reformat` does not finish until `Input_Line_Task`, `Word_Task`, and `Output_Line_Task` have all completed their sequences of statements. In this case, all the work is done by the three tasks, so the main program's sequence of statements consists of a single `NULL` statement.

Here is the subunit for `Input_Line_Task`:

```
WITH Text_IO; USE Text_IO;
SEPARATE (Reformat)
TASK BODY Input_Line_Task IS
   Buffer      : String (1 .. 132);
   Line_Length : Natural;
```

```
BEGIN
   WHILE NOT End_Of_File LOOP
      Get_Line (Buffer, Line_Length);
      FOR i IN 1 .. Line_Length LOOP
         Word_Task.Deliver_Character ( Buffer (i) );
      END LOOP;
      Word_Task.Deliver_Character (' ');
         -- Extra blank at end of line
   END LOOP;
   Word_Task.Deliver_Character (ASCII.NUL);
      -- End-of-stream character
END Input_Line_Task;
```

Input_Line_Task will rendezvous with Word_Task once for every character in the stream of characters.

Here is the Word_Task subunit:

```
SEPARATE (Reformat)

TASK BODY Word_Task IS

   Next_Character : Character;
   Word_Buffer    : String (1 .. 65);
   Word_Length    : Integer RANGE 0 .. Word_Buffer'Last;

BEGIN

   ACCEPT Deliver_Character (c : IN Character) DO
      Next_Character := c;
   END Deliver_Character;

   LOOP
      -- Scan past blanks:
      WHILE Next_Character = ' ' LOOP
         ACCEPT Deliver_Character (c : IN Character) DO
            Next_Character := c;
         END Deliver_Character;
      END LOOP;
      EXIT WHEN Next_Character = ASCII.NUL;
      -- Scan nonblanks and deliver word:
      Word_Length := 0;
      LOOP
         Word_Length := Word_Length + 1;
         Word_Buffer (Word_Length) := Next_Character;
         ACCEPT Deliver_Character (c : IN Character) DO
            Next_Character := c;
         END Deliver_Character;
         EXIT WHEN Next_Character = ' ';
      END LOOP;
```

```
        Output_Line_Task.Deliver_Word
           ( Word_Buffer (1 .. Word_Length) );
     END LOOP;

     Output_Line_Task.Deliver_Word ("");
        -- End-of-stream word

  END Word_Task;
```

Since Input_Line_Task places a space after each line, there is at least one space following the last word in the stream of characters. This makes it unnecessary to check for ASCII.NUL in the second WHILE loop (which scans past nonblank characters). Word_Task will rendezvous with Output_Line_Task once for each word it finds.

Finally, here is the Output_Line_Task subunit:

```
WITH Text_IO; USE Text_IO;
SEPARATE (Reformat)
TASK BODY Output_Line_Task IS
   SUBTYPE Size_Subtype IS Integer RANGE 0 .. 65;
   TYPE Word_Type (Size : Size_Subtype := 0) IS
      RECORD
         String_Part : String (1 .. Size);
      END RECORD;
   Line_Length   : Size_Subtype;
   Needed_Length : Positive;
   Next_Word     : Word_Type;
   End_Word      : CONSTANT Word_Type := (0, "");
BEGIN
   ACCEPT Deliver_Word (Word : IN String) DO
      Next_Word := (Word'Length, Word);
   END Deliver_Word;
   WHILE Next_Word /= End_Word LOOP
      -- Start a new line:
      Put (Next_Word.String_Part);
      Line_Length := Next_Word.Size;
      -- Output as many words as will fit on the line:
      LOOP
         ACCEPT Deliver_Word (Word : IN String) DO
            Next_Word := (Word'Length, Word);
         END Deliver_Word;
         Needed_Length := Line_Length + 1 + Next_Word.Size;
         EXIT WHEN
            Next_Word = End_Word OR
            Needed_Length > Size_Subtype'Last;
         Put (' ');
         Put (Next_Word.String_Part);
         Line_Length := Needed_Length;
      END LOOP;
```

```
        New_Line;
     END LOOP;
  END Output_Line_Task;
```

The `WHILE` loop is executed once for each output line, and the inner loop is executed once for each word on the line.

Each of these transformations is simple by itself, but together they perform a complex job. The simplicity comes from the independence of the transformations. Each task has differently structured loops, and each rendezvous plays a role both in the loop of the calling task and the loop of the called task.

From the point of view of `Input_Line_Task`, a `Deliver_Character` rendezvous occurs once for each character in each input line and one extra time at the end of each line. From the point of view of `Word_Task`, these rendezvous repeatedly take place once for each character in a run of blanks and then once for each character in a run of nonblanks. From the point of view of `Word_Task`, `Deliver_Word` rendezvous occur every time a run of nonblanks is encountered. From the point of view of `Output_Line_Task`, `Deliver_Word` rendezvous occur once for each word in each output line.

A similar pattern can be found in most well-written multitask programs. Rendezvous play distinct roles in the calling and called tasks, but the division of the computation into separate tasks allows each task to be understood, independently of the other task, as a single conceptual "thread" of events.

18.5 SUMMARY

A *task* performs actions one after the other. In an Ada program, several tasks may execute concurrently. Tasks normally execute *asynchronously,* meaning that one task's rate of progress is not related to another's. However, tasks can synchronize through *rendezvous* to work cooperatively. Different tasks may execute the same sequence of statements at the same time, each at its own pace.

Each task is associated with a data object called a *task object.* Task objects belong to types called *task types.* Tasks in the same type execute the same sequence of statements, manipulate their own copies of identically declared variables, and have the same interface for communication with other tasks. Task types are limited, meaning that task objects cannot be copied or compared for equality. Like any type, a task type can be used in object declarations and in declarations of other types.

To declare a task type, you must write a *task-type declaration* and a *task body.* Together, these constitute a *task unit.* The typical form of a task-type declaration is

```
TASK TYPE identifier IS
   entry declaration
        ~~~
   entry declaration
END identifier ;
```

where an entry declaration has the form

```
ENTRY identifier
    [ ( parameter specification ; ~~~ ; parameter specification ) ] ;
```

(For a task type with no entry declarations, a task-type declaration of the form

```
TASK TYPE identifier ;
```

is allowed.) The typical form of a task body is as follows:

```
TASK BODY identifier IS
    declarative part
BEGIN
    sequence of statements
[ EXCEPTION
    handler
      ~~~
    handler ]
END identifier ;
```

After a task object in a particular type is created, the declarative part of the type's task body is elaborated and its sequence of statements is executed, concurrently with other tasks. This is done every time a task object of that type that is created, and each elaboration of the task body's declarative part creates a new set of variables for use by the newly created task.

A task-type declaration may appear in a package specification, with the task body in the corresponding package body. Any program unit using the package may contain declarations of objects in the task type provided by the package. A task-type declaration may be used in a package's private part as the full declaration of a limited private type.

A task-type declaration may also appear in the declarative part of a subprogram body, a package body, a block statement, or an outer task body. The task body corresponding to the task-type declaration must follow in the same declarative part. The task-type declaration is a basic declaration, and the task body is a later declaration.

A body stub of the form

```
TASK BODY identifier IS SEPARATE ;
```

may appear in the declarative part of a compilation unit in place of a task body. The task body is then compiled separately as a subunit. Task units cannot be compiled separately as library units. Neither are there generic task units, although a generic package can provide a task-type declaration.

A *single task declaration* of the form

```
TASK identifier IS
    entry declaration
        ~~~
    entry declaration
END identifier ;
```

(identical to a task-type declaration except that the word TYPE does not appear after the word TASK) is equivalent to the declaration of an *anonymous task type* followed by the declaration of a single object in that type. In this case, the identifier names the object itself rather than a task type. This is useful in declaring one-of-a-kind task objects. Like a task-type declaration, a single-task declaration must be accompanied by a task body. A one-of-a-kind task object with no entries may be declared as follows:

```
TASK identifier ;
```

Two tasks communicate when the first task *calls* an entry of the second and the second task *accepts* the entry call. This is called a rendezvous. Whichever task initiates the rendezvous waits until the other task is ready to complete the rendezvous, then both tasks resume asynchronous execution. If more than one task has called the same entry, the entry calls are queued and accepted on a first-come-first-served basis.

The first task calls the second by executing an *entry call statement,* which is similar to a procedure call statement. However, the procedure name is replaced by an entry name of the form

```
task object name . entry identifier
```

or, in the case of an object designated by an access value,

```
access value . entry identifier
```

The second task accepts the call by executing an ACCEPT statement, typically of the form

```
ACCEPT identifier
   ( parameter specification ; ~~~ ; parameter specification )  DO
   sequence of statements
END identifier ;
```

An ACCEPT statement plays a role in an entry call similar to the role played by a procedure body in a procedure call, except that it can only be executed when it is reached by the called task. The called task's body may have several ACCEPT statements for the same entry. Each entry has formal parameters, declared in its entry declaration in the same way that subprogram parameters are declared. Each ACCEPT statement for that entry has identical parameters. ACCEPT statements are allowed only within task bodies, but not within a subprogram body nested inside a task body.

A rendezvous consists of three steps:

1. For entry parameters of mode IN or IN OUT, the values of the actual parameters in the entry call are copied into the corresponding formal parameters of the ACCEPT statement.
2. The sequence of statements inside the ACCEPT statement is executed.
3. For entry parameters of mode IN OUT or OUT, the values of the formal parameters in the ACCEPT statement are copied into the corresponding actual parameters of the entry call.

An ACCEPT statement of the form

```
ACCEPT identifier ;
```

is equivalent to one of the form

```
ACCEPT identifier DO
   NULL;
END identifier ;
```

It is appropriate if a rendezvous is to be used only to synchronize tasks and not to pass data between them.

A task-type declaration or single-task declaration may have more than one entry with the same name, provided that the entries have different parameter and result type profiles. Similarly, a renaming declaration of the form

```
PROCEDURE identifier
   ( parameter specification ; ... ; parameter specification )
   RENAMES entry name ;
```

(where the entry name is an expanded name consisting of a task object or access value name and an entry identifier) may be used to rename an entry of a particular task object as a procedure. The renaming may overload other subprograms, enumeration literals, and renamed entries.

A DELAY statement causes the task executing it to become idle for *at least* the duration specified in the DELAY statement. The task becomes *eligible* to resume execution as soon as the specified amount of time passes, but a processor might not be available at the moment this happens. A loop of the form

```
Next_Iteration_Time := Calendar.Clock;
LOOP
   ...
   Next_Iteration_Time :=
      Next_Iteration_Time + Iteration_Interval;
   DELAY Next_Iteration_Time - Calendar.Clock;
END LOOP;
```

is executed every `Iteration_Interval` seconds *on the average.* Some cycles may be longer than average, but these are followed by `DELAY` statements for shorter-than-average delays. In the long run, the loop stays "on schedule."

Sometimes an apparently sequential problem is simplified by decomposing it into pieces, each piece performing a straightforward transformation on a stream of input values to produce a stream of output values. The transformations can be implemented as tasks that send or receive data through rendezvous. Each task can be kept simple because it need not be concerned with the progress of the other tasks.

EXERCISES

18.1 Below is a description of a computer-controlled heating system. Describe (in English, not the Ada language) the tasks that you would use to build the control program for the system. Explain the purpose of each task. Tell which tasks will communicate with which and what kind of data they will exchange.

The heating system has ten zones, each with its own temperature sensor and its own vent. The temperature sensor can be read, and the vent can be opened or closed, by appropriate procedure calls. All vents are fed with warm air from one central heater. The heater has four settings—*off, low, medium,* and *high*—that can be controlled by a procedure call. The heater should be set to *off* when all vents are closed, to *low* when from one to three vents are open, to *medium* when from four to seven vents are open, and to *high* when from eight to ten vents are open. The system maintains a 24-hour schedule of the desired temperature in each zone at each time of the day. (Different temperatures may be desired in different zones at the same time, and different temperatures may be desired in the same zone at different times.) When the temperature in a zone falls below the desired temperature for that time (or a new desired temperature, higher than the current temperature, takes effect), that zone's vent is opened. It remains opened until the temperature rises to at least two degrees above the current desired temperature for the zone (or until a new desired temperature, two or more degrees below the current temperature, takes effect). It is sufficient to check a zone's temperature once every five seconds on the average. There is a terminal from which an operator can change the schedule of desired temperatures. By entering a carriage return, the operator initiates a dialogue in which he specifies that the desired temperature for a particular zone is to be changed to a particular value at a particular time of day. All of the operator's input should be checked for validity, and the operator should be asked to reenter data when invalid input is found.

18.2 Write the declaration for a library package providing task type and task-object declarations for the tasks described in the answer to Exercise 18.1.

18.3 Write a package providing a task `Blank_Condenser_Task`. This task should have one entry named `Get_Character`. Each call on this entry should set the actual parameter of the entry call to the next character from the standard input file, except that consecutive blanks in the standard input file should be condensed to a single blank. For example, if the input file contains the characters 'X', ' ', ' ', ' ', 'Y', the calls

```
Blank_Condenser_Task.Get_Character (C1);
Blank_Condenser_Task.Get_Character (C2);
Blank_Condenser_Task.Get_Character (C3);
```

should leave 'X' in C1, ' ' in C2, and 'Y' in C3.

18.4 Suppose you are given the following package:

```
PACKAGE Speed_Package IS

   TASK Speed_Task IS
      ENTRY Get_Speed (Speed : OUT Float);
   END Speed_Task;

END Speed_Package;
```

Each second, a speedometer measures a vehicle's speed in feet per second and waits for a call on Speed_Task.Get_Speed. The measured speed is placed in the entry parameter. Use this package to write a package Acceleration_Package that provides a task Acceleration_Task with an entry Get_Acceleration. This entry should have one parameter of type Float. Every time a call on Speed_Task.Get_Speed is accepted, Acceleration_Task should compute the current acceleration in feet per second per second (by subtracting the previous speed reading from the current speed reading), accept a call on Get_Acceleration, and place the computed acceleration in the entry parameter.

18.5 Suppose you are given the following package:

```
PACKAGE Matrix_Package IS

   TYPE Matrix_Type IS ARRAY (1 .. 30, 1 .. 30) OF Float;

   PROCEDURE Read_Matrix (Matrix : OUT Matrix_Type);
   PROCEDURE Invert_Matrix (Matrix : IN OUT Matrix_Type);
   PROCEDURE Print_Matrix (Matrix : IN Matrix_Type);

END Matrix_Package;
```

Write a main program that will read ten matrix values, invert them, and print their inverses, but will allow input, computation of inverses, and output to proceed concurrently. (Then the program will not be forced to wait idly for input and output operations to complete if there is useful work for it to do computing inverses.)

18.6 Solve the reformatting problem described in Section 18.4.2 without using tasks. Compare the two solutions. Which is simpler, and why?

18.7 Modify the Reformat program of Section 18.4.2 so that the output file is broken into pages. Each page should contain three blank lines, a line containing only a page number right-justified in columns 76 though 78, two more blank lines, up to 54 lines of text, and six more blank lines.

18.8 Rewrite the Reformat program of Section 18.4.2 so that the rendezvous go in the opposite direction. Word_Task should call an entry of Input_Line_Task to obtain a character. Output_Line_Task should call an entry of Word_Task to obtain a 65-character string and an integer giving the length of the word stored in that string.

18.9 In the Reformat program of Section 18.4.2, suppose that Input_Line_Task were designed to call an entry Deliver_Character to place a character in the output stream and Word_Task were designed to call an entry Obtain_Character to obtain a character from the input stream. Write a task Stream_Task with entries Obtain_Character and Deliver_Character so that Input_Line_Task and Word_Task can communicate indirectly through Stream_Task.

18.10 Suppose the two tasks provided by the following package have been independently designed;

```
PACKAGE Signal_Package IS

   TASK Sensor_Task IS
      ENTRY Wait_For_Signal;
   END Sensor_Task;

   TASK Processing_Task IS
      ENTRY Report_Signal;
   END Processing_Task;

END Signal_Package;
```

`Sensor_Task` accepts a call on `Wait_For_Signal` every time a signal is detected. `Processing_Task` expects its `Report_Signal` entry to be called every time a signal is detected. Write the declaration and body of a third task that calls `Processing_Task.Report_Signal` every time a signal has been detected by `Sensor_Task`. (The `Signal_Package` body should contain body stubs for the `Sensor_Task` and `Processing_Task` bodies.)

CHAPTER

NINETEEN

CONTROLLING TASK INTERACTION

Section 18.3 introduced the simplest form of interaction between tasks—a *rendezvous* that occurs when one task calls an entry and another task reaches an **ACCEPT** statement for that entry. In this chapter, we examine more sophisticated interactions among tasks. Section 19.1 explains how tasks synchronize when they begin and end their execution. Section 19.2 describes more flexible forms of rendezvous. These forms allow a task to wait simultaneously for a call on any of several entries, to accept a call on a particular entry only when specified conditions hold, to terminate automatically after it has received its last entry call, to limit the amount of time it will wait for a rendezvous, or to perform an alternative action if a rendezvous cannot take place immediately. Section 19.3 describes how to assign priorities to tasks, how to declare "arrays" of entries, and how to terminate tasks abnormally. Section 19.4 describes how exceptions behave in multitask programs. Section 19.5 fills in remaining details to complete the description of the Ada language's multitasking features.

19.1 ACTIVATION AND TERMINATION OF TASKS

Like other objects, task objects may be either declared or allocated. A declared task begins execution after the declarative part containing the task-object declaration is completely elaborated. An allocated task begins execution upon evaluation of the allocator that creates the task object.

A running task may eventually terminate. This can happen, for example, when it reaches the end of its sequence of statements. (In Sections 19.2, 19.3, and 19.4 we shall see other ways in which a task can terminate.) When a task *t* is declared in a subprogram, block statement, or the body of another task, departure from that subprogram, block statement, or task body cannot occur until *t* has terminated.

When an access type designating task objects is declared in a subprogram, block statement, or the body of another task, departure from that subprogram, block statement, or task body cannot occur until termination of all allocated tasks designated by values in that access type. A task object is said to *depend* on that part of the program that cannot be exited until the task terminates. Task dependence will play an important role in Section 19.2.

The rest of this section explains the rules for task activation and termination in greater detail, first for declared tasks and then for allocated tasks. Sections 19.1.1 and 19.1.2 consider only task objects and access types declared in subprograms, block statements, and task bodies. The rules for task objects and access types declared in packages are more complicated and are addressed separately in Section 19.1.3.

19.1.1 Tasks Created by Object Declarations

Suppose a task object is declared in some declarative part *d* that corresponds to a sequence of statements *s*. The task begins execution just after *d* has been elaborated and just before *s* begins execution. Execution of *s* does not begin until after all tasks declared in *d* have elaborated the declarative parts of their task bodies. For example, in the program below, the task `Next_Position` begins executing just before the call on `Get_Time_Of_Day`.

```
PROCEDURE Track_Aircraft IS

   TASK TYPE Position_Type IS
      ENTRY Initialize (x, y : IN Float := 0.0);
      ENTRY Change
         (Delta_X, Delta_Y : IN Float;
          New_X, New_Y     : OUT Float);

   END Position_Type;
      ...
   Next_Position : Position_Type; -- Task object declaration
      ...
   TASK BODY Position_Type IS
      ...
   BEGIN
      ...
   END Position_Type;

BEGIN

   -- Next_Position starts executing at this point.
   Get_Time_Of_Day (Time_Of_Day);
   ...

END Track_Aircraft;
```

The procedure Track_Aircraft waits while Next_Position elaborates the declarative part of the Position_Type task body. Then Track_Aircraft resumes execution while Next_Position concurrently executes the statements in the Position_Type task body, as shown in Figure 19.1. (Section 19.4 explains how this sequence of events is affected by exceptions arising during elaboration of a declarative part.)

If the declarative part of the frame includes a declaration for a composite object containing one or more task objects, the effect is the same as if these task objects were declared directly in object declarations. For example, if the Track_Aircraft procedure had included the declarations

```
TYPE Position_List_Type IS
   ARRAY (Positive RANGE <>) OF Position_Type;
Position_List : Position_List (1 .. 4);
```

then Position_List (1), Position_List (2), Position_List (3), and Position_List (4) would each begin elaborating their declarative parts just before the call on Get_Time_Of_Day. Track_Aircraft could not begin executing its sequence of statements until all these task objects had elaborated the declarative part of the Position_Type task body, as shown in Figure 19.2.

When a task object, or a composite object containing a task object, is declared in the declarative part of a subprogram, block statement, or task body, the task *depends* on that frame. Departure from the frame's sequence of statements cannot occur until all tasks depending on it have terminated. For example, as indicated in Figure 19.1, the procedure Track_Aircraft cannot return until the task Next_Position has terminated. The statements

```
DECLARE
   TASK A_Task;
   TASK BODY A_Task IS
   BEGIN
      a;
   END A_Task;
   TASK B_Task;
   TASK BODY B_Task IS
   BEGIN
      b;
   END B_Task;
BEGIN
   c;
END;
d;
```

cause procedures a, b, and c to be executed in parallel, with procedure d beginning only after a, b, and c have finished. Because A_Task and B_Task depend on the block statement, departure from the block statement cannot occur until A_Task and B_Task have terminated.

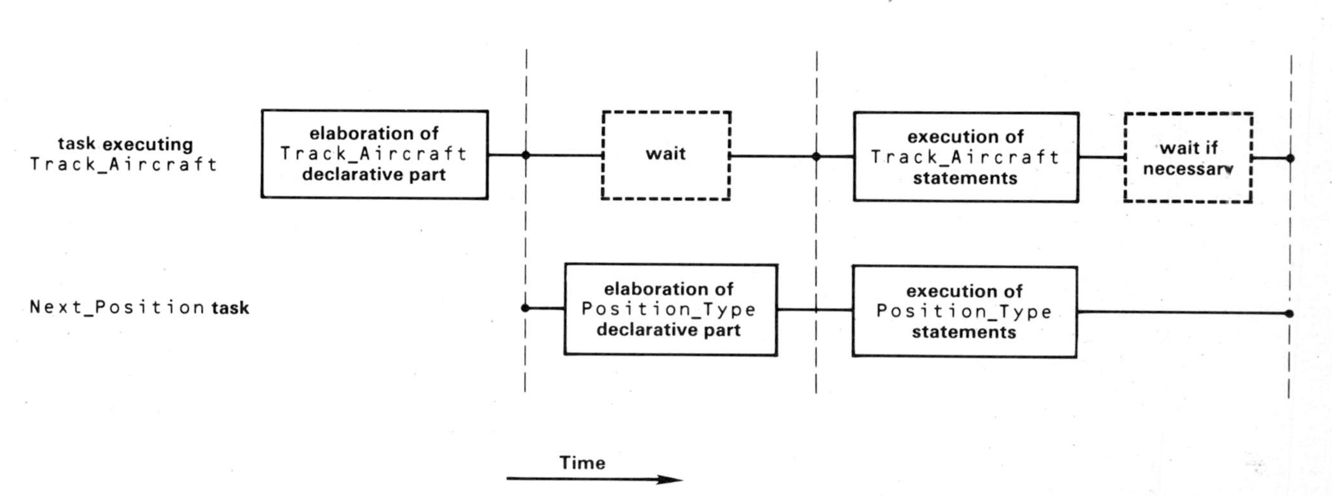

Figure 19.1. Sequence of events when task Next_Position is created. First, the surrounding procedure elaborates its declarative part, then Next_Position elaborates the declarative part of its task type's task body. Finally, the statements in the surrounding procedure and the statements in the task body are executed concurrently. The "wait if necessary box" following the execution of the procedure's statements will be explained later.

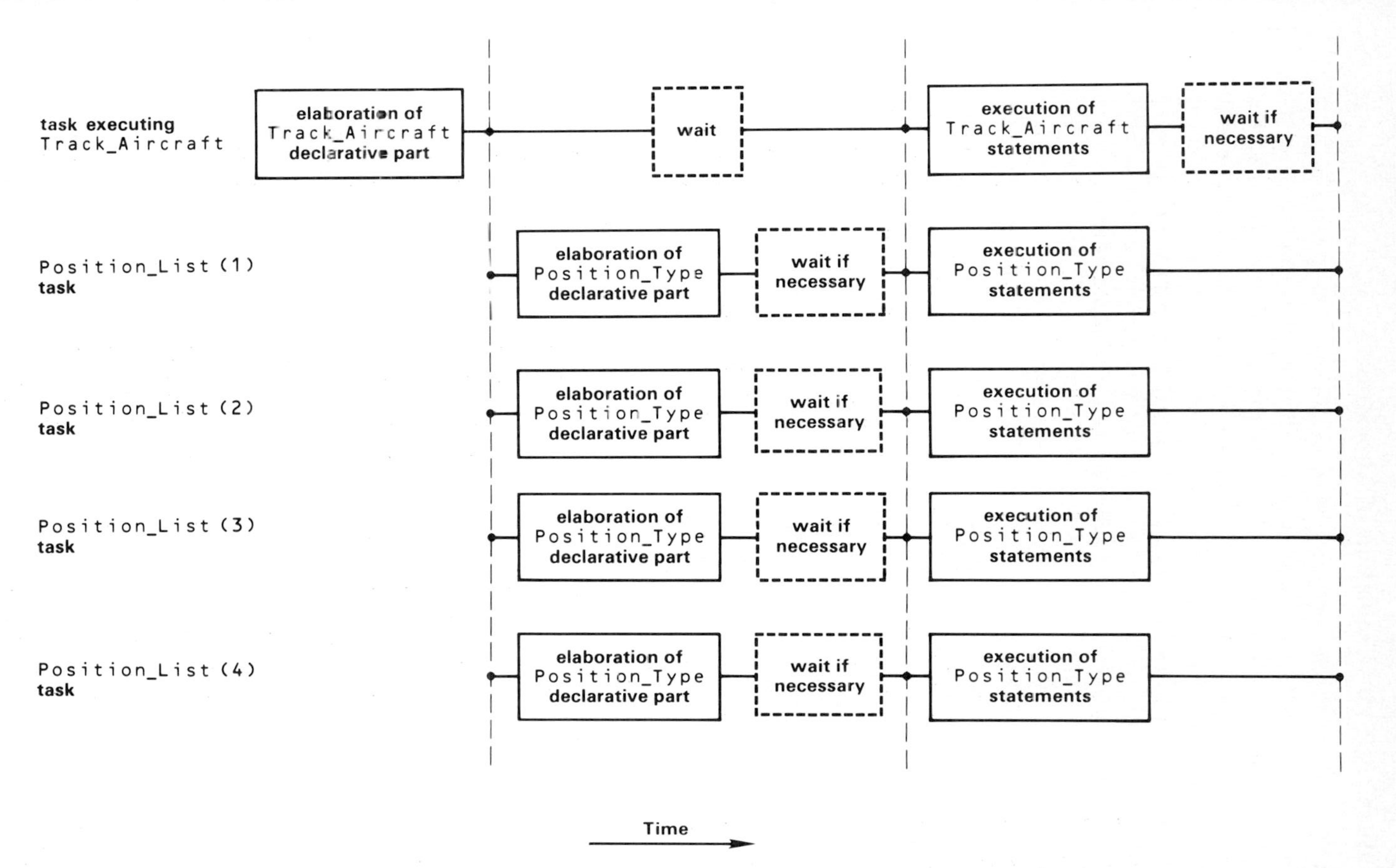

Figure 19.2 Sequence of events when task `Position_Task (1)`, `Position_Task (2)`, `Position_Task (3)`, and `Position_Task (4)` are created. First, the surrounding procedure elaborates its declarative part. Next, each component of `Position_Task` elaborates the declarative part of the task type's task body. After all four tasks have completed this step, the task executing the surrounding procedures executes the task body's statements, and the four tasks declared inside the procedure each independently execute the task body's statements, all in parallel.

19.1.2 Tasks Created by Evaluation of Allocators

When a task object is created by evaluation of an allocator, the allocated task first elaborates the declarative part of its task body. Then the allocator evaluates to an access value designating the allocated task. At this point, the task may begin executing the sequence of statements in its task body. If a composite object containing one or more task objects is allocated, similar rules apply. All component tasks created by the allocation first elaborate the declarative parts of their task bodies. Then the allocator evaluates to an access value designating the composite object, and the new tasks begin executing the statements in their task bodies.

If an access type designating a task type is declared in a subprogram, block body, or task body, all allocated tasks designated by values in the access type depend on that frame. Departure from the frame cannot occur until all these allocated tasks have terminated. Consider the following example:

```
PROCEDURE Track_Aircraft IS
   TASK TYPE Position_Type IS
      ...
   END Position_Type;
   TYPE Position_Pointer_Type IS ACCESS Position_Type;
   ...
   TASK BODY Position_Type IS
      ...
   BEGIN
      ...
   END Position_Type;
BEGIN
   ...
   DECLARE
      p : Position_Pointer_Type;
      ...
   BEGIN
      ...
      p := NEW Position_Type;  -- Task p.ALL depends on
                               -- Track_Aircraft, where the
                               -- access type is declared.
      ...
   END;

END Track_Aircraft;
```

The task that is eventually named `p.ALL` begins execution upon evaluation of the allocator in the block statement. The block statement can be exited as soon as all its statements have been executed. However, because the access type `Position_Pointer_Type` is declared in the declarative part of `Track_Aircraft`, departure from `Track_Aircraft` cannot take place until the allocated task has terminated.

19.1.3 Tasks and Access Types Declared in Packages

Suppose a task object (or a composite object containing a task object) is declared in either a package specification or a package body. The rules for task activation depend on whether or not the package in which the task object is declared has a package body. If the package has a body, the task begins execution just after the declarative part of the package body is elaborated. (If there are any initialization statements in the package body, these statements are not executed until after the declared task has elaborated its declarative part.) For example, given the packages

```
PACKAGE Position_Type_Package IS
   TASK TYPE Position_Type IS
      ...
   END Position_Type;
END Position_Package;


WITH Position_Type_Package;
PACKAGE Tracking_Package IS
   ...
   Visible_Position : Position_Type_Package.Position_Type;
   ...
END Tracking_Package;


PACKAGE BODY Tracking_Package IS
   ...
   Hidden_Position : Position_Type_Package.Position_Type;
   ...
BEGIN
   -- Visible_Position and Hidden_Position begin execution
   --  here.
   ... [initialization statements]
END Tracking_Package;
```

`Visible_Position` and `Hidden_Position` elaborate the `Position_Type` declarative part after the `Tracking_Package` body's declarative part has been elaborated. Once both these tasks have elaborated their declarative parts, they begin to execute the `Position_Type` statement sequence, and the task elaborating the `Tracking_Package` body begins executing the `Tracking_Package` initialization statements (see Figure 19.3).

In the case of a library package with no package body, such as

```
WITH Position_Type_Package;
PACKAGE Position_List_Package IS
   Position_List :
      ARRAY (1 .. 4) OF Position_Type_Package.Position_Type;
END Position_List_Package;
```

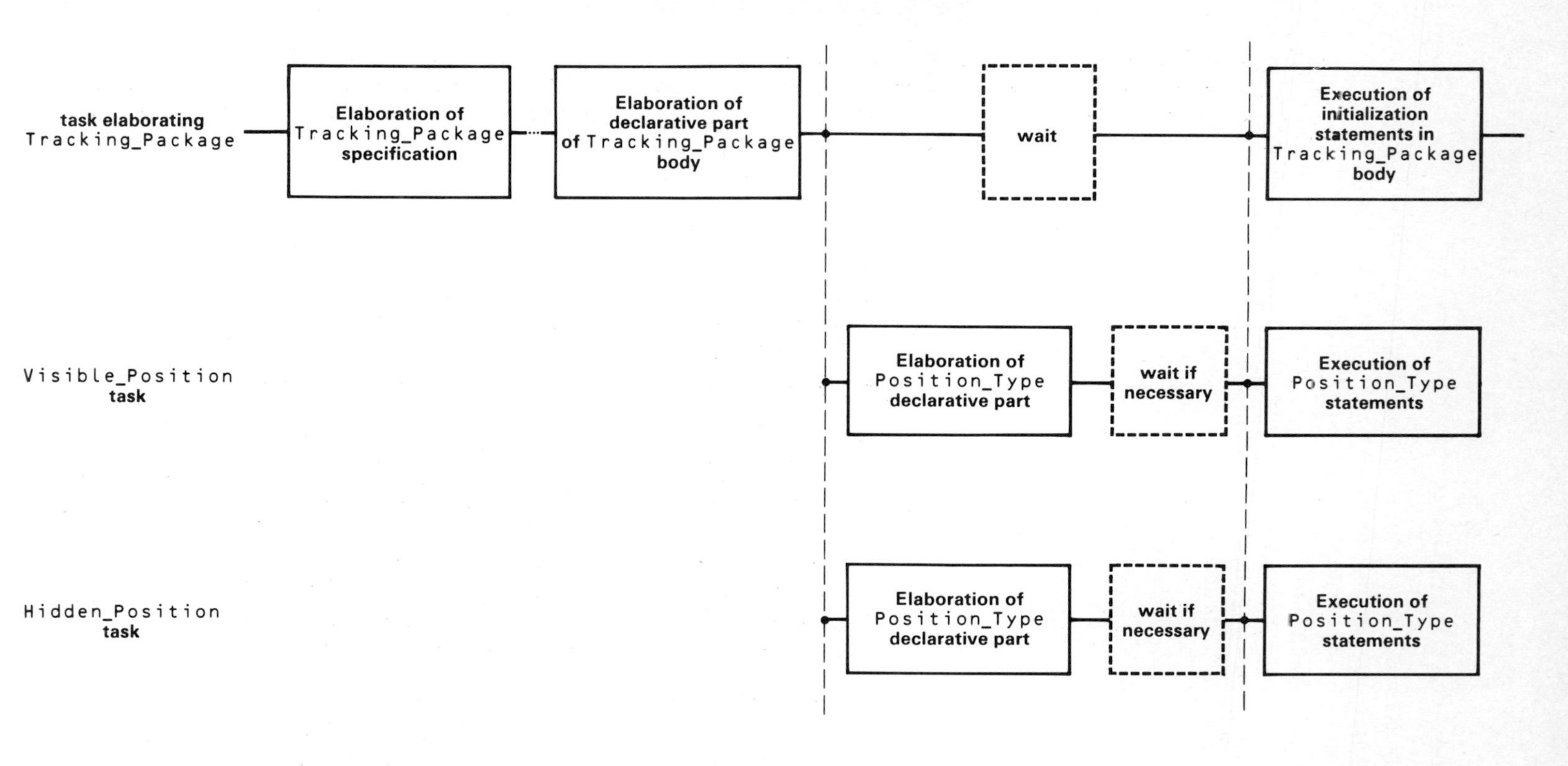

Figure 19.3 Creation of tasks declared in a package. After the task elaborating the package elaborates the declarative part of the package body but before the initialization statements of the package body are executed, each task declared in either the package specification or package body elaborates the declarative part of its task type's body.

the task begins execution sometime after the package specification has been elaborated but before the main program has begun.

In the case of a declarative part *d* containing a package specification but no package body, any task object declared in the package specification begins execution just after all declarations in *d* have been elaborated. For example, the procedure

```
PROCEDURE Track_Aircraft_Version_2 IS

   TASK TYPE Position_Type IS
      ENTRY Initialize (x, y : IN Float := 0.0);
      ENTRY Change
         (Delta_X, Delta_Y : IN Float;
          New_X, New_Y     : OUT Float);
   END Position_Type;

   ...

   PACKAGE Next_Position_Package IS
      Next_Position : Position_Type;
   END Next_Position_Package;

   ...

   TASK BODY Position_Type IS
      ...
   BEGIN
      ...
   END Position_Type;

BEGIN

   -- Next_Position starts executing at this point.
   Get_Time_Of_Day (Time_Of_Day);
   ...

END Track_Aircraft_Version_2;
```

behaves in exactly the same manner as the version of `Track_Aircraft` at the beginning of Section 19.1.2 (in which the declaration of `Next_Position` was not enclosed in a package).

The rules for dependence and termination are based on when declared task objects and access types cease to exist. Types and objects declared in a subprogram, block statement, or task body cease to exist upon departure from that frame. That is why departure from such a frame does not occur until all tasks declared in the frame, or designated via an access type declared in the frame, have terminated.

Packages are different from other frames because the objects declared in packages continue to exist after departure from the sequence of statements in the package body. Types and objects declared in a library package continue to exist for the life of the main program. If a package is declared in the declarative part of some outer frame, types and objects declared in the package continue to exist for as long as types and objects declared directly in that outer frame.

A task declared in a library package is said to depend on the library package. Since a library package remains alive for the duration of the main program, however, no part of the program ever waits for completion of such a task. In fact, depending on the Ada implementation, a task declared in a library package may be allowed to continue executing even after the main program has terminated. Similar rules apply to tasks designated via access types declared in a library package.

A task declared in an inner package depends on the innermost frame surrounding it that is not an inner package. This surrounding frame may be a subprogram, block statement, task body, or the body of a library package. When the surrounding frame is a subprogram, block statement, or task body, the inner package ceases to exist upon departure from the surrounding frame. Thus the frame cannot be exited until the task declared in the inner package terminates. For example, `Track_Aircraft_Version_2` does not terminate until `Next_Position_Package.Next_Position` has terminated. When the surrounding frame is a library package, as in

```
WITH Position_Type_Package;
PACKAGE Outer_Package IS
   PACKAGE Inner_Package IS
      Position : Position_Type_Package.Position_Type;
   END Inner_Package;

END Outer_Package;
```

the inner package remains in existence for the lifetime of the main program, so no part of the program ever waits for the task to terminate. Again, similar rules apply to tasks designated via access types declared in an inner package.

19.2 MAKING RENDEZVOUS MORE USEFUL

The basic rendezvous mechanism described in Section 18.3 is rather rigid. A calling task calls a specific entry and waits for it to be accepted. A called task waits for a call on a specific entry. This requires a high level of coordination between calling tasks and called tasks and can make it difficult to consider each task independently.

Fortunately, rendezvous can be made more flexible. This section describes how a task can wait for calls on several entries at once, accepting whichever call arrives first; how it can restrict which of these calls may be accepted under which conditions; how a called task can be made to terminate automatically when there is no more work for it to do; and how either a called or calling task can go on to do other work if a rendezvous is not possible immediately or within a specified amount of time. These capabilities make entry calls and `ACCEPT` statements capable of solving a wide variety of problems.

19.2.1 Selective Waits

19.2.1.1 Basic selective waits. The Ping-Pong video game has a task named `Screen_Task` responsible for continually updating the video display. It is declared inside the library package `Screen_Package` as follows:

```
WITH Global_Types_Package; USE Global_Types_Package;
PACKAGE Screen_Package IS

   TASK Screen_Task IS
      ENTRY Reset_Screen;
      ENTRY Display_Ball
         (x : IN Game_X_Type; y : IN Game_Y_Type);
      ENTRY Erase_Ball
         (x : IN Game_X_Type; y : IN Game_Y_Type);
      ENTRY Display_Racquet
         (x : IN Game_X_Type; y : IN Game_Y_Type);
      ENTRY Erase_Racquet
         (x : IN Game_X_Type; y : IN Game_Y_Type);
   END Screen_Task;

END Screen_Package;
```

The `Display_Racquet` and `Erase_Racquet` entries are called by the tasks that keep track of the current position of each racquet. The `Display_Ball` and `Erase_Ball` entries are called by the task that determines the path of the ball.

To keep the display current, `Screen_Task` should service each entry call within a very short time after the call is made. This suggests that `Screen_Task` should execute `ACCEPT` statements for its various entries in the order in which the other tasks call those entries. Unfortunately, there is no simple way for `Screen_Task` to predict the order in which its entries will be called.

The solution to this problem is a *selective wait,* which allows a task to wait simultaneously for calls on several entries and to accept whichever call arrives first. This can be specified by a statement like the following:

```
SELECT
   ACCEPT Display_Ball
      (x : IN Game_X_Type; y : IN Game_Y_Type) DO
      ...
   END Display_Ball;
   [statements to display a circle symbol at the appropriate place]
OR
   ACCEPT Erase_Ball (x : IN Game_X_Type; y : IN Game_Y_Type) DO
      ...
   END Erase_Ball;
   [statements to display a space at the appropriate place]
```

```
OR
    ACCEPT Display_Racquet
        (x : IN Game_X_Type; y : IN Game_Y_Type) DO
        ...
    END Display_Racquet;
    [statements to display two rectangular blocks at the appropriate place]
OR
    ACCEPT Erase_Racquet
        (x : IN Game_X_Type; y : IN Game_Y_Type) DO
        ...
    END Display_Racquet;
    [statements to display two spaces at the appropriate place]
END SELECT;
```

More generally, a selective wait can take the following form:

```
SELECT
    ACCEPT statement
    sequence of statements
OR
        ~~~
OR
    ACCEPT statement
    sequence of statements
END SELECT;
```

(This is the simplest form of the selective wait. Variations on this form will be introduced in subsequent sections.) The combination

```
ACCEPT statement
sequence of statements
```

is called a SELECT *alternative.*

If none of the entries named in the ACCEPT statements have been called when a task reaches the selective wait, the task waits for one of them to be called. It then executes the corresponding SELECT alternative, starting with the ACCEPT statement. If any SELECT alternatives can be executed immediately when a task reaches the selective wait, one of these alternatives is chosen and executed. The choice of an alternative in this case depends on the implementation. A good implementation will choose "fairly," so that if the selective wait is executed repeatedly, any alternative ready to be executed will eventually be chosen. However, fairness is hard to measure.

Different SELECT alternatives can start with ACCEPT statements for the same entry. When that entry is called, the implementation has the option of choosing either SELECT alternative. The sequence of statements following the ACCEPT statement in a SELECT alternative may contain another ACCEPT statement. Such an ACCEPT statement is executed as part of the SELECT alternative when that SELECT alternative is chosen, but it plays no role in determining when the alternative is chosen.

Selective waits are typically executed inside basic loops. A task executing a selective wait in a loop acts as a server to other tasks. Each of the task's entries corresponds to one of the services that the task provides. The task repeatedly waits for a request for any one of these services and then acts upon the request.

Here is the body of Screen_Package in its entirety:

```
WITH Display_Package;
PACKAGE BODY Screen_Package IS

   TASK BODY Screen_Task IS

    Column : Display_Package.Column_Subtype;
    Line   : Display_Package.Line_Subtype;
    X_Copy : Game_X_Type;
    Y_Copy : Game_Y_Type;
    X_Offset : CONSTANT := 40.5; -- Screen coordinate of X=0
    Y_Offset : CONSTANT := 12.5; -- Screen coordinate of Y=0

   BEGIN

      LOOP

         SELECT

            ACCEPT Display_Ball
               (x : IN Game_X_Type; y : IN Game_Y_Type) DO
               X_Copy := x;
               Y_Copy := y;
            END Display_Ball;
            Column :=
               Display_Package.Line_Subtype(X_Copy+X_Offset);
            Line :=
               Display_Package.Column_Subtype
                  (Y_Copy + Y_Offset);
            Display_Package.Position_Cursor
               (Line, Column);
            Display_Package.Write_Symbol
               (Display_Package.Circle);
```

```
OR

   ACCEPT Erase_Ball
      (x : IN Game_X_Type; y : IN Game_Y_Type) DO
      X_Copy := x;
      Y_Copy := y;
   END Erase_Ball;
   Column :=
      Display_Package.Line_Subtype(X_Copy+X_Offset);
   Line :=
      Display_Package.Column_Subtype
         (Y_Copy + Y_Offset);
   Display_Package.Position_Cursor (Line, Column);
   Display_Package.Write_String (" ");

OR

   ACCEPT Display_Racquet
      (x : IN Game_X_Type; y : IN Game_Y_Type) DO
      X_Copy := x;
      Y_Copy := y;
   END Display_Racquet;
   Column :=
      Display_Package.Line_Subtype(X_Copy+X_Offset);
   Line :=
      Display_Package.Column_Subtype
         (Y_Copy + Y_Offset - 0.5);
   Display_Package.Position_Cursor(Line,Column);
   Display_Package.Write_Symbol
      (Display_Package.Block);
   Display_Package.Position_Cursor
      (Line + 1, Column);
   Display_Package.Write_Symbol
      (Display_Package.Block);

OR

   ACCEPT Erase_Racquet
      (x : IN Game_X_Type; y : IN Game_Y_Type) DO
      X_Copy := x;
      Y_Copy := y;
   END Erase_Racquet;
```

```
            Column :=
               Display_Package.Line_Subtype (X_Copy + X_Offset);
            Line :=
               Display_Package.Column_Subtype
                  (Y_Copy + Y_Offset);
            Display_Package.Position_Cursor (Line, Column);
            Display_Package.Write_String (" ");
            Display_Package.Position_Cursor
               (Line + 1, Column);
            Display_Package.Write_String (" ");

         END SELECT;

      END LOOP;
   END Screen_Task;
END Screen_Package;
```

The package `Display_Package` provides primitive operations for manipulating the video display. It is declared as follows:

```
PACKAGE Display_Package IS
   SUBTYPE Line_Subtype IS Integer RANGE 1 .. 25;
   SUBTYPE Column_Subtype IS Integer RANGE 1 .. 80;
   TYPE Symbol_Type IS ( ..., Circle, ..., Block, ... );
   PROCEDURE Position_Cursor
      (Line : IN Line_Subtype; Column : IN Column_Subtype);
   PROCEDURE Write_String (s : IN String);
   PROCEDURE Write_Symbol (Symbol : IN Symbol_Type);
END Display_Package;
```

The video display has 25 lines of eighty characters each and is capable of displaying either ordinary ASCII characters or a limited number of special symbols. `Symbol_Type` has one enumeration literal for each such symbol. (We have only shown two of the symbols above. The `Circle` symbol is used to depict a ball. A `Block` symbol is a completely filled-in character position. Two `Block` symbols, one directly below the other, are used to depict a racquet.) `Position_Cursor` positions the cursor at a specified line and column. `Write_String` writes the specified screen starting at the current cursor position, wrapping around to the next line if necessary. (Wrapping around from line 25 causes the screen to scroll upward one line.) `Write_Symbol` writes the specified special symbol at the current cursor position. `Write_String` and `Write_Symbol` leave the cursor positioned just after the last character written.

19.2.1.2 Monitors. At first, `Screen_Task` may seem unnecessary. It is simpler to have `Screen_Package` provide seven ordinary subprograms, one for each of the services now provided by an entry of `Screen_Task`. Unfortunately, this will not work, because these services are requested asynchronously by three different tasks (tasks keeping track of the two racquets and a task keeping track of the ball). Two or three of these subprograms could be active at the same time, invoked by different tasks, each trying to position the cursor in preparation for writing a character. Depending on the way execution of the various tasks is interleaved, this could result in the following sequence of events:

1. The task tracking racquet one positions the cursor at line five, column 1.
2. The task tracking the ball positions the cursor at line ten, column twenty.
3. The task tracking racquet one, having just positioned the cursor at line five, column one, writes a `Block` symbol, but this symbol comes out at line ten, column twenty instead.
4. The task tracking racquet one now positions the cursor at line six, column one, and writes a `Block` symbol (for the bottom half of the racquet) at that position. This leaves the cursor at line six, column two.
5. The task tracking the ball, having just positioned the cursor at line ten, column twenty, writes a `Circle` symbol, but this symbol comes out at line six, column two instead.

This is an example of a *race condition,* or *simultaneous update.* When concurrent tasks try to manipulate the same device or update the same variable, these manipulations may be interleaved in unpredictable ways. Unless special measures are taken, the writer of a task cannot assume that the state established in one statement will still exist when the next statement is reached.

`Screen_Task` is an example of such a special measure. `Screen_Task` is the only task that manipulates the screen directly. All other tasks call entries of `Screen_Task` to obtain services related to the video display. This eliminates the simultaneous update problem. `Screen_Task` completes an entire abstract operation (possibly involving several positioning and writing operations) before beginning another abstract operation. This ensures that parts of different operations are not interleaved and thus that the operations work as intended.

`Screen_Task` is an example of a *monitor.* A monitor is a mechanism for avoiding race conditions. It is used under the following conditions:

There is a resource, such as a cursor or a variable, shared by several tasks.

There are one or more *abstract operations* on that shared resource that may not work correctly if parts of operations being carried out by different tasks are interleaved.

A monitor is invoked to carry out an entire abstract operation on the shared resource, as an indivisible operation.

In the Ada language, a monitor is easily implemented by a task whose body contains a basic loop with a selective wait. The task has one entry for each abstract operation. Each SELECT alternative in the selective wait carries out a different abstract operation in it entirety. The loop causes the selective wait to be executed repeatedly. Thus the monitor task acts as a *server,* repeatedly waiting to receive another request to carry out.

Sometimes race conditions are not evident. For example, consider a program to keep track of the total number of people in a building with several doors. A device at each door detects each person entering or leaving the building and drives a task that increments or decrements the total number of people in the building, respectively. That is, each task executes the statement

```
Total_People := Total_People + 1;
```

whenever someone enters through its door, or the statement

```
Total_People := Total_People - 1;
```

whenever someone leaves through its door. Another task periodically examines the value of Total_People and displays it on a security console. The race condition arises from the fact that a compiler may translate a single Ada statement into many machine-language instructions, so that parts of the execution of one statement by one task may be interleaved with parts of the execution of another statement by another task. Consider the following scenario, for example:

1. With Total_People containing the value ten, two people enter the building at about the same time, through doors one and two.
2. The task for door one evaluates the expression Total_People + 1, obtaining the value eleven.
3. The task for door two evaluates the expression Total_People + 1, also obtaining the value eleven.
4. The task for door one completes its assignment statement by copying the value eleven into Total_People.
5. The task for door two completes its assignment statement by copying the value eleven into Total_People

Thus Total_People ends up with the value eleven instead of twelve.

A solution is to write a monitor task for the count shared by several tasks. The abstract operations are incrementing the common count, decrementing the common count, and reporting the current value of the common count. Thus the task declaration is as follows:

```
TASK Common_Count_Monitor IS
   ENTRY Increment;
   ENTRY Decrement;
   ENTRY Get_Current_Count (Count : OUT Natural);
END Common_Count_Monitor;
```

The task body follows the same pattern as the `Screen_Task` body:

```
TASK BODY Common_Count_Monitor IS
   Total : Natural := 0;
BEGIN
   LOOP
      SELECT
         ACCEPT Increment;
         Total := Total + 1;
      OR
         ACCEPT Decrement;
         Total := Total - 1;
      OR
         ACCEPT Get_Current_Count (Count : OUT Natural) DO
            Count := Total;
         END Get_Current_Count;
      END SELECT;
   END LOOP;
END Common_Count_Monitor;
```

Since the variable `Total` is declared inside the `Common_Count_Monitor` body, it can only be named directly by that task. Since all statements naming `Total` are executed by the same task, each of these statements is executed in its entirety before another one starts. Now if two tasks try to increment the common count at the same time, one will have to wait at its entry call on `Common_Count_Monitor.Increment` until `Common_Count_Monitor` finishes its rendezvous with the other task and is ready to accept a new entry call.

A monitor serves two purposes. Like a package, it protects a data structure declared inside of it from being manipulated arbitrarily. The data structure can be manipulated only according to certain abstract operations that the monitor provides to the rest of the program through its entries. Unlike a package, a monitor also protects the data structure against concurrent update by two or more tasks. *Whenever a data structure is to be manipulated by two or more tasks, it ought to be protected by a monitor.* In particular, if a package body contains a variable declaration and the package provides a subprogram whose body changes the value of that variable, then a race condition can result if the subprograms provided by the package can be called by more than one task. In such cases, a monitor is appropriate.

19.2.1.3 Guards. Sometimes it is desirable for one task to send data to another task and to continue about its business even if the other task is not yet ready to receive the data. The rendezvous mechanism does not provide this capability directly, since a task issuing an entry call cannot proceed until the called task is ready to accept that entry call. However, the rendezvous mechanism can be used to build a *message-buffer* task, which does provide this capability. (The item of data sent, whatever its type, is referred to as a *message*.)

A message-buffer task is a monitor that protects a first-in, first-out queue and provides two abstract operations: adding an item to the back of the queue and removing an item from the front of the queue. To send data to a receiving task, a sending task inserts the data at the back of the queue. Following the rendezvous with the message-buffer task, but possibly before the data item is received by the receiving task, the sending task goes on to do other work. The receiving task, when it is ready to receive data, enters a rendezvous with the message-buffer task to obtain and remove the item at the back of the queue. If each message were to consist of a single `Integer` value, a task type for message buffers could be declared as follows:

```
TASK TYPE Integer_Message_Buffer_Type IS
   ENTRY Send (Message : IN Integer);
   ENTRY Receive (Message : OUT Integer);
END Integer_Message_Buffer_Type;
```

There is one complication. When a message buffer is empty, the receiving task must wait for another call on the buffer's `Send` entry before entering a rendezvous with the message-buffer task. Similarly, an upper limit is usually placed on the size of the message buffer's queue, large enough so that the queue rarely becomes filled; but when the queue does become filled, an entry call to send a message must wait until the receiving task receives one of the backlogged messages and thus frees up space in the queue.

To write the `Integer_Message_Buffer_Type` task body, we must be able to control the conditions under which an entry call is accepted. We would like to write the task body with a basic loop that contains a `SELECT` statement with alternatives for the `Send` and `Receive` entries. However, a call on `Send` should only be accepted when the queue is not full, and a call on `Receive` should only be accepted when the queue is not empty.

This control is provided by *guards*. A guard is a construct of the form

`WHEN` *condition* `=>`

that may precede some or all of the alternatives of a selective wait. Each condition is an expression of type `Boolean` evaluated at the beginning of the selective wait. Only those alternatives that are preceded by true guards or by no guard at all may be accepted during execution of that selective wait.

The `Integer_Message_Buffer_Type` task body may be written as follows with guards, assuming an upper limit of ten on the size of the queue:

```
TASK BODY Integer_Message_Buffer_Type IS
   SUBTYPE Queue_Index_Subtype IS Integer RANGE 1 .. 10;
   Circular_Queue : ARRAY (Queue_Index_Subtype) OF Integer;
   Next_Insertion, Next_Removal : Queue_Index_Subtype := 1;
   Current_Size :
      Integer RANGE 0 .. Queue_Index_Subtype'Last := 0;
```

```
BEGIN
   LOOP
      SELECT
         WHEN Current_Size < Queue_Index_Subtype'Last =>
            ACCEPT Send (Message : IN Integer) DO
               Circular_Queue (Next_Insertion) := Message;
            END Send;
            IF Next_Insertion = Queue_Index_Subtype'Last THEN
               Next_Insertion := Queue_Index_Subtype'First;
            ELSE
               Next_Insertion := Next_Insertion + 1;
            END IF;
            Current_Size := Current_Size + 1;

      OR

         WHEN Current_Size > 0 =>
            ACCEPT Receive (Message : OUT Integer) DO
               Message := Circular_Queue (Next_Removal);
            END Receive;
            IF Next_Removal = Queue_Index_Subtype'Last THEN
               Next_Removal := Queue_Index_Subtype'First;
            ELSE
               Next_Removal := Next_Removal + 1;
            END IF;
            Current_Size := Current_Size - 1;

      END SELECT;

   END LOOP;

END Integer_Message_Buffer_Type;
```

When the queue is full, then `Current_Size = Queue_Index_Subtype'Last`, only a call on `Receive` can be accepted, and calls on `Send` must wait. When the queue is empty, then `Current_Size = 0`, only a call on `Send` can be accepted, and a call on `Receive` must wait. In all other cases, a call on either entry can be accepted. (The array `Circular_Queue` is viewed as a circle in which the last component is followed by the first component. This means that the queue can be extended whenever it is not already filled to capacity, possibly by wrapping around to the beginning of the array. In a nonempty queue, `Next_Insertion` indexes the empty array component at which the next item will be inserted, and `Next_Removal` indexes the full array element from which the next item will be removed. See Figure 19.4.)

19.2.1.4 The `TERMINATE` Alternative. Like many task bodies, the `Integer_Message_Buffer_Type` task body contains a basic loop that in turn contains a `SELECT` statement. This means that a task of type `Integer_Message_Buffer_Type` never terminates. Consider the following procedure:

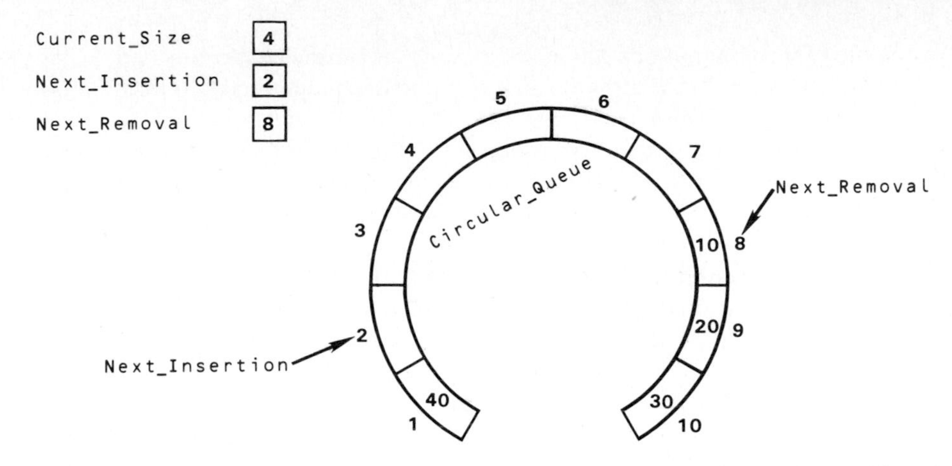

Figure 19.4 Representation of a circular queue containing the values ten, twenty, thirty, and forty, in that order. Physically, `Circular_Queue` is a one-dimensional array with index values ranging from one to ten. Abstractly, we view it as a circle in which component ten follows component one.

```
PROCEDURE Main IS

   ...
   Buffer_1, Buffer_2 : Integer_Message_Buffer_Type;
   ...

BEGIN

   ...

END Main;
```

Since the tasks declared in the declarative part of `Main` never terminate, the procedure `Main` can never terminate (according to the rules explained in Section 19.1.1).

This problem is easily solved with a `TERMINATE` *alternative.* A selective wait may include an alternative of the form

```
WHEN condition =>
   TERMINATE ;
```

(Although it is allowed, the guard is rarely used on a `TERMINATE` alternative.) Selection of this alternative causes the task to terminate. A task *t* can accept a terminate alternative only under certain circumstances in which termination of *t* will allow immediate departure from a subprogram, block statement, or other task that is done with its own work but cannot be left until *t* terminates.

Specifically, a task *t* *depends* on any subprogram, block statement, or other task which, according to the rules explained in Section 19.1, cannot be left until *t* terminates. Dependence may be direct or indirect. (For example, if task *t1* depends on subprogram *s* and task *t2* depends on *t1,* then *t2* indirectly depends on *s.*) A `TERMINATE` alternative may be selected when the following conditions hold:

1. Some subprogram, block statement, or task has finished executing its sequence of statements but is waiting for one or more dependent tasks to terminate so that it too may terminate.
2. All tasks that directly or indirectly depend on this subprogram, block statement, or task either have finished executing their statement sequences or are waiting at selective waits with TERMINATE alternatives.

When both these conditions hold, the TERMINATE alternatives referred to in condition 2 are *all* selected. This causes the completed subprogram, block statement, or task and all its dependent tasks to terminate together. This can only happen under circumstances in which none of the tasks waiting at selective waits would ever again receive an entry call. All tasks that might make such calls are themselves either finished executing their statement sequences or waiting at a SELECT alternative none of whose entries will ever be called.

The rules for selection of a TERMINATE alternative are based on the assumption that a task dependent on some subprogram, block statement, or task was created to serve that frame. In fact, the frame is called a *master* of the tasks that depend on it. When the master has finished its work and there is nothing left for its dependent tasks to do, those dependent tasks executing basic loops can select TERMINATE alternatives. This allows departure from the master that those tasks were created to serve.

A selective wait with a TERMINATE alternative usually occurs in a basic loop of a task body. It is appropriate when some object of the corresponding task type will either be declared in a subprogram body, block statement, or task body or pointed to via an access type declared in one of those places. Without the TERMINATE alternative, that subprogram body, block statement, or task body could never be left.

Here is the Integer_Message_Buffer_Type task body with a TERMINATE alternative added:

```
TASK BODY Integer_Message_Buffer_Type IS
   SUBTYPE Queue_Index_Subtype IS Integer RANGE 1 .. 10;
   Circular_Queue : ARRAY (Queue_Index_Subtype) OF Integer;
   Next_Insertion, Next_Removal : Queue_Index_Subtype := 1;
   Current_Size :
      Integer RANGE 0 .. Queue_Index_Subtype'Last := 0;

BEGIN
   LOOP
      SELECT
         WHEN Current_Size < Queue_Index_Subtype'Last =>
            ACCEPT Send (Message : IN Integer) DO
               Circular_Queue (Next_Insertion) := Message;
            END Send;
```

```
            IF Next_Insertion = Queue_Index_Subtype'Last THEN
               Next_Insertion := Queue_Index_Subtype'First;
            ELSE
               Next_Insertion := Next_Insertion + 1;
            END IF;
            Current_Size := Current_Size + 1;

      OR

         WHEN Current_Size > 0 =>
            ACCEPT Receive (Message : OUT Integer) DO
               Message := Circular_Queue (Next_Removal);
            END Receive;
            IF Next_Removal = Queue_Index_Subtype'Last THEN
               Next_Removal := Queue_Index_Subtype'First;
            ELSE
               Next_Removal := Next_Removal + 1;
            END IF;
            Current_Size := Current_Size - 1;

      OR

         TERMINATE;

      END SELECT;

   END LOOP;

END Integer_Message_Buffer_Type;
```

A `TERMINATE` alternative is not appropriate if all objects of the corresponding task type will be declared in library packages (or pointed to via an access type declared in a library package). In such a case, all objects of the task type depend *only* on library packages. No part of the program will ever wait for termination of such a task, so the `TERMINATE` alternative is unnecessary. In fact, the `TERMINATE` alternative will never be selected, because no subprogram, block statement, or task body will ever fulfill conditions 1 and 2 for such a task. The video game task `Screen_Task` presented at the beginning of Section 19.2.1 is declared in the library package `Screen_Package`. Therefore, even though its task body contains a selective wait within a basic loop, this selective wait should not be given a `TERMINATE` alternative.

19.2.1.5 `DELAY` Alternatives. Sometimes a task must wait for whichever entry call arrives first, but it must do something else if no entry call arrives within a specified amount of time. This capability is needed, for example, if a task must perform some activity on a periodic basis, but also accept entry calls as they arise. A selective wait with a `DELAY` *alternative* provides this capability.

A `DELAY` alternative is an alternative in a selective wait that begins with a `DELAY` statement rather than an `ACCEPT` statement:

```
  ..................
  :WHEN condition =>:
  ..................
        DELAY expression ;
       ......................
       : sequence of statements :
       ......................
```

A DELAY statement in this context has a special meaning. If no other alternative in the selective wait is selected before the amount of time specified in the DELAY statement, the DELAY alternative is selected. When a DELAY alternative is selected, the statements following the DELAY statement are executed, completing execution of the selective wait. The expression in the DELAY statement of a DELAY alternative is evaluated at the time the selective wait is entered.

A selective wait may not contain both a TERMINATE alternative and a DELAY alternative. However, it may contain more than one DELAY alternative. If two DELAY alternatives expire at the same time, the implementation selects one according to its own criteria.

As an example, consider a more realistic version of the Ping-Pong video game task Joystick_Task, introduced in Chapter 18. Joystick_Task is declared in a library package as follows:

```
WITH Global_Types_Package; USE Global_Types_Package;
PACKAGE Joystick_Package IS

   TYPE Coordinate_Type IS DELTA 0.01 RANGE -1.0 .. 1.0;

   TASK Joystick_Task IS
      ENTRY Get_Coordinates
         (Player_ID : IN Player_ID_Type;
          x, y      : OUT Coordinate_Type);
      ENTRY Wait_For_Button_1;
      ENTRY Wait_For_Button_2;
   END Joystick_Task;

END Joystick_Package;
```

Joystick_Task maintains current data on the status of both joysticks by polling (i.e., requesting new data from) the joysticks every fifty milliseconds. A call on Get_Coordinates provides current X and Y coordinates for the specified player's joystick. A call on Wait_For_Button_1 or Wait_For_Button_2 is accepted only when the trigger button on the corresponding joystick is found to be down. By calling Wait_For_Button_1, for example, a task forces itself to wait until the trigger button on joystick 1 has been pressed.

We assume that the computer receives data from both joysticks through a single controller. This controller simultaneously provides the program with the X and Y coordinates of the two sticks and the status of the trigger buttons on the two sticks. Data is obtained from the controller by a call on the following procedure:

```
PROCEDURE Read_Stick_Controller
   (x1, y1, x2, y2                      : OUT Coordinate_Type;
    Button_1_Pressed, Button_2_Pressed : OUT Boolean);
```

(It is because a single operation is used to examine both joysticks that there is one task for both joysticks rather than a separate task for each one.)

Here is the `Joystick_Package` body:

```
WITH Calendar, Read_Stick_Controller; USE Calendar;
PACKAGE BODY Joystick_Package IS
   TASK BODY Joystick_Task IS
      Polling_Interval                     : CONSTANT := 0.05;
      Next_Scheduled_Poll                  : Time;
      x1, y1, x2, y2                       : Coordinate_Type;
      Button_1_Pressed, Button_2_Pressed   : Boolean;
   BEGIN
      Next_Scheduled_Poll := Clock + Polling_Interval;
      Read_Stick_Controller
         (x1, y1, x2, y2,
          Button_1_Pressed, Button_2_Pressed);
      LOOP
         SELECT
            ACCEPT Get_Coordinates
               (Player_ID : IN Player_ID_Type;
                x, y      : OUT Coordinate_Type) DO
               CASE Player_ID IS
                  WHEN 1 =>
                     x := x1;
                     y := y1;
                  WHEN 2 =>
                     x := x2;
                     y := y2;
               END CASE;
            END Get_Coordinates;
         OR
            WHEN Button_1_Pressed =>
               ACCEPT Wait_For_Button_1;
         OR
            WHEN Button_2_Pressed =>
               ACCEPT Wait_For_Button_2;
```

```
            OR

               DELAY Next_Scheduled_Poll - Clock;
               Read_Stick_Controller
                  (x1, y1, x2, y2,
                  Button_1_Pressed, Button_2_Pressed);
               Next_Scheduled_Poll :=
                  Next_Scheduled_Poll + Polling_Interval;
            END SELECT;
         END LOOP;
      END Joystick_Task;
   END Joystick_Package;
```

The selective wait is executed, and the loop containing it repeated, every time the task accepts an entry or polls for new data. Before entering the loop for the first time, and each time it polls for data, the task computes the exact time at which it is next scheduled to poll for data. The expression in the `DELAY` statement is reevaluated each time the selective wait is encountered. The time at which the next poll is scheduled is subtracted from the time at which the selective wait is entered (and the expression is evaluated), obtaining the duration after which the `DELAY` alternative should be selected if no entry call arrives first.

The *decision* to select a `DELAY` alternative is made at the instant that the duration specified in the `DELAY` statement expires. However, a processor might not be allocated to the task containing the `DELAY` alternative at the moment this decision is made. Like the ordinary `DELAY` statement, a `DELAY` alternative in a selective wait may thus result in a delay longer than that requested. `Joystick_Task` may occasionally go more than fifty milliseconds without obtaining new data, but it will still poll every fifty milliseconds *on the average*. `Joystick_Task` computes its delays in terms of the exact time at which each poll is scheduled (reflected in the variable `Next_Scheduled_Poll`). If the task falls behind on one cycle, this does not affect the scheduled time of the next poll. Rather, the next cycle specifies a correspondingly shorter delay.

19.2.1.6 `ELSE` Parts. `DELAY` alternatives specify an action to be taken in a selective wait if no entry call arrives within a specified amount of time. Sometimes we need a greater degree of control—the ability to perform a particular action if no entry call can be accepted *immediately*. A selective wait with an `ELSE` part provides this capability. Such a selective wait has the following form:

```
SELECT
   [WHEN condition =>]
         ACCEPT statement
         [sequence of statements]
OR
   ~~~
```

```
OR
    ..................
    : WHEN condition => :
    ..................
        ACCEPT statement
        ....................
        : sequence of statements :
        ....................
ELSE
    sequence of statements
END SELECT ;
```

When such a selective wait is encountered and one of the ACCEPT alternatives can be accepted immediately (i.e., a call on one of the specified entries has already been issued and the corresponding ACCEPT alternative does not have a false guard), an entry with a waiting call is selected according to the implementation's own criteria, as usual. However, if none of the alternatives can be selected immediately, the statements following the word ELSE are executed.

A selective wait with an ELSE part may not contain a TERMINATE alternative or DELAY alternatives. TERMINATE alternatives, DELAY alternatives, and ELSE parts specify three incompatible responses to the absence of an entry call. Therefore, they are mutually exclusive.

ELSE parts are useful for tasks that perform routine repetitive processing but respond to certain entry calls by departing momentarily from the routine processing. The statements in the ELSE part specify the routine processing, and the ACCEPT alternatives specify the more urgent special actions to be taken when an entry is called. Each time the selective wait is encountered, the routine processing in the ELSE part is carried out unless an entry call is waiting. If an entry call is waiting, the special processing in its ACCEPT alternative is carried out instead.

As an example, consider a task in a nautical navigation system responsible for displaying the craft's current position every second. The position is reported in terms of nautical miles east and north of some fixed reference point. Most of the time, the position is computed by periodically computing the X and Y components of the craft's velocity and updating the position accordingly. (The computation is based on the speed of the craft with respect to the water, the craft's compass heading, and the presumed velocity of the water current.) This method is subject to inaccuracy due to sudden fluctuations in the craft's velocity between sample times or misestimation of the water current. Therefore, the task has an entry Set_Position that can be called to initialize or readjust the position. (The position might be readjusted when a landmark is sighted, for example.) The task is provided by the following library package:

```
PACKAGE Position_Package IS

   TYPE Nautical_Miles_Type IS
      DELTA 0.001 RANGE -5000.0 .. 5000.0;
```

```
      TASK Position_Task IS
         ENTRY Set_Position (x, y : IN Nautical_Miles_Type);
      END Position_Task;

   END Position_Package;
```

The task has a selective wait executed once per second on the average. The selective wait has an `ACCEPT` alternative for the `Set_Position` entry and an `ELSE` part that computes an updated position for the craft based on velocity. Except in the special case that `Set_Position` has been called, it is the `ELSE` part of the selective wait that is executed. In either case, execution of the selective wait has the effect of obtaining a new value for the craft's position. We assume that another library package, `Speed_Package`, provides a fixed-point type `Knots_Type` and a task `Speed_Task`, and that `Speed_Task` provides an entry `Sample_Speed` with three parameters: the X and Y components of the craft's velocity plus the time of the sensor readings from which those components were derived.

Here is the body of `Position_Package`:

```
WITH Calendar, Speed_Package, Display_Position; USE Calendar;
PACKAGE BODY Position_Package IS

   SUBTYPE Knots_Type IS Speed_Package.Knots_Type;
   FUNCTION "+"
      (Left, Right : Knots_Type) RETURN Knots_Type
      RENAMES Speed_Package."+";
   FUNCTION "/"
      (Left : Knots_Type; Right : Integer)
      RETURN Knots_Type
      RENAMES Speed_Package."/";

   TYPE Interval_Length_Type IS
      DELTA 1.0E-5 RANGE 0.000 .. 0.003; -- in hours

   TASK BODY Position_Task IS
      Next_Update_Time, Old_Sample_Time, Sample_Time : Time;
      X_Position, Y_Position : Nautical_Miles_Type;
      Old_X_Speed,
         Old_Y_Speed,
         X_Speed_Midpoint,
         Y_Speed_Midpoint : Knots_Type;
      X_Speed, Y_Speed     : Knots_Type := 0.0;
      Actual_Interval      : Interval_Length_Type;
      Seconds_Per_Hour     : CONSTANT := 3600.0;
   BEGIN
      Sample_Time := Clock;
      Next_Update_Time := Sample_Time;
```

```
    LOOP
        DELAY Next_Update_Time - Clock;
        SELECT
            ACCEPT Set_Position
                (x, y : IN Nautical_Miles_Type) DO
                X_Position := x;
                Y_Position := y;
            END Set_Position;

        ELSE
            Old_Sample_Time := Sample_Time;
            Old_X_Speed := X_Speed;
            Old_Y_Speed := Y_Speed;

            Speed_Package.Speed_Task.Sample_Speed
                (X_Speed, Y_Speed, Sample_Time);

            X_Speed_Midpoint := (Old_X_Speed + X_Speed) / 2;
            Y_Speed_Midpoint := (Old_Y_Speed + Y_Speed) / 2;

            Actual_Interval :=
                Interval_Length_Type
                    ( (Sample_Time -Old_Sample_Time) /
                       Seconds_Per_Hour );

            X_Position :=
                X_Position +
                Nautical_Miles_Type
                    (X_Speed_Midpoint * Actual_Interval);

            Y_Position :=
                Y_Position +
                Nautical_Miles_Type
                    (Y_Speed_Midpoint * Actual_Interval);

        END SELECT;

        Display_Position (X_Position, Y_Position);
        Next_Update_Time := Next_Update_Time + 1.0;

    END LOOP;

  END Position_Task;

END Position_Package;
```

The position computation averages successive velocity measurements and uses the average as an estimate of the average velocity between the time the two measurements were taken. This is multiplied by the length of time between the two measurements (which may vary since the effect of the DELAY statement is not exact) to obtain the distance traveled between the two measurements. The difference between successive sampling times is measured in seconds. This must be converted to hours so that it can be multiplied by a speed measured in knots (nautical miles per hour) to obtain a distance in nautical miles. (The versions of "+" and "/" used to compute the average are for Knots_Type, which is originally declared in Speed_Package.

The renaming declarations make those versions visible within the Position_Task body.)

19.2.2 Making Entry Calls More Flexible

Selective waits give a task flexible control over which entry calls it will accept and how long it will wait for an entry call to arrive. *Timed entry calls* and *conditional entry calls* provide a *calling* task with flexible control over how long it will wait for an entry call that it has issued to be accepted. Superficially, timed entry calls and conditional entry calls look like selective waits, but with ACCEPT statements at the beginning of alternatives replaced by entry *call* statements. However, the form of a timed entry call or a conditional entry call is more restricted than that of a selective wait. There are also differences in meaning.

19.2.2.1 Timed entry calls. A timed entry call is an entry call that is *cancelled* if it is not accepted within a specified amount of time. When a call on some entry is cancelled, it is removed from the queue of waiting calls on that entry. To the called task, the effect is as if the call had never been issued.

The form of a timed entry call is similar to a selective wait with a DELAY alternative:

```
SELECT
   entry call statement
   sequence of statements
OR
   DELAY expression ;
   sequence of statements
END SELECT ;
```

There are always exactly two alternatives, the first of which begins with an entry *call* statement and the second of which always begins with a DELAY statement. The alternatives never have guards.

The meaning of the DELAY statement in a timed entry call is similar to its meaning in the DELAY alternative of a selective wait. If the entry call cannot be accepted within the amount of time specified in the DELAY statement, it is cancelled, and the sequence of statements following the DELAY statement is executed. Otherwise, the entry call and the statements following it are executed.

A program to control a railroad train might contain a loop like the following to monitor the speed of the train:

```
LOOP
   Obtain_Speed (Speed);
   IF Speed > Maximum_Safe_Speed THEN
      SELECT
         Control_Task.Reduce_Speed;
         Warning_Lamp_Package.Turn_On (Speed_Lamp);
      OR
         DELAY 1.0;
         RAISE Emergency_Shutdown;
      END SELECT;
   ELSE
      Warning_Lamp_Package.Turn_Off (Speed_Lamp);
   END IF;
   Next_Poll_Time := Next_Poll_Time + Polling_Interval;
   DELAY Next_Poll_Time - Clock;
END LOOP;
```

If the train is found to be going too fast, the entry `Control_Task.Reduce_Speed` is called to reduce power and apply brakes. After this call has been accepted, the program lights a warning light. If, for some reason, `Control_Task` does not accept this entry call within one second, `Control_Task` is bypassed and the exception `Emergency_Shutdown` is raised, to bring the train to an emergency stop via a backup mechanism.

19.2.2.2 Conditional entry calls. A conditional entry call is an entry call that is cancelled if it cannot be accepted immediately. Its form is similar to a selective wait with one alternative and an `ELSE` part:

```
SELECT
     entry call statement
    ......................
    : sequence of statements :
    :                        :
    ......................
ELSE
     sequence of statements
END SELECT ;
```

The entry call can be accepted immediately if, at the time the conditional entry call is executed, the called task is waiting at an `ACCEPT` statement for the called entry. The entry call can also be accepted immediately if the called task is waiting at a selective wait, at least one of the `SELECT` alternatives begins with an `ACCEPT` statement for the called entry, and the alternative is not preceded by a false guard. In either of these cases, the entry call statement and the statements following it are executed. In any other case, the statements in the `ELSE` part are executed instead.

The following conditional entry call uses `Joystick_Task` (given in Section 19.2.1.5) to test whether the trigger button on joystick 1 is currently pressed. The Boolean variable `Currently_Pressed` is set appropriately. If the button is not currently pressed, the task executing the conditional entry call does not wait for it to be pressed.

```
SELECT
   Joystick_Package.Joystick_Task.Wait_For_Button_1;
   Currently_Pressed := True;
ELSE
   Currently_Pressed := False;
END SELECT;
```

As another example, consider the following declarations:

```
TASK TYPE Printer_Task_Type IS
   ENTRY Obtain_Printer;
   ENTRY Release_Printer;
END Printer_Task_Type;

Printer_Task_List : ARRAY (1 .. 5) OF Printer_Task_Type;
```

The `Printer_Task_Type` body can be written so that once a task of that type accepts a call on `Obtain_Printer`, it will not accept another call on `Obtain_Printer` until it has accepted a call on `Release_Printer`. (The task body is left as an exercise for the reader.) In a program in which many tasks share five printers, a task can gain exclusive access to a printer if all tasks call

```
Printer_Task_List (i).Obtain_Printer
```

before using printer number *i* and

```
Printer_Task_List (i).Release_Printer
```

afterward. An ordinary call on

```
Printer_Task_List (i).Obtain_Printer
```

forces the calling task to wait until printer number *i* is available. The following loop searches for any printer currently available and waits only if all printers are currently in use:

```
Printer_Search:
   LOOP
      FOR p IN Printer_Task_List'Range LOOP
         SELECT
            Printer_Task_List (p).Obtain_Printer;
            Printer_Obtained := p;
            EXIT Printer_Search;
         ELSE
            NULL;
         END SELECT;
      END LOOP;
      DELAY 5.0;
   END LOOP;
```

The `FOR` loop attempts an entry call for each printer, exiting the outer loop when a call succeeds. Each time an entry call is attempted that cannot be accepted immediately, the conditional entry call executes its `ELSE` part, which does nothing. If all printers are found to be busy, the outer loop waits at least five seconds and tries again. (The reason for the delay is so that the task executing the loop can be "put to sleep" while it waits for a printer, rather than consuming processor time with "busy waiting.")

19.3 ADVANCED TASKING FEATURES

19.3.1 Priorities

A task type may be assigned a *priority*. This is a number specifying the urgency of executing tasks in that type, compared with tasks in other types. Priorities help determine the task to which a processor will be assigned when there is more than one task ready to execute. Priorities are not meant to provide precise control over which tasks will be executing at a particular time.

Priorities are specified by the `Priority` pragma. The form of this pragma is

```
PRAGMA Priority ( expression ) ;
```

This pragma normally goes in a task-type declaration or single-task declaration (along with the entry declarations). In addition, the pragma may appear in the declarative part of the main program to specify the priority of the task executing the main program.

The expression must be of type `Integer`, and a *higher number* indicates a *higher degree of urgency*. The allowable range of priority numbers depends on the implementation. The predefined package `System`, discussed in Chapter 20, provides a subtype of type `Integer` named `Priority`. This subtype consists of the priority values allowed by the implementation.

The expression in the `Priority` pragma must be static (see Section 8.3.5). This means that a task's priority is fixed at the time its task-type declaration or task declaration is compiled. A task's priority cannot be changed while the program is executing.

The effect of task priorities is narrowly defined: *If two tasks of different priorities are both ready to execute, then the higher-priority task will not be kept waiting while the lower-priority task executes.* A task is "ready to execute" if it is not completed, it is not blocked, and there are sufficient computing resources available (a suitable processor and enough storage, for example). A task is *blocked* when it is waiting for a rendezvous, waiting at a `DELAY` statement that has not expired, or waiting for a dependent task to terminate. A rendezvous is executed at the higher of the calling and called tasks' priorities.

In a typical implementation, in which tasks are interleaved on a single processor and all tasks require the same computing resources, this means that a task is suspended when a higher-priority task becomes unblocked. For example, if a task is waiting for a rendezvous and a lower-priority task begins this rendezvous, then both tasks will be unblocked upon the completion of the rendezvous. At that point, the lower-priority task will be suspended and the task that had been waiting will execute. Similarly, if a task is waiting at a `DELAY` statement, a selective wait with a `DELAY` alternative, or a timed entry call, and a lower-priority task is executing when the delay expires, then the lower-priority task is suspended so that the newly unblocked task can execute. Lower-priority tasks get a chance to execute when higher-priority tasks block themselves. Of the lower-priority unblocked tasks, one with at least as high a priority as the others is chosen for execution.

For different kinds of implementations, priorities may have different consequences. In particular, for an implementation with more than one processor, priorities govern what happens when there are more unblocked tasks than processors. Two tasks of different priorities may be executing at the same time, provided that both tasks have a higher priority than any other task that is ready to execute.

When several tasks call the same entry, priorities *do not* determine which entry call is accepted first. Entry calls are always queued in order of arrival, regardless of the priorities of the calling tasks. Similarly, priorities do not necessarily affect which alternative in a selective wait is chosen. The tasks that have called the entries in the selective wait do not become "ready to execute" until *after* the selective wait chooses one of the entries, so their priorities are irrelevant. Since an implementation makes this choice according to its own criteria, it is *possible* that an implementation will base this choice on the priorities of the calling tasks, but the rules of the Ada language do not require this.

Consider the task `Speed_Package.Speed_Task` alluded to in Section 19.2.1.5. This task had an entry `Sample_Speed` returning the X and Y coordinates of a craft's velocity and the time of the sensor readings from which the velocity was computed. The time of the sensor readings is critical in the computation of the craft's position from its velocity. Most likely, `Speed_Task` has a loop of the following form:

```
LOOP
   [obtain sensor readings]
   Clock_Reading := Clock;
   [compute X_Speed and Y_Speed from readings]
   ACCEPT Sample_Speed
      (x, y : OUT Knots_Type; Reading_Time : OUT Time) DO
      x := X_Speed;
      y := Y_Speed;
      Reading_Time := Clock_Reading;
   END Sample_Speed;
END LOOP;
```

Unfortunately, the value of Reading_Time will be inaccurate if the implementation switches to another task just before the assignment to Clock_Reading. By the time Speed_Task regains control, Clock may return a significantly later time than the time of the sensor readings. This can be avoided by giving Speed_Task a higher priority than any other task in the program. Then the implementation may not switch to another task until Speed_Task starts waiting for a call on Sample_Speed.

High priorities should be reserved for urgent tasks that become eligible for execution relatively rarely and make themselves ineligible for execution again after a short time. Otherwise, high-priority tasks will monopolize the processor and low-priority tasks will rarely get a chance to execute. In the Speed_Task example above, if the computation of X and Y velocity components from sensor readings is long, it would be better to write a separate task to read the sensors and the clock at the highest priority:

```
TASK Sensor_Reading_Task IS
   ENTRY Obtain_Readings ( ... ; Reading_Time : OUT Time);
   PRAGMA Priority (System.Priority'Last);
END Sensor_Reading_Task;

TASK BODY Sensor_Reading_Task IS
   Clock_Reading : Time;
   ...
BEGIN
   LOOP
      [obtain sensor readings]
      Clock_Reading := Clock;
      ACCEPT Obtain_Readings
         ( ... ; Reading_Time : OUT Time) DO
         ...
         Reading_Time := Clock_Reading;
      END Obtain_Readings;
   END LOOP;
END Sensor_Reading_Task;
```

Then `Speed_Task` can execute at a lower priority, repeatedly calling `Sensor_Reading_Task.Obtain_Readings` (to obtain sensor readings and a timely clock reading) and then computing `X_Speed` and `Y_Speed` from the raw sensor readings.

19.3.2 Entry Families

An *entry family* is, in essence, a one-dimensional "array" of entries. Entry families allow a task to have many entries that are treated in a uniform manner. The entry to be used in an `ACCEPT` statement or an entry call is determined by an index value that can be computed by the program. Long, repetitive sequences of similar operations on different entries of the same task can be replaced by a `FOR` loop in which the loop parameter is used as an index to select a member of an entry family.

An entry family is declared by an entry declaration of the following form:

```
ENTRY identifier ( discrete range )
    [ ( parameter specification ; ~~~ ; parameter specification ) ] ;
```

This declaration goes in a task or task-type declaration, just like other entry declarations. (Discrete ranges were described in Section 4.2.5.)

The typemark `Player_ID_Type` (naming an integer type with a range of `1 .. 2`) is used as a discrete range in the following task declaration:

```
TASK Joystick_Task IS
   ENTRY Get_Coordinates (Player_ID_Type)
      (x, y : OUT Coordinate_Type);
   ENTRY Wait_For_Button (Player_ID_Type);
END Joystick_Task;
```

This declaration describes a version of `Joystick_Task` with four entries:

```
Get_Coordinates (1)
Get_Coordinates (2)
Wait_For_Button (1)
Wait_For_Button (2)
```

Each of these entries is a *member* of the entry family `Get_Coordinates` or the entry family `Wait_For_Button`. A member of an entry family is a full-fledged entry, with its own queue of entry calls.

In this version of `Joystick_Task`, a call on entry `Get_Coordinates (i)` sets that entry's `OUT` parameters to the current coordinates of joystick *i*, where *i* is in the range `1 .. 2`. Similarly, a call on `Wait_For_Button (i)` causes the calling task to wait until the trigger button on joystick *i* is pressed. A call on `Wait_For_Button (1)` and a call on `Wait_for_Button (2)` may both be pending at the same time, each waiting in its own entry queue.

In an entry call or ACCEPT statement, a member of an entry family is identified by a name of the form

entry-family-name (*expression*)

The expression, known as an *entry index,* must be a value in the range specified in the entry family declaration. The value of this expression determines which entry family member is named. For example, the following function returns the current Y coordinate of a specified joystick:

```
WITH Joystick_Package, Global_Types_Package;
USE Joystick_Package, Global_Types_Package;

FUNCTION Current_Y_Coordinate
   (Stick : Player_ID_Type) RETURN Coordinate_Type IS

   x, y : Coordinate_Type;

BEGIN

   Joystick_Task.Get_Coordinates (Stick) (x, y);
   RETURN y;

END Current_Y_Coordinate;
```

In the first statement of this function,

```
Joystick_Task.Get_Coordinates (Stick)
```

is the name of the entry being called, and x and y are the actual parameters to the entry call. The ACCEPT statement

```
ACCEPT Get_Coordinates (1) (x, y : OUT Coordinate_Type) DO
   x := x1;
   y := y1;
END Get_Coordinates;
```

accepts a call on entry Get_Coordinates (1). Like other entries, members of entry families can be renamed as procedures. The renaming declaration

```
PROCEDURE Get_Stick_1_Coordinates
   (X_Coordinate, Y_Coordinate : OUT Coordinate_Type)
   RENAMES Joystick_Task.Get_Coordinates (1);
```

renames the entry family member Get_Coordinates (1) as a procedure.

A call on an entry family member with no parameters looks like a call on an ordinary entry with one parameter:

```
Joystick_Task.Wait_For_Button (1);
```

You must examine the declaration of Joystick_Task to determine that Wait_For_Button is an entry family name rather than an entry name, and thus that the 1 is an entry index rather than an actual parameter.

Matters could get quite confusing if a family of entries with no parameters had the same name as a single entry with one parameter declared in the same task. Fortunately, this is not allowed. Entry names may be overloaded, but entry *family* names may not be. That is, two entries in the same task may have the same name (provided that their parameter types are different), but an entry family may never have the same name as another entry family or another single entry in the same task.

The entry index in an ACCEPT statement need not be static. The first step in executing a standalone ACCEPT statement with an entry index is to evaluate the index. Once the index has been evaluated, the ACCEPT statement waits for a call on a particular member of an entry family. In a selective wait, the first step is to evaluate all guards. Then, if any of the ACCEPT alternatives without a false guard has an entry index in its opening ACCEPT statement, the entry index is evaluated. From that point until the completion of the selective wait, each ACCEPT alternative corresponds to a particular entry—either an ordinary entry or a particular member of an entry family.

Suppose a task controlling access to a printer had an entry family declared as follows:

```
ENTRY Request_Printer (1 .. 5);
```

Other tasks could call members of this entry family to request exclusive use of the printer. These entry calls could have an entry index corresponding to the *precedence level* of the request. The following loop accepts one call on a member of Request_Printer, assuming one is waiting, making sure that an entry call is accepted only if no calls with a higher precedence level are waiting:

```
-- This point reached only when the printer is available and
--   a call on some member of the Request_Printer entry
--   family is known to be waiting.

FOR Precedence_Level IN REVERSE 1 .. 5 LOOP
   SELECT
      ACCEPT Request_Printer (Precedence_Level);
      Printer_In_Use := True;
      EXIT;
   ELSE
      NULL;
   END SELECT;
END LOOP;
```

Each time through the loop, the entry index Precedence_Level is evaluated to determine which entry is named by the ACCEPT alternative. If a call on that entry family member is not already waiting, the ELSE part of the selective wait is executed, doing nothing. The next iteration of the loop will look for a waiting call on the member of Request_Printer corresponding to the next lower level of precedence.

This example illustrates an important use of entry families: providing a task with more control over the order in which entry calls are accepted. Had `Request_Printer` been a single entry, with the precedence level passed as an entry parameter, there would have been a single queue of calls on this entry. The accepting task would have had no choice but to accept calls in the order they were made, regardless of precedence level. With `Request_Printer` declared as an entry family, each member of the family has its own queue of entry calls. Calls on a given entry family member must be accepted in the order in which they were made, but the accepting task can choose the queue from which it removes the front entry call.

Do not confuse entry families with arrays of task objects. If *a* is an array of task objects with single entries named *e*, then there is a group of entries that can be named by names of the form *a* (*i*) . *e*, where *i* is an array index. If *t* is a single task with an entry family named *f*, then there is a group of entries that can be named by names of the form *t* . *f* (*i*), where *i* is an entry index. However, there is an important distinction. In an array of task objects, each object is associated with a different thread of control (that is, with a different sequence of actions). An entry family is an "array" of entries for one task with one thread of control. Calls on members of an entry family are accepted in strict sequence by one task.

While it is convenient to think of entry families as "arrays of entries," an entry family is not, strictly speaking, an array. An array is a data object that belongs to some array type and has components that are also data objects. An array may have many dimensions. An array's index values can be described by the array's `'First`, `'Last`, `'Range`, and `'Length` attributes. None of this is true of an entry family.

19.3.3 Aborting Tasks

In rare circumstances it may be necessary to stop a task in its tracks and prevent it from interfering with other tasks in the program. The `ABORT` statement is used to prevent a task from continuing to communicate or synchronize with the other tasks in a program. The `ABORT` statement is intended for use only as a measure of last resort, not for routine task management. Even then, an `ABORT` statement should be used only if its consequences have been carefully considered.

The form of an `ABORT` statement is as follows:

`ABORT` *task–object–name* , ~~~ , *task–object–name* ;

Strictly speaking, this statement does not abort the tasks listed! Rather, it renders them *abnormal.* Depending on the implementation, an abnormal task may continue to execute for a while, but it must become completed by the time it does one of the following:

begin or complete elaboration of its task body's declarative part
reach an entry call
reach a `DELAY` statement

reach a selective wait or an ACCEPT statement
reach the end of an ACCEPT statement
cause another task to become active, either by allocating a task object or completing
the elaboration of a declarative part in which a task object is declared
reach an exception handler

A *completed* task is one that is done performing actions and will terminate as soon as its dependent tasks terminate. When a task becomes abnormal, all of its dependent tasks also become abnormal. If the "aborted" task and all of these dependent abnormal tasks eventually complete, the "aborted" task will eventually terminate.

If a task is *already* waiting to begin elaboration of its declarative part, waiting for a rendezvous, or waiting at a DELAY statement when it becomes abnormal, the task becomes completed immediately, and may be considered "aborted" by the time the ABORT statement is over. In contrast, if a calling task becomes abnormal while in a rendezvous, it *must not* become completed until the rendezvous is over. The ACCEPT statement completes normally, and the called task remains oblivious to the demise of its partner. This allows the called task to continue to receive and service entry calls from other tasks.

If a task is not already waiting for one of the events previously listed when it becomes abnormal, the effect of the ABORT statement depends on the implementation. An implementation may cause an "aborted" task to become completed immediately, it may wait for one of the events listed, or it may cause the "aborted" task to become completed sometime in between. If the "aborted" task is stuck in an infinite loop in which it never tries to do any of the things listed above, an implementation is not required to ever make the task completed.

The ABORT statement is inappropriate for achieving routine task termination when a task has completed its work. An aborted task may be cut off at an inopportune time, such as in the middle of manipulating a data structure. This can leave the data structure in an inconsistent state. Furthermore, an aborted task has no chance to "clean up" after itself, deallocating variables it allocated, closing files it opened, and so forth.

Preferable alternatives include using the TERMINATE alternative in tasks that repeatedly service entry calls and giving tasks special entries that request the called task to terminate. Either of these alternatives gives the task to be terminated some control over when termination will take place. The task can complete its data structure manipulations and perform cleanup actions before it completes.

The ABORT statement is rarely useful even in emergency situations. Blindly aborting a task when it appears to have gone out of control is like trying to bring a misdirected car under control by removing the steering wheel. Tasks are placed in programs to serve specific purposes, and they are almost always indispensable to the programs in which they occur. Unless a program designer gives very careful thought to how the program can proceed (perhaps in a degraded mode) once a particular task is aborted, aborting that task is likely to lead to a ripple effect, fouling up other tasks that try to communicate with the aborted task.

19.4 TASKS AND EXCEPTIONS

Chapter 15 described how exceptions work in single-task programs. All the rules described there remain valid for multitask programs, but there are additional cases that must be considered. Different rules govern the propagation of exceptions raised in the declarative part of a task body and the statements of a task body. In addition, there are special rules for exceptions raised during intertask communication. There is a predefined exception, `Tasking_Error`, raised when certain problems occur in the interaction between tasks.

19.4.1 Exceptions in Task Bodies

An exception arising at the top level of a task body's statement sequence is never propagated out of the task body. If the task body has a handler for the exception, the handler is executed and the task becomes completed. If there is no handler, the task becomes completed immediately. No other task is directly affected. Like a task that becomes completed for any other reason, a task that becomes completed because of an exception waits for its dependent tasks to terminate. When all of its dependent tasks have terminated, the task itself terminates.

Consider the following somewhat contrived task-type declaration and task body:

```
TASK TYPE Multiplier_Task_Type IS
   ENTRY Deliver_Factor (Factor : IN Positive);
   ENTRY Obtain_Product (Product : OUT Positive);
END Multiplier_Task_Type;

TASK BODY Multiplier_Task_Type IS

   TYPE Positive_Pointer_Type IS ACCESS Positive;
   Product_Pointer :
      Positive_Pointer_Type := NEW Positive'(1);
   Factor_Pointer :
      Positive_Pointer_Type := NEW Positive;

   TASK Journal_Task IS
      ENTRY Record_Event (Event : IN String);
   END Journal_Task;

   TASK BODY Journal_Task IS
      ...
   END Journal_Task;
```

```
BEGIN

   LOOP
      SELECT
         ACCEPT Deliver_Factor (Factor : IN Positive) DO
            Factor_Pointer.ALL := Factor;
         END Deliver_Factor;
         Journal_Task.Record_Event ("DF");
         Product_Pointer.ALL :=
            Product_Pointer.ALL * Factor_Pointer.ALL;
         Factor_Pointer := NEW Positive;

      OR

         ACCEPT Obtain_Product (Product : OUT Positive) DO
            Product := Product_Pointer.ALL;
         END Obtain_Product;
         Journal_Task.Record_Event ("OP");
      OR
         TERMINATE;
      END SELECT;
   END LOOP;

EXCEPTION

   WHEN Storage_Error =>
      Journal_Task.Record_Event ("SE");

END Multiplier_Task_Type;
```

If the allocator in the first `ACCEPT` alternative raises `Storage_Error`, the handler will be invoked. Once the handler is finished, the `Multiplier_Task_Type` task will wait for its dependent task `Journal_Task` to terminate. Then the `Multiplier_Task_Type` task will terminate. If the multiplication in the first `ACCEPT` alternative raises `Numeric_Error` (for which there is no handler), the `Multiplier_Task_Type` task will immediately become completed. Once `Journal_Task` terminates (for instance, because of a `TERMINATE` alternative), then the `Multiplier_Task_Type` task will also terminate. No exceptions are raised elsewhere in the program.

When an exception is raised in the declarative part of a task body, the task becomes completed and the exception `Tasking_Error` is raised at the place the task was activated. For a task declared in some declarative part *d,* the exception is raised just after the `BEGIN` following *d.* This point is within the statement sequence corresponding to *d,* so `Tasking_Error` can be handled by an exception handler for that statement sequence. If an *allocated* task raises an exception while elaborating its declarative part, `Tasking_Error` is raised by the allocator. (Whenever a task object is allocated, evaluation of the allocator does not finish until after the allocated task emhas successfully elaborated its declarative part. This allows the allocator to raise Tasking_Error if the allocated task raises an exception in its declarative part.)

Consider the following procedure, which uses the task type Multiplier_Task_Type declared above:

```
PROCEDURE Multiply IS
   ...
   Multiplier : Multiplier_Task_Type;
BEGIN
   ...
EXCEPTION
   WHEN Tasking_Error =>
      RAISE Unanticipated_Error;
END Multiply;
```

If the initialization of Product_Pointer in the Multiplier_Task_Type task body raises Storage_Error, the task Multiplier will immediately become completed and will terminate as soon as its dependent task Journal_Task terminates. (The task body's handler for Storage_Error is not invoked because the handler applies only to the statements in the task body, not the declarations. See Section 15.1.2.) The exception Tasking_Error is raised just after the BEGIN in procedure Multiply. This causes the handler in Multiply to be invoked.

Sometimes several tasks are activated together, as when several task objects are declared in the same declarative part or an array of task objects is allocated. If more than one of these tasks raises an exception while elaborating its declarative part, Tasking_Error is only raised once at the point of activation. If some of these tasks complete elaboration of their declarative parts and others do not, the ones that do will proceed normally.

For example, suppose the procedure Multiply were modified as follows:

```
PROCEDURE Multiply IS

   Multiplier_List :
      ARRAY (1 .. 3) OF Multiplier_Task_Type;
BEGIN
   ...
EXCEPTION
   WHEN Tasking_Error =>
      RAISE Unanticipated_Error;
END Multiply;
```

Suppose Storage_Error is raised only when Multiplier_List (3) elaborates its declarative part. Then Multiplier_List (3) becomes complete as before, but Multiplier_List (1) and Multiplier_List (2) proceed normally. Tasking_Error is again raised just after the BEGIN in Multiply, causing the handler for Tasking_Error to raise Unanticipated_Error. (However, Multiply does not propagate this exception until after its two dependent tasks Multiplier_List (1) and Multiplier_List (2) have terminated.)

Section 15.3 described some circumstances in which the predefined exception Program_Error is raised. There is another such circumstance that arises only in task bodies: If a selective wait has no ELSE part and each of its alternatives has a false guard, then the selective wait raises Program_Error. For example, the selective wait

```
SELECT
   WHEN Current_Count > 0 =>
      ACCEPT Decrement;
      Current_Count := Current_Count - 1;
OR
   WHEN Current_Count < 0 =>
      ACCEPT Increment;
      Current_Count := Current_Count + 1;
END SELECT;
```

raises Program_Error when it is executed with Current_Count equal to zero. (If a selective wait has an ELSE part and each of its alternatives has a false guard, it simply executes the ELSE part, and no exception is raised.)

19.4.2 Exceptions During Task Interaction

When an exception is raised during a rendezvous, further execution of the ACCEPT statement is abandoned, and the same exception is reraised in both the called task and the calling task. In the called task, the exception is raised by the ACCEPT statement itself within the surrounding sequence of statements. In the calling task, the exception is reraised by the entry call statement. Each raising of the exception is independent of the raising in the other task. The exception might be handled in one task and go unhandled in the other, for example.

Consider the following package declaration:

```
PACKAGE Altitude_Package IS

   TYPE Altitude_Type IS DELTA 16.0 RANGE 0.0 .. 120_000.0;

   TASK Altitude_Task IS
      ENTRY Get_Smoothed_Altitude
         (Altitude : OUT Altitude_Type);
   END Altitude_Task;
```

```
      Invalid_Altitude : EXCEPTION;

   END Altitude_Package;
```

`Altitude_Task` reads an altitude sensor once every fifth of a second on the average. The altitude sensor has self-testing hardware. Each time it is read, the sensor provides both an altitude reading and a flag indicating whether the reading can be considered reliable. Whenever the three most recent readings can be considered reliable, a call on `Get_Smoothed_Altitude` sets its parameter to the average of those three readings. When two of the three most recent readings can be considered reliable, the call yields the average of those two readings only. Otherwise, a call on `Get_Smoothed_Altitude` raises the exception `Invalid_Altitude`.

Unreliable readings may result from transient conditions such as sudden acceleration or fluctuations in power supply. Therefore, the proper response to an `Invalid_Altitude` exception may be for the caller of `Get_Smoothed_Altitude` to try again several times before concluding that the altitude sensor is broken. It follows that `Altitude_Task` should continue to operate normally even after it raises `Invalid_Altitude`.

The task body below allows this. The procedure `Read_Sensor`, which obtains raw altitude readings and validity flags, is not shown here.

```
WITH Calendar; USE Calendar;
PACKAGE BODY Altitude_Package IS
   PROCEDURE Read_Sensor
      (Altitude : OUT Altitude_Type; Valid : OUT Boolean)
      IS SEPARATE;
   TASK BODY Altitude_Task IS

      Next_Poll_Time     : Time;
      Valid_Count        : Integer RANGE 0 .. 3 := 0;
      Valid_Sum          : Altitude_Type := 0.0;
      Next               : Integer RANGE 1 .. 3 := 1;
      Reading            : ARRAY (1 .. 3) OF Altitude_Type;
      Is_Valid           : ARRAY (1 .. 3) OF Boolean :=
                              (1 .. 3 => False);
      Polling_Interval : CONSTANT Duration := 0.2;
   BEGIN
      Next_Poll_Time := Clock;
      LOOP
         BEGIN
            SELECT
               ACCEPT Get_Smoothed_Altitude
                  (Altitude : OUT Altitude_Type) DO

                  IF Valid_Count >= 2 THEN
                     Altitude := Valid_Sum / Valid_Count;
                  ELSE
                     RAISE Invalid_Altitude;
                  END IF;
               END Get_Smoothed_Altitude;
```

```
            OR
               DELAY Next_Poll_Time - Clock;
               -- Remove the oldest reading:
               IF Is_Valid (Next) THEN
                  Valid_Count := Valid_Count - 1;
                  Valid_Sum := Valid_Sum - Reading (Next);
               END IF;
               -- Replace it with the newest reading:
               Read_Sensor
                  ( Reading (Next), Is_Valid (Next) );
               IF Is_Valid (Next) THEN
                  Valid_Count := Valid_Count + 1;
                  Valid_Sum := Valid_Sum + Reading (Next);
               END IF;
               -- Advance to the next oldest reading:
               IF Next = 3 THEN
                  Next := 1;
               ELSE
                  Next := Next + 1;
               END IF;
               Next_Poll_Time :=
                  Next_Poll_Time + Polling_Interval;
            END SELECT;
         EXCEPTION
            WHEN Invalid_Altitude =>
               NULL;
         END;
      END LOOP;
   END Altitude_Task;
END Altitude_Package;
```

To propagate `Invalid_Altitude` to the entry call, `Altitude_Task` must raise the exception within the `ACCEPT` statement. This also causes the exception to be propagated to the `ACCEPT` statement itself, so the selective wait is enclosed in a block statement that handles the local raising of `Invalid_Altitude` by doing nothing. This allows `Altitude_Task` to continue with the next iteration of the loop. (The block is placed around the selective wait rather than the `ACCEPT` statement, because an `ACCEPT` alternative may only begin with an `ACCEPT` statement, not a block statement. An exception arising in an alternative of a selective wait is propagated to the selective wait itself.)

An entry call statement raises `Tasking_Error` if the called task becomes completed before accepting the entry call. It does not matter whether the called task was already completed at the time it was called or if it became completed some time after the call was made but before it got around to accepting the call. Similarly, an entry call statement raises `Tasking_Error` if an `ABORT` statement renders the called task abnormal before the task accepts the entry call.

In fact, an entry call statement raises Tasking_Error if the called task becomes abnormal *during* a rendezvous. However, if a *calling* task becomes abnormal during a rendezvous, the ACCEPT statement completes normally and the called task is unaffected. (Recall from Section 19.3.3 that a task that becomes abnormal during a rendezvous does not become completed until the rendezvous is over.) This asymmetric treatment of tasks aborted during a rendezvous reflects the view that accepting tasks are servers and calling tasks are clients. A client task cannot continue after its server has been aborted; but when one of its clients is aborted, a server task should remain alive to serve other clients.

When a subprogram, block statement, or task body is the master of some task, it cannot be left until that task terminates. This rule applies even if an exception is raised in the subprogram, block statement, or task body. If there is a handler for the exception, it is executed. The master then waits for the termination of its dependent tasks. If there is no handler, a subprogram or block statement does not propagate the exception until the dependent tasks have terminated.

19.5 FURTHER DETAILS

19.5.1 Shared Variables

Ada tasks were designed to communicate through rendezvous. It is also possible for two tasks to communicate through a global variable whose scope includes both tasks. This is dangerous because it introduces the possibility of race conditions (see Section 19.2.1.2). It makes the program harder to understand because the interaction between the two tasks becomes implicit. However, if suitable precautions are taken, communication through *shared variables* may save time. In rare situations where a program is found to run too slowly because it spends too much time in rendezvous, it may be appropriate to introduce shared variables.

Consider a package to manage telecommunications:

```
PACKAGE Telecommunications_Package IS
   PROCEDURE Get (Item : OUT Character);
   PROCEDURE Put (Item : IN Character);
END Telecommunications_Package;

PACKAGE BODY Telecommunications_Package IS
   TASK Transmitter_Task IS
      ENTRY Put (Item : IN Character);
      ENTRY Pause;
      ENTRY Resume;
   END Transmitter_Task;

   TASK Receiver_Task IS
      ENTRY Get (Item : OUT Character);
   END Receiver_Task;

   PROCEDURE Get(Item : OUT Character) IS
   BEGIN
      Receiver_Task.Get (Item);
   END Get;
```

```
      PROCEDURE Put (Item : IN Character) IS
      BEGIN
         Transmitter_Task.Put (Item);
      END Put;

      PROCEDURE Transmit_Character (c : IN Character)
         IS SEPARATE;

      PROCEDURE Receive_Character (c : OUT Character)
         IS SEPARATE;

      TASK BODY Transmitter_Task IS SEPARATE;

      TASK BODY Receiver_Task IS SEPARATE;

   END Telecommunications_Package;
```

A call on the procedure `Telecommunications_Package.Put` sends a character along a telecommunications line, and a call on the procedure `Telecommunications_Package.Get` receives a character from a telecommunications line. The actual input/output device manipulation is done by the procedures `Send_Character` and `Receive_Character`, not shown here. The purpose of `Transmitter_Task` and `Receiver_Task` is to implement a simple communications protocol to ensure that the device at the other end of the telecommunications line does not fall too far behind.

The protocol is known as XOFF/XON. The device at the other end of the line places characters in a buffer as they are received and removes them from the buffer as quickly as it can process the characters. If the buffer begins to get too full, the device sends the program an *XOFF signal* consisting of the character `ASCII.DC3` (control-S), and the program stops sending characters. When the buffer becomes sufficiently empty, the device sends the program an *XON signal* consisting of the character `ASCII.DC1` (control-Q), and the program resumes transmission of characters.

The role of `Receiver_Task` is to obtain characters received from the device. Ordinary characters are passed on to calls on `Get`, but the XOFF/XON control characters are intercepted. `Receiver_Task` calls the `Transmitter_Task` entries `Pause` and `Resume`, respectively, when the XOFF and XON signals are received. `Transmitter_Task` normally accepts calls on its `Put` entry and transmits the character passed as a parameter; but when the `Pause` entry is called, `Transmitter_Task` does not accept any more calls on `Put` until the `Resume` entry is called.

Here are the task bodies:

```
SEPARATE (Telecommunications_Package)

TASK BODY Receiver_Task IS

   X_Off : CONSTANT Character := ASCII.DC3;
   X_On  : CONSTANT Character := ASCII.DC1;
   c     : Character;
```

```
BEGIN
   LOOP
      Receive_Character (c);
      CASE c IS
         WHEN X_Off =>
            Transmitter_Task.Pause;
         WHEN X_On =>
            Transmitter_Task.Resume;
         WHEN OTHERS =>
            ACCEPT Get (Item : OUT Character) DO
               Item := c;
            END Get;
      END CASE;
   END LOOP;
END Receiver_Task;
-- -- -- -- -- -- -- -- -- -- --
SEPARATE (Telecommunications_Package)
TASK BODY Transmitter_Task IS
   TYPE Mode_Type IS (Off, On);
   Current_Mode : Mode_Type := On;
   c            : Character;
BEGIN
   LOOP
      SELECT
         -- A waiting call on Pause takes precedence over
         --  any other call.
         ACCEPT Pause;
         Current_Mode := Off;
      ELSE
         SELECT
            WHEN Current_Mode = On =>
               ACCEPT Put (Item : IN Character) DO
                  c := Item;
               END Put;
               Transmit_Character (c);
         OR
            ACCEPT Pause;
            Current_Mode := Off;
         OR
            ACCEPT Resume;
            Current_Mode := On;
         END SELECT;
      END SELECT;
   END LOOP;
END Transmitter_Task;
```

(In Transmitter_Task, the outer SELECT statement with an ELSE part guarantees that a pending call on Pause is accepted before a pending call on either other entry, so that XON signals are acted on promptly. If no call on Pause is waiting, but a call on some other entry is waiting, the call is accepted in the inner SELECT statement. If no call at all is waiting, the inner SELECT statement waits for a call on any entry.)

Suppose that the program runs too slowly. The first response should be to find out where the program is spending its time. Suppose a metering tool reveals that the program is spending a significant portion of its time executing the ACCEPT statement for Receiver_Task.Get, which copies every character ever received. The copying can be eliminated by declaring a variable New_Character in the Telecommunications_Package specification, so that it is visible to users of the package. Receiver_Task is modified to read characters directly into this variable, where they can be examined directly by the task using the received data.

To synchronize Receiver_Task and the task using the received data, we replace the entry Get with two parameterless entries. The using task will call an entry named Request_Character to signal that it is ready for the previous contents of the variable New_Character to be overwritten. After accepting a call on this entry, Receiver_Task will read characters into New_Character until a character other than the XOFF or XON signal has been placed there. Then it will accept a call on the entry Wait_For_Character to signal to the using task that New_Character is ready for examination. The using task does not examine New_Character until a call on this entry has been accepted. Since Receiver_Task now reads new characters only when the using task has requested a character, prompt processing of XOFF and XON signals depends on the using task requesting characters at frequent intervals.

The new package specification looks like this:

```
PACKAGE Telecommunications_Package IS

   New_Character : Character;
      -- set by a call on Get_New_Character

   PROCEDURE Get_New_Character;
   PROCEDURE Put (Item : IN Character);

END Telecommunications_Package;
```

To process a new character, a user of the package calls Get_New_Character and then examines New_Character.

Internally, Get_New_Character first calls the Request_Character entry of Receiver_Task, then calls the Wait_For_Character entry of Receiver_Task, then returns. The new package body looks like this:

```
PACKAGE BODY Telecommunications_Package IS

   TASK Transmitter_Task IS
      ENTRY Put (Item : IN Character);
      ENTRY Pause;
      ENTRY Resume;
   END Transmitter_Task;
```

```
   TASK Receiver_Task IS
      ENTRY Request_Character;
      ENTRY Wait_For_Character;
   END Receiver_Task;

   PROCEDURE Get_New_Character IS
   BEGIN
      Receiver_Task.Request_Character;
      -- Receiver_Task may now begin updating New_Character.
      Receiver_Task.Wait_For_Character;
      -- The update is now complete.
   END Get_New_Character;

   PROCEDURE Put (Item : IN Character) IS
   BEGIN
      Transmitter_Task.Put (Item);
   END Put;

   PROCEDURE Transmit_Character (c : IN Character)
      IS SEPARATE;

   PROCEDURE Receive_Character (c : OUT Character)
      IS SEPARATE;

   TASK BODY Transmitter_Task IS SEPARATE;

   TASK BODY Receiver_Task IS SEPARATE;

END Telecommunications_Package;
```

The revised `Receiver_Task` subunit is as follows:

```
SEPARATE (Telecommunications_Package)

TASK BODY Receiver_Task IS

   X_Off : CONSTANT Character := ASCII.DC3;
   X_On  : CONSTANT Character := ASCII.DC1;

BEGIN

   LOOP

      ACCEPT Request_Character;
      -- New_Character may now be overwritten.

      LOOP -- Repeatedly read characters into New_Character
           --    until the character read is a data character,
           --    informing Transmitter_Task of any XON or XOFF
           --    characters read first.

         Receive_Character (New_Character);

         CASE New_Character IS

            WHEN X_Off =>
               Transmitter_Task.Pause;

            WHEN X_On =>
               Transmitter_Task.Resume;

            WHEN OTHERS =>
               EXIT;

         END CASE;

      END LOOP;
```

```
      -- New_Character now contains the next data character.
      ACCEPT Wait_For_Character;
   END LOOP;
END Receiver_Task;
```

A rendezvous with a single parameter has been replaced by two rendezvous without parameters or ACCEPT statement bodies. Depending on the implementation of rendezvous, the two new rendezvous may be more or less efficient than the one original rendezvous. Perhaps more significantly, Receiver_Task has substantially less work to do because it no longer copies each character it receives. Whatever the impact on program performance, the new task interaction is certainly harder to understand than the original, so shared variables should not be used routinely.

The entries Request_Character and Wait_For_Character prevent race conditions. After a Request_Character rendezvous and before a Wait_For_Character rendezvous, only Receiver_Task uses the shared variable New_Character (by updating it). After a Wait_For_Character rendezvous and before the next Request_Character rendezvous, only a user of Telecommunications_Package uses the shared variable (by examining it). These rendezvous are called *synchronization points* for Receiver_Task and the user task.

Usually, such synchronization points are necessary for tasks to share variables safely. In fact, the rules of the Ada language allow a compiler to assume when generating machine code that synchronization points have been used in this way to prevent race conditions. Specifically, a compiler may assume that whenever one task updates a shared noncomposite variable between two synchronization points, no other task uses the variable between those points.

One consequence of this assumption is that a compiler may manipulate its own *copy* of a noncomposite global variable rather than the global variable itself between two synchronization points. For example, a Request_Character rendezvous and the next Wait_For_Character rendezvous are consecutive synchronization points. Because Receiver_Task updates New_Character between these two points, the compiler is permitted to assume that no other task uses New_Character between these two points. Thus the compiler could have the call on Receive_Character place the value of its parameter directly in a fast register and have the CASE statement examine the contents of this register rather than the variable New_Character itself. It is not necessary to copy the contents of the register into New_Character until the loop is exited and the ACCEPT statement for Wait_For_Character is reached.

This efficient code-generation scheme would not be valid if another task could examine New_Character after a call on Request_Character and before a call on Wait_For_Character, because it would not be examining the most recent value for New_Character computed by Receiver_Task. Similarly, if another task could update New_Character between those two points, the deferred copying of the register contents into New_Character could overwrite a value placed in

New_Character more recently by another task. Nonetheless, the compiler is permitted to generate code for Receiver_Task in this way, on the assumption that no other task can examine or update New_Character after a call on Request_Character but before a call on Wait_For_Character.

There are circumstances in which tasks can safely share variables without synchronizing. Suppose, for example, that the task actually producing characters to be sent handled transmission of the characters itself and the task actually examining received characters handled the receipt of characters itself. This would eliminate the need for the entries Put, Request_Character, and Wait_For_Character. To eliminate the need for the remaining entries, Pause and Resume, a shared variable declared in a library package could be used to communicate XOFF and XON signals. The library package might look like this:

```
PACKAGE Shared_Data_Package IS
   TYPE Mode_Type IS (Off, On);
   Current_Mode : Mode_Type := On;
END Shared_Data_Package;
```

The task processing received characters would have a loop of the following form:

```
LOOP
   LOOP -- Repeatedly read characters into New_Character
        --  until the character read is a data character,
        --  informing the transmitting task of any XON or
        --  XOFF characters read first.
     Receive_Character (New_Character);
     CASE New_Character IS
        WHEN X_Off =>
           Shared_Data_Package.Current_Mode := Off;
        WHEN X_On =>
           Shared_Data_Package.Current_Mode := On;
        WHEN OTHERS =>
           EXIT;
     END CASE;
   END LOOP;
   -- New_Character now contains the next data character.
   -- [statements to process the new data character]
END LOOP;
```

The task producing and sending characters would have a loop of the following form:

```
LOOP
    -- [statements to produce a new character and place it in the variable c ]
    -- Busy wait until Shared_Data_Package.Current_Mode = On:
    WHILE Shared_Data_Package.Current_Mode = Off LOOP
        DELAY 0.1;
    END LOOP;
    Transmit_Character (c);
END LOOP;
```

Every time this task has a character ready to transmit, it checks the value of the shared variable `Current_Mode`. If it is `Off`, the task delays itself for at least a tenth of a second and then checks again.

Since the receiving task is the only one that updates the shared variable, there can be no simultaneous update problem. The only race condition we have to worry about is one where the transmitting task examines the value of the shared variable an instant before the receiving task updates it, then proceeds to act upon this now obsolete value. For this particular program, such a race condition presents no problem. It just means that the transmitting task gets to transmit one more character before the XOFF signal takes effect. Since the device at the other end of the telecommunications line transmits an XOFF signal well before its buffer becomes completely full, this is harmless.

Nonetheless, this solution may not work correctly with certain compilers. Each task executes a loop containing no synchronization points. A compiler is permitted to generate optimized machine code based on the assumption that, between synchronization points, no task updates a variable being used by another task. A clever optimizing compiler could do two things, either of which by itself would be enough to make the program work incorrectly. First, when compiling the receiving task, the compiler could observe that the task updates but never examines the variable `Current_Mode`, assume since there are no intervening synchronization points that no other task ever examines the variable, and eliminate the assignments to `Current_Mode`! Second, when compiling the transmitting task, the compiler could observe that the task examines but never updates the variable `Current_Mode`, assume since there are no intervening synchronization points that no other task ever updates the variable, conclude that `Current_Mode` retains its initial value, `On`, and thus that the `WHILE` loop can never be executed, and eliminate the `WHILE` loop!

The `Shared` pragma can be used to prevent such an occurrence. The form of the `Shared` pragma is:

```
PRAGMA Shared ( identifier ) ;
```

The identifier must be a noncomposite variable name introduced earlier by an object declaration (not a renaming declaration). The pragma appears later in the same sequence of declarations as the object declaration.

The pragma stipulates that, when dealing with the specified variable, the compiler may not make the assumption described earlier. That is, the compiler must account for the possibility that the variable may be updated by one task and read or updated by another task without an intervening synchronization point.

You *must* use the `Shared` pragma for any variable that is written by one task and read or written by another task between the same pair of synchronization points. Otherwise the compiler may generate code based on false assumptions about your program. Thus `Shared_Data_Package` should be changed to read as follows:

```
PACKAGE Shared_Data_Package IS
   TYPE Mode_Type IS (Off, On);
   Current_Mode : Mode_Type := On;
   PRAGMA Shared (Current_Mode);
END Shared_Data_Package;
```

This forces the compiler to generate code that really updates `Current_Mode` when the receiving task reaches its assignment statements and really examines `Current_Mode` when the transmitting task reaches the top of the `WHILE` loop.

19.5.2 Attributes of Tasks And Entries

There are three attributes whose values describe the state of a task and its entries. All of these attributes are of limited use because the values returned by them are subject to race conditions. That is, between the time a task evaluates one of these attributes and the time it takes some action based on that value, some other task may perform an action that makes that value obsolete.

A task may be in progress, *abnormal, completed,* or *terminated.* A task becomes abnormal when an `ABORT` statement naming it is executed. It becomes completed when it is done performing all the actions it will ever perform and is waiting for its dependent tasks to terminate. When a task is completed and all its dependent tasks terminate, the task itself becomes terminated.

If *T* is a task object, the attribute *T*`'Callable` returns a value of type `Boolean`. The value is `True` if entries of *T* can be called without immediately raising `Tasking_Error`; the value is `False` otherwise. Specifically, *T*`'Callable` is true if *T* is in progress and false if *T* is abnormal, completed, or terminated. Even if *T*`'Callable` is true, a call on one of *T*'s entries can *eventually* raise `Tasking_Error` if *T* becomes abnormal or completed before accepting the call.

The attribute *T*`'Terminated` is similar. It too returns a value of type `Boolean`. In this case, the value of the attribute is `False` if *T* is in progress, abnormal (but not yet completed), or completed (but not yet terminated); and it is `True` if *T* is terminated.

In a statement such as

```
IF Sensor_Task'Callable THEN
   Sensor_Task.Read_Sensor (x);
ELSE
   RAISE Sensor_Error;
END IF;
```

`Sensor_Task` can become uncallable between the time the attribute evaluates to `True` and the time the entry call inside the `IF` statement is executed. The `'Terminated` attribute suffers from a similar problem. A safer way to achieve the intended effect of the previous `IF` statement is as follows:

```
BEGIN
   Sensor_Task.Read_Sensor (x);
EXCEPTION
   WHEN Tasking_Error =>
      RAISE Sensor_Error;
END;
```

Within the body of a task with an entry named *E*, the attribute *E*`'Count` returns the number of calls on that entry currently waiting to be accepted. This attribute may be used as a value of any integer type. The attribute *E*`'Count` is not allowed outside the task body for which *E* is declared.

Between the time this attribute is evaluated and the time the value is acted upon, *E*`'Count` may get either larger or smaller. It will get larger if other tasks call the entry. More subtly, it will get smaller if timed calls on the entry are cancelled, or if an entry call is cancelled because the calling task has been aborted. Like the `'Callable` and `'Terminated` attributes, the `'Count` attribute must be used with caution.

19.5.3 More on `ACCEPT` Statements

The sequence of statements in an `ACCEPT` statement may include a `RETURN` statement of the form

```
RETURN ;
```

If this statement is executed, it completes execution of the sequence of statements. Otherwise, execution of the sequence of statements is completed when the last statement in the sequence is executed. Because the sequence of statements in an `ACCEPT` statement is usually short and simple, a `RETURN` statement there is rarely useful.

Section 18.3.2.3 introduced `ACCEPT` statements of the form

`ACCEPT` *identifier* `;`

In fact, an ACCEPT statement without any "body" may have formal parameters:

ACCEPT *identifier* (*parameter specification list*) ;

Parameters in such an ACCEPT statement are useless, because there are no statements to examine or set them. However, calls on some entry with parameters might be accepted from several places, with the parameters ignored in only some of those places. If an entry has formal parameters, they must be listed on each ACCEPT statement for that entry, even if a given ACCEPT statement ignores them.

19.5.4 Matching Identifiers

We have described task-type declarations, task declarations, task bodies, and ACCEPT statements as ending with a line of the form

END *identifier* ;

The identifier must be identical to that given at the top of the declaration, body, or ACCEPT statement. The matching identifiers help a reader to find the beginning and end of the construct. They make it easier to keep track of nesting. They can also make it easier for a compiler to reorient itself after encountering a syntax error, so that it can provide accurate error messages.

Actually, the identifier following the END is optional in each of these places. You may find it omitted in programs written by others. However, there is never any good reason for you to omit the identifier in a program that you write. Omitting the identifier buys you nothing (beyond a few keystrokes), but makes your program harder to read.

19.5.5 Scope and Visibility

The scope and visibility rules of Chapter 14 apply to task-type declarations, task-object declarations, entry declarations, and parameter specifications in entry declarations. The scope and visibility rules of a task-type declaration or a task-object declaration are the same as for any type or object declaration. The scope rules for entry declarations and entry parameter specifications follow from the scope rules given in Section 14.1, but we introduce four new visibility rules in this section to supplement the visibility rules in Section 14.2.

An entry declaration is an auxiliary declaration of the task or task-type declaration in which it occurs. According to Scope Rule 2 of Section 14.1, this means that the scope of an entry declaration starts at the beginning of the entry declaration and includes the rest of the scope of the enclosing task or task-type declaration. This explains, for example, why an entry can be named in an ACCEPT statement, in the 'Count attribute, or outside the task body in an entry call.

A parameter specification *in an entry declaration* is an auxiliary declaration of that entry declaration. Thus its scope starts at the beginning of the parameter specification and includes the rest of the scope of the entry declaration—that is, the rest of the scope of the enclosing task or task-type declaration. This explains why the formal parameter of an entry can be named in an `ACCEPT` statement or, outside the task body, in an entry call with named parameter associations. An entry parameter specification *in an* `ACCEPT` *statement* repeats information given in the entry declaration but does not introduce a new entity. Therefore, no scope is defined for it.

Now let us turn to visibility rules, first for entry declarations and then for entry parameter specifications. In each case, there are two rules—one describing where the declaration is directly visible and one describing where it is visible by selection (see Section 14.2.3).

Visibility Rule 14:

An entry declaration is directly visible from the end of the entry declaration to the end of the enclosing task or task-type declaration and throughout the corresponding task body, except where it is hidden.

Visibility Rule 14 explains, for example, why an entry can be named by its identifier alone in an `ACCEPT` statement or in the `'Count` attribute (which can only occur within a task body).

Visibility Rule 15:

A declaration for entry *e* is visible by selection just after the dot in an expanded name of the form *t*. *e*, where *t* is a name denoting a task object or an access value pointing to a task object.

Visibility Rule 15 explains how an entry is usually named in an entry call. However, in the unusual case that one task body is nested within another, Visibility Rule 14 tells us that the inner task may call an entry of the outer task by giving only the entry name, without the task name.

Visibility Rule 16:

A parameter specification occurring in an entry declaration is directly visible within `ACCEPT` statements for that entry, except where hidden by an inner declaration within the `ACCEPT` statement.

An inner declaration within an `ACCEPT` statement can only occur directly or indirectly inside a block statement or another `ACCEPT` statement:

```
ACCEPT Get_Total (Total : OUT Integer) DO
   ...
   DECLARE
      Total : Float;
   BEGIN
      ... -- The entry parameter is hidden here.
   END;
   ...
END Get_Total;
```

Within an ACCEPT statement, an entry parameter specification is considered an inner declaration, hiding any outer declaration of the same identifier:

```
TASK BODY Shared_Total_Type IS
   Total : Integer := 0;
BEGIN
   LOOP
      SELECT
         ACCEPT Change_Total (Change : IN Integer) DO
            -- The variable Total declared in the task body is
            --    directly visible here, and the parameter
            --    Total of the Get_Total entry is not visible.
            Total := Total + Change;
         END Change_Total;
      OR
         ACCEPT Get_Total (Total : OUT Integer) DO
            -- The variable Total declared in the task body is
            --    hidden here, and the entry parameter Total is
            --    directly visible.
            Total := Shared_Total_Type.Total;
         END Get_Total;
      OR
         TERMINATE;
      END SELECT;
   END LOOP;
END Shared_Total_Type;
```

To avoid the need for selected names such as that in the ACCEPT statement for Get_Total, you should not use the same name as both an entry parameter and a task-body variable.

Visibility Rule 17:

A parameter specification occurring in an entry declaration is visible by selection in a named call on that entry.

Visibility Rule 17 explains the occurrence of the entry formal parameter `Total` in the entry call

```
Shared_Total_1.Get_Total (Total => x);
```

19.6 SUMMARY

When a declarative part corresponding to some statement sequence *s* contains declarations of task objects, the tasks begin execution as soon as the declarative part has been elaborated. First, the tasks all elaborate the declarative parts of their task bodies. When all have done so, the statements of the task bodies and the statements of *s* begin execution in parallel. Departure from the block statement, subprogram body, or task body containing *s* cannot occur until all the declared tasks have terminated. Any task raising an exception while elaborating its task body's declarative part completes immediately, and the exception `Tasking_Error` is raised in *s*.

A dynamically allocated task object begins execution when the allocator creating it is evaluated. First, the task elaborates the declarative part of its task body; then the allocator returns the access value designating the task object; and then the task begins executing the statements of its task body in parallel with the task that evaluated the allocator. Departure from the block statement, subprogram body, or task body containing the corresponding access-type declaration cannot take place until all tasks pointed to by values in that access type have terminated. If a dynamically allocated task raises an exception while elaborating its task body's declarative part, the task completes immediately and `Tasking_Error` is raised by the allocator.

When a task object is declared in a library package, it begins execution when the package is elaborated (before the main program starts). No part of the program is forced to await the termination of the task. Similarly, if an access type designating a task object is declared in a library package, no part of the program is forced to await the termination of the task.

When a task object is declared in an inner package, the task begins execution when the package is elaborated. If the package is directly or indirectly surrounded by a block statement, subprogram body, or task body, departure from the innermost such frame must await termination of the task. Similarly, if an access type designating task objects is declared in a package directly or indirectly surrounded by such a frame, departure from the innermost such frame must await the termination of all tasks pointed to by values in that access type.

A task can achieve greater control over the entry calls it accepts by executing a *selective wait*. The general form of a *selective wait* is

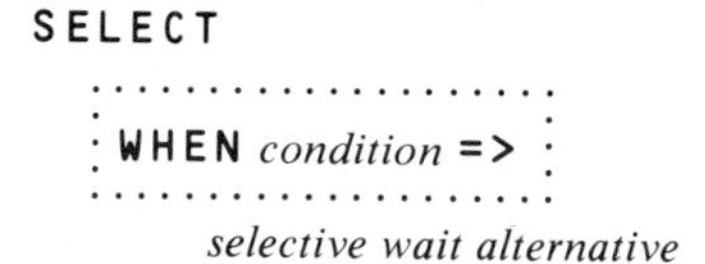

```
OR
    ~~~

OR
   ....................
   : WHEN condition => :
   ....................
         selective wait alternative

 .........................
 :ELSE                    :
 :    sequence of statements :
 .........................

 END SELECT ;
```

A selective wait alternative may take one of three forms:

```
 ACCEPT statement
 ...................
 :sequence of statements:
 ...................

 DELAY expression ;
 ...................
 :sequence of statements:
 ...................

 TERMINATE ;
```

At least one of the alternatives must be of the first form. Optionally, a selective wait may also contain *either* one or more alternatives of the second form, *or* exactly one alternative of the third form, *or* an **ELSE** part. No more than one of these options may be exercised in a single selective wait.

Upon execution of a selective wait, the conditions following the word **WHEN** (known as *guards*) are evaluated, and any alternatives preceded by guards that evaluate to **False** are removed from further consideration. Then, if there are any alternatives of the second form remaining, the expressions in the **DELAY** statements are evaluated. If there are any remaining alternatives of the first form with calls waiting on the entries corresponding to the **ACCEPT** statements, one of these is chosen and executed, completing execution of the selective wait. The criterion for making this choice depends on the implementation, so the programmer should view the choice as arbitrary. If there are no entry calls waiting, the behavior of the selective wait depends on its form:

If all selective wait alternatives begin with an **ACCEPT** statement and the selective wait has no **ELSE** part, the task waits until an entry call arrives corresponding to one of those **ACCEPT** statements. The corresponding alternative is then executed, completing execution of the selective wait.

If the selective wait contains an **ELSE** part, the statements in the **ELSE** part are executed to complete execution of the selective wait.

If the selective wait contains one or more alternatives of the second form, the task waits until either an entry call arrives that allows an alternative of the first form to be executed or the amount of time specified in one of the DELAY statements expires, allowing the alternative beginning with that DELAY statement to be executed.

If the selective wait contains an alternative of the third form, and there is some part of the program from which departure can take place as soon as certain tasks, all waiting at selective waits of this form, terminate, then all such tasks choose the TERMINATE alternative and terminate. Otherwise, the selective wait statement waits until an entry call arrives that allows one of the alternatives of the first form to be executed.

If all selective wait alternatives have false guards and there is an ELSE part, the statements in the ELSE part are executed; if there is no ELSE part, the exception Program_Error is raised.

Just as selective waits give a task control over the way it *accepts* entry calls, *timed entry calls* and *conditional entry calls* give a task control over the way it *issues* entry calls and waits for them to be accepted. The form of a timed entry call is

```
SELECT
    entry call statement
    sequence of statements
OR
    DELAY expression ;
    sequence of statements
END SELECT ;
```

If the entry call is accepted before the amount of time specified in the DELAY statement passes, the sequence of statements following the entry call is executed. Otherwise, the entry call is cancelled, and the sequence of statements following the DELAY statement is executed. The form of a conditional entry call is

```
SELECT
    entry call statement
    sequence of statements
ELSE
    sequence of statements
END SELECT ;
```

If the entry call can be accepted immediately, it and the statements following it are executed. Otherwise, the statements following the word ELSE are executed.

A programmer may specify the *priority* of a task. This helps an implementation choose which task to execute when more than one task is ready. It does not provide precise control over which tasks will execute when. Priorities are specified by a pragma of the form

PRAGMA Priority (*expression*) ;

This pragma goes in a task or task-type declaration or in the declarative part of the main program. The expression is a static expression of type Integer and must lie within a range defined by the implementation. Tasks with higher priority numbers are given preference when an implementation decides which tasks should execute and which should wait for a processor to become available.

A task type may have a number of entries with identical parameters, distinguished from each other by the value of an *entry index* computed during program execution. An *entry family* is declared by a declaration of the form

ENTRY *identifier* (*discrete range*)
[(*parameter specification* ; ~~~ ; *parameter specification*)] ;

An entry family is, in essence, a one-dimensional "array" of entries, known as *members* of the entry family. Each member of an entry family is an ordinary entry. An entry family member is identified by a name of the form

entry family name (*expression*)

In an entry call, the value of the expression determines which entry family member is being called. In an **ACCEPT** statement, the value of the expression determines the entry on which a call will be awaited. In a selective wait, such expressions are evaluated before any waiting begins.

The **ABORT** statement, whose form is

ABORT *task object name* , ~~~ , *task object name* ;

is a means of last resort for controlling an uncooperative task. Execution of an **ABORT** statement causes the tasks listed in the statement to become *abnormal*. An abnormal task becomes completed by the time it synchronizes in some way with other tasks, or, depending on the implementation, perhaps sooner. A calling task that becomes abnormal in the middle of a rendezvous does not become completed until the rendezvous is over.

An aborted task has no control over when it is interrupted, so it cannot arrange to put partially updated data structures in a consistent state or to perform clean-up actions. Furthermore, most tasks play essential roles in their programs, and it is difficult to design programs to behave sensibly after tasks have been aborted. Therefore, **TERMINATE** alternatives and specially designated entries are usually better means for causing a task to terminate.

Special rules apply to exceptions in multitask programs. When an exception is propagated to a task body, the task becomes completed, possibly after a handler has been executed. The exception is not propagated further. When an exception is raised in a rendezvous, the exception is re-raised twice—in the calling task at the point of the entry call statement and in the called task at the point of the `ACCEPT` statement. An entry call raises `Tasking_Error` if the called task becomes completed or abnormal before it accepts the call or if the called task becomes abnormal during the rendezvous. (However, if a calling task becomes abnormal during a rendezvous, the rendezvous completes normally and the called task is unaffected.)

Some programs can be sped up—usually at the cost of clarity and with greater risk of subtle programming errors—by having tasks communicate through shared variables rather than through entry parameters. Often, rendezvous are still needed to synchronize the tasks so that they do not use shared data at the same time. In the rare case that it is not necessary to synchronize the tasks sharing a variable, the variable must be named in a pragma of the following form:

```
PRAGMA Shared ( identifier ) ;
```

The identifier must be the name of a noncomposite variable introduced in an object declaration. If this pragma is not used, a compiler may generate object code based on the assumption that rendezvous are used to synchronize access to the shared variable, and that if one task updates the shared variable, no other task uses it in any way until a rendezvous occurs.

Certain attributes are defined for task objects and entries. If *T* is a task object, the Boolean attribute *T*`'Callable` is true if *T* is in progress and false if *T* is abnormal, completed but waiting for other tasks to terminate, or terminated; the Boolean attribute *T*`'Terminated` is true if *T* is terminated, but false if *T* is in progress, abnormal, or completed but waiting for other tasks to terminate. If *E* is an entry identifier, the attribute *E*`'Count` may only appear within the task body corresponding to *E*'s entry declaration. Its value is the number of calls on that entry currently waiting to be accepted. All of these attributes must be used with care, because their values can be changed by the actions of other tasks an instant after they are evaluated.

EXERCISES

19.1 Suppose that the following functions are all separately compiled and take a long time to execute:

```
FUNCTION e (x : IN Float) RETURN Float;
FUNCTION f (x : IN Float) RETURN Float;
FUNCTION g (x : IN Float) RETURN Float;
FUNCTION h (x : IN Float) RETURN Float;
```

Write a function that takes a `Float` parameter `x` and returns the value

```
h ( f(e(x)), g(e(x)) )
```

This value should be computed in such a way that `e` is only called once and `f` and `g` are called concurrently (so that, on a multiprocessor system, `f` and `g` could execute simultaneously).

19.2 A parking garage has room for 500 cars. There are sensors that report each time a car enters or leaves the garage. The data gathered by these sensors are used to control a gate that blocks the entrance when the garage becomes full and opens again when parking space becomes available. The package `Interface_Package` provides four parameterless procedures: `Wait_For_Arrival`, `Wait_For_Departure`, `Close_Gate`, and `Open_Gate`. A call on `Wait_For_Arrival` waits until a car is detected entering the garage; the procedure then returns. `Wait_For_Departure` works analogously for cars leaving the garage. The names `Close_Gate` and `Open_Gate` are self-explanatory. Write the program to control the gate. (*Hint:* Write a task that repeatedly waits for a call on `Wait_For_Arrival` to complete and then issues an entry call. Do the same for `Wait_For_Departure`. This will cause arrivals and departures to be manifested by entry calls that can be waited for in a selective wait and serviced in the order they arise.)

19.3 Write a program to monitor a patient's resting pulse and to display an updated value approximately once each second. The value displayed each second should be a cumulative average based on the number of heartbeats detected since the program began running and the length of time the program has been running. Assume that the following library package is available:

```
PACKAGE Interface_Package IS

   TYPE Pulse_Type IS DELTA 0.1 RANGE 0.0 .. 200.0;
      -- in beats per minute

   PROCEDURE Display_Pulse (Pulse : IN Pulse_Type);
   PROCEDURE Wait_For_Heartbeat;

END Interface_Package;
```

A call on `Wait_For_Heartbeat` returns when a heartbeat is detected.

19.4 Rewrite the pulse monitoring program described in the previous question so that it displays nothing for the first fifteen seconds and then, every second thereafter, displays four times the number of heartbeats detected during the immediately preceding fifteen seconds. (*Hints:* Write a task that calls an entry of a second task each time a heartbeat is detected. The second task should maintain a list of the number of heartbeats detected during each of the fifteen preceding seconds. This list should be updated every time another second passes or another heartbeat is detected.)

19.5 Write a generic package for message buffers. The type of the items to be buffered and the size of the buffer are generic parameters. An instance of the package should provide a limited private type for message buffers, an operation to add a specified item to a message buffer as soon as there is room for it, and an operation to remove an item from a message buffer as soon as an item becomes available.

19.6 Explain the difference in behavior between the following two statements:

(*a*)
```
SELECT
   Alarm_Task.Wait_For_Alarm;
OR
   DELAY 1.0;
   Report_Normal_Conditions;
END SELECT;
```

(*b*)
```
SELECT
   Alarm_Task.Wait_For_Alarm;
ELSE
   DELAY 1.0;
   Report_Normal_Conditions;
END SELECT;
```

19.7 Write the body for the task type `Printer_Task_Type` described in Section 19.2.2. (*Hint:* The solution is surprisingly short and simple.)

19.8 Suppose `Task_1`, `Task_2`, and `Task_3` have priorities one, two, and three, respectively. `Task_3` has called entry `Task_2.E` and is waiting for the call to be accepted. There are two processors in the system, scheduling is preemptive, and `Task_1` and `Task_2` are both executing at the same time. What will happen after `Task_2` executes an `ACCEPT` statement for entry `E`?

19.9 Implement the heating system described in Exercise 18.1, using the following hardware interface package:

```
PACKAGE Heating_Equipment_Package IS

   TYPE Zone_Type IS RANGE 1 .. 10;
   TYPE Heater_Setting_Type IS (Off, Low, Medium, High);
   TYPE Degrees_Type IS DELTA 1.0 RANGE -50.0 .. 150.0;

   FUNCTION Current_Temperature
      (Zone : Zone_Type) RETURN Temperature_Type;

   PROCEDURE Open_Vent (Zone : IN Zone_Type);
   PROCEDURE Close_Vent (Zone : IN Zone_Type);

END Heating_Equipment_Package;
```

19.10 The heating system implemented in the previous exercise has an undesirable effect. If a zone becomes too cold while the heater is off, the zone's vent is opened and cold air is fed through the vent until the heater has a chance to warm up. Modify the program so that a zone needing heat turns on the heater if necessary but does not open the zone's vent until the heater has been on for two minutes. (If the heater has already been on for two minutes or longer, the vent should be opened immediately. If the heater has already been on for thirty seconds, the program should wait another ninety seconds before opening the vent.)

CHAPTER

TWENTY

LOW-LEVEL PROGRAMMING

One of the goals of the Ada language is to allow programs controlling hardware to be written entirely in a high-level language. The language has features specifically designed for direct interaction with hardware and assembly-language-level software. These *low-level programming* features allow a programmer to specify the exact bit-by-bit data representations and machine instructions required for such interaction. If used properly, these features do not bring a high-level program down to the bit level, but allow bit-level and device-level operations to be described abstractly.

The low-level programming features allow a program to determine properties of the machine running the program. A program can also examine the internal data representations chosen by a compiler. When a specific internal representation is required by an application, this representation can be specified by the program. There is a way to bypass type restrictions in the rare case that it is necessary to view the same sequence of bits as, for example, a collection of flags and a binary integer. Programs can be made to execute specific machine instructions, including device-level input and output operations.

Because low-level features refer directly to the underlying hardware, their meaning varies from one compiler to another. The rules of the Ada language give an implementation considerable leeway in defining the allowable forms of low-level features and their meaning for a particular machine. Each implementation has its own version of the *Ada Language Reference Manual*'s Appendix F, describing that implementation's rules for the low-level features. In this book, we describe low-level features in general terms and illustrate them for hypothetical implementations. You should consult your compiler's Appendix F to learn the forms allowed by your compiler and the meaning that your compiler attaches to them.

An Ada program that uses low-level features and runs on one computer cannot generally be made to run on another kind of computer without some changes. (That is, the program is not *portable*.) This is partly because the low-level specifications that are accepted by one compiler may be rejected by another. For example, a request to place certain data in bits 0 through 34 of a word may be accepted by a compiler for a machine with 36-bit words but rejected by a compiler for a machine with 32-bit words. A more fundamental problem is that programs using low-level features may use algorithms based on characteristics of the underlying hardware.

A degree of portability can be salvaged by using low-level features in a disciplined way. First, they should be used only when it is necessary to interact with hardware or with assembly-level software. Second, this interaction should be confined to a few *interface packages*. Low-level features should be confined to these packages, and the rest of the program should interact with the hardware and low-level software indirectly through the facilities provided by the interface packages. This approach allows the bulk of a program, not concerned with low-level interactions, to remain portable. The program can be moved to another machine by reimplementing the interface packages and keeping the rest of the program unchanged. Besides keeping most of the program portable, this approach keeps most of the program at a high level. Most of the program manipulates the hardware abstractly, through the facilities of the interface packages, without referring to specific bit-by-bit data representations.

20.1 THE PACKAGE `System`

Each implementation of the Ada language provides its own version of a predefined package named `System`. This package provides named numbers, types, subtypes, and constants that reflect characteristics of the machine that will run the program. Depending on the implementation, certain of these characteristics can sometimes be changed by the use of pragmas. A compilation unit referring to this package must name it in a `WITH` clause.

The named numbers provided by the package `System` describe the range and precision of numeric types supported by the implementation, the number of bits in a storage unit, the number of storage units in the machine's memory, and the precision of the time reported by the function `Calendar.Clock` (see Section 12.3). There is a type for representing machine addresses, a subtype for task priorities, a type with one value for each configuration for which the compiler can generate machine code, and a constant whose value during any compilation indicates the configuration for which it *is* generating code.

Section 20.1.1 describes the facilities provided by the package `System`; Section 20.1.2 describes how the definition of this package can be altered by pragmas; and Section 20.1.3 discusses how the package can be used.

20.1.1 Facilities Provided by the Package

This section describes the facilities that must be provided by any implementation's version of the package `System`. A particular version may provide additional facilities as well. An implementation's Appendix F will describe its version of the package.

One of the facilities provided by the package System is the subtype Priority, consisting of those values of type Integer that may be used as task priority levels. This subtype was described in Section 19.3.1, and it will not be described further here.

20.1.1.1 Alternative runtime configurations. A *runtime configuration* consists of both the *target machine* that will run a program and the environment in which the program will operate. This environment includes the operating system, peripheral devices, and so forth. Some Ada implementations can generate machine code for more than one runtime configuration.

For example, there might be several operating systems that run on the same machine, and a compiler might be capable of placing different system calls in the object program, depending on the operating system under which the program will run. Alternatively, a computer manufacturer might produce a new model of a computer, which executes all the instructions of the old model plus some new, more powerful instructions. A compiler might be capable of generating object code either for the old model (not using any of the new instructions) or the new model (taking advantage of the new instructions to produce a better object program). Finally, an Ada Programming Support Environment might provide cross-compilers for several target machines. These can be viewed as a single compiler capable of generating machine code for several runtime configurations.

Each version of System provides an enumeration type called Name with one value for each runtime configuration handled by the implementation. (For some implementations, this enumeration type has only one value.) Each version of System also provides a constant called System_Name of type Name. Although the rules of the Ada language say nothing about the meaning of this constant, the obvious intention is for its value to indicate the runtime configuration for which code is being compiled. The pragma System_Name (discussed further in Section 20.1.2) can change the constant System_Name to a specified value of type Name. For some implementations, this allows a program to specify the runtime configuration for which a compiler is to generate code.

By referring to the value of System.System_Name, a program can make its algorithm dependent on the runtime configuration. For example, a compiler for a personal computer might support three different operating systems—DOS, CP/M, and Unix, for instance. Thus its version of the package System might contain the following type declaration:

```
TYPE Name IS (DOS, CP_M, Unix);
```

A program written for this compiler could contain a statement like the following:

```
CASE System.System_Name IS
   WHEN System.DOS =>
      Put_Line ("Insert COMMAND.COM disk in drive A.");
   WHEN System.CP_M =>
      Put_Line ("Warm Boot");
   WHEN System.Unix =>
      NULL;
END CASE;
```

The behavior of this program may depend on the value that has been specified by the System_Name pragma or in the operating system command invoking the Ada compiler. This makes it possible to maintain a single source program that can be compiled for different runtime configurations and behave differently for each configuration. The System_Name pragma may be the only part of the source program requiring change.

(Do not confuse the expanded name System.Name with the simple name System_Name: System.Name is an enumeration type provided by the package System, and System_Name is a constant of that type also provided by the package System. The constant's expanded name is System.System_Name.)

20.1.1.2 Hardware addresses. Some low-level features refer to specific memory locations. The package System provides a type Address, whose values identify memory locations. Typically, Address is an integer type with a nonnegative range, but addresses may have other forms on certain architectures. For example, if the target machine has a segmented architecture, Address might be a record type consisting of a segment name plus an offset into that segment. In a distributed system, an address might consist of the name of a processor in the system plus an address into that processor's storage.

Each value of type Address identifies a different *storage unit.* In the IBM 370 architecture, for example, the storage unit is an eight-bit byte; in the Univac 1100 architecture, the storage unit is a 36-bit word (because each address refers to a different word and bytes within a word are not individually addressable). The package System provides a named number Storage_Unit whose value is the number of bits in each addressable storage unit on the machine that will run the program. System.Storage_Unit equals eight when a program is being compiled for an IBM 370, and it equals 36 when a program is being compiled for a Univac 1100.

The package System also provides a named number Memory_Size giving the number of storage units in the runtime configuration. Typically, this depends not on the model of the processor that will run the program, but on the individual hardware configuration. When Address is an integer type, Address'Last will typically be the highest address allowed by the processor architecture. Memory_Size may be a much smaller number, especially if the machine supports some sort of virtual addressing.

There are pragmas named Storage_Unit and Memory_Size that can be used to change the values of the corresponding named numbers. These pragmas are discussed in Section 20.1.2.

20.1.1.3 Numeric capabilities. Numeric-type declarations allow a programmer to specify a type's range and precision abstractly rather than in terms of bytes or words. This allows a program to be written in terms of its logical properties rather than in terms of a particular machine and thus makes it more portable. For example, the integer-type declaration

```
TYPE Large_Natural_Type IS RANGE 0 .. 2 ** 35;
```

might cause Large_Natural_Type to be represented in one 36-bit word on one machine or in two 32-bit words on another.

An Ada compiler is required to accept a numeric-type declaration only if its target machine has an efficient representation for that type. The declaration

```
TYPE Precise_Number_Type IS DIGITS 20;
```

for example, might be accepted by one compiler but flagged as an error by another. The package System provides five named numbers indicating the maximum range and precision that the compiler will accept in numeric-type declarations.

The named numbers Min_Int and Max_Int specify the smallest and largest integers, respectively, that may be specified in an integer-type declaration. The named number Max_Digits specifies the maximum number of significant digits that can be specified in a floating-point type declaration. The named numbers Fine_Delta and Max_Mantissa describe the limits on fixed-point type declarations.

Limits on fixed-point types are difficult to characterize because there is a tradeoff between range and precision. The smaller the delta of the type (i.e., the higher the precision), the smaller the range that can be covered with the same number of internal representations. Fine_Delta gives the smallest delta that can appear in a fixed-point type declaration with the range -1.0 .. 1.0. Max_Mantissa is defined in terms of the model numbers of a fixed-point type. (Model numbers were described in Section 8.3.3.) For each nonnegative model number n * T'Small of the fixed-point type T, the unsigned integer n must be representable using at most Max_Mantissa bits. This means that for any value of i, a delta as small as 2^{-i} and a range as large as

$$-2^{\text{Max\_Mantissa}-i} \;..\; 2^{\text{Max\_Mantissa}-i}$$

may appear in the same fixed-point type declaration. By setting i equal to Max_Mantissa, we see that Fine_Delta is always equal to $2^{-\text{Max\_Mantissa}}$.

20.1.1.4 Precision of the computer's clock. The named number Tick specifies the smallest granule of time that can be distinguished by the machine that will run the program, the length of one "tick" of the machine's clock. The value returned by the function Calendar.Clock (described in Section 12.3) changes every Tick seconds. When a DELAY statement is executed, the minimum delay effectively requested is some whole number of ticks.

Tick is not necessarily identical to Duration'Small, the smallest granule of time that can be represented by type Duration. For example, if Tick is 25.0E-6 (25 microseconds) and Duration'Small is 50.0E-6 (50 microseconds), the statements

```
t := 125.0E-6; -- t is of type Duration
DELAY t;
```

might cause t to be represented internally either as 100.0E-6 (so that a four-tick delay is requested) or as 150.0E-6 (so that a six-tick delay is requested). On the other hand, if Tick were 25.0E-6 and Duration'Small were 10.0E-6, the statements

```
t := 10.0E-6;
DELAY t;
```

might have the same effect as the statements

```
t:= 20.0E-6;
DELAY t;
```

—namely to request a delay of at least one tick. Nonetheless, type Duration's extra precision in this case can be useful. Consider the declarations

```
Reset_Time        : CONSTANT Duration := 115.0E-6;
Number_Of_Resets : Integer;
```

If Number_Of_Resets holds 1,000, the statement

```
DELAY Number_Of_Resets * Reset_Time;
```

will compute a duration between 110,000 and 120,000 microseconds, or between 4,400 and 4,800 ticks. Had Duration'Small been larger, the number of ticks could have varied over a wider range.

20.1.2 Altering the Definition of the Package

Each implementation comes with a "standard" version of the package System, but it is possible to alter the definition of this package by use of the following pragmas:

```
PRAGMA System_Name ( enumeration literal ) ;
PRAGMA Memory_Size ( numeric literal ) ;
PRAGMA Storage_Unit ( numeric literal ) ;
```

The enumeration literal passed to the System_Name pragma must be of type System.Name. Each of these pragmas creates a new version of the package System, in which the named number or constant with the same name as the pragma is given a specified value.

Compiling one of these pragmas is equivalent to modifying and recompiling the predefined package System. The compilation order rules of Section 13.4 apply as if this recompilation had actually occurred. Thus any compilation unit compiled earlier with a WITH clause for System must be recompiled after one of these pragmas is compiled.

These pragmas can only occur at the beginning of a compilation. That is, they can only occur at the top of a file submitted to a compiler, before any compilation units. A particular implementation may impose further restrictions, such as disallowing some of these pragmas or allowing them only in the first compilation with a new program library.

An implementation may require that the target configuration be described in the operating system command that invokes the Ada compiler. Such an implementation may still allow the System_Name, Memory_Size, or Storage_Unit pragmas, but require that they specify the same information as the operating system command. The pragmas can be used to document the fact that a program makes certain assumptions about the runtime configuration and to generate a warning if the compiler is invoked to compile a program for a different configuration.

20.1.3 Use of the Package

Most program components can be written without referring to properties of the runtime configuration. In the unusual case that an algorithm depends on the runtime configuration, this dependency should be expressed in terms of the package System. This increases reliability, abstraction, maintainability, and portability.

By writing System.Memory_Size instead of, for example, 131_172, a programmer avoids having to memorize specific configuration-dependent numbers and eliminates the risk of getting it wrong. Furthermore, like other named numbers, System.Memory_Size conveys more useful information to a reader than the numeric literal 131_172. It provides an abstract description of the quantity being used, conveying its significance rather than its value.

As Section 20.1.1.1 explained, the package System (and particularly the constant System_Name) can be used to maintain a single source program that can be compiled for different target machines, even if the versions for different machines have certain differences. If the program must be changed, that change need only be made in one source program. This decreases the effort required to make modifications and avoids version control problems.

Given that a program component must rely on a property of the runtime configuration, use of the package System can actually *increase* portability. Suppose that specifications call for a floating-point type Measurement_Type with the maximum precision allowed by the target machine. A programmer who knows that "the" target machine can support up to sixteen digits of precision might write

```
TYPE Measurement_Type IS DIGITS 16;
```

If this program is later moved to another target machine, this type declaration could be flagged as an error (if the new target did not support sixteen digits of precision), or it could specify less than the maximum available precision, thus violating the specifications. A programmer who recognizes that the program might be compiled for another machine some day would write

```
TYPE Measurement_Type IS DIGITS System.Max_Digits;
```

instead.

20.2 Representation Attributes

The constants and named numbers of package `System` allow a program to refer to implementation-dependent properties of the runtime configuration as a whole. A set of attributes called *representation attributes* provide a program with similar information about individual objects, types, and program units. There are representation attributes that give the address or size of an entity, the amount of storage available for dynamic allocation or execution of a task, and the underlying representation of particular types. Like the values provided by the package `System`, these attributes allow a program to name implementation-dependent values abstractly, preserving the portability of a program.

20.2.1 The Use of Storage

If *X* is a subprogram, task unit, or package, *X*`'Address` is the address of the first machine instruction of the subprogram, the task body, or the initialization statements of the package body. If *X* is a constant or a variable, *X*`'Address` is the address at which its value is stored. The value of this attribute belongs to the type `System.Address`.

If *X* is a constant or variable, *X*`'Size` is the number of bits used to hold that object. If *X* is a type or subtype, *X*`'Size` is the minimum number of bits required to hold all objects of this type or subtype. In the case of an unconstrained type or subtype, different objects may have different sizes. It is the size of the largest possible object of the type or subtype that is given by this attribute. *X*`'Size` can be used as a value in any integer type.

For each access-type declaration, there is a pool of storage units set aside for allocating variables that will be pointed to by values of the access type. (The same pool is used for allocating variables that will be pointed to by types derived from the access type.) If *T* is a subtype of an access type, *T*`'Storage_Size` is the number of addressable storage units in the pool associated with the base type of *T*.

Every time a task is activated, a pool of storage units is set aside to hold the objects declared in program units invoked by the task. The size of this pool is the same for all tasks in a given task type. If *T* is a task object, *T*`'Storage_Size` is the number of storage units in the task's pool. If *T* is a task type, *T*`'Storage_Size` is the number of objects in each pool for a task object of type *T*. Whether *T* is a subtype of an access type, a task object, or a task type, *T*`'Storage_Size` can be used as a value in any integer type.

The `'Size` attribute measures storage in bits, but the `'Storage_Size` attribute measures storage in *addressable storage units.* As explained in Section 20.1.1.2, an addressable storage unit is whatever a single address refers to—a byte on most machines but a word on some other machines. There are `System.Storage_Unit` bits in an addressable storage unit.

The `'Address` and `'Size` attributes may be applied to any subtype and any object. This includes private types and objects belonging to private types. It also includes objects belonging to access types. For most attributes, if *v* is an access value and *d* is an attribute designator, then the attribute *v*`'`*d* names the *d* attribute of the

```
TYPE List_Cell_Type IS
   RECORD
      Character_Part : Character;
      Link_Part      : List_Type;
   END RECORD;

Cell : List_Cell_Type;
```

Storage Unit 0								Storage Unit 1								Storage Unit 2								Storage Unit 3							
Bit 0	Bit 1	Bit 2	Bit 3	Bit 4	Bit 5	Bit 6	Bit 7									Bit 0	Bit 1	Bit 2	Bit 3	Bit 4	Bit 5	Bit 6	Bit 7	Bit 8	Bit 9	Bit 10	Bit 11	Bit 12	Bit 13	Bit 14	Bit 15
unused	Character_Part							unused								Link_Part															

Cell.Character_Part'Position = 0	Cell.Link_Part'Position = 2
Cell.Character_Part'First_Bit = 1	Cell.Link_Part'First_Bit = 0
Cell.Character_Part'Last_Bit = 7	Cell.Link_Part'Last_Bit = 15

Figure 20.1 An illustration of the `'Position`, `'First_Bit`, and `'Last_Bit` attributes for a hypothetical representation of the record `Cell`. The `'Position` attribute returns the offset in storage units of the first storage unit containing part of the specified record component. The `'First_Bit` and `'Last_Bit` attributes return an offset in bits from the start of that storage unit. The bit numbering used to determine `Cell.Link_Part'Last_Bit` is relative to the beginning of storage unit 2, which is the first storage unit containing part of the `Link_Part` component.

variable pointed to by *v*. However, the `'Address` and `'Size` attributes work differently. The attributes *v*`'Address` and *v*`'Size` give the address and size of *v* itself. You must write *v*`.ALL'Address` and *v*`.ALL'Size` to get the address and size of the variable pointed to by *v*.

20.2.2 The Physical Layout of Record Components

If *R* is an object in a record type with component *C*, *R*`.`*C*`'Position` is the offset of the first storage unit occupied by the component *C*, relative to the first storage unit occupied by the entire record *R*. This offset is measured in *addressable storage units*. *R*`.`*C*`'First_Bit` is the offset within this storage unit of the first bit of the storage unit occupied by *C*. This offset is measured in *bits*. *R*`.`*C*`'Last_Bit` is the offset from the start of that same storage unit of the last bit occupied by *C*. This offset is also measured in *bits* and may be greater than the number of bits in one storage unit. Figure 20.1 illustrates these attributes.

20.2.3 Floating-Point and Fixed-Point Arithmetic

The rules presented in Section 8.3.3 require the results of floating-point and fixed-point arithmetic to lie within specified model intervals. An implementation may perform the arithmetic in any way that meets this requirement. In particular, when the true mathematical result of an operation does not have an exact representation, some machines may *truncate* the mathematical result (i.e., ignore the least significant digits) to obtain a nearby approximation; other machines may *round* the result to the *nearest* value with an exact representation. Different types may have different representations, so that results in one type are truncated while results in another type are rounded. (For example, an implementation might use a central processing unit that truncates for short floating-point types and a separate floating-point coprocessor that rounds for long floating-point types.) If *T* is a floating-point subtype or a fixed-point subtype, the attribute *T*`'Machine_Rounds` evaluates to `True` if the implementation rounds all results in the base type of *T*; it evaluates to `False` otherwise.

Overflow is said to occur when the result of an operation in a floating-point or fixed-point type lies outside the range of representable values. An implementation *may* raise the exception `Numeric_Error` when overflow occurs. However, it is not required to do so because the check for overflow would be very expensive on some machines. If *T* is a floating-point or fixed-point type, the attribute *T*`'Machine_Overflows` evaluates to `True` if every overflow in the base type of *T* either yields a correct result or raises `Numeric_Error`. Otherwise, `T'Machine_Overflows` evaluates to `False`.

There are four attributes concerned with the internal representation of floating-point types. The typical machine representation of a floating-point value consists of a sign, an exponent, and a mantissa. The mantissa is a sequence of bits representing a fraction between 0.5 and 1.0. This fraction is understood to be expressed in some radix that is a power of two. (For example, on different machines, a 24-bit mantissa might be viewed as 24 binary digits, as eight octal digits, or as six hexadecimal digits.) The effective value of the number is obtained by multiplying the mantissa by that power of the radix indicated by the exponent. (Thus the exponent tells how many binary, octal, or decimal digits the mantissa should be shifted left or right.) A larger radix yields a larger range (since the exponent specifies multiplication of the mantissa by a higher number) but less precision (since a radix of 2^n requires some mantissas to begin with up to n-1 zero bits, thus reducing the number of significant bits in the mantissa).

If *T* is a floating-point subtype, then *T*`'Machine_Radix` evaluates to the radix used in the machine representation of *T*'s base type; *T*`'Machine_Mantissa` evaluates to the number of digits *in that radix* contained in the mantissa; and *T*`'Machine_EMin` and *T*`'Machine_EMax` give the lower and upper bounds, respectively, of the exponent. The value of any of these attributes can be used as a value of any integer type.

For example, the IBM 370 has a 32-bit floating-point representation consisting of a sign bit, a seven-bit exponent ranging from -64 to 63 and specifying a power of 16, and a 24-bit mantissa treated as six hexadecimal digits. If this representation is used for the predefined type `Float`, then `Float'Machine_Radix = 16`, `Float'Machine_Mantissa = 6`, `Float'Machine_EMin = -64`, and `Float'Machine_EMax = 63`.

(The `'Machine_EMax` attribute should not be confused with the `'EMax` and `'Safe_EMax` attributes described in Section 8.3.4. *T*`'Machine_EMax` is the largest power of *T*`'Machine_Radix` that can be expressed in the machine representation of *T*; *T*`'EMax` and *T*`'Safe_EMax` are the powers of two by which the mantissa is multiplied in the largest model number and the largest safe number of *T*, respectively.)

20.3 REPRESENTATION CLAUSES AND PRAGMAS

The representation attributes allow a program to *examine* internal representations. The Ada language also provides mechanisms for a program to *control* internal representations. *Representation clauses* order an implementation to use specific internal representations. An implementation will flag a program as illegal if the program contains a representation clause that the implementation does not support. *Representation pragmas* specify the criteria that an implementation should use in selecting a representation on its own. An implementation may *ignore* a representation pragma, but it will never flag one as illegal. Both representation clauses and representation pragmas can affect the values of representation attributes.

20.3.1 Representation Clauses

Representation clauses control various aspects of internal representation. The general form of a representation clause is

```
FOR aspect to be controlled USE desired representation ;
```

The representation clause usually goes in either a package specification or in a declarative part. In a package specification, the representation clause may appear in either the visible part or the private part, and the effect is the same. In a declarative part, the representation clause is a *basic declaration,* so it must appear before any bodies or body stubs. (Basic declarations were described in Section 9.1.) There is a special case, described in Section 20.5, in which a representation clause may appear after the entry declarations in a task declaration.

There are four kinds of representation clauses—length clauses, enumeration clauses, record representation clauses, and address clauses. A length clause specifies the value for some attribute of a type. It may take any of three forms, where *T* is the name of a type:

```
FOR T'Size USE expression ;
FOR T'Storage_Size USE expression ;
FOR T'Small USE expression ;
```

In a representation attribute, *T* may be a name introduced in a subtype declaration. In a length clause, it may not be. The three forms of length clauses are discussed in Sections 20.3.1.1, 20.3.1.2, and 20.3.1.3, respectively.

An enumeration clause specifies the integers to be used internally to specify each value in an enumeration type. It has the following form:

FOR *enumeration type name* **USE** *array aggregate* **;**

Section 20.3.1.4 discusses enumeration representation clauses.

A record representation clause specifies the position of each component in a record and may restrict the addresses at which a record can start. Its form is

FOR *record type name* **USE** *record description* **;**

The form of a record description is given in Section 20.3.1.5.

An address clause specifies the location of an entity or stipulates that a particular kind of hardware interrupt should cause a particular task entry to be called. An address clause has the following form:

FOR *identifier* **USE AT** *address* **;**

Address clauses specifying the location of an entity are described in Section 20.3.1.6. Address clauses associating hardware interrupts with task entries are discussed in Section 20.5.

20.3.1.1 Controlling the size of objects in a type. Just as the representation attribute *T*'Size evaluates to the maximum number of bits in all objects of type *T*, a length clause of the form

FOR *T*'Size **USE** *expression* **;**

specifies that number. The expression may belong to any integer type, and it is evaluated at the time the representation clause is elaborated. The implementation will reject the representation clause if it does not have a way of representing all values of the type in the specified number of bits.

With some implementations, when a size is specified for an array or record type, it does not determine the size of the components. Rather, the implementation assumes some size for the components and tries to alter the gaps between components if necessary to fit the array or record in the required number of bits. Before specifying a size for an array or record type under such an implementation, you should specify the size of each component type. Otherwise, the implementation may not be able to squeeze all the components into the size you specify.

For example, an operating system for a personal computer maintains a *file allocation table* on each diskette. This is an array of 316 *cluster numbers,* each of which is a twelve-bit unsigned integer. To save space on the diskette, the twelve bits of one table entry are immediately followed by the twelve bits of the next. Thus every three eight-bit bytes contain two table entries. The operating system might have to keep an exact copy of this table in memory.

The first step is to declare the type for the table entries and specify that it should be twelve bits long:

```
TYPE Cluster_Number_Type IS RANGE 0 .. 16#FFF#;
FOR Cluster_Number_Type'Size USE 12;
```

(We use the based literal `16#FFF#` rather than the equivalent decimal literal `4095` because it more directly expresses the abstract requirement to use the highest unsigned integer that can be expressed in twelve bits. Based literals were introduced in Section 8.3.2.) The next step is to declare the type for the table itself and specify that it should be just big enough to contain all the bits of its components:

```
TYPE File_Allocation_Table_Type IS
   ARRAY (Cluster_Number_Type RANGE 0 .. 315) OF
      Cluster_Number_Type;
FOR File_Allocation_Table_Type'Size USE
   File_Allocation_Table_Type'Length *
      Cluster_Number_Type'Size;
```

The attribute `File_Allocation_Table'Length` gives the number of components in the array (316) and the attribute `Cluster_Number_Type'Size` gives the number of bits required for each component (twelve, as determined by the earlier length clause), so their product (3,792) is the number of bits in a `File_Allocation_Table_Type` object if all bits are to be occupied by component values. The length clause

```
FOR File_Allocation_Type'Size USE 3792;
```

would have had the same effect, but the rationale would have been much less evident to someone reading the program.

On many machines it is expensive to fetch or update a value that occupies all of one storage unit and part of another. In the absence of a length clause for `Cluster_Number_Type`, an implementation might well choose to represent each `Cluster_Number_Type` value in an easily accessible sixteen-bit word. Then the length clause

```
FOR File_Allocation_Type'Size USE 3792;
```

would cause an error, because there is no way to squeeze 316 sixteen-bit words into 3,792 bits. If the size of the component type `Cluster_Number_Type` had been specified but the the size of the array type `File_Allocation_Table_Type` had not, an implementation might still place four "padding bits" before each twelve-bit array component, so that each component value would be right-justified in its own sixteen-bit word.

20.3.1.2 Controlling the allocation of storage. Typically, for each access type, an implementation reserves an area of storage for the allocation of variables that will be pointed to by values in that access type. Similarly, for each task object, an implementation reserves an area of storage for the objects that will be created by the execution of that task. When storage is scarce and a programmer has some idea of how big each of these areas should be, he can stipulate that certain areas be large (so that allocation of a variable or execution of a task will not raise `Storage_Error`) and that other areas be small (so that storage can be saved for other purposes).

Just as the representation attribute *T*`'Storage_Size` *evaluates to* the number of storage units in the area reserved for access type *T* or for objects of task type *T*, a length clause of the form

```
FOR T'Storage_Size USE expression ;
```

specifies that number. The expression may be of any integer type and is evaluated when the representation clause is elaborated.

The precise effect of specifying the size of storage areas depends on how the implementation uses them. For instance, when an access type is declared inside a task body, some implementations may set aside part of the area reserved for the task object and use it as the area reserved for the access type; other implementations may find a separate region of storage to use as the area reserved for the access type. Some implementations may allow every storage unit in the area reserved for an access type to be used as part of an allocated variable; other implementations may use some of the area for internal control information. See your implementation's Appendix F for details.

Suppose that you wanted to allow allocation of up to 500 variables of type `Integer`. First, you would declare an access type whose values point to allocated integer variables:

```
TYPE Integer_Pointer_Type IS ACCESS Integer;
```

Next, you would specify the value of `Integer_Pointer_Type'Storage_Size` through a length clause. The number of bits in an `Integer` variable is `Integer'Size`. The number of bits in a storage unit is `System.Storage_Unit`. Assuming that `Integer'Size` is an even multiple of `System.Storage_Unit`, each variable of type `Integer` occupies

```
Integer'Size / System.Storage_Unit
```

storage units. Assuming that all the storage units in the area reserved for `Integer_Pointer_Type` can be used to hold allocated variables, the desired length clause is

```
FOR Integer_Pointer_Type'Storage_Size USE
   500 * (Integer'Size / System.Storage_Unit);
```

20.3.1.3 Controlling the approximations in a fixed-point type. A fixed-point type consists of evenly spaced approximations to real numbers. The space between approximations in a fixed-point type *T* is given by the attribute *T*`'Small` (which was introduced in Section 8.3.4). An implementation is required to provide exact representations only for certain numbers of the form *n* * *T*'Small. (These are the *model numbers* of *T*, as explained in Section 8.3.3.1.)

Normally, *T*'Small is the highest positive or negative power of two that is less than or equal to the delta specified in the declaration of *T*. Thus the declaration

```
TYPE Money_Type IS DELTA 0.01 RANGE 0.0 .. 1.0E6;
```

normally results in a value of 0.0078125 (i.e., 1/128) for Money_Type'Small. This causes money to be counted in 128ths of a dollar rather than in exact numbers of cents and could lead to roundoff errors.

To avoid problems of this kind, a length clause of the form

```
FOR T'Small USE expression ;
```

where *T* is a fixed-point type, can be used to specify a different value for *T*'Small. The expression may belong to any floating-point or fixed-point type, but it must be static. (Static expressions were described in Section 8.3.5.) For the example above, we would want to write the following length clause:

```
FOR Money_Type'Small USE 0.01;
```

This would force an exact representation for each whole number of cents.

20.3.1.4 Controlling the encoding of an enumeration type. In languages without enumeration types, programmers often simulate enumeration types by declaring a series of integer objects with different values. That is essentially what typical Ada implementations do internally. The differences are that the programmer need not be aware of the correspondence between enumeration literals and internal integer codes; and that the programmer may not use the enumeration literal as an arithmetic quantity, but only as a value in its enumeration type.

Sometimes it is desirable to specify the integer encoding to be used for each enumeration literal—not to make the logic of the program dependent on the encoding, but to provide an abstract view of integer codes used by the hardware or operating system. For example, suppose a low level operating system routine to perform an input or output operation at a specific disk address returns a status byte indicating whether or not the operation completed successfully. All eight bits of the byte are set to zero if the operation completes successfully. Otherwise, exactly one of the bits is set to one to indicate why the operation failed, as follows:

Bit zero (least significant bit):	write-protection violation
Bit one:	disk drive not ready
Bit two:	error reading data
Bit three:	unable to find track
Bit four:	unable to find sector
Bit five:	error writing data
Bit six:	invalid disk address
Bit seven (most significant bit):	hardware failure

Suppose we want to write a higher-level disk access subprogram that examines this status byte after each call on the low-level routine. Rather than keeping track of each of the nine possible bit patterns throughout the subprogram, we can declare a nine-value enumeration type and then provide an enumeration representation clause specifying the internal bit pattern for each enumeration literal. This enables us to view the low-level routine as returning status information as a value in this enumeration type. In the rest of our program, we can use the status information without regard to the integer encoding. We can use the status value as we would any other enumeration value, for example in a `CASE` statement.

The form of an enumeration representation clause is

FOR *enumeration type name* **USE** *array aggregate* **;**

The array aggregate is for an imaginary one-dimensional array type indexed by the enumeration type, such that the component indexed by enumeration value x contains the internal integer encoding of x. The aggregate may be positional or named. The component values in the array must be specified by static *universal integer* expressions, such as integer literals. (See Sections 8.3.5 and 8.3.6 for a complete description of static and universal expressions, respectively.) The array must be sorted in strict ascending order.

For the disk status example, we would use the following type declaration and representation clause:

```
TYPE Disk_Status_Type IS
   (Normal_Completion,Write_Protect_Error,Not_Ready_Error,
    Reading_Error,Track_Error,Sector_Error,Writing_Error,
    Disk_Address_Error, Hardware_Error);
FOR Disk_Status_Type USE
   (Normal_Completion   => 2#0000_0000#,
    Write_Protect_Error => 2#0000_0001#,
    Not_Ready_Error     => 2#0000_0010#,
    Reading_Error       => 2#0000_0100#,
    Track_Error         => 2#0000_1000#,
    Sector_Error        => 2#0001_0000#,
    Writing_Error       => 2#0010_0000#,
    Disk_Address_Error  => 2#0100_0000#,
    Hardware_Error      => 2#1000_0000#);
```

(The component values in the array aggregate are written in base two to emphasize the correspondence with the bit patterns described earlier. The enumeration representation clause could also have been written simply

```
FOR Disk_Status_Type USE (0, 1, 2, 8, 16, 32, 64, 128);
```

but the correspondence to the specifications of the low-level disk routine would have been less clear.)

As this example illustrates, the encoding of an enumeration type may contain gaps. In the absence of an enumeration representation clause, an implementation typically encodes an enumeration value x in type t by the number `t'Pos(x)`. This makes it simple to compute `t'Pred(x)`, `t'Succ(x)`, and of course `t'Pos(x)` in terms of the internal representation. It is also easy to compute the address of an array component indexed by x. When an enumeration representation clause specifies gaps in the internal encoding, these operations may become considerably slower.

20.3.1.5 Controlling the positions of record components. Hardware specifications and interfaces to low-level software often specify the bit-by-bit layout of certain "blocks" of storage. The blocks are divided into fields of bits that contain different kinds of information. Such blocks can be modeled in an Ada program by records, with each field of the block corresponding to a component of the record. A record representation clause specifies the exact position of each record component in a record type. This allows the rest of the program to refer to treat the block of storage abstractly as an ordinary record, without further reference to the location of each bit field. The physical order of components in the internal representation of a record need not correspond to the logical order that appears in the record-type declaration and in positional record aggregates.

On some machines, data spanning more than one storage unit may be more quickly accessible if the data is *aligned* in a particular way—that is, if the address of its first storage unit is evenly divisible by a particular number. Some implementations allow a record representation clause also to specify the required alignment of all records in a record type. This does not affect the internal structure of objects in the type, but rather their placement.

The form of a record representation clause roughly parallels the form of a record-type declaration:

```
FOR record type name USE
    RECORD  [AT MOD storage unit multiple]

      [ component name AT storage unit offset RANGE bit range ;
            ~~~
        component name AT storage unit offset RANGE bit range ; ]

END RECORD ;
```

The storage unit multiple following `AT MOD` controls alignment. It is a static expression of any integer type. A typical implementation will permit only certain values for this expression or none at all. When the storage unit multiple is specified, objects of the named record type may only begin at addresses that are multiples of the specified number.

For example, on an IBM 370, each address corresponds to a byte, the two consecutive bytes starting at an even address constitute a half-word, the two consecutive half-words starting at an address divisible by four constitute a word, and the two consecutive words starting at an address divisible by eight constitute a double word. Thus `AT MOD 2` specifies alignment on a half-word boundary,

`AT MOD 4` specifies alignment on a word boundary, and `AT MOD 8` specifies alignment on a double-word boundary.

The storage unit offsets and bit ranges specify the positions of the named components. The order in which components are listed is irrelevant and need not correspond to either the order in the record-type declaration or the order in the internal representation. Some component positions can be left unspecified, in which case the implementation selects a position for the component.

The storage unit offset specified for each component is a static expression of any integer type. It specifies the storage unit in which a record component starts, relative to the beginning of the record. (This is the information provided by the `'Position` representation attribute described in Section 20.2.2.) The bit range has the form

expression **. .** *expression*

where each expression is static and belongs to some integer type. It indicates the bit within the specified storage unit at which the record component starts and the bit at which it ends. There must be enough bits in the range to represent every value of the component's subtype.

The bits of a storage unit are numbered starting with zero, but the direction of the numbering depends on the implementation. On some machines, bits are conventionally numbered from left to right (so that the most significant bit is bit zero), and on others they are conventionally numbered from right to left (so that the least significant bit is bit zero). An Ada implementation is free to follow the conventions of the target machine, in order to ensure a clear correspondence between hardware and low-level software specifications and the bit positions in a record representation clause.

Some implementations may not allow a record representation clause to specify a component spanning more than one storage unit. Those that allow it define their own conventions for the second expression of the bit range when the first and last components of a record lie in different storage units. Typically, this convention is to keep assigning numbers to bits of successive storage units relative to bit zero of the first storage unit. Many machines allow two adjacent bytes to be viewed as parts of a single number; but some (e.g., the IBM 370 and the Motorola MC68000) use the lower-addressed byte as the most significant byte and others (e.g., the DEC PDP-11 and the Intel 8086) use the higher-addressed byte as the most significant byte. Machines treating the lower-addressed byte as most significant generally have bits numbered from left to right, and machines treating the higher-addressed byte as most significant generally have bits numbered from right to left. Either way, if bytes are eight bits long, then bits zero through seven of storage unit $n+1$ can be viewed as bits eight through fifteen, respectively, of the two-byte value starting at storage unit n. See Figure 20.2.

Let us look at two examples of record representation clauses. First, consider a machine whose storage unit is an eight-bit byte and that represents a time of day in a two-byte word as shown in Figure 20.3: Bits in a word are numbered left to right

Lower-addressed byte most significant:

Byte 0								Byte 1								Byte 2								Byte 3							
Bit 0	Bit 1	Bit 2	Bit 3	Bit 4	Bit 5	Bit 6	Bit 7	Bit 0	Bit 1	Bit 2	Bit 3	Bit 4	Bit 5	Bit 6	Bit 7	Bit 0	Bit 1	Bit 2	Bit 3	Bit 4	Bit 5	Bit 6	Bit 7	Bit 0	Bit 1	Bit 2	Bit 3	Bit 4	Bit 5	Bit 6	Bit 7

two-byte value at location 0																two-byte value at location 2															
Bit 0	Bit 1	Bit 2	Bit 3	Bit 4	Bit 5	Bit 6	Bit 7	Bit 8	Bit 9	Bit 10	Bit 11	Bit 12	Bit 13	Bit 14	Bit 15	Bit 0	Bit 1	Bit 2	Bit 3	Bit 4	Bit 5	Bit 6	Bit 7	Bit 8	Bit 9	Bit 10	Bit 11	Bit 12	Bit 13	Bit 14	Bit 15

Higher-addressed byte most significant:

Byte 3								Byte 2								Byte 1								Byte 0							
Bit 7	Bit 6	Bit 5	Bit 4	Bit 3	Bit 2	Bit 1	Bit 0	Bit 7	Bit 6	Bit 5	Bit 4	Bit 3	Bit 2	Bit 1	Bit 0	Bit 7	Bit 6	Bit 5	Bit 4	Bit 3	Bit 2	Bit 1	Bit 0	Bit 7	Bit 6	Bit 5	Bit 4	Bit 3	Bit 2	Bit 1	Bit 0

two-byte value at location 2																two-byte value at location 0															
Bit 15	Bit 14	Bit 13	Bit 12	Bit 11	Bit 10	Bit 9	Bit 8	Bit 7	Bit 6	Bit 5	Bit 4	Bit 3	Bit 2	Bit 1	Bit 0	Bit 15	Bit 14	Bit 13	Bit 12	Bit 11	Bit 10	Bit 9	Bit 8	Bit 7	Bit 6	Bit 5	Bit 4	Bit 3	Bit 2	Bit 1	Bit 0

Figure 20.2 Some machines use lower addresses for the most significant bytes. Others use higher addresses for the most significant bytes. Since we are used to writing numbers with the most significant digits on the left, the first kind of machine is most easily visualized as having storage units numbered from left to right and the second kind as having storage units numbered from right to left. Bits within storage units (or groups of consecutive storage units) are usually numbered in the same direction as the storage units.

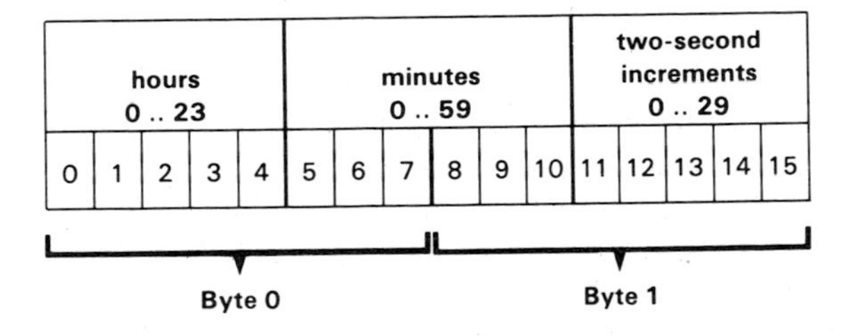

Figure 20.3 A two-byte representation for the time of day.

from zero to fifteen. The more significant byte in the word has the lower address, which must be an even number. Bits zero through four hold a number of hours from zero to 23, bits five through ten hold a number of minutes from zero to 59, and bits eleven through fifteen hold a number of two-second increments from zero to 29, all as unsigned binary numbers.

The following declarations provide an abstract view of this word as a record with three components:

```
TYPE Seconds_Type IS DELTA 2.0 RANGE 0.0 .. 58.0;
TYPE Time_Type IS
   RECORD
      Hours_Part   : Integer RANGE 0 .. 23;
      Minutes_Part : Integer RANGE 0 .. 59;
      Seconds_Part : Seconds_Type;
   END RECORD;
```

The declaration of `Seconds_Type` as a fixed-point type allows a value such as thirty seconds to be represented in program text by the literal `30.0` rather than by `15`. The fact that the number of seconds is represented internally in two-second increments is a detail of the implementation, irrelevant to the user of `Seconds_Type` except insofar as he depends on the accuracy of the value. (We have presumed that each value *n* * *T*'`Small` in a fixed-point type *T* is represented internally by the integer *n*. This is the usual representation of a fixed-point type. It provides an exact representation for each model number and makes the arithmetic operations allowed for fixed-point types very easy to implement in terms of integer arithmetic. Since `Seconds_Type'Delta` is a power of two, it is used directly as the value of `Seconds_Type'Small`, so the internal representation is as a number of two-second increments.)

An Ada implementation might allow the following representation clauses to specify the internal structure of a `Time_Type` value:

```
FOR Seconds_Type'Size USE 5;
FOR Time_Type USE
   RECORD AT MOD 2
      Hours_Part   AT 0 RANGE 0 .. 4;
      Minutes_Part AT 0 RANGE 5 .. 10;
      Seconds_Part AT 0 RANGE 11 .. 15;
   END RECORD;
```

The length clause for `Seconds_Type` ensures that only the required five bits are used, so that the subsequent record representation clause can be obeyed. The bit ranges for `Minutes_Part` and `Seconds_Part` continue to number bits of storage unit one as though they were part of storage unit zero. The position of `Seconds_Part` could also have been specified as

```
Seconds_Part AT 1 RANGE 3 .. 7;
```

Depending on the implementation, there may be be no other way to represent the position of `Minutes_Part`, which extends from one storage unit to another.

We could provide a public package to make `Time_Type` available to any program using the package:

```
PACKAGE Time_Package IS
   TYPE Seconds_Type IS DELTA 2.0 RANGE 0.0 .. 58.0;
   TYPE Time_Type IS
      RECORD
         Hours_Part   : Integer RANGE 0 .. 23;
         Minutes_Part : Integer RANGE 0 .. 59;
         Seconds_Part : Seconds_Type;
      END RECORD;
PRIVATE
   FOR Seconds_Type'Size USE 5;
   FOR Time_Type USE
      RECORD AT MOD 2
         Hours_Part   AT 0 RANGE 0 .. 4;
         Minutes_Part AT 0 RANGE 5 .. 10;
         Seconds_Part AT 0 RANGE 11 .. 15;
      END RECORD;
END Time_Package;
```

This package has no body. Since it does not declare a private type, it is not required to have a private part; the representation clauses could have followed the type declarations in the visible part of the package. They are placed in a private part only for reasons of style: The internal representation of `Seconds_Type` and `Time_Type` should be of no concern to the user of the package. As with a package providing a private type, the visible part of the `Time_Package` specification tells a programmer what he must know to use the package, and the private part tells a compiler what it must know about the internal representation of certain types to compile program components using those types.

Now let us consider another machine with eight-bit bytes and two-byte words, but with the more significant byte in a word having the higher address. On this machine, bits are numbered right to left. We want to manipulate the *table of contents* on a mountable disk. The table of contents lists all the files on the disk and may also contain a *disk label* identifying the disk. Each file is identified by a *file name* of up to eight characters followed by an *extension* of up to three characters. The table of contents consists of a series of fourteen-byte *file descriptions* formatted as shown in Figure 20.4: Normally, bytes zero through seven hold the characters of the file name, bytes seven through ten hold the characters of the extension, byte eleven holds a set of flags, and bytes twelve and thirteen form a word holding the starting position of the file (from zero to 500). The flags in byte eleven are as follows:

Bit zero: the file can be read but not updated
Bit one: the file is "hidden" so that it will not appear in
the list of a disk's contents

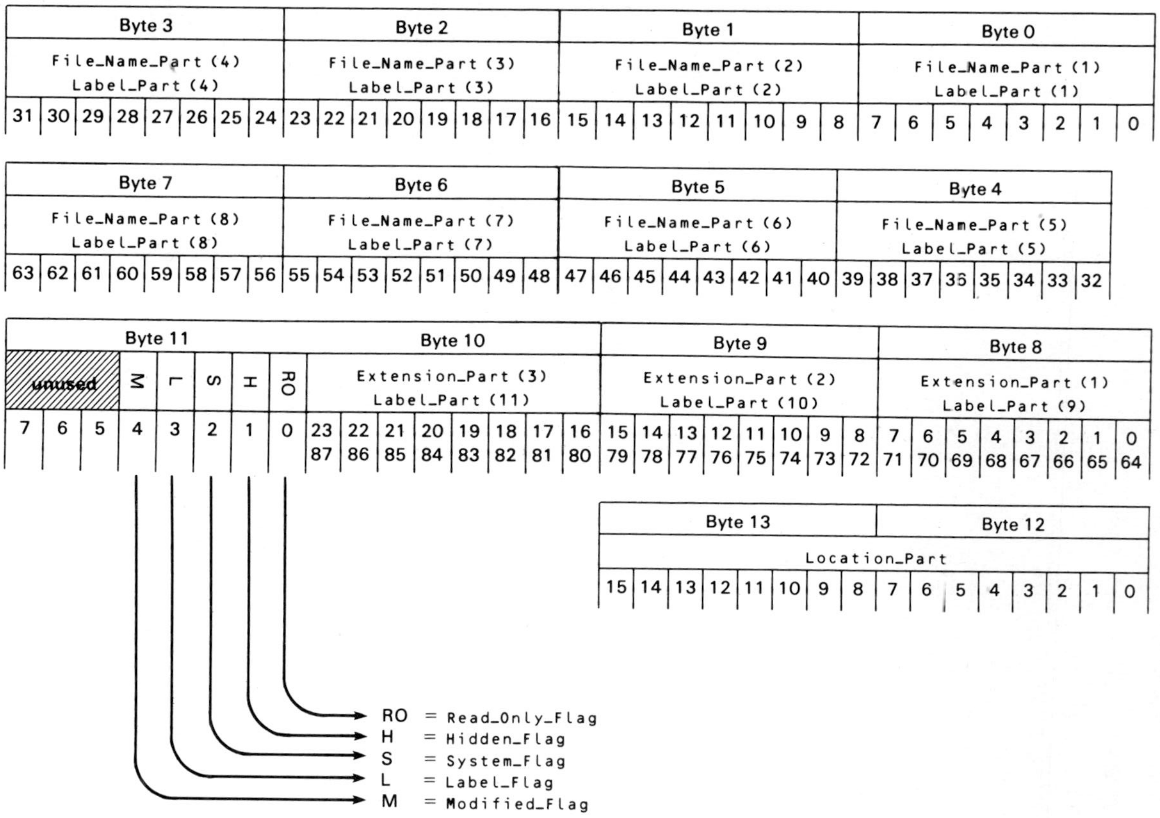

Byte 3	Byte 2	Byte 1	Byte 0
File_Name_Part (4) Label_Part (4)	File_Name_Part (3) Label_Part (3)	File_Name_Part (2) Label_Part (2)	File_Name_Part (1) Label_Part (1)
31 30 29 28 27 26 25 24	23 22 21 20 19 18 17 16	15 14 13 12 11 10 9 8	7 6 5 4 3 2 1 0

Byte 7	Byte 6	Byte 5	Byte 4
File_Name_Part (8) Label_Part (8)	File_Name_Part (7) Label_Part (7)	File_Name_Part (6) Label_Part (6)	File_Name_Part (5) Label_Part (5)
63 62 61 60 59 58 57 56	55 54 53 52 51 50 49 48	47 46 45 44 43 42 41 40	39 38 37 36 35 34 33 32

Byte 11								Byte 10	Byte 9	Byte 8
unused			M	L	S	H	RO	Extension_Part (3) Label_Part (11)	Extension_Part (2) Label_Part (10)	Extension_Part (1) Label_Part (9)
7	6	5	4	3	2	1	0	23 22 21 20 19 18 17 16 87 86 85 84 83 82 81 80	15 14 13 12 11 10 9 8 79 78 77 76 75 74 73 72	7 6 5 4 3 2 1 0 71 70 69 68 67 66 65 64

Byte 13	Byte 12
Location_Part	
15 14 13 12 11 10 9 8	7 6 5 4 3 2 1 0

RO = Read_Only_Flag
H = Hidden_Flag
S = System_Flag
L = Label_Flag
M = Modified_Flag

Figure 20.4 Structure of a file description. Because bytes are numbered right to left, array components appear to be listed right to left.

Bit two: the file is a system file and cannot be deleted
Bit three: the directory entry actually contains a disk label
Bit four: the file has been changed since it was last archived

Bits five, six, and seven are unused. When bit three is true, the file description has a different meaning. The first eleven bytes of the directory entry contain the disk label instead of the file name and extension, and the rest of the entry is unused.

Since a file description can have two different forms, depending on the value of the disk label flag, the type for file descriptions should be a record type with two variants. The disk label flag acts as a discriminant, indicating which variant exists in a given record. The following declarations give the logical structure of a file description:

```
TYPE File_Description_Type (Label_Flag : Boolean := False) IS
   RECORD
      CASE Label_Flag IS
         WHEN True =>
            Label_Part : String (1 .. 11);
         WHEN False =>
            File_Name_Part : String (1 .. 8);
            Extension_Part: String (1 .. 3);
            Read_Only_Flag : Boolean;
            Hidden_Flag    : Boolean;
            System_Flag    : Boolean;
            Modified_Flag  : Boolean;
            Location_Part  : Integer RANGE 0 .. 500;
      END CASE;
   END RECORD;
```

An implementation might allow us to specify the physical structure of a `File_Description_Type` record as follows:

```
FOR File_Description_Type USE
   RECORD
      Label_Part     AT  0 RANGE 0 .. 87;
      File_Name_Part AT  0 RANGE 0 .. 63;
      Extension_Part AT  8 RANGE 0 .. 23;
      Read_Only_Flag AT 11 RANGE 0 .. 0;
      Hidden_Flag    AT 11 RANGE 1 .. 1;
      System_Flag    AT 11 RANGE 2 .. 2;
      Label_Flag     AT 11 RANGE 3 .. 3;
      Modified_Flag  AT 11 RANGE 4 .. 4;
      Location_Part  AT 12 RANGE 0 .. 15;
   END RECORD;
```

As this example shows, a position may be specified for a discriminant just as for any other record component. Since the physical location of a component is unrelated to its logical location, the discriminant need not be physically located at the beginning of the record. When a record type has variants, overlapping positions may be specified for components in different variants, but overlapping is not allowed in any other case. In `File_Description_Type`, `Label_Part` overlaps with `File_Name_Part` and `Extension_Part`. A record component that is one bit long has a bit range in which the lower and upper bounds are identical.

20.3.1.6 Controlling the address of an entity. Some computers reserve certain addresses to serve special purposes. For example, the hardware may branch to a certain address each time the machine is reset, or it may save status information at a certain address each time an interrupt occurs. An address clause can be used to specify that a program unit or an object will begin at a particular address. Its form is

> **FOR** *identifier* **USE AT** *expression* **;**

The expression must be of type `System.Address`, but it need not be static. A `WITH` clause for package `System` is required in order to use an address clause, even if the expression in the address clause is an integer literal.

If the identifier names a subprogram or task unit, the address specifies where the first machine instruction of the subprogram or task body will go. If the identifier names a package, the address specifies where the first machine instruction for the package's initialization statements will go. If the identifier is declared in an object declaration, it specifies where the object will be located. This allows a memory location with a special hardware function to be used as an ordinary variable in an Ada program, as will be illustrated in the next subsection. Address clauses are also used to associate a hardware interrupt with an entry of an Ada task. This will be explained in Section 20.5.

An identifier introduced in a renaming declaration may not be used as the identifier in an address clause. Address clauses are not meant to be used to make different data objects or program units occupy the same storage location (or overlapping storage locations). It is an error to use address clauses in that way.

20.3.1.7 An example: Specifying a video display interface. In an IBM Personal Computer with a Monochrome Display Adapter, there is a 4,000-byte buffer at location B0000 hexadecimal whose contents control what appears on the display screen. The display has 25 lines of eighty characters each, and the buffer has two bytes corresponding to each position on the screen. The first byte for each position specifies the character to be displayed, and the second controls the manner in which it is displayed.

The byte specifying the character may hold any value from zero to 255. The numbers 32 through 126 cause the corresponding character in the ASCII character set to be displayed. The numbers zero through 31 and 127 (corresponding to the ASCII control characters) and 128 through 255 (not part of the ASCII code) cause various special characters to be displayed, as shown in Figure 20.5. We declare a new 256-value character type to represent the displayable characters:

```
TYPE Display_Character_Type IS
   (Space_0, Face, Reversed_Face, Heart, Diamond, Club, Spade,
    Spot, Reversed_Spot, Circle, Reversed_Circle, Male,
    Female, Eighth_Note, Sixteenth_Notes, Sun, Right_Triangle,
    Left_Triangle, Up_Down_Arrow, Double_Exclamation,
    Paragraph, Section, Cursor, Underlined_Up_Down_Arrow,
    Up_Arrow, Down_Arrow, Right_Arrow, Left_Arrow,
    Bottom_Right_Corner, Left_Right_Arrow, Up_Triangle,
    Down_Triangle, ' ', '!', '"', '#', '$', '%', '&', ''',
    '(', ')', '*', '+', ',', '-', '.', '/', '0', '1', '2',
    '3', '4', '5', '6', '7', '8', '9', ':', ';', '<', '=',
    '>', '?', '@', 'A', 'B', 'C', 'D', 'E', 'F', 'G', 'H',
    'I', 'J', 'K', 'L', 'M', 'N', 'O', 'P', 'Q', 'R', 'S',
    'T', 'U', 'V', 'W', 'X', 'Y', 'Z', '[', '\', ']', '^',
    '_', '`', 'a', 'b', 'c', 'd', 'e', 'f', 'g', 'h', 'i',
    'j', 'k', 'l', 'm', 'n', 'o', 'p', 'q', 'r', 's', 't',
    'u', 'v', 'w', 'x', 'y', 'z', '{', '|', '}', '~', House,
    Printed_Delta, UC_C_Cedilla, LC_u_Dieresis, LC_e_Acute,
    LC_a_Circumflex, LC_a_Dieresis, LC_a_Grave, LC_a_Circle,
    LC_c_Cedilla, LC_e_Circumflex, LC_e_Dieresis, LC_e_Grave,
    LC_i_Dieresis, LC_i_Circumflex, LC_i_Grave, UC_A_Dieresis,
    UC_A_Circle, UC_E_Acute, LC_ae, UC_AE, LC_o_Circumflex,
    LC_o_Dieresis, LC_o_Grave, LC_U_Circumflex, LC_U_Grave,
    LC_y_Dieresis, UC_O_Dieresis, UC_U_Dieresis, Cent, Pound,
    Yen, Peseta, Franc, LC_a_Acute, LC_i_Acute, LC_o_Acute,
    LC_u_Acute, LC_n_Tilde, UC_N_Tilde, LC_a_Underline,
    LC_o_Underline, Inverted_Question_Mark, Top_Left_Corner,
    Top_Right_Corner, One_Half, One_Quarter,
    Inverted_Exclamation_Point, Left_Quotation_Brackets,
    Right_Quotation_Brackets, Light_Shading, Medium_Shading,
    Dark_Shading, NS_Junction, NSW_Junction, NSWW_Junction,
    NNSSW_Junction, SSW_Junction, SWW_Junction,
    NNSSWW_Junction, NNSS_Junction, SSWW_Junction,
    NNWW_Junction, NNW_Junction, NWW_Junction, SW_Junction,
    NE_Junction, NEW_Junction, SEW_Junction, NSE_Junction,
    EW_Junction, NSEW_Junction, NSEE_Junction, NNSSE_Junction,
    NNEE_Junction, SSEE_Junction, NNEEWW_Junction,
    SSEEWW_Junction, NNSSEE_Junction, EEWW_Junction,
    NNSSEEWW_Junction, NEEWW_Junction, NNEW_Junction,
    SEEWW_Junction, SSEW_Junction, NNE_Junction, NEE_Junction,
    SEE_Junction, SSE_JunctionNNSSEW_Junction, NW_Junction,
    SE_Junction, Whole_Block, Bottom_Half_Block,
    Left_Half_Block, Right_Half_Block, Top_Half_Block, Alpha,
    Beta, Gamma, Pi, Printed_Sigma, Script_Sigma, Mu, Tau,
    Printed_Phi, Theta, Omega, Script_Delta, Infinity,
    Script_Phi, Epsilon, Intersection, Equivalent,
    Plus_Or_Minus, Greater_Than_Or_Equal, Less_Than_Or_Equal,
    Integral_Top, Integral_Bottom, Divided_By,
    Approximately_Equal, Degrees, Large_Dot, Small_Dot,
    Square_Root, Eta, Squared, Box, Space_255);
```

We specify the representation of this type as follows:

```
FOR Display_Character_Type USE
   (0, 1, 2, 3, 4, 5, 6, 7, 8, 9, 10, 11, 12, 13, 14, 15, 16,
    17, 18, 19, 20, 21, 22, 23, 24, 25, 26, 27, 28, 29, 30,
    31, 32, 33, 34, 35, 36, 37, 38, 39, 40, 41, 42, 43, 44,
    45, 46, 47, 48, 49, 50, 51, 52, 53, 54, 55, 56, 57, 58,
    59, 60, 61, 62, 63, 64, 65, 66, 67, 68, 69, 70, 71, 72,
    73, 74, 75, 76, 77, 78, 79, 80, 81, 82, 83, 84, 85, 86,
    87, 88, 89, 90, 91, 92, 93, 94, 95, 96, 97, 98, 99, 100,
    101, 102, 103, 104, 105, 106, 107, 108, 109, 110, 111,
    112, 113, 114, 115, 116, 117, 118, 119, 120, 121, 122,
    123, 124, 125, 126, 127, 128, 129, 130, 131, 132, 133,
    134, 135, 136, 137, 138, 139, 140, 141, 142, 143, 144,
    145, 146, 147, 148, 149, 150, 151, 152, 153, 154, 155,
    156, 157, 158, 159, 160, 161, 162, 163, 164, 165, 166,
    167, 168, 169, 170, 171, 172, 173, 174, 175, 176, 177,
    178, 179, 180, 181, 182, 183, 184, 185, 186, 187, 188,
    189, 190, 191, 192, 193, 194, 195, 196, 197, 198, 199,
    200, 201, 202, 203, 204, 205, 206, 207, 208, 209, 210,
    211, 212, 213, 214, 215, 216, 217, 218, 219, 220, 221,
    222, 223, 224, 225, 226, 227, 228, 229, 230, 231, 232,
    233, 234, 235, 236, 237, 238, 239, 240, 241, 242, 243,
    244, 245, 246, 247, 248, 249, 250, 251, 252, 253, 254,
    255);

FOR Display_Character_Type'Size USE 8;
```

Bits in a byte are numbered from right to left, and the byte controlling how a character is displayed has the form described in Figure 20.6: Bits zero through two control the *foreground*—the character itself—and bytes four through six control the *background*—the box in which the character is displayed. The foreground and background bits are intended to be used in one of the following four combinations:

Foreground (bits 0–2)	Background (bits 4–6)	
000	000	black on black (invisible)
001	000	underlined white on black
111	000	white on black
000	111	black on white (reversed video)

Other combinations of these bits duplicate one of these effects. When bit three is set, it causes a white-on-black character (underlined or not) to be displayed more intensely. Otherwise, bit three has no effect. When bit seven is set, it causes the foreground character to blink.

There are only six meaningful combinations for bits zero through six, while the meaning of bit seven is independent of the other seven bits. Thus we can view bit seven as representing a one-bit flag and bits zero through six as representing an enumeration type:

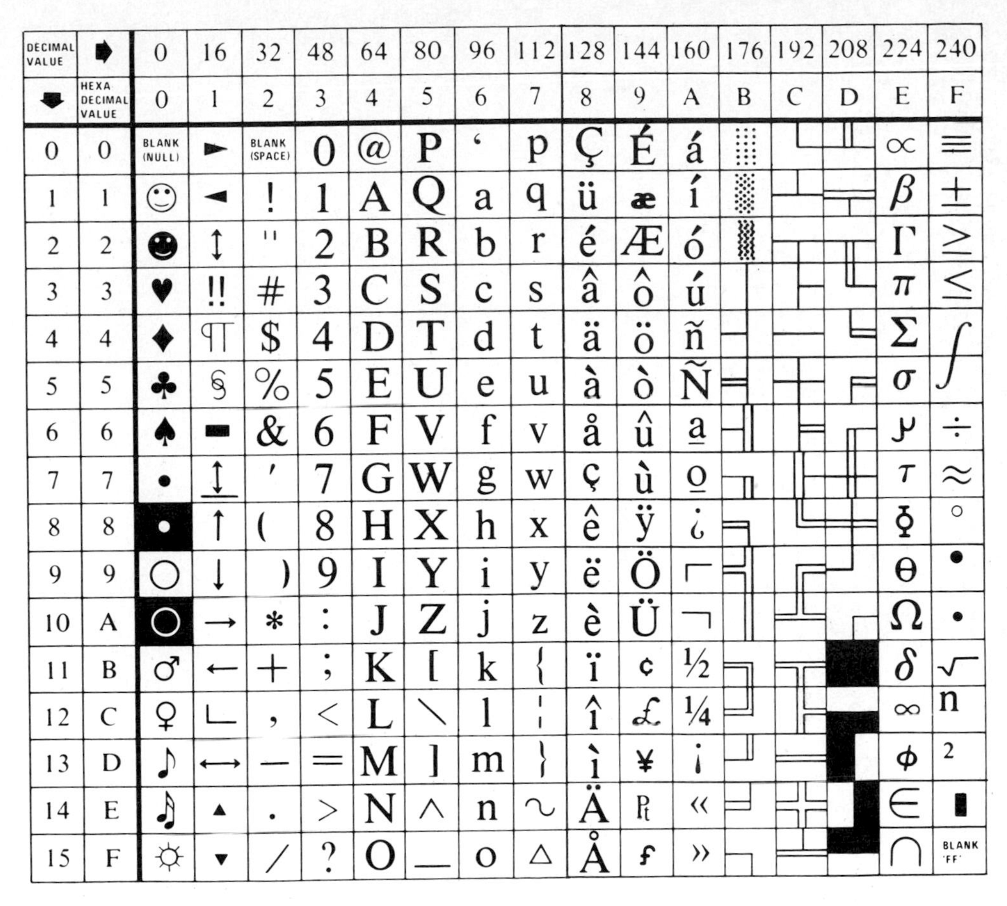

DECIMAL VALUE	➡	0	16	32	48	64	80	96	112	128	144	160	176	192	208	224	240
⬇	HEXA DECIMAL VALUE	0	1	2	3	4	5	6	7	8	9	A	B	C	D	E	F
0	0	BLANK (NULL)	►	BLANK (SPACE)	0	@	P	‘	p	Ç	É	á	░	└	╨	∝	≡
1	1	☺	◄	!	1	A	Q	a	q	ü	æ	í	▒	┴	╤	β	±
2	2	☻	↕	"	2	B	R	b	r	é	Æ	ó	▓	┬	╥	Γ	≥
3	3	♥	‼	#	3	C	S	c	s	â	ô	ú	│	├	╙	π	≤
4	4	♦	¶	$	4	D	T	d	t	ä	ö	ñ	┤	─	╘	Σ	⌠
5	5	♣	§	%	5	E	U	e	u	à	ò	Ñ	╡	┼	╒	σ	⌡
6	6	♠	▬	&	6	F	V	f	v	å	û	ª	╢	╞	╓	µ	÷
7	7	•	↨	'	7	G	W	g	w	ç	ù	º	╖	╟	╫	τ	≈
8	8	◘	↑	(	8	H	X	h	x	ê	ÿ	¿	╕	╚	╪	Φ	°
9	9	○	↓	)	9	I	Y	i	y	ë	Ö	⌐	╣	╔	┘	Θ	•
10	A	◙	→	*	:	J	Z	j	z	è	Ü	¬	║	╩	┌	Ω	·
11	B	♂	←	+	;	K	[	k	{	ï	¢	½	╗	╦	█	δ	√
12	C	♀	∟	,	<	L	\	l	¦	î	£	¼	╝	╠	▄	∞	ⁿ
13	D	♪	↔	-	=	M	]	m	}	ì	¥	¡	╜	═	▌	φ	²
14	E	♫	▲	.	>	N	∧	n	∼	Ä	₧	«	╛	╬	▐	∈	■
15	F	☼	▼	/	?	O	_	o	△	Å	ƒ	»	┐	╧	▀	∩	BLANK 'FF'

Figure 20.5 The 256 characters generated by the IBM Personal Computer monochrome display adapter. (Reproduced with permission from International Business Machines.)

```
TYPE Display_Mode_Type IS
   (Invisible, Underlined, Normal, Underlined_Intense,
    Intense, Reversed);
FOR Display_Mode_Type USE
   (Invisible            => 2#000_0_000#,
    Underlined           => 2#000_0_001#,
    Normal               => 2#000_0_111#,
    Underlined_Intense   => 2#000_1_001#,
    Intense              => 2#000_1_111#,
    Reversed             => 2#111_0_000#);
FOR Display_Mode_Type'Size USE 7;
TYPE Display_Element_Type IS
   RECORD
      Character_Part : Display_Character_Type;
      Mode_Part      : Display_Mode_Type;
      Blinking_Flag  : Boolean;
   END RECORD;
```

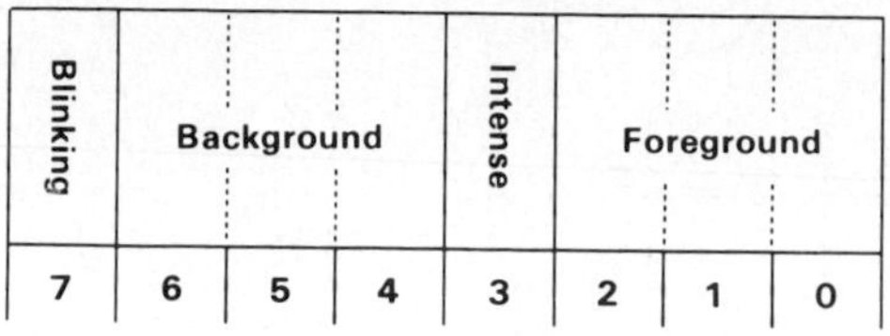

Blinking	Background			Intense	Foreground		
7	6	5	4	3	2	1	0

Figure 20.6 Structure of the byte controlling how a character is displayed.

```
FOR Display_Element_Type USE
   RECORD AT MOD 2
      Character_Part AT 0 RANGE 0 .. 7;
      Mode_Part      AT 1 RANGE 0 .. 6;
      Blinking_Flag  AT 1 RANGE 7 .. 7;
   END RECORD;

FOR Display_Element_Type'Size USE 16;
```

Finally, we can declare a type for 25-by-80 arrays of `Display_Element_Type` values, and declare `Display_Buffer` to be a variable of this type residing at the special address B0000 hexadecimal:

```
SUBTYPE Line_Number_Subtype IS Integer RANGE 1 .. 25;
SUBTYPE Column_Number_Subtype IS Integer RANGE 1 .. 80;

TYPE Display_Type IS
   ARRAY (Line_Number_Subtype, Column_Number_Subtype)
      OF Display_Element_Type;

FOR Display_Buffer_Type'Size USE
   Display_Type'Length(1) * Display_Type'Length(2) *
   Display_Element_Type'Size;

Display_Buffer : Display_Buffer_Type;

FOR Display_Buffer USE AT 16#B0000#;
```

(There are two reasons for not declaring `Display_Buffer` as an object in an anonymous array type. First, there would have been no way to specify its representation, since length clauses apply only to types, not objects. Second, other objects in the type can be used to hold predetermined display formats. A single assignment of one of these other objects to `Display_Buffer` will replace the contents of the entire display screen.)

These declarations and representation clauses can be combined into a single package with the following specification and no body:

```
WITH System; -- needed to use an address clause

PACKAGE Display_Buffer_Package IS

   TYPE Display_Character_Type IS ( ... );

   TYPE Display_Mode_Type IS
      (Invisible, Underlined, Normal, Underlined_Intense,
       Intense, Reversed);
```

```
   TYPE Display_Element_Type IS
      RECORD
         Character_Part : Display_Character_Type;
         Mode_Part      : Display_Mode_Type;
         Blinking       : Boolean;
      END RECORD;

   SUBTYPE Line_Number_Subtype IS Integer RANGE 1 .. 25;
   SUBTYPE Column_Number_Subtype IS Integer RANGE 1 .. 80;

   TYPE Display_Buffer_Type IS
      ARRAY (Line_Number_Subtype, Column_Number_Subtype)
         OF Display_Element_Type;

   Display_Buffer : Display_Buffer_Type;

PRIVATE

   FOR Display_Character_Type USE ( ... );
   FOR Display_Character_Type'Size USE 8;
   FOR Display_Mode_Type USE ( ... );
   FOR Display_Mode_Type'Size USE 7;
   FOR Display_Element_Type USE
      RECORD AT MOD 2
         ...
      END RECORD;
   FOR Display_Element_Type'Size USE 16;
   FOR Display_Buffer_Type'Size USE
      Display_Type'Range (1) * Display_Type'Range (2) *
      Display_Element_Type'Size;
   FOR Display_Buffer USE AT 16#B0000#;

END Display_Buffer_Package;
```

The interface, described in the visible part of the package, is as simple and abstract as it can be while allowing the hardware to be manipulated in most meaningful ways. It is certainly possible to write a package providing higher-level operations on the display, such as displaying a string or scrolling. However, some applications require direct access to the full capability of the hardware (e.g., to create full-screen displays or animation). `Display_Buffer_Package` provides most of the full capability of the hardware in terms of abstract Ada declarations. The actual bit patterns and addresses hidden in the private part are irrelevant to a user of the package. In effect, `Display_Buffer_Package` allows an Ada programmer to throw away the Monochrome Display Adapter hardware specifications and replace them with abstract software specifications. Packages providing higher-level screen operations could use `Display_Buffer_Package` and avoid direct reference to the hardware.

20.3.2 Representation Pragmas

Representation clauses provide exact control over internal representations of types. For some applications it is sufficient to indicate only the general strategy that an implementation should follow in choosing representations. Representation pragmas provide this ability. Like representation clauses, representation pragmas can go in a package specification or in a declarative part.

There is only one representation pragma, the `Pack` pragma, that all implementations of the Ada language are required to recognize. Its form is

```
PRAGMA Pack ( composite type name ) ;
```

It specifies that the implementation should choose a representation for the named array or record type that minimizes the gaps between components. This can save space, but it may cause a single addressable storage unit to contain part of the representation of one component and part of the representation of another component. This can increase the number of machine instructions required to examine or update a component.

An implementation treats the `Pack` pragma as general advice and may follow this advice to a greater or lesser degree. Unlike a length clause specifying a `'Size` attribute, however, a grammatically correct `Pack` pragma can never be flagged as an error. Because of this, and because the `Pack` pragma does not depend on the storage units of a particular target machine, the `Pack` pragma provides a greater degree of portability than a length clause.

An implementation is required to ignore a pragma that it doesn't recognize, rather than flagging it as an error, so an implementation-defined representation pragma will normally not decrease portability. The only danger in moving a program with an implementation-defined pragma to another implementation is that the new implementation will have a pragma of its own with the same name but a different meaning. It is wise to check each implementation's Appendix F, which lists the implementation-defined pragmas, before moving such a program from one implementation to another.

There is another pragma, `Optimize`, that is not, strictly speaking, a representation pragma. Nonetheless, its purpose is similar. It takes one of two forms:

```
PRAGMA Optimize (Space);
PRAGMA Optimize (Time);
```

The first form advises the compiler to generate code that minimizes storage requirements, even at the cost of making the program run more slowly. The second form advises the compiler to generate fast code, even if it requires more storage. Unlike the `Pack` pragma, the `Optimize` pragma does not apply to a particular type. Rather, it goes in the declarative part of a block statement, subprogram body, package body, or task body and applies to that part of the program as a whole.

20.3.3 Types and Representations

At most, one representation may be specified, using representation clauses and representation pragmas, for each type. Sometimes it is desirable to have two representations, such as a packed and unpacked representation, for the same abstract data. This can be achieved by declaring a derived type and specifying different representations for the derived type and the parent type. Then type conversion from the parent type to the derived type or vice versa will translate from one representation to the other.

If a representation clause or representation pragma is specified for the parent type before the derived-type declaration, it will apply to both types, and a separate representation cannot be specified for the derived type. If the derived-type declaration occurs first, the representations of the derived type and parent type are independent. The programmer can specify representations for either or both of the types. When no representation is specified, the implementation's standard representation is used.

For example, let us revisit the type `File_Allocation_Table_Type` of Section 20.3.1.1. This was an array of 316 twelve-bit unsigned integers, packed so that every three bytes contained two components. Access to these array components can be slow, so we might find it necessary to define both a packed representation of a file allocation table, matching its representation on disk, and an unpacked representation, permitting efficient access:

```
TYPE Cluster_Number_Type IS RANGE 0 .. 16#FFF#;
FOR Cluster_Number_Type'Size USE 12;
TYPE Packed_File_Allocation_Table_Type IS
   ARRAY (Cluster_Number_Type RANGE 0 .. 315) OF
      Cluster_Number_Type;
TYPE Unpacked_File_Allocation_Table_Type IS
   NEW Packed_File_Allocation_Table_Type;
FOR Packed_File_Allocation_Table_Type'Size USE
   File_Allocation_Table_Type'Length *
      Cluster_Number_Type'Size;
-- Use default representation for
--   Unpacked_File_Allocation_Table_Type.
```

Suppose that the following procedures read a packed file allocation table directly from a disk and wrote a packed file allocation table directly to the disk:

```
PROCEDURE Read_Packed_Table
   (Table : OUT Packed_File_Allocation_Table_Type);
PROCEDURE Write_Packed_Table
   (Table : IN Packed_File_Allocation_Table_Type);
```

An algorithm to read a file allocation table from a disk, rearrange it, and write it back out to the disk could take the following general form:

```
PROCEDURE Rearrange_Table IS
   ...
   Old_Table, New_Table : Packed_File_Allocation_Table_Type;
   Scratch_Table        : Unpacked_File_Allocation_Table_Type;
```

```
BEGIN
    Read_Packed_Table (Old_Table);
    Scratch_Table :=
       Unpacked_File_Allocation_Table_Type (Old_Table);
       -- type conversion to "unpack" the table
```

[statements to rearrange Scratch_Table*]*

```
    New_Table :=
       Packed_File_Allocation_Table_Type (Scratch_Table);
       -- type conversion to "pack" the table
    Write_Packed_Table (New_Table);
END Rearrange_Table;
```

20.3.4 Placement of Representation Clauses and Pragmas

Representation clauses and representation pragmas may go in the sequence of declarations of a package specification or a declarative part. A representation clause must appear after the declaration of the type, object, or program unit whose representation it determines and before any body or body stub.

When no representation clause or representation pragma is given for an entity, the implementation chooses a *default representation* for it. Normally, this happens at the end of the package specification or declarative part in which the entity is declared. However, certain constructs in a sequence of declarations refer implicitly or explicitly to the representation of an entity declared earlier in the sequence. If such a construct occurs before a representation clause or representation pragma for the entity, the compiler commits itself to the default representation *at that point.* Any subsequent representation clause or representation pragma for that entity will be illegal, since a representation has already been chosen.

If a sequence of declarations contains an object declaration and the name of the object occurs later in the same sequence of declarations, an address clause for the object can only occur between those two points:

```
Interrupt_Queue_Length : Natural;
FOR Interrupt_Queue_Length USE AT 16#40#;
Current_Interrupt_Count : Natural := Interrupt_Queue_Length;
```

If a sequence of declarations contains a subprogram declaration, package specification, or task declaration and a representation attribute for that program unit occurs later in the same sequence of declarations, an address clause for the program unit can only occur between those two points:

```
PROCEDURE Timer_Interrupt_Handler;
FOR Timer_Interrupt_Handler USE AT 16#100#;
Timer_Interrupt_Handler_Address :
   CONSTANT System.Address :=
      Timer_Interrupt_Handler'Address;
```

The restrictions for specifying the representation of a type are more complex. A type *t* declared in a sequence of declarations can be named later in the same sequence of declarations without forcing a representation to be chosen, providing that the occurrence is in one of the following contexts and not within an expression:

in the declaration of another type or subtype
in the formal parameter specification of a subprogram or entry
in a deferred constant declaration
in a pragma
in a representation clause controlling one aspect of *t*'s representation

However, if *t*, a subtype of *t*, or any other type or subtype directly or indirectly containing components of type *t* is named in any other context in the sequence of declarations, the default representation for *t* is chosen at that point, and no representation clauses or representation pragmas for *t* may follow.

20.4 DEVICE-LEVEL INPUT AND OUTPUT

Chapter 17 discussed input to and output from files. The files are typically provided by an operating system, which acts as an intermediary between the Ada program and the physical devices reading and writing data. The operating system translates high-level operations on files (e.g., "read the next file element") to low-level operations on devices (e.g., "read the 256 bytes starting at track 40, sector 10, on disk drive 2 into the buffer at address 2000"). An Ada program can also use input and output devices directly, to perform low-level operations. This is useful when a program is running on a "bare machine"—that is, without an operating system to provide services for it. Programs for embedded computers generally fall into this category. So do operating systems themselves (viewed as programs). Device-level operations are also useful for attaching special-purpose devices, such as a joystick, to a single-user computer.

Large mainframe computers usually distinguish between privileged machine instructions that can only be executed by the operating system and ordinary operations that can be executed by any program. Device-level input and output operations typically use privileged instructions. Therefore, application Ada programs that are to run on a multiuser mainframe computer will probably not be able to perform device-level input and output. Application programs that are to run on a single-user microcomputer may be able to do so.

Device-level input and output operations are provided by the predefined library package `Low_Level_IO`. The devices that can be manipulated and the information that can be received from or sent to a device vary from implementation to implementation. `Low_Level_IO` provides one or more types whose values correspond to devices and one or more types corresponding to the data received from and sent to devices. The package uses these types to declare some number of overloaded versions of the procedures `Receive_Control` and `Send_Control`.

`Receive_Control` is a low-level input operation, and `Send_Control` is a low-level output operation. All versions of these procedures have declarations of the following form:

```
PROCEDURE Receive_Control
   (Device : IN [some type for devices];
    Data   : IN OUT[some type for data]) ;
PROCEDURE Send_Control
   (Device : IN [some type for devices];
    Data   : IN OUT [some type for data]) ;
```

For example, the Intel 8086 has two kinds of addresses— memory addresses ranging from zero to $2^{20} - 1$ and input/output addresses ranging from zero to $2^{16} - 1$. Every device connected to the 8086 processor communicates with it through one or more of these input/output addresses. There is an IN machine instruction to read either one or two bytes from a specified input/output address and an OUT instruction to write either one or two bytes to a specified input/output address. Thus a version of `Low_Level_IO` for programs to run on the Intel 8086 might look like this:

```
PACKAGE Low_Level_IO IS
   -- Hypothetical version for the Intel 8086
   TYPE Device_Type IS RANGE 0 .. 16#FFFF#;
   TYPE Byte_Type IS RANGE 0 .. 16#FF#;
   TYPE Word_Type IS RANGE 0 .. 16#FFFF#;
   PROCEDURE Receive_Control
      (Device : IN Device_Type; Data : IN OUT Byte_Type);
   PROCEDURE Receive_Control
      (Device : IN Device_Type; Data : IN OUT Word_Type);
   PROCEDURE Send_Control
      (Device : IN Device_Type; Data : IN OUT Byte_Type);
   PROCEDURE Send_Control
      (Device : IN Device_Type; Data : IN OUT Word_Type);
PRIVATE
   FOR Byte_Type'Size USE 8;
   FOR Word_Type'Size USE 16;
END Low_Level_IO;
```

In this hypothetical implementation, a call on `Receive_Control` corresponds to an IN operation, and a call on `Send_Control` corresponds to an OUT operation.

In addition to the video display buffer described in Section 20.3.1.7, the Motorola 6845 CRT Controller used in the IBM Personal Computer Monochrome Display Adapter has eighteen internal eight-bit registers. The contents of these registers control such things as the size and position of the cursor and the size of the image on the screen. Two other registers in the CRT controller—the *index register*

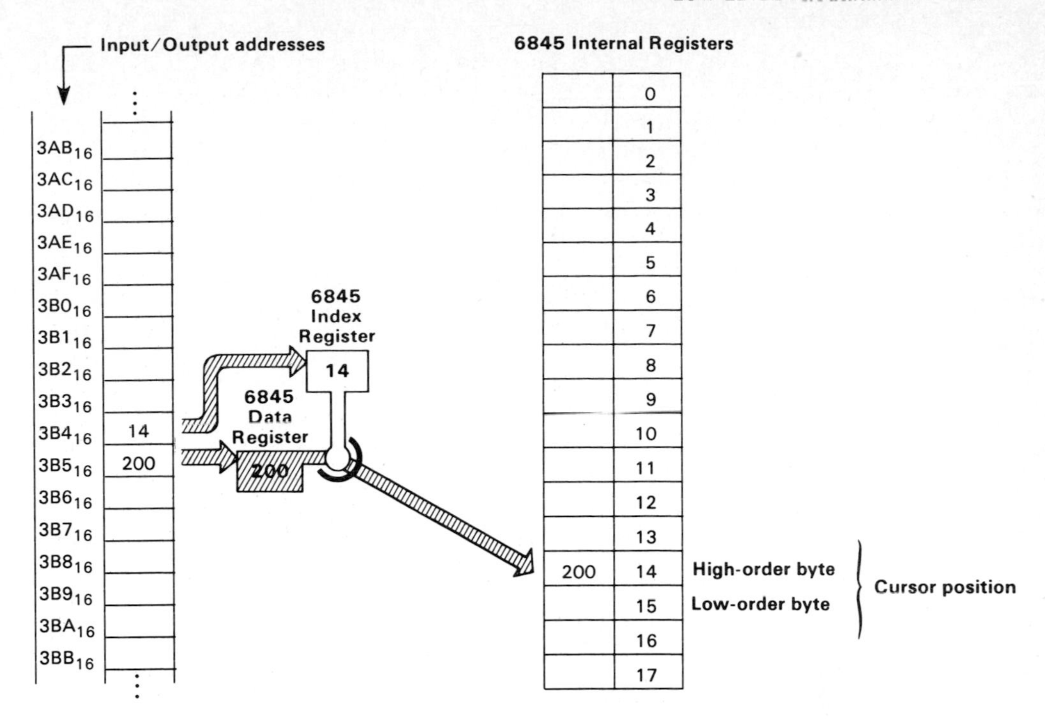

Figure 20.7 An OUT operation to input/output address 3B4 hexadecimal causes the 6845 index register to point to a specified internal register. An OUT operation to input/output address 3B5 hexadecimal places data in the 6845 register, from where it is copied to the internal register currently pointed to by the index register.

and the *data register*—are used to alter the contents of the internal registers. First, an internal register number (from zero to seventeen) is placed in the index register. Then the value to be placed in the specified internal register is inserted in the data register. An OUT operation to input/output address 3B4 hexadecimal sends a specified byte to the 6845 index register, and an OUT operation to input/output address 3B5 hexadecimal sends a specified byte to the 6845 data register. (See Figure 20.7.)

Suppose we wish to augment `Display_Buffer_Package` (as given in Section 20.3.1) with a procedure `Set_Cursor` to move the cursor to a specified line and column:

```
WITH System;
PACKAGE Display_Buffer_Package IS
   TYPE Display_Character_Type IS ( ... );
   TYPE Display_Mode_Type IS ( ... );
   TYPE Display_Element_Type IS
      RECORD
         ...
      END RECORD;
```

```
      SUBTYPE Line_Number_Subtype IS Integer RANGE 1 .. 25;
      SUBTYPE Column_Number_Subtype IS Integer RANGE 1 .. 80;

      TYPE Display_Buffer_Type IS
         ARRAY (Line_Number_Subtype, Column_Number_Subtype)
            OF Display_Element_Type;

      Display_Buffer : Display_Buffer_Type;

      PROCEDURE Set_Cursor
         (Line_Number   : IN Line_Number_Subtype;
          Column_Number : IN Column_Number_Subtype);

   PRIVATE

      ...

   END Display_Buffer_Package;
```

The package must be given a body with the implementation of `Set_Cursor`. `Set_Cursor` must compute the offset of the cursor from the start of the screen (a number from zero to 1,999) and place this value in the appropriate internal registers of the CRT controller. The high-order byte of the cursor position offset (viewed as a sixteen-bit binary integer) goes in internal register fourteen, and the low-order byte goes in internal register fifteen. `Set_Cursor` is easily implemented in terms of the version of `Low_Level_IO` hypothesized previously:

```
   WITH Low_Level_IO;

   PACKAGE BODY Display_Buffer_Package IS

      PROCEDURE Set_Cursor
         (Line_Number   : IN Line_Number_Subtype;
          Column_Number : IN Column_Number_Subtype) IS

         SUBTYPE Screen_Position_Subtype IS
            Integer RANGE 0 .. 25 * 80 - 1;

         Motorola_6845_Index_Register :
            CONSTANT Low_Level_IO.Device_Type := 16#3B4#;

         Motorola_6845_Data_Register :
            CONSTANT Low_Level_IO.Device_Type := 16#3B5#;

         Cursor_Position_High_Register : CONSTANT := 14;

         Cursor_Position_Low_Register : CONSTANT := 15;

         Line_Starting_Position, Cursor_Position :
            Screen_Position_Subtype;

    Low_Order_Byte, High_Order_Byte : Low_Level_IO.Byte_Type;
```

```
BEGIN
   -- Compute high- and low-order bytes of cursor offset:
   Line_Starting_Position := 80 * (Line_Number - 1);
   Cursor_Position :=
      Line_Starting_Position + Column_Number - 1;
   Low_Order_Byte :=
      Low_Level_IO.Byte_Type ( Cursor_Position MOD 256 );
   High_Order_Byte :=
      Low_Level_IO.Byte_Type ( Cursor_Position / 256 );
   -- Place high-order byte in 6845 internal register 14:
   Low_Level_IO.Send_Control
      (Motorola_6845_Index_Register,
       Cursor_Position_High_Register);
   Low_Level_IO.Send_Control
      (Motorola_6845_Data_Register, High_Order_Byte);
   -- Place low-order byte in 6845 internal register 15:
   Low_Level_IO.Send_Control
      (Motorola_6845_Index_Register,
       Cursor_Position_Low_Register);
   Low_Level_IO.Send_Control
      (Motorola_6845_Data_Register, Low_Order_Byte);
 END Set_Cursor;
END Display_Buffer_Package;
```

20.5 INTERRUPT ENTRIES

Some implementations allow an address clause to appear after all the entry declarations in a task declaration. This address clause associates an entry of the task with a particular machine interrupt, so that the entry is called each time the interrupt takes place. This allows an interrupt handler to be written in the Ada language in the form of a task. The entry associated with an interrupt is called an *interrupt entry*.

The form of the address clause is

FOR *identifier* USE AT *expression* ;

where the identifier names an entry declared earlier in the same task declaration (not an entry family and not a member of an entry family). The expression is of type

`System.Address` and need not be static. Like any address clause, this address clause requires a `WITH` clause for the package `System`.

The meaning of the address depends on the implementation. Typical machines associate each kind of interrupt with an *interrupt vector*. This is a fixed memory location containing the address to which the hardware branches when a certain kind of interrupt occurs. An Ada implementation might associate an entry with a particular kind of interrupt by specifying the address of the corresponding interrupt vector as the "address of the entry."

For example, suppose a computer embedded in an electrocardiogram machine received an interrupt with interrupt vector 10 hexadecimal every time a heartbeat was detected. We could write a function to return thc number of heartbeats detected since the previous call on the function by having the function call an entry of an interrupt handling task:

```
PACKAGE Heartbeat_Package IS
   FUNCTION New_Beats RETURN Natural;
END Heartbeat_Package;

WITH System; -- needed to use an address clause
PACKAGE BODY Heartbeat_Package IS
   TASK Heartbeat_Interrupt_Handler IS
      ENTRY Heartbeat_Interrupt;
      ENTRY Read_And_Reset_Interrupt_Count
         (Number_Of_New_Interrupts : OUT Natural);
      FOR Heartbeat_Interrupt USE AT 16#10#;
   END Heartbeat_Interrupt_Handler;
   FUNCTION New_Beats RETURN Natural IS
      Result : Natural;
   BEGIN
      Heartbeat_Interrupt_Handler.
         Read_And_Reset_Interrupt_Count
            (Result);
      RETURN Result;
   END New_Beats;
   TASK BODY Heartbeat_Interrupt_Handler IS
      Unreported_Interrupt_Count : Natural := 0;
   BEGIN
      LOOP
         SELECT
            ACCEPT Heartbeat_Interrupt;
            Unreported_Interrupt_Count :=
               Unreported_Interrupt_Count + 1;
```

```
        OR
           ACCEPT Read_And_Reset_Interrupt_Count
              (Number_Of_New_Interrupts : OUT Natural) DO
              Number_Of_New_Interrupts :=
                 Unreported_Interrupt_Count;
           END Read_And_Reset_Interrupt_Count;
           Unreported_Interrupt_Count := 0;
        END SELECT;
     END LOOP;
  END Heartbeat_Interrupt_Handler;

END Heartbeat_Package;
```

The `Heartbeat_Interrupt_Handler` task body looks just like the task body of an ordinary monitor task. (See Section 19.2.1.2.) There are two operations on a shared count—one is incrementing the count, and the other is reading the count and resetting it to zero. The monitor prevents race conditions (e.g., reading the count, incrementing it, and then resetting it to zero, so that the last increment is never reported). The only difference is that the incrementing operation is not invoked by another task, but by the hardware. Every time an interrupt with interrupt vector 10 hexadecimal occurs, the entry

```
Heartbeat_Interrupt_Handler.Heartbeat_Interrupt
```

is automatically called. Since this entry is not intended to be part of the software interface of `Heartbeat_Package`, the task declaration is hidden in the package body. The function `New_Beats` provides an abstract interface that does not reflect the underlying implementation.

Some computers make control information available when an interrupt occurs. This control information may, for example, describe the exact cause of an interrupt or identify the peripheral device that generated the interrupt. An Ada implementation may stipulate that interrupt entries for certain kinds of interrupts have entry parameters. These parameters are always of mode `IN` and are used to convey control information. If your implementation requires or allows interrupt entries to have parameters, the parameters will be described in Appendix F.

Entry calls generated by hardware interrupts are treated as though made by "hardware tasks" with higher priorities than the priority of any software task. (Priorities were explained in Section 19.3.1.) Since a rendezvous is executed at the higher of its two participants' priorities, this means that, for implementations using preemptive task scheduling, the rendezvous resulting from an interrupt always takes place immediately, unless another interrupt rendezvous is already in progress or the interrupt handler is not waiting for a call on the interrupt entry. An implementation may assign different priority levels to the "hardware tasks" that generate different kinds of interrupts. These priorities may model priorities that the hardware assigns to different kinds of interrupts.

Interrupt entries can also be called by software using ordinary entry calls. This allows the simulation of an interrupt. However, the resulting rendezvous takes place at the priority of the calling task or the priority of the interrupt handler, whichever is higher, not at the priority of some "hardware task."

An interrupt entry is an entry of a particular task object. No more than one interrupt entry may be associated with a given kind of interrupt at a given time. This restriction allows interrupt entries to be implemented quite efficiently, by altering an interrupt vector so that the hardware branches directly to the appropriate `ACCEPT` statement when an interrupt occurs. As a result of this restriction, it almost never makes sense to declare an interrupt entry in a task type declaration.

20.6 UNCHECKED CONVERSION

The type rules of the Ada language are based on the principle that a type consists of a set of values plus a set of operations on those values. Normally, an Ada value can only be manipulated in accordance with the operations defined for its type. Occasionally, in low-level programming, it is necessary to treat the same sequence of bits as a value in more than one type. For example, a sequence of four bytes might be viewed as a character string, an unsigned integer, a signed integer, or a floating-point number. The bits have different and possibly unrelated meanings in each case—for example, the bit pattern representing the floating-point value 65.25 might also represent the integer 1,076,106,240—and the applicable operations are different.

This language provides the capability to view the bits representing a value in one type as the representation of a value in some other type. This capability should only be used in rare circumstances, such as when interacting with hardware or low-level software that views the same bits in different ways. Abuse of this capability can subvert the elaborate consistency-checking mechanisms built into the Ada language and lead to improper internal representations for data.

A predefined library generic function called `Unchecked_Conversion` can be instantiated with a specified *source type* and *target type*. When called with a parameter of the source type, the instance returns that value in the target type that has the same internal bit representation. This requires no computation when a program runs, but the function parameter and function result are viewed as belonging to two different types when the program is being compiled. An unchecked conversion function is different from all the type conversions we have seen so far because the parameter and result values may not have any abstract relationship to each other. The name `Unchecked_Conversion` reflects the dangers inherent in the use of this facility.

The declaration of `Unchecked_Conversion` is as follows:

```
GENERIC
   TYPE Source IS LIMITED PRIVATE;
   TYPE Target IS LIMITED PRIVATE;
FUNCTION Unchecked_Conversion (s : Source) RETURN Target;
```

An implementation may restrict the types that can be used as generic actual parameters to `Unchecked_Conversion`. For instance, it may require `Source'Size` and `Target'Size` to be equal. To perform unchecked conversion, you must mention the generic template `Unchecked_Conversion` in a `WITH` clause, instantiate it, and call the instance.

For example, the interface to the 6845 CRT controller presented in Section 20.4 required two views of a sixteen-bit integer: as a number in the range zero to 1,999 and as a pair of bytes holding the high-order and low-order eight bits. The `Set_Cursor` procedure of Section 20.4 used integer division by 256 and the `MOD` operator to separate the two-byte number arithmetically into numbers represented by the low-order and high-order bytes. In this case, it would actually be clearer (as well as more efficient) to express the decomposition directly in terms of the bit patterns.

This requires the declaration of a new record type, for example, `Byte_Pair_Type`, representing the view of a sixteen-bit word as a pair of bytes. We use a record representation clause and a length clause for `Byte_Pair_Type` to guarantee the correspondence between the representation of the record type and the representation of type `Integer` (which we assume uses sixteen bits). Then we instantiate `Unchecked_Conversion` to obtain a function, `Byte_Pair_From_Integer`, taking a value of type `Integer` and returning the `Byte_Pair_Type` value with the same underlying bit representation. The function call

```
Byte_Pair_From_Integer (x)
```

returns a `Byte_Pair_Type` record whose components represent the low-order and high-order bytes in the representation of *x*:

```
WITH Low_Level_IO, Unchecked_Conversion;
PACKAGE BODY Display_Buffer_Package IS
   TYPE Byte_Pair_Type IS
      RECORD
         High_Byte, Low_Byte : Low_Level_IO.Byte_Type;
      END RECORD;
   FOR Byte_Pair_Type USE
      RECORD
         Low_Byte AT 0 RANGE 0 .. 7;
         High_Byte AT 1 RANGE 0 .. 7;
      END RECORD;
   FOR Byte_Pair_Type'Size USE 16;
   FUNCTION Byte_Pair_From_Integer IS
      NEW Unchecked_Conversion
         (Source => Integer, Target => Byte_Pair_Type);
```

```
   PROCEDURE Set_Cursor
      (Line_Number   : IN Line_Number_Subtype;
       Column_Number : IN Column_Number_Subtype) IS
      SUBTYPE Screen_Position_Subtype IS
         Integer RANGE 0 .. 25 * 80 - 1;
      Motorola_6845_Index_Register :
         CONSTANT Low_Level_IO.Device_Type := 16#3B4#;
      Motorola_6845_Data_Register :
         CONSTANT Low_Level_IO.Device_Type := 16#3B5#;
      Cursor_Position_High_Register : CONSTANT := 14;
      Cursor_Position_Low_Register : CONSTANT := 15;
      Line_Starting_Position, Cursor_Position :
         Screen_Position_Subtype;
      Low_Order_Byte, High_Order_Byte : Low_Level_IO.Byte_Type;
   BEGIN
      Line_Starting_Position := 80 * (Line_Number - 1);
      Cursor_Position :=
         Line_Starting_Position + Column_Number - 1;
      Low_Level_IO.Send_Control
         (Motorola_6845_Index_Register,
          Cursor_Position_High_Register);
      Low_Level_IO.Send_Control
         (Motorola_6845_Data_Register,
          Byte_Pair_From_Integer (Cursor_Position). High_Byte);
      Low_Level_IO.Send_Control
         (Motorola_6845_Index_Register,
          Cursor_Position_Low_Register);
      Low_Level_IO.Send_Control
         (Motorola_6845_Data_Register,
          Byte_Pair_From_Integer (Cursor_Position).Low_Byte);
   END Set_Cursor;
END Display_Buffer_Package;
```

20.7 USING THE ADA LANGUAGE TOGETHER WITH ANOTHER LANGUAGE

With some implementations, it is possible to write a program written partly in the Ada language and partly in some other language. This could allow an Ada program to use a statistical function library written in FORTRAN, for example. It may also be possible, if it is found that a large Ada program is running too slowly and spending most of its time executing the same small subprogram, to rewrite that subprogram in assembly language. Even if over 95 percent of the program remains written in the Ada language, this is likely to speed up the entire program significantly. You can simultaneously benefit from both the efficiency of assembly-language programming and the readability and abstraction of a high-level language. Finally, short sequences of machine-language instructions can be inserted directly in an Ada program to use specific hardware functions in special circumstances.

The `Interface` pragma is used to call subprograms written in another high-level language or in assembly language. *Code procedures* are procedures consisting of specific machine-language instructions. These features are only provided by some implementations, and the details vary from one implementation to another. Code procedures are intended for specifying very short sequences of machine-language instructions (e.g., five or ten instructions) without using another language processor. If a longer sequence of instructions is to be specified, it will be clearer and less cumbersome to code it in assembly language and use the `Interface` pragma.

20.7.1 The `Interface` Pragma

The `Interface` pragma allows an Ada program to call a program written in another language. It directs the implementation to generate subprogram calls in accordance with the calling conventions of the other language. (There is no standard mechanism defined to allow a program written in another language to call a subprogram written in the Ada language.) An Ada program calling a subprogram written in another language must contain a declaration for that subprogram, written in the usual Ada notation for subprogram declarations. The code in the other language plays the role of an Ada subprogram body, so the Ada program contains an `Interface` pragma *instead of* the subprogram body.

The form of an `Interface` pragma is:

```
PRAGMA Interface ( language name, subprogram name ) ;
```

If the subprogram declaration is separately compiled, the pragma must be compiled after the subprogram declaration but before any other compilation unit. If the subprogram is declared in a declarative part, the pragma must follow later in the same declarative part. If the subprogram is declared in a package specification, the pragma must follow later in the package specification. (Because the pragma describes the implementation of the subprogram rather than its interface, it is stylistically more appropriate to place the pragma in the private part of the package specification than in the visible part.) If the subprogram name given in the `Interface` pragma is overloaded, the pragma applies simultaneously to all subprograms declared earlier in the same sequence of declarations with that name.

Suppose some Ada function `Cable_Tension` requires the use of a hyperbolic sine function, and suppose this function is available only in the FORTRAN subroutine library. If the implementation allowed it, `Cable_Tension` might be written like this:

```
FUNCTION Cable_Tension
   (x, y1, y2, Density : Float) RETURN Float IS
   ...
   PROCEDURE Sinh (x : Float) RETURN Float;
   PRAGMA Interface (Sinh, FORTRAN);
   ...
BEGIN
   ...
   a := Sinh (b);
   ...
END Cable_Tension;
```

An implementation may restrict the use of the `Interface` pragma. For example, it might establish a correspondence between certain predefined Ada types and types in the other language and require that each subprogram parameter and function result belong to one of these types. There might also be restrictions on parameter modes, for example.

20.7.2 Code Procedures

An implementation allowing code procedures has a predefined library package named `Machine_Code`. This package provides one or more record types whose values correspond to machine-language instructions. Record components correspond to fields of the machine-language instruction. On machines with different formats for different "opcodes," the opcode component may act as a discriminant in a record type with variants. The package may also provide other facilities, such as enumeration types whose values name machine instructions or registers.

A code procedure has the following form:

```
PROCEDURE identifier [ ( formal parameter list ) ] IS
   [ USE clause
        ~~~
     USE clause ]
BEGIN
   qualified record aggregate ;
        ~~~
   qualified record aggregate ;
END [ identifier ] ;
```

Only `USE` clauses are allowed in the declarative part. Instead of statements, the procedure body contains a sequence of qualified expressions followed by semicolons. Each qualified expression contains a record aggregate of one of the machine instruction types provided by the package `Machine_Code`. The procedure body may not contain exception handlers. An implementation may impose further restrictions, such as requiring expressions in the record aggregate to be static or prohibiting parameters.

Here is a hypothetical example, placing the contents of the parameter `Argument` in register R0, issuing supervisor call twelve hexadecimal to obtain some operating system service, and placing the resulting contents of register R1 in the parameter `Result`:

```
WITH Machine_Code; USE Machine_Code;
PROCEDURE Obtain_Service
   (Argument : IN Integer; Result : OUT Integer) IS
   USE Machine_Code;
BEGIN
   Machine_Instruction'(LOAD, R0, Argument'Address);
   Machine_Instruction'(SVC, 16#12#);
   Machine_Instruction'(STORE, R1, Result'Address);
END Obtain_Service;
```

20.8 SUMMARY

The Ada language provides a set of *low-level programming* features that allow a program to deal with hardware or assembly-language-level software abstractly. These features allow a program to specify bit-by-bit data representations and manipulations in terms of high-level Ada constructs. Different Ada compilers have different rules governing the use and meaning of low-level features. Each compiler comes with its own version of Appendix F of the Ada Reference Manual, giving these rules. The examples given in this section have been for hypothetical Ada compilers.

The package `System` provides declarations of named numbers, types, subtypes, and constants describing characteristics of the machine that will run the program. A program using this package can refer to these characteristics abstractly, in a way that remains valid when compiled for other implementations. The types and subtypes include the following:

`Name` — An enumeration type with one value for for each runtime configuration handled by the implementation.

`Address` — A type (most often an integer type) whose values are hardware addresses.

`Priority` — A subtype of type `Integer` whose values may be used in the `Priority` pragma to specify task priorities.

The constants and named numbers include the following:

`System_Name` — A constant of type `Name`, typically indicating the runtime configuration for which code is being compiled.

`Storage_Unit`	The number of bits in the storage unit corresponding to a single address.
`Memory_Size`	The number of storage units in the runtime configuration.
`Min_Int`	The smallest integer that may be specified in an integer-type declaration.
`Max_Int`	The largest integer that may be specified in an integer-type declaration.
`Max_Digits`	The largest number of digits of precision that can be named in a floating-point type declaration.
`Fine_Delta`	The smallest delta that can be specified in a fixed-point type declaration with a range of `-1.0 .. 1.0`.
`Max_Mantissa`	The logarithm to the base two of `1.0/Fine_Delta`.
`Tick`	The number of seconds in each "tick" of the machine that will run the program.

(`System_Name` is a constant, and the others are named numbers.) In addition to these declarations, provided by all implementations, a particular compiler's package `System` may provide additional declarations.

Some implementations allow the values of `System_Name`, `Memory_Size`, and `Storage_Unit`, respectively, to be altered by the following pragmas:

```
PRAGMA System_Name ( enumeration literal ) ;
PRAGMA Memory_Size ( numeric literal ) ;
PRAGMA Storage_Unit ( numeric literal ) ;
```

These pragmas must occur at the beginning of a compilation, before any compilation units, and some implementations may allow them only with a new program library into which no units have been compiled. Use of these pragmas requires recompilation of any compilation unit containing a `WITH` clause for package `System`.

Representation attributes provide information about low-level, implementation-dependent properties of objects, subtypes, and program units. The representation attributes are as follows:

X`'Address`	If *X* is a subprogram, task unit, or package, the address of the first machine instruction of the subprogram, the task body, or the package's initialization statements. If *X* is a constant or a variable, the address at which its value is stored.

X`'Size`	If *X* is a constant or a variable, the number of bits used to hold that object. If *X* is a subtype, the minimum number of bits required to hold all objects in this subtype.
X`'Storage_Size`	If *X* is an access type, the number of storage units set aside for allocating variables pointed to by values of type *X*. If *X* is a task type, the number of storage units set aside for the execution of each task of that type.
R.*C*`'Position`	The offset in storage units of the first storage unit of component *C* from the first storage unit occupied by the entire record *R*.
R.*C*`'First_Bit`	The offset in bits of the beginning of record component *R*.*C* from the beginning of the storage unit in which it is contained.
R.*C*`'Last_Bit`	The offset in bits of the end of record component *R*.*C* from the beginning of the storage unit containing the first bit of the component.
T`'Machine_Rounds`	`True` if operations in the base type of floating-point or fixed-point subtype *T* round to the nearest approximation to the result; `False` if these operations truncate to obtain an approximation.
T`'Machine_Overflows`	`True` if every overflowing operation in the base type of floating-point or fixed-point subtype *T* raises `Numeric_Error`; `False` otherwise.
T`'Machine_Radix`	The radix used in the machine representation of the base type of floating-point type *T*.
T`'Mantissa`	The number of digits in radix *T*`'Machine_Radix` used to represent values in the base type of floating-point type *T*.
T`'Machine_EMin`	The lowest exponent in the machine representation of the base type of floating-point type *T*.
T`'Machine_EMax`	The highest exponent in the machine representation of the base type of floating-point type *T*.

An implementation may provide additional representation attributes of its own.

Just as representation attributes *report* internal representations, *representation clauses* and *representation pragmas* request particular representations. A representation clause demands that an implementation use a particular internal representation for some entity. It will be flagged as illegal if the implementation does not support that representation. A representation pragma recommends a general strategy for choosing representations. An implementation may ignore a representation pragma, but it will not reject it as illegal.

Three kinds of representation clauses are called *length clauses.* A length clause of the form

```
FOR T'Size USE expression ;
```

specifies the maximum number of bits to be used to represent all objects of type *T*. A length clause of the form

```
FOR T'Storage_Size USE expression ;
```

specifies the number of storage units to be set aside for allocating variables to be pointed to by values in access type *T;* or the number of storage units to be set aside for the execution of a task of task type *T*. A length clause of the form

```
FOR T'Small USE expression ;
```

specifies the interval between exactly represented values in fixed-point type *T*.

An *enumeration representation clause* of the form

```
FOR enumeration type name USE array aggregate ;
```

specifies the internal integer encodings of enumeration-type values. The array aggregate's index values are the enumeration values of the named type. The aggregate's components are the corresponding integer encodings.

A *record representation clause* of the form

```
FOR record type name USE
      RECORD [ AT MOD storage unit multiple ]
        [ component name AT storage unit offset RANGE bit range ;
            ~~~
          component name AT storage unit offset RANGE bit range ; ]
END RECORD ;
```

controls the internal representation of values in a record type. The first storage unit occupied by a record component, and the offset of the component's first and last bits from the start of that storage unit, can be specified for zero or more record components. The storage unit multiple following **AT MOD** can be used to specify that all objects in the record type begin at addresses evenly divisible by that multiple. Rules restricting the storage unit multiple and conventions for numbering bits vary from implementation to implementation.

An *address clause* of the form

```
FOR identifier USE AT expression ;
```

specifies an address for the first machine instruction of a subprogram, a task body, or a package body's initialization statements; or the address of an object. In addition, an address clause for an entry can be specified in a task declaration. This links the entry with a hardware interrupt, so that the entry is automatically called every time the interrupt occurs. The entry is then called an *interrupt entry*. Interrupt handlers can be written abstractly as Ada tasks that accept calls on interrupt entries, and very efficient implementations are possible.

The only representation pragma defined for all Ada implementations is the `Pack` pragma:

```
PRAGMA Pack ( composite type name ) ;
```

It recommends that the implementation minimize the gaps between components in the named array or record type, even if this entails slower access to the components. A related pragma, not strictly a representation pragma, is the `Optimize` pragma:

```
PRAGMA Optimize ( Time );
PRAGMA Optimize ( Space );
```

It indicates whether the block statement, subprogram body, package body, or task body in whose declarative part it is placed should be compiled in a way that reduces execution speed at the cost of storage space or vice versa. An implementation is allowed to define representation pragmas of its own.

Sometimes it is desirable to have two internal representations for the same data, for instance, a packed and unpacked representation. This can be achieved by declaring a derived type and specifying different representations for the derived type and its parent type. Conversion between these two types then results in a change of representation.

Device-level input and output operations may be supplied in an implementation-defined package named `Low_Level_IO`. This package provides types whose values represent devices and types whose values are data sent to or received from devices. The package also provides overloaded versions of the following procedures:

```
PROCEDURE Receive_Control
    (Device : IN [some type for devices];
     Data   : IN OUT [some type for data]) ;
PROCEDURE Send_Control
    (Device : IN [some type for devices];
     Data   : IN OUT [some type for data]) ;
```

Each version of Receive_Control corresponds to a low-level input operation, and each version of Send_Control corresponds to a low-level output operation.

The predefined library generic function Unchecked_Conversion allows the same pattern of bits to be viewed as representing values in more than one type. Its generic declaration is as follows:

```
GENERIC
   TYPE Source IS LIMITED PRIVATE;
   TYPE Target IS LIMITED PRIVATE;
FUNCTION Unchecked_Conversion (s : Source) RETURN Target;
```

An implementation may restrict allowable instantiations. Given a value in the source type, an instance of the generic function returns that value in the target type represented by the same sequence of bits. Appropriate uses of Unchecked_Conversion are rare.

Some implementations allow parts of Ada programs to be written in another language or specified at the machine instruction level. The pragma

```
PRAGMA Interface ( language name, subprogram name ) ;
```

specifies that a particular subprogram is written in another language. This pragma takes the place of a subprogram body. Some implementations have a predefined package Machine_Code providing one or more record types whose values correspond to machine-language instructions. Such implementations may allow *code procedures,* which are procedures of the form

```
PROCEDURE identifier [ ( formal parameter list ) ] IS

  [ USE clause
       ~~~
    USE clause ]

BEGIN
   qualified record aggregate ;
       ~~~
   qualified record aggregate ;
END [ identifier ] ;
```

Each record aggregate specifies a machine-language instruction. The rules governing such procedures are highly implementation-dependent.

EXERCISES

20.1 Rewrite the package Time_Package given in Section 20.3.1.5 under the assumption that bits are numbered from right to left on the target machine. Assume that, as before, the most significant five bits give the number of hours, the next six bits give the number of minutes, and the least significant five bits give the number of two-second increments in a time of the day.

20.2 Suppose the type `Display_Element_Type` declared in Section 20.3.1.7 is to be used with a color monitor. In the byte controlling how each character is displayed, bits zero through two (controlling the foreground color) and bits four through six (controlling the background color) are given the following meanings:

Bit 0: Blue on in foreground
Bit 1: Green on in foreground
Bit 2: Red on in foreground

Bit 4: Blue on in background
Bit 5: Green on in background
Bit 6: Red on in background

The eight possible combinations of the primary colors red, green, and blue produce the following colors:

Red	Green	Blue	
Off	Off	Off	black
Off	Off	On	blue
Off	On	Off	green
Off	On	On	cyan
On	Off	Off	red
On	Off	On	violet
On	On	Off	yellow
On	On	On	white

Write two new declarations for `Display_Element_Type` providing different abstract views of this byte. The first view is that the eight colors above are independent basic values. The second view is that every color is some combination of primary colors. (The second view is appropriate, for example, if one region of the screen is to be colored blue and another region of the screen is to be colored red, with the places at which these regions overlap colored violet.) Provide representation clauses based on the assumptions given in Section 20.3.1.

20.3 Assuming the version of `Low_Level_IO` and the description of the 6845 CRT controller given in Section 20.4, write a subprogram `Set_Register` to place an arbitrary byte in an arbitrary register of the 6845. Rewrite the `Set_Cursor` subprogram to use `Set_Register`.

20.4 Write a terminal input handler assuming that your implementation provides the hypothetical version of `Low_Level_IO` given in Section 20.4. Each character typed at the terminal causes an interrupt associated with address 10 hexadecimal. Following this interrupt, a low-level input instruction from input/output address 124 hexadecimal yields the ASCII code of the character that was typed. A backspace (character `ASCII.BS`) should cancel the most recent character in the line, and a control-X (character `ASCII.CAN`) should cancel the entire line. A carriage return (character `ASCII.CR`) ends a line. Characters entered after a line already contains 132 characters (other than backspace, control-X, and carriage return) should be ignored, as should backspace and control-X characters entered for an empty line. The abstract interface of the terminal handler should provide a procedure with two `OUT` parameters—a 132-character string containing the characters of a complete line (not containing any backspace, control-X, or carriage return characters) and an integer giving the logical length of the line. A call on this procedure waits until a line has been completely typed in. Assume that the procedure is called often enough so that a call is always waiting to complete whenever a carriage return is entered.

20.5 Given your implementation's Appendix F and a guide to your operating system's assembly language system calls, write an Ada package providing an abstract interface for a group of related system calls. Select a set of calls that use a block of storage with a particular bit-by-bit format.

APPENDIX

THE PACKAGE Basic_IO

This is the package Basic_IO that provides the primitive input and output facilities used until Chapter 15. The facilities provided by Basic_IO are restricted versions of some of the more advanced facilities provided by the predefined package Text_IO. They are implemented in terms of the more advanced facilities.

```
WITH IO_Exceptions;
PACKAGE Basic_IO IS
   PROCEDURE Get (Item : OUT Integer);
   PROCEDURE Get (Item : OUT Character);
   PROCEDURE Get (Item : OUT String);

   PROCEDURE Put (Item : IN Integer);
   PROCEDURE Put (Item : IN Character);
   PROCEDURE Put (Item : IN String);

   PROCEDURE Get_Line
      (Item : OUT String; Last : OUT Natural);

   PROCEDURE New_Line;

   PROCEDURE New_Page;

   FUNCTION End_Of_File RETURN Boolean;

   Device_Error  : EXCEPTION RENAMES IO_Exceptions.Device_Error;
   End_Error     : EXCEPTION RENAMES IO_Exceptions.End_Error;
   Data_Error    : EXCEPTION RENAMES IO_Exceptions.Data_Error;
END Basic_IO;
```

```
WITH Text_IO;
PACKAGE BODY Basic_IO IS
   PACKAGE Type_Integer_IO IS
      NEW Text_IO.Integer_IO (Integer);
   PROCEDURE Get (Item : OUT Integer) IS
   BEGIN
      Type_Integer_IO.Get (Item);
   END Get;
   PROCEDURE Get (Item : OUT Character) IS
   BEGIN
      Text_IO.Get (Item);
   END Get;
   PROCEDURE Get (Item : OUT String) IS
   BEGIN
      Text_IO.Get (Item);
   END Get;
   PROCEDURE Put (Item : IN Integer) IS
   BEGIN
      Type_Integer_IO.Put (Item);
   END Put;
   PROCEDURE Put (Item : IN Character) IS
   BEGIN
      Text_IO.Put (Item);
   END Put;
   PROCEDURE Put (Item : IN String) IS
   BEGIN
      Text_IO.Put (Item);
   END Put;
   PROCEDURE Get_Line
      (Item : OUT String; Last : OUT Natural) IS
   BEGIN
      Text_IO.Get_Line (Item, Last);
   END Get_Line;
   PROCEDURE New_Line IS
   BEGIN
      Text_IO.New_Line;
   END New_Line;
   PROCEDURE New_Page IS
   BEGIN
      Text_IO.New_Page;
   END New_Page;
   FUNCTION End_Of_File RETURN Boolean IS
   BEGIN
      RETURN Text_IO.End_Of_File;
   END End_Of_File;
END Basic_IO;
```

SUBJECT INDEX

PROGRAM UNIT INDEX